INEQUALITY AND THE FADING OF REDISTRIBUTIVE POLITICS

INEQUALITY AND THE FADING OF REDISTRIBUTIVE POLITICS

Edited by Keith Banting and John Myles

UBCPress · Vancouver · Toronto

© UBC Press 2013

All rights reserved. No part of this publication may be reproduced, stored in a retrieval system, or transmitted, in any form or by any means, without prior written permission of the publisher, or, in Canada, in the case of photocopying or other reprographic copying, a licence from Access Copyright, www.accesscopyright.ca.

21 20 19 18 17 16 15 14 13   5 4 3 2 1

Printed in Canada on FSC-certified ancient-forest-free paper
(100% post-consumer recycled) that is processed chlorine- and acid-free.

Library and Archives Canada Cataloguing in Publication

    Inequality and the fading of redistributive politics / edited by Keith Banting and John Myles.

Includes bibliographical references and index.
Issued in print and electronic formats.
ISBN 978-0-7748-2599-3 (bound). – ISBN 978-0-7748-2600-6 (pbk.). –
ISBN 978-0-7748-2601-3 (pdf). – ISBN 978-0-7748-2602-0 (epub)

    1. Canada – Social policy. 2. Equality – Canada. 3. Welfare economics.
4. Distributive justice – Canada. I. Banting, Keith G., author, writer of introduction, editor of compilation. II. Myles, John author, writer of introduction, editor of compilation

| HN107.I54 2013 | 361.6'10971 | C2013-904111-7 |
| | | C2013-904112-5 |

Canadä

UBC Press gratefully acknowledges the financial support for our publishing program of the Government of Canada (through the Canada Book Fund), the Canada Council for the Arts, and the British Columbia Arts Council.

This book has been published with the help of a grant from the Canadian Federation for the Humanities and Social Sciences, through the Awards to Scholarly Publications Program, using funds provided by the Social Sciences and Humanities Research Council of Canada.

UBC Press
The University of British Columbia
2029 West Mall
Vancouver, BC V6T 1Z2
www.ubcpress.ca

Contents

Acknowledgments / ix

Acronyms / xi

1 Introduction: Inequality and the Fading of Redistributive Politics / 1
KEITH BANTING AND JOHN MYLES

Part 1: Politics

2 Historical Transformations of Canada's Social Architecture: Institutions, Instruments, and Ideas / 43
JANE JENSON

3 Drivers of Increasing Market Income Inequality: Structural Change and Policy / 65
DAVID A. GREEN AND JAMES TOWNSEND

4 Business, Labour, and Redistributive Politics / 93
WILLIAM D. COLEMAN

5 Restructuring Civil Society: Muting the Politics of Redistribution / 116
SUSAN D. PHILLIPS

6 Public Opinion on Social Spending, 1980-2005 / 141
ROBERT ANDERSEN AND JOSH CURTIS

7 Multicultural Diversity and Redistribution / 165
KEITH BANTING, STUART SOROKA, AND EDWARD KONING

8 The Party System, Elections, and Social Policy / 187
RICHARD JOHNSTON

9 The New Bureaucratic Politics of Redistribution / 210
DAVID A. GOOD

10 Territorial Politics and the New Politics of Redistribution / 234
GERARD W. BOYCHUK

11 Quebec's New Politics of Redistribution / 256
ALAIN NOËL

Part 2: Policy

12 Health Care Policy after Universality: Canada in Comparative Perspective / 285
CAROLYN HUGHES TUOHY

13 Income Security for Seniors: System Maintenance and Policy Drift / 312
JOHN MYLES

14 The Recent Evolution of Tax-Transfer Policies / 335
ROBIN BOADWAY AND KATHERINE CUFF

15 Childcare, New Social Risks, and the New Politics of Redistribution in Ontario / 359
RIANNE MAHON

16 Labour Market Income Transfers and Redistribution: National Themes and Provincial Variations / 381
RODNEY HADDOW

Part 3: Conclusion

17 Canadian Social Futures: Concluding Reflections / 413
KEITH BANTING AND JOHN MYLES

Contributors / 429

Index / 433

Acknowledgments

This project began with a workshop supported by the Social Sciences and Humanities Research Council of Canada (SSHRC) in May 2010, at which authors presented initial drafts of their chapters. We owe a special debt of thanks to Deanna Pikkov, who helped organize both the workshop and the successful SSHRC grant application that funded it.

Numerous colleagues and graduate students from across Canada and the United States joined us as discussants at the workshop, including Ito Peng, J.J. Huo, Martin Hering, Richard Simeon, Sujit Choudry, Paul Armstrong, Holly Grinwald, Deanna Pikkov, Norah MacKendrick, and Mai Phan.

Martin Rhodes and George Ross played a particularly important role. Their task was to provide us with a discussion of the project from an international perspective and to advise us on its overall structure. Their comments were extremely influential with regard to the way we have developed the themes of the volume. Our colleagues at Statistics Canada, Feng Hou and Garnett Picot, provided important interventions that kept us from making silly mistakes in our reading of the data.

In 2011, a set of the revised chapters was presented in linked panels during the annual meetings of the Canadian Political Science Association. Special thanks to our discussants, Michael Prince, Stephen McBride, and Kent Weaver, whose comments enriched not only the individual chapters but also the collective enterprise.

Along the way, we benefitted from the professional assistance of several talented people. Elizabeth Thompson edited each chapter to enhance its readability for a broad audience. Valerie Jarus managed the electronic challenges involved in consolidating sixteen chapters into a single text. Thank you, Elizabeth and Valerie.

At UBC Press, our editor, Emily Andrew, was a superb and supportive guide through the editorial process. As usual, peer review greatly enhanced the quality of the final product, and thanks are due to the two anonymous reviewers for UBC Press who had a lot of reading to do.

Our deepest expression of gratitude goes to the chapter authors. Following the conference, they returned to their offices to draft full papers. We then submitted them to several merciless rounds of revisions. Like true professionals, they responded to our demands as well as to comments from external reviewers with alacrity and grace. The end result was worth the effort. Many of their chapters will become instant "classics."

This book has been published with the help of a grant from the Canadian Federation for the Humanities and Social Sciences, through the Awards to Scholarly Publications Program, using funds provided by SSHRC.

At its best, social policy reform is aimed at enhancing the well-being of the members of the next generation. We dedicate this volume to them, in the hope that the insights gathered here will contribute to fresh thinking about redistributive politics in Canada during the decades to come.

Acronyms

ALMPs	active labour market policies
AWPS	Annual Work Patterns Survey
BCNI	Business Council on National Issues
CACSW	Canadian Advisory Council on the Status of Women
CAP	Canada Assistance Plan
CCAAC	Childcare Advocacy Alliance of Canada
CCC	Canadian Chamber of Commerce
CCCE	Canadian Council of Chief Executives
CCED	Child Care Expense Deduction
CCSD	Canadian Council of Social Development
CCTB	Canada Child Tax Benefit
CES	Canadian Election Study
CFIB	Canadian Federation of Independent Business
CHST	Canada Health and Social Transfer
CHT	Canada Health Transfer
CLC	Canadian Labour Congress
CMA	Canadian Manufacturers Association
CME	Canadian Manufacturers and Exporters
C/QPP	Canada/Quebec Pension Plans

CPP	Canada Pension Plan
CPQ	Conseil du Patronat du Québec
CST	Canada Social Transfer
CSOs	civil society organizations
CUSFTA	Canada-US Free Trade Agreement
ECEC	early childhood education and care
EI	Employment Insurance
ELCC	early learning and childcare
ESCS	Equality, Security, and Community Survey
FAP	Family Allowance Program
GAI	Guaranteed Annual Income
GIS	Guaranteed Income Supplement
GST	Goods and Services Tax
HRDC	Human Resources Development Canada
HST	Harmonized Sales Tax
HRSDC	Human Resources and Skills Development Canada
LEAF	Women's Legal and Education Action Fund
LFS	Labour Force Survey
LMAS	Labour Market Activity Surveys
LICO	low-income cut-off
LIM	low-income measure
NAC	National Action Committee on the Status of Women
NAFTA	North American Free Trade Agreement
NAPO	National Anti-Poverty Organization
NCB	National Child Benefit
NCBS	National Child Benefit Supplement
NCW	National Council of Welfare
NDP	New Democratic Party
NIT	negative income tax
OAS	Old Age Security
OCBCC	Ontario Coalition for Better Child Care
OECD	Organisation for Economic Cooperation and Development
OLS	ordinary least squares
PCO	Privy Council Office

PMO	Prime Minister's Office
PQ	Parti québécois
PRSPs	Pooled Retirement Savings Plans
PRT	power resources theory
QPP	Quebec Pension Plan
RESP	Registered Education Savings Plan
RPPs	Registered Pension Plans
RRSPs	Registered Retirement Savings Plans
SA	social assistance
SCF	Survey of Consumer Finances
SLID	Survey of Labour and Income Dynamics
SMEs	small and medium-sized enterprises
SPP	Security and Prosperity Partnership of North America
SSR	Social Security Review
SUM	Survey of Union Membership
SWA	Survey of Work Arrangements
TFSAs	Tax Free Savings Accounts
UCCB	Universal Child Care Benefit
UI	Unemployment Insurance
VSI	Voluntary Sector Initiative
VSR	Voluntary Sector Roundtable
WITB	Working Income Tax Benefit
WVS	World Values Survey

INEQUALITY AND THE FADING OF REDISTRIBUTIVE POLITICS

1

Introduction
Inequality and the Fading of Redistributive Politics

KEITH BANTING AND JOHN MYLES

The redistributive state is fading in Canada. Until the mid-1990s, the consensus was that Canada was not following the lead of the United States and the United Kingdom, where the level of inequality began to grow in the late 1970s and accelerated dramatically in the 1980s. By contrast, inequality in the incomes Canadians derived from the market was rising, but government programs, especially the tax-transfer system, offset this development, even during the harsh recession of the early 1990s. This has changed. The tax-transfer system is no longer offsetting the growth in inequality generated by the market, and Canadian society is more unequal. The celebration of Canada as the kinder and gentler nation on the North American continent is now fading.

Politics has been critical to the redistributive fade. All advanced democracies have faced the pressures of globalization, technological change, and new family forms, which have generated higher levels of inequality in market incomes almost everywhere. But countries have responded differently, reflecting differences in their domestic politics. In some countries, changes in public policy have accentuated the growth of inequality; in others, policy has mitigated it. What has been the Canadian response? A major study by the Organisation for Economic Cooperation and Development (OECD) found that, in the period between the mid-1980s and the mid-1990s, the redistributive impact of the tax-transfer system was strongest in Canada, Denmark, Finland, and Sweden. But by the period between the mid-1990s and the mid-2000s, Canada had joined Switzerland and the US as the countries with the smallest redistributive impact (OECD 2011, 271).

The surge in inequality in the past several decades has posed a puzzling new question for policy makers in many countries. Income inequality can rise because the rich are getting richer or because the poor are getting poorer relative to those in the "middle." As we shall see in more detail below, much of the rise in income inequality in recent decades has been driven by the former trend. The rich have gotten dramatically richer, as the Occupy Movement highlighted in 2011, and higher-income groups generally have done well. By contrast, Canadians in the middle, especially those in the lower middle of the wage distribution, have been struggling in the wake of economic change and have not received their fair share of the benefits of economic growth for a generation. In Canada, however, the burden of growing inequality has not been concentrated at the bottom, among the poor. Compared to other OECD countries, Canada continues to tolerate high levels of poverty. But during the recent growth of inequality, poverty has been stable or even declining, depending on how it is measured. All this simply means that recent economic gains have gone disproportionately to high-income earners, while both the middle and the bottom have been losing ground in relative terms. Policy makers in many countries have had to decide whether and how to adapt their redistributive strategies to the contemporary form of inequality. Canada, however, seems to have done less well in this regard than many.

This book analyzes the changes in the politics of social policy that have contributed to the redistributive fade in Canada. There is no smoking gun to be found in the story that emerges. The politics of redistribution are too multidimensional for simple explanations. According to our authors, a complex mix of forces has reshaped the politics of social policy: global economic pressures, ideological change, shifts in the influence of business and labour, the decline of equality-seeking civil society organizations and think tanks, realignment in the party system, shifting bureaucratic politics, and decentralization in the federation. While it is impossible to disentangle the independent effect of these diverse changes, their cumulative impact has transformed the politics of redistribution. On one side, organizations that speak for the economic interests of lower-middle income groups and poor Canadians – mobilizing resources, expertise, and attention on their behalf – have been weakened; on the other side, changes in the distribution of power within our political institutions have made concerted action to tackle inequality more difficult. The result is a mutually reinforcing political syndrome that is less sensitive to the economic needs of lower-income individuals and families.

Changed politics generate changed policies. As we shall see, the policy trajectory in recent decades combines three elements: system maintenance, policy change, and policy drift. System maintenance has sustained universal programs such as pensions and health care that benefit the entire population, including the broad middle classes. While these programs were not designed primarily with redistribution to the poor in mind, they do have important redistributive impacts, which have also largely been maintained. Policy change and policy drift, however, have had the opposite effect. Policy restructuring shrank programs that provided support to vulnerable Canadians, such as unemployment benefits and social assistance, and reduced the progressivity of the tax system. As we shall see, Canada experienced a "neoliberal moment" during the 1990s, when the federal and provincial governments made dramatic changes. During the 2000s, governments continued to weaken the redistributive impact of the tax-transfer system in more incremental ways.

Policy drift also matters. There is a tendency to equate "retrenchment" with authoritative changes in formal rules, policies, and procedures. But an exclusive focus on action ignores the consequences of inaction. As the economic and social world changes, new risks and pressures are created for important parts of the population. If public policy fails to keep pace, social programs "come to cover a declining portion of the salient risks faced by citizens" (Hacker 2004, 243; Hacker and Pierson 2010). As we shall see, the Canadian story includes serious policy drift. Governments have not responded energetically to the evidence of growing inequality, and they have not modernized the policy architecture in light of new social risks confronting Canadian families. Action and inaction, sins of omission and sins of commission, have weakened the redistributive state.

This Introduction has two purposes. It seeks to integrate the findings in the chapters that follow into a comprehensive overview of the changing politics of redistribution. In addition, it puts Canadian experience in a broader perspective by drawing on insights emerging from comparative research on the politics of the welfare state. The Introduction comprises four sections. The first section sets the background context by briefly examining the welfare state that emerged in Canada during the postwar era and the politics that shaped it. The second section explores the ways in which Canadian politics has changed in the decades since 1980, altering the balance of political pressures on social policy. The third section examines the impact of the new politics on social programs, tracing system maintenance, policy change, and policy drift. The fourth analyzes the impact of change and drift on the redistributive role of the state in Canada, analyzing the extent and timing of the decline in redistribution in greater detail. The concluding chapter of this volume, Chapter 17, extends the discussion by reflecting on the importance of the findings, both for the scholarly literature on the politics of social policy and for the future of social well-being in Canada.

The Postwar Politics of Redistribution

Canadians built their version of the welfare state during the middle decades of the twentieth century. The remarkably innovative postwar era saw the introduction of programs to address a wide range of social needs: income protection for the elderly, the disabled, and the unemployed; support for families with children; health care for Canadians as a whole; and social services for those in need. These programs transformed Canadian society, reducing poverty and inequality, and making critical services such as health care accessible to everyone. As Hanratty and Blank (1992, 237-38) have shown, Canadian poverty rates declined dramatically in the 1970s, falling below US levels for the first time in 1974.

The postwar welfare state clearly made Canada a fairer place, and many Canadians began to think of their social model as a mid-point between Europe and the US. In reality, however, the Canadian model was always comparatively modest. In his typology of welfare states, Esping-Andersen (1990) classifies Canada, along with the US and other English-speaking democracies, as a "liberal" welfare state, in contrast to the more expansive corporatist or Christian-Democratic welfare states of Continental Europe and the social-democratic welfare states of Scandinavia. For Esping-Andersen, the term "liberal" has a nineteenth-century meaning: individualistic rather than solidaristic. Liberal welfare states are reluctant to replace market relations with social rights; instead, they seek to provide a safety net for the "poor" and to encourage the bulk of the population to rely as much as possible on private sources of economic security, including occupational benefits and personal savings.

Liberal welfare states are characterized by comparatively low levels of welfare spending. Table 1.1 tracks the growth in total social expenditures on income transfers and health care (excluding education) among democratic countries between 1960 and 2012. In 1960, no one was spending very much by contemporary standards. The countries of Continental Europe (where welfare state innovation began in the late nineteenth century) were the

TABLE 1.1
Total public social expenditure as a percentage of GDP, selected OECD countries, 1960-2007

Country	1960	1980	1990	2000	2007	2012*
Anglo-Saxon countries						
Australia	7.4	10.6	13.1	17.3	16.0	18.7
Canada	**9.1**	**13.7**	**18.1**	**16.5**	**16.9**	**18.2**
United Kingdom	10.2	16.7	16.8	18.6	20.5	23.9
United States	7.3	13.1	13.5	14.5	16.2	19.4
Mean	*8.5*	*13.5*	*15.4*	*16.7*	*17.4*	*20.1*
Scandinavian countries						
Denmark	10.6	25.1	25.1	25.7	26.1	30.5
Finland	8.8	24.1	24.1	24.2	24.8	29.0
Norway	7.8	22.3	22.3	21.3	20.8	22.1
Sweden	10.8	30.2	30.2	28.4	27.3	28.2
Mean	*9.5*	*25.4*	*25.4*	*24.9*	*24.8*	*27.5*
Continental Europe						
Austria	15.9	23.8	23.8	26.7	26.4	28.3
Belgium	13.8	24.9	24.9	25.4	26.3	30.0
France	13.4	24.9	24.9	27.7	28.4	32.1
Germany	18.1	21.7	21.7	26.6	25.2	26.3
Netherlands	11.7	25.6	25.6	19.8	20.1	24.3
Mean	*14.6*	*24.2*	*24.2*	*25.2*	*25.3*	*28.2*
Southern Europe						
Italy	13.1	20.0	20.0	23.3	24.9	28.1
Spain	3.2	19.9	19.9	20.4	21.6	26.3

* Projected

Sources: Data for 1960 from OECD, "New Orientations for Social Policy," *Social Policy Studies* 12 (Paris: OECD, 1994). Data for 1980-2012, downloaded from OECD, Social Expenditure Database (SOCX), March 2013.

welfare state leaders, while both Scandinavian and Anglo-Saxon nations were relative laggards. However, expenditures in Scandinavia and the Continental countries exploded between 1960 and 1980 and then levelled off. Canadian spending peaked in 1990 at 18 percent of gross domestic product (GDP), slightly higher than in the US but well below typical European levels. Canadian expenditures then faded somewhat to 16.9 percent in 2007, only trivially higher than in the US (16.2 percent). Provisional OECD estimates for 2012 show the lingering impact of the recession that began in 2008, with spending levels increased in almost all countries. The data suggest that, by that point, Canada (at 18.2 percent of GDP) had actually fallen behind the US (19.4 percent), no doubt due to a sharper US recession. By any international standard, however, Canada is not especially generous.

How to explain these differences? Power resource theory (Stephens 1979; Korpi 1983; Myles 1984; Esping-Andersen 1985) provided the dominant approach in the 1980s and 1990s, and it provides an important framework for several of our authors (see especially the chapters by Richard Johnston and Rodney Haddow). Studies in this tradition argue that differences in welfare state spending and entitlements can be explained by the relative success of left political parties, particularly social-democratic parties, and the strength of organized labour. Countries with strong left parties and powerful trade unions were more likely to develop expansive welfare states in the postwar era; countries in which parties of the right and the centre dominated and trade unions were weak developed more modest welfare states.

As Richard Johnston's chapter demonstrates, the postwar Canadian experience fits this model. Class-based voting was particularly limited in Canada compared to other Western democracies, and left political parties enjoyed only modest success at the polls. Founded in the 1930s by a coalition of farmer organizations, labour unions, and socialist intellectuals, the Co-operative Commonwealth Federation (CCF) was restructured in the early 1960s as the New Democratic Party (NDP), a more conventional social-democratic party with organic links to organized labour. Although the CCF/NDP has governed in five of the ten provinces at various times, it has never held power at the national level. During the postwar decades, it introduced important innovations at the provincial level and put pressure on centrist and conservative federal governments from the opposition benches in Parliament. Its overall role, however, has been secondary and indirect. Similarly, labour unions have been comparatively weak in Canada. Unionization of the labour force peaked at about 35 percent of the non-agricultural labour force in the early 1970s and declined slowly thereafter. Moreover, in contrast to European countries, organized labour in Canada remained decentralized and ideologically divided.

Nevertheless, an exclusive focus on comparative theory misses much that is distinctive about Canada. As Jane Jenson observes in her chapter: "An initial puzzle for the Canadian literature was, then, what were the politics that got it there? If they were not the class-based and class-organized politics ... what were the political drivers?" More than in most countries, Canadian politics is territorial politics, rooted in linguistic and regional divisions. Territorial divisions cross-cut class-based politics at the national level, and the politics of equality has always centred as much on regional inequalities as on class inequalities. Territorial politics generated a distinctively Canadian dynamic of expansion in social policy in the postwar period. Ever since Bismarck introduced social insurance in Germany in the 1880s, the welfare state has been recognized as an instrument of social integration in divided societies. In most countries, attention focuses on the role of social policy in bridging class divisions. In postwar Canada, however, social programs were seen as an instrument of territorial integration (Banting 1995, 2005). In the 1960s, for example, federal Liberals expanded social programs as "part of a strategy to strengthen the presence of the federal government and encourage 'nation' building in Canada" (Maioni 1998, 132). Over time, many Canadians, especially in English Canada, came to see national social programs as part of the Canadian identity, something distinguishing them from their powerful neighbours to the south, and part of the social glue holding their vast country together (Boychuk 2008; Johnston et al. 2010).

As the chapter by Jenson demonstrates, the social model that emerged from this distinctive combination of class and territorial politics is best characterized as a modified or hybrid version of the liberal welfare state (also Tuohy 1993). Income security programs were a thoroughly liberal component of the social architecture. Universal benefits such as Family Allowances provided modest benefits compared to the programs developing in many European countries. Pension programs protected poorer Canadians but were not designed to meet in full the retirement income needs of the middle class. In combination, Old Age Security (OAS), Canada/Quebec Pension Plans (C/QPP), and the Guaranteed Income Supplement (GIS) replaced approximately 40 percent of earnings for the average wage earner, a modest amount by European or even US standards. Similarly, Unemployment Insurance provided lower benefits for shorter periods of time than did the unemployment benefits in most European welfare states. Although postwar social planners hoped that the new income security programs would end reliance on traditional welfare programs (Marsh 1943), Canada continued to rely more heavily than did many Western nations on means-tested programs, such as social assistance.

The major exception was health care. Its more social-democratic character flowed from a distinctive interaction between power resource politics and territorial politics in the health sector. Pioneered in Saskatchewan by the CCF government, the universal model of health care was extended across the country by federal efforts to build a national approach to the issue. Coverage for core diagnostic, medical, and hospital services was universal; funding came from general tax revenues; there were no charges at the point of service – no co-payments, no user fees. The public system was not fully comprehensive. Such important items as prescription drugs outside the hospital context, dentistry, and long-term care were not covered; these areas follow a liberal model with a complex mix of private plans and public programs for the elderly and the poor. Nevertheless, in core elements of the health care system, social-democratic principles predominate.

In short, the Canadian social model became a hybrid – essentially liberal but modified by social-democratic elements in health care.

The New Politics of Redistribution

Major turning points in history rarely announce themselves as such. In retrospect, it is clear that the politics that built the postwar welfare state were transformed in the last two decades of the twentieth century. The 1980s represented a transitional decade in Canadian social policy. In programmatic terms, the welfare state actually grew stronger. Parliament unanimously approved the Canada Health Act, 1984, reinforcing the universal model and strengthening the prohibition of financial charges at the point of service. In 1985, the federal Progressive Conservative government extended the Spouse's Allowance incrementally to all low-income widows and widowers aged 60 to 64. In some provinces, especially Ontario, social assistance benefit levels were raised sharply, and caseloads jumped. Both levels of government, struggling to reduce growing deficits, introduced surtaxes for high-income earners. As we shall see, the redistributive impact of the tax-transfer system actually strengthened over the decade.

However, the 1980s also saw growing pressures for a new politics of social policy. In the US and the UK, the election of the governments of Ronald Reagan and Margaret Thatcher, respectively, shifted political discourse dramatically. In typically Canadian fashion, this country's transition was more evolutionary. Over the course of the decade, conservative ideological challenges to the welfare state, fiscal pressures facing both levels of government, and regional challenges to the federal role in social policy all grew stronger. Explicit policy moves in these directions were largely repulsed in the 1980s, as John Myles's chapter on pensions indicates. Nevertheless, a new politics was emerging, and burst into full force in the 1990s, as federal and provincial governments retrenched and restructured. To understand these transitions, we start with comparative insights into the politics of retrenchment and then turn to Canada and the findings of our authors.

Comparative Perspectives

There is striking variation in the extent to which the redistributive role of the state has weakened in contemporary democracies, and much research has been directed to understanding this variation. Most discussions of the restructuring of the welfare state start with the impact of global economic changes. Initially, many analysts were convinced that globalization and technological change were eroding the foundations of the welfare state, forcing governments of both the left and the right to give priority to economic competitiveness, low levels of taxation, and a flexible labour force (Rhodes 1996; Strange 1996). The result, it was thought, would be a "race to the bottom" in which generous welfare states would be forced to adopt market-friendly social programs. Another school of thought, following Polanyi (1944), countered that globalization would trigger an expansion of the welfare state, especially in more open economies, as governments sought to protect their publics from the volatility inherent in the global economy (Cameron 1978; Katzenstein 1985; Garret 1998). But the dominant view was that globalization was weakening the welfare state. After several decades of further research, the evidence points to a more nuanced interpretation. Most analysts agree that large government debts create real vulnerability to global financial pressures, irrespective of the governments in power, as is illustrated by the fiscal crises that racked Canada in the 1990s and the European Union more recently. Beyond the vulnerability of large debts, however, comparative studies tend to conclude that, on average, the effects of trade openness and capital mobility are relatively weak. But they also find that the impact varies considerably and that domestic politics matters a lot when it comes to how different countries respond (Swank 2010, 2002; Brady, Beckfield, and Seeleib-Kaiser 2005; Busemeyer 2009; Huber and Stephens 2001).

A second common starting point in discussions of restructuring is ideological or ideational change. As Jenson argues in her chapter, "the way in which political actors interpret problems and identify solutions is important" (see also Heclo 1974; Béland 2009; Prince 2001). Recent decades have seen several changes in prevailing ideological currents. The 1980s and 1990s saw a return to classical liberal ideas about the relation between state and economy – a return usually identified as "neoliberalism" (McBride 1992).

Neoliberalism holds that countries with high minimum wages, generous social benefits, and "rigid" labour market institutions fare poorly in the global economy; and the neoliberal prescription calls for reducing income transfers such as unemployment insurance and social assistance and making labour markets more flexible. This strategy was advocated by international agencies such as the OECD, whose 1994 Jobs Study framed the social policy debate in democratic countries over the decade (OECD 1994; Mahon and McBride 2008). However, these ideas did not go uncontested. As Mahon (2008) argues, "liberalism" has always come in a variety of forms. Classical liberalism, with its emphasis on negative freedoms and a limited state, has had to jostle with currents of social liberalism, which are focused on positive freedoms of opportunity and personal development. In the contemporary period, this social side of liberalism has emphasized a more inclusive strategy of building the "human capital" of the next generation. Jenson's chapter highlights a "social investment" paradigm that emphasizes empowering people to meet the challenges of technological change and globalization by investing in early childhood education, life-long learning, and "helping parents to parent." Since the 1990s, these ideas have spread internationally (Esping-Andersen et al. 2002; Huo 2009; Morel, Palier, and Palme 2012). As in the case of economic pressures, however, the impact of new ideological currents is filtered through domestic politics. New ideas must be injected into policy debates by powerful political advocates; and the extent to which those ideas are implemented depends on domestic political battles (Hall 1993; Blyth 2002). As a result, the imprint of both neoliberalism and the social investment paradigm varies considerably from country to country.

What are the domestic factors that condition the impact of globalization and neoliberalism? There is intense debate about whether strong labour unions and left parties remain central. Analysts in the power resource tradition insist that the strength of left political parties largely explains why some countries have retrenched more than others (Brady 2009; Korpi and Palme 2003; Allan and Scruggs 2004). But others disagree. Most prominently, Paul Pierson (1994, 1996) argues that power resource theory cannot explain the relative durability of the welfare state in the 1980s. In the US and the UK, the Reagan and Thatcher governments attempted to reduce the welfare state at a time when organized labour was in retreat and the parties of the left were in disarray. In the end, they had limited impact on their respective welfare states because, according to Pierson, mature welfare states have sources of support well beyond those of left parties and unions.

Cutbacks to programs that benefit large parts of the population, such as pensions and health care, are unpopular with the electorate, and well-organized groups, representing both the providers and the beneficiaries of social services, patrol the boundaries of the welfare state. Changing social programs can impose high political costs on governments, and direct assaults are often defeated.

The structure of political institutions also filters the impact of globalization and neoliberalism. Cross-national studies suggest that resistance to retrenchment has been strongest in countries with corporatist institutions, common in Europe. In these systems, both business and organized labour are represented by strong national organizations, and are seen by the government as "social partners" who are directly involved in policy development and the management of social protection programs. In effect, such institutions build the direct representation of economic interest into the policy process and make it more difficult for governments to ignore organized labour (Huber and Stephens 2001). Other studies highlight the importance of other political institutions. Comparative evidence suggests that the electoral system matters a lot and that first-past-the-post electoral systems give less voice to low-income groups than do electoral systems based on proportional representation. Proportional systems allow the representation of more parties and more interests, and tend to facilitate alliances between those representing middle-class voters and those representing working-class voters with an interest in redistribution (Iverson and Soskice 2006; van Kersbergen and Manow 2009). In addition, constitutional structures that generate multiple "veto points" privilege interests that wish to block government intervention in health and social policy (Lijphart 1999; Immergut 1992, 2010). Federal institutions can create such veto points, and cross-national studies conclude that federalism constrains social spending, especially if both taxation and spending are highly decentralized (Rodden 2003). Finally, the form of the welfare state itself seems to matter: universal welfare states seem more resistant to retrenchment politics than do liberal welfare states (Rothstein 1998).

Sorting out the relative impact of each of these institutional factors is difficult. But their cumulative weight is clear. Countries characterized by corporatism, centralized government institutions, and universal welfare states have resisted retrenchment pressures more successfully than have other countries. Retrenchment has been more common in countries with pluralist rather than corporatist politics, majoritarian rather than proportional electoral systems, decentralized political institutions, and liberal welfare programs (Swank 2002, 2010; Beramendi and Anderson 2008; Brady, Beckfield, and Seeleib-Kaiser 2005; Huber and Stephens 2001; Hicks 1999). It is notable that Canada falls in the second group of countries on virtually all of these dimensions. Not surprisingly, the contributors to this volume echo many of the themes in the comparative literature.

The New Politics of Redistribution in Canada

In comparative terms, Canada seems vulnerable to globalization and neoliberalism. The Canadian economy depends heavily on international trade and is among the most open in the OECD. Globalization in the Canadian case has meant deeper integration with the American economy, which absorbed over 80 percent of Canadian exports in the 1990s. The adoption of the 1988 Canada-US Free Trade Agreement and the 1994 North American Free Trade Agreement triggered intense political controversy about whether deeper economic integration would require Canada to adopt the US social model (Banting 1997). Canadian vulnerability was enhanced by heavy debt levels, which comparative experience suggests is critical. Beginning in the late 1970s, governments regularly incurred deficits, and, by the 1990s, the accumulated debt was squeezing budgets at both federal and provincial levels. At the worst point, Canada was among the most indebted of the G7 nations; approximately 35 percent of all federal revenue was pre-empted by interest payments on its debt, and at least one province faced problems placing its bonds in financial markets.

Several of our chapters explore how the combination of globalization and neoliberalism has shaped the politics of Canadian social policy. In their chapter, David Green and James Townsend track the economic turbulence of the 1980s and early 1990s, characterized by high unemployment levels, stagnant wage growth, and a shift towards less stable forms of employment. The problems were pervasive throughout the Western world, but, in these years, the US seemed to fare particularly well (especially after 1990) and Europe particularly poorly. However, the underlying causes of these economic failings were not self-evident, and the key question was how they were interpreted. As Green and Townsend demonstrate, Canadian policy makers reinterpreted the economic world in those years. They fully embraced the interpretation advanced by the OECD, among others, assuming that Canada was living through a skills-biased technological transformation that favoured skilled over unskilled workers. These ideas permeated official Canadian policy discourse in the 1990s, appearing in key government documents, budget statements, and ministerial speeches at both the federal and provincial levels (Jackson 2008). Policy makers also adopted the neoliberal policy agenda implicit in this paradigm, pressing for cuts in "passive" benefits such as unemployment insurance and social assistance, and advocating flexible labour markets and activation programs that encourage movement into the labour force. Green and Townsend argue that this interpretation was actually wrong, a misreading of the ongoing economic transition in Canada and other Western nations. Right or wrong, however, these views profoundly shaped policy strategies in the 1990s, especially in the case of unemployment insurance and social assistance.

The chapter by Robin Boadway and Katherine Cuff also emphasizes the global transmission of policy ideas, especially in reshaping taxation. Elite ideas about tax policy have changed dramatically over the past half century, and taxation has been on "the leading edge of the new political tide" (Steinmo 2003, 217). Before the 1970s, the pervasive assumption was that taxes could and should be an instrument of redistribution and that the anchor of a fair tax system was a comprehensive and progressive system of income taxes, a belief captured in Canada by the mantra that "a dollar is a dollar no matter what its source" (Canada 1966). The 1970s and 1980s saw the erosion of these core beliefs in elite opinion, beginning in the first instance in the US and the UK. New doctrines argued that the tax system should be concerned more with efficiency than with equity; that capital should be taxed at lower rates, if at all; that progressive income taxes have disincentive effects; and that the tax mix should shift from income to consumption taxes. In Boadway and Cuff's view, "the case in favour of limited progressivity has been fairly widely accepted by dominant countries and imitated by others," including Canada. With few exceptions, the overall direction of Canadian tax policy has faithfully reflected these ideas.

As we have seen, in many countries domestic political institutions and processes have limited the impact of globalization and ideological change. However, Canadian politics posed fewer barriers than was the case in many countries. To start, Canada lacks corporatist institutions that have mattered elsewhere. In his chapter on the role of business and labour organizations, Will Coleman tracks how globalization has shifted the balance between economic interests, accentuating close ties between business representatives and government, and marginalizing labour from the policy process. Business associations have used their access to the highest reaches of government to promote market-oriented policies, emphasizing economic competitiveness in the American and global marketplaces, tax reductions, and limits to the social role of the state. Meanwhile, organized labour has been weakened by declining membership, especially in the private sector.[1] Old links with government departments such as the Department of Labour have been disrupted by the restructuring of government bureaucracies and the shift of power over social policy to the Department of Finance. Lacking close links to government, labour leaders have had to advocate greater social equality from the outside.

Civil society organizations have also weakened. Susan Phillips's chapter traces the rise and fall of civil society organizations (CSOs), including women's organizations, voluntary associations, welfare rights groups, and other social movements. During the 1960s and 1970s, they carved out a visible presence in the politics of social policy. However, they were never mass membership organizations; they found it hard to mobilize the individuals on whose behalf they spoke; and they could not sustain themselves based on membership dues. Instead, their growth and viability depended on financial support from the federal government. As the politics of restraint took hold in the late 1980s, social policy groups increasingly moved into oppositional politics, and the federal government responded by cutting their funding, destabilizing and dooming many. In Phillips's view, internal divisions also weakened the sector. The growth of identity politics rooted in language, gender, class, and race fuelled internal tensions within important organizations such as the women's movement; another schism developed between advocacy groups and service-providing organizations seeking closer links with government. Slowly but surely, equality-seeking CSOs faded from federal politics, weakening the support for redistributive initiatives.

This pattern has been reinforced by the decline in the vigorous network of government advisory bodies, research institutes, and think tanks that once populated the sector. The list of victims that have been decisively weakened or closed completely after cuts by the federal government includes the National Council of Welfare, the Canadian Council on Social Development, Canadian Policy Research Networks, the National Aboriginal Health Organization, and Rights and Democracy. The availability of quality data on social issues, the primary resource of equality-seeking groups, has also been compromised by cuts to Statistics Canada and the elimination of the mandatory long-form census. The resulting impoverishment of social policy analysis sucks the oxygen out of the social policy advocacy community.

The weakening of organizations speaking on behalf of the economic interests of lower-income groups is compounded by their own political passivity. Lower-income Canadians are less likely to turn out to vote or join either a political party or an interest group (Gidengil et al. 2004). Historically, the poor and disenfranchised made their voice heard through protests and demonstrations, but protest politics today is now largely the preserve of those who are comfortably well off: "In Canada, as in other advanced industrial democracies, the affluent and the highly educated are the most likely to sign petitions, join in boycotts, and attend lawful demonstrations, just as they are more likely to vote, to become members of political parties, and to join interest groups. They have voice, and those with voice are more likely to be heard" (ibid., 153).

What of public opinion more generally? In their chapter, Robert Andersen and Josh Curtis show that support for redistribution policy closely tracks national economic trends. When times are good, Canadians are more supportive of income redistribution than they are when times are bad. During the 1990s, as the recession took hold, opinion polls recorded more resistance to social benefits and greater support for tax cuts. But this pattern peaked in the mid-1990s and faded as the economy grew and public finances returned to surplus. By 2000, public support for social programs had returned to historic levels. Andersen and Curtis find no evidence of a long-term trend in public opinion supporting reductions in redistribution.

The chapter written by Keith Banting, Stuart Soroka, and Edward Koning drills down into one specific aspect of public opinion, examining the impact of growing ethnic diversity on public attitudes towards redistribution. In the US and Europe, many commentators fear that ethnic and racial diversity is eroding the sense of community, weakening feelings of trust in fellow citizens, and fragmenting the historic coalitions that built the welfare state. They fear that members of the majority public might withdraw support from social programs that give money to "outsiders" who are not part of "us" (Gilens 1999; Alesina and Glaesar 2004). Banting, Soroka, and Koning dig into Canadians' views of minority use of welfare and find that immigration is not eroding support for redistribution in this country (see also Banting 2010; Banting et al. 2010). But their chapter also documents a darker side to Canadian attitudes. Respondents who believe Aboriginal peoples are heavily dependent on welfare tend to reduce their support not only for social assistance itself but also for the redistributive state as a whole. This reaction is strongest in western Canada, where support for social assistance is lowest.

Shifts in organized politics and public attitudes have been amplified by changes in core political institutions such as the party system and the bureaucracy. As Johnston's chapter highlights, the Canadian party system shifted to the right in the 1990s, and party manifestos reflected an anti-welfare bias. Moreover, the Liberal government, elected in 1993, enjoyed unparalleled electoral freedom. Its historic enemy, the Progressive Conservative Party, was broken in two, while the social-democratic NDP fell to its lowest level of political support in a generation, barely surviving as an officially recognized political party. The gap in seats between the government and the Official Opposition was wider than at any time in Canadian history, a condition that Johnston, following Pierson, calls "electoral slack." Although freed from tight electoral constraints, the Liberals were under intense fiscal pressure resulting from cumulative debt levels. In response, the Liberals cut deeply into programs they had introduced during the postwar era. A similar process unfolded in many provinces.

A new bureaucratic politics also weakened the politics of redistribution. Traditionally, according to the chapter by David Good, redistributive policy making comprised three players: (1) the "advocates," the ministers and senior officials in social departments such as National Health and Welfare and its successor, Human Resources and Skills Development Canada; (2) the "restrainers," the minister and officials in the Department of Finance; and (3) the "gatekeepers" in the Prime Minister's Office (PMO) and the Privy Council Office (PCO), who kept track of priorities. This pattern of bureaucratic politics has been replaced by a centralized and politicized process. Line ministers and departments who were policy advocates and policy developers in the postwar era are now primarily delivery agents. Today, not only does the Department of Finance set fiscal parameters for program initiatives, but it has also become the undisputed policy designer. The PCO and, especially, the PMO, once the gatekeepers of priorities, are now mostly political communicators, shaping priorities through the lens of political strategy and messaging. This transformation has powerful implications. Inside government, redistributive policies are driven by fiscal and tax policy considerations, not by program departments and their constituencies, which led developments in the postwar era. As a result, redistributive policy making now focuses more on adapting past programs and less on responding to new needs (also Hale 2002).

The changing roles of business, labour, CSOs, political parties, and bureaucracies have parallels in many countries, but the distinctively Canadian *territorial* politics also shifted in this era. During the postwar years, the federal government saw national social programs as one of few instruments available to knit together a country divided by linguistic and regional conflicts. During recent decades, this tradition has been challenged by

Quebec nationalism and the rise to power of the sovereigntist Parti québécois. Regional economic conflicts also deepened when the energy crisis of the 1970s and free trade in the 1980s pitted region against region. In response to these pressures, the federation has become more decentralized, and the federal government's ability to steer provincial programs has been reduced. In addition, Quebec has carved out an increasingly asymmetrical place in the federation, expanding its autonomy in social policy beyond that of other provinces. In the field of social policy, Canada is now one of the most decentralized welfare states in the OECD (Obinger, Liebfried, and Castles 2005, Table 1.6). It is particularly decentralized in fiscal terms, with federal transfers representing a comparatively small portion of provincial revenues, which, as we saw above, is precisely the pattern that comparative evidence suggests most dampens spending (Rodden 2003).

Several chapters ask whether decentralization and asymmetry have changed redistributive politics in Canada. Gerard Boychuk argues that, at the federal level, the imperatives of territorial politics remain vigorous. In his view, the federal government still wishes to touch the lives of individuals and families through its social programs. In the mid-1990s, the federal government cut unemployment benefits and terminated the Canada Assistance Plan, but it also expanded benefits for a bigger constituency as its fiscal position improved. The National Child Benefit, in particular, expanded benefits for a larger number of families, including not just the poor but also lower-middle-income families.

Nevertheless, decentralization has decisively shifted much of the action to provincial politics and has accentuated regional variation in social programs. Quebec has seized the opportunity to build a stronger model of social protection, as the chapter by Alain Noël demonstrates (see also Béland and Lecours 2008). While support for redistributive policies was weakening elsewhere, Quebec introduced a family policy that included universal childcare, active labour market policies, and a strategy against poverty and social exclusion. These changes increased redistribution and helped Quebec defy the country-wide trend towards greater inequality (see also Fortin 2010). The distinctive politics of Quebec lay behind the growing divide. In the middle of the 1990s, Quebec still had a strongly organized society, with powerful trade unions, a solid women's movement, and a dense network of social and community organizations. As a result, the political dynamic resembled the politics of welfare state reform in many European countries, where governments seeking to reform their welfare states built coalitions among historic social partners (Häusermann 2010). In 1996 and

1997, the Quebec government and its social partners built such a reform coalition around innovations in public finance, employment, and family policies, including childcare. Quebec represents the road not taken by the rest of Canada. It also demonstrates that social policy is not driven exclusively by impersonal economic forces and that politics matters to our social future.

The distinctiveness of Quebec is underscored by Mahon's chapter on childcare in Ontario. In comparison with Quebec's universal approach to the issue, expansion in Ontario has been limited. Without the coalitional politics that exist in Quebec, policy has been more sensitive to shifts in party politics, with the Conservative government, elected in 2006, reversing the efforts of previous Liberal and NDP governments. In addition, progress has been slowed by the tendency of childcare activists and politicians in the province to play multi-level politics, seeking pan-Canadian solutions and funding for childcare. Waiting for the magic combination of sympathetic governments at both federal and provincial levels has delayed action and repeatedly dashed activists' hopes. Signs that Ontario is going its own way in early childhood development, discussed more fully below, point to an escape from the complexities of federalism.

Finally, Haddow's chapter also highlights the extent of regional variation in redistribution. He concludes that the difference between Canada's most and least redistributive provinces is strikingly large. Consistent with the power resources approach, his analysis shows that, over the past fifteen years, the redistributive impact of taxes and transfers has been higher in provinces with greater union density and more left-party governments. Provinces dominated by conservative parties have moved in the opposite direction.

What, then, is the cumulative impact of decentralization on redistribution in Canada? Optimists point to the Quebec experience as a path for other provinces. However, Haddow finds little evidence of convergence in provincial redistributive regimes. Pessimists fear that Quebec's distinctive language and culture give it greater flexibility in taxation, that other provinces are much more constrained by tax competition among each other, and that the imposition of a cap on growth in the equalization program, which supports have-not provinces, will weaken the scope for innovation in poorer regions. As we see below, redistribution has declined more at the provincial level than at the federal level; and, in their chapter, Boadway and Cuff conclude that decentralization and inter-regional competition are part of the explanation for the overall decline in redistribution in Canada.

In summary, a powerful confluence of changes has reshaped the politics of redistribution. As noted at the outset, no single factor represents a smoking gun, but the various changes have coalesced into two broad trends. First, the organized politics of social policy has been transformed. The displacement of organized labour, the decline of equality-seeking social movements and CSOs, and the crippling of advisory bodies and think tanks have weakened the traditional advocates of the economic interests of less affluent Canadians. This fading attention in public discourse, coupled with the lower propensity of the poor to vote, has reduced the incentives of political parties to worry about the less affluent compared to the highly attentive and vociferous middle-class and more affluent voters. Second, these shifts in organized politics have been reinforced by shifts in the distribution of power within our political institutions that further raise the barriers to concerted action against inequality. Within governments, power has shifted from social policy departments to departments of finance; between governments, power has shifted from the federal to the provincial level. In combination, these changes have weakened the politics of redistribution in Canada.

Restructuring the Model: System Maintenance, Policy Change, and Policy Drift

New politics generate new policies. The Canadian social model has been reshaped through system maintenance, policy change, and policy drift. Once again insights from comparative research help put Canadian experience in perspective.

Comparative Perspectives

The new institutionalist literature provides several distinctive interpretations of *how* welfare states change. Early contributions highlight the importance of path dependency and the resilience of policy structures, even "a 'frozen' welfare state landscape" (Esping-Andersen 1996, 24). In these interpretations, the past weighs heavily on the present. Over time, Pierson and others argue, social programs become progressively more "locked-in" as past commitments and program design narrow the options for the future. Pensions represent a classic example, as governments must manage commitments promised by their predecessors as much as forty years ago (Myles and Pierson 2001). From our perspective, it is important to note that such stability can require positive action and the injection of substantial resources, a pattern we describe as *system maintenance*.

By the 2000s, it became clear that welfare states were not frozen but, rather, were evolving, and two theoretical approaches have emerged to explain this process of *policy change*. One interpretation sees a process of "punctuated equilibrium," in which a pattern of long continuity suddenly gives way to a sharp burst of radical change, which, in turn, locks in a new trajectory that persists for a long time. In Pempel's (1998, 3) words, "path-dependent equilibrium is periodically ruptured by radical change, making for sudden bends in the path of history" (see also Tuohy 1999). A second interpretation anticipates a more evolutionary process. This approach assumes that policies and institutions are the subject of ongoing political contestation and that they evolve incrementally through a long succession of reforms (Palier 2010; Thelen 2004; Streeck and Thelen 2005; Mahoney and Thelen 2010). In this interpretation, governments employ strategies of "blame avoidance" (Weaver 1986), or what has been dubbed in Canada "the politics of stealth" (Battle 2001), adopting changes that are less visible to the public and are phased in slowly. Governments also seek to protect themselves by negotiating packages with opposition parties and/or associations representing labour and business (Myles and Pierson 2001). Because of the consensus-building process associated with such bipartisan agreements, dramatic change is unlikely. Moreover, such packages often combine cuts in old programs with innovations in new fields, such as child and elder care, to win support from emerging constituencies for reform (Häusermann 2010).

Finally, the historical record also contains considerable *policy drift*. As noted at the outset, Hacker (2004) argues that program effectiveness can fade through processes of drift. Drift occurs when policy makers choose not to reinforce programs with new resources, as in system maintenance, or to update them in response to changing external circumstances. Failing to increase benefit levels to reflect inflation or overall wage growth is the simplest form of drift. But failing to respond to emerging social problems and new social risks is also powerful. The danger is that social programs "mirror a society that no longer obtains" (Esping-Andersen 1996, 5). Deliberate inaction and neglect in the face of social change is a way of slowly marginalizing the welfare state.

Restructuring the Policy Model in Canada

The shifting political dynamics in Canada has led to a complex mix of system maintenance, policy change, and policy drift. While system maintenance has helped preserve universal programs, policy change and policy drift have weakened the redistributive role of governments. Both action and inaction have mattered.

System Maintenance

System maintenance characterizes two core programs that benefit both the middle class and the poor – health care and pensions. As the chapter by Carolyn Tuohy shows, neoliberal politics have not made much of a dent in the core health care model. The single-payer system of universal insurance for hospital and physician services enjoys iconic status in the Canadian psyche, and elected leaders trifle with it at their peril. Health care did come under serious pressure during the 1990s. Costs in the sector were growing faster than the general rate of inflation; and federal transfers to provincial programs were cut in 1995, exacerbating the restraint already under way at the provincial level. By the late 1990s, newspaper reports described the closing of hospital wards, the slower acquisition of new technologies, declining staffing levels, long waiting times for non-emergency surgical procedures, and crowded emergency departments. Polls suggested that Canadian faith in health care had fallen more rapidly than in other Western nations. Governments quickly responded: retrenchment was superseded by a "catch-up" phase of dramatic reinvestment in the 2000s. Health care rose from 13.3 to 17.8 percent of government spending between 1995 and 2007. In 2004, an "Accord" between Ottawa and the provinces guaranteed annual increases of 6 percent in federal health transfers until 2014; and, in 2012, the federal government announced an extension until 2024, although with a less generous formula governing increases after the third year.

The politics of system maintenance was equally marked in pensions. As John Myles shows in his chapter, attempts to cut old-age benefits were unsuccessful in the 1980s and 1990s. In 1985, the Progressive Conservatives proposed partial de-indexation of OAS but backed down quickly in the face of angry elderly voters. A decade later, the Liberal government proposed replacing OAS and the GIS with an integrated income-tested seniors' benefit, but it also abandoned the idea under withering political fire. In March 2012, the Harper government launched a new effort to cut future spending on OAS and the GIS by proposing to increase the age of eligibility for benefits from sixty-five to sixty-seven. But in a classic case of blame mitigation, the government plans to phase in the increases between 2023 and 2029 (Canada 2012, 197). If these changes are not reversed by a subsequent government, they will represent the first significant retrenchment in the pension sector.

In the case of contributory pensions, significant effort in the 1990s was devoted to stabilizing the C/QPP. A federal-provincial review was launched in 1996 in response to actuarial reports questioning the long-term financial status of the program. From the outset, however, negotiations focused on a narrow range of options; the governments did not even try for dramatic retrenchment. The electoral sensitivity of pensions was undoubtedly important, but federal-provincial decision making also led to a consensus-driven, incremental politics. The Province of Quebec announced that it would not consider significant reductions in benefits, a position supported by NDP governments in Saskatchewan and British Columbia. In the end, the federal and provincial governments agreed to accelerate increases in contribution rates from 5.5 percent to 9.9 percent of earnings over a ten-year period. There was a modest trimming of some benefits, and the two NDP governments refused to sign the final agreement. But the final changes largely stabilized the role of contributory pensions in the retirement income system through a major steady injection of new resources.

Policy Change
In comparison with the tender treatment of programs critical to the middle class, benefits for the unemployed and other vulnerable Canadians experienced deep cuts. The Canadian response here reflects a combination of "punctuated equilibrium" followed by incremental change. The "sudden bend in the path of history" – to borrow Pempel's words – came in the mid-1990s, with cuts falling most sharply on unemployment benefits and social assistance. Unemployment benefit levels were reduced and more restrictive eligibility requirements contributed to the decline in the proportion of the unemployed actually receiving benefits; in the late 1980s, over 80 percent of unemployed Canadians were in receipt of unemployment benefits; by the late 1990s, the number had dropped to 40 percent. Part of the drop reflected changes in the labour market, such as the growth of contract workers who are not covered by Employment Insurance (a clear case of policy drift). But a significant part resulted from formal changes in the program. The impact did vary by region as the cuts generated intense opposition in eastern Canada. As a result, the proportion of the unemployed receiving benefits in Atlantic Canada remained relatively high but plummeted to approximately 30 percent in Ontario and British Columbia in the early 2000s (Battle, Mendelson, and Torman 2006).

Social assistance programs underwent similar cuts. In 1990, the federal Progressive Conservative government imposed a cap on the Canada Assistance Plan (CAP) for the three richest provinces, limiting growth in the federal contribution for social assistance to 5 percent a year. In 1995, the Liberal government abolished CAP altogether, shifting its funding to a new block grant and dramatically cutting the funds being transferred. The federal government also took the opportunity to eliminate most of the conditions attached to its funding for social assistance, and provinces used the new flexibility. The intensity of retrenchment varied across the country, with the steepest reductions made in Ontario, when the Progressive Conservative government cut benefits by 20 percent in 1996. Nevertheless, the direction of change was consistent across the country (Kneebone and White 2008). The real value of benefits fell by large amounts. Caseloads dropped dramatically as eligibility conditions were tightened and beneficiaries came under increasing pressure to participate in employability programs and to move into employment.

At the federal level, the impact of retrenchment was partially mitigated by investment in other transfer programs. As federal finances came back into balance in the late 1990s, the federal government increased the Canada Child Tax Benefit, an income-tested payment delivered each month to all low- and middle-income families. The goal was to "make work pay" by narrowing the gap between the income of families on welfare and those living on wages from low-paid jobs. In the case of welfare families, the federal government urged provinces to offset the increase by reducing the child component of their social assistance benefits by the same amount and to reinvest the savings in child-related services, such as childcare. In this way, social assistance recipients would not lose all their child-related benefits when moving into low-paid work, and low-wage workers with children would have less financial incentive to leave work for welfare.

The period of deep and rapid retrenchment lasted only until the late 1990s. Thereafter, Canada's public finances moved into surplus, public resistance to social spending softened, and the electoral slack of the mid-1990s declined as federal politics once again became competitive. In the 2000s, Canada shifted into a period of incremental change along the trajectories established in the 1990s (Prince 2002). Even the sharp recession that began in 2008 did not shift the country onto a new path. The federal Conservative government extended unemployment benefits for an additional five weeks and increased retraining and work-sharing. But these initiatives were carefully designed to be temporary, lapsing within two years. After winning a majority government in 2012, the Conservatives returned to incremental retrenchment, introducing more stringent requirements relating to the nature of alternative employment that Employment Insurance (EI) recipients would be required to accept (Banting 2012, 27-28).

Finally, taxation policy has also evolved dramatically (for an overview, see Kerr, McKenzie, and Mintz 2012). As Boadway and Cuff note in their chapter, the income tax system became considerably less progressive in this period. In the case of income taxes, the surtaxes on higher-income individuals were steadily reduced, and the top marginal rate of combined federal and provincial taxes fell from 80 percent in 1971 to 51 percent in 1987 to 43 percent in 2009 (Treff and Ort 2010; Fortin et al. 2012). Once again the most dramatic changes came between 1995 and 2000, especially at the provincial level. Ontario reduced its provincial income tax rate by over 30 percent, but it was not unique; every province lowered its rates in these years, and Alberta eventually adopted a flat tax (Frenette, Green, and Milligan 2009). Since coming to power in 2006, the federal Conservatives have continued to give priority to tax cuts. They enhanced the sheltering of capital income and reduced federal corporate tax rates from 19.5 percent in 2008 to 15 percent by 2012, urging provincial governments to do the same (Treff and Ort 2009, 4.3). In addition, the federal government cut the Goods and Services Tax. While the GST was never a progressive tax, the reductions further reduced the fiscal capacity of the federal government to support social programs.[2] Overall, the role of the tax system for reducing inequality has been muted over most of the income range. When combined with changes in transfers, which they also survey, Boadway and Cuff conclude that "redistribution policy has become, if anything, less redistributive," and for "the neediest persons ... redistributive policy has become particularly harsh."

Policy Drift
Finally, the Canadian welfare state has been weakened by the failure to respond to emerging social problems, new social risks, and new policy ideas. At the simplest level, many provinces allowed social assistance to decline by not adjusting benefit levels for inflation for almost a decade between the mid-1990s and the mid-2000s (National Council of Welfare 2010). But Canadian governments have also shown limited taste for serious policy innovation in the 2000s, and the resulting drift is clear on both the old and the new frontiers of the welfare state.

Drift on old frontiers can be seen in the limited response to growing social risks on the margins of the core programs in health care and pensions. In the case of health care, technology and population aging are enhancing the risks not covered by the universal, single-payer program. Technological developments have enhanced the importance of pharmaceuticals in the health consumption patterns of Canadians. Except for those in hospital, however, pharmaceuticals are not covered by the universal program. Population aging has also driven up demand for both home care and long-term institutional care services, which are also not included in the single-payer model. Responses across the provinces to these technological and demographic shifts have varied. In the case of pharmaceuticals, for example, Quebec introduced universal "pharmacare" in 1996, but elsewhere governments moved selectively. In Ontario, for example, government took responsibility for covering "catastrophic" drug care costs in addition to its established programs for seniors and social assistance recipients; and several western provinces moved from age-based to income-based drug coverage. However, as Tuohy shows, these programs have not been sufficient to fully offset the "passive privatization" of health care at the margins.

Drift has also characterized old frontiers in pension policy. During the 2000s, attention shifted from the core public programs to workplace pensions (Registered Pension Plans [RPPs]) and individual retirement accounts (Registered Retirement Savings Plans [RRSPs]). As Myles points out, the concern here was not about today's seniors but those of the future. Workplace pensions have been in decline, especially among younger workers; risk has been shifted from employers to workers; and administrative costs for these private retirement vehicles are high. As a result, there is a real danger that many of today's middle-income earners will not be adequately protected when they retire. Four provincial reports and a federal-provincial summit put a number of innovative proposals on the table, and a proposal to expand the C/QPP was widely discussed. At the end of the day, however, bold action fizzled. The federal government introduced a modest proposal for a pooled retirement savings plan, a strategy about which many observers are sceptical.

The new frontiers of social policy have also seen drift, as Mahon's chapter highlights. Social change is exposing young families to new risks and pressures. The "old politics" of the postwar welfare state were focused on the male-headed, single wage-earner family model. At that time, families faced economic catastrophe if "dad" was unemployed, disabled, or faced with retirement. The gender revolution in women's education and employment has changed the risk structure facing individuals and families (Esping-Andersen and Myles 2009; Goldin 2006). In our education-driven economy, young adults – who bear the responsibilities for young children – begin their work careers much later. The relative earnings and accumulated assets of these young adults have also fallen sharply since 1980, placing new pressures on efforts to contain or reduce child poverty. Access to a middle-class lifestyle now depends on the dual wage-earner family, generating additional pressures for childcare, income support for single-earner households (especially single mothers), and policies to help reconcile work and family life. In all of these areas, the response of Canadian governments, outside of Quebec, has been tepid.

Nor have Canadian governments embraced new ideas in bold ways. As Jenson's chapter demonstrates, their response to the new social investment paradigm has disappointed its advocates. The federal Liberal government adopted the language of social investment in the late 1990s and early 2000s (Jenson and Saint Martin 2003, 2006), but concrete action was limited. Jenson sees the National Child Benefits and the Working Income Tax Benefit as expressions of the social investment approach. But investment in learning and early childhood development falls largely within provincial jurisdiction, and the federal government has little influence. Federal initiatives to promote early learning and childcare in 2000 and 2003 were short-term efforts with diffuse effects. A major effort in 2005 to establish a pan-Canadian childcare system through federal-provincial agreements did not survive the change in government in 2006. The incoming Conservative government cancelled the shared-cost agreements, replacing them with a small universal payment sent directly to all parents with young children (Prince and Teghtsoonian 2007). Since then, action has depended on provincial initiatives. Quebec established its universal childcare, and Ontario announced the phasing-in of all-day kindergarten. Nevertheless, these initiatives remain modest in international terms. In the euphemistic words of an OECD review team, outside Quebec, Canadian policy on early childhood education remains "in its initial stages" (OECD 2004, 6). In a 2008 report by UNICEF (2008) on childhood development, Canada tied with Ireland for last place among twenty-five economically advanced countries. More generally, OECD analysis of spending patterns actually suggests that Canadian public spending on education as a whole has declined significantly since 1980 (Nikolai 2012).

Finally, and most generally, Canadian governments have failed to respond to the evidence of growing inequality in Canada. As Good's chapter argues, governments seldom focus on inequality as such; in his words, no single institution in government is responsible "for monitoring and managing the Gini coefficient." But governments make decisions every day that alter the distribution of advantage and disadvantage in society. They can launch new initiatives to combat poverty and unequal life chances or they can chose to ignore the issues. In these matters, Canadian governments – again with the exception of Quebec – have been passive, taking only timid steps to help the disadvantaged and ignoring the broader dimensions of the new inequality.

In combination, system maintenance, policy change, and policy drift have redefined the aspirations of Canadian governments, with retrenchment and drift in particular weakening the redistributive role of the state. It is now time to examine the impacts on redistribution in detail.

The Fading Redistributive Impact: Inequality and Poverty

After four decades of relative stability, income inequality in Canada surged upward in the latter half of the 1990s. Between the mid-1990s and the mid-2000s, inequality increased more in Canada than in other OECD countries, and the redistributive impact of the tax-transfer system in Canada declined (OECD 2008, fig. 4.7). As we saw at the outset, by the mid-2000s, the redistributive impact of Canadian taxes and transfers was among the smallest among OECD countries (OECD 2011, 271).

The big surge in *market* income inequality began during the recession of the early 1980s and continued until the end of the 1990s. Rising market inequality reflects several distinct but powerful trends. Most attention has focused on the stunning rise in the proportion of income captured by the top 1 percent of income-earners, reflecting changing norms about compensation for the highly paid (Saez and Veal 2005; Fortin et al. 2012). The share of income captured by the top 1 percent is now approaching the levels reached in the "Gilded Age" of the 1920s and the Great Depression of the 1930s, generating an intense debate about the division between the rich and the rest, which was highlighted by the Occupy Movement in 2011. However, other trends have also mattered. One is the loss of solid middle-income jobs as a result of a combination of technological change, outsourcing, and declining unionization. According to one analysis, "the young and the poorly educated have borne the brunt of these forces, but significant numbers of those previously in the middle and lower middle of the occupational skill and wage distribution have also been adversely affected" (Fortin at al. 2012, 133). Finally, social changes have been important. Women and men increasingly choose spouses with similar educational levels, a process known as marital homogamy, or educational assortative mating. This trend tends to increase family income inequality as high-income earners increasingly marry each other and lower-income earners do likewise. Figure 1.1 captures the impact of these wider trends, demonstrating the strong rise in the real

FIGURE 1.1

Family market incomes by percentile, all persons, 1976-2004

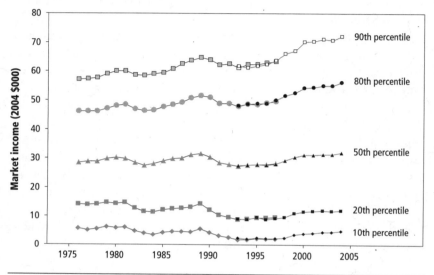

Note: The series shown in the graph combines results from the Survey of Consumer Finance for 1978-97 (when the survey was terminated) and the Survey of Labour and Income Dynamics (1993-2004) that replaced it. Hence, two data observations are charted for the period of overlap (1993-97). The results indicate that the change in design had little impact.
Source: Heisz (2007, Figure 13.1).

income of families at the 80th and 90th percentile, compared to the stagnation in the incomes of families in the middle and lower levels of the income distribution.

The fading redistributive impact of the tax-transfers system can be seen in Figure 1.2. The top line shows the long-term increase in inequality in the market income of families from 1976 to 2010. The redistributive impact of government is captured in the bottom line, which tracks disposable income (after transfers and taxes). Note the relative stability of inequality in disposable income through 1995, when the Gini coefficient for disposable income (.293) had scarcely changed from its 1979 level (.286). After 1995, however, inequality in disposable income rose over the remainder of the decade.

While the drivers of growing inequality have reshaped the distribution of income generally, including in the middle and at the top, the effects have not been concentrated at the bottom, among the poor. Comparative analysis

FIGURE 1.2

Inequality by income type, 1976-2010 (Gini coefficients)

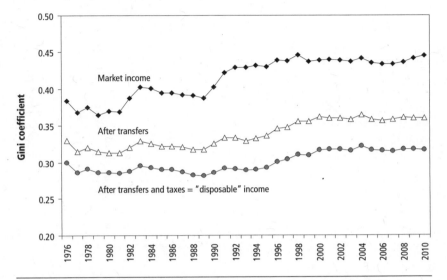

Source: Statistics Canada, Table 202-0709, "Gini coefficients of market, total and after-tax income of individuals," CANSIM (database), http://www.statcan.gc.ca/cansim/home-accueil?lang=eng.

does confirm that, by international standards, Canada is still stuck near the bottom of the pack in combating poverty. Using the standardized estimates of poverty and inequality from the Luxembourg Income Study, Table 1.2 shows that, in the mid-2000s, poverty rates were twice as high in Canada and other Anglo-Saxon countries as they were in Scandinavia and Continental Europe. Child poverty rates were two to four times as high. The main exception is the dramatic decline in poverty rates among Canada's elderly since 1980, Canada's one big success story.

Nevertheless, viewed over time, poverty levels in Canada have not been increasing as inequality has been growing. Of course, much depends on how poverty is measured. Figure 1.3 presents two different patterns in the low-income ("poverty") series published by Statistics Canada. The low-income measure (or LIM) is much like an inequality measure. It is a calculation of the share of population with incomes less than 50 percent of the median for all families and does not register the effect of rising incomes. By this standard, there was little or no change in Canadian poverty rates between the mid-1990s and 2010. The low-income cut-off (or LICO) series, in

TABLE 1.2

Poverty rates, selected OECD countries, 2004 or near date

Country	Poverty rate		
	All	Children	Seniors
Anglo-Saxon countries			
Australia (2003)	12.2	14.0	22.3
Canada (2004)	**13.0**	**16.8**	**6.3**
United Kingdom (2004)	11.6	14.0	16.3
United States (2004)	17.3	21.2	24.6
Mean	*13.5*	*16.5*	*17.4*
Scandinavian countries			
Denmark (2004)	5.6	3.9	8.5
Finland (2004)	6.5	3.7	10.1
Norway (2004)	7.1	4.8	6.3
Sweden (2005)	5.6	4.7	6.6
Mean	*6.2*	*4.3*	*7.9*
Continental Europe			
Austria (2004)	7.1	7.0	9.4
Belgium (2000)	8.1	7.2	15.4
France (2000)	7.3	7.9	8.5
Germany (2004)	8.5	10.7	8.6
Netherlands (1999)	4.9	6.3	1.6
Mean	*7.2*	*7.8*	*8.7*
Southern Europe			
Italy (2004)	12.1	18.4	11.2
Spain (2004)	14.1	17.2	23.4

Source: Luxembourg Income Study (LIS), Key Figures, June 2010.

contrast, uses a "fixed" cut-off (in this case living standards in 1992), and when real incomes at the bottom rise, the poverty rate declines. Although redistributive programs weakened in the 1990s, labour markets and labour market policy took up some of the slack in the following decade. After three decades of virtually no growth, real hourly wages started rising, especially after 2005 (Morissette, Picot, and Lu 2012). At the same time, there were noteworthy increases in the minimum wage in virtually all provinces, with particularly large increases after 2008. Minimum wages declined in real value in the 1980s and 1990s, but by 2010 the national average minimum wage had increased again close to its 1976 peak (Battle 2011), contributing

FIGURE 1.3

Low-income rate, 1976-2010

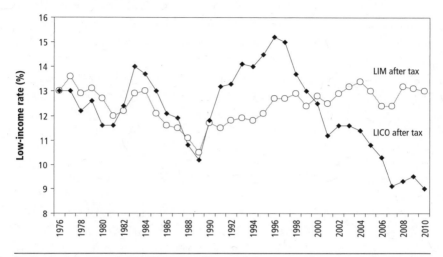

Source: Statistics Canada, Table 202-0804, "Persons in low income, by economic family type, annual," CANSIM (database), http://www.statcan.gc.ca/cansim/home-accueil?lang=eng.

to real wage increases at the lowest end of the distribution (Fortin et al. 2012). Consequently, the LICO fell after 2000. It rose again during the recession that began in late 2008, but it had fallen again to a historic low of 9 percent by 2010. Moreover, both data series reported, for the first time, significant declines in "lone mother" poverty in the 2000s as a result of rising employment and earnings. Thus part of the paradox of the contemporary period has been the combination of rising inequality and stable or declining poverty. We return to these apparently contradictory trends in "poverty" and "inequality" in our conclusion.

What do the data say about the tax-transfer policies that mattered most to the fading redistributive impact of the state? Given the decentralized nature of the federation, the trends were strongly influenced by provincial decisions. Indeed, in their detailed analysis, Frenette and his colleagues conclude that "most of the 'action' in changes in the redistributiveness of tax and transfer systems over this period took place at the provincial level" (Frenette, Green, and Milligan 2009, 408). Rising transfers under social assistance and surtaxes on top-earning families at the provincial level increased redistribution through 1995; but cuts to social assistance and the elimination of surtaxes and reduction of general tax rates reversed the process after 1995.

Several provinces did proclaim anti-poverty initiatives in the 2000s, but, except for Quebec, their effects were not strong enough to offset the larger pattern. Haddow reaches the same conclusion in his chapter. From 2000 to 2007, the *federal* impact on redistribution remained stable; as noted earlier, cuts to EI were offset by the expansion of child benefits. In contrast, the redistributive impact of *provincial* programs, outside Quebec, declined.

What do the data say about the relative importance of policy change, on one hand, and policy drift, on the other? Explicit welfare state "retrenchment" by cutting EI and social assistance and eliminating surtaxes on high-income individuals is part of the story (see Finnie and Irvine 2011; Heisz 2007; Frenette, Green, and Milligan 2009). But it is not the entire story. Frenette, Green and Milligan (2009) show that, even in the absence of cuts, family income inequality would have increased over the decade. *Market income inequality was simply moving too fast for the existing policy framework.* In short, *policy drift* – policy inaction in the face of changing labour markets and family structures – is a major theme in the Canadian story.

We can demonstrate this conclusion by comparing the offsetting effects of taxes and transfers on rising market inequality for the country as a whole with the experience of Quebec, where government took a more proactive role (Table 1.3). Because redistribution tends to increase during recessions, we follow Heisz (2007) and calculate changes in redistribution for three peaks in the business cycle: 1979, 1989, and 2004. The key question is the extent to which the tax-transfer system managed to keep pace with and *offset* the rise in market inequality. The bottom line is that Quebec offset more than 100 percent of the increase in market inequality in the critical period from 1989 to 2004. In Canada as a whole, the figure was 24 percent. Politics and their policy outcomes matter.

Conclusion

The politics of redistribution in Canada have changed in the last twenty years. The organized voices defending the economic interests of lower-middle income groups and poor Canadians have weakened, and power shifts within our political institutions have raised the barriers to concerted action. Changed politics produced policy changes and policy drift, and a weakening of the capacity of the welfare state to narrow growing gaps in income and life chances of Canadians. Big changes in the economy, family structures, and compensation for top earners have driven the growth in market inequality across the OECD region, and welfare states have had to run faster simply to keep the income distribution standing still. In the 1980s, the Canadian

TABLE 1.3

Change in income inequality and redistribution in Canada and Quebec, 1979-2004

	Canada	Quebec
1. Change in family market inequality (Gini coefficent × 100)		
1979-89	2.3	1.7
1989-2004	5.4	4.7
2. Change in family income inequality after transfers and taxes (Gini coefficent × 100)		
1979-89	0.5	2.3
1989-2004	4.1	−0.9
3. Increase in market income inequality offset by redistribution (%)		
1979-89	−122	+35
1989-2004	−24	−119

Source: Calculated by the authors from Statistics Canada, Table 202-0709, "Gini coefficients of market, total and after-tax income of individuals," CANSIM (database), http://www.statcan.gc.ca/cansim/home-accueil?lang=eng.

welfare state did run faster: the increase in the redistributive effect of taxes and transfers more than offset the increase in market inequality in that decade. But, since then, Canadian governments have stopped trying to keep up with rising inequality: between 1989 and 2004, the increase in the redistributive effect of taxes and transfers offset less than a quarter of the increase. Action and inaction – policy change and policy drift – are at the heart of growing inequality in Canada.

The composition of the surge in inequality of the past several decades is new. The rich have gotten richer; the middle has been weakened; but there is little evidence to indicate that the poor have gotten poorer. As noted earlier, recent economic gains have gone disproportionately to the "top," while both the middle and the bottom have been losing ground in relative terms. Egalitarians in Canada have traditionally relied on an anti-poverty discourse and evidence of surges in poverty levels to mobilize supporters. For egalitarians, the upside of the new pattern of inequality is that it provides a material base for new political coalitions between the middle and the bottom, coalitions that have traditionally been absent from redistributive politics in Canada. We pursue this reflection further in the final chapter of this volume.

NOTES

1 The decline in unionization has a double impact on inequality, increasing inequality in market earnings (Fortin et al. 2012, 133) and also weakening a political champion of the redistributive role of the state.
2 Tax revenues have declined as proportion of GDP throughout this period. In 2000, Canadian tax revenues as a proportion of GDP were above the OECD average; by 2010, the Canadian ratio (31.0 percent) had fallen below the OECD average (33.8 percent). See OECD (2012).

REFERENCES

Alesina, Alberto, and Edward Glaeser. 2004. *Fighting Poverty in the US and Europe: A World of Difference.* Oxford: Oxford University Press.

Allen, James, and Lyle Scruggs. 2004. "Political Partisanship and Welfare State Reform in Advanced Industrial Societies." *American Journal of Political Science* 48: 493-512.

Banting, Keith. 1995. "The Welfare State as Statescraft: Territorial Politics and Canadian Social Policy." In Stephan Leibfried and Paul Pierson, eds., *European Social Policy: Between Fragmentation and Integration,* 269-300. Washington, DC: Brookings Institution.

–. 1997. "The Social Policy Divide: The Welfare State in Canada and the United States." In Keith Banting, George Hoberg, and Richard Simeon, eds., *Degrees of Freedom: Canada and the United States in a Changing World,* 267-309. Montreal and Kingston: McGill-Queen's University Press.

–. 2005. "Canada: Nation-Building in a Federal Welfare State." In Herbert Obinger, Stephan Leibfried, and Frank G. Castles, eds., *Federalism and the Welfare State: New World and European Experiences,* 89-137. Cambridge: Cambridge University Press.

–. 2010. "Is There a Progressive's Dilemma in Canada? Immigration, Multiculturalism and the Welfare State." *Canadian Journal of Political Science* 43(4): 797-820.

–. 2012. "Introduction: Debating Employment Insurance." In Keith Banting and Jon Medow, eds., *Making EI Work: Research from the Mowat Centre Employment Insurance Task Force,* 1-34. Montreal and Kingston: McGill-Queen's University Press.

Banting, Keith, Richard Johnston, Will Kymlicka, and Stuart Soroka. 2010. "Are Diversity and Solidarity Incompatible? Canada in Comparative Context." *Inroads: The Canadian Journal of Opinion* 29: 36-48.

Battle, Ken. 2001. "Relentless Incrementalism: Deconstructing and Reconstructing Canadian Income Security Policy." In Keith Banting, Andrew Sharpe, and France St-Hilaire, eds., *The Review of Economic and Social Progress: The Longest Decade – Canada in the 1990s,* 183-229. Montreal: Institute for Research on Public Policy.

–. 2011. *Restoring Minimum Wages in Canada.* Ottawa: Caledon Institute of Social Policy.

Battle, Ken, Michael Mendelson, and Sherri Torjman. 2006. *Towards a New Architecture for Canada's Adult Benefits.* Ottawa: Caledon Institute of Social Policy.

Béland, Daniel. 2009. "Ideas, Institutions, and Policy Change." *Journal of European Public Policy* 16(5): 701-18.

Béland, Daniel, and André Lecours. 2008. *Nationalism and Social Policy: The Politics of Territorial Solidarity*. Oxford: Oxford University Press.

Beramendi, Pablo, and Christopher Anderson, eds., 2011. *Democracy, Inequality and Representation: A Comparative Perspective*. New York: Russell Sage Foundation.

Blyth, Mark. 2002. *Great Transformations: Economic Ideas and Institutional Change in the Twentieth Century*. Cambridge: Cambridge University Press.

Boychuk, Gerard. 2008. *National Health Insurance in the United States and Canada: Race, Territory, and the Roots of Difference*. Washington, DC: Georgetown University Press.

Brady, David. 2009. *Rich Democracies, Poor People: How Politics Explain Poverty*. Oxford: Oxford University Press.

Brady, David, Jason Beckfield, and Martin Seeleib-Kaiser. 2005. "Economic Globalization and the Welfare State in Affluent Democracies, 1975-2001." *American Sociological Review* 70: 921-48.

Busemeyer, Marius. 2009. "From Myth to Reality: Globalization and Public Spending in OECD Countries Revisited." *European Journal of Political Research* 48(4): 455-82.

Cameron, David. 1978. "The Expansion of the Public Economy: A Comparative Analysis." *American Political Science Review* 72: 1243-61.

Canada. 1996. Royal Commission on Taxation. *Report*. Ottawa: Queen's Printer.

–. 2012. *Jobs, Growth and Long-Term Prosperity: Economic Action Plan 2012*. Ottawa: Public Works and Government Services Canada.

Esping-Andersen, Gøsta. 1985. *Politics against Markets: The Social Democratic Road to Power*. Princeton, NJ: Princeton University Press.

–. 1990. *The Three Worlds of Welfare Capitalism*. Princeton, NJ: Princeton University Press.

–. 1996. "After the Golden Age? Welfare State Dilemmas in a Global Economy." In Gøsta Esping-Andersen, ed., *Welfare States in Transition: National Adaptations in Global Economies*, 1-31. London: Sage.

Esping-Andersen, Gøsta, Duncan Gallie, Anton Hemerijck, and John Myles. 2002. *Why We Need a New Welfare State*. Oxford: Oxford University Press.

Esping-Andersen, Gøsta, and John Myles. 2009. "Economic Inequality and the Welfare State." In W. Salvadera, B. Nolan, and T. Smeeding, eds., *The Oxford Handbook of Economic Inequality*, 639-64. Oxford: Oxford University Press.

Finnie, Ross, and Ian Irvine. 2011. "The Redistributive Impact of Canada's Employment Insurance Program." *Canadian Public Policy* 37(2): 201-18.

Fortin, Nicole, David Green, Thomas Lemieux, Kevin Milligan, and Craig Riddell. 2012. "Canadian Inequality: Recent Developments and Policy Options." *Canadian Public Policy* 38(2): 121-45.

Fortin, Pierre. 2010. "Quebec Is Fairer." *Inroads: The Canadian Journal of Opinion* 26: 58-65.

Frenette, Marc, David A. Green, and Kevin Milligan. 2009. "Taxes, Transfers, and Canadian Income Inequality." *Canadian Public Policy* 35(4): 389-411.

Garrett, Geoffrey. 1998. *Partisan Politics in the Global Economy.* Cambridge: Cambridge University Press.

Gidengal, Elisabeth, André Blais, Neil Nevitte, and Richard Nadeau. 2004. *Citizens.* Vancouver: UBC Press.

Gilens, Martin. 1999. *Why Americans Hate Welfare: Race, Media and the Politics of Antipoverty Policy.* Chicago: University of Chicago Press.

Goldin, Claudia. 2006. "The Quiet Revolution That Transformed Women's Employment, Education, and Family." *American Economic Review, Papers and Proceedings* 96: 1-21.

Hacker, Jacob S. 2004. "Privatizing Risk without Privatizing the Welfare States: The Hidden Politics of Social Policy Retrenchment in the United States." *American Political Science Review* 98(2): 243-60.

Hacker, Jacob, and Paul Pierson. 2010. *Winner-Take-All Politics: How Washington Made the Rich Richer – and Turned Its Back on the Middle Class.* New York: Simon and Schuster.

Hale, Geoffrey. 2002. *The Politics of Taxation in Canada.* Peterborough, ON: Broadview Press.

Hall, Peter. 1993. "Policy Paradigms, Social Learning, and the State: The Case of Economic Policy-making in Britain." *Comparative Politics* 25(3): 275-96.

Hanratty, Maria, and Rebbeca Blank. 1992. "Down and Out in North America: Recent Trends in Poverty Rates in the United States and Canada." *Quarterly Journal of Economics* 107: 233-54.

Häusermann, Silja. 2010. *The Politics of Welfare State Reform in Continental Europe.* Cambridge: Cambridge University Press.

Heclo, Hugh. 1974. *Modern Social Politics in Britain and Sweden: From Relief to Income Maintenance.* New Haven, CT: Yale University Press.

Heisz, Andrew. 2007. *Income Inequality and Redistribution in Canada: 1976 to 2004.* Analytical Studies Branch Research Paper Series. Ottawa: Statistics Canada.

Hicks, Alexander. 1999. *Social Democracy and Welfare Capitalism: A Century of Income Security Policies.* Ithaca, NY: Cornell University Press.

Huber, Evelyne, and John Stephens. 2001. *Development and Crisis of the Welfare State: Parties and Policies in Global Markets.* Chicago: University of Chicago Press.

Huo, Jingjing. 2009. *Third Way Reforms: Social Democracy after the Golden Age.* Cambridge: Cambridge University Press.

Immergut, Ellen. 1992. *Health Politics: Interests and Institutions in Western Europe.* Cambridge: Cambridge University Press.

–. 2010. "Political Institutions." In Francis Castles, Stephan Leibfried, Jane Lewis, Herbert Obinger, and Christopher Pierson, eds., *The Oxford Handbook of the Welfare State,* 227-40. Oxford: Oxford University Press.

Iverson, Torben, and David Soskice. 2006. "Electoral Institutions and the Politics of Coalitions: Why Some Democracies Redistribute More Than Others." *American Political Science Review* 100(2): 165-81.

Jackson, Andrew. 2008. "Crafting the Conventional Economic Wisdom: The OECD and the Canadian Policy Process." In Rianne Mahon and Stephen McBride, eds., *The OECD and Transnational Governance*, 170-87. Vancouver: UBC Press.

Jenson, Jane, and Denis Saint-Martin. 2003. "New Routes to Social Cohesion? Citizenship and the Social Investment State." *Canadian Journal of Sociology* 28(1): 77-99.

–. 2006. "Building Blocks for a New Social Architecture: The LEGO™ Paradigm of an Active Society." *Policy and Politics* 34(3): 429-51.

Johnston, Richard, Keith Banting, Will Kymlicka, and Stuart Soroka. 2010. "National Identity and Support for the Welfare State." *Canadian Journal of Political Science* 43(2): 349-77.

Katzenstein, Peter. 1985. *Small States in World Markets*. Ithaca, NY: Cornell University Press.

Kerr, Heather, Ken McKenzie, and Jack Mintz. 2012. *Tax Policy in Canada*. Toronto: Canadian Tax Foundation.

Kneebone, Ronald, and Katherine White. 2008. "Fiscal Retrenchment and Social Assistance in Canada." *Canadian Public Policy* 34(4): 419-40.

Korpi, Walter. 1983. *Democratic Class Struggle*. London: Routledge and Kegan Paul.

Korpi, Walter, and Joakim Palme. 2003. "New Politics and Class Politics in the Context of Austerity and Globalization: Welfare State Regress in 18 Countries, 1975-95." *American Political Science Review* 97(3): 425-46.

Lijphart, Arend. 1999. *Patterns of Democracy: Government Forms and Performance in Thirty-Six Countries*. New Haven, CT: Yale University Press.

Mahon, Rianne. 2008. "Varieties of Liberalism: Canadian Social Policy from the 'Golden Age' to the Present." *Social Policy and Administration* 42: 342-61.

Mahon, Rianne, and Stephen McBride, eds. 2008. *The OECD and Transnational Governance*. Vancouver: UBC Press.

Mahoney, James, and Kathleen Thelen, 2010. *Explaining Institutional Change: Ambiguity, Agency and Power*. Cambridge: Cambridge University Press.

Maioni, Antonia. 1998. *Parting at the Crossroads: The Emergence of Health Insurance in the United States and Canada*. Princeton, NJ: Princeton University Press.

Marsh, Leonard. [1943] 1975. *Report on Social Security in Canada*. Toronto: University of Toronto Press.

McBride, Stephen. 1992. *Not Working: State, Unemployment and Neo-conservatism in Canada*. Toronto: University of Toronto Press.

Morel, Nathalie, Bruno Palier, and Joakim Palme. 2012. *Towards a Social Investment Welfare State*. Bristol, UK: The Policy Press.

Morissette, Rene, Garnett Picot, and Yuqian Lu. 2012. "Wage Growth over the Past 30 Years: Changing Wages by Age and Education." In *Economic Insights*. Ottawa: Statistics Canada. http://www.statcan.gc.ca/pub/11-626-x/11-626-x2012008-eng.pdf.

Myles, John. 1984. *Old Age in the Welfare State: The Political Economy of Public Pensions*. Boston: Little Brown.

Myles, John, and Paul Pierson. 2001. "The Comparative Political Economy of Pension Reform." In Paul Pierson, ed., *The New Politics of the Welfare State*, 305-33. Oxford: Oxford University Press.

National Council of Welfare. 2010. *Welfare Incomes 2009*. Ottawa: The Council.
Nikolai, Rita. 2012. "Towards Social Investment? Patterns of Public Policy in the OECD World." In Nathalie Morel, Bruno Palier, and Joakim Palme, eds., *Towards a Social Investment Welfare State*, 91-116. Bristol, UK: The Policy Press.
Obinger, Herbert, Stephan Leibfried, and Frank Castles, eds. 2005. *Federalism and Social Policy: Comparative Perspectives on the Old and New Politics of the Welfare State*. Cambridge: Cambridge University Press.
Organisation for Economic Cooperation and Development [OECD]. 1994. *The OECD Jobs Study: Facts, Analysis, Strategies*. Paris: OECD.
–. 2004. "Early Childhood Education and Care Policy: Canada Country Note." Directorate for Education. Paris: OECD.
–. 2008. *Growing Unequal? Income Distribution and Poverty in OECD Countries*. Paris: OECD.
–. 2011. *Divided We Stand: Why Inequality Keeps Rising*. Paris: OECD.
–. 2012. Revenue Statistics. Paris: OECD.
Palier, Bruno, ed. 2010. *A Long Goodbye to Bismarck? The Politics of Welfare Reform in Continental Europe*. Amsterdam: University of Amsterdam Press.
Pempel, T.J. 1998. *Regime Shift: Comparative Dynamics of the Japanese Political Economy*. Ithaca, NY: Cornell University Press.
Pierson, Paul. 1994. *Dismantling the Welfare State? Reagan, Thatcher and the Politics of Retrenchment*. Cambridge: Cambridge University Press.
–. 1996. "The New Politics of the Welfare State." *World Politics* 48: 143-79.
Polanyi, Karl. 1944. *The Great Transformation*. Boston: Beacon Press.
Prince, Michael. 2001. "How Social Is Social Policy? Fiscal and Market Discourse in North American Welfare States." *Social Policy and Administration* 35(1): 2-13.
–. 2002. "The Return of Directed Incrementalism: Innovating Social Policy in Canada." In G.B. Doern, ed., *How Ottawa Spends, 2002-03: The Security Aftermath and National Priorities*, 176-95. Toronto: Oxford University Press.
Prince, Michael J., and Katherine Teghtsoonian. 2007. "The Harper Government's Universal Child Care Plan: Paradoxical or Purposeful Social Policy?" In G.B. Doern, ed., *How Ottawa Spends, 2007-08: The Harper Conservatives – Climate of Change*, 180-99. Montreal and Kingston: McGill-Queen's University Press.
Rhodes, Martin. 1996. "Globalization and the Welfare State: A Critical Review of Recent Debates." *Journal of European Social Policy* 6(4): 305-27.
Rodden, Jonathan. 2003. "Reviving Leviathan: Fiscal Federalism and the Growth of Government." *International Organization* 57: 695-29.
Rothstein, Bo. 1998. *Just Institutions Matter: The Moral and Political Logic of the Universal Welfare State*. Cambridge: Cambridge University Press.
Steinmo, Sven. 2003. "The Evolution of Policy Ideas: Tax Policy in the 20th Century." *British Journal of Politics and International Relations* 5(2): 206-36.
Stephens, John. 1979. *The Transformation from Capitalism to Socialism*. Chicago: University of Illinois Press.
Strange, Susan. 1996. *The Retreat of the State: The Diffusion of Power in the World Economy*. New York: Cambridge University Press.

Streeck, Wolfgang, and Kathleen Thelen. 2005. *Beyond Continuity: Institutional Change in Advanced Political Economies.* Oxford: Oxford University Press.

Saez, Emmanuel, and Michael Veall. 2005. "The Evolution of High Incomes in North America: Lessons from Canadian Evidence." *American Economic Review* 95(3): 831-49.

Swank, Duane. 2002. *Global Capital, Political Institutions and Policy Change in Developed Welfare States.* Cambridge: Cambridge University Press.

–. 2010. "Globalization." In Francis Castles, Stephan Leibfried, Jane Lewis, Herbert Obinger, and Christopher Pierson, eds., *The Oxford Handbook of the Welfare State,* 318-30. Oxford: Oxford University Press.

Thelen, Kathleen. 2004. *How Institutions Evolve: The Political Economy of Skills in Germany, Britain, the United States and Japan.* Cambridge: Cambridge University Press.

Treff, Karin, and Deborah Ort. 2009. *Finances of the Nation 2008.* Toronto: Canadian Tax Foundation.

–. 2010. *Finances of the Nation 2009.* Toronto: Canadian Tax Foundation.

Tuohy, Carolyn. 1993. "Social Policy: Two Worlds." In Michael Atkinson, ed., *Governing Canada: Political Institutions and Public Policy,* 275-305. Toronto: Harcourt Brace Jovanovich.

–. 1999. *Accidental Logics: The Dynamics of Change in the Health Care Arena in the United States, Britain, and Canada.* New York: Oxford University Press.

UNICEF. 2008. "The Child Care Transition: A League Table of Early Childhood Education and Care in Economically Advanced Countries." Innocenti Research Centre. *Report Card 8.* Florence: UNICEF.

Van Kersbergen, Kees, and Philip Manow, eds. 2009. *Religion, Class Coalitions and Welfare States.* Cambridge: Cambridge University Press.

Weaver, R. Kent. 1986. "The Politics of Blame Avoidance." *Journal of Public Policy* 6: 371-98.

PART 1

POLITICS

2

Historical Transformations of Canada's Social Architecture
Institutions, Instruments, and Ideas

JANE JENSON

One of the challenges for understanding Canada's social architecture is that the political contours of both its establishment and recent modifications seem to conform very little to what happened elsewhere. It is hard to find the class politics that shaped Western European politics through the twentieth century and laid the foundation for social policy. Yet there is no doubt that, after 1945, Canada developed a welfare regime of the "liberal" type, according to the well-known typology (Myles 1998). A puzzle for Canadian researchers is, then, what were the political drivers of this welfare regime? More recently, Canada's social architecture has been redesigned, taking directions similar to those taken by other postindustrial societies. Specifically, Canada was an early adopter of the social investment perspective used by other countries to modernize practices of redistribution and social citizenship (Jenson and Saint-Martin 2003; Morel, Palier, and Palme 2012). But what is driving these changes?

This chapter addresses the puzzle about the drivers of policy change by analyzing institutions, instruments, and ideas. I argue that Canadian policy makers act within institutions, using a toolbox of available policy instruments. Canada's "fading redistributive politics" follows, therefore, from policy challenges and conundrums generated within the institutions of earlier decades and by existing policy instruments. I also argue that policy makers act with two sorts of ideas, one concerning federalism (or the constitutional division of powers and relationships among communities and cultures) and the other centring on the social role of the state, particularly the proper mix of responsibilities among markets, families, the voluntary sector, and the state. Ideally, policy makers will reinterpret their world and generate novel solutions to new problems. But as they work on this sense-making, they do so within institutions that use policy instruments that may have been created for other ends and that, therefore, may need to be redesigned.

Thinking about Old and New Politics of Redistribution

Many have tried to account for the characteristics of modern social policy and the redistribution that it involves. Early commentators took a functionalist approach, claiming that the transition to an industrial society generated public spending on education, health, and so on. In this view, the main drivers of redistribution were economic and social rather than political. Thus, countries at similar levels of economic and social development were expected to converge (Myles and Quadagno 2002, 36-37). Theoretical claims about a converging trend were soon contested by those who saw *politics* as more important to the story and sought to understand *differences* across time and space. This chapter – and this book – is located within the second tradition.

Social Architecture over Time: Institutions and Instruments

The claim that "politics matters" gave rise to several theoretical perspectives (Myles and Quadagno 2002, 37ff). One is the power-resource approach, which claims that levels of spending on social programs are explained by success rates of left parties aligned with unions.[1] Another way of demonstrating "politics matters" comes from new institutionalism, with its focus on politics structured within and by government institutions (e.g., Weir, Orloff, and Skocpol 1988). Gøsta Esping-Andersen's typology of welfare regimes is a marriage of the power-resource approach and new institutionalism. He identifies three factors shaping regimes: "the nature of class mobilization (especially of the working class); class-political coalition structures; and the historical legacy of regime institutionalization" (Esping-Andersen 1990, 29). The Canadian literature makes use of both the power-resource approach and new institutionalism.

Despite the long-standing weaknesses of the Canadian left, some have applied the power-resource approach to explain its influence,[2] often as a theoretical expression of the political chestnut: "the CCF/NDP made the Liberals do it."[3] This approach helps to explain events in the 1940s and the wave of reforms in the mid-1960s that consolidated the post-1945 social architecture. In both periods, the Liberals were being harassed from the left: an up-start left party, the Co-operative Commonwealth Federation (CCF), in the 1940s; the New Democratic Party (NDP) and a modernizing Quebec in the 1960s (e.g., Maioni 1997, 414ff; Banting 2005, 18-19). But the power-resource approach leaves much unaccounted for.

More compelling are arguments relying on institutional explanations, particularly the effects of institutions and instruments of federalism on social policy development. Antonia Maioni (1997, 412) examines parliamentary institutions as well as federalism to account for the capacity of the CCF-NDP as a third party to be a policy entrepreneur with respect to health policy.[4] Keith Banting (2006, 140-41) argues for dissecting the impact of institutions on public policy because "reformist pressures were refracted through federal institutions ... In effect, the struggle was for control over the Canadian welfare state."[5]

These arguments improve upon functionalist accounts. Their attention to history, to the early decades of social reform, and to the constraints imposed by institutional arrangements confirms the utility of analyzing both institutions and choice of instruments within a welfare regime. However, they are less helpful in accounting for change over time.

Adding Ideas

A second wave of analyses of the politics of redistribution moved away from the emergence of social architecture after 1945 towards globalization and the effects, beginning in the 1980s, of the neoliberal assault on the welfare state, with a focus on accounting for the difficulty of effecting change. Paul Pierson describes a "new politics of the welfare state," thereby differentiating the years of welfare state crisis and neoliberalism from the earlier, more creative, years when social architecture was built out of class politics.[6] The mechanism of blame-avoidance, combined with politics dominated by interest groups such as pensioners rather than trade unions, explains "how hard it is to find *radical* changes in advanced welfare states." For Pierson (1996, 174), the "new politics of the welfare state" makes virtually impossible anything more than "a tightening of eligibility."[7]

Often missing from these analyses of a "new politics," however, is attention to goals. If earlier analysts recounted the post-1945 histories of social architecture as political projects whose purpose was to achieve objectives such as equality, Catholic solidarity, or support for male breadwinners, the "new politics" writers tended to put aside ideas, ideology, and values, asking instead: "Given that retrenchment is so difficult, what are the conditions under which it is done?"

Not surprisingly, others have chosen to go beyond this limited question. For them, as in the closing decades of the nineteenth and the mid-twentieth centuries, the current conjuncture is "an era in which rival forces, once again, promote their blueprints for a Good Society" (Esping-Andersen et al. 2002, 2). From this perspective, there are competing visions not only of the goals social policy should promote but also of how to design that policy.

This chapter sides with the notion that visions of social architecture matter, and it pays attention to the ideas of actors. While accepting that material interests and institutional effects cannot be ignored, I argue that the ways in which political actors interpret problems and identify solutions are important. For example, while, after 1945, numerous countries implemented "Keynesian" macro-economic policies, they neither identified the same challenges nor proposed the same solutions (Hall 1989). Similarly, after 1945, Christian Democrats influenced by social Catholicism and Social Democrats influenced by class analysis both sought to improve their societies. They did not, however, propose the same institutions or instruments. Christian Democrats tended towards institutions and instruments based on social insurance principles, while Social Democrats preferred universalism. Their choices derived from fundamentally different ideas about social solidarity. For Christian Democrats the main idea was to preserve a status hierarchy by distributing social benefits, such as pensions, based on earnings and therefore status, while Social Democrats promoted the idea of equality of citizenship (Esping-Andersen 1990, 23-26).

If ideas mattered when the social architecture of welfare regimes was designed, I argue that they still do.[8] In addition to analyzing institutions and instruments, therefore, I trace two congeries of ideas: the first is about the distribution of responsibilities among the producers of welfare; the second is about constitutional arrangements and federalism.

As Esping-Anderson notes: "The basic issue for any aspiring welfare architect is how to allocate welfare production. This means deciding on the division of responsibilities between markets, families, and governments" (Esping-Andersen et al. 2002, 11). Instead of this three-sided image, I use the concept of "welfare diamond" as a heuristic aid. This four-sided image depicts the allocation of responsibility among four possible sources of well-being – markets, families, the voluntary sector, and the state (Jenson 2009). Each welfare regime reflects the institutionalization of ideas about, for example, what markets should do; the family's responsibility for, among other things, the intergenerational distribution of welfare; the role of the voluntary sector in delivering services (whether such services are financed by charitable donations or public funding); and the role of the state in the distribution of income and access to services. Taking this a step farther, I describe how changing ideas about individual and collective responsibility, as well as the respective roles of markets, families, voluntary associations, and states, have driven the recent redesign of the Canadian social architecture.

Ideas about federalism have always played a role in Canada's politics of redistribution. Federalism shapes institutions and instruments, as already noted. But Canadian federalism has also been profoundly shaped by ideas and debates about ideas. Interpretations of the constitutional division of powers, recognition of national identities, and the ways to accommodate difference and diversity are notions that have been extensively debated and have shifted over time. Such ideas have shaped the politics of redistribution precisely because pressures for change are refracted through them as well as through the institutions of federalism.

Ideas may be the property of citizens, politicians, policy experts, or bureaucrats. They may be unexamined assumptions or carefully derived policy diagnostics. Whatever their form, they cannot be ignored in an analysis of the politics of redistribution.

Building Canada's Social Architecture

Early institutions and instruments of Canada's liberal welfare regime appeared in the 1940s; the next two decades consolidated the regime. A key principle throughout was the "preference for market solutions to welfare problems" (Myles 1998, 342), and this orienting idea directly shaped the main goal of social policy after 1945. The goal was to increase the economic security of all categories of the population rather than to undertake a major redistribution of income from rich to poor (Banting 2006, 431). Achieving this version of Canada's politics of redistribution involved adapting institutions, particularly those of federalism, expanding the responsibility of the state within the welfare diamond, and creating new instruments for redistributing income to provincial governments as well as individuals.

The British North America Act, 1867, left any public support for individuals' welfare to the provinces and, especially, their wards, the municipalities. The Depression of the 1930s, however, revealed a depth of need that could not be satisfied by limited public assistance programs such as mothers' allowances and municipal relief for the poor.[9] Therefore, politicians and policy experts promoting a broadening of the state sector of the welfare diamond often also advocated a greater involvement of the federal government, with its richer coffers and wider tax base. Defenders of provincial prerogative thus frequently found themselves opposing the creation of social policy instruments.

Even during the height of the Second World War, policy reflection was ongoing. Political parties, including the Progressive Conservatives, accepted the idea advanced by policy experts that there would have to be more social policy activity. Both the Rowell-Sirois Royal Commission (1940) and the Marsh Report (1943) proffered ideas about the organization of federal-provincial relations and the role of the state so that the misery of the Depression could be avoided in future. Influenced by these ideas, the federal government made a wartime announcement of a "grand design" for a new social security system (Boychuk 1998, 42; Rice and Prince 2000, chap. 3).

Instead of being implemented in one fell swoop, the regime was built slowly, institutionalizing a set of policy instruments: contributory unemployment insurance (UI) (1940) under the federal government's jurisdiction; universal flat-rate family allowances (1944); a universal flat-rate old-age pension (Old Age Security - OAS) and a needs-based pension whose costs were shared with the provinces (1952); universal hospital insurance (1957); public assistance, with federal-provincial cost-sharing of the Unemployment Assistance Act (for the unemployed not eligible for UI, 1956); and support for the blind (1951) and the disabled (1954).[10]

Provinces were prodded towards new social programs by the expansive federal government. It had two basic political resources with which to do this. The first was an idea about federalism: Ottawa claimed that the British North America Act gave it a constitutional prerogative. More specifically, its spending power allowed it to "make grants for any purpose," including within areas of acknowledged provincial jurisdiction. The second was a financing instrument: shared-cost programs allowed the federal government to create pan-Canadian programs in areas of provincial jurisdiction by offering conditional matching funds.[11] Faced with an offer of a substantial sum of money, it was difficult for provinces to stick to traditional political conservatism or principled views about the constitutional division of powers. Only Quebec, under the right-wing government of Maurice Duplessis in the 1950s, resisted the siren call, refusing shared-cost funding for postsecondary education. But even Quebec could not always resist popular pressure; it had to line up with the other provinces and accept a constitutional amendment in 1952 to allow for the creation of the OAS (Banting 2005, 21, 25).

There were consequences to institutionalizing ideas about a larger role for the state via federal-provincial politics and within its institutions, and these shaped Canada's politics of redistribution in at least three ways. First, even if, in 1945, the Liberal government, having supposedly driven back the CCF threat, considered itself to have an electoral mandate to install its grand design, the real politics of redistribution were such that the two largest provinces could block its initiatives for years simply because they disagreed with its financial design (Banting 2005, 21). Second, since federal-provincial institutions move according to a rhythm of negotiations rather than elections, and since innovation requires widespread agreement, the Canadian social architecture was drawn up slowly. Britain and other liberal welfare regimes provided health insurance in the 1940s, but it took Canada twenty years longer. Third, policy instruments have effects. Building pan-Canadian social programs via conditional grants meant that the generosity of benefits depended less on the real needs of a province's population than on the fiscal capacity of its government; thus, regional inequalities and inequities were reproduced. Nonetheless, the offer of "50¢ dollars" was a strong inducement for a provincial government to follow the federal lead. In short, provincial priorities were being sculpted by the federal government instead of by the electorate.

In the mid-1960s, three major and virtually simultaneous reforms replaced the piecemeal and leisurely approach to provincial-federal relations. In 1966, several programs were folded into the Canada Assistance Plan (CAP) to support social assistance benefits for the disabled, lone parents, and poor families, and to provide a range of social services, including daycare (Haddow 1993, chap. 3; Mahon 2000, 595-96). Financing was still shared, but provinces gained significant autonomy in choosing how to spend. Moreover, and importantly, the federal government was committed to matching every dollar a province decided to spend under CAP.

The Canada/Quebec Pension Plans (C/QPP) also date from 1966. Compulsory social insurance plans, they cover virtually the whole of the regular labour force. They oblige employees and employers to contribute towards a wage-related retirement pension as well as towards long-term disability and survivor's benefits. Their creation marked an innovation in intergovernmental relations by permitting Quebec to "opt out" of the Canada Pension Plan (CPP) and to establish its own Quebec Pension Plan (QPP). This insurance approach was complemented by the simultaneous addition of a guaranteed income supplement and the gradual reduction to age sixty-five of the universal OAS pension (Myles 1984).

Finally, building on the Hospital Insurance and Diagnostic Act, 1957, which gave the federal government authority to enter into an agreement with the provinces to establish a comprehensive, universal plan covering acute hospital care and laboratory and radiology diagnostic services, the Medical Care Act, 1966, extended health insurance to cover doctors' services (Maioni 1997, 417ff).

This consolidation of three decades of social policy action marked the completion of the grand design promised during the Second World War. Two factors account for it: changed ideas and altered institutions. First, "from the 1940s to the 1970s a broadly shared set of beliefs on building a progressive system of social security" (Rice and Prince 2000, 78) was diffused across key institutions of the federal government and within provinces.[12] CAP, C/QPP, and medicare distilled ideas about the proper role of the public sector in ensuring a citizen's well-being, albeit within the constraints of a liberal approach to welfare.[13] Second, with the Quiet Revolution launched in 1960, there was a sea-change in ideas about the role of the state and social policy in Quebec. As one of the two largest provinces, Quebec's ongoing opposition not only to federal intervention in areas of provincial jurisdiction but also to any enlargement of the state's role had been a significant drag on development of the welfare regime through the 1950s. With the explosion of enthusiasm for state action in all sectors – from energy to education – the balance of forces within federal-provincial politics shifted significantly. Instead of braking change, Quebec became a leader, although demanding important concessions to protect its constitutional authority, as in the pension debate that resulted in the asymmetric design of the C/QPP. Quebeckers also contributed to federal-provincial discussions of modernized ideas on how to balance the welfare diamond as they shed the influence of the Roman Catholic Church, promoted community development practices, mobilized a second-wave women's movement, and so on.

Along with their ideas, the provinces changed their institutions. Through the 1950s, the federal government's influence was, in large part, founded on its virtual monopoly of the capacity for policy thinking. But by the 1960s, "province-building" was in full swing, as provincial governments expanded their civil services and developed their ability to participate fully in the numerous intergovernmental bodies that policy developments required. Like Quebec, they could contest and offer resistance in the ideational contests about how to design social policy (Young et al. [1984] review the literature on province-building even if they are ultimately critical of the concept). And they could insist on institutions within federalism that respected this new capacity. Of these years, Banting (2005, 22) writes: "Programmes enacted in the 1940s and 1950s tended to give Ottawa the dominant role, whereas those introduced in the 1960s gave more scope to provincial governments."

It is important to note, however, that this consolidation, provincial activism, and explosion of programs did not significantly alter the ideas underlying the liberal welfare regime, and the preference for market solutions remained strong. Social assistance, if more easily accessible to more people with the creation of CAP, nonetheless remained primarily a residual program for those without labour market attachments. Some support of labour force participation in order to maximize employability was built into CAP, whose funds could be used to extend financial and other assistance to individuals and families "likely to fall into dependency." This was generally taken to mean that, where income from work was clearly insufficient to meet basic needs, public spending could be used to aid the working poor (Guest 1985, 116).

Other instruments were deployed within this liberal logic. For example, when policy makers learned from, among others, the Royal Commission on the Status of Women (1970) and various women's movements, how many families were struggling to juggle work and family life, three new instruments were adopted in the early 1970s. One involved provinces using CAP funds to offer childcare subsidies to low-income families so that they would be able to establish and maintain labour force participation (Mahon and Phillips 2002, 199). The second, clearly reflecting the strong preference for supporting market choices, was the 1971 creation of a Child Care Expense Deduction (CCED), administered through the tax system. Here the federal government explicitly chose a fiscal instrument rather than funding or even promoting universal public childcare services directly. The third, the contributory UI system, open to those active in the labour market, was re-jigged to provide paid maternity benefits in 1971.

Therefore, even if the state sector of the welfare diamond pushed out its borders, it never displaced, or even threatened to displace, the market sector, which was also providing substantial benefits via Canada's "private welfare state." Collective agreements continued to provide private health insurance, pensions, and other benefits to union members and their families at a time when union membership rates were on the rise. This private welfare state was an important component of income security for the retired and supplemented universal health benefits.

Choosing New Instruments

The institutions and instruments consolidated by the completion of the grand design promised in the 1940s soon generated a set of policy challenges and conundrums for those responsible for social policy. In the case of health insurance, for example, the decision not to cover pharmaceuticals prescribed outside hospitals, despite the recommendation of the 1964 Royal Commission on Health Services, meant that governments deprived themselves of an instrument to control health costs; it also generated piecemeal solutions. There is now a debate about whether or not to move towards universal pharmacare, and there are wide disparities in practices across provinces. Other examples for each of the three big reforms of the mid-1960s could be provided, and each would require a detailed analysis to document how responses to the challenges and conundrums were developed. For reasons of space, only the case of income security, primarily shaped by CAP, is analyzed here.[14]

The Cap on CAP: Ending an Instrument, Remaking an Institution

Beginning in the mid-1960s, a major part of Canada's programs for income security was housed within CAP and therefore involved the federal government matching provincial social expenditures. Provinces' spending on social assistance and services rose steeply from the mid-1950s until the mid-1970s. Part of this increase was due to higher case loads and part of it reflected an increased generosity, especially in the decade after the introduction of CAP. Nevertheless, the availability of federal funds for cost-sharing was also a driver. Indeed "the increase was larger in programmes eligible for cost-sharing than in non-shareable services; and federal and provincial officials certainly believed the federal transfers were critical, especially in poorer provinces" (Banting 2005, 38).

Simply stated, by selecting cost-sharing as the financial instrument for implementing CAP, the federal government lost control of its expenditures. By the 1980s, this choice of instrument was one of the reasons the federal government had difficulty controlling its deficit. The solution selected to meet this challenge involved a fundamental alteration in federal-provincial relations. After various skirmishes, in 1990, the first volley was fired in what became an upheaval in intergovernmental relations in the realm of income security. The Conservative government's budget imposed a "cap on CAP." Instead of open-ended financing in which it matched the spending choices of the provinces, the federal government imposed a limit of 5 percent annually on any increase in transfers to the three richest provinces (Alberta, British

Columbia, and Ontario). As Battle (1998, 329) notes: "The 'cap on CAP' decapitated the Canada Assistance Plan and put all the provinces on notice that they too could no longer count on the same level of federal largesse." The institutionalized rules of the intergovernmental game were even more dramatically transformed in 1995, when the Liberal government unilaterally ended CAP. In its place, the Department of Finance announced the Canada Health and Social Transfer (CHST) and released the provinces from almost all conditions for spending any funds transferred to them.[15] In exchange, they lost billions of dollars of transfers from Ottawa (Battle 1998, 330).

These changes to the instruments and the ways of doing federal-provincial politics meant that even provinces with little ideological enthusiasm for cutting social assistance rolls were forced to rethink their social policies. One result has been a significant reduction in levels of disposable income available to social assistance receipts (NCW 2006, 48). A second result is that the role of provincial governments in redistribution is more limited than it was before (Boychuk, Chapter 10, this volume). But beyond the monetary effects are the changes in ideas about what social programs can and should do. Cuts to recipients real incomes, which were below the poverty line at the best of times, effectively informed them that they would have to rely increasingly on family solidarity, where it was available, and on the voluntary sectors' food banks and other charitable supports (Phillips, Chapter 5, this volume). Such ideas and the instruments enacting them meant that the state sector of the welfare diamond had shrunk and that redistribution had diminished.[16]

New Instruments for the Federal Government

In these same years, the income security programs that the federal government controlled were reformed. The Liberal government elected in 1993 undertook a significant overhaul and redesign of UI, renaming the program Employment Insurance (EI) and reducing coverage. According to Banting (2006, 426): "The changes contributed to a sharp drop in the portion of the unemployed who receive unemployment benefits." If remodelling had stopped there, we might conclude that the only goal was to shrink the space occupied by the state in the welfare diamond.

However, more was going on. The institutions and instruments resulting from this reform mimicked ideas then widely circulating in international policy communities and networks about labour-market policy and families. Particularly within the OECD, criticisms of so-called passive benefits, such as unemployment payments and social assistance, flourished (Green and

Townsend, Chapter 3, this volume). There was enthusiasm for "active labour-market policies" (ALMPs) in order to increase employment rates of women as well as of men. Employment Insurance (EI) incorporated such ideas by, for example, setting lower replacement rates for repeat claims for benefits, extending coverage to part-time workers (a heavily feminized category), and improving parental benefits to encourage women to combine family and employment rather than choosing one over the other.

In these years, other instruments were initiated, often in the form of tax credits that enabled the federal government to redirect its spending (in the area of retirement income and the unemployed) or to redesign it (in the area of family benefits) (Myles and Pierson 1997). As the standard post-1945 programs and instruments, such as UI and social assistance, were criticized and lost their popular legitimacy, there was political pressure to use new instruments to target spending to low-income Canadians rather than making universal payments that went to the "wealthy banker's wife."[17] When UI became EI and eligibility rules were tightened in the name of ALMP, there was a simultaneous introduction of an instrument to ensure that children would not be unduly penalized. Low-income unemployed workers (earning under $25,921) with dependent children became eligible to receive the EI Family Supplement; it could raise the reimbursement rate as high as 80 percent instead of the usual 55 percent.

Indeed, as the federal government moved in the second half of the 1990s into a phase labelled "repairing the social union" (Prince 2002, 127), child benefits became the focus of federal-provincial politics. This new politics of redistribution emerged in part from provincial anger over the unilateral creation of the CHST. Another source was the federal government's desperation to gain a modicum of influence over the direction of social policy development as its financial levers were attenuated and it lost touch with individual Canadians (Boychuk, Chapter 10, this volume). But the direction chosen, and particularly child-centred policy, is not explained by these two motives. Understanding the focus on children requires considering ideas coming from within Canadian society and international policy communities. Both were advocating a redesign of the responsibility mix in the welfare diamond to achieve what Esping-Andersen, quoted above, terms the "Good Society."

Building New Instruments with New Ideas: The Social Investment Perspective
After 1995, Canada's federal government and some provinces, along with an increasing number of other countries and international organizations,

justified the politics of redistribution from a social investment perspective (Jenson and Saint-Martin 2003; Jenson 2010; Morel, Palier, and Palme 2012). For more than fifteen years, welfare regimes, especially liberal and social democratic ones, have converged around ideas for modernization of social models via labour market involvement of all adults and new forms of investment, especially in human capital and including early childhood education and care, and "children" more generally. The perspective has three salient and interrelated features (Jenson and Saint-Martin 2006). The first is an emphasis on education and learning to ensure that adults in the present and children in the future will be able to adapt to a knowledge-based economy that demands flexibility in employment relations and that offers many precarious jobs. The second is an orientation to the future: there is greater concern for setting the conditions for future success for individuals and countries as a whole than there is for achieving equality in the present. Finally, it is suggested that successful individuals enrich our common future and that ensuring their success is beneficial for the community as a whole, now and into the future.

Translating these ideas into social policy has consequences. Implementation of all three implies a change in the welfare diamond, with the state sector removing, for example, portions of early childhood education and care from the market and emphasizing earlier kindergarten. It also means that labour markets and not a male breadwinner will provide most women with their income security. And it implies that, as has been the case in Nordic countries for decades, ALMPs will propel unemployed and undertrained workers into the labour market after skill upgrading (although sometimes this does not happen). A foundational idea is that all adults (with the exception of some persons with disabilities) *should* participate in the paid labour force. Beyond the liberal principle that earning income is a good in itself, this policy prescription rests on the idea that poverty interferes with children's cognitive development. Therefore, fostering parental employment is an investment in human capital as well as a way to break the intergenerational cycle of poverty (e.g., Esping-Andersen et al. 2002, 9; Jenson and Saint-Martin 2003, 72).

These ideas were not home-grown in Canada, although Canadians contributed to their development; rather, they circulated within international networks to which the federal government (and some provinces) sent representatives, and they percolated through policy communities in the late 1990s, all of which were in search of responses to the challenges and conundrums created by earlier institutions and instruments. Policy instruments that failed to encourage, and even actively discouraged, labour-market participation were particularly criticized. So, too, was marketized childcare if quality services became too expensive for parents to afford; such a situation encouraged reliance on informal care, with fewer positive results for human capital acquisition.[18]

Initiatives within federal-provincial relations need to be interpreted in this context of new ideas about the proper directions of social policy and how to rebalance the welfare diamond. To be sure, the actions of provincial and federal actors within the new institutions of intergovernmental relations were driven by their understanding of those institutions, but they were also affected by their ideas about social policy. Both sets of ideas had altered and were pushing policy makers towards taking up new instruments.

Federalism without a Leader
The federal government quickly tamed the deficit after 1995. Then its conversion to the social investment perspective made it eager to actively re-engage in the politics of redistribution. It did so via transfers to individuals in the form of tax credits; this allowed it to take on a role larger than that of all provinces but Quebec with regard to redistribution across income categories (Boychuk, Chapter 10, this volume). Nevertheless, since the 1995 budget, in which the federal government announced a unilateral decision to cancel CAP, federal-provincial relations are no longer what they were. The new configuration is less shaped by federal-provincial negotiations than at any time since the 1940s. The elimination of any conditionality allowed the provinces maximum autonomy of action and considerably reduced the federal government's influence over policy design. The result for the federal government was, in comparison to an earlier moment of federalism, a major difficulty in sculpting provinces' social policy. The politics of redistribution in some key areas of income security, such as social assistance, have become, therefore, more varied, responding more clearly to the political imperatives in each province.[19]

Experimentation with a new kind of relationship took place over the next years. The policy terrain on which experiments were tried was child-centred, in line with the ideas about social investment. Chief among these experiments was the National Child Benefit (NCB) initiative, a classic example of this perspective (Jenson and Saint-Martin 2003). The NCB is an innovation both in how governments work together and in the objectives they pursue. Its goals are to "help prevent and reduce the depth of child poverty; promote attachment to the work force; and reduce overlap and duplication between Canadian and provincial/territorial programs." The NCB also promises "to remove child benefits from welfare."[20]

The NCB is as much about intergovernmental relations as it is about redistribution and labour-force participation. With respect to the relationship between Quebec and others, the NCB involves something we may call "asterisk federalism" (Jenson 2001). Quebec does not officially participate in initiatives undertaken by the other governments because they infringe on provincial jurisdiction, but it does attend meetings, engage in discussion, and monitor decisions.[21]

A second aspect of the NCB that is important for intergovernmental relations is its seeming ability to offer a clear division of labour between the two levels of government. The federal government's role, justified by its spending power, consists of paying two benefits directly to families with children. The first is the income-tested Canada Child Tax Benefit (CCTB). The cut-off is high, and 80 percent of families receive something. The second is the National Child Benefit Supplement (NCBS), available to families with very low incomes. The provinces' role in the NCB was originally described as "reinvesting in services" to support the objectives listed above, the money for which would become available when the federal government took over the supplementary portion paid to families with dependent children in provincial social assistance programs. This would allow governments to claim "to remove child benefits from welfare."

The NCB initiative was clearly aligned with that part of the social investment perspective that focused on increasing employment by "making work pay," along with the notion that living in poverty interferes with healthy child development and cognition. The route to these ends was to dismantle the "welfare wall" built by the instruments of CAP. The basic idea was that social assistance too often discouraged parents from accepting a low-paying job. Whereas social assistance recipients had their benefits cut if they earned income, working would not reduce the CCTB or even the NCBS if the job was low-paid. Parents moving off social assistance also lost their supplementary health and dental benefits, and few low-paying jobs provided such benefits privately. Therefore, the provincial portion of the NCB initiative incorporated the idea that provinces would take the money saved by not paying social assistance to cover children (this now being paid as the NCBS) and would instead "reinvest" it in extended benefits to ease the transition from welfare to work. And, in fact, many provinces did so.[22]

But, if they did so, it was because the choice was theirs. Implementation of the NCB has amply demonstrated that Ottawa has little influence on provincial policy choices, such as whether to claw back the NCBS.[23] Nor is there any way to ensure that the initial logic of "reinvesting in services" is followed. Several provinces prefer to provide their own child tax credits rather than to spend on services (Mahon and Jenson 2006, 13; Mahon, Chapter 15, this volume).

Experimentation with post-1995 federal-provincial relations in social policy has brought several other initiatives; they, too, demonstrate that the federal government has few levers for exercising leadership over provincial policy choices. It has been particularly difficult to entice the provinces into providing particular kinds of services. For example, as part of its conversion to the social investment perspective, the federal government tried to promote early learning and childcare (ELCC).[24] The same model was used over and over: the federal government offered extra funding to the provinces via an intergovernmental agreement in the hope that they would develop programs in designated areas. But some provinces resisted these suggestions. The 2000 Early Child Development Initiatives listed early learning and childcare as one of four areas in which the provinces and territories could spend federal money, but they did not require spending in all four areas. Initially, less than 10 percent of the funding was used for childcare, and only six of thirteen governments invested in regulated care. None of the biggest provinces (Alberta, British Columbia, and Ontario) did so. Next, the 2003 Multilateral Framework Agreement on Early Learning and Child Care focused directly on preschool childcare, and funding was promised for five years. However, the agreement offered a broad spending menu: information provision, fee subsidies, quality assurance systems, capital and operating grants, training and professional development, and wage enhancements, with funds for both commercial and non-profit providers (Mahon and Jenson 2006, 13). In other words, virtually any form of care, informal as well as early learning, could be sheltered under this umbrella.

The last effort by the Liberal government to promote a pan-Canadian childcare system came in 2005. After a half decade of trying to induce the provinces and territories to improve childcare services in both quantity and quality, it managed to convince all ten provinces to sign individual agreements to open more childcare spaces in exchange for a federal transfer.

These instruments of negotiated agreements and "initiatives" were often ineffective when it came to meeting federal goals, and they were fragile. Provinces had autonomy to construct their own menu of services, even to the exclusion of those most valued by the federal government. The agreements were for a fixed term, and renewal was not guaranteed. And, as seen with the election of the Harper Conservatives in 2006, even a duly signed agreement could be cancelled if the new government had different ideas.

Looking Forward

The dramatic cancellation of the childcare agreements after the 2006 election might seem to have sounded the death knell for the social investment perspective, but this has not been the case. First, the relative lack of conditionality within these types of institutions allowed provinces to continue on the social investment path. The Ontario Liberal government, for example, repudiated the opposition to expanding regulated childcare often expressed by the Harris Conservatives and instituted "Best Start," emphasizing healthy early development and investments in human capital via ELCC and full-day kindergarten.[25] Second, some of the instruments developed after 1995 were not cancelled. The Multilateral Framework Agreement continued through 2008, providing provinces with some predictability in their planning.

Of course, the cancelled childcare agreements and their replacement by the more costly Universal Child Care Benefit (UCCB) was a dent in the logic of social investment. Since respecting their campaign promise, however, the Conservatives have done several things less dramatically, which suggests that the social investment perspective on social policy retains some legitimacy inside and outside the federal government. The government slightly redesigned the UCCB, giving more support to lone-parent families, a major target from the social investment perspective. It also introduced and then extended a new instrument that reflects one of the "big ideas" of social policy "modernizers" – the need to provide supplements to low-income earners, usually relying on a tax-credit as the policy instrument.

Many countries now provide such in-work benefits, promoted by, among others, the OECD, as a useful tool for achieving activation goals. In the 2007 budget, the Conservatives unveiled a refundable tax credit, the Working Income Tax Benefit (WITB), intended to "make work pay."[26] It, too, is child-tested, providing significantly higher benefits to families with children than to low-wage earners without dependent children. The initial tiny amounts of the WITB have been increased in subsequent budgets.

A significant characteristic of the WITB is that it, like the NCB and subsequent programs, was designed to facilitate alignment with provincial priorities rather than to encourage an alignment around federal government priorities as in the post-1945 decades. Provinces and territories may alter the instrument so as to harmonize it with their own income security systems, something that Quebec, British Columbia, and Nunavut immediately did (Caledon 2008, 2).

That this design was selected with little public discussion or intergovernmental negotiation suggests that policy instruments of this type will continue to shape and reinforce a federalism in which the federal government finds less possibility for leadership in areas of provincial jurisdiction than it did in earlier periods. It must content itself with looking after its own programs, such as EI and the child benefits, and making limited interventions in areas of provincial responsibility. Thus, in 2012 the federal government unilaterally announced two significant reforms that provoked consternation in the provinces. Without warning, in April it took back responsibility for immigrant integration services, much to the dismay of Manitoba and British Columbia, which had been constructing a provincial regime around them (Paquet 2012). In May it was the turn of EI; benefits were redesigned to discourage repeat users and to encourage job take-up.

In the end, the new politics of redistribution have not diverged from the track of a liberal welfare regime: market solutions to welfare problems remain the priority, even as ideas and instruments for implementing them have changed over time. However, the institutions of federalism in which these relations play out are quite different today. The provinces have the initiative, and federal spending does less to shape their actions than it did in the post-1945 decades. The result for the politics of redistribution is likely to be wide variety, as the fourteen provincial and territorial governments each chooses its own road to follow.

NOTES

1 Classic studies using this approach are Korpi (1980), Myles (1984), and Esping-Andersen (1985). A counter-claim focusing on the fundamental difficulties of class mobilization comes from Przeworski (1985), upon whom Brodie and Jenson (1988) draw.
2 See, for example, Alain Noël (Chapter 11, this volume), and Rodney Haddow (Chapter 16, this volume).
3 One of the first versions of this argument by an academic is Underhill (1943, 308); it was taken up by John Porter (1965) and Gad Horowitz (1966, 162, 167, and passim), in their analyses of "creative politics" in the 1950s and 1960s.
4 John Myles (Chapter 13, this volume) develops an argument about the weight of instrument design over time.
5 See also his important earlier work (Banting 1987).

6 Of course, Pierson's position never achieved consensus. Some argue explicitly that the basic pattern of class-based politics still operates. See, for example, Korpi and Palme (2003). For a recent critique of Pierson's argument, see Bonoli and Natali (2012).
7 The resulting notion of "permanent austerity" achieved numerous followers, who explained *how* change occurs. For example, Myles and Pierson (1997) describe the turn to negative income taxes (NIT) as a new policy instrument, arguing that, in liberal welfare regimes, these instruments could be introduced because they make change opaque, and thus a politics of stealth becomes possible.
8 Green and Townsend (Chapter 3, this volume), for example, also argue for the importance of ideas, or what they term the intellectual discourse of economics. Mahon (Chapter 15, this volume) also discusses changing policy ideas about childcare over time in Ontario.
9 One of the first provincewide public assistance programs of the twentieth century was for poor mothers of young children who had been widowed or abandoned by their male partners. Beginning in Manitoba in 1933, the programs finally reached the last province, Prince Edward Island, in 1949 (Boychuk 1998, 28ff).
10 Mothers' allowances remained an exclusively provincial responsibility.
11 There were exceptions to this form of financing: UI was funded by contributions from employers and employees as well as by the federal government; OAS was paid from an Old Age Security Fund created with earmarked taxes.
12 Haddow (1993, chap. 3) describes the construction of agreement about reform within the federal government and across federal-provincial politics that generated CAP.
13 As Carolyn Tuohy (Chapter 12, this volume) describes in detail, these constraints led to a single-payer system with significant characteristics of a universal welfare regime.
14 For health care see Tuohy (Chapter 12, this volume) and for pensions see Myles (Chapter 13, this volume).
15 CAP transfers came with three conditions: provinces provide income assistance only on the basis of need; they have an appeals system in place for the use of applicants and recipients; no minimum residence requirements would be imposed. Only the third was carried over to the CHST (Battle 1998, 331).
16 Noël (Chapter 11, this volume) argues that Quebec has been an exception to this generalization.
17 In the 1980s, the "wealthy banker's wife" was symbolically famous in debates over universality versus targeting, as in this formulation: why squander family allowance payments on the wealthy banker's wife when the money could be targeted to low-income families that really need it. The symbol endures in the title of McQuaig (1993).
18 The OECD particularly insisted that good quality, affordable services were investments in human capital (see Jenson 2010, 65).
19 Noël and Mahon (Chapters 11 and 15, this volume) particularly emphasize this variation.
20 This is from http://www.nationalchildbenefit.ca/eng/98/q_a.shtml (viewed 31 October 2010).

21 This is known as "asterisk federalism" because key documents include a footnote (originally in the form of an asterisk) indicating that, while Quebec shares most of the goals of the initiative, it refuses to participate because to do so would be to accept an intrusion into areas of provincial competence (Jenson 2001). See, for example, the description of the National Child Benefit at http://www.nationalchildbenefit.ca/eng/06/ncb.shtml (viewed 31 October 2010).

22 For the details of provincial spending see the annual progress reports, prepared since 2000 as well as the archives in general, at http://www.nationalchildbenefit.ca/eng/06/archives.shtml, consulted 31 October 2010.

23 The NCB design legitimated provinces and territories that were simply treating the CCTB and NCBS as "income" and reducing social assistance payments accordingly (Banting 2006, 428). All but New Brunswick and Newfoundland and Labrador initially applied the clawback, provoking a storm of protest among advocates for the poor and poor families. For one of many critical discussions, see NCW (2006, 56ff).

24 Whereas in the rest of the world the preferred terminology is "early childhood education and care" (ECEC), in Canada that terminology cannot be used when the federal government is involved because "education" is a domain of exclusive provincial competence.

25 See http://www.children.gov.on.ca/htdocs/English/topics/earlychildhood/index.aspx (viewed 31 October 2010). For the details, see Mahon (Chapter 15, this volume). Quebec had been following its own road on childcare since 1997 (Noël, Chapter 11, this volume).

26 See http://www.servicecanada.gc.ca/eng/goc/witb/index.shtml, consulted 31 October 2010.

REFERENCES

Banting, Keith. 1987. *The Welfare State and Canadian Federalism*. 2nd ed. Montreal and Kingston: McGill-Queen's University Press.

–. 2005. "Canada: Nation-Building in a Federal Welfare State." In Herbert Obinger, Stephan Leibfried, and Frank G. Castles, eds., *Federalism and the Welfare State: New World and European Experiences*, 89-137. Cambridge: Cambridge University Press.

–. 2006. "Dis-embedding Liberalism? The New Social Policy Paradigm in Canada." In David A. Green and Jonathan R. Kesselman, eds., *Dimensions of Inequality in Canada*, 417-52. Vancouver: UBC Press.

Battle, Ken. 1998. "Transformation: Canadian Social Policy since 1985." *Social Policy and Administration* 32(4): 321-40.

Bonoli, Guiliano, and David Natali. 2012. *The Politics of the New Welfare State*. Oxford: Oxford University Press.

Boychuk, Gerald W. 1998. *Patchworks of Purpose: The Development of Provincial Social Assistance Regimes in Canada*. Montreal and Kingston: McGill-Queen's University Press.

Brodie, Janine, and Jane Jenson. 1988. *Crisis, Challenge and Change: Party and Class in Canada*. Ottawa: Carleton University Press.

Caledon. 2008. *Make Work Pay.* A Caledon Commentary. Ottawa: Caledon Institute. September.
Esping-Andersen, Gøsta. 1985. *Politics against Markets.* Princeton, NJ: Princeton University Press.
—. 1990. *The Three Worlds of Welfare Capitalism.* Princeton, NJ: Princeton University Press.
Esping-Andersen, Gøsta, Duncan Gallie, Anton Hemerijck, and John Myles. 2002. *Why We Need a New Welfare State.* Oxford: Oxford University Press.
Guest, Dennis. 1985. *The Emergence of Social Security in Canada.* 2nd rev. ed. Vancouver: UBC Press.
Haddow, Rodney. 1993. *Poverty Reform in Canada, 1958-78: State and Class Influences on Policy Making.* Toronto: University of Toronto Press.
Hall, Peter A., ed. 1989. *The Political Power of Economic Ideas: Keynesianism across Nations.* Princeton, NJ: Princeton University Press.
Horowitz, Gad. 1966. "Conservatism, Liberalism, and Socialism in Canada: An Interpretation." *Canadian Journal of Economics and Political Science* 32(2): 143-71.
Jenson, Jane. 2001. "Canada's Shifting Citizenship Regime: The Child as Model Citizen." In Michael Keating and Trevor C. Salmon, eds., *The Dynamics of Decentralization: Canadian Federalism and British Devolution.* Montreal and Kingston: McGill-Queen's University Press.
—. 2009. "Lost in Translation: The Social Investment Perspective and Gender Equality." *Social Politics: International Studies in Gender, State and Society* 16(4): 446-83.
—. 2010. "Diffusing Ideas for After Neo-liberalism: The Social Investment Perspective in Europe and Latin America." *Global Social Policy* 10(1): 59-84.
Jenson, Jane, and Denis Saint-Martin. 2003. "New Routes to Social Cohesion? Citizenship and the Social Investment State." *Canadian Journal of Sociology* 28(1): 77-99.
—. 2006. "Building Blocks for a New Social Architecture: The LEGO™ Paradigm of an Active Society." *Policy and Politics* 34(3): 429-51.
Korpi, Walter. 1980. "Social Policy and Distributional Conflict in the Capitalist Democracies: A Preliminary Framework." *West European Politics* 3(3): 296-316.
Korpi, Walter, and Joakim Palme. 2003. "New Politics and Class Politics in the Context of Austerity and Globalization: Welfare State Regress in 18 Countries, 1975-95." *American Political Science Review* 97(3): 425-46.
Mahon, Rianne. 2000. "The Never Ending Story: The Struggle for Universal Child Care Policy in the 1970s." *Canadian Historical Review* 81(4): 582-615.
Mahon, Rianne, and Jane Jenson. 2006. *Learning from Each Other: Early Learning and Child Care Experiences in Canadian Cities.* Toronto: City of Toronto.
Mahon, Rianne, and Susan Phillips. 2002. "Dual-Earner Families Caught in a Liberal Welfare Regime? The Politics of Child Care Policy in Canada." In Sonya Michel and Rianne Mahon, eds., *Child Care Policy at the Crossroads: Gender and Welfare State Restructuring,* 191-218. New York: Routledge.

Maioni, Antonia. 1997. "Parting at the Crossroads: The Development of Health Insurance in Canada and the United States, 1940-65." *Comparative Politics* 29(4): 411-31.

McQuaig, Linda. 1993. *The Wealthy Banker's Wife: The Assault on Equality in Canada*. Toronto: Penguin.

Morel, Nathalie, Bruno Palier, and Joakim Palme. 2012. *Towards a Social Investment Welfare State? Ideas, Policies and Challenges*. Bristol, UK: The Policy Press.

Myles, John. 1984. *Old Age in the Welfare State: The Political Economy of Public Pensions*. Boston: Little Brown.

—. 1998. "How to Design a 'Liberal' Welfare State: A Comparison of Canada and the United States." *Social Policy and Administration* 32(4): 341-64.

Myles, John, and Paul Pierson. 1997. "Friedman's Revenge: The Reform of 'Liberal' Welfare States in Canada and the United States." *Politics and Society* 25(4): 443-72.

Myles, John, and Jill Quadagno. 2002. "Political Theories of the Welfare State." *Social Service Review* 76(1): 34-57.

NCW (National Council of Welfare). 2006. *Welfare Incomes 2005*. Ottawa: NCW. http://www.ncwcnbes.net/en/research/welfare-bienetre.html.

Paquet, Mireille. 2012. "Federalisation and Province-Building: Immigration and Integration in Canada, 1990-2010." Paper presented to the Annual Meeting of the Canadian Political Science Association. Edmonton, Alberta, June.

Pierson, Paul. 1996. "The New Politics of the Welfare State." *World Politics* 48(2): 143-79.

Prince, Michael. 2003. "SUFA: Sea Change or Mere Ripple for Canadian Social Policy?" In Sarah Fortin, Alain Noël, and France St-Hilaire, eds., *Forging the Canadian Social Union: SUFA and Beyond*, 125-56. Montreal: Institute for Research on Public Policy.

Porter, John A. 1965. *The Vertical Mosaic: An Analysis of Social Class and Power in Canada*. Toronto: University of Toronto Press.

Przeworski, Adam. 1985. *Capitalism and Social Democracy*. New York: Cambridge University Press.

Rice, James J., and Michael Prince. 2000. *The Changing Politics of Canadian Social Policy*. Toronto: University of Toronto Press.

Underhill, F.H. 1943. "The Canadian Party System in Transition." *Canadian Journal of Economics and Political Science* 9(3): 300-16.

Weir, Margaret, Ann Orloff, and Theda Skocpol, eds. 1988. *The Politics of Social Policy in the United States*. Princeton, NJ: Princeton University Press.

Young, Robert A., Philippe Faucher, and André Blais. 1984. "Province-Building: A Critique." *Canadian Journal of Political Science* 17(4): 783-818.

3 Drivers of Increasing Market Income Inequality
Structural Change and Policy

DAVID A. GREEN AND JAMES TOWNSEND

As emphasized in Boadway and Cuff (Chapter 14, this volume), the Canadian tax and transfer system underwent a substantial shift in the mid-1990s. In an attempt to explain this shift, we examine the main patterns in employment and earnings outcomes over the thirty-year period (between 1980 and 2010) leading up to, including, and following that change. We hypothesize that labour market developments from 1980 to the mid-1990s led successive Canadian governments to believe they were witnessing the effects of a combination of increased globalization and technological change. The subsequent shift in policy was a relatively coherent attempt to respond to this perceived new state of the world. Thus – without denying the importance of political driving forces emphasized in much of the rest of this book – we take what Jensen (Chapter 2, this volume) calls a functionalist approach to understanding Canada's mid-1990s policy shift.

We begin by establishing what policy makers in the mid-1990s were witnessing in the Canadian and international labour markets, starting with discussions of employment rates, wages, and trends in "non-standard" employment. We demonstrate that the 1980s and early 1990s were characterized by poor employment outcomes and stagnant wages, along with a move towards less stable jobs. Internationally, the US fared particularly well (especially after 1990), and Europe particularly poorly. To illuminate the Canadian situation, we discuss these trends in international labour markets, and we consider other major domestic economic trends (i.e., Canada's increased exposure to foreign trade and the shift away from manufacturing).

The second step in our argument is to establish the intellectual link between the labour market patterns just described and the policies that followed. We argue that the intellectual discourse in economics in the mid-1990s was dominated by a paradigm that was given concrete form in the OECD Jobs Strategy. According to this paradigm, the world was experiencing a technological change that favoured skilled over unskilled workers. Economies with "rigid" labour market institutions would fare particularly poorly in this environment as these rigidities would amplify the effects of reduced demand for low-skilled workers. The logical policy response was twofold: (1) alter policies such as unemployment insurance to make the labour market more flexible; and (2) increase the level of human capital in the economy. The latter implies that education and training policy should become a key part of redistributive policy, especially as educating workers affects the remaining unskilled workers by reducing the supply pressures holding down their wages. As Jensen (Chapter 2, this volume) describes, Canada's mid-1990s policy shift involved a move towards exactly these types of policies – what she calls the "social investment" perspective. She fully develops the idea of this perspective and its impact on policy.

Of course, showing that the dominant economic model can rationalize the policies Canada adopted in the mid-1990s does not prove that Canadian policy makers actually accepted and used this model. However, evidence gleaned from major policy documents of the time shows that policy discussions did refer directly to the key elements of this model. It is still possible that Canadian policy makers adopted the model's language because it implied an ideal message for a policy-making community: that Canada had some work to do but that it had not made terrible decisions up to this point. In any event, the evidence suggests that understanding the dominant model and its relationship to Canadian labour market patterns is important for understanding the mid-1990s shift in policy – regardless of whether that model was a driving force or a rationalization.

It is also important to determine whether that view of the Canadian labour market is the right one. If the dominant model is incorrect in its assumptions, the accompanying policy shifts may have been ineffective or even damaging. In the third section of the chapter, we take advantage of the fact that we can see patterns over a longer time period (another fifteen years) to assess the applicability of the dominant paradigm to Canada. Our main conclusion is that the model does not provide a good explanation for patterns in Canada's labour market over the last three decades. We argue instead that the data fit with a model of technological change in which the pace of adoption of new technologies is determined endogenously by the relative supply of skilled and unskilled labour and capital. Significantly, such a model has very different policy implications from the dominant model: education policy may lead to an exacerbation of, not a reduction in, inequality. The extent to which it results in increased inequality will depend, partly, on whether there is enough physical capital per worker, leading to another policy that is not emphasized in the dominant approach: that investment in human capital should be complemented with investment in physical capital. We argue, further, that once one allows for imperfections in labour market contracts, the conclusion that more flexibility in labour market policy is always a good goal comes into question. Thus, we conclude that the thinking behind the mid-1990s policy shift, which continues to inform policy making today, is flawed.

Patterns and Trends

Data

We begin by describing the main data we use to portray patterns in Canadian labour market outcomes. No single database provides information on wages, employment, industry of employment, and so on from the early 1980s to the late 2000s. However, we can piece together data from a series of datasets, all of which are based on the common sampling frame provided by the Labour Force Survey (LFS). In particular, we use the 1981 Annual Work Patterns Survey (AWPS), the 1984 Survey of Union Membership (SUM), the 1986-87 and 1988-90 Labour Market Activity Surveys (LMAS), and the 1995 Survey of Work Arrangements (SWA) – all of which were special surveys attached to the LFS. The LFS itself has included wage data since 1997. We combine the earlier datasets with the LFS for the years 1997 through 2009.[1] These surveys utilize a relatively consistent set of questions, allowing us to construct comparable wage measures over time. We mainly focus on individuals between the ages of twenty and sixty-four.

Labour Market Trends

Employment and Unemployment
In Figure 3.1, we present unemployment rates for Canada and the US for 1980 to 2008.[2] The figure tells an important story. After decades of similar values, the Canadian and US unemployment rates diverged in the early

FIGURE 3.1

Unemployment rates, Canada and the US, 1980-2008

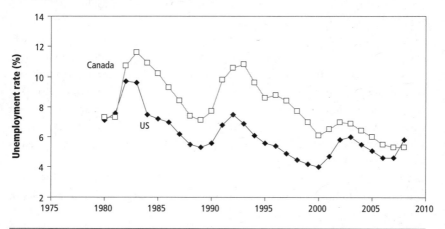

Source: US Bureau of Labour Statistics, International Labour Comparisons (various years), http://www.bls.gov/fls/tables.htm.

1980s' recession. Canada's unemployment rate was over three percentage points above that in the US by 1984 and remained about two percentage points higher during the boom period of the late 1980s. This raised serious questions about whether Canada's labour market had become too rigid relative to that of the US and, in particular, whether Canadian unemployment insurance and social assistance (SA) programs were generating high costs for the Canadian economy (Card and Riddell 1993; Riddell 2005). These concerns heightened when Canada's unemployment rate rose even further above the American rate in the recession of the early 1990s and remained there for years. The persistence of this differential may have contributed to policy makers' thinking about structural, as opposed to cyclical, factors causing trouble in the labour market when they considered policy reforms in the mid-1990s.

In Figure 3.2, we plot the employment rates for Canada and the US over our period. While Canada again fared somewhat worse in the early 1980s recession, by 1989 the employment rates in the two countries were nearly identical. At this point, one might argue that the remaining difference in unemployment rates was just a measurement issue and not consequential. But the large gap in employment rates that emerged in the early 1990s made such arguments moot and again raised the question of whether Canada was experiencing a structural problem or a cyclical downturn.

FIGURE 3.2

Employment rates, Canada and the US, 1980-2008

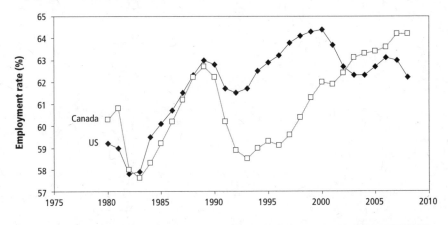

Source: US Bureau of Labour Statistics, International Labour Comparisons (various years), http://www.bls.gov/fls/tables.htm.

Non-standard Employment and Employment Instability

Perceptions about structural change were also influenced by changes in the nature of employment in the early 1990s. In particular, "non-standard" employment, sometimes defined as self-employment, part-time employment, or temporary full-time employment (Vosko, Zukewich, and Cranford 2003), was on the rise. Analysts suggested that this heralded the demise of the "standard" full-year, full-time job with benefits and that it was occurring because the forces of globalization and technical change were imposing greater flexibility on work arrangements (Krahn 1995). In Figure 3.3, we present the time pattern of the inverse of non-standard employment: the proportion of all employment accounted for by full-time, paid employees.[3] Note the substantial decline in standard jobs in the first part of the 1990s. From the standpoint of analysts in the mid-1990s, this could easily be seen as evidence of structural change.[4]

Education Differentials in Wages and Employment

Differentials in wages and employment between workers with different levels of education are considered a key piece of evidence for understanding the labour market. In Figure 3.4, we present plots of the difference in mean log hourly wages between workers with a BA or higher education and workers with some or completed high school education separately for men and

FIGURE 3.3

Proportion of jobs that are standard, Canada, 1987-2009

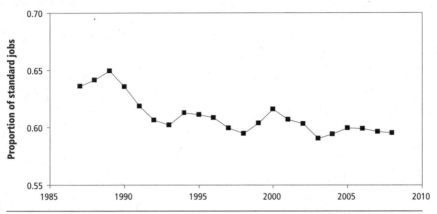

Source: Statistics Canada, Labour Force Survey (various years).

women. For men, the overall pattern can be divided into three sub-periods. The first is between 1981 and approximately 1986, during which the differential grew by over .1 log points. The second is between 1986 and 2000, during which it grew, but by a smaller amount. Boudarbat, Lemieux, and Riddell (2008), using census data, show that the latter increase occurred mainly in the second half of the 1990s. During the last sub-period (the years since 2000), the skill premium declined slightly. Analysts argued that the flat skill premium trend was evidence in support of a skill-biased demand shift favouring more educated workers because, by itself, the increase in the relative employment of university- versus high-school-educated men should have reduced the skilled premium (Freeman and Needels 1993; Murphy, Riddell, and Romer 1998).[5]

The skill premium line for women in Figure 3.4 reveals a larger premium in all years, but its long-run profile is essentially flat. Whatever was going on in the labour market was not affecting men and women in the same manner.

In Figure 3.5, we present the ratio of the number of university-educated employed workers to the number of high-school-or-less-educated workers separately for men and women. For both genders, the ratio nearly doubles over the 1980s then grows at an even faster rate in the 1990s and 2000s.[6] This constant growth is important because it implies that the increase in the education level of the workforce cannot explain the pattern of growth then decline in the skill premium for men in Figure 3.4.

FIGURE 3.4

Canadian skill premia for men and women workers, university vs. high school eduation, 1981-2009

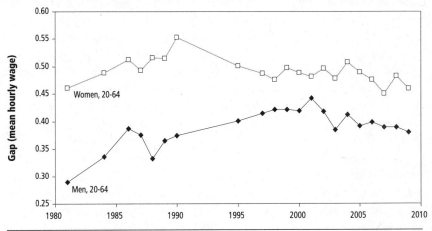

Source: Statistics Canada, Survey of Annual Work Patterns (1981); Labour Force Survey (various years); Survey of Union Membership (1984); Longitudinal Market Activity Survey (1986-90); Survey of Work Arrangements (1995).

FIGURE 3.5

Canadian skill employment ratios for men and women workers, university vs. high school education, 1981-2009

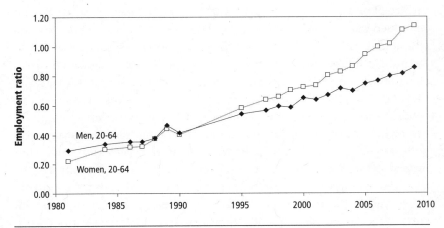

Source: See Figure 3.4.

Differentials across Cohorts

The other key "skill" dimension examined in empirical investigations is work experience. As we have seen, initial discussions of education differentials argued that they did not rise in Canada in the 1980s. The same studies indicated that, in contrast, returns to experience increased substantially, with some argument that this was part of the general "skill biased technical change" (Freeman and Needels 1993). However, such conclusions depend crucially on how the data are organized. The earlier studies examined wage differences between workers with different experience (roughly speaking, workers with the same education but different ages) within a given cross-section of data; they then considered how that differential evolved across cross-sections. To call this differential a "return to experience," one must assume that the wages earned by, say, a fifty-year-old in a given year are what a thirty-year-old in the same year will expect to earn in twenty years' time. The fact that these cross-sectional differentials were changing over time suggests this is not the case.

In Green and Townsend (2010), we investigate the declining real wages of high school-educated men using the LFS based data described in Section 2. These data include a consistent question on the length of time a worker has been in his job across the sample period (1981 to 2009). Using this, we assemble workers into "job entry cohorts" (groups of workers who started their job in the same pair of years and who have the same education level) and follow the evolution of their wages with job tenure. This allows us to see the actual returns to experience for each cohort. In Figure 3.6a, we present smoothed wage-tenure profiles by job entry cohort for high-school-or-less-educated men.[7] For job entry cohorts starting work before the mid-1990s, the profiles follow the same pattern as found in Beaudry and Green (2000) using other data: they shift down in parallel, with the real entry wages of the 1995-96 cohort being over 20 percent lower than those of the 1980-81 cohort. This implies that the increase in the experience differential witnessed in cross-sectional data does not reflect an increase in returns to experience (since each cohort had the same increase in wages with tenure) but instead a sharp trend downward in the wages of newer job entrants. For the late 1990s cohorts, in contrast, the entry wage stops falling and the slopes of the profiles begin to increase. In the 2000s, this pattern continues, with entry wages rising slightly and profiles twisting up. It is worth noting, though, that the wage profiles of the earliest cohorts (entering their jobs in the early 1980s) are unaffected by the changes in the labour market in the late 1990s and 2000s.

FIGURE 3.6

Smoothed wage profiles for men, by education and job entry cohorts, 1980-2010

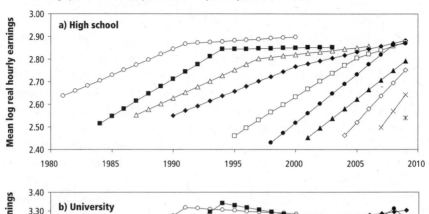
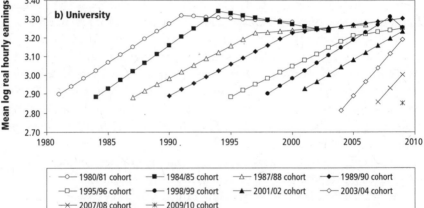

Source: See Figure 3.4.

Figure 3.6b contains wage-tenure profiles for university-educated men. Entry wages vary over a much smaller range for this group, and the patterns in profile slopes are unclear. What is clear is that there are no substantial gains in entry wages or increasing returns to experience, even for the more educated workers. Similar figures for women (for the sake of brevity, not shown here) reveal the same cross-cohort patterns. The main differences are that the female wages are at a lower level, and the decline in entry wages is much smaller than it is for men.

Overall, successive cohorts of labour market entrants have done badly, with only a mild benefit in terms of entry wages in the tight labour markets of the mid-2000s. Certainly, the data do not reveal a winning group of workers, benefitting from, say, skill-biased technical change.

Unionization and Industrial Composition
One potential explanation for the decline in real wages is a shift in unionization and the industrial composition of the workforce. It is interesting, again, to organize our discussion by job entry cohort since features like industrial composition change slowly for the whole labour force, but changes in trends show up immediately for new entrants. In Table 3.1, we present unionization rates, industrial composition (using fourteen consistently defined categories), and the mean log wage for male new job starters (workers with up to one year of job tenure) in 1981, 1989, 2000, 2007, and 2009, respectively. The years 1981, 1989, and 2000 all have unemployment rates of approximately 7.5 percent, and all correspond to cyclical peaks just preceding a downturn. The year 2007 has a lower unemployment rate but is a similarly defined cyclical peak. We include 2009 in order to provide a picture of our most recent data year. For less skilled men, the most striking pattern is the decline in unionization among new job starters, showing a seven percentage point drop between 1981 and 1989 and an even stronger 14 percentage point drop between 1989 and 2000. The pattern is relatively flat in the 2000s. While the overall unionization rate remains near 30 percent because older cohorts are more unionized than are younger cohorts, the rates among new job entrants indicate that, within one to two decades, Canada will have an overall unionization rate as low as that in the US.

Almost as striking is the shift of low-skilled men away from manufacturing. It is worth noting, though, that the decline in manufacturing was not large over the 1980s and was still not dramatic over the 1990s. The real decline came between 2000 and 2007, when the percentage in manufacturing fell from 21 percent to 14 percent. At the same time, however, employment in construction grew somewhat, so that the overall employment in these two blue-collar sectors declined by only two percentage points between 2000 and 2007. There have been further cyclical declines in both sectors in the current recession.

A key point for our discussion is that, by the mid-1990s, policy analysts might have viewed the loss of manufacturing jobs as an issue but not as the main problem in the labour market. Moreover, because unionization rates and industrial composition were presented for the overall labour force rather than for new entrants, the downward shift was masked by the slow-moving nature of changes in stocks. Thus, the economics literature of the

TABLE 3.1

Unionization rates, industry composition of employment, and log mean earnings of male job starters in Canada, selected years

	Start year				
	1981	1989	2000	2007	2009
I. Some high school					
Unionized	35.3	27.8	14.0	13.6	14.4
Agriculture	1.5	1.9	1.5	2.2	1.3
Primary	7.7	5.2	5.9	5.1	4.4
Construction	18.8	20.9	14.3	18.7	22.8
Manufacturing	23.5	22.4	21.3	14.3	12.2
Trade	17.7	18.7	17.3	18.5	21.0
Utilities	0.9	0.6	0.3	0.3	1.1
Transportation and storage	9.4	9.5	9.9	9.5	7.7
Finance, insurance, and real estate	1.8	1.5	1.8	3.3	2.4
Education	1.4	1.9	1.0	1.5	1.7
Public administration	3.4	3.5	1.2	1.7	1.1
Accommodations/food	5.8	5.0	8.2	6.9	9.5
Health care and social assistance	1.5	1.3	1.1	0.8	1.4
Professional services	2.7	2.8	9.3	10.6	8.4
Other services	4.0	4.8	6.9	6.7	5.0
Mean log wage	*2.64*	*2.56*	*2.43*	*2.50*	*2.55*
II. University educated					
Unionized	31.7	25.2	12.0	13.5	19.3
Agriculture	0.3	0.2	0.8	0.0	0.4
Primary	2.7	3.2	1.0	2.3	1.9
Construction	2.8	3.9	3.1	3.8	4.2
Manufacturing	16.6	16.4	17.3	12.7	11.9
Trade	6.4	8.8	8.1	12.2	9.1
Utilities	0.8	0.4	0.9	0.4	2.1
Transportation and storage	4.7	5.4	2.2	4.1	2.5
Finance, insurance, and real estate	6.5	6.7	8.2	6.8	10.5
Education	27.5	17.2	9.6	11.5	16.6
Public administration	8.3	9.3	7.1	5.6	5.2
Accommodations/food	2.2	2.6	2.5	3.9	3.5
Health care and social assistance	5.6	2.9	5.2	4.3	6.4
Professional services	12.7	18.5	25.2	20.6	19.6
Other services	2.8	4.5	8.8	11.7	6.2
Mean log wage	*2.88*	*2.93*	*2.90*	*2.85*	*2.87*

Sources: Statistics Canada, Survey of Annual Work Patterns (1981); Longitudinal Market Activity Survey (1989); Labour Force Survey (2000, 2007, 2009).

FIGURE 3.7

Canadian merchandise imports as a share of GDP, by region, 1980-2009

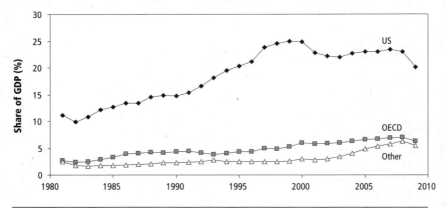

Sources: Statistics Canada, assorted CANSIM datasets: V183400, Canada, balance of payments, imports, US, including Puerto Rico and Virgin Islands; V183401, Canada, balance of payments, imports, United Kingdom; V183402, Canada, balance of payments, imports, European Union, excluding the UK; V183403, Canada, balance of payments, imports, Japan; V183404, Canada, balance of payments, imports, other OECD countries; V183405, Canada, balance of payments, imports, other countries; V646925, Canada, GDP at market prices.

time concluded that these were not the main driving forces behind the wage structure changes (e.g., DiNardo, Fortin, and Lemieux 1996).

The second part of Table 3.1 contains information on the same compositional shifts for university-educated men. Consistent with Figure 3.6b, this group did not experience large wage losses. As with high school men, university-educated job starters experienced rapid de-unionization, with most of the decline occurring between 1989 and 2000. Employment in manufacturing fell as well, with all of the change occurring between 2000 and 2007.

Trade

Some analysts attributed Canada's high unemployment in the 1990s to structural adjustments in response to the Canada-US Free Trade Agreement (CUSFTA), 1989, and the North American Free Trade Agreement (NAFTA), 1994. Figure 3.7 shows the volume of merchandise imports to Canada from the US, the remaining OECD countries, and the remaining non-OECD countries, as a share of GDP.[8] This figure highlights the dominant role of the US with regard to Canada's imports. Imports from the US were trending up during the 1980s. This trend accelerated in the 1990s, in the wake of the Canada-US Free Trade Agreement, 1989, but came to an abrupt halt after 2000 as new border security measures following 9/11 were implemented (Globerman and Storer 2008).

A series of papers have examined the consequences of CUSFTA for the Canadian labour market. Beaulieu (2000) and Trefler (2004) find that sectors facing large tariff cuts also experienced employment losses, primarily among production workers. Trefler concludes that, for sectors facing the deepest tariff cuts, employment contracted by 12 percent. In addition, after controlling for changes in the composition of the labour force, Townsend (2007) finds wage declines of up to 9 percent for workers in sectors facing the largest tariff cuts. However, as only a small fraction of workers in manufacturing were employed by firms in these industries, he concludes that the overall impact of CUSFTA on the wage structure was small. While CUSFTA clearly had an impact on the labour market, these types of calculations suggest that it was not sufficiently large to account for the labour market developments of the 1990s. This has been the consensus among economists. We return to the question of the size of trade impacts in the last section of the chapter.

International Comparisons

International comparisons have played an important role in Canadian policy debates in recent decades. In Figure 3.8, we plot the US unemployment rate

FIGURE 3.8

Unemployment rates, US, France, and Germany, 1980-2008

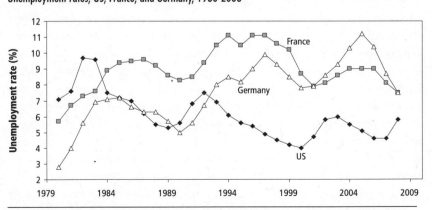

Sources: US Bureau of Labour Statistics, International Labor Comparisons (various years), http://www.bls.gov/fls/tables.htm.

along with the rates for France and Germany over the period from 1980 to 2008. The figure shows that the US moved from being a relatively high unemployment rate country in 1980 (as it had been in the preceding decades) to having much lower unemployment rates than France and Germany. Moreover, the separation of the unemployment rates coincided with an emerging difference in unemployment dynamics as Europe came to be characterized by a greater proportion of long unemployment spells than the US (Riddell 1999). Together, these were seen as a sign of "Eurosclerosis" versus the "US Miracle."

The US and Europe provide an important context for our study in terms of their employment and wage differentials by education group. For the US, a set of seminal papers (including Katz and Murphy [1992]; and Bound and Johnson [1992]) followed by a huge volume of other research established two main facts. First, in the 1980s, the wage differential between university- and high school-educated workers increased dramatically. Second, the relative employment of university- versus high school-educated workers also increased, albeit less dramatically than in the 1970s. Plotted as points in a diagram, with the ratio of university to high school average wages on the vertical axis and the ratio of university to high school employment on the horizontal axis, the conclusion was clear: the US was witnessing a skill-biased demand shift favouring more educated workers (Katz and Murphy 1992).

But the question remained: what was driving the demand shift? Three hypotheses were advanced. The first was that increased trade with less developed (and, hence, less skilled) countries had reduced the demand for lower-educated American workers. This was given some credence but was generally viewed as a secondary factor by economists for the same reasons discussed in the preceding section on the impacts of NAFTA. While the average wage for US high school-educated men dropped by approximately 20 percent in the 1980s (Beaudry and Green 2005), standard decomposition exercises indicated that trade shifts could account for, at most, a 4 percent drop (Bound and Johnson 1992; DiNardo, Fortin, and Lemieux 1996). Based on this, most economists rejected "globalization" as a main driving force behind what was happening in the labour market. Indeed, while much about the shifts in the wage structure remained contentious, this conclusion with regard to globalization reached near consensus among economists.

The second possible driving force was the decline of "institutions" that held up wages in low-skilled labour markets, particularly unions and minimum wages. The average real minimum wage declined by 30 percent over the 1980s, and the unionization rate declined by 25 percent. Decomposition exercises again suggest that these declines had important effects, but they leave much of the wage pattern unexplained (DiNardo, Fortin, and Lemieux 1996; DiNardo and Lemieux 1997; Donald, Green, and Paarsch 2000).

The third potential explanation for the relative wage and employment patterns was skill-biased technical change. We discuss this in more detail in the next section.

At the same time as the US was experiencing increased educational wage and employment differentials, European countries witnessed increased employment of more educated workers but no increase in wage differentials (Beaudry and Green 2003). Using other measures, European income inequality remained relatively unchanged over the 1980s and early 1990s, while US inequality grew tremendously (Gottschalk and Smeeding 1997). Overall, as is shown in Figure 3.8, unemployment grew in Europe but declined in the US.

Summary
It is worth recapping the patterns that policy makers in Canada faced (or thought they faced) in the mid-1990s. First, employment outcomes were troubling. This was true in an immediate sense – unemployment rates remained persistently high through the first half of the 1990s – and in the longer term. The late 1980s boom did not reduce unemployment rates to the levels seen in previous booms, raising concerns about a ratcheting-up of unemployment with each new recession. The fact that Canada had fallen substantially behind the US in terms of the employment rate in the 1990s made these concerns more pressing. Second, increases in non-standard employment in the early 1990s, combined with comparisons of US versus European outcomes, seemed to show that developed countries were facing a shift to a labour market in which more flexible work arrangements were required. Third, differentials in wages and employment by education level were increasing or, in cases where they were not, the evidence was interpreted as reflecting underlying forces that would eventually drive the differentials up. Fourth, trade, industrial composition, and unionization were all moving, but none appeared to be the main driving force behind the trends. Fifth, the US was characterized as having good employment outcomes but sharply rising inequality, while Europe was characterized as having high unemployment but little or no rise in inequality.

Standard Interpretation of the Patterns

The Dominant Theory

The various observations set out in the last section were unified by economists and policy analysts using a simple, yet powerful model, and this became the dominant theory. For Canada, this model was given its most complete expression in Murphy, Riddell, and Romer (1998). It had two components, which were not always combined.

The first was the hypothesis that the world was facing a skill-biased demand shift. In explicit formulations of the model, firms produce output by using unskilled labour, skilled labour, and capital. Over time, new inventions have become available that allow firms to produce more efficiently. The classic example is computers, which are often seen as replacing less skilled workers in performing routine tasks while enhancing the productivity of skilled workers. Thus, for example, computers reduce the need for clerical workers while allowing analysts to make sophisticated calculations faster than they could before. Such a technical change (referred to as "skill-biased technical change") naturally implies an increase in the demand for skilled labour relative to unskilled labour and, therefore, an increase in skilled relative to unskilled wages.

In some periods, shifts in the supply of skilled relative to unskilled labour (e.g., the US in the 1970s and Canada in the 1980s) meant that relative wages did not change much, and so the relative demand shift was hard to see. In the absence of policy changes and supply responses, the ongoing skill-biased technical change implied increasing inequality as skilled wages rose relative to wages for the unskilled (Katz and Murphy 1992). At the same time, the technical changes arising from the computer revolution were seen as driving the perceived increase in non-standard work.[9] Thus, these technical changes were perceived to be changing the structures of work and wages.

Importantly, the main models used in economics by the mid-1990s were not specific about the source of the technological change. In the main empirical work, technological change was not directly observed but, rather, inferred from the remaining movements in relative wages and relative employment after accounting for trade and institutional change. Thus, whatever could not be directly related to measurable variables was attributed to skill-biased technical change. This made the theory virtually impossible to refute, and it gained power as an explanation.

The second component of the dominant theory had to do with the effects of labour market policies. Governments, it was argued, could choose between policies that propped up wages in the face of the declining demand for low-skilled labour (e.g., high minimum wages or generous unemployment benefits) but yielded higher unemployment rates, and more flexible policies that would yield lower wages but more employment.[10] This was the explanation for the differences in outcomes between the US and Europe (Card, Kramarz, and Lemieux 1999). In the US, with its increasingly flexible labour markets, this showed up as declining wages for low-skilled workers, rising wages for high-skilled workers, and reduced unemployment. In Europe, rigid labour market institutions prevented low-skilled wages from falling and the relative demand shift was revealed as increased unemployment. These observations were combined into what Riddell (1999) called the "Krugman/OECD" hypothesis.[11]

However, the two components of the unified theory were not always combined in discussions. The Krugman/OECD hypothesis was based on the existence of a skill-biased demand shift that could stem from technological change or changes in trade patterns. But, as described earlier, based on decomposition exercises, economists rejected trade as a major driving force. Thus, the paradigmatic model came to be one in which exogenous technological change shifted relative to demand in favour of more skilled workers, with the precise effects of that shift on unemployment and wages depending on a combination of offsetting supply shifts and the flexibility of the labour market.

Did Canadian Policy Makers Buy into the Dominant Theory?

Rhetoric
Did the Canadian policy community "buy into" the dominant theory as a way of framing Canada's experience in the 1980s and early 1990s? The rhetoric in several key documents certainly suggests that it did. In 1994, the Department of Finance published *A New Framework for Economic Policy* (the Purple Book), which set out the policy direction for the newly elected Liberal government. The Purple Book pointed to "a revolution in technology, based on the microchip and related innovations, that has put knowledge and information at the cutting edge of economic progress" (Department of Finance 1994a, 1). Similarly, in a document heralding substantial changes in the unemployment insurance system, *From Unemployment Insurance to Employment Insurance*, Human Resources Development Canada described the need "to enable workers and employees to adapt to rapid technological change" (HRDC 1994b). Thus, the same message was coming from two very

different parts of the federal government. In fact, similar phrases describing ubiquitous technological change and the related rise in demand for skills can be found in a number of provincial government and policy think tank publications (e.g., Caledon Institute 1993; Ontario 1990). The only real contrast to what was being said among academic economists was that many of these documents placed equal emphasis on technological change and increased trade with lower wage countries, while we argue that economists largely dismissed trade as an explanation.

The rhetoric in policy-related documents placed a similar emphasis on the second component of the unified theory, with many directly referencing the OECD Jobs Study (e.g., Department of Finance 1994a; HRDC 1994b). The Purple Book directly states that the US has more inequality but less unemployment than Europe because it has "given much freer rein to market forces" (Department of Finance 1994a, 48-49). Importantly, the discussion in the Purple Book puts Canada together with European countries in terms of unemployment outcomes. As we have seen, Canadian unemployment rates were well above those in the US, raising concerns that we were too much like the Europeans and not enough like the Americans.

Policies

Did the rhetoric translate into actual policies? The dominant theory has two clear implications. First, it implies a trade-off between inequality and unemployment. To get less of the latter, countries must adopt more flexible labour market policies. The federal government placed more emphasis on employment than wage outcomes and so adopted these policies. This showed up in changes to the UI system which echoed the OECD language of shifting from "passive" to "active" programs (OECD 1994) – words that frequently show up in policy documents from the mid-1990s (e.g., the 1995 federal budget speech). Active programs emphasized getting benefit recipients back to work, providing training, and, in some cases, reducing access to benefits. At the same time, a number of provinces (most notably Ontario, Alberta, and British Columbia) moved towards reducing labour market regulation in an attempt to make their labour markets "flexible." As Boadway and Cuff (Chapter 14, this volume) discuss, this was complemented by changes in federal and especially provincial policies reducing both taxes at the top end and transfers at the bottom.

Given the theory and the international evidence, focusing on employment meant accepting high and rising inequality. But the new policies also focused on human capital. Again, the Purple Book led the way, calling for increased training and "lifelong learning" (Department of Finance 1994a, 38). Life-long learning focused on training while also emphasizing that workers needed to be flexible, in keeping with the first set of policies. The call for increased training was widespread, coming from governments and think tanks on the left and the right (HRDC 1994a, 1994b; Department of Finance 1994a, 1994b; Caledon Institute 1993; Ontario 1990). As Banting (2005) argues, Canada tended to talk about human capital policy rather than to enact it, but the proclaimed policy direction was clear. Overall, while we cannot prove that Canadian policies in the crucial mid-1990s period were derived from the dominant theory, they certainly fit with it.

Problems with the Dominant Theory

The dominant theory played an important role in either motivating or rationalizing the policy changes of the mid-1990s, and its impact continues to be felt today. More specifically, the policies adopted in the mid-1990s are still with us, and they continue to inform policy decisions. *Advantage Canada*, the 2006 document setting out the Conservative government's policy direction, analyzes labour market policy challenges in dominant theory terms: "Globalization and the growth of the knowledge-based economy are also sharply increasing the importance of the skills, education and adaptability of our workforce for global competitiveness" (Department of Finance 2006, 11). It goes on to say that "Canada's Knowledge Advantage will create the best-educated, most-skilled and most flexible workforce in the world" (Department of Finance 2006, chap. 3). These same phrases appear throughout documents written in the mid-1990s, the chief difference being that the more recent ones also emphasize new problems, especially looming skill shortages.

Given this ongoing impact, it is important to assess the validity of the dominant theory for Canada. We argue that the theory doesn't fit the Canadian data in a number of key dimensions. As we have seen, the lack of movement in the ratio of university- to high-school-educated average wages in the Survey of Consumer Finances (SCF) data from the 1980s, combined with a surge in university enrolment in that decade, were interpreted in the mid-1990s as implying that Canada was experiencing a skill-biased demand shift, exactly offset by a relative supply shift. However, as Figure 3.4 shows, a more careful examination of the data reveals that the wage differential actually rose sharply in the early 1980s, particularly for young people (Boudarbat, Lemieux, and Riddell 2008). Thus, the group facing the largest relative supply shift (those in their twenties) experienced the largest increase in the education-wage differential. This is not to say that there was no skill-biased demand shift (a relative rise in both wages and employment for the university-educated necessarily implies such a shift), but a model in which that shift is created by an exogenous skill-biased technological change offset for some groups by relative supply shifts cannot fit this data. Moreover, as Figure 3.6 shows, real entry wages for high school-educated males have declined dramatically since 1980, and the real entry wages of the university-educated have not risen. If there is a skill-biased demand shift directly raising the productivity and wages of the most skilled and, ultimately, raising the wages of the less skilled through general equilibrium effects, it is hard to find it in Canadian wage data.

Beaudry and Green (2005) examine the fit of the exogenous skill-biased technical change model for wage patterns in the US – whose economy the model was created to explain. They show that, in the period between the mid-1970s and the early 2000s – the period during which computer technology came online – the relative supply of skills was positively correlated with the skilled-unskilled wage differential. This is the exact opposite of what the theory predicts.[12] In an online appendix to Green and Townsend (2010), we show that their conclusions hold for Canada.

These arguments have pushed proponents of the skill-biased technical change model to develop more nuanced versions of the theory. For example, Autor, Katz, and Kearney (2008) and Autor, Levy, and Murnane (2003) argue that new computer technologies bias demand towards skilled workers and unskilled service workers performing tasks that cannot be done by computers, while reducing demand for semi-skilled workers (e.g., production line operatives). Their policy prescription continues to be increased education. So far, there has been no investigation of whether this new version of the theory fits Canadian data.

Another important piece of evidence underlying the theorizing about labour markets is the relative performance of the American and European labour markets. As we have seen, several analysts have argued that Europe and the US have been facing the same skill-biased demand shift, but, because of rigidities in the labour market, it has showed up in increased unemployment rather than in wage inequalities in the European economies. The hypothesis needs to be stated more clearly. What should have happened in Europe since 1980, according to this theory, is a relative increase in unemployment, with less-skilled workers performing relatively worse. However, Card et al. (1999) show that relative employment outcomes for less- versus more-educated individuals moved in a similar way in France, Canada, and the US. There is no evidence of a relative worsening in employment outcomes for less-skilled workers in more regulated economies. It is true that unemployment was higher in France by the end of the 1990s, and perhaps labour market policies played a role, but this is not evidence of a skill-biased demand shift.

Finally, changes in the extent of non-standard employment helped convince analysts that the labour market was changing in such a way as to require more flexibility from workers in the future. However, the increase in non-standard employment was confined to the early part of the 1990s. Since then, as Figure 3.3 shows, the proportion of jobs that are non-standard has remained virtually unchanged. Moreover, Brochu (2004) shows that the probability that a job in place in one year will continue to the following year rose in the mid-1990s to levels above those witnessed at any time since the mid-1970s (when data on this began) and stayed high up to the current recession. This is a case in which perceptions about what was going on were muddied by the prolonged labour market recession in the 1990s. The probability of a job's ending tends to decline during recessions because of reductions in quit rates, so it was not clear, even by the end of the 1990s, whether the measured increase in job stability reflected a cyclical effect hiding a long-term trend towards instability or, as turned out to be the case, if it reflected a long-term trend towards greater job stability (Heisz 2005).

Alternative Views on Labour Market Patterns

In this section, we touch on alternate models for explaining patterns in the Canadian labour market and their implications for policy. The first model we consider is a model of technological change, which Beaudry and Green (2003, 2005) argue fits the US data from the mid-1970s through the 1990s. In the online appendix to Green and Townsend (2010), we show that it also fits the Canadian data between 1980 and 2007. This model considers an economy in transition between an older and a newer general purpose technology. Both technologies employ capital, unskilled labour, and skilled labour to produce a common output. The older technology makes relatively greater use of unskilled labour, while the newer technology makes greater use of skilled labour. In this scenario, capital and unskilled labour work together to enhance each other's productivity, and the same is true for capital and skilled labour (i.e., capital complements both types of labour). Now, consider an entrepreneur who is deciding whether to invest her capital in the new or old technology. If the education level of the economy is increasing, more entrepreneurs will choose to produce with the new technology since its defining factor (skilled labour) is becoming more abundant. As a result, we will observe a decline in high-skilled wages because of the increased supply of skilled labour, but we will also observe a decline in the wages of unskilled workers because there is less demand for their services. In fact, under conditions that Beaudry and Green (2005) show hold for the US in this period, unskilled wages will fall, and we will witness an increase in the skilled wage differential. This pattern of increases in the skilled wage differential, coinciding with increases in the relative supply of skills, with neither skilled nor unskilled workers experiencing substantial wage increases, is exactly what we see in the Canadian data.

The model in Beaudry and Green (2003, 2005) has very different policy implications from the standard skill-biased technical change model. In the latter model, increases in education are beneficial for the less skilled because they become a relatively scarce factor. However, the technology selection model points to the opposite conclusion: increasing the education level will benefit the specific workers who obtain the education, but the remaining unskilled workers will have less capital to work with and will be left further behind as the number of skilled workers increases. Thus, human capital policy will not have the inequality-decreasing effect that the dominant model implies. What will help unskilled workers are increases in physical capital, which, broadly speaking, will allow the expanding group of skilled workers to be outfitted with capital without taking capital away from the unskilled. Indeed, after 1997, a combination of increased capital flows into Canada and a slowdown in the expansion of the number of skilled workers resulted in a turnaround in the downward trend in unskilled wages. The overall conclusion is not to deny the usefulness of investing in human capital but, rather, to emphasize that such investments need to be accompanied by investment in physical capital in order to avoid greater inequality.

Other models of the labour market advise similar caution in following the dominant theory. Beaudry, Green, and Sand (2012) show that a search and bargaining model with multiple sectors and multiple cities has tight testable implications that fit with US data over the last quarter century. In their model, firms and workers meet and bargain over wages. The bargaining outcome depends on the outside options of both the firms and the workers. For workers, their outside option depends, in part, on the set of other jobs available in their city; workers in high-wage cities will view themselves as having better outside options than workers in low-wage cities. Using US data, Beaudry, Green, and Sand (2012) show that, in fact, wages within a given industry (e.g., construction) increase in cities that experience a shift in their industrial composition towards a set of industries that pay relatively high wages (typically, heavy industry for low-skilled workers) even if construction's share of employment in the city is held constant.

This result has two implications for our discussion. The first is that shifts in industrial composition have spill-over effects on wages in other industries. Economists who conclude that trade shifts played a relatively minor role in declining real wages in recent decades do not take account of such spill-overs; if a steel industry job, say, is lost because of trade effects, standard investigations merely count that lost job in their tally of trade impacts. But if wage setting in the rest of the economy is also affected, the total impact could be much larger. Indeed, Beaudry, Green, and Sand (2012) conclude that the total impact of these kinds of changes could be three times what was previously measured. Trade and globalization may have a more direct impact on the labour market than economists – and, it would seem, Canadian policy makers – have assumed.

The results also suggest a rethinking of changes in SA and UI policies. These policies form part of workers' outside options when bargaining since leaving the current match could involve a period of unemployment. Reduced access to SA and UI benefits after the mid-1990s implies reductions in wages for low-skilled workers in all industries. This indicates a greater link between policy decisions and wages than typically appears in the economics literature. Moreover, if both trade and policy explain more of the wage structure shifts, this means that technical change, since it is essentially a residual explanation, necessarily explains less. This is troubling if, as we argue, policy decisions were based on the belief that the wage structure was being driven by technical change.

Conclusion

In this chapter, we argue that a combination of perceptions of trends in the Canadian labour market up to the mid-1990s and economic theorizing led to a dominant story about the forces driving the Canadian wage and employment structure. In that story, technological change was improving outcomes for skilled workers, worsening outcomes for less-skilled workers, and imposing more flexibility on workers of all skill levels. On the one hand, if this force were allowed to operate unhindered, the result would be increasing inequality but better employment outcomes and improved international competitiveness. This route was seen to be exemplified by the US. On the other hand, if a country resisted the implications for low-skilled wages, the effects of the technological change would show up in higher unemployment. This is how Europe was perceived. We argue that Canada adopted a consistent set of policies within the context of this dominant theory. Whether these policies followed from the theory or the theory was used to justify previously determined policy directions cannot be determined, but, in either case, policy documents from the mid-1990s are replete with statements consistent with the dominant theory.

A key part of the declared policy response (if not always the actual policy action) was increased investment in human capital. The idea was that the inequality effects of technological change could be offset by increasing the supply of skills; this would dampen rising skilled wages and raise low-skilled wages. Investing in human capital would also make the economy more productive and, hence, competitive. Therefore, the second policy prescription was to make the labour market more "flexible"; at the federal level this showed up most clearly in changes in the UI system. Both sets of policy responses had long-lasting impacts, and the main ideas underlying the dominant theory continue to show up in recent policy documents, implying that it is important to examine whether the theory really fits Canadian data.

In fact, we argue that the perceptions about the labour market that underlie the dominant story are incorrect. Granted, some of this only became evident after the smoke of the prolonged early- and mid-1990s labour market recession cleared away. We argue, further, that the basic model of the impact of technological change on the labour market does not fit the data for Canada. In its stead, we posit labour market models that incorporate wage bargaining, with technological change determined endogenously by movements in relative factor shares. In this approach, human capital policies are shown to increase inequality rather than to decrease it, and trade impacts on the labour market appear as much larger than economists have typically assumed. To the extent that this is true, it calls into question the validity of the substantial package of labour market reforms put in place in the mid-1990s; instead, it implies that policies designed to increase human capital investment need to be accompanied by policies targeting increased physical capital investment. With more physical capital, the increasing numbers of skilled workers can essentially be outfitted with capital without having to reduce capital per unskilled worker and, with it, unskilled wages. In addition, these alternate models suggest the need to pay attention to the impacts of cutting income support programs on unskilled wages and to ask whether we have gone too far in pursuit of higher employment policies. To phrase it differently, it raises a question recently posed by John Myles: Should we adopt a set of policies to make Canada a high-wage economy instead of the policies pursued since the mid-1990s, which seem to have had the opposite effect?

NOTES

1. We discuss the comparability of these datasets at length in Green and Townsend (2010).
2. These adjusted series are from the US Bureau of Labor Statistics, which has corrected them for definitional differences.
3. These data come from the LFS. "Full-time" is defined as thirty or more hours per week.
4. It continued to be viewed this way for quite some time (e.g., Vosko, Zukevich, and Cranford 2003).
5. It is important to point out that, until recently, the broad over time pattern would have been characterized quite differently. Using data from the Survey of Consumer Finances, Freeman and Needels (1993), Murphy, Riddell, and Romer (1998), and Burbidge, Magee, and Robb (2002) all portray the skill premium as essentially flat through the 1980s. Boudarbat, Lemieux, and Riddell (2008) argue that this finding actually reflects a combination of the dataset being used, the use of weekly rather than hourly wages, and a lack of controls for shifts in the age structure. Once they take account of these factors, Boudarbat, Lemieux, and Riddell find the same pattern as is described here.
6. A simple regression of the ratio for men and women combined on an intercept and a linear trend yields an R-squared of .99.
7. Each cohort is fitted to a separate spline, which allows the slope of the wage profile to change after ten years of tenure.
8. Import volumes were obtained from series on import values using a common price deflator as deflators specific to each region are not available.
9. For example, computers enable employees to work from home.
10. As Boadway and Cuff (Chapter 14, this volume) show, the same outlook emerged in the intellectual discussions surrounding tax and transfer policies.
11. Since it was suggested in the OECD (1994) Jobs Paper and in Krugman (1994), among other places.
12. Card and DiNardo (2002) also argue that the exogenous skill-biased technological change model does not fit the US data well.

REFERENCES

Autor, David H., Lawrence F. Katz, and Melissa S. Kearney. 2008. "Trends in US Wage Inequality: Revising the Revisionists." *Review of Economics and Statistics* 90(2): 300-23.

Autor, David H., Frank Levy, and Richard J. Murnane. 2003. "The Skill Content of Recent Technological Change: An Empirical Exploration." *Quarterly Journal of Economics* 118(4): 1279-333.

Banting, Keith G. 2005. "Do We Know Where We Are Going? The New Social Policy in Canada." *Canadian Public Policy* 31(4): 421-29.

Beaudry, Paul, and David A. Green. 2000. "Cohort Patterns in Canadian Earnings: Assessing the Role of Skill Premia in Inequality Trends." *Canadian Journal of Economics* 33(4): 907-36.

—. 2003. "Wages and Employment in the United States and Germany: What Explains the Differences?" *American Economic Review* 93(3): 573-602.

—. 2005. "Changes in US Wages, 1976-2000: Ongoing Skill Bias or Major Technological Change?" *Journal of Labor Economics* 23(3): 609-48.

Beaudry, Paul, David A. Green, and Ben Sand. 2012. "Does Industrial Composition Matter? An Empirical Evaluation Based on Search and Bargaining Theory." *Econometrica* 80(3): 1063-104.

Beaulieu, Eugene. 2000. "The Canada-US Free Trade Agreement and Labour Market Adjustments in Canada." *Canadian Journal of Economics* 33: 540-63.

Boudarbat, B., T. Lemieux, and W.C. Riddell. 2008. "The Evolution of the Returns to Human Capital in Canada, 1980-2006." Working paper, Canadian Labour Market and Skills Researcher Network.

Bound, John, and George Johnson. 1992. "Changes in the Structure of Wages in the 1980s: An Evaluation of Alternative Explanations." *American Economic Review* 82(3): 371-92.

Brochu, Pierre. 2004. "Explaining the Canadian Job Stability Paradox." Department of Economics working paper, University of British Columbia.

Burbidge, J.B., L. Magee, and A.L. Robb. 2002. "The Education Premium in Canada and the United States." *Canadian Public Policy* 28(2): 203-17.

Caledon Institute. 1993. *Federal Social Policy Agenda*. Caledon Institute, Ottawa.

Card, David, and John DiNardo. 2002. "Skill Biased Technical Change and Rising Wage Inequality: Some Problems and Puzzles." *Journal of Labor Economics* 20(4): 733-81.

Card, David, Francis Kramarz, and Thomas Lemieux. 1999. "Changes in the Relative Structure of Wages and Employment: A Comparison of the United States, Canada, and France." *Canadian Journal of Economics* 32(4): 843-77.

Card, David, and W. Craig Riddell. 1993. "A Comparative Analysis of Unemployment in Canada and the United States." In D. Card and R.B. Freeman, eds., *Small Differences That Matter: Labor Markets and Income Maintenance in Canada and the United States*, 149-90. Chicago: University of Chicago Press for National Bureau of Economic Research, Inc.

Department of Finance. 1994a. *A New Framework for Economic Policy*. Ottawa: Supply and Services Canada.

—. 1994b. *Building a More Innovative Economy*. Ottawa: Supply and Services Canada.

—. 2006. *Advantage Canada*. Ottawa: Supply and Services Canada.

DiNardo, John, Nicole Fortin, and Thomas Lemieux. 1996. "Labour Market Institutions and the Distribution of Wages, 1973-92: A Semiparametric Approach." *Econometrica* 64(5): 1001-44.

DiNardo, John, and Thomas Lemieux. 1997. "Diverging Male Wage Inequality in the United States and Canada, 1981-88: Do Institutions Explain the Difference?" *Industrial and Labour Relations Review* 50(4): 629-51.

Donald, Stephen G., David Green, and Harry J. Paarsch. 2000. "Differences in Wage Distributions between Canada and the United States: An Application of a Flexible Estimator of Distribution Functions in the Presence of Covariates." *Review of Economic Studies* 67(4): 609-33.

Freeman, Richard B., and Karen Needels. 1993. "Skill Differentials in Canada in an Era of Rising Labor Market Inequality." In D. Card and R.B. Freeman, eds., *Small Differences That Matter: Labor Markets and Income Maintenance in Canada and the United States*, 45-68. Chicago: University of Chicago Press for National Bureau of Economic Research, Inc.

Globerman, Steven, and Paul Storer. 2008. *The Impacts of 9/11 on Canada-US Trade*. Toronto: University of Toronto Press.

Gottschalk, Peter, and Timothy M. Smeeding. 1997. "Cross-National Comparisons of Earnings and Income Inequality." *Journal of Economic Literature* 35(2): 633-87.

Green, David A., and James Townsend. 2010. "Understanding the Wage Patterns of Canadian Less Skilled Workers: The Role of Implicit Contracts." *Canadian Journal of Economics* 43(10): 373-403.

Heisz, Andrew. 2005. "The Evolution of Job Stability in Canada: Trends and Comparisons with US Results." *Canadian Journal of Economics* 38(1): 105-27.

HRDC. 1994a. *From Unemployment Insurance to Employment Insurance*. Ottawa: Supply and Services Canada.

–. 1994b. *Improving Social Security in Canada: A Discussion Paper*. Ottawa: Supply and Services Canada.

Katz, Lawrence F., and Kevin M. Murphy. 1992. "Changes in Relative Wages, 1963-1987: Supply and Demand Factors." *Quarterly Journal of Economics* 107: 35-78.

Krahn, H. 1995. "Non-Standard Work on the Rise." *Perspectives on Labour and Income, Statistics Canada* 7(4): 35-42.

Krugman, Paul. 1994. "Past and Prospective Causes of High Unemployment." *Proceedings*, Federal Reserve Bank of Kansas, January, 49-98.

Murphy, Kevin M., W. Craig Riddell, and Paul M. Romer. 1998. "Wages, Skills and Technology in Canada and the United States." In Elhanen Helpman, ed., *General Purpose Technologies and Economic Growth*, 283-309. Cambridge: MIT Press.

OECD. 1994. *The OECD Jobs Study*. Paris: Organisation for Economic Cooperation and Development.

Ontario. 1990. "People and Skills in the New Global Economy." Ontario Premier's Council, Toronto.

Riddell, W. Craig. 1999. "Canadian Labour Market Performance in International Perspective." *Canadian Journal of Economics* 32(5): 1097-134.

–. 2005. "Why Is Canada's Unemployment Rate Persistently Higher Than in the United States?" *Canadian Public Policy* 31(1): 93-100.

Townsend, James. 2007. "Do Tariff Reductions Affect the Wages of Workers in Protected Industries? Evidence from the Canada-US Free Trade Agreement." *Canadian Journal of Economics* 40(1): 9-92.

Trefler, Daniel. 2004. "The Long and Short of the Canada-US Free Trade Agreement." *American Economic Review* 94(4): 870- 95.
Vosko, L.F., N. Zukewich, and C. Cranford. 2003. "Precarious Jobs: A New Typology of Employment." *Perspectives on Labour and Income* 4(10): 16-26.

4 Business, Labour, and Redistributive Politics

WILLIAM D. COLEMAN

Analysts of the role of the state have long argued that the relative balance in political influence between business and labour is critical to explaining the differences that emerged in welfare states during the postwar era. Accordingly, understanding the contemporary politics of redistribution in Canada should include an examination of the specific interests of the political organizations representing business and labour, their relative strengths, and their capacity to engage in political debates about the social role of the state over the longer term. In its analysis of the balance between business and labour, this chapter considers both classes in light of their respective organizational capacities. These capacities, in turn, are mapped on to their reactions to globalization and changes in the policy process arising from the centralization of power within the federal and provincial governments.

Crucial to the creation of a useful dialogue on redistribution is the existence of encompassing representative associations, that is, associations whose membership structures permit them to represent all or a large majority of employees, on the one side, or business firms, on the other (see Olson 1982, 47-53). In an ideal world, working through such organizations, labour and business could reach agreement on the importance of reducing inequalities in society and find a general approach to policy that they might discuss with politicians.[1] Unfortunately, cooperation between business and labour, so typical of the robust redistributive policies of other countries, is absent in Canada. Neither business nor labour has built vertically integrated,[2] highly representative, encompassing organizations to define and support such policies. Furthermore, unlike some other OECD countries, in Canada, business has long been considerably more influential than labour. Finally, over the past fifteen years, the potential for business-labour cooperation has declined due to deep differences in their understanding of the advantages and disadvantages of economic globalization.

In this chapter, I argue the following. First, when political organizations representing business and labour cooperate as integrated, economy-wide interest associations, they are more likely to find common interests, developing synergies between economic and social (redistributive) policies. These synergies lead to more robust distributive and redistributive policies to support those of modest means. When one or both is weaker in building such associations, however, as in Canada, policies are less robust, less universal, and take less account of the problems of those with modest incomes. Because Canadian group politics has lacked strong economy-wide organizations for business, and as those associations seeking to represent labour as a class tend to be less encompassing and more divided than those in many other OECD states, building a policy consensus has been difficult, if not impossible.

Second, as contemporary globalizing processes have deepened since 1980 (Castells 1999; Scholte 2005; Sassen 2007), the divide between labour and business has widened. (For a discussion about how globalization has affected Canadian labour markets, see Chapter 3, this volume.) Generally speaking, business organizations support globalization and argue that economic and social policies must give precedence to Canada's efforts to engage with the global economy. The two most encompassing business associations, the Canadian Council of Chief Executives (CCCE) and the Canadian Federation of Independent Business (CFIB) agree on the importance of focusing on economic policies that maximize the role of market forces and put less emphasis on redistribution, even though they do not always agree on the mechanics of redistributive policies. They also agree on the need to coordinate policies with the approaches taken in other countries, particularly in the US. This agreement reinforces their capacity to exert pressure on governments. In contrast, labour groups find contemporary "neoliberal" globalization a threat to policies aimed at reducing social and economic inequality; in their view, redistribution policies should be prioritized and globalization challenged (see Swank 2002).

Finally, centralization of policy making has meant an increasing concentration of authority in the hands of the prime minister and of the provincial premiers, and this development has advantaged business associations over labour organizations. This institutional development reinforces the strong influence of business, particularly transnational corporations, on public policy related to redistribution in Canada.

The argument is developed in three steps. The first section of the chapter reviews two theoretical arguments that underline the importance of political organizations of business and labour in determining how and to what extent governments address social inequality. The second section builds on this theory and suggests a methodology to assess the organizational capacity of representative groups of business and labour to influence politics. The third section reviews changes in how these representative groups have engaged the policy process since 1990, highlighting the weakening position of labour and the deepening cleavage between business and labour over globalization.

Theorizing Political Organizations of Business and Labour

The argument in this chapter draws its inspiration from the idea that political organizations of business and labour are crucial to their success or failure in influencing public policy. Policies are not developed overnight, nor do governments automatically know what different social classes want; rather, policies emerge as the product of intensive discussions, debates, and lobbying over many months, if not years. As Hacker and Pierson (2010, 172) note: "These are struggles that involve drawn out conflicts in multiple arenas, extremely complicated issues where only full-time, well-trained participants are likely to be effective, and stakes that can easily reach hundreds of billions of dollars. Inevitably, organized groups are crucial actors, and usually *the* crucial actors, in these struggles." Given this observation, one widely shared by students of public policy, which organizational attributes are most important for understanding a group's capacity to influence social policy outcomes? Both the *corporatism* approach and *power resources* theory attempt to answer this question.

Before discussing the corporatist approach, it is useful to set it against another type of interaction involving organized groups: *pluralism*. In pluralist associational systems, power is diffused widely within the state and among interest groups representing particular interests of small populations in society. This dispersal of power prevents coordinated policy making between business and labour as a whole and invites policies focused on the short term, catering to individual power centres in society (Coleman 1988, 70-72). In pluralist systems, individual organizations act independently rather than in concert. Given social actors may have a variety of associations from which to choose, each with a specialized purpose and often in competition with one another

In contrast, corporatist systems create environments through encompassing associations for reconciling conflicting interests, sometimes from different classes, and sometimes from fractions within the same class. When these systems bring together encompassing organizations representing business and labour, business is forced to take the interests of labour into account and vice versa. Corporatism thus usually involves a three-cornered configuration of conflicting social interests and state intermediation (Coleman 1988, 76). The policies conducive to corporatism are not so much regulatory or allocative as redistributive: "Redistribution generates the conflict that gives rise to the corporatist 'temptation'" (ibid.).

The corporatist approach hypothesizes that economies progress most successfully when institutional arrangements encourage individuals and organizations to work together and when business and labour agree on sufficiently strong distributive and redistributive polices to address economic security (Hicks and Kenworthy 1998, 1633-34; see also Hollingsworth and Boyer 1997; Lehmbruch and Schmitter 1982; Katzenstein 1984; Streeck and Schmitter 1985). Speaking at a general level, Hicks and Kenworthy opine that, when business organizations are grouped into centralized confederations, they are able to reduce rent-seeking by individual firms and sectors. By "confederations" they mean that these overarching associations include as their members more specialized associations representing different sectors of business or, in the case of labour, different, more specialized unions. In this respect, the specialized groups federate to the overarching ones, delegating to the latter the responsibility for engaging with the state on economy-wide questions. When the degree of integration of the specialized groups into representative associations is high, and when these groups represent all or most of their business firms or workers in their given sector of specialization, the policy capacity of the overarching associations is high, and they have more influence on governments (Atkinson and Coleman 1990, 81-82).

Hicks and Kenworthy add that, when governments and interest groups cooperate in policy making, more productive and coherent state policies follow. Moreover, there is some evidence that the policies agreed upon between business and government are anticipatory and long term, rather than reactive and able to address short-term crises only (Atkinson and Coleman

1990, 87-93). Agreeing upon anticipatory, longer-term policies is more likely when the relevant government agencies concentrate authority in autonomous, policy capable units.

Drawing on a large corporatism literature, Hicks and Kenworthy (1998) also note two special roles played by labour organizations. First, when the labour movement has built highly representative, centralized encompassing organizations, then wage bargaining encourages wage restraint, which, in turn, favours more effective redistributive policies. Second, when labour organizations and business associations cooperate and engage with the state on policy, they create what Hicks and Kenworthy call a "tripartite corporatism." When such organizations exist for business and labour, and when they are willing to negotiate with one another and the state, they set the stage for economic policies sustaining employment, on the one side, and restraining inflation, on the other. Hicks and Kenworthy (1659-60) find that, when these conditions are met, distributive/redistributive policies and outcomes are enhanced, investment levels and trade performance improve, and inflation is reduced.[3]

For its part, power resources theory (PRT) focuses on how labour organizes to face the capitalist class, the most powerful actor in society given its control over economic resources. The opening premise of PRT is the following: "Wage and salary-earners who are relatively disadvantaged in terms of economic resources to be used on the markets can be expected to attempt – with varying degrees of success – to act collectively via democratic politics, where the universal and equal right to vote, at least in principle, is the most important power resource" (Korpi 1998, ix; see also Stephens 1979). PRT proponents see the balance of power between business and labour as fluid and as dependent on the kinds of political organizations and strategies employed by the two social classes. Labour can enhance its influence by forming a political party and by drawing on its large population base to vote that party into power. Once in power, the party can develop effective redistributive policies. A necessary condition for success, however, is effective organization, including high rates of unionization and "the organization of unions into a cohesive labour central or confederation" (Olsen and O'Connor 1998, 6). PRT theorists hypothesize that the better this condition is met, the stronger the welfare state.

Esping-Andersen (1990) builds on both approaches in his widely cited typology of welfare states. In his analysis, the type of welfare state that has emerged in any country reflects the nature of class coalitions constructed at critical historical junctures, with the social-democratic model predominating in Scandinavian societies characterized by strong labour movements allied with social democratic parties and engaging with encompassing business interest associations.

Both the corporatist and the power resources theoretical approaches put considerable emphasis on the capacity of labour to develop encompassing, confederal peak organizations that represent a significant percentage of the potential membership base. This emphasis is not surprising because labour is the only organized interest whose focus is on the "broad economic concerns of those with modest incomes" (Hacker and Pierson 2010, 182). The corporatist approach departs from PRT in emphasizing the additional advantages that come from centralized organizations for business and their willingness to engage with organizations that represent all or most of labour.

Both theoretical approaches make assumptions about economic policy making that are challenged by globalization: advanced capitalist nation-states retain sufficient sovereignty and control to define economic policy autonomously from other states. But Hicks and Kenworthy (1998) and Olsen and O'Connor (1998) worry that this assumption might not hold under economic globalization. In his study of economic policy making and globalization, Reinicke (1998) argues that globalization has led to the emergence of a parallel, even competing, set of linkages at the level of production that are transnational and global rather than international in form. Reinicke concludes that "global public policy" is the only strategy that is sustainable in the long term. He doubts the long-term viability of strategies of protectionism (defensive intervention) or countries trying to set up the most welcoming domestic environment possible for attracting global corporations (offensive intervention). Instead, he recommends a movement towards global public policy: "the delinking of some elements of the operational aspects of internal sovereignty (governance) from its territorial foundation (the nation-state) and its institutional and legal environment (the government) and their reapplication on a sectoral – that is, functional – basis" (Reinicke 1998, 87). In this way, policies could "cut across" state boundaries to match political geography with the increasingly global economic geography.

Globalization has generated considerable debate, with scholars like Linda Weiss (1998, 2003) arguing that welfare state policies remain robust even under globalization. But even Weiss (2005) sees globalization changing the politics of how states and groups define welfare state policies. For our purposes, as Reinicke observes, economic globalization forces states to cooperate more fully with other states on regional and global scales. In pursuing these engagements systematically and energetically, they change the ground rules for political organizations representing business and labour. Business organizations will reflect the changing interests of their members and will focus on "competitiveness" of the nation-state in the global domain. In contrast, recognizing the significant threats to domestic economic and social policies from globalization, labour will oppose engagement with the global economy. These changes in emphasis on the part of business and labour will lower significantly the likelihood of their cooperating on economic and social policies. Cerny (1997) summarizes these developments as a move away from the welfare state to the "competition state."

Methodology

Consistent with the corporatism and PRT literatures, I am particularly interested in those interest associations that seek to represent and speak for business and labour as a whole or as social classes. There are hundreds of associations representing business interests in particular sectors (see Coleman 1988), and many union organizations speak for workers in different niches of the private and public sectors. Generally speaking, these specialized associations and unions leave broader policy debates to more encompassing groups and only intervene when there is a particular policy provision that directly affects their members.

In previous research, I have operationalized some of the above theoretical thinking about political organizations and their influence by assessing the "power capacity" of representative groups (Coleman 1996). I focus on several aspects of associational systems related to the kinds of integration of interests in encompassing associations discussed in the two theoretical approaches above: the degree of competition among associations for members, the presence of horizontal bridges between associations, and the level of vertical integration in the associational system. By the latter, I mean the extent to which smaller, specialized groups are integrated into larger, more inclusive and encompassing groups – perhaps industry-wide or representing all sectors of the economy

My selection of these variables grows out of my participation in the Organization of Business Interests project in the 1980s. Headed by Philippe Schmitter and Wolfgang Streeck, the project built an analytical framework for the study of corporatism. In choosing these three aspects of associational systems, I assume that the less competition between associations, the more horizontal coordination between them, and the higher the level of vertical integration, the more capacity business and labour organizations will have to influence and then participate in political decision making related to distributive and redistributive policies.

Labour

Generally speaking, workers or employees of private businesses, governments, or organizations active in the non-profit private sector turn to their unions to represent their particular economic and social interests. As a preliminary step to the analysis of power capacity, it is useful to look at union density: the percentage of the labour force represented by unions. The higher the percentage of workers represented by unions, the more power capacity we can expect encompassing union organizations to have. Statistics on density have been kept by Statistics Canada for many years. Over the past two decades, union density in Canada has fallen slowly (HRSDC 2010). In 1991, union membership as a percentage of the civilian labour force was 28.6, and for non-agricultural paid workers it was 34.8. In 2008, these percentages were 25.6 and 30.4 percent, respectively. The majority of the decline, however, had occurred by 2002; since then, the decline has stabilized, and figures have changed very little.

Analysts also speak of "union coverage," which considers situations in which workers in particular sectors of the economy who are not members of a union are nevertheless "covered" by an agreement made between a union and firms in the given sector. In some states, like France, this coverage is required under "extension laws," that is, laws that require labour agreements reached in a sector to be "extended" to all workers in the sector, whether they belong to the union or not. In Canada, however, no such extension laws exist, and most collective bargaining takes place between single firms and the unions representing their employees rather than between all firms in a sector (OECD 2004, 146-50). For this reason, "union coverage" and "union density" are close to the same number. For example, in 2007, union density for non-agricultural workers was 30.3 percent, and union coverage was 31.5 percent (Statistics Canada 2008).

The gradual decline of union density is a concern to labour because, without strong union representation, workers will "lack a collective democratic voice and the collective power to influence economic outcomes and workplace governance" (Jackson 2004, 25). Union membership has declined significantly for men but has remained relatively stable for women. The decline is more significant in the private sector than in the public sector.[4] Finally, it is more significant for younger than for older workers (Jackson 2006, 67).

There has been considerable debate about the permanence of decline in density in Canada and how to reverse the situation (Rose and Chaison 2000; Jackson 2004, 2006; Murray 2004). Part of the discussion has focused on structural factors, in particular the highly decentralized and enterprise-based pattern of organization and collective bargaining. As noted, there is little centralized and coordinated bargaining between employer and union peak organizations in whole sectors of the economy of the type found in many European countries. Generally speaking, union density is higher where this kind of centralization exists: "The absence of centralized bargaining structures has been the principle barrier to expanding union influence, membership and density in Canada" (Rose and Chaison 2000, 45). More important for our purposes, unions represent less than one-third of the labour force, thus weakening their power capacity.

In his extensive comparative studies of macro-corporatism and labour in OECD countries, Traxler classifies Canada as having a "pluralist" system (Traxler 2004; Traxler, Kittel, and Blaschke 2001). In my own approach to corporatism, I break this analysis down to speak of several factors. First, there is the degree of competition between peak-like organizations. Corporatist systems tend to have very little competition, whereas pluralist ones have much more. Canada comes closer to the pluralist end of the scale. Assessing this factor requires us to consider the role of the Canadian Labour Congress (CLC) and the degree of competition for members. In 2008, through its affiliate unions, the CLC represented 70.7 percent of unionized workers. It faced competition from independent Quebec union centrals, which organized 10.4 percent of unionized workers, with another 13 percent in "independent" national unions (HRSDC 2010). These figures show that the CLC has been relatively successful in becoming a single representative of labour in Canada outside Quebec. It has a place in Quebec, but its affiliated provincial organization competes with the Confédération des syndicats nationaux and two smaller union centrals. In addition to provincial affiliates in each province, the CLC has four regional offices. It retains a small research staff at its central office in Ottawa.

In a corporatist system, there will be institutionalized horizontal bridges between associations that permit the associational system to speak with a collective voice when needed. Such arrangements are missing in the Canadian labour representative system. The separate Quebec groups are not linked in any systematic way to the CLC, and they focus their efforts on the Quebec government. If we move down into the system and look at the relationships between the unions that are members of the CLC, there is little evidence of coordination. In fact, they have recently become more competitive with one another. The largest private-sector unions, for example, the auto workers and the steel workers, have absorbed many other unions outside their traditional fields, placing them in competition not only with one another for members but also with large public-sector unions (Jackson and Baldwin 2007, 479). Another obstacle to horizontal coordination is the breakaway group from the American Federation of Labor–Congress of Industrial Organizations, Change to Win, which is being established in Canada. Its Canadian affiliates include unions that are independent of the CLC, and these have become more competitive with one another.

Obviously, the competition for union members reduces labour unions' capacity to work together. It also makes it difficult for the CLC to devise acceptable common policy stances for the whole of labour. Moreover, as these member unions, like the Canadian Auto Workers, become larger and more diverse in their membership, they take on broader issues that can put them into direct competition with the CLC in advocating public policies.

In the confederal structures highlighted by the corporatist and PRT approaches, there are strong dimensions of vertical integration as well: the member unions are integrated fully as members of the peak associations. This form of integration permits the peak associations to take strong positions on general issues, to bargain occasionally for all unionized workers, and to mobilize support systematically from workers across the economy. Such vertical integration is absent from the Canadian system, rendering the CLC merely one representative of labour among many, albeit the most important one. In fact, the CLC is really only a lobbying group for labour: it has no power to engage in any aspect of collective bargaining, as would be expected in a corporatist arrangement.

Finally, the PRT approach emphasizes the importance of the labour movement having a close relationship with a political party to promote and defend its interests. When the New Democratic Party was created in 1961 following the dissolution of the Co-operative Commonwealth Federation, both union leaders and party officials envisioned a successful social-democratic party of the type found in Europe. Their dream, however, was not fulfilled. Union affiliation with the NDP peaked immediately after the party's founding and has declined ever since (Savage 2008, 177). Labour leadership has failed to deliver the votes of rank-and-file union members in any significant way. Even when the NDP has been in power (British Columbia, Saskatchewan, Manitoba, Ontario, and Nova Scotia), the respective provincial governments maintained a distance from the union movement. Changes in party funding at the federal level first by the Liberal Party and then by the Conservative Party in 2006 effectively prevented labour organizations from directly financing the NDP.

In summation, the combination of weak confederal organizations and the failure to build a social-democratic party strong enough to assume power after elections places strong limitations on labour's capacity to influence the politics of redistribution.

Business

The system of encompassing business associations in Canada is also pluralistic in form. Until the 1970s, it was dominated by the Canadian Chamber of Commerce (CCC), provincial chambers (independent of the national body), and the Canadian Manufacturers Association (CMA). Although the CMA represented industrial firms only, secondary (branch plant) industry was sufficiently important in the Canadian economy through the first half of the twentieth century that the CMA was an important national voice for business. This landscape changed significantly in the late 1960s and the 1970s. In 1969, a new comprehensive association emerged in Quebec, the Conseil du Patronat du Québec (CPQ), in response to the conflict between business and an increasingly radicalized Quebec labour movement and to the challenges of the nationalist advance. A year later, John Bulloch, a teacher and son of a politically outspoken Toronto tailor, formed the Canadian Council on Fair Taxation to protest a federal white paper on tax reform. As a result of his successful campaign, Bulloch set up the Canadian Federation of Independent Business (CFIB), which became the country's largest direct-member business association within a decade and the principal representative of small and medium-size enterprises (SMEs). Five years later, the chief executives of the country's largest corporations decided they needed their own voice, one that would adopt a less strident position on key national issues than those voiced by the CCC and the CMA. The unruly response of the labour movement to wage and price controls in 1975 reinforced their perception, leading to the creation of the Business Council on National Issues (BCNI) in 1976.

With the economic changes stemming from the processes of globalization, this landscape has changed in two ways in the past twenty years. The idea of a protected manufacturing sector, which lay at the heart of Macdonald's National Policy and was the long-standing raison d'être of the CMA, ended with the signing of CUSFTA and NAFTA. With branch plants of US firms either closing or restructuring, it no longer made sense to have manufacturers and exporters represented in separate associations. The CMA merged with the Canadian Export Association in May 1996, creating the Canadian Manufacturers and Exporters (CME). At this point, it effectively shed its role as an encompassing business association.

In 2001, the BCNI changed its name to the Canadian Council of Chief Executives, consciously dropping the word "national." What might seem to be a trivial change was sparked by the council's wish to be "thinkers and players in Canada, in North America and on a global basis," to quote its chair, Jean C. Monty, also chair and chief executive officer of BCE Inc. (CCCE 2001). Further signalling its intention to focus globally as well as nationally, the CCCE established a global policy committee to address international finance, trade, investment and development policy, and key multilateral, regional, and bilateral relationships beyond North America.

With several encompassing business associations in play, the associational system again is pluralist rather than corporatist, similar to labour. It differs from labour in being better integrated and in representing higher proportions of its potential membership domains. Consistent with a pluralist system, vertical integration is absent because none of the encompassing associations is a peak association whose members are sectoral associations representing different parts of the economy, as occurs in many European countries (see Coleman and Grant 1988). CCCE members are individual persons, the chief executive officers of the largest private corporations in the country; the CFIB speaks for small and medium-sized firms, the CME for manufacturing and exporting enterprises, and the CCC for local (but not provincial) chambers of commerce. The CPQ has a peak association structure along European lines, but it functions only in Quebec.

Although vertical integration is not possible in such a pluralist structure, horizontal integration is minimally present. The CCCE has taken small steps in this direction by having the elected chairpersons of the CME, the CCC, and the CPQ declared "associate members." But the associations led by these chairpersons remain fully independent of the CCCE. The CCCE thus has the potential to mobilize considerable business support across the economy – resources, manufacturing, construction, services, banking and finance – when needed. Admittedly, small business sits outside this alliance in the form of the CFIB, but such separate representation of small firms is also common in many of the European corporatist systems (Coleman 1990; Coleman and Grant 1988). The CFIB now represents over 105,000 firms across Canada and effectively uses member surveys and internet consultation to anchor its lobbying, drawing on support in all provinces. Its positions do not necessarily compete with or contradict the CCCE-based alliance; rather, they add a small business perspective to policy debates.

In summary, both the business and labour associational systems feature considerable competition for members; there is no systematic vertical integration in either, and very little systematic horizontal coordination. In the absence of these properties, it is virtually impossible for business and labour to play the roles outlined by corporatist theory. These properties of labour organizations, when coupled to a relatively weak social-democratic party, also suggest that labour has little capacity to gain the influence projected by power resources theory.

Labour, Business, and the Policy Process

The method of gaining access to the policy process at the federal level in Canada has changed in the past twenty years. As globalization intensified during the 1970s and 1980s, governments focused less on fostering and protecting domestic industries. The government's attention shifted from devising a Canada-specific policy for given sectors to fostering competitiveness and innovation across all sectors in order to be successful in the "global economy." Older departments gradually changed; for example, the former Industry, Trade and Commerce in the federal government lost officers who specialized according to sector and who had worked more closely with industry associations. And departments with particular clientele like agriculture and labour declined in importance.

Paralleling these processes was an intensification of the changes begun in the 1970s that strengthened central agencies, particularly the Privy Council Office, the Prime Minister's Office, and the role of the prime minister as an individual actor (Savoie 2008). This type of centralization of authority took place in many OECD countries, not just Canada, over this period. (For more discussion of the changes leading to greater power of central agencies, see Chapter 9, this volume.)

Finally, with the increasing need to design policies in cooperation with other governments, the development of regional and global policy forums and networks has led to the establishment of internationally networked working groups of officials (Slaughter 2004). These processes require horizontal collaboration among various departments at the nation-state level, contributing to a blurring of long-standing distinctions between domestic policy and foreign policy. The regional and global networks of public officials, in combination with horizontal decision making at home, creates obstacles for political organizations representing business and labour seeking to "lobby" in usual ways. These obstacles have proved more prohibitive to labour, however. While labour's access to policy making has been undermined, organizations like the CCCE, which is composed of chief executive officers of transnational corporations and whose political activities focus on central agencies and the prime minister, have gained advantages.

Labour

In the postwar period up to the mid-1970s, labour engaged in a kind of bipartite politics centred on contacts between the CLC and ministers and departments of labour. This approach began to fray around the edges during struggles over wage and price controls in the 1970s. Governments dealt with this conflict by setting up bipartite labour-business bodies, culminating in the creation of the Canadian Labour Market and Productivity Centre in 1984 (Jackson and Baldwin 2007, 476). These efforts gradually dissembled as business and labour fought strongly on opposite sides of the Canada-US, and later NAFTA, trade policy debates. These conflicts were an indication of the growing division between business and labour over whether to engage with or to oppose economic globalization: "In this context of fundamental disagreement, continued participation in consultative and formal policy processes became highly problematic within the labour movement. The explicitly anti-union content of economic orthodoxy and its rejection of most of organized labour's policy agenda for labour market regulation and income security made critical distance all but inevitable" (ibid., 482).

These trends in policy arising from neoliberal thinking were translated differently across the Canadian provinces, making it more difficult for labour to speak with a single policy voice (Kumar and Murray 2006, 84). Adding to the challenges were the changing demographics of the persons interested in joining unions: many more women, persons from visible minorities, and immigrants. These members were more likely to stress "dignity of work" issues and human rights concerns than the more traditional focus on pensions, benefits, pay, and job security (Murray 2004, 162).

The combination of these various changes has led to a movement from "social unionism" towards "social movement unionism." The former is predicated on a broad definition of solidarity in which unions represent the interests of the worker as citizen and as wage earner (Kumar and Murray 2006, 82). The latter builds on this tradition but emphasizes the social transformation of the market as the way to advance worker interests. This philosophy takes unionism away from traditional social-democratic parties, which are seen as insufficiently critical of markets to focus on social movements that are seeking broader changes in the economy and society (Kumar and Murray 2006, 84, 87).[5]

In the social movement unionism approach, developing union power and, thus, influence on policy requires a focus on external solidarity: working with a variety of community groups and social movements in pursuit of change. Paradoxically, as Lévesque and Murray (2006, 123-25) note, the kinds of networks needed at local, regional, national, and international scales for this kind of grassroots politics are enabled by the improved means of communication and travel accompanying contemporary globalization. Lévesque and Murray's research is particularly persuasive for Quebec, where there is a long tradition of union engagement with other progressive political organizations and coalition politics. In Chapter 11 (this volume), Alain Noël offers a more extended discussion of the kind of coalition building that occurs among social justice groups in Quebec. In addition, Haddow (Chapter 16, this volume) notes the importance of labour's cooperation with other social groups when it comes to sustaining redistributive policies.

In Canada outside Quebec, the evidence of social movement unionism is less strong, but there are some innovative examples of labour working with other political organizations. Two relatively recent "campaigns" by the CLC are indicative of a change in thinking. The CLC decided to concentrate increased resources on municipal-level politics by mobilizing its local members to support candidates opposed to neoliberalism. The labour movement saw local governments becoming agents of neoliberal globalization: cities and towns were increasingly neoliberal, seeking to privatize services and to enter into private-public partnerships. In Chapter 5 (this volume), Phillips notes a similar change to a more local scale on the part of civil society organizations after 2000.

Therefore, in 2006, the CLC concentrated considerable resources in "Municipalities Matters" campaigns,[6] supporting candidates opposed to such privatization initiatives and supportive of public social welfare services. The campaigns involved five stages: (1) visioning (bringing together a wide variety of people at public meetings), (2) training activists, (3) endorsing progressive candidates, (4) mobilizing voters and getting them out to vote, and finally (5) introducing accountability (keeping in touch with elected candidates). The activities took place in twenty-one key cities, involving fifty labour councils and resulting in the endorsement of 438 candidates in sixty different municipalities. Of these, 217 were successful in elections in October

2006 (Savage 2008, 174). The greatest success occurred in Guelph, where a labour-endorsed mayor and eight labour-endorsed ward councillors were elected, representing a majority of council. The CLC worked closely with the Guelph Civic League, a coalition of local members of the Council of Canadians, various neighbourhood groups, supporters of the public library, and environmentalists (see http://www.guelphcivicleague.ca).

A second campaign took place in 2009-10; although this one was on a national level, it again involved politicking in municipalities. Entitled "Retirement Security for Everyone!," the campaign had three goals: (1) doubling benefits for the Canada Pension Plan over a seven year period, (2) increasing the Guaranteed Income Supplement to Old Age Security pensions, and (3) introducing a federal system of pension insurance (http://www.canadian labour.ca/action-center/retirement-security-for-everyone). In carrying out the campaign, the CLC obtained an endorsement from the Federation of Canadian Municipalities and worked with other non-governmental actors like the Council of Canadians with Disabilities and the Canadian Association of Retired Persons. Of course, local labour councils provided crucial support across the country.

In becoming part of broader coalitions, labour has been able to enhance its policy breadth and sophistication by drawing on the support of progressive think tanks. The CLC helped set up the Canadian Centre for Policy Alternatives (CCPA) in 1980, and it has remained a supporter of this successful think tank. The CCPA's work covers a number of issues of interest to labour in economic, social, and environmental policy areas. Labour can also make use of the excellent research of the Caledon Institute of Social Policy and the Canadian Council on Social Development. Finally, the labour movement has set up the Columbia Institute, which sponsors the Centre for Civic Governance. The centre concentrates its efforts on research to support community leadership in meeting contemporary social and environmental challenges: global warming, Canada's increasing equity gap, the impact of technology, and changing social trends (http://www.civic governance.ca/about). The creation of the institute and the support of such a broad research agenda indicate labour's strategy of reaching out to other social movements while working towards its own goals.

These changes in labour's engagement with the state have contradictory implications for the pursuit of their views on redistributive politics. On the one hand, they may compensate for their gradual decline in close contacts with federal and provincial authorities by engaging in broader-based contentious politics to increase pressure in favour of policies targeting inequality in society; on the other hand, by becoming more distant and less able to influence political leaders directly, they lose the capacity to preserve, let alone renew, redistributive social and economic policies in ways they might have pursued in the past.

Business

Changes in the policy process have had relatively little impact on small businesses as represented by the CFIB, while creating new opportunities for policy access for large corporations. The CFIB now includes over 107,000 small firms as members. Consistent with its founding as an anti-tax movement, it focuses on reducing costs due to taxation for small businesses, while working towards policies that permit small business owners to have the kind of social protection available to workers in public institutions. It carries out campaigns based on large numbers of supporters voicing support and contacting relevant government officials. It keeps a close eye on the Canada Revenue Agency, the federal finance department, and provincial finance ministers. Its direct membership approach has become even stronger with the arrival of contemporary communication technologies.

In contrast, the increasing centralization of power in the hands of first ministers or presidents in OECD countries and the rapid development of intergovernmental networks across many policy areas have created new opportunities for large business representatives. All of the leading capitalist countries have seen the formation of powerful associations of chief executive officers like the Business Council on National Issues/Canadian Council of Chief Executives. The membership structure of these associations – personal membership of chief executives rather than firms more broadly – has facilitated person-to-person communication with first ministers or heads of state. Many of these chief executives come from transnational corporations, which are part of transnational business associations. These associations, in turn, permit corporations to monitor goings-on in the expanding intergovernmental networks (Coleman 2006).

The choice of John Manley – former minister of industry, minister of foreign affairs, deputy prime minister, and minister of finance in the Liberal governments of Jean Chrétien – as president and CEO of the CCCE in January 2010 indicates the importance of maintaining close connections to central agencies.

Over the past fifteen years, the CCCE (2000, 2006) has issued two major policy documents outlining its support for globalization: *Global Champion or Falling Star? The Choice Canada Must Make* in April 2000 and *From*

Bronze to Gold: A Blueprint for Canadian Leadership in a Transforming World in 2006. Briefly stated, the association's position on redistributive politics can be summarized as follows. The CCCE has little sympathy for more classic redistributive policies. It believes that focusing on economic growth and productivity is the key first step that governments must take. It focuses on individuals and looks for economic incentives to support their education, skills development, and risk-taking behaviour. It recognizes the need for social safety-nets but argues that the financing of these policies cannot take away from economic development and individual entrepreneurship. And, wherever possible, it would prefer private enterprise to provide social safety-net policies. In all these respects, it implicitly accepts inequalities, perhaps very large ones, in Canadian society. Equality of condition, in particular, can never be a goal in itself. The same is likely true for equality of opportunity.

Evidence of privileged access for business under executive dominant state governance can be drawn from the establishment of the North American Security and Prosperity Initiative (SPI). Alarmed at the tightening of the Canada-US border following the attack on the World Trade Center in September 2001, the CCCE launched its SPI in January 2003. It published a major document, *New Frontiers: Building a 21st Century Canada-United States Partnership in North America*, in April 2004 (CCCE 2004).[7] Following the setting up of the SPI, the leaders of Canada, Mexico, and the US created a trilateral advisory panel, the North American Competitiveness Council, which was composed of business leaders. The CCCE provided the Canadian secretariat for the council.

The SPI is a good example of executive led policy making outside of Parliament. It is not a signed treaty. It has never been brought before legislatures for discussion and approval. It is driven by the executive levels of government, thus the prime minister and the PMO in Canada. Government leaders seek advice directly from corporate executives and use this advice to direct the working groups in the bureaucracy of Canada, the US, and Mexico. As Teresa Healy (2007, 8) of the CLC comments: "This is what plutocracy looks like." In another document, the CLC argues that giving corporate executives such a role in governance is an "affront to democracy." It adds: "Instead of cooperating on public health insurance, the SPP limits the health care discussion to regulations about bio-terrorism and epidemics" (CLC 2007).

Over the same period, the CCCE has worked closely with "chief executive" organizations from other OECD countries to issue documents in support of economic globalization, including one on the importance of concluding the Doha Round at the World Trade Organization. These include the Business Council of Australia, the Business Roundtable (US), Consejo Mexicano de Hombres de Negocios, the European Roundtable of Industrialists, and Nippon Keidanren (Japan). Given the transnational character of many corporate members of these organizations, some large corporations belong to more than one group. For example, General Electric, IBM, Johnson and Johnson, KPMG, PriceWaterhouseCoopers, SAP, and Sieman's Corporation belong to both the CCCE and the US Business Roundtable.

Conclusion

In Canada, there is little evidence of cooperation between business and labour with respect to the issue of redistribution. Neither has built the vertically integrated, highly representative, encompassing trans-class organization needed to define and support strong redistributive policies. Admittedly, when it comes to encompassing associations, business has greater capacity than labour. Relatively low union density and less cohesive and integrated organizations weaken labour's influence, while higher density of representation, less competition between groups, and more horizontal coordination when necessary strengthens business.

In any event, over the past fifteen years, the already minimal potential for business-labour cooperation has declined even further as a result of deep differences over the advantages and disadvantages of economic globalization. Business associations, such as the CCCE, are engaging in international coordination with cognate groups to influence domestic policies of concern. They eschew deeper redistributive policies while promoting economic policies that support market development and individual initiative. In contrast, labour organizations continue to promote social equality as a central goal and support the development of strong redistribution policies to reach that goal.

Important changes in policy making and executive centralization by states in response to globalizing processes have led to more changes in approaches to influencing policy by labour than by business. Labour now enters into more alliances with relevant social partners, both nationally and globally, and engages in direct action initiatives. In contrast, business associations have consolidated access to government, with the CCCE having especially close ties to the top ministers.

The immediate prospect of change either in the organizational capacity of business and labour or in their ability to talk to one another about policy is dismal. If robust redistributive policies are to emerge in Canada, it will be despite the contributions of business and labour.

NOTES

I would like to thank Verónica Rubio Vega for her research assistance, and Keith Banting and John Myles for their helpful advice in revising this chapter.

1 In an alternative scenario, these two classes would not be able to construct the political organizations needed to build intra-class consensus or engage in inter-class discussions of inequality on a society-wide basis. In this alternative situation, introducing and putting into practice effective redistributive policies becomes unlikely.
2 An example will illustrate what I mean by vertical integration. Take the automobile sector as one sector or slice of the economy. In that sector, there are likely to be separate associations representing the big firms assembling the cars, the manufacturers of automobile parts, the producers of electronic components, specialized plastics firms, the dealers that sell the cars, and so on. If all of these associations are members of a more encompassing organization that represents the whole of the automobile sector, they are said to be vertically integrated into that industry-wide organization. And if that industry-wide organization is a member, in turn, of an even more encompassing association that represents all sectors of the economy, we speak of deeper vertical integration. Often, these more encompassing associations are referred to as peak associations.
3 Looking at similar variables as they apply to the labour movement, Wallerstein (1999, 672) finds that wage-setting tends to be more egalitarian across the board.
4 Union density in the private sector is not all that different from the rates in the US (Murray 2004, 159).
5 It also supports notions of the transformative potential of conflict.
6 These "Municipalities Matters" campaigns were tested in BC in 2003 and in Ontario in 2005 before the strong effort in 2006.
7 The CCCE also prominently supported the report of the Council on Foreign Relations, *Building a North American Community*, published in May 2005. John Manley was one of the chairs of the report, and Thomas D'Aquino, CCCE president, was one of its vice-chairs.

REFERENCES

Atkinson, Michael, and William D. Coleman. 1990. *The State, Business and Industrial Change in Canada*. Toronto: University of Toronto Press.
Canadian Council of Chief Executives (CCCE). 2000. *Global Champion or Falling Star? The Choice Canada Must Make*. Ottawa: CCCE.
–. 2001. "Organizational Structure." Press Release. Ottawa: CCCE.
–. 2004. *New Frontiers: Building a 21st Century Canada-United States Partnership in North America*. Ottawa: CCCE.
–. 2006. *From Bronze to Gold: A Blueprint for Canadian Leadership in a Transformng World*. Ottawa: CCCE.

Canadian Labour Congress (CLC). 2007. *This Is What Plutocracy Looks Like: The Upcoming Meeting of the North American Competitiveness Council with North American Government Ministers.* Ottawa: CLC.

Castells, Manuel. 1999. *The Rise of the Network Society.* 2nd ed. Cambridge, MA: Blackwell.

Cerny, Philip G. 1997. "Paradoxes of the Competition State: The Dynamics of Political Globalization." *Government and Opposition* 32(2): 251-74.

Coleman, William. 1988. *Business and Politics: A Study of Collective Action.* Montreal and Kingston: McGill-Queen's University Press.

–. 1990. "State Traditions and Comprehensive Business Associations: A Comparative Structural Analysis." *Political Studies* 38(2): 231-52.

–. 1996. *Financial Services, Globalization, and Domestic Policy Change: A Comparison of North America and the European Union.* Basingstoke: Macmillan.

–. 2006. "Global Public Policy, Associative Orders and Business Interest Associations." In Wolfgang Streeck, Jürgen Grote, Volker Schneider, and Jesse Visser, eds., *Governing Interests: Business Associations Facing Internationalization,* 199-218. London: Routledge.

Coleman, William, and Wyn P. Grant. 1988. "The Class Cohesion and Political Influence of Business: A Study of Comprehensive Associations." *European Journal of Political Research* 16: 467-87.

Esping-Andersen, Gøsta. 1990. *The Three Worlds of Welfare Capitalism.* Princeton, NJ: Princeton University Press

Hacker, Jacob S., and Paul Pierson. 2010. "Winner-Take-All Politics: Public Policy, Political Organization, and the Precipitous Rise of Top Incomes in the United States." *Politics and Society* 38(2): 152-204.

Healy, Teresa. 2007. *Deep Integration in North America: Security and Prosperity for Whom?* Ottawa: Canadian Labour Congress.

Hicks, Alexander, and Lane Kenworthy. 1998. "Cooperation and Political Economic Performance in Affluent Democratic Capitalism." *American Journal of Sociology* 103(6): 1631-72.

Hollingsworth, J. Rogers, and Robert Boyer. 1997. *Contemporary Capitalism: The Embeddedness of Institutions.* Cambridge, UK: Cambridge University Press.

Human Resources and Skills Development Canada (HRSDC). 2010. *Union Membership in Canada.* http://www.rhdcc-hrsdc.gc.ca/eng/labour/labour_relations/info_analysis/union_membership/index.shtml.

Jackson, Andrew. 2004. "Solidarity Forever: Trends in Canadian Union Density." *Studies in Political Economy* 74: 125-46.

–. 2006. "Rowing against the Tide: The Struggle to Raise Union Density in a Hostile Environment." In Pradeep Kumar and Christopher Schenk, eds., *Paths to Union Renewal: Canadian Experiences,* 61-77. Peterborough, ON: Broadview Press.

Jackson, Andrew, and Bob Baldwin. 2007. "Policy Analysis by the Labour Movement in a Hostile Environment." In Laurent Dobuzinskis, Michael Howlett, and David Laycock, eds., *Policy Analysis in Canada: The State of the Art,* 473-96. Toronto: University of Toronto Press.

Katzenstein, Peter J. 1984. *Corporatism and Change: Austria, Switzerland, and the Politics of Industry*. Ithaca, NY: Cornell University Press.

Korpi, Walter. 1998. "The Iceberg of Power below the Surface: A Preface to Power Resources Theory." In Julia S. O'Connor and Gregg M. Olsen, eds., *Power Resources Theory and the Welfare State: A Critical Approach*, vii-xiv. Toronto: University of Toronto Press.

Kumar, Pradeep, and Gregor Murray. 2006. "Innovation in Canadian Unions: Patterns, Causes and Consequences." In Pradeep Kumar and Christopher Schenk, eds., *Paths to Union Renewal: Canadian Experiences*, 79-102. Peterborough, ON: Broadview Press.

Lehmbruch, Gerhard, and Philippe C. Schmitter, eds. 1982. *Patterns of Corporatist Policy-Making*. London: Sage.

Lévesque, Christian, and Gregor Murray. 2006. "Globalization and Renewal: Perspectives from the Quebec Labour Movement." In Pradeep Kumar and Christopher Schenk, eds., *Paths to Union Renewal: Canadian Experiences*, 113-26. Peterborough, ON: Broadview Press.

Murray, Gregor. 2004. "Union Myths, Enigmas and Other Tales: Five Challenges for Union Renewal." *Studies in Political Economy* 74: 157-69.

Olsen, Gregg M., and Julia S. O'Connor, 1998. "Introduction – Understanding the Welfare State: Power Resources Theory and Its Critics." In Julia S. O'Connor and Gregg M. Olsen, eds., *Power Resource Theory and the Welfare State*, 3-33. Toronto: University of Toronto Press.

Olson, Mancur. 1982. *The Rise and Decline of Nations: Economic Growth, Stagflation, and Social Rigidities*. New Haven: Yale University Press.

Organisation for Economic Cooperation and Development (OECD). 2004. *Employment Outlook 2004*. Paris: OECD.

Reinicke, Wolfgang. 1998. *Global Public Policy: Governing without Government?* Washington, DC: Brookings Institution Press.

Rose, Joseph B., and Gary N. Chaison. 2001. "Unionism in Canada and the United States in the 21st Century: The Prospects for Revival." *Relations industrielles / Industrial Relations* 56(1): 34-65.

Sassen, Saskia. 2007. *A Sociology of Globalization*. New York: W.W. Norton.

Savage, L. 2008. "Organized Labour and Local Politics: Ontario's 2006 Municipal Elections." *Labour/Le Travail* 62: 171-84.

Savoie, Donald J. 2008. *Court Government and the Collapse of Accountability in Canada and the United Kingdom*. Toronto: University of Toronto Press.

Scholte, Jan Aart. 2005. *Globalization: A Critical Introduction*. 2nd ed. Basingstoke, UK: Palgrave Macmillan.

Slaughter, Anne-Marie. 2004. *A New World Order*. Princeton, NJ: Princeton University Press.

Statistics Canada 2008. "Union Coverage Rates." http://www.statcan.gc.ca/pub/71-222-x/2008001/sectionk/k-rates-taux-eng.htm.

Stephens, John. 1979. *The Transition from Capitalism to Socialism*. Urbana: University of Illinois Press.

Streeck, Wolfgang, and Philippe C. Schmitter, eds. *Private Interest Government: Beyond Market and the State.* London: Sage.
Swank, Duane. 2002. *Global Capital, Political Institutions, and Policy Change in Developed Welfare States.* Cambridge, UK: Cambridge University Press.
Traxler, Frans. 2004. "The Metamorphoses of Corporatism: From Classical to Lean Patterns." *European Journal of Political Research* 43: 571–98.
Traxler, Frans, Sabine Blaschke, and Bernhard Kittel. 2001. *National Labour Relations in Internationalized Markets.* Oxford: Oxford University Press.
Wallerstein, Michael. 1999. "Wage-Setting Institutions and Pay Inequality in Advanced Industrial Societies." *American Journal of Political Science* 43(3): 649-80.
Weiss, Linda. 1998. *The Myth of the Powerless State: Governing the Economy in a Global Era.* Cambridge, UK: Polity Press.
–. 2003. "Introduction: Bringing Domestic Institutions Back In." In Linda Weiss ed., *States in the Global Economy: Bringing Domestic Institutions Back In,* 1-33. Cambridge, UK: Cambridge University Press.
–. 2005. The State-Augmenting Effects of Globalization. *New Political Economy* 10(3): 345-53.

5

Restructuring Civil Society
Muting the Politics of Redistribution

SUSAN D. PHILLIPS

The nature of political representation in Canada has changed dramatically over the past three decades so that civil society now has less impact on social policy. This, in turn, has weakened the redistributive role of the state: with less resistance from civil society and fewer sources of fresh ideas, the federal government has steered a course in social policy towards greater inequality. With few exceptions, however, analysis of Canadian social policy has lacked serious discussion of the part played by civil society organizations – variously known as interest groups, voluntary associations, nonprofits, NGOs, social movements, or the third sector – in shaping policy directions and outcomes. When told at all, the story has had a very simple plot: the neoliberal politics that took hold in the late 1980s delegitimated representation and cut funding to civil society organizations (CSOs), producing an "advocacy chill" and leading to the demise of many. While the essence of this is true – social policy groups were branded as "special interests" and their funding was cut – the story is more complex than convention suggests.

The purpose of this chapter is to provide a fuller account of the involvement of social policy and related organizations – broadly defined to include anti-poverty, childcare, disability, and women's groups – in the politics of redistribution since the mid-1980s and to explore the consequences for both redistributive politics *and* policy outcomes. The roles and influence of

CSOs depend to varying degrees on exogenous factors such as governing arrangements and political opportunities and on internal capacities and strategies chosen by individual organizations and by CSOs collectively. The collective capacity of CSOs to make a difference in the politics of redistribution, particularly in a federal system, depends on the strength of both a *vertical* and a *horizontal* dimension of representation. *Vertical* refers to the connections between the leadership of CSOs and their memberships and those that integrate grassroots groups into regional, provincial, and national organizations, or umbrellas. This dimension taps into the extent to which CSOs are capable of engaging and mobilizing their memberships and the degree to which coordinating structures are able to provide policy leadership at various levels in a federal system. *Horizontal* refers to the networks in which CSOs are embedded, including not only other citizen groups and movements but also a variety of supporting intermediaries such as think tanks and foundations and allies such as unions, business, and professional associations, all of which may be sources of ideas, research, finance, or influence.

What does it mean to influence public policy? In a narrow sense, influence is having one's ideas and preferences reflected in policy outcomes. More broadly, influence is felt in how ideas are debated and accepted as part of dominant policy discourses, how allies and networks are forged, and how access to policy making is attained. For CSOs "success" can also be measured by the ability to contribute to democratic processes and societal change by mobilizing and engaging citizens. Advocacy of governments is not the only route of influence for CSOs in liberal welfare states, however, as many deliver services to citizens, either as agents of the state or independent of it. In this way, they are gatekeepers of social citizenship, determining who gets what level and quality of services, and their strategies for balancing and connecting service provision with advocacy affect the routes through which influence is exercised.

The story told in this chapter concerns how changes, both imposed by governments and emerging from within civil society itself, weakened the capacity of CSOs to maintain a forceful presence in the politics of redistribution. The story has its roots in the fragility of Canadian CSOs, even in their most activist period. Coleman's (Chapter 4, this volume) observation that the associational systems for business and labour lacked vertical integration and strong horizontal bridges among organizations and suffered from competition for members and representation applies equally to CSOs.

Few CSOs were mass membership organizations; they often found it hard to mobilize the individuals on whose behalf they spoke and could not sustain themselves on the basis of membership dues alone. Their growth was therefore heavily dependent on financial support from the federal government. In addition, it proved difficult to build enduring, cross-cutting networks that could generate new policy ideas and alternatives that had to be taken seriously, a problem exacerbated by the relative weakness of Canadian foundations and think tanks. Arguably, federalism – which is reflected in the structure of CSOs – added to the fragility, making it difficult for most to be effective advocates at both national and provincial/local scales.

As a result, the sector was highly vulnerable when its relations with the federal government polarized in the late 1980s. The federal government responded by cutting funding to its critics, destabilizing and ultimately dooming many social policy organizations. Tensions within civil society also weakened the sector. The growth of identity politics rooted in language, gender, class, and race fuelled internal divisions within important organizations, weakening their ability to command attention. A growing schism emerged between advocacy groups and service-providing organizations that sought a closer link with government based on new models of service delivery. Increasingly, many CSOs became overwhelmed with delivering services or projects, both in response to increased demand and as a means of organizational survival, rather than concentrating on policy at all.

The pattern has not been a steady or inevitable decline from a "golden age" of activism in the 1970s to the present – one that could be readily explained by path dependency or incremental adjustments. Nor has it simply followed the contours of partisan politics. Rather, it has been marked by four distinct periods of major realignments: (1) a polarization of relationships between the federal government and social policy groups from 1985 to 1989, (2) a major restructuring of civil society during the 1990s, (3) a struggle for survival and a widening of the schism between service provision and "big identity" politics from 2000 to 2006, and (4) a reinvention of CSOs and government espousal of social enterprise during the current period.[1]

Canadian Civil Society before 1985: The Myth of a "Golden" Age

Before examining these periods in more detail, it is useful to get a sense of how Canadian civil society developed as the welfare state matured and as these foundational patterns created vulnerabilities. The 1970s and early 1980s are nostalgically portrayed as a golden era for civil society representation in

Canada, characterized by citizen activism, networks of supportive allies, and regular opportunities to be consulted in policy making. But this popular image masks an underlying fragility that became more evident as the politics of redistribution played out.

From early on, Canada's mixed economy of welfare has involved service provision by families, charities, and other non-profits (and, to an increasing degree, for-profits), the specific mix of responsibilities varying in different components of the welfare state (see Jenson, Chapter 2, this volume). As the modern welfare state matured with the introduction of new shared-cost programs, a broader array of social services was provided, extensive contracting regimes developed with provincial (and municipal) governments (Panet and Trebilcock 1998), and the number of CSOs grew substantially between 1960 and 1975 (Pross 1992, 65). This was paralleled by a rise in advocacy organizations as part of the "associational revolution" (Salamon 1994) felt in most developed countries. The "New Social Movements" – the second wave of the women's movement and peace, environmental, and student movements – sparked emphasis on identity politics and transformational societal change (see Smith 2008).[2] At the same time, anti-poverty and welfare rights organizations sprang up across the country. By the mid-1980s, then, the associational system in social policy was quite large, albeit fragmented (Haddow 1990).

Such growth was enabled by federal funding. The federal government began providing operational funding – in contrast to simply contracting for services – to select CSOs in the mid-1940s as part of the establishment of a Canadian citizenship regime (Pal 1993). Funding was a vehicle for the Citizenship Branch of the Department of the Secretary of State to help disadvantaged Canadians, but, as Pal (1993) notes, it was also intended to build the loyalty of immigrant groups that, after the Second World War, were seen as potentially dissident. More pragmatically, the ability to work through voluntary associations allowed the newly established Citizenship Branch to achieve more than it could by relying solely on its own limited staff. This initial experimentation with funding was expanded under Prime Minister Trudeau's "Just Society," which emphasized social action and citizen participation led by an activist, animating state. Linked to a nation building project, Secretary of State created new programs in the 1970s aimed at providing core funding to groups supporting the enrichment of a "Canadian identity" (official language minorities; women; multicultural organizations; political Aboriginal organizations; and, in the 1980s, persons with disabilities).

Starting in 1969, the Department of Health and Welfare initiated the National Welfare Grants, thereby stimulating a burst of anti-poverty organizing (Finkel 2006; Haddow 1993). The attention to specific population groups within government was reinforced by the creation of independent advisory bodies of which the National Council of Welfare (NCW) and the Canadian Advisory Council on the Status of Women (CACSW) were the most significant. When the Liberal government woke up in 1972 with a "hangover of a minority administration" (Bernard Ostry quoted in Pal 1993, 118), however, federal attention again turned to the preoccupation with national unity. Although the funding programs remained in place for more than a decade, their political support dissipated and Canada never returned to a well-articulated grand vision for the role of civil society.

Canadian Exceptionalism: The Foundations of an Underlying Fragility
In Canada, unlike in the US and UK, several factors rendered fragile an apparently activist civil society. The downside of substantial federal funding was vulnerability as it impeded incentives for the diversification of financing and risked sanctions if advocacy tactics displeased funders. The ability to attract diverse sources of revenue for advocacy CSOs is not easy under the best of conditions, and Canada is further hampered by a weak, undercapitalized foundation sector. While a few foundations have actively worked to develop CSO capacity and helped to launch coalitions, their grant-making ability is limited and the majority are more interested in supporting services and safe, middle-of-the-road issues. United Way support has been vital to many social service agencies, but it too is centred on services and its sudden withdrawal can be devastating, as experienced by the social planning councils (which partnered with and were paid by the United Way to identify community needs) when the funder severed their relationship in the 1980s (Levens 2006).

The weakness of the Canadian foundation sector has been compounded by the dearth and limited capacity of think tanks. Canada has proportionally fewer think tanks than the US, and they have a modest presence in the policy community (Abelson and Carberry 1998; Lindquist 1993; Tupper 1993). As Howlett (2009) suggests, governments have come to dominate the policy analytical community, but neither they nor Canadian CSOs have the kind of evidence needed to design effective long-term policy measures.

Finally, the imperatives of federalism have shaped the national CSOs. Many were established as federations themselves, with memberships comprised of subnational organizations. Unlike the US, Canada has not had large mass membership advocacy organizations capable of sophisticated lobbying and outreach to people across the country. National offices generally run on a shoestring, making it easy to become dependent on federal funding and forcing a choice of policy arenas as they can realistically only play in one. Many initially chose the federal, but when the locus of policy making shifted to the provincial level (Boychuck, Chapter 10, this volume), it was difficult for the national CSOs to nimbly refocus their efforts.

In short, many features of organized civil society that were built in as the welfare state was expanding have now been exposed as liabilities.

Polarizing Relationships: 1985-89

In social policy terms, the period 1985 to 1989 is book-ended by debates on de-indexing, opened by the 1985 budget and closed by the clawbacks to Family Allowances and Old Age Security. In terms of civil society organizing, the period is demarcated by the twin realizations that major social policy change would not be consultative and that government would punish its critics.

The Politics of Stealth

The Mulroney Progressive Conservatives' initial social policy master plan included economic equality for women, support for the family, and pension reform, thereby seeming to satisfy many constituencies. In January 1985, the Mulroney government issued the *Child and Elderly Benefits, Consultation Paper* setting out a range of options for social policy (with a focus on reducing benefits to high-income citizens and increasing those for low-income citizens) and promising far-reaching consultation. The NCW hailed the consultation document as a "breakthrough in the history of Canadian public policy" (quoted in Rice 1987, 218). Both social policy and business groups entered into discussion with government about changes to social security, and government signalled that it was prepared to listen.

Given this spirit of collaboration, the budget delivered by Finance Minister Wilson in 1985 came as a shock. The indexation formula for personal transfers was to be altered so that expenditures would be contained while tax revenues increased. In effect, the deficit would be tamed "on the backs of the poor and disadvantaged" (Rice 1987, 219). The ensuing protests by seniors, social policy groups, unions, and citizens from across the political spectrum generated spectacular media coverage and forced government to withdraw the proposal (see Myles, Chapter 13, this volume). The sense that social policy reform would be forged out of a national consensus was lost, however, and radical transformation of both CSOs and social policy had begun.

Over the next few years, as Good explains so well in Chapter 9 (this volume), social policy was dominated by the Department of Finance and characterized by cost containment through technical, almost invisible, program adjustments that produced major change (see also Battle 1993; Prince 1999; Prince and Rice 2000). Although social policy advocates lost ground, given the deepening discordance of relationships with the federal government, the character of redistributive politics still had two distinct advantages. First, it was national in scope so advocacy efforts could be concentrated at one level; second, political representation was relatively "thick," with overlapping networks of CSOs able to coalesce on different sets of issues. Following the de-indexing debate, for example, a loose coalition of groups came together as the Social Policy Reform Group to lobby the Department of Finance (Haddow 1990, 228); this included anti-poverty organizations (Canadian Council of Social Development [CCSD] and the National Anti-Poverty Organization [NAPO]), the National Action Committee on the Status of Women (NAC), CACSW, and the professional association of social workers. The anti-poverty groups were divided on the question of universality of social programs: CCSD supported the principle, while NAPO was more willing to consider targeting benefits to the most needy. Yet they were able to unite in opposition to the government and to communicate an alternative perspective.

Similarly, mobilization against the Progressive Conservatives' 1988 childcare bill, which avoided setting any national standards and permitted funding of for-profit care, brought together an array of childcare, anti-poverty, and women's organizations, and unions (Mahon, Chapter 15, this volume; Mahon and Phillips 2002; Teghtsoonian 1993). Although such widespread collective action was a major factor in killing the bill, the government was annoyed by its critics, and this drove a stake through future relationships with parts of the childcare community. Meanwhile, organizations that supported traditional families, some with ties to the Christian right such as REAL Women, had the ear of government and reinforced the social conservative agenda of the Mulroney government and the later Harper government.

Wedge Politics and the Women's Movement
In much of the organizing around social policy in the mid-1980s, women's groups were the "strength of weak ties" (Granovetter 1973) that connected many other types of organizations in broad coalitions. They (along with

childcare groups) were particularly successful in enlisting the support of unions, given the involvement of activists with a foot in both camps and the relevance of gender issues to unions. Although none was richly resourced, the ability of women's groups to forge extensive connections was aided by federal funding of their core operations as they did not need to risk mission drift to pursue earned income: in the 1980s, NAC received 60 percent of its $680,000 budget as federal grants (Vickers, Rankin, and Appelle 1993, 141). The diversity of women's groups on the national scene also allowed specialization, with some working inside the system (increasingly difficult after the locus of social policy migrated to the Department of Finance), and others engaging in "outsider" strategies and protest tactics (Dobrowolsky 2000). Women's organizations were among the most effective early adopters of rights-based arguments under the Charter of Rights and Freedoms, and, with assistance from the Court Challenges Program, they often achieved through the courts what they could not achieve through advocacy. As Manfredi (2004) notes, the Women's Legal and Education Action Fund (LEAF) won over 80 percent of its thirty-six cases during the 1980s and early 1990s.

In the late 1980s, the leadership of NAC, dominated by socialist feminists (McKeen 2004), chose to vocally oppose the Meech Lake Accord on constitutional reform, and NAFTA. Its stance on the former created a permanent rift in the already tenuous relationships with Quebec women, and the latter caused many liberal women to leave (Rebick 2005, 192). NAC had always been a somewhat uneasy amalgam of institutionalized and radical women's groups; during the 1980s, as Bashevkin (1996, 223) observes, "The fact that newer, protest-oriented elements grew more influential than older lobbyist ones meant that NAC functioned less and less as a moderate but critical interest group, and became increasingly identified as an oppositional protest group." By 1989, NAC's relationship with the federal government was poor: for the first time in twenty-five years, the federal minister responsible for the Status of Women refused to meet the NAC lobby on Parliament Hill (Bashevkin 1996; Vickers et al. 1993).

United We Stand
Despite the crafting of options, presentation of briefs to parliamentary committees, and protests, the positions of CSOs were virtually ignored in the outcomes of social policy during this period. Ken Battle (1993, 439) observes: "Social policy groups were vocal and analytically sophisticated in their criticisms, but they were ineffective in communicating their concerns

to the media and the public, and powerless to alter the course of social policy under the Tories. They cast no fear into a government which believed (with good reason) that social advocates have little or no capacity to mobilize significant numbers of voters." This reflected the fact that the national groups were not mass membership organizations but federations or umbrellas of other organizations. In particular, NAPO and the CCSD were never able to mobilize disadvantaged Canadians and, while extensive organizing occurred in several cities in the mid-1980s, local energy did not feed into the national scene (Greene 2008; Haddow 1990).

By the end of the 1980s, tired of its critics, the Progressive Conservative government not only ignored them in policy making but retaliated with funding cuts aimed at advocacy organizations (Phillips 1991). When clawbacks to transfers were again introduced in 1989, they came abruptly with no consultation or public debate, imposed by fiat in the budget (Battle 1993, 427). Although social policy groups may not have influenced outcomes during this period, they still played an active role in public debate about redistribution. But such participation became more difficult.

Restructuring Representation: 1990-99

Between 1990 and 1999 virtually every aspect of social policy was dramatically restructured, with the largest restraint measures ever imposed via the 1995 budget and further constraint of the federal role in shaping social policy. The 1990s also saw a transformation of civil society through funding cuts and a realignment of concerns and identities from within. By the late 1990s, social policy organizing was characterized by even greater fragmentation, not only between radical and pragmatic elements but also between the local and national, and between charitable organizations and social justice advocates. The women's movement was no longer a serious player nationally, and the unions were less engaged with the rest of the social policy community (albeit still involved with the childcare movement). Although income inequality rose sharply (Banting 2006), social policy groups were increasingly ill-equipped to make a coordinated case for more effective policy responses.

The Height of Rights: A Marketplace of Ideas

The latter years of the Mulroney era were consumed with the high politics of constitutional reform and the Charlottetown Accord, adding a rights-based discourse to social policy with the idea of enshrining a social charter in the Constitution. Although the discussion engaged a broad spectrum of social movements (Jenson 1995; Smith 1993), the vigorous opposition of NAC, aligned with Aboriginal women, to the Accord, and the support of labour for a social charter, divided the social policy community. The notion of a charter as a foundation for advancing social policy was the high point of a collective rights approach to social policy (Smith 1993), and, when it faded, groups seeking credibility needed to make more evidence-based claims, thus stretching their limited capacity for policy research.

The changes in civil society in this period took some time to be fully realized, but they had profound effects. The retaliatory funding cuts of the early 1990s directed largely at organizations critical of government averaged 15 percent per year. NAC lost 70 percent of its core federal funding between 1987 and 1995 (MacIvor 1996), and NAPO and the CCSD lost all core funding in 1994 (Cardozo 1996). As the Program Review of 1994 made clear, ideas about public funding had changed: the preference was to fund services over advocacy and to give priority to groups serving a broad public benefit and/or government's priorities (Cardozo 1996; Jenson and Phillips 1996). It was presumed to be a marketplace of ideas in which organizations with good ideas would find other support. However, membership dues, foundation funds, and other funding sources did not make up the shortfall, so many turned to earned income through services and projects, and all tightened their belts through cost reductions. Although most CSOs made it through the 1990s, the loss of infrastructure on an already thin base made them highly unstable – a "series of projects connected to a hollow foundation" (Scott 2003, 4).

The very legitimacy of advocacy organizations, now branded as "special interest groups," came under attack from the right, notably the Reform Party and REAL Women, which was persistent in making the case that NAC and other feminist organizations did not represent all women. It was also evident that some parliamentarians saw CSOs as unwanted competition in the representation of citizens. The discourse of special interests was picked up by the media, and the general public began attributing the paralysis of policy making to lobbying by these groups, making it easy to dismiss their claims and research supporting them. The legitimacy of CSOs was further diminished by changes in how representation was structured to and within the federal government. Beginning in the early 1990s with the Citizens' Forum on Canadian Unity (Spicer Commission), the government moved to a practice of engaging "ordinary" citizens as well as – and often instead of – representatives of organized groups.[3] This preference was followed by the Panel on Violence against Women in 1994 (Phillips 2002), the Royal Commission on New Reproductive Technologies (Montpetit, Scala, and Fortier 2004), and the 1994 Social Security Review (SSR), a mega-consultation that prided itself on hearing from 100,000 Canadians (Rice 1995; Lindquist 2005). While the SSR raised expectations of a return to more consultative politics, its implementation inspired serious questions about the government's genuine interest in engaging on important policy matters. The process began with confusion as to what government was proposing, and the "staggering numbers of requests from interest groups to appear before the committee swamped an under-resourced and ill-prepared process" (Rice 1995, 189). Thus, an important review of social policy ended in debacle, the attempt at consultative policy change was quickly abandoned in favour of the closed process of the 1995 budget, and a consultation of this scale on social policy has not been attempted since.[4]

The identities of CSOs were being crafted externally but also realigned from within. During this period NAC, one of the few CSOs to take diversity of representation seriously at the time, faced an internal challenge from women of colour who had been organizing at the local level and mobilizing within NAC. The organization was already split between more radical members and pragmatists when a minority woman became president in 1993; the internal politics related to her presidency further divided it (Bashevin 1996). NAC never regained internal coherence or reclaimed its leadership role; a close observer pegged this as "a combination of the victory of conservative governments, the fact that the abortion fight had been won, the aging of the NAC leadership and the gap between us and the next generation." By 1998, NAC was effectively gone from the policy scene, but because it had been a weak national player for several years, its demise was hardly noticed. A similar struggle for "authenticity" to ensure that organizations were representative of their users and members occurred within national organizations of anti-poverty and disabled persons. This caused their attention to turn inward for a substantial period but, in the case of the latter, ultimately produced stronger organizations (Hutchinson et al., 2007).

Anti-Poverty Activism Refocused
A major influence on the politics of redistribution was the shift among the anti-poverty CSOs from a concern with poverty in general to a focus on child poverty. In the late 1980s, as the effects of targeting benefits were debated, a number of social policy groups took up the cause of child poverty. In 1988, Canada's Child Poverty Action Group (founded in Toronto in 1983) joined other groups concerned with children and families to form a

coalition with a specific focus on children in poverty. Following its failed childcare bill, the Mulroney government shifted its attention to children "at risk" and then to children in poverty, supporting a successful 1989 all-party resolution in the House of Commons to end child poverty by 2000. The coalition, with support from several foundations, quickly transformed itself into Campaign 2000 with a goal of monitoring and publicly reporting on progress towards this target. Several characteristics distinguished Campaign 2000 from the existing anti-poverty CSOs: it worked as a network rather than as a formal federation, which enabled it to be more outward than inward looking; with a membership of seventy (now 120) national, provincial, and community organizations, it was considerably larger than earlier coalitions, and it was prepared to use a mix of tactics, including protest, as needed.[5]

The narrowing of the policy discourse from income inequalities across the general population to child poverty was facilitated by other factors. First, the cuts to social assistance in Ontario and the general tone of "welfare bashing" pursued by the Harris government soon after its 1995 election sparked a new cycle of provincial activism, distracting many Ontario-based anti-poverty and childcare organizations from participation in the national scene. In addition, as Mahon (Chapter 15, this volume) notes, the downloading of childcare costs to municipalities meant that to preserve services and funding, childcare advocates needed to concentrate on urban governments, especially Toronto.

Second, notwithstanding the momentary attention gained by seniors with the 1985 protests that prevented the first attempt at de-indexing Old Age Security (OAS), there has not been a consistently strong voice for seniors or consumers. Canada has never had an equivalent to the American Association of Retired Persons, which claims 40 million members and is one of the most sophisticated lobbies in Washington. And the national anti-poverty organizations that might have taken up the cause for poor people other than children were sidelined: NAPO had internal challenges related to representation and, by the late 1990s, was in free-fall (Greene 2008, 113), and the CCSD was concentrating on research, including research for the Campaign 2000 report cards. Hence, government faced little external pressure to focus on poverty issues across the lifespan.

Third, the paradigm shift from adult to child and from poverty to child development was facilitated by a fortuitous alignment of government, advocates, and experts. Through its annual reports and vociferous criticism of governments, Campaign 2000 made it clear that the number of children living in poverty was rising quite significantly. Uncomfortable with the social justice rhetoric and tactics of Campaign 2000, some more conservative organizations and professional associations (teachers, nurses, public health, and childcare providers) who wanted to move towards implementing a broader children's agenda, formed the National Children's Alliance in 1996. Happy to have an alternative, the federal government put substantial funding behind the alliance to enable it to conduct consultations and to expand its networks. Legitimacy was added by expert evidence stressing the importance of children's early years to their later success, thereby creating the right conditions for a paradigm shift from addressing poverty through redistribution to a social investment state (Jenson 2004; Dobrowolsky and Saint-Martin 2002).[6] For once, key advocates and government were more or less in sync; in May 1999, the federal-provincial/territorial Ministerial Council endorsed a coordinated National Children's Agenda and initiated the joint National Child Benefit (NCB), a major refundable tax credit payable to all low- and middle-income families with children (see Jenson, Chapter 2, this volume).

Muting Advocacy, Shifting Scale: 2000-06

The early years of this century are characterized by the dominance of a social investment perspective – the idea that investment in human capital, particularly in children, will pay off in the future for both individuals and society (Banting 2006; Jenson 2004). In a climate of improved intergovernmental relations and budget surpluses, substantial federal transfers (over $3.2 billion over five years) were allocated under the Early Childhood Development Initiative and the Multilateral Framework on Early Learning and Child Care in 2000 and 2003, respectively. In 2005, the Liberal government negotiated a series of bilateral agreements with the provinces and territories, supported by $5 billion, to establish the foundations of a national system of early learning and childcare (Collier and Mahon 2008, 121). In terms of service delivery, social investment created opportunities for new projects, particularly in early childhood learning, but from an advocacy perspective it had several disadvantages. As a tax transfer, the NCB runs more or less on autopilot from the Canada Revenue Agency and Department of Finance; opportunities for substantial ongoing discussion about the design or impact of the instrument are limited. As an intergovernmental agenda, the real policy decisions had migrated to the tables of executive federalism, from which third parties are excluded. In addition, the focus on children, coupled with the more limited ability of the federal government to shape social policy after the retrenchment of the 1995 budget, squeezed out other redistributive issues.[7]

Finally, social investment compels sophisticated measurement, often over a long time horizon, to determine if investments are paying off. This is more complicated than counting new childcare spaces or the number of people on (or off) social assistance benefits in a given year. As a result, organizations put increased emphasis on research and public reporting, such as the annual "report cards" produced by Campaign 2000 or the recent Vital Signs annual reports on quality of life generated by community foundations.

The 2006 election campaign demonstrated that, while the Conservatives shared an interest in children, they had a very different view on childcare, and on federalism. The Harper government swiftly implemented its agenda on both, cancelling the bilateral agreements (as being too directive from the federal level) and introducing a universal childcare benefit.[8] This ended the dominance of a social investment perspective as an integrating theme for the distribution of social benefits, although, as Jenson (Chapter 2, this volume) observes, subsequent tinkering with benefits has not been out of line with it.

The Cumulative Effect of Shrinking Capacity

The underlying weaknesses of Canadian civil society were increasingly exposed after the early 1990s, and, with additional cutbacks and excessive accountability constraints on federal grants and contributions following the Human Resources Development Canada (HRDC) scandal in 2000 (Good 2003), organizations began to crumble. The effects are well documented (Eakin 2007; Scott 2006): organizations cut costs, laid off staff, and turned to earned income and provision of services to replace lost revenues. The turnover in staff created by gaps in project funding produced enormous volatility for many CSOs. The inter-organizational environment became more competitive and groups self-regulated their participation in policy advocacy and modified their tactics for fear of losing both government and foundation funding (Pross and Webb 2003; Scott 2003, 2006).

In other countries, an important trend was the growing hybridization of organizational forms to suit a more complex mix of activities, take advantage of a wider range of financing instruments (tax credits, vouchers), and better manage advocacy alongside service provision (Brandsen, van de Donk, and Putters 2005; Smith 2010). In Canada, laws governing non-profit incorporation and federal regulations on registered charities have deterred extensive hybridization, with the potential implication that Canadian CSOs are more susceptible to mission drift. The hybrid form used extensively in Canada is the coalition. Although coalitions may look impressive, their capacity is often limited. For instance, the National Children's Alliance, once the federal darling of the children's agenda (reconstituted as the National Alliance for Children and Youth) reported total revenues in 2008-09 of just $16,000.

Recasting the Players
The changes during this period cannot be explained by diminished capacity alone; they were also affected by a continued restructuring of relationships that opened a chasm between charities and the "big" identity organizations, and brought actors with quite different views on social policy to the stage. Recognizing the vacuum of policy leadership at the national level on cross-cutting issues affecting CSOs, a loose coalition had formed in 1995 as the Voluntary Sector Roundtable (VSR), which attempted to get CSOs to think of themselves as a "sector" (the "voluntary" sector). While a positive move towards creating a stronger voice for CSOs and trying to build a more constructive relationship with the federal government, the VSR was driven by charity leaders and, for the most part, excluded the movements and advocacy organizations that had long been core to the social policy community of the 1980s. For several years, the VSR successfully engaged in a form of elite accommodation with ministers of the Chrétien government (White 2008), who came to see the advantages of better relationships with this sector. Realizing that relationship building could not be imposed by fiat but had to unfold as a joint process, in 2000 the Chrétien government launched a unique two year collaborative exercise, the Voluntary Sector Initiative (VSI). This produced some important new research and a variety of special projects, but got bogged down in process and operational issues rather than dealing with higher-level policy; indeed, several of the key policy issues (financing, limits on advocacy, major regulatory reform) were excluded from joint consideration (Social Development Canada 2004).[9]

Despite its good intentions, the VSI had damaging consequences. With its focus on charities, it sharpened the public image of CSOs as service delivery agents and widened the division with advocacy organizations. How representatives of visible minority and Aboriginal groups were invited to engage created tensions and served as a reminder that minorities are not well represented in Canadian CSOs (Social Development Canada 2004). In addition, the intensity of the VSI drained many participating CSOs, leaving little energy for other policy issues and prompting key individuals to move out of active policy leadership roles. The leadership capacity of this part of civil society was weaker after the VSI than it had been going into it, and remains so today. And the connections among different types of organizations, as limited as they were in the mid-1990s, were even more tenuous a decade later.

Other players gained prominence, however. The 2005 debate over same-sex marriage increased the policy activism of both evangelical and Roman Catholic churches; several strenuously pushed the rules over political activities of registered charities, rules that other charities had long argued were too stringent, and apparently came close to being sanctioned by the Canada Revenue Agency (Valpy 2005). The evangelical Christian right has expanded with the rise of new CSOs, such as the Institute for Canadian Values and Concerned Christians Canada, which reportedly have close personal and ideological connections with senior members of the Conservative Party. Just how influential are such ties is a matter of debate: Marci McDonald's 2010 book caused a sensation with its assessment of how deeply the evangelical right has penetrated the Conservative Party; Malloy (2009) remains sceptical, however, arguing that, in Canada, the Christian right lacks a broad leadership or membership base and that, given institutional constraints of a parliamentary system, its long-term prospects are limited. Although the influence and potential of these organizations is difficult to assess (most have not been transparent in identifying their directors, size of membership, or funding), their presence is a reminder that the social policy "community" is by no means cohesive, with minor variations among like-minded equality-seeking organizations, and that the fissures among CSOs in the politics of redistribution can be deep.

Shifting Scale

By the early 2000s, many CSOs had given up on the federal level, realizing that the kind of major social policy change they wanted was not likely to be achieved, and they turned their attention to provincial and urban governments.[10] A shift had already occurred among Ontario's childcare advocates who worked at all three levels (Mahon, Chapter 15, this volume), and local anti-poverty advocacy flourished when national activity was weak (Greene 2009). As Coleman notes (Chapter 4, this volume), local coalitions of citizen groups worked closely with the Canadian Labour Congress in a number of cities during the 2006 municipal elections to support social services and to oppose privatization initiatives by local governments. A particularly successful refocusing was achieved by the movement of disabled persons in Ontario, which, after recognizing that years of working towards a national strategy on disability had not produced the desired results, concentrated its efforts on the passage, in 2005, of the Access for Ontarians with Disabilities Act (Chivers 2008). Coterminous with the VSI, new cross-cutting networks were created subnationally, loosely knit together as the Canadian Federation of Voluntary Sector Networks; their research and policy capacity is very limited, but they have promoted local awareness of common interests. In several provinces, the importance of the voluntary sector has been formally recognized with the establishment of ministers or departments responsible (Elson 2010). Overall, the emerging trend is one of growing variation and unevenness in civil society organizing across the country.

In sum, the policy voices of CSOs became even more constricted in the early 2000s: evidence made little difference, protest even less, and, in trying to work conventional inside routes, they found access closed (Pross and Webb 2003) because the federal government was either not open to new social policy ideas or because it no longer had the latitude to act. In the absence of visible protest actions, the media became disinterested in the messages of CSOs and did not carry their issues. The growth of the service delivery role of CSOs also restricted broader debates about redistribution. Although governments, mainly provincial, still set the criteria for, and monitor, social program delivery, the reality on the ground is that CSOs decide who to serve and how to do so, pushing the real allocation decisions from government into civil society. And the invisibility of these tough decisions has enabled governments to avoid dealing publicly with the full implications of redistribution.

Social Enterprise and Value Politics: 2006 and Beyond

One striking feature of the current environment is how many national CSOs have collapsed or are in serious trouble. In a surprise move in September 2006, the Harper government surgically cut $1 billion in funding, while simultaneously announcing a $13.2 billion budget surplus (Minister of Finance 2006), targeting initiatives with a distinctive Liberal stamp (Canada Volunteerism Initiative), organizations supporting advocacy and research (literacy coalitions, Canadian Policy Research Networks, the Court Challenges Program, and the Law Reform Commission), those transferrable to the provinces (literacy programs) – and those they simply wanted to silence ("feminist" groups) (Phillips 2009). Although it took a year or two for some defunded organizations to collapse, collapse they did.

Although the fate of many CSOs was sealed before the 2008 financial crisis, the crisis added stress, especially for smaller organizations. A national survey in late 2009 (Imagine Canada 2010) revealed that one-third of CSOs had difficulty covering their expenses because revenues had declined (on average, 17.5 percent) while expenditures and demand had increased (on average, by 1.6 percent). One-quarter had cut services, and one-quarter said that their existence was at risk, a proportion about the same a year later (Imagine Canada, 2010, 2011). Those that have survived, even done well, are the large multi-service organizations with diverse membership or client bases; indeed, in late 2010, 70 percent of large charities (annual revenues over $5 million) said they were not stressed by the economic situation (Imagine Canada 2011, 5).

A second noteworthy feature of the current period is the new-found interest in social enterprise. The buzz is not about creativity in pursuit of policy issues but innovation in blending social benefit with commercial activity. As Jackson (2008) observes, social enterprise is still finding its way in Canada (in Quebec it has a long history) and deciding if it is really in the business of significant social transformation. Finally, under the Harper government, evidence-based policy making is taking a backseat to values-based decisions. As the 2010 imbroglio over the cancelling of the long-form census illustrates, the government is prepared to take and defend policy decisions on the basis of values, no matter the evidence. Whether an organization can demonstrate its case through solid research, as the plethora of poverty and community report cards attempt to do, may have less import federally now than in any other period. Thus, some CSOs will be on the winning side on the basis of their values alone, while others will be ignored no matter how good they are at advocating. While not a new occurrence, this is now more overt than it was in the past.

The terrain for CSOs in Canada is at once more barren, given the loss of infrastructure organizations and the vulnerability of many others, and more diverse, given the potential for new forms of hybrid organizational forms propelled by the social enterprise movement. How this landscape will develop is unclear, but we know from other countries that, if CSOs are to flourish, governments must lead in articulating a vision for the role of civil society in governance and citizenship, creating appropriate enabling regulatory environments and developing a flexible array of financing instruments (Phillips and Smith 2011). In this regard, Canada has lagged for three decades.

Conclusion

Have CSOs significantly influenced the new politics of redistribution and its outcomes? Yes and no. In terms of policy outcomes, the effects are minimal. The policy paths followed by the federal government were not what most social policy advocates, at least those who might be called "equality seeking," wanted: benefits have been targeted, a national childcare program was almost won but lost, the role of a national redistributive state has diminished, and income inequality has increased. In effect, the federal government has acted as it thought necessary in spite of any opposition from civil society.

In terms of contributing ideas and shaping policy debate, the evidence is mixed. CSOs have repeatedly raised concerns about growing inequality and rising poverty but have been forced into self-perpetuating reactive and oppositional politics. When they became vocal critics of the federal government, it shut them out of consultation and policy development. When key women's organizations absented themselves from debates on income security and childcare – and their political influence dwindled – policy thinking lost an important gender component. The only real "success" occurred in the late 1990s when CSO concerns with child poverty converged with governmental interests and expert advice stressing the importance of early childhood development, thereby shaping the social investment perspective.

If influence is measured by the ability to forge strong networks and to mobilize allies and citizens, CSO effectiveness has also been varied. At the height of oppositional and identity politics from the mid-1980s to the early 1990s, CSOs were able to stand together as diverse but united coalitions and to engage in collective action, but this diminished over time, and the ability to engage poor and disadvantaged Canadians at the national level has always been weak. In general, Canadian civil society has suffered from a lack of strong national federations, supported by robust think tanks, foundations, and other infrastructure organizations that could sustain a policy presence in national and provincial policy making. CSOs were badly hurt by repeated cuts to their federal government support; some of the earliest casualties were the organizations best able to connect and bridge issues – for example, women's equality and childcare, or disability and poverty. Consequently, the politics of redistribution became compartmentalized as narrower issues and, as conservative groups gained a greater (although still minor) presence, became more deeply divided. Finally, as the locus of policy making migrated to the provinces, many national CSOs were unable to reorient or operate at both scales, so Canadian redistributive politics became even more isolated by geography.

The main challenges in coming years are to rebuild some of the lost capacity, to make productive use of the growing interest in social innovation and social enterprise so that CSOs can be more flexible in responding to a changing environment, and to develop a greater policy presence at provincial and urban levels.

NOTES

1 This chapter does not account for developments at provincial or local levels, particularly in Quebec, where government-civil society relationships have evolved in a very different way. See Noël (Chapter 11, this volume); Laforest (2006); White (2008).
2 For instance, the largest umbrella group representing women, the National Action Committee on the Status of Women (NAC), established in 1972, grew to more than 450 affiliated organizations within a decade and then to more than seven hundred (Vickers, Rankin, and Appelle 1993, 139).
3 The ongoing pre-budget consultations that started in the 1980s remain a way for organized groups to be heard, although their impact is difficult to assess.
4 Many advisory councils and ministries of state that provided representation within government of the interests of particular populations were dismantled (Jenson and Phillips 1996), and the office responsible for disabled persons was downsized and moved from Secretary of State to the new behemoth Human Resources Development Canada (HRDC) where its presence was greatly diminished; disability issues and their connection to poverty lost the visibility they had in the late 1980s (Enns and Neufeldt 2003; Prince 2009).
5 Because women's organizations abandoned income security as a means of advancing women's equality and were weak players in social policy, the analysis of child poverty became gender-neutral (McKeen 2007; Jenson 2009).
6 The two important inputs from experts were the 1999 study by Margaret McCain and Fraser Mustard (with the Canadian Institute for Advance Research) on children's early years and the work of Ken Battle from the Caledon Institute on reducing the barriers between welfare and work (see Jenson 2004).
7 By the early years of 2000, Campaign 2000 was fully on board with the social investment language and had modified its messaging (Dobrowolsky and Saint-Martin 2002), NAPO was in the process of recreating itself to become Canada Without Poverty, and the CCSD was absorbed with the voluntary sector (it is now in financial difficulty and barely alive).
8 Collier and Mahon (2008) argue that the Universal Child Care Benefit (UCCB) is a market-based mechanism that supports the notion of "parental choice"; limited state involvement in regulated childcare plays well with the "family values," social-conservative base of the Harper government.
9 An accord governing the whole-of-government and whole-of-sector relationship, modelled after the 1997 English Compact, was signed but lacked the institutional

and political support for implementation. As a result, it was never widely used, and when the government changed in 2006, it was abandoned.

10 Quebec CSOs always focused on "their" government, and, as Nöel notes in Chapter 11 (this volume), in contrast to the national level Quebec social movements were actually strengthened during this period by "their" government's commitment to social democracy and the coalition politics it encouraged (see also Laforest 2006).

REFERENCES

Abelson, Donald E., and Christine E. Carberry. 1998. "Following Suit or Falling Behind? A Comparative Analysis of Think Tanks in Canada and the United States." *Canadian Journal of Political Science* 31(3): 525-55.

Banting, Keith G. 2006. "Dis-embedding Liberalism? The New Social Policy Paradigm in Canada." In David A. Green and Jonathan R. Kesselman, eds., *Dimensions of Inequality in Canada*, 417-52. Vancouver: UBC Press.

Bashevkin, Sylvia. 1996. "Losing Common Ground: Feminists, Conservatives and Public Policy in Canada during the Mulroney Years." *Canadian Journal of Political Science* 29(2): 211-42.

Battle, Ken. 1993. "The Politics of Stealth: Child Benefits under the Tories." In Susan D. Phillips, ed., *How Ottawa Spends: A More Democratic Canada?*, 417-48. Ottawa: Carleton University Press.

Brandsen, Taco, W. van de Donk, and K. Putters. 2005. "Griffins or Chameleons? Hybridity as a Permanent and Inevitable Characteristic of the Third Sector." *International Journal of Public Administration* 28(9/10): 749-66.

Cardozo, Andrew. 1996. "Lion Taming: Downsizing the Opponents of Downsizing." In Eugene Swimmer, ed., *How Ottawa Spends, 1996-1997: Life under the Knife*, 303-36. Ottawa: Carleton University Press.

Chivers, Sally. 2008. "Barrier by Barrier: The Canadian Disability Movement and the Fight for Equal Rights." In Miriam Smith, ed., *Group Politics and Social Movements in Canada*, 307-28. Peterborough, ON: Broadview.

Collier, Cheryl, and Rianne Mahon. 2008. "One Step Forward, Two Steps Back: Child Care Policy from Martin to Harper." In Allan M. Maslove, ed., *How Ottawa Spends, 2008-2009: A More Orderly Federalism?*, 110-133. Montreal and Kingston: McGill-Queen's University Press.

Dobrowolsky, Alexandra. 2000. *The Politics of Pragmatism: Women, Representation and Constitutionalism in Canada*. Toronto: Oxford University Press.

Dobrowolsky, Alexandra, and Denis Saint-Martin. 2002. "Agency, Actors and Change in a Child-Focused Future: Problematizing Path Dependency's Past and Statist Parameters." Working Paper No. 3, Fostering Social Cohesion: A Comparison of New Policy Strategies, Université de Montréal.

Eakin, Lynn. 2007. *We Can't Afford to Do Business This Way: A Study of the Administrative Burden Resulting from Funder Accountability and Compliance Practices*. Toronto: Wellesley Institute.

Elson, Peter R. 2010. "A Slice of the Pie: An Overview of Provincial Non-Profit-Sector-Government Relations in Canada." Paper presented to the VSSN Conference, London.

Enns, Henry, and Aldred H. Neufeldt. 2003. *In Pursuit of Equal Participation: Canada and Disability at Home and Abroad.* Concord, ON: Captus.

Finkel, Alvin. 2006. *Social Policy and Practice in Canada: A History.* Waterloo, ON: University of Waterloo Press.

Good, David A. 2003. *The Politics of Public Management.* Toronto: IPAC.

Granovetter, Mark S. 1973. "The Strength of Weak Ties." *American Journal of Sociology* 78(6): 1360-80.

Greene, Jonathan. 2008. "Boardrooms and Barricades: Anti-Poverty Organizing in Canada." In Miriam Smith, ed., *Group Politics and Social Movements in Canada,* 107-28. Peterborough, ON: Broadview.

Haddow, Rod. 1990. "The Poverty Policy Community in Canada's Liberal Welfare State." In William D. Coleman and Grace Skogstad, eds., *Policy Communities and Public Policy in Canada: A Structural Approach,* 212-37. Mississauga, ON: Copp Clark Pitman.

–. 1993. *Poverty Reform in Canada, 1958-1978: State and Class Influences on Policy Making.* Montreal and Kingston: McGill-Queen's University Press.

Howlett, Michael. 2009. "Policy Analytical Capacity and Evidence-Based Policy Making: Lessons from Canada." *Canadian Public Administration* 52(2): 153-75.

Hutchison, Peggy, Susan Arai, Alison Pedlar, John Lord, and Colleen Whyte. 2007. "Leadership in the Canadian Consumer Disability Movement: Hopes and Challenges." *International Journal of Disability, Community & Rehabilitation* 6 (1). http://www.ijdcr.ca/VOL06_01_CAN/articles/hutchison.shtml.

Imagine Canada. 2010. *Sector Monitor,* 1, 1, April. http://www.imaginecanada.ca/sector_monitor.

–. 2011. *Sector Monitor,* 1, 3, February. http://www.imaginecanada.ca/sector_monitor.

Jackson, Edward. 2008. "How Ottawa Doesn't Spend: The Rapid Appearance and Disappearance – and Possible Reappearance – of the Federal Social Economy Initiative." In Allan M. Maslove, ed., *How Ottawa Spends, 2008-2009: A More Orderly Federalism?* 163-78. Montreal and Kingston: McGill-Queen's University Press.

Jenson, Jane. 1995. "What's in a Name? Nationalist Movements and Public Discourse." In Hank Johnston and Bert Klandermans, eds., *Social Movements and Culture,* 107-26. London: UCL Press.

–. 2004. "Changing the Paradigm: Family Responsibility or Investing in Children." *Canadian Journal of Sociology* 29(2): 169-84.

–. 2009. "Lost in Translation: The Social Investment Perspective and Gender Equality." *Social Politics: International Studies in Gender, State and Society* 16(4): 446-83.

Jenson, Jane, and Susan D. Phillips. 1996. "Regime Shift: New Citizenship Practices in Canada." *International Journal of Canadian Studies* 14: 11-36.

Laforest, Rachel. 2004. "Governance and the Voluntary Sector: Rethinking the Contours of Advocacy." *International Journal of Canadian Studies* 30: 185-203.

–. 2006. "State and Community Sector Relations: Crisis and Challenges in Quebec." *The Philanthropist* 20(4): 171-84.

Levens, Bruce R. 2006. "In Search of Relevance: Observations on United Way Funding Distribution." *The Philanthropist* 20(3): 185-97.

Lindquist, Evert. 1993. "Think Tanks or Clubs: Assessing the Influence and Role of Canadian Policy Institutes." *Canadian Public Administration* 36(4): 547-79.

—. 2005. "Organizing for Megaconsultation: HRDC and the Social Security Reform." *Canadian Public Administration* 48(3): 348-85.

MacIvor, Heather. 1996. *Women and Politics in Canada*. Peterborough, ON: Broadview.

Mahon, Rianne, and Susan D. Phillips. 2002. "Dual-Earner Families Caught in a Liberal Welfare Regime? The Politics of Child Care in Canada." In Sonya Michel and Rianne Mahon, eds., *Child Care Policy at the Crossroads: Gender and Welfare State Restructuring*, 191-218. New York: Routledge.

Malloy, Jonathan. 2009. "Jesusland North? The Christian Right in Canadian Politics." Presentation to Center for Canadian Studies, Duke University.

Manfredi, Christopher. 2004. *Feminist Activism in the Supreme Court: Legal Mobilization and the Women's Legal Education and Action Fund*. Vancouver: UBC Press.

McDonald, Marci. 2010. *The Armageddon Factor: The Rise of Christian Nationalism in Canada*. Toronto: Random House.

McKeen, Wendy. 2004. *Money in Their Own Name: The Feminist Voice in Poverty Debate in Canada, 1970-1995*. Toronto: University of Toronto Press.

Minister of Finance. 2006. *Canada's New Government Cuts Wasteful Programs, Refocuses Spending on Priorities, Achieves Major Debt Reduction as Promised*. Ottawa: Finance.

Montpetit, Éric, Francesca Scala, and Isabelle Fortier. 2004. "The Paradox of Deliberative Democracy: The National Action Committee on the Status of Women and Canada's Policy on Reproductive Technology." *Policy Sciences* 37: 137–57.

Pal, Leslie A. 1993. *Interests of State: The Politics of Language, Multiculturalism and Feminism in Canada*. Montreal and Kingston: McGill-Queen's University Press.

Panet, Philip de L., and Michael J. Trebilcock. 1998. "Contracting Out Social Services." *Canadian Public Administration* 41(1): 21-50.

Phillips, Susan D. 1991. "How Ottawa Blends: Shifting Government Relationships with Interest Groups." In Frances Abele, ed., *How Ottawa Spends: The Politics of Fragmentation*, 183-228. Ottawa: Carleton University Press.

—. 2002. "Political Strategies of the Canadian Women's Movement: Who's Speaking? Who's Listening?" In Radha Jhappan, ed., *Women's Legal Strategies*, 379-407. Toronto: University of Toronto Press.

—. 2009. "Canada's 'New Government' and the Voluntary Sector: Whither a Policy Agenda." In Rachel Laforest, ed., *The New Federal Policy Agenda and the Voluntary Sector*. Montreal and Kingston: McGill-Queen's University Press.

Phillips, Susan D., and Steven Rathgeb Smith. 2011. "Between Governance and Regulation: Evolving Government-Third Sector Relationships." In Susan D. Phillips and Steven Rathgeb Smith, eds., *Governance and Regulation in the Third Sector: International Perspectives*. London: Routledge.

Prince, Michael J. 1999. "From Health and Welfare to Stealth and Farewell: Federal Social Policy, 1980-2000." In Leslie A. Pal, ed., *How Ottawa Spends, 1999-2000: Shape Shifting – Canadian Governance toward the 21st Century*, 151-96. Toronto: Oxford University Press.

—. 2009. *Absent Citizens: Disability Politics and Policy in Canada*. Toronto: University of Toronto Press.

Prince, Michael J., and James J. Rice. 2000. *Changing Politics of Canadian Social Policy*. Toronto: University of Toronto Press.

Pross, A. Paul. 1992. *Group Politics and Public Policy*. Toronto: Oxford University Press.

Pross, A. Paul, and Kernaghan R. Webb. 2003. "Embedded Regulation: Advocacy and the Federal Regulation of Public Interest Groups." In Kathy L. Brock, ed., *Delicate Dances: Public Policy and the Nonprofit Sector*, 63-121. Montreal and Kingston: McGill-Queen's University Press.

Rebick, Judy. 2005. *Ten Thousand Roses: The Making of a Feminist Revolution*. Toronto: Penguin.

Rice, James J. 1987. "Restitching the Safety Net: Altering the National Social Security System." In Michael J. Prince, ed., *How Ottawa Spends, 1987-1988: Restraining the State*, 211-36. Toronto: Methuen.

—. 1995. "Redesigning Welfare: The Abandonment of a National Commitment." In Susan D. Phillips, ed., *How Ottawa Spends, 1995-1996: Mid-Life Crises*, 185-208. Ottawa: Carleton University Press.

Salamon, Lester M. 1994. "The Rise of the Nonprofit Sector." *Foreign Affairs* 73(4): 109-22.

Scott, Katherine. 2003. *Funding Matters: The Impact of Canada's New Funding Regime on Nonprofit and Voluntary Organizations*. Ottawa: Canadian Council on Social Development.

—. 2006. *Pan-Canadian Funding Practice in Communities: Challenges and Opportunities for the Government of Canada*. Ottawa: Canadian Council on Social Development.

Smith, Miriam. 1993. "Constitutionalizing Economic and Social Rights in the Charlottetown Round." In Susan D. Phillips, ed., *How Ottawa Spends: A More Democratic Canada?*, 83-108. Ottawa: Carleton University Press.

—, ed. 2008. *Group Politics and Social Movements in Canada*. Peterborough, ON: Broadview.

Smith, Steven Rathgeb. 2010. "Structural Complexity and Funding Diversification in Nonprofit Organizations: The Governance Challenge." *Policy and Society*, Special Issue on Financing Civil Society.

Social Development Canada. 2004. *The Voluntary Sector Initiative Process Evaluation*. Ottawa: Social Development Canada. http://www.hrsdc.gc.ca/eng/cs/sp/sdc/evaluation/sp-ah213e/page00.shtml.

Teghtsoonian, Katherine. 1993. "Neo-Conservative Ideology and Opposition to Federal Regulation of Child Care Services in the United States and Canada." *Canadian Journal of Political Science* 26: 97-121.

Tupper, Allan. 1993. "Think Tanks, Public Debt and the Politics of Expertise in Canada." *Canadian Public Administration* 36(4): 530-46.

Valpy, Michael. 2005. "Bishop Blasted for Calling on the State to Target Gays." *Globe and Mail*, 18 January.

Vickers, Jill, Pauline Rankin, and Christine Appelle. 1993. *Politics as if Women Mattered: A Political Analysis of the National Action Committee on the Status of Women.* Toronto: University of Toronto Press.

White, Deena. 2008. "Can Advocacy Survive Partnership? Representing the Clients of the Welfare State." Paper presented to the annual meeting of ISA RC19, Stockholm, September.

Public Opinion on Social Spending, 1980-2005

ROBERT ANDERSEN AND JOSH CURTIS

This chapter considers the relationship between social spending and public opinion in Canada between 1980 and 2005. We ask whether the gradual move to the right in Canadian politics and the concomitant decrease in public spending are justified on the grounds that politicians and policy makers have given Canadians what they want. Have Canadians really become more conservative in their views of social spending? Or have patterns in public opinion followed trends in the economy?

We begin by arguing that public opinion tracked quite closely with changes in the economy, in particular the unemployment rate, median income, and income inequality. We then explore the relationship between individual economic conditions and attitudes towards the government's responsibility to provide for citizens. To shed light on how political conditions might also matter, we compare attitudes in Canada and the United States. We conclude that the gradual erosion of the Canadian welfare state reflects politicians' attempts to influence, rather than accommodate, public opinion. We find no evidence that Canadians have become increasingly conservative in their views of social spending; instead, both spending and support for spending follow the business cycle.

Social Context and Public Opinion

Before discussing our findings in greater detail, it is helpful to discuss relevant research on public opinion, on social spending, and on welfare states more generally. With this in mind, this section has three objectives. We start by putting Canadian public opinion into a larger context. Next, we discuss the ways in which *national context* might influence public opinion. We then explore how people's attitudes might be shaped by their *own* economic conditions.

Public Opinion on Social Spending in Canada
Esping-Andersen's (1990) widely used typology identifies three types of welfare state regimes: social democratic, conservative, and liberal. Social democratic regimes (e.g., the Scandinavian countries) are characterized by extensive, generous, and universal social spending programs; liberal regimes (e.g., Australia, Canada, the United States) tend to have only limited social spending; conservative regimes (e.g., Germany, the Netherlands) fall somewhere between the two. Canada is typically considered a liberal social welfare regime characterized by fairly limited social spending (Esping-Andersen 1990; Myles 1998; Svallfors 1997). Despite this label, Canada is clearly more statist than the United States (Grabb and Curtis 2005), which is often deemed the best example of a liberal welfare state. The two countries have many differences in social expenditures (both in type and extent), most notably with respect to health care, where Canada's universal health care system stands in stark contrast to the privatized health care system of the US.

Although empirical research has yielded mixed results (e.g., Jaeger 2006, 2009; Svallfors 2008; Matthews and Erickson 2008), many suggest that differences in welfare state regimes reflect public demand (Esping-Andersen 1990; Korpi and Palme 1998). This argument would expect, then, that Canadians are less supportive of social spending than are citizens of countries with less liberal market economies. Moreover, although systematic research on the topic is scarce, anecdotal evidence suggests that Canadians highlight themselves as "kinder" than Americans when it comes to redistribution policies. The empirical evidence that does exist suggests that a large majority of Canadians feel that the government should be responsible for reducing poverty through social programs and redistribution policies (Blekesaune and Quadagno 2003; Matthews and Erickson 2008). There is also some evidence that Canadians have relatively egalitarian views, given Canada's level of social spending (Svallfors 2008). But other research suggests that different types of social spending receive different levels of support. For example, Reutter, Harrison, and Neufeld (2002) demonstrate that spending on childcare programs receives far greater support than does spending on welfare. Studies specifically comparing Canada and the US further suggest that Canadian public opinion is no more generous than is American public opinion. For example, Adams (1990) argues there is very little difference between Canadians and Americans in attitudes towards policies regarding the redistribution of social spending. Others posit that differences in public opinion within the two countries are almost as great as are the differences between them (Grabb and Curtis 2005).

Contextual Effects on Public Opinion

Opinions about what should be considered an acceptable level of inequality vary across time, social groups, and cultures (Noll and Roberts 2003; Osberg and Smeeding 2006). For example, research suggests that national differences in acceptance of inequality are negatively related to economic development, welfare state involvement (Kelley and Evans 1993; Weakliem, Andersen, and Heath 2005), and a Soviet-communist past (Kelley and Zagorski 2005; Fisher and Heath 2006). Public opinion on social spending differs in a similar manner (Kenworthy and McCall 2008). Gallie (1983, 268) argues that, when analyzing differences in public support for social expenditures, it is important to consider "the profound institutional differences that can exist between capitalist societies at a broadly similar level of economic development."

Other research looks specifically at the role of welfare states. In this regard, social spending both reflects public desires and influences it. The argument for the role of the welfare states is straightforward: political regimes are characterized by distinct "historical and institutional compromises between state, market, and family" (Jaeger 2006, 157) that profoundly shape public support for redistribution. Most studies find only limited evidence of such a relationship, but this could be due to methodological limitations (see Jaeger 2006 for a detailed discussion). Svallfors (1997) is an exception (see also Papadakis 1993), finding that social democratic countries are characterized by strong public support for welfare-state intervention and income equality. Countries with more liberal economies, meanwhile, tend to have very little public support for government redistribution and income distribution.

The idea that public opinion is influenced by political and economic context is given credence by the fact that support for redistribution policies fluctuates within countries. Using individual-level survey data collected in Finland between 1975 and 1993, Shivo and Uusitalo (1995) demonstrate that public opinion tends to be more favourable towards redistribution in times of economic recession. Svallfors (1991, 1995) shows similar findings for Sweden. Moreover, while Soroka and Wlezien (2004, 533) emphasize the role of policy, they suggest that Canadian public opinion responds to the structuring role of institutions, noting: "As in the US and the UK, the Canadian public appears to respond thermostatically to changes in social spending, and Canadian policymakers appear to respond to public preferences. The underlying details are not the same, however, and the pattern of results across the three countries is suggestive about the structuring role of institutions."

Individual Economic Conditions

If economic conditions influence aggregate public opinion, it follows that they also affect the attitudes of individuals. In this regard, the "economic-utilitarian" hypothesis provides a possible explanation. This rational choice argument holds that people are motivated by self-interest and, thus, support social spending if they feel they might potentially benefit from it (Kaltenthaler and Ceccoli 2008; Jaeger 2006; Schneider and Jacoby 2007). It follows, then, that those with lower incomes or from lower social classes will tend to be most favourable towards social spending. Kaltenthaler and Ceccoli (2008) find support for this hypothesis when they consider welfare state policy in seven West European countries – Finland, France, Germany, Spain, Sweden, Switzerland, and the United Kingdom. They propose two explanations for the relationship. First, individuals of higher socio-economic status tend to rely less on the welfare state than do the poor. Second, welfare state provisions redistribute wealth from individuals with higher incomes to those with lower incomes, meaning that those with higher incomes stand to lose more if welfare expenditures increase.

Others suggest that political values or political party preferences have an important influence on attitudes. Of course, values and party preferences are not completely disconnected from economic conditions, but this argument focuses largely on the notion that attitudes towards redistribution result from adhering to the political principles and values of the welfare state institutions one experiences (Van Oorschot 2002; Jaeger 2006). Using panel data to support his claims, Jaeger (2006) demonstrates that Canadian attitudes towards the welfare state are influenced by both political ideology and self-interest.

Still other research suggests that how one's economic position affects one's attitude depends on the type of political regime. In this regard, Korpi and Palme (1998, 2003) argue that targeting benefits at the poor rather than offering universal transfers is less likely to reduce poverty and inequality, thus resulting in a "paradox of redistribution." The rationale for the paradox of redistribution is based on the reaction of public opinion, especially that of the middle classes, to social spending policies. As an example, consider unemployment benefits. If one provides benefits to all regardless of personal economic situation, and if one gives everyone a level of benefits that allows them to remain reasonably close to the standard of living they enjoyed while working, then support for spending will come from all social classes. In a similar vein, Iversen and Soskice (2006) suggest that redistribution is most likely in proportional representation electoral systems because political parties that espouse redistribution policies have a better chance of having candidates elected under these systems.

An Analysis of Public Opinion on Social Spending in Canada, 1980-2005

Simple Trends in Public Opinion and Social Spending

The goal of the present chapter is to determine whether Canadian public opinion was shaped by economic and political conditions during the period from 1980 to 2005. Using aggregate data from yearly opinion polls conducted by Environics, we explore simple trends in public opinion on social spending in three areas: (1) general welfare spending, (2) social services for the poor, and (3) child daycare. The questionnaire item was identical for all three issues and in all years under study. The wording is as follows:

> Keeping in mind that increasing services could increase taxes, do you think the federal government is spending too much, just the right amount, or should be spending more on each of the following: welfare, social services for the poor, child day care.[1]

In total, eighteen polls were conducted on general welfare, from 1980 to 2001; fifteen polls were conducted on social services for the poor, from 1988 to 2005; and sixteen polls were conducted on child daycare, from 1988 to 2004.

Before proceeding to a more rigorous analysis of correlates of public opinion, it is useful to graphically explore whether the trends in public opinion match trends in government social spending. Figure 6.1(a) displays average public opinion (scored 1 for "too much," 2 for "just right," and 3 for "not enough") regarding social spending on welfare, poverty, and childcare in Canada from 1980 to 2004. One is immediately struck by the lack of a

FIGURE 6.1

(a) Canadian public opinion on social spending; (b) social expenditures as a percentage of GDP, 1980-2005

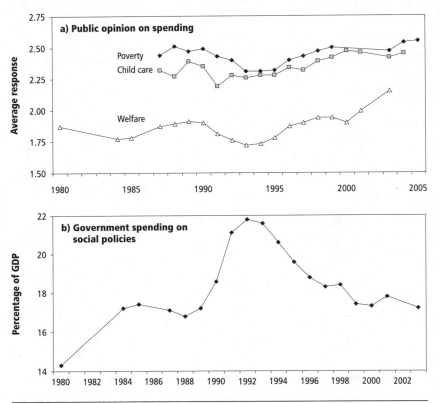

secular trend in public opinion on any of the three social spending issues. Simply put, there is no indication that the Canadian public became less supportive of social spending over time. Although public opinion fluctuated, each issue displays a cyclical pattern attuned to the business cycle, falling when the economy performs poorly and rising when it does well. There are two distinct business cycles, one peaking in the late 1980s and the other in the late 1990s, with a big dip in the early 1990s.

Figure 6.1(b) displays government spending on social policies (as a percentage of GDP). Consistent with findings from other research on social spending in Canada (Picot, Morissette, and Myles 2002), we see a rising trend in spending from the early 1980s until 1994, with a following sharp decline until spending reaches approximately the same level as in the 1980s.

Other research indicates that this decline stemmed from paring back benefits for the unemployed and single parents (Battle, Mendelson, and Torjman 2005; Banting 2006; Osberg 2007). Although these benefits are primarily a provincial responsibility, the replacement of the Canada Assistance Program with the Canada Health and Social Transfer suggests that the federal government played a role in the decline (e.g., see Johnston, Chapter 8, this volume; Frenette, Green, and Milligan 2009). In short, preliminary evidence suggests that 1994 was a turning point for social spending in Canada.

The two panels of Figure 6.1 demonstrate that the trends in public opinion on social spending mirror the trend in social expenditures. For example, the early 1990s are characterized by a precipitous decline in support for spending until 1994, after which support rises sharply until reaching – and even slightly surpassing – the level of the late 1980s and early 1990s. In other words, there is some evidence that the preference for spending among the Canadian population increased during times of declining spending. At the very least, these data fail to support the argument that the decline in social expenditures reflects Canadians' preferences. Still, this finding is not inconsistent with Wlezien's (1995) idea of a responsive public: "when policy increases (decreases), the preference for more policy decreases (increases)" (Soroka and Wlezien 2004).

Contextual Factors Associated with Spending and Public Opinion

Having shown that trends in public opinion are cyclical in nature, our next goal is to test the extent to which particular economic conditions and political contexts might account for these fluctuations. To this end, we explore three sets of research questions.

The first set pertains to the role of political context. Specifically, is there a relationship between public opinion and political context? In particular, did public opinion move in tandem with the political regime (i.e., Liberal versus Conservative federal governments) and the level of social expenditures?

The second set of questions considers the role of the economy. Did support for spending correspond to changes in median income, income inequality, and unemployment? If there is a relationship between public opinion and income inequality, we posit the following: (1) people with higher incomes feel morally obligated to help eradicate inequality or to keep it under control to limit some of the ills of inequality (e.g., crime, a lack of social cohesion); (2) those with lower incomes favour income social spending for instrumental reasons, particularly because they stand to benefit. We have two competing arguments regarding a possible relationship between public opinion and median income: (1) as median income increases, the public becomes more affluent generally and is more willing to spend on social programs; or (2) preferences for spending decrease as median income rises because less social spending is needed. We also have two competing hypotheses regarding the role of unemployment, both of which relate to the business cycle: (1) the public is most in favour of social spending when the economy is doing well (i.e., when unemployment is low) because there is more money to spread around; or (2) the public responds to growing needs (i.e., a growth in the number of people who need assistance) by favouring increases in spending when the economy is performing badly (i.e., unemployment is high).

Finally, we also assess how one's personal economic situation affects one's opinion of the welfare state. To this end, we compare the relationship between income and attitudes towards the government's responsibility to provide for its citizens in Canada and the US. The comparison of these two countries also allows insight into the role of political context. We expect to find a stronger relationship between income and public opinion in Canada on the grounds that the Canadian working class has greater awareness of the issues because of the New Democratic Party, which, unlike any US party, emphasizes the importance of social spending for working-class families (Andersen and Fox 2001; Johnston, Chapter 8, this volume).

Aggregate Public Opinion on Redistribution

Using data from Human Resources and Skills Development Canada (2010), we examine the extent to which changes in the average median family income, level of income inequality, the unemployment rate, and amount of social expenditures relative to GDP can account for variations in public opinion over time. We also explore whether political regime (Liberal versus Conservative federal governments) affected public opinion. Table 6.A1 (located in the appendix at the end of this chapter) provides a detailed description of the polling data and the contextual variables employed in the analysis.

Figure 6.2 displays trends in some important economic indicators during the same 1980 to 2004 period. Particularly interesting are the increases in both median income and income inequality in the mid-1990s. With respect to median incomes, it is striking how the rising trend occurs after a gradual decline that began in 1980. On the other hand, the level of income inequality remained relatively stable until around 1995. Although the trend in unemployment rate bears little resemblance to the trends in public expenditure

FIGURE 6.2

Trends in (a) median family income, (b) income inequality, and (c) the unemployment rate, 1980-2005

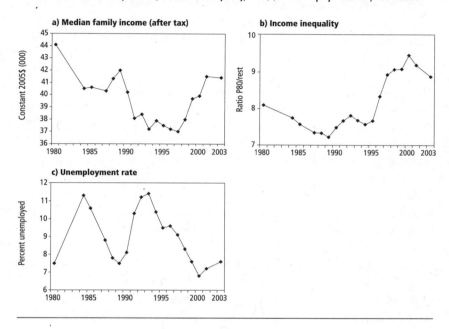

and support for social spending before 1990, it looks remarkably similar to these trends thereafter. Finally, although not shown in Figure 6.2, the marked change in the patterns corresponds to the period of Liberal government from 1993 on.

The correlation coefficients shown in Table 6.A2 provide more evidence of a relationship between public opinion and the context variables. Consistent with the information shown in Figure 6.1, public opinion on social spending is negatively correlated with actual social expenditures. In other words, as expenditures went *down*, public preferences for spending went *up*. Also important are the very strong negative correlations between the unemployment rate and all three public opinion measures. Median income and income inequality are related to public opinion in the expected direction, though the correlations are not always statistically significant. There is no clear relationship between governing party and public opinion, however. Moreover, although the Liberals tended to spend less than the Conservatives, the difference in spending between the two parties is not statistically significant. Taken together, these findings suggest that people are influenced by their personal economic conditions. Nevertheless, the strong correlations between many of the context variables and the fact that these are only bivariate correlations suggest that some of these relationships may be spurious. We thus wait to discuss these relationships in further detail until after carrying out more sophisticated analyses below.

Multinomial Log-Linear Models Predicting Public Opinion
We now turn to more rigorous tests of the relationships between the national context variables and public opinion. Although we do not discount the possibility that public opinion influences – either directly or indirectly – many of the context variables, we proceed on the assumption that the contextual variables influence public opinion. Given that each public opinion dependent variable has three response categories, we employ multinomial log-linear models to carry out our tests. These models assess the partial effects of the context variables on the number of respondents who fall into each category. In other words, the models allow us to estimate the effects of one context variable controlling for values of the others. Although we fit several models, the best fitting model for all three dependent variables includes both the political and economic context variables. Likelihood ratio tests for the terms in the various models and measures of fit are shown in Table 6.A1. From this point forward, we put most emphasis on the best fitting model.

To better comprehend the effects of each of the three context variables, we calculate predicted percentages for each category of the dependent variable rather than displaying the coefficient estimates (Fox and Andersen 2006). The resulting effect displays appear in Figures 6.3-6.5. We concentrate on Figure 6.3, which displays the relationship between public opinion and general welfare spending. Starting with panel (a), we see that the lines representing the three response categories converge at high levels of median income, suggesting that, as median family income rises, public opinion becomes more favourable to redistribution. Most striking is the large increase in the percentage of people who feel that too much is being spent on welfare as incomes decline. Just as important, unemployment rate has a strong effect: as unemployment increases, the public is less in favour of social spending. In other words, we find more support for the business cycle thesis.

The relationship between income inequality and public opinion on spending is very similar. That is, as income inequality rises, the Canadian public

FIGURE 6.3

Predicted public opinion regarding social spending on welfare by median income, income inequality, unemployment rate, and governing party

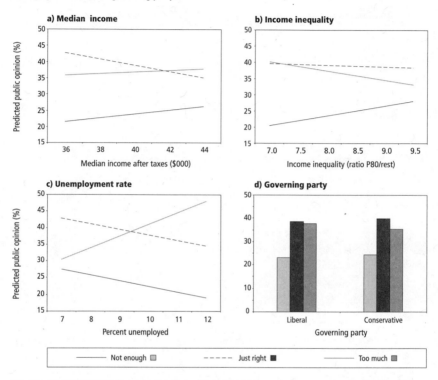

Note: Predicted values are derived from the final multinomial log-linear model.

appears to feel that more spending is needed. Still, interpretation of this result is complicated by the fact that the increase in inequality was almost entirely driven by growth in incomes at the very top. Moreover, it is likely that the general Canadian public is less aware of changes in income inequality than they are of the business cycle as captured by the unemployment rate and median income. We can speculate, then, that the effect of income inequality on public opinion largely reflects changes in the opinions of those with higher incomes. That is, it is possible that these people became more generous in their views on social spending as their own incomes rose drastically. The data we have here, however, do not allow us to test this conjecture.

FIGURE 6.4

Predicted public opinion regarding social spending on poverty by median income, income inequality, unemployment rate, and governing party

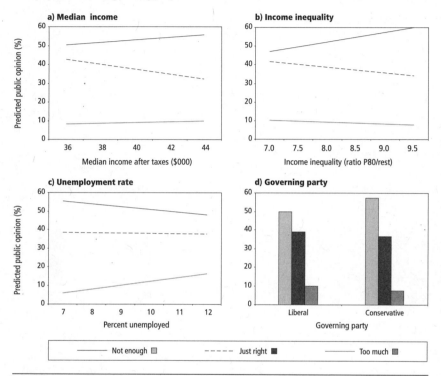

Note: Predicted values are derived from the final multinomial log-linear model.

Finally, it is important to note that political context appears to have had little impact on trends in public opinion during the period under investigation. After controlling for economic conditions, the relationship between actual government spending on social programs and public opinion regarding that spending is weak (and statistically insignificant) (see Table 6.A2). Moreover, although the relationship between public opinion and governing party is statistically significant, it is substantively weak (see Figure 6.3[d]).

By and large, the contextual variables have a similar influence on public opinion towards spending on the poor and childcare. A possible exception is the role of the unemployment rate. In contrast to the negative relationship between unemployment rate and public opinion on general welfare spending, there is no apparent relationship between unemployment and

FIGURE 6.5

Predicted public opinion regarding social spending on childcare by median income, income inequality, unemployment rate, and governing party

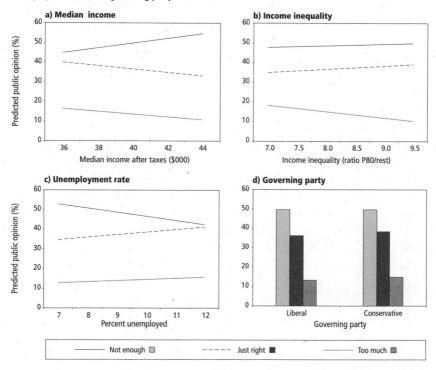

Note: Predicted values are derived from the final multinomial log-linear model.

public opinion on spending on childcare or poverty. These results are consistent with other research that suggests people perceive spending on welfare in a slightly different light than they do other social issues (Jacoby 1994). People tend to see welfare recipients in a more negative light than they see recipients of other social spending programs (MacLeod, Montero, and Speer 1999; Will 1993). Possibly, the public is more willing to support welfare recipients, who are more likely to be considered responsible for their own plight than are the poor or children, when there is plenty of money to go around. On the other hand, the public responds to the worsening conditions of children and the poor – which is reflected by higher unemployment – by favouring increased spending to help them. We must be careful not to over-interpret these results, however, especially because of the relatively few data points for public opinion on childcare and poverty.

Individual-Level Conditions and Attitudes

The previous analyses demonstrate a clear link between national-level economic conditions and aggregate public opinion on redistribution. The next stage of analysis concerns the relationship between individual-level economic conditions and attitudes towards income inequality and redistribution. Our goal is to assess how individual-level economic conditions are related to attitudes towards government spending in Canada, but we also consider whether Canadians are more favourable towards government intervention than Americans and whether income has different effects in the two countries.

For this analysis, we utilize individual-level survey data from the World Values Survey (WVS) collected in 1990 and 2000 (Inglehart et al. 2001). Our dependent variable asks respondents about the role of the welfare state. Respondents were presented with the following two extremes:

- People should take more responsibility to provide for themselves (coded 1);
- The government should take more responsibility to ensure that everyone is provided for (coded 10).

The main explanatory variable, income, is measured in deciles. We include controls for age, gender, religion, marital and family status, and education. We fit separate models for Canada and the US but test for an interaction between country and income on the pooled data. Estimates are found using ordinary least squares (OLS) regression.

An analysis of variance for the regression fitted to the pooled data suggests a significant interaction between country and income (p = .002). To better understand the income effect, we explore the models fitted separately to the data for each country. The model summaries are shown in Table 6.A3. Rather than discuss the coefficients, we calculate fitted values across the ten categories of income for both Canada and the US and plot them in the effect displays shown in Figure 6.6. These fitted values are calculated with all other explanatory variables set to typical values (e.g., the sample proportion for each category). In other words, the lines in Figure 6.6 represent the average attitude score at particular values of income, controlling for other important predictors. The points and the solid lines represent the

FIGURE 6.6

Effect of income on attitudes towards government responsibility to provide for its citizens, Canada and the United States

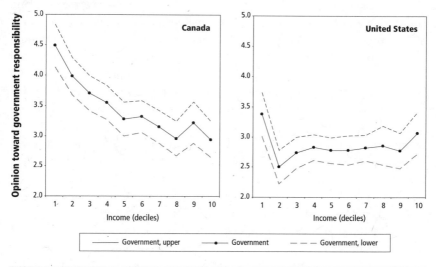

fitted values; the dashed lines represent the 95 percent confidence envelopes for the fitted values.

Figure 6.6 shows that attitudes have a different relationship with income in Canada and the US. In Canada, people with lower than median incomes tend to be supportive of government redistribution; they become less so as income rises until it reaches the approximate median income, at which point income has no further effect. In the US, on the other hand, income has far less influence on attitudes. Consistent with previous research (see, for example, Epstein 2004), we find a large difference in opinions between the very highest and the very lowest deciles. Aside from those at very low incomes, all other income groups tend to be most similar to the richest group. It is noteworthy that, while there is no significant difference in attitudes between Canadians and Americans with high incomes, Canadians with lower incomes are much more favourable towards government intervention than are Americans with lower incomes. We suspect that this reflects the greater politicization of the Canadian working class. Whereas the US lacks a working-class party, Canada has the NDP, thus making issues of government intervention and redistribution more salient in this country.

Conclusion

This chapter explores the relationship between economic and political conditions and public opinion towards social spending in Canada. Our analysis suggests that changes in public opinion reflect cyclical changes in economic conditions. In other words, we find no evidence that Canadians are generally becoming more conservative in their preferences for social spending. Our findings also contrast with popular (mis)conceptions that the decline in social spending since the mid-1990s reflected public opinion on the issue. In fact, there is little evidence that public opinion on spending was related to actual levels of spending. Still, our finding that Canadians are more accepting than are Americans of the government's responsibility for its citizens and the fact that this distinction is more often seen at lower income levels suggest that the Canadian working class is more aware than is its American counterpart of the benefits it may reap from redistribution policies.

Our conclusion that public opinion follows the business cycle is supported by the trends in median income and unemployment, two measures widely considered to reflect the health of the economy. The relationship between median income and public opinion suggests that the public is most supportive of social spending when there is more money to spread around. Put otherwise, a rise in median income typically implies a rise in the overall standard of living, resulting in public opinion more likely to favour social spending. We are not suggesting that most people are aware of the median income at any given point in time; rather, enough people are aware of the general economic conditions influencing the country for aggregate public opinion to reflect these trends.

An interesting finding is that the unemployment rate (i.e., the business cycle) has a different impact on the public opinion of welfare policies than it does on the public opinion of policies for the poor or childcare. More specifically, when the economy is performing poorly, people are less likely to support increases in social spending on welfare benefits and more likely to support spending on childcare and the poor. Consistent with other research on attitudes towards welfare recipients (MacLeod, Montero, and Speer 1999; Will 1993), these findings suggest that some people see welfare recipients as responsible for their plight and therefore as less deserving of assistance than others. Unfortunately, limitations in the data do not allow us to pursue this question.

We propose a different story for the mechanisms underlying the relationship between income inequality and public opinion on spending. In this case, people appear to want to remedy rising inequality through increased spending. We posit two possible reasons for the increasing desire to eradicate inequality as it rises, both based on the premise that people become more aware of inequality and its effects as it becomes larger. First, people of higher incomes may feel increasingly obligated, on moral grounds, to help those in poor economic conditions as the level of inequality becomes more apparent. Second, as inequality increases, those at the bottom of the income distribution may become more aware of their own position and thus become increasingly likely to support social spending on the grounds that it might help them or people like them.

Finally, our analysis of the individual-level data for Canada and the US suggests that politics matters. Canadians with low incomes are much more likely than are Canadians with high incomes to believe that the government should ensure that everyone is provided for. We find little evidence of a relationship between income and attitudes in the US, however. We argue that income plays a lesser role in the US because there is no true working-class party that champions income-related issues. We suspect that working-class Canadians have a greater awareness of economic issues because of the presence of the NDP, which, although it has had little success in federal elections, puts issues of inequality on the political agenda. We should point out that our findings contrast with some recent research suggesting that poorer Americans are more likely to favour welfare spending (Soroka and Wlezien 2008), making it possible that, on this issue, Canadians and Americans are similar. Nevertheless, our findings show very clearly that, in terms of general government intervention to ensure the general welfare of citizens, Canadians tend to be more favourable than Americans, especially Canadians with lower incomes. Nevertheless, the difference is at lower incomes rather than at higher incomes, leading us to conclude that Canadians are not "kinder" or more "generous" than Americans but, rather, more informed and more instrumental.

TABLE 6.A1

Values of predictors and dependent variables by year, 1980-2005

		1980	1981	1982	1983	1984	1985	1986	1987	1988	1989	1990	1991	1992
Median income		44.1	43	41.7	40.1	40.5	40.6	40.4	40.3	41.3	42	40.2	38.1	38.4
Income inequality		8.09	7.48	7.60	8.04	7.75	7.56	7.48	7.34	7.32	7.22	7.48	7.67	7.81
Unemployment rate		7.5	7.6	11	12	11.3	10.6	9.7	8.8	7.8	7.5	8.1	10.3	11.2
Social expenditures		14.3	14.7	17.2	17.4	17.2	17.4	17.4	17.1	16.8	17.2	18.6	21.1	21.8
Public opinion measures														
Spending on welfare (%)	"Too much"	36	–	–	–	42	43	–	–	33	35	33	41	44
	"Just right"	41	–	–	–	39	36	–	–	42	39	44	37	36
	"Not enough"	23	–	–	–	19	21	–	–	24	26	23	22	20
	Average score	1.92	–	–	–	1.74	1.71	–	–	1.98	1.95	2.01	1.77	1.68
Spending on poor (%)	"Too much"	–	–	–	–	–	–	–	–	6	8	7	10	11
	"Just right"	–	–	–	–	–	–	–	–	37	34	37	40	38
	"Not enough"	–	–	–	–	–	–	–	–	57	57	56	51	51
	Average score	–	–	–	–	–	–	–	–	2.82	2.73	2.79	2.73	2.67
Spending on childcare (%)	"Too much"	–	–	–	–	–	–	–	–	18	16	14	22	16
	"Just right"	–	–	–	–	–	–	–	–	40	29	37	37	40
	"Not enough"	–	–	–	–	–	–	–	–	43	55	49	41	44
	Average score	–	–	–	–	–	–	–	–	2.49	2.52	2.58	2.34	2.52

Years 1993-2005 ▶

▼ TABLE 6.A1 *Years 1980–92*

	1993	1994	1995	1996	1997	1998	1999	2000	2001	2002	2003	2004	2005
Median income	37.2	37.9	37.5	37.2	37	38	39.7	39.9	41.5	41.5	41.4	41.7	42.7
Income inequality	7.68	7.57	7.67	8.34	8.94	9.08	9.09	9.47	9.20	8.99	8.89	9.20	9.37
Unemployment rate	11.4	10.4	9.5	9.6	9.1	8.3	7.6	6.8	7.2	7.7	7.6	7.2	6.8
Social expenditures	21.6	20.6	19.6	18.8	18.3	18.4	17.4	17.3	17.8	17.1	17.2	16.6	16.5
Public opinion measures													
Spending on welfare (%)													
"Too much"	47	44	41	36	36	32	31	34	29	–	29	–	–
"Just right"	37	36	40	41	38	42	41	42	43	–	30	–	–
"Not enough"	17	19	19	23	26	26	27	24	28	–	42	–	–
Average score	*1.62*	*1.65*	*1.77*	*1.92*	*1.92*	*2.04*	*2.04*	*1.98*	*2.13*	*–*	*2.16*	*–*	*–*
Spending on poor (%)													
"Too much"	14	13	12	11	10	7	6	–	–	–	8	8	7
"Just right"	41	43	44	41	37	39	38	–	–	–	37	33	31
"Not enough"	45	44	44	49	53	54	56	–	–	–	55	60	62
Average score	*2.58*	*2.61*	*2.64*	*2.7*	*2.7*	*2.79*	*2.82*	*–*	*–*	*–*	*2.76*	*2.79*	*2.79*
Spending on childcare (%)													
"Too much"	19	17	17	13	14	11	11	9	8	–	10	10	–
"Just right"	36	38	38	40	40	39	36	35	38	–	35	35	–
"Not enough"	45	45	45	47	46	50	53	56	54	–	54	55	–
Average score	*2.43*	*2.49*	*2.49*	*2.61*	*2.58*	*2.67*	*2.67*	*2.73*	*2.76*	*–*	*2.67*	*2.7*	*–*

TABLE 6.A2

Likelihood ratio tests for terms and measures of fit for multinomial log-linear models fitted to public opinion data

		Spending issue		
		Welfare	Poor	Childcare
Model 0: Intercept only				
Measures of fit	Residual deviance	1238	1520	1218
	AIC	1711	1922	1634
Model 1: Political climate				
Social expenditures		166.4***	162.5***	123.8***
Liberal government		17.0***	58.8***	60.9***
Measures of fit	Residual deviance	899	898	767.2
	AIC	1383	1312	1195
	Pseudo-R^2	.68	.89	.89
Model 2: Economic conditions				
Median income		3.2***	24.1***	8.4*
Income inequality		19.8***	75.8***	85.0***
Unemployment rate		129.5***	9.9**	7.7*
Measures of fit	Residual deviance	504	408	362
	AIC	994	827	796
	Pseudo-R^2	.82	.95	.95
Model 3: Final model				
Social expenditures		4.0	0.0	2.9
Liberal government		13.9***	25.1***	12.1**
Median income		6.8*	9.5**	16.8***
Income inequality		30.1***	77.7***	42.0***
Unemployment rate		118.6***	3.6	6.0*
Measures of fit	Residual deviance	418	270	308
	AIC	921	701	753
	Pseudo-R^2	.85	.97	.96
Number of respondents		34,020	28,386	29,140
Number of polls		18	15	16

*$p < .05$; **$p < .01$; ***$p < .001$
Note: All tests for model terms have two degrees of freedom.

TABLE 6.A3

OLS regressions predicting public opinion towards government responsibility in Canada and the US, World Values Survey, 1990 and 2000

	Canada		US	
	Estimate	Standard error	Estimate	Standard error
Intercept	154.99***	20.45	157.68***	22.79
Year (2000 = 1)	−0.075***	0.010	−0.076***	0.011
Men	0.079	0.096	0.249**	0.086
Age	0.014***	0.004	0.010***	0.003
Marital status				
Married	0.253	0.151	0.478***	0.133
Other	0.297	0.157	0.020	0.149
Single	0	–	0	–
Children	0.003	0.035	0.015	0.029
Religion				
Practising Catholic	−0.019	0.143	0.139	0.137
Non-practising Catholic	0.048	0.135	0.201	0.177
Practising Protestant	−0.143	0.154	0.284*	0.118
Non-practising Protestant	0.117	0.159	0.071	0.149
Other	−0.408	0.276	−0.119	0.193
None	0	–	0	–
Education	−0.011	0.009	0.006	0.008
Income (deciles)				
1st	0	–	0	–
2nd	−0.507*	0.229	−0.881***	0.225
3rd	−0.786***	0.228	−0.640**	0.221
4th	−0.938***	0.226	−0.551**	0.211
5th	−1.205***	0.229	−0.599**	0.212
6th	−1.163***	0.228	−0.597**	0.223
7th	−1.337***	0.230	−0.561**	0.216
8th	−1.529***	0.238	−0.520*	0.251
9th	−1.265***	0.254	−0.603*	0.243
10th	−1.543***	0.242	−0.311	0.260
R^2	0.067		0.045	
N	3,070		3,753	

*$p < .05$; **$p < .01$; ***$p < .001$

NOTE

1 A bit awkward for our argument is the fact that the question asks respondents about federal government spending when these issues fall under provincial jurisdiction. We suspect, however, that most people are unaware that these issues come under provincial jurisdiction.

REFERENCES

Adams, Michael. 1990. "Canadian and American Attitudes toward the Role of the Government and the Private Enterprise System." *International Journal of Public Opinion Research* 2: 53-70.

Andersen, Robert, and John Fox. 2001. "Pre-election Polls and the Dynamics of the 1997 Canadian Federal Election." *Electoral Studies* 20: 87-108.

Banting, Keith G. 2006. "Dis-embedding Liberalism? The New Social Policy Paradigm in Canada." In David A. Green and Jonathan R. Kesselman, eds., *Dimensions of Inequality in Canada*, 417-52. Vancouver: UBC Press.

Battle, Ken, Michael Mendelson, and Sherri Torjman. 2005. "The Modernization Mantra: Toward a New Architecture for Canada's Adult Benefits." *Canadian Public Policy/Analyse de Politiques* 31: 431-37.

Blekesaune, Morten, and Jill Quadagno. 2003. "Public Attitudes toward Welfare State Policies: A Comparative Analysis of 24 Nations." *European Sociological Review* 19(5): 415-27.

Epstein, William M. 2004. "Cleavage in American Attitudes toward Social Welfare." *Journal of Sociology and Social Welfare* 31: 177-201.

Esping-Andersen, Gøsta. 1990. *The Three Worlds of Welfare Capitalism.* Princeton. NJ: Princeton University Press.

Fisher, Stephan, and Anthony Heath. 2006. "Decreasing Desires for Income Inequality?" In Peter Esther, Michael Braun, and Peter Mohler, eds., *Globalization, Value Change, and Generations: A Cross-National and Intergenerational Perspective.* Amsterdam: Brill Academic Publishers.

Fox, John, and Robert Andersen. 2006. "Effect Displays for Multinomial and Proportional-Odds Logit Models." *Sociological Methodology* 36: 225-56.

Frenette, Marc, David A. Green, and Kevin Milligan. 2009. "Taxes, Transfers, and Canadian Income Inequality." *Canadian Public Policy/Analyse de Politiques* 35: 389-411.

Gallie, Duncan. 1983. *Social Inequality and Class Radicalism in France and Britain.* Cambridge: Cambridge University Press.

Grabb, Edward, and James Curtis. 2005. *Regions Apart: The Four Societies of Canada and the United States.* Toronto: Oxford University Press.

Human Resources and Skills Development Canada. 2010. http://www.hrsdc.gc.ca/.

Inglehart, Ronald, et al. 2001. "World Values Surveys and European Values Surveys, 1981-1984, 1990-1993, 1995-1997 and 1999-2000 [Computer file]. ICPSR version. Ann Arbor, MI: Institute for Social Research [producer]." Ann Arbor, MI: Inter-University Consortium for Political and Social Research (distributor).

Iversen, Torben, and David Soskice. 2006. "Electoral Institutions and the Politics of Coalitions: Why Some Democracies Redistribute More Than Others." *American Political Science Review* 100(2): 165-81.

Jacoby, William G. 1994. "Public Attitudes toward Government Spending." *American Journal of Political Science* 38(2): 336-61

Jaeger, M.M. 2006. "What Makes People Support Public Responsibility for Welfare Provision: Self-interest or Political Ideology?" *Acta Sociologica* 49(3): 321-38.

—. 2009. "United But Divided: Welfare Regimes and the Level and Variance in Public Support for Redistribution." *European Sociological Review* 25(6): 723-37.

Kalterthaler, Karl, and Stephen Ceccoli. 2008. "Explaining Patterns of Support for the Provision of Citizen Welfare." *Journal of European Public Policy* 15(7): 1041-68.

Kelley, Jonathan, and M.D.R. Evans. 1993. "The Legitimation of Inequality: Occupational Earnings in Nine Nations." *American Journal of Sociology* 99(1): 75-125.

Kelley, Jonathan, and Krzysztof Zagorski. 2005 "Economic Change and the Legitimation of Inequality: The Transition from Socialism to the Free Market in Poland and Hungary, 1987-1994." *Research in Social Stratification and Mobility* 22: 321-66.

Kenworthy, Lane, and Leslie McCall. 2008. "Inequality, Public Opinion and Redistribution." *Socio-Economic Review* 6: 35–68.

Korpi, Walter, and Joakim Palme. 1998. "The Paradox of Redistribution and Strategies of Equality: Welfare State Institutions, Inequality, and Poverty in the Western Countries." *American Sociological Review* 63(5): 661-87.

—. 2003. "New Politics and Class Politics in the Context of Austerity and Globalization: Welfare State Regress in 18 Countries, 1975-95." *American Political Science Review* 97: 425-46.

MacLeod, Laurie, Darrel Montero, and Alan Speer. 1999. "America's Changing Attitudes toward Welfare and Welfare Recipients, 1938-1995." *Journal of Sociology and Social Welfare* 26-2: 175-86.

Matthews, J., and L. Erickson. 2008. "Welfare State Structures and the Structure of Welfare State Support: Attitudes towards social spending in Canada, 1993-2000." *European Journal of Political Research* 47: 411-35.

Myles, John. 1998. "How to Design a Liberal Welfare State: A Comparison of Canada and the United States." *Social Policy and Administration* 32: 341-64.

Noll, Heinz-Herbert, and Lance W. Roberts. 2003. "The Legitimacy of Inequality on Both Sides of the Atlantic. A Comparative Analysis of Attitudes in Canada and Germany." *Tocqueville Review* 24(2): 154-89.

Osberg, Lars. 2007. "A Quarter Century of Economic Inequality in Canada, 1981-2006." Halifax: Dalhousie University, unpublished manuscript.

Osberg, Lars, and Timothy Smeeding. 2006. "'Fair' Inequality? Attitudes toward Pay Differentials: The United States in Comparative Perspective." *American Sociological Review* 71(3): 450–73.

Papadakis, Elim. 1993. "Class Interests, Class Politics and Welfare State Regime." *British Journal of Sociology* 44(2): 249-70.

Picot, Garnett, Rene Morissette, and John Myles. 2003. "Low Income Intensity during the 1990s: The Role of Economic Growth, Employment Earnings, and Social Transfers." *Canadian Public Policy* 29: S15-S40.

Reutter, Linda, Margaret Harrison, and Anne Neufeld. 2002. "Public Support for Poverty-Related Policies." *Canadian Journal of Public Health* 93(4): 297-304.

Schneider, Saundra K., and William G. Jacoby. 2007. "Reconsidering the Linkage between Public Assistance and Public Opinion in the American Welfare State." *British Journal of Political Sociology* 37: 555-66.

Sihvo, T., and H. Uusitalo. 1995. "Economic Crises and Support for the Welfare State in Finland: 1975-1993." *Acta Sociologica* 38: 251-62.

Soroka, Stuart N., and Christopher Wlezien. 2004. "Opinion Representation and Policy Feedback: Canada in Comparative Perspective." *Canadian Journal of Political Science* 37: 531-59.

—. 2008. "On the Limits to Inequality in Representation." *PS: Political Science and Politics* 41(2): 319-27.

Svallfors, Stefan. 1991. "The Politics of Welfare Policy in Sweden: Structural Determinants and Attitudinal Cleavages." *British Journal of Sociology* 42(4): 609-34.

—. 1995. "The End of Class Politics? Structural Cleavages and Attitudes to Swedish Welfare Policies." *Acta Sociologica* 38(1): 53-74.

—. 1997. "Worlds of Welfare and Attitudes to Redistribution: A Comparison of Eight Western Nations." *European Sociological Review* 13(3): 283-304.

—. 2008. "Worlds of Welfare and Attitudes to Redistribution: A Comparison of Eight Western Nations." *European Sociological Review* 13(3): 283-304.

Van Oorschot, W. 2002. "Individual Motives for Contributing to Welfare Benefits in the Netherlands." *Policy and Politics* 30: 31-46.

Weakliem, David, Robert Andersen, and Anthony Heath. 2005. "By Popular Demand: The Effect of Public Opinion on Income Inequality." *Comparative Sociology* 4: 261-84.

Will, Jeffry A. 1993. "Dimensions of Poverty: Public Perceptions of the Deserving Poor." *Social Science Research* 22: 312-32.

Wlezien, Christopher. 1995. "The Public as Thermostat: Dynamics of Preferences for Spending." *American Journal of Political Science* 39: 981–1000.

—. 2004. "Patterns of Representation: Dynamics of Public Preferences and Policy." *Journal of Politics* 66: 1-24.

7
Multicultural Diversity and Redistribution

KEITH BANTING, STUART SOROKA,
AND EDWARD KONING

Students of social policy have long argued that the welfare state was built on, and can only be sustained by, a strong sense of community and associated feelings of trust, reciprocity, and mutual obligation. An early expositor of this view was T.H. Marshall, who wrote his most definitive work on social citizenship in Britain during the postwar expansion of social programs. For Marshall, entitlement to an expanded range of social benefits reflected the emergence of a national consciousness, a consciousness that began to develop before the extension of modern social programs, and that sustained their development in the twentieth century. "Citizenship," Marshall (1950, 8) argues in an oft-quoted passage, "requires a bond of a different kind, a direct sense of community membership based on loyalty to a civilisation that is a common possession."

In recent years, however, analysts have increasingly argued that immigration and ethnic diversity are eroding the sense of a common community and identity, and weakening the sense of trust in fellow citizens, with potentially debilitating consequences for the politics of social policy. These analysts have pointed to a number of potential dangers. They cite evidence from other countries that growing ethnic or racial diversity fragments the historic coalitions that supported the welfare state and make it more difficult for the new minority groups to cooperate in a common fight for redistributive agendas. They argue that members of the majority public withdraw support from social programs that redistribute resources to people they regard as "strangers" or "outsiders" whom they do not see as part of "us;" or, the majority might support the exclusion of newcomers from popular social benefits. In addition, they note that members of the majority sometimes vote for conservative or radical right parties that oppose immigration, thereby contributing to a retrenchment in the welfare state they may not have sought while in the voting booth.

If diversity really is the enemy of redistribution, then the Canadian welfare state is in serious trouble. Canada is one of the most multicultural countries in the world. A plurinational country, it incorporates English- and French-speaking communities and distinct Aboriginal peoples. To these historic differences, immigration is adding new forms of diversity: today, about 20 percent of the population was born outside the country, and each year Canada admits around 250,000 more permanent migrants, about 80 percent of whom are of non-Western origin, plus even more temporary foreign workers.

This chapter asks whether ethnic diversity weakens public support for redistribution in Canada. It finds that, unlike in many other countries, in Canada ethnic diversity in general does not seem to significantly erode social solidarity. However, this general conclusion is subject to an important qualification, namely, the dramatic difference in public attitudes towards immigrants and Aboriginal peoples. People who believe that immigrants rely heavily on welfare are less likely to support social assistance as such, but they are more likely to support redistribution and the welfare state generally. In effect, a sense that immigrants are in growing economic trouble tends to nudge Canadians towards, not away from, supporting redistribution. The same is not true for Aboriginal peoples. Here we find the toxic effects found in other countries: people who believe that Aboriginal peoples are heavily dependent on welfare tend to reduce their support not only for social assistance but also for a redistributive state as a whole, a corrosive impact with important regional dimensions.

A Comparative Perspective

Considerable research has been devoted to the relationship between immigration, racial diversity, and redistribution. The racialization of welfare has been a prominent theme in the US literature, where attitudes about welfare combine negative stereotypes about beneficiaries' presumed lack of motivation or ambition with deeply embedded racial stereotypes about African Americans. Gilens (1995, 1996b) finds that attitudes about race are *the single most important factor* in opposition to welfare in that country – more than economic self-interest and attitudes about individualism, for instance – and that these views are supported by media content that overrepresents blacks in reporting on welfare (Gilens 1996a). Gilens's findings are supported by a wide range of survey research (e.g., Bobo and Kleugel 1993; Frederico 2004, 2005; Goren 2003; Peffley, Hurwitz, and Sniderman 1997) and by experimental laboratory research (Mendelberg 2001; Huber and Lapinski 2006).[1] Moreover, the link between race and welfare appears not to be exclusive to blacks; Fox (2004) finds a similar dynamic in the case of Latinos, for instance.

Similar reactions emerge in Europe with respect to immigration. Until very recently, European countries did not actively recruit highly skilled immigrants. As a result, large parts of the immigrant population in Europe are low-skilled, and many immigrants do not speak the language of their new country. The result is a large and persistent socio-economic gap between immigrants and native-born Europeans. Not surprisingly, therefore, immigrants tend to be overrepresented among welfare recipients in virtually every European country (Boeri, Hanson, and McCormick 2002; Hjerm 2005; Blume, et al. 2007; Voges, Frick, and Büchel 1998). The problems are compounded in the so-called corporatist welfare states, such as Germany and France, where highly regulated labour markets make it even more difficult for outsiders to integrate into the economy and to escape reliance on welfare (Esping-Andersen 1996; Miller and Neo 2003; Kogan 2007; Jurado and Brochmann 2013).

The problems facing immigrants in Europe are politically combustible. Immigrants are widely seen as the least deserving of all social groups (van Oorschot 2006), and radical anti-immigrant parties frequently politicize their use of welfare (Menz 2006; Green-Pedersen and Odmalm 2008; Guibernau 2010; Kitschelt 1995). Welfare dependency is not the sole or even the primary source of backlash as anti-immigrant parties also depict migrants as posing a general threat to national identity or liberal values (Leiken 2005; Oesch 2008; Chebel D'Appollonnia and Reich 2008). But the image of immigrants as welfare "parasites" is part of xenophobic discourse in Europe. For example, before the 2007 elections in Switzerland, the anti-immigrant SVP (Schweizerische Volkspartei) had a video game on its party website in which voters had to prevent immigrants from stealing tax-payers' money. Similarly, during the 2010 election in the Netherlands, a manifesto of the PVV (Partij voor de Vrijheid) demanded that immigrants be banned from any social service for the first ten years after admission to the country. Reflecting this opposition to newcomers' use of welfare services, immigrant eligibility is increasingly being cut in European countries (Sainsbury 2012; Mynott, Humphries, and Cohen 2002; Ireland 2004; Minderhoud 1999) or made conditional on cultural integration programs (Hagelund 2005; Dwyer 2006).

Canadian Experience

In contrast with the United States and Europe, research on the Canadian experience has found little tension between immigration, ethnic diversity, and public attitudes towards redistribution. Unlike other leading OECD countries, in Canada support for immigration and immigrants is strikingly positive. Canadians are much more likely to believe that immigrants are good for the economy, much less likely to believe that immigrants cause crime, and much less committed to reducing immigration (Banting 2010).

This comfort level holds when attention focuses more tightly on the relationship between ethnic diversity and support for social programs, examining factors that scholars argue contribute to a toxic relationship elsewhere (for a review of Canadian evidence, see Banting et al. 2011). For example, Robert Putnam (2007) argues, on the basis of research in the US, that ethnic and racial diversity erodes interpersonal trust, not just in members of ethnic outgroups but also in members of one's own ethnic group, leading people living in ethnically diverse areas to "hunker down" in social isolation and to lose faith in government solutions to social problems. Research in Canada also finds that interpersonal trust declines in ethnically diverse neighbourhoods. But, strikingly, support for redistribution is resistant to this dynamic: support for social programs does not decline in diverse neighbourhoods in Canada (Soroka, Johnston, and Banting 2007).

Other factors that help sustain a multicultural welfare state are relevant here. For example, Bo Rothstein (1998) and others argue that support for redistribution depends more on trust in government institutions than on interpersonal trust, and that trust in government is less sensitive to changes in the ethnic composition of society. Research results for Canada confirm such arguments. Trust in government is positively associated with support for health care and pensions, and, unlike interpersonal trust, trust in government is not lower in ethnically diverse neighbourhoods in this country (Soroka, Helliwell, and Johnston 2007).

Other scholars, such as David Miller (1995), argue that a common sense of national identity can be the cultural glue binding a diverse society. Canadian research also finds partial support for such an argument. Those with the strongest sense of Canadian identity embrace immigration and immigrants more warmly than do their less nationalist neighbours, a pattern not found in most other countries. And, while people who hold anti-immigrant views tend to be more opposed to redistribution, a strong sense of national identity offsets this, helping to insulate the welfare state from the corrosive impact of nativism (Johnston et al. 2010).

While this suggests that immigration is not undermining support for redistribution in Canada, there are important gaps in the evidence. First, existing research has largely ignored Aboriginal peoples. Second, we know little about whether public perceptions of welfare recipients are as racialized here as in the US. We know that support for welfare policy in Canada, as elsewhere, is conditioned by the public's impressions of who receives benefits (Harrell, Soroka, and Mahon 2008). But we do not know whether the public sees immigrants or racial minorities as heavy users of welfare and whether such perceptions weaken support for the welfare state.

This chapter seeks to deepen our knowledge by exploring the extent to which Canadians perceive these groups as heavily dependent on welfare and asking whether such perceptions influence support for social programs in this country. We also consider whether negative effects are focused tightly on social assistance ("welfare") or whether the full range of social programs, including universal programs such as health care, is vulnerable. Before starting the analysis, however, the next section sets the context, looking at the demographic presence of immigrants and Aboriginal peoples in Canada and the extent to which they turn to welfare programs.

Immigrants, Aboriginal Peoples, and Welfare

Canada has one of the largest immigrant populations in the world. As noted earlier, 20 percent of the population was born outside the country, a number that is expected to rise to between 25 and 28 percent by 2031 (Statistics Canada 2010). Moreover, immigrants to Canada come from many parts of the world, creating a multicultural diversity of ethnicities, races, and religions. The presence of immigrants is highly uneven across the country. According to the 2006 census, close to 30 percent of the population of Ontario and British Columbia were born outside the country, followed by Alberta at 16 percent and Quebec at 11 percent. Immigrant presence in Atlantic Canada, by contrast, is much lower.

In contrast to the European experience, the use of welfare programs among immigrants in Canada has traditionally been strikingly low. Indeed,

FIGURE 7.1

Percentage of population receiving social assistance, by country of origin, 1999-2009

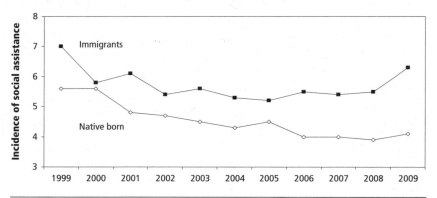

Source: Statistics Canada, Survey of Labour and Income Dynamics, various years.

until recently, immigrants used social assistance and unemployment benefits less than did native-born Canadians (Akbari 1989; Baker and Benjamin 1995a, 1995b; Sweetman 2001). These low recipiency rates are not accidental; rather, they reflect an immigration policy designed to minimize immigrants' reliance on welfare programs. In the case of economic migrants, the largest group of newcomers, immigration policy has selected people on the basis of language and work skills, thereby increasing their chances of finding work. In the case of family reunification, Canada requires sponsorship; to be admitted, family migrants must be sponsored by someone in Canada with the resources and the willingness to support them. Traditionally, only refugees have been likely to need social assistance, and they only make up about one in ten of all incoming newcomers to Canada. In recent years, however, immigrants have been experiencing greater difficulty in entering the labour force, despite having higher levels of education and training than previous immigrant cohorts. As a result, there has been some increase in immigrants' reliance on welfare programs. As Figure 7.1 indicates, immigrant use of social assistance is now somewhat higher than for the native-born population, a gap that widened during the recession that began in late 2008 and hit immigrants hard (see also DeVoretz and Pivnenko 2004; Baker, Benjamin, and Fan 2009; Picot, Lu, and Hou 2009; De Silva 1997).

The Aboriginal population in Canada is much smaller than the immigrant population. According to the 2006 census, people with an Aboriginal identity, including First Nations, Métis, and Inuit, represented approximately 4 percent of the total population. Approximately half of First Nations people and Métis live in urban areas; many others live in rural non-reserve areas, and only about one-quarter live on reserves. While Aboriginal peoples live in all regions of the country, they have a much larger presence in the west and comprise the largest minority group in many Prairie cities. The Aboriginal population is also very young, with Aboriginal youth representing over one-quarter of the younger generation in Saskatchewan and Manitoba.

The economic condition of Aboriginal peoples stands in stark contrast to that of the population as a whole. In the words of the Royal Commission on Aboriginal Peoples, these communities endure conditions "normally associated with impoverished developing countries" (RCAP 1996, vol. 3, sec. 1.0). In comparison with the population as a whole, educational levels are low and unemployment rates are high. The 2001 census revealed that 31 percent of Aboriginal families were living in poverty, compared to 12 percent of non-Aboriginal people; and 41 percent of Aboriginal children were poor, as opposed to 18 percent of Canadian children generally (National Council of Welfare 2007). The unsurprising result of these grim realities is greater need for welfare support, a pattern with deep historic roots (Shewell 2004; Timpson 1995; Dussault and Erasmus 1997).

The federal government is responsible for income assistance on reserves, and Table 7.1 compares the proportion of Aboriginals receiving income assistance on reserves with the proportion of the general population receiving social assistance in 2003, approximately when our data on perceptions of dependency were gathered (see below). Clearly, welfare plays a significant role on reserves, supporting about one-third of the population. However, this represents the most extreme case: the much larger group of Aboriginals who do not live on reserves must turn to provincial social assistance in times of need, and, while comparable data on the extent of support are not available, the levels are certainly lower. Indirect evidence comes from Table 7.2, which draws on census data to compare the contribution of government transfer programs to the total income of Aboriginals on and off reserve. Focusing on selective benefits such as child benefits and "other" programs, including social assistance, confirms that such programs provide a much smaller proportion of the total incomes of Aboriginals living in urban or rural non-reserve areas. As a result, the overall level of Aboriginal use of welfare will be lower than the levels shown in Table 7.1 but still considerably higher than that of non-Aboriginal Canadians.

TABLE 7.1

Social assistance coverage rates, general and on-reserve Aboriginal population, 2003

	Population (%)	
Territory	General	On-reserve
Canada	5.5	34.8
British Columbia	4.3	22.5
Manitoba	5.1	43.9
Atlantic	7.0	64.2
Ontario	5.5	22.5

Source: National Council of Welfare (2007, Table 2.1).

TABLE 7.2

Government transfers as percentage of income of Aboriginals, by area of residence, 2006

	Total Aboriginal	Residence		
		On-reserve	Rural	Urban
OAS/GIS	2.6	5.2	2.8	1.8
CPP/QPP	2.2	1.6	2.8	2.2
Child benefits	4.4	10.1	3.4	3.2
EI	2.6	3.0	3.6	2.1
Other	6.3	8.3	5.1	6.2
Total transfers	18.1	28.2	17.7	15.5

OAS/GIS: Old Age Security pensions/Guaranteed Income Supplement; CPP/QPP: Canada/Quebec Pension Plan benefits; EI: Employment Insurance benefits.
Source: Census of Canada, 2006.

Patterns of economic inequality and welfare use have no intrinsic political meaning. They must be perceived, interpreted, and injected into public debates. Canadian history provides ample evidence of racial stereotypes of Aboriginal people as lazy or unintelligent (Zion 1992, 191; Shewell 2004, 328). Our questions are whether such stereotypes remain alive today, whether they apply to immigrants as well, and whether they shape the politics of social policy in contemporary Canada.

Perceptions of Welfare Dependence and Support for Redistribution

Support for welfare programs has long been sensitive to stereotypes of the poor and to popular views about whether recipients are "worthy" or "unworthy." People who believe that welfare recipients are lazy and likely to depend on support for long periods tend to be much less supportive of welfare programs (see, for example, Appelbaum 2001; Cnaan 1989; Cozzarelli, Wilkinson, and Tagler 2001). Such perceptions, myths, and stereotypes about welfare recipients can be lethal if they become racialized, with racial minorities or newcomers seen as heavily dependent on welfare.

We examine the impact of such perceptions on support for welfare as such and for redistribution more generally. For data on public perceptions, we draw on the second wave of the Equality, Security, and Community Survey (ESCS) conducted in 2002-03. A detailed description of the ESCS can be found in Soroka, Helliwell, and Johnston (2007) and Soroka, Johnston, and Banting (2007). A strength of the ESCS for our purposes is its combination of questions on respondents' economic circumstances, their attitudes towards immigrants and Aboriginals, and their support for a variety of social programs. Moreover, the survey includes questions that directly capture respondents' perceptions of welfare dependence among immigrants and Aboriginals. To conduct our analysis, we build on a model of support for social programs developed in our earlier studies, adding measures that capture such perceptions.

We begin with some basic patterns. Table 7.3 shows the distribution of responses from two survey questions that capture understandings of immigrant and Aboriginal reliance on welfare:

- How many recent immigrants are on welfare? Would you say one-quarter, one-half, three-quarters, or most of them?
- How many Aboriginal persons are on welfare? Would you say one-quarter, one-half, three-quarters, or most of them?

These questions are hardly ideal as they do not allow respondents to say less than one-quarter (which, in most cases, is the correct answer). The questions therefore bias the responses upwards. Certainly, the perceived level of use is much higher than are actual utilization levels discussed above. Accordingly, we do not emphasize the absolute levels in our analysis; instead, we array the responses on a continuum from "low" to "high."

Table 7.3, which reports the results of the majority (non-immigrant/non-Aboriginal) population only,[2] shows that Aboriginals are seen to be much more reliant on welfare than immigrants. Roughly 46 percent of the respondents picked the lowest answer option for immigrants ("one-quarter is on welfare"), while only 22 percent gave that answer for Aboriginals.

TABLE 7.3
"Majority" perceptions of immigrants and Aboriginals

	How many ... on welfare? (%)				
	LOW			HIGH	
	"One-quarter"	"One-half"	"Three-quarters"	"Most of them"	N
Aboriginals on welfare	22.0	38.4	19.8	18.9	2,282
Immigrants on welfare	45.6	32.4	9.2	12.7	2,058

Note: Based on perceptions of "majority" (non-immigrant, non-Aboriginal) respondents only.

Perceptions of Aboriginals are clearly worse, and, as we shall see, this matters. (These differences remain in a regression setup, even when other demographics factors, including age, education, and income are controlled for.)[3]

Our central question is whether these perceptions matter for public support for welfare. Despite the findings in the US literature, it is possible that the patterns are different in Canada. Perhaps welfare support is driven mainly by economic or broader ideological factors, and perceptions about who is a beneficiary matter little. Do perceptions of immigrant and Aboriginal welfare use have an impact on overall support for welfare in Canada?

We capture support for welfare using two questions:

- Which is closer to your own view: One, refusing welfare to single parents is unfair to their children, OR two, giving welfare to single parents rewards irresponsible behaviour?
- People on welfare should be required to work for the community. Do you agree or disagree?

The two questions cover different elements of what we might call "welfare generosity." Since preliminary analyses suggest that the drivers of both measures are very similar, we combine the two measures in a single ordinal index, where respondents receive a score of 0 if they are less generous on both questions, 1 if they select the more generous option on one question, and 2 if they select the more generous option on both. The overall distribution of this measure is: low support (0), 32 percent; medium support (1), 50 percent; and high support (2), 18 percent.

It is crucial for our analysis to distinguish between a general suspicion of all welfare recipients, on the one hand, and particular concerns about immigrant and Aboriginal use, on the other. To make this distinction, we include a control variable that taps general attitudes about welfare recipients and is not directly related to race or ethnicity. The question is:

- Which is closer to your own view: One, people on welfare are usually there for a short time and are unlikely to be on it again, OR, two, once people get on welfare they usually stay on it.

Responses to this question are coded as 1 for the less generous option and 0 for the first, more generous option. The results are striking: 74 percent of respondents say that once people get on welfare, they usually stay on. Not surprisingly, responses to this question are strongly related to those for the two welfare support measures. We nevertheless see this variable as capturing a distinct component of welfare support – attitudes towards recipients – and one worth controlling for in an analysis focused on the relevance of the ethnicity of recipients to overall support for welfare.[4]

The remainder of our model of welfare support builds on previous work (Soroka et al. 2006 as refined in Johnston et al. 2010). This model includes the following measures: gender, age, education, income, employment status (employed, unemployed, other), union membership, perceptions that one's own economic situation has worsened over the past year, and fear of job loss. We add one variable to this model, namely, whether the respondent has a friend who is or was recently on welfare. We expect that friends' need for assistance will affect support for welfare, just as we expect that respondents' own economic situations may affect their support. Detailed information on the coding of each of these variables is included in the appendix.

Results from the full model are reported in the appendix in Table 7.A1. Here, in Figure 7.2, we focus just on the impact that perceptions of immigrant and Aboriginal welfare use have on welfare support (controlling for the other variables listed above). In short, respondents who think most immigrants are on welfare are 25 percent less likely to support welfare.[5] A perception of high Aboriginal welfare dependence has a somewhat greater impact: it is associated with a 37 percent decrease in welfare support.

The full results in Table 7.A1 point towards some other interesting findings. Both education and union membership tend to increase support for welfare, for instance. The currently unemployed are almost 140 percent more likely to support welfare. Perceptions of recipients (our ethnicity-neutral measure of attitudes) also have a powerful effect. Believing that recipients generally tend to stay on welfare makes one 62 percent less likely

FIGURE 7.2

Impact of perceptions of immigrants and Aboriginals on support for welfare

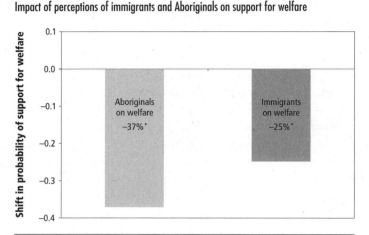

* Statistically significant at $p < .05$.

to be one unit higher on the welfare support measure. Clearly, the notion that those on welfare are on it repeatedly matters a lot. But the most salient results for our purposes here are captured in Figure 7.2. *Ceteris paribus*, the belief that immigrants and/or Aboriginals are on welfare is associated with decreased support for that program.

While Figure 7.2 shows average estimated effects across Canada, the effects of perceptions of immigrants and Aboriginals on welfare do vary somewhat geographically.[6] Even though perceptions of reliance on welfare do not differ dramatically across regions, their implications for public support for welfare do. Figure 7.3 illustrates these regional differences. As in the case of Figure 7.2, Figure 7.3 shows odds ratios for the two perceptions variables.[7]

Note first that a good number of the odds ratios in Figure 7.3 are statistically insignificant. This is not surprising, considering that we split the sample in five and introduce collinearity through interactions. Nevertheless, all coefficients point in the same (negative) direction, and there are some statistically significant differences in coefficients across regions. Attitudes about immigrants (in the left panel of Figure 7.3) matter most to welfare support in Quebec, where the result is statistically significant; that is, Quebec respondents show the strongest connection between perceptions of immigrants as welfare-dependent and lower overall support for welfare. Perceived

FIGURE 7.3

Impact of perceptions of immigrants and Aboriginals on support for welfare, by region

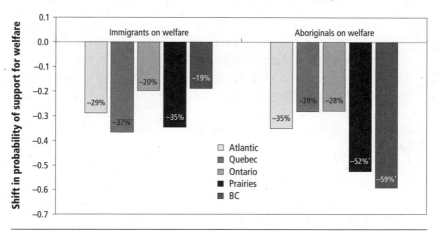

* Statistically signifcant at $p < .05$.

Aboriginal welfare dependency (in the right panel of Figure 7.3) matters most in the Prairies and in British Columbia.

This negative connection between Aboriginals and support for welfare may help to explain overall regional differences in welfare support more generally. Support for welfare, according to our measure, is at its lowest in Saskatchewan (a mean of .81) and Manitoba (.83) and at its highest in Ontario (.86) and BC, Quebec, and the combined eastern provinces (.90). This statistically significant drop in support in the two Prairie provinces is consistent with what we see in our individual-level models. The provinces with the largest Aboriginal populations in proportionate terms show somewhat lower levels of support for welfare.

So far, our focus has been only on welfare. We now explore whether the effects of perceived minority dependence spill over onto other social policies and the wider redistributive goals of the welfare state. Some scholars argue that means-tested programs such as welfare are especially vulnerable to perceptions of the "worthiness" of recipients, whereas more universal policies are comparatively immune (Rothstein 1998; Swank and Betz 2003; Crepaz 2008). We are interested, then, in whether the effects spill over to a wider commitment to redistribution through a wider set of policy instruments. To test this possibility, we conduct the same analysis using two other measures of support for social policy. First, general orientations towards redistribution are captured in a two-item index (scored as above) based on the following questions:

- Which is closer to your own view: One, the government should see to it that everyone has a decent standard of living, OR, two, the government should leave it to people to get ahead on their own; and,
- The government must do more to reduce the income gap between rich and poor Canadians. Do you agree or disagree?

Support for health care, a (binary) measure, is determined based on the following:

- Which is closer to your own view: One, everyone should have equal access to health care, even if that means waiting for treatments, OR, [two, if you can afford it you should be able to buy faster access to health care] OR [two, if you are willing to pay for it you should be able to buy faster access to health care].[8]

Again, the full models are included in the appendix in Table 7.A1. The results for controls are roughly as we have seen elsewhere (Soroka et al. 2006; Johnston et al. 2010). Figure 7.4 shows odds ratios for the two variables most critical for the current discussion.

The left panel of Figure 7.4 shows results for redistribution. Strikingly, the perception that immigrants rely heavily on welfare has a *positive* effect on general support for social policies. More specifically, believing that immigrants make much use of welfare is positively and significantly related to support for redistribution generally; in the right panel of Figure 7.4, it is positively related to support for health care as well (the coefficient for health care comes close to statistical significance, $p = .15$). Perceived economic difficulties for immigrants appear, then, to move respondents *towards* rather than away from support for redistribution. As we have seen, the relationship between perceived welfare use by immigrants and support for social assistance specifically is negative. The implication seems to be that the modal Canadian respondent does see immigrant use of welfare as a problem; however, the preferred solution is not reliance on welfare, per se, but a broader approach to the redistribution of income.

The opposite appears to be true for Aboriginals. Indeed, perceptions of high Aboriginal welfare dependence permeate the full sweep of the social role of the state. Such perceptions are significantly and negatively related to

FIGURE 7.4

Impact of perceptions of immigrants and Aboriginals on support for redistribution and health care

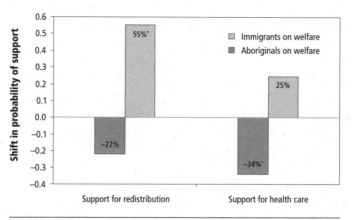

* Statistically signifcant at $p < .05$.

support for universal health care and are negatively related to support for redistribution (the coefficient narrowly misses statistical significance). There are strong hints of a consistent, negative effect of perceptions of Aboriginals on welfare driving not just attitudes about welfare specifically but also attitudes on a wide range of social welfare domains.

Discussion

Canadians can be harsh critics of welfare recipients. As we have seen, three-quarters of respondents believe that people on welfare usually stay there. Moreover, for many Canadians, these perceptions have an ethnic content. Simply stated, these perceptions matter: Canadians who hold them are much less likely to support welfare. Respondents who believe recipients linger on welfare are dramatically less supportive of welfare, and this has a more powerful direct impact than their level of education, their income, or whether they are worried about the economic future. Among our controls, only being unemployed has a bigger impact. More critically for our current concerns, perceptions of immigrant and Aboriginal reliance on welfare appear to further erode support for welfare. The impact is less dramatic than the general perception of dependence, and the effect is certainly not enough to move the median voter to a completely different level of support for welfare. Nevertheless, it is not trivial.

Even more apparent is the difference between immigrants and Aboriginal peoples. The toxic effects of negative views of Aboriginal reliance on welfare spreads throughout the entire welfare state, including universal programs such as health care. The reverse is true for images of immigrant dependence. The belief that immigrants must turn to welfare in large numbers reduces support for social assistance itself but increases support for redistribution generally and for health care in particular. Immigrants clearly benefit from a more privileged space in Canadian cultural imagery. Nationalism in Canada embraces a conception of the country as a multicultural society that successive waves of immigrants have helped to build. Diversity and multiculturalism are seen as distinctly Canadian virtues, and this highly multicultural form of nationalism mitigates the toxic effects that anti-immigrant sentiment might otherwise have for the welfare state (Johnston et al., 2010). This protection does not overcome resentment about social assistance itself, but it does extend to the wider redistributive role of the state. Tragically, it does not seem to embrace Canada's first peoples.

APPENDIX: VARIABLES USED IN MODELS OF WELFARE SUPPORT

Female: a binary variable equal to 1 if the respondent is female.

Age: captured using three binary variables equal to 1 if the respondent is (a) 30-49 yrs old, (b) 50-64 yrs old, and (c) 65 or older, where the residual category is less than 30 yrs old.

Education: a binary variable equal to 1 if the respondent has more than a high school education.

Income: income, in 100,000s, with missing data imputed as in Johnston et al. (2010).

Labour status: captured using (a) a binary variable equal to 1 if the respondent is currently unemployed, and (b) a binary variable equal to 1 if the respondent is not in the labour force (e.g., student, homemaker, retired), where the residual category is respondents who are currently employed.

Union member: a binary variable equal to 1 if the respondent is a member of a union.

Economic situation worse: a binary variable equal to 1 if the respondent answered "worsened" in response to: Thinking about the past twelve months, has your household's economic situation improved, stayed about the same, or worsened?

Have friend on welfare: a binary variable equal to 1 if the respondent answered "yes" in response to: Do you have a friend who has been on welfare?

TABLE 7.A1

Support for welfare, general orientations, health care, and pensions

	Dependent variable					
	Welfare		General orientations		Health care	
Immigrants on welfare	-.286** (.132)	*.751** *	.440*** (.129)	*1.553*** *	.220 (.150)	*1.246*
Aboriginals on welfare	-.463*** (.129)	*.629*** *	-.127 (.125)	*.881*	-.419*** (.145)	*.658*** *
... on it again?	-.944*** (.105)	*.389*** *	-.209** (.098)	*.811** *	-.209* (.116)	*.812* *
Female	.038 (.085)	*1.039*	.398*** (.082)	*1.489*** *	.352*** (.095)	*1.421*** *
Age (30-49)	-.026 (.103)	*.975*	-.324*** (.101)	*.724*** *	.157 (.114)	*1.170*
Age (50-64)	.045 (.131)	*1.046*	-.352*** (.127)	*.703*** *	.054 (.144)	*1.056*
Age (65+)	-.064 (.176)	*.938*	-.389** (.168)	*.678** *	.191 (.195)	*1.211*
Education (> high school)	.315*** (.090)	*1.370*** *	-.133 (.087)	*.875*	-.423*** (.103)	*.655*** *
Income (imputed)	-.002 (.066)	*.998*	-.228*** (.063)	*.796*** *	-.129* (.067)	*.879* *
Unemployed	.858** (.436)	*2.358** *	.198 (.403)	*1.219*	.159 (.485)	*1.172*
Not in labour force	-.038 (.118)	*.962*	.107 (.114)	*1.113*	-.062 (.130)	*.940*
Union member	.218** (.106)	*1.244** *	.436*** (.104)	*1.546*** *	.409*** (.123)	*1.506*** *
Economic situation worse	.198* (.112)	*1.219* *	.083 (.107)	*1.087*	.109 (.127)	*1.115*
Fear of job loss	-.128 (.176)	*.880*	.395** (.171)	*1.484** *	.011 (.198)	*1.011*
Friend on welfare	.106 (.086)	*1.112*	.140* (.082)	*1.150* *	.174* (.096)	*1.191* *
Cut 1	-.522*** (.147)		-1.556*** (.148)	*.211*** *		
Cut 2	2.403*** (.159)		.268* (.143)	*1.307*		
Constant					.831*** (.163)	*2.294*** *
N	2,243		2,260		2,260	

Note: Cells contain coefficients and standard errors in parentheses, with odds ratios in italics, from an ordered logit regression model for general orientations and pensions, and a binary logit model for health care.

* $p < .10$; ** $p < .05$; *** $p < .01$.

NOTES

1 For more extended accounts of the relationship between race and welfare in the US, see Lieberman (1998); Misra, Moller, and Karides (2003); Schram, Soss, and Fording (2003); Williams (2003).
2 For the purpose of this chapter, we are mostly interested in reactions to diversity among the majority population. Results for immigrants and Aboriginals are available upon request.
3 Regression results are available upon request.
4 As it turns out, including this item as a control strengthens the effects we observe for the questions about immigrants and Aboriginals. The differences are minimal, however. Overall, the effect of other variables in the models changes only slightly with the inclusion of this variable.
5 Technically such respondents have, on average, a 25 percent lower probability to be one unit higher on overall welfare support than do respondents who think only one-quarter of immigrants are on welfare.
6 Our preliminary tests did not reveal significant contextual effects; living in a census tract or subdivision in which there is a greater proportion of immigrants or Aboriginals appears not to be systematically connected to perceptions of welfare dependence for either group. Results are available upon request.
7 The model we use here allows the perceptions variables to take on different coefficients in each of the five regions in Canada. Complete results, including the ratios for the control variables, are available upon request.
8 Note that survey respondents received one of two possible wordings for the second option, one focused on being able to afford care, and the other focused on willingness to pay. We do not use this wording experiment here; we focus only on the likelihood of expressing support for equal access, regardless of wording.

REFERENCES

Akbari, Ather H. 1989. "The Benefits of Immigrants to Canada: Evidence on Tax and Public Services." *Canadian Public Policy* 15(4): 424-35.

Appelbaum, Lauren. 2001. "The Influence of Perceived Deservingness on Policy Decisions Regarding Aid to the Poor." *Political Psychology* 22(3): 419-42.

Baker, Michael, and Dwayne Benjamin. 1995a. "Labor Market Outcomes and the Participation of Immigrant Women in Canadian Transfer Programs." In Don J. DeVoretz, ed., *Diminishing Returns: The Economics of Canada's Recent Immigration Policy*, 209-42. Toronto: C.D. Howe Institute.

–. 1995b. "The Receipt of Transfer Payments by Immigrants to Canada." *Journal of Human Resources* 30(4): 650-76.

Baker, Michael, Dwayne Benjamin, and Elliott Fan. 2009. *Public Policy and the Economic Wellbeing of Elderly Immigrants*. Working paper 52. Vancouver: Canadian Labour Market and Skills Researcher Network.

Banting, Keith. 2010. "Is There a Progressives' Dilemma in Canada? Immigration, Multiculturalism and the Welfare State." *Canadian Journal of Political Science* 43(4): 797-820.

Banting, Keith, Richard Johnston, Will Kymlicka, and Stuart Soroka. 2011. "Are Diversity and Solidarity Incompatible? Canada in Comparative Context." *Inroads: The Canadian Journal of Opinion* 29: 36-48.

Blume, Kræn, Björn Gustafsson, Peder J. Pedersen, and Mette Verner. 2007. "At the Lower End of the Table: Determinants of Poverty among Immigrants to Denmark and Sweden." *Journal of Ethnic and Migration Studies* 33(3): 373-96.

Bobo, Lawrence, and James Kleugel. 1993. "Opposition to Race-Targeting: Self-Interest, Stratification Ideology, or Racial Attitudes." *American Sociological Review* 58(4): 443-64.

Boeri, Tito, Gordon Hanson, and Perry McCormick. 2002. *Immigration Policy and the Welfare System*. Oxford: Oxford University Press.

Chebel d'Appollonia, Ariane, and Simon Reich, eds. 2008. *Immigration, Integration, and Security. America and Europe in Comparative Perspective*. Pittsburgh: University of Pittsburgh Press.

Cnaan, Ram. 1989. "Public Opinion and the Dimensions of the Welfare State." *Social Indicators Research* 21(3): 297-314.

Cozzarelli, Catherine, Anna Wilkinson, and Michael Tagler. 2001. "Beliefs about the Poor: Attitudes toward the Poor and Attributions of Poverty." *Journal of Social Issues* 57(2): 207-27.

Crepaz, Markus. 2008. *Trust beyond Borders: Immigration, the Welfare State and Identity in Modern Societies*. Ann Arbor: University of Michigan Press.

De Silva, Arnold. 1997. "Immigrant Participation in the Unemployment Insurance System." *Canadian Public Policy* 23(4): 375-97.

DeVoretz, Don, and Sergiy Pivnenko. 2004. "Immigrant Public Finance Transfers: A Comparative Analysis by City." *Canadian Journal of Urban Research* 13(1): 155-69.

Dussault, Hon. René, and George Erasmus. 1997. "Allocution à l'occasion de la parution du Rapport de la Commission royale sur les peuples autochtones." *Canadian Public Administration* 40(1): 108-22.

Dwyer, Peter. 2006. "Governance, Forced Migration and Welfare." In Catherine Jones Finer, ed., *Migration, Immigration and Social Policy*, 63-80. Malden, MA: Blackwell.

Esping-Andersen, Gøsta. 1996. "Welfare States without Work: The Impasse of Labour Shedding and Familialism in Continental European Social Policy." In Gøsta Esping-Andersen, ed., *Welfare States in Transition: National Adaptations in Global Economies*, 66-87. London: Sage.

Fox, Cybelle. 2004. "The Changing Color of Welfare? How White's Attitudes toward Latinos Influence Support for Welfare." *American Journal of Sociology* 110(3): 580-625.

Frederico, Christopher. 2004. "When Do Welfare Attitudes Become Racialized? The Paradoxical Effects of Education." *American Journal of Political Science* 48(2): 374-91.

—. 2005. "Racial Perceptions and Evaluative Responses to Welfare: Does Education Attenuate Race-of-Target Effects?" *Political Psychology* 26(5): 683-97.

Gilens, Martin. 1995. "Racial Attitudes and Opposition to Welfare." *Journal of Politics* 57(4): 994-1014.
–. 1996a. "Race and Poverty in America: Public Misperceptions and the American News Media." *Public Opinion Quarterly* 60(4): 515-41.
–. 1996b. "'Race Coding' and White Opposition to Welfare." *American Political Science Review* 90(3): 593-604.
Goren, Paul. 2003. "Race, Sophistication and White Opinion on Government Spending." *Political Behavior* 25(3): 201-20.
Green-Pedersen, Christoffer, and Pontus Odmalm. 2008. "Going Different Ways? Right-Wing Parties and the Immigrant Issue in Denmark and Sweden." *Journal of European Public Policy* 15(3): 367-81.
Guibernau, Montserrat. 2010. "Migration and the Rise of the Radical Right: Social Malaise and the Failure of Mainstream Politics." Policy Network Paper, March 9.
Hagelund, Anniken. 2005. "Why It Is Bad to Be Kind – Educating Refugees to Life in the Welfare State: A Case Study from Norway." *Social Policy and Administration* 39(6): 669-83.
Harell, Allison, Stuart Soroka, and Adam Mahon. 2008. "Is Welfare a Dirty Word? Canadian Public Opinion on Social Assistance Policies." *Policy Options* (September): 53-56.
Hjerm, Mikael. 2005. "Integration into the Social Democratic Welfare State." *Social Indicators Research* 70(2): 117-38.
Huber, Gregory, and John Lapinski. 2006. "The 'Race Card' Revisited: Assessing Racial Priming in Policy Contests." *American Journal of Political Science* 50(2): 421-40.
Ireland, Patrick. 2004. *Becoming Europe: Immigration, Integration, and the Welfare State*. Pittsburgh, PA: University of Pittsburgh Press.
Johnston, Richard, Keith Banting, Will Kymlicka, and Stuart Soroka. 2010. "National Identity and Support for the Welfare State." *Canadian Journal of Political Science* 43(2): 349-77.
Jurado, Elena, and Grete Brochmann. 2013. *Europe's Immigration Challenge: Reconciling Work, Welfare and Mobility*. London: I.B. Tauris.
Kitschelt, Herbert. 1995. *The Radical Right in Western Europe: A Comparative Analysis*. Ann Arbor: University of Michigan Press.
Kogan, Irena. 2007. *Working through Barriers: Host Country Institutions and Immigrant Labour Market Performance in Europe*. Dordrecht: Springer.
Leiken, Robert S. 2005. "Europe's Angry Muslims." *Foreign Affairs* 84(4): 120-35.
Lieberman, Robert. 1998. *Shifting the Color Line: Race and the American Welfare State*. Cambridge, MA: Harvard University Press.
Marshall, T.H. 1950. "Citizenship and Social Class." In T.H. Marshall and T. Bottomore, eds., *Citizenship and Social Class*. London: Pluto Press.
Mendelberg, Tali. 2001. *The Race Card: Campaign Strategy, Implicit Messages, and the Norm of Equality*. Princeton, NJ: Princeton University Press.
Menz, Georg. 2006. "'Useful' Gastarbeiter, Burdensome Asylum Seekers, and the Second Wave of Welfare Retrenchment: Exploring the Nexus between Migration and the Welfare State." In Craig A. Parsons and Timothy M. Smeeding, eds., *Immigration and the Transformation of Europe*, 393-418. Cambridge: Cambridge University Press.

Miller, David. 1995. *On Nationality.* Oxford: Oxford University Press.
Miller, P.W., and L.M. Neo. 2003. "Labour Market Flexibility and Immigrant Adjustment." *Economic Record* 79: 336-56.
Minderhoud, Paul E. 1999. "Asylum Seekers and Access to Social Security: Recent Developments in the Netherlands, United Kingdom, Germany, and Belgium." In Alice Bloch and Carl Levy, eds., *Refugees, Citizenship, and Social Policy in Europe,* 132-48. Basingstoke, UK: Macmillan.
Misra, Joya, Stephanie Moller, and Marina Karides. 2003. "Envisioning Dependency: Changing Media Depictions of Welfare in the 20th Century." *Social Problems* 50(4): 482-504.
Mynott, Ed, Beth Humphries, and Steve Cohen. 2002. "Introduction: Locating the Debate." In Steve Cohen, Beth Humphries, and Ed Mynott, eds., *From Immigration Controls to Welfare Controls,* 1-8. London: Routledge.
National Council of Welfare. 2007. *First Nations, Métis and Inuit Children and Youth: Time to Act.* Vol. 127. Ottawa: National Council of Welfare.
Oesch, Daniel. 2008. "Explaining Workers' Support for Right-Wing Populist Parties in Western Europe: Evidence from Austria, Belgium, France, Norway, and Switzerland." *International Political Science Review* 29: 349-73.
Peffley, Mark, Jon Hurwitz, and Paul Sniderman. 1997. "Racial Stereotypes and Whites' Political Views of Blacks in the Context of Welfare and Crime." *American Journal of Political Science* 41(1): 30-60.
Picot, Garnett, Yuqian Lu, and Feng Hou. 2009. "Immigrant Low-Income Rates: The Role of Market Income and Government Transfers." *Perspectives.* Statistics Canada report 75-001, 13-27.
Putnam, Robert. 2007. "E Pluribus Unum: Diversity and Community in the Twenty-First Century – The 2006 Johan Skytte Prize Lecture." *Scandinavian Political Studies* 30(2): 137-74.
Rothstein, Bo. 1998. *Just Institutions Matter: The Moral and Political Logic of the Universal Welfare State.* Cambridge: Cambridge University Press.
Royal Commission on Aboriginal Peoples. 1996. *Gathering Strength.* Vol. 3. Ottawa: Canada Communication Group Publishing.
Sainsbury, Diane. 2012. *Welfare States and Immigrant Rights: The Politics of Inclusion and Exclusion.* Oxford: Oxford University Press.
Schram, Sanford, Joe Soss, and Richard Fording, eds. 2003. *Race and the Politics of Welfare Reform.* Ann Arbor: University of Michigan Press.
Shewell, Hugh. 2004. *"Enough to Keep Them Alive": Indian Welfare in Canada, 1873-1965.* Toronto: University of Toronto Press.
Soroka, Stuart N., John F. Helliwell, and Richard Johnston. 2007. "Measuring and Modelling Interpersonal Trust." In Fiona Kay and Richard Johnston, eds., *Social Capital, Diversity, and the Welfare State,* 95-132. Vancouver: UBC Press.
Soroka, Stuart N., Richard Johnston, and Keith Banting. 2007. "Ethnicity, Trust, and the Welfare State." In Fiona Kay and Richard Johnston, eds., *Social Capital, Diversity, and the Welfare State,* 279-303. Vancouver: UBC Press.
Statistics Canada. 2010. *Projections of the Diversity of the Canadian Population: 2006-31.* Catalogue #91-551-X. Ottawa.

Swank, Duane, and Hans-Georg Betz. 2003. "Globalization, the Welfare State and Right-Wing Populism in Western Europe." *Socio-Economic Review* 1: 215-45.

Sweetman, Arthur. 2001. "Immigrants and Employment Insurance." In Saul Schwartz and Abdurranhman Aydemir, eds., *Essays on the Repeat Use of Unemployment Insurance*, 123-54. Ottawa: Social Research and Demonstration Corporation.

Timpson, Joyce. 1995. "Four Decades of Literature on Native Canadian Child Welfare: Changing Themes." *Child Welfare* 74(3): 525-46.

Van Oorschot, Wim. 2006. "Making the Difference in Social Europe: Deservingness Perceptions among Citizens of European Welfare States." *Journal of European Social Policy* 16(1): 23-42.

Voges, Wolfgang, Joachim Frick, and Felix Büchel. 1998. "The Integration of Immigrants into West German Society: The Impact of Social Assistance." In Hermann Kurthen, Jürgen Fijalkowski, and Gert G. Wagner, eds., *Immigration, Citizenship, and the Welfare State in Germany and the United States: Immigrant Incorporation*, 159-74. Stamford, CT: JAI Press.

Williams, Linda. 2003. *The Constraint of Race: Legacies of White Skin Privilege in America*. University Park, PA: Penn State UniversityPress.

Zion, James W. 1992. "North American Indian Perspectives on Human Rights." In Abdullahi Ahmed An-Naim, ed., *Human Rights in Cross Cultural Perspectives: A Quest for Consensus*, 191-220. Philadelphia: University of Pennsylvania Press.

The Party System, Elections, and Social Policy

RICHARD JOHNSTON

The Canadian party system has only weakly and sporadically engaged with social policy. Yet precisely for this reason the Canadian case illustrates the power of the major politically focused theories of the growth and retrenchment of the welfare state. Although the growth of the Canadian welfare state conforms to the "power resources" model in both its overall modesty and the dynamics of its elaboration, the system's retrenchment in the 1990s is best understood as an interaction of the mechanisms in the power resources model with those in a recent rival, the "new politics" model. Now with a Conservative majority in power, the power resources perspective, arguably, is back in force, and the prospects for Canada's welfare state are bleak.

Theoretical Debates

The Power Resources Model

Everywhere in the rich, capitalist world, the welfare state has grown, but the system started earlier and went further in some places than in others. It seems clear that a critical factor in the size and universality of the welfare state is the relative political strength of labour and capital (Korpi 1983, 1989; Stephens 1979; Huber and Stephens 2001), with the continuing power of socially traditional pre-capitalist formations also relevant (Esping-Andersen 1990). The political expression of the capital-labour struggle is the balance of electoral forces and the implications of that balance for power in or over government. The greater the parliamentary weight of the political left, the larger and more elaborate is the welfare state. Unsurprisingly, a major factor in the power of the left is the degree of labour mobilization, usually captured by union density (Bartolini 2000).

The New Politics of the Welfare State

Just as the welfare state is ubiquitous, so are pressures for cutting it back. As with growth, so with retrenchment: some attempts at cutting social programs have been more successful than others. But the pattern of retrenchment may not be just the mirror image of the pattern of growth. A redistributive and social insurance regime creates a clientele independent of the power resources that created the regime in the first place. Indeed, the welfare state itself may be empowering. Serious cutbacks may require patience and a fundamental reshaping of the electoral landscape (Pierson 1994).[1]

Nonetheless, Pierson (1996) identifies conditions for sudden major cutbacks. One is *electoral slack,* "when governments believe that they are in a strong enough position to absorb the electoral consequences of unpopular decisions" (ibid., 176). Another is *fiscal crisis:* "Moments of budgetary crisis may open opportunities for reform. Advocates of retrenchment will try to exploit such moments to present reforms as an effort to save the welfare state rather than destroy it. Framing the issue in this manner may allow governments to avoid widespread blame for program cutbacks" (ibid.).

Power Resources in the Party System, 1940-93

It may seem odd to assert that parties and elections in Canada have any relevance for social policy. Party competition is said to be constituted on cultural rather than on economic foundations, and the two parties that actually govern tend not to differ widely over the welfare state. In this, the Canadian party system is an outlier. In Lijphart's (1999, Table 5.3) landmark comparative account of democratic party systems, the "socioeconomic" dimension is highly salient for thirty-two of thirty-six cases. Only for four systems is the dimension merely moderately salient, and Canada is among these.[2] But to infer from this that the party system does not matter for social policy is to miss the point. The historically modest gap between the major parties helps explain the relative weakness of the Canadian welfare state. And at key points, the dynamics of government formation explain much of the growth that did occur.

The core parties in the Canadian system have differed over social spending in a fairly consistent way – if we accept that the core parties include not

FIGURE 8.1

The party system and the welfare state, 1945-2008

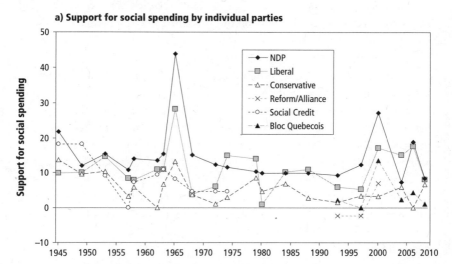

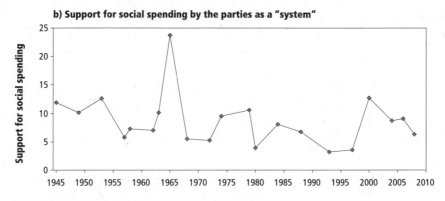

Source: Manifesto Research Group, analyses by the author.

just the Conservatives and Liberals but also the NDP. Almost without fail, the NDP (and its predecessor the Co-operative Commonwealth Federation or CCF) has anchored the left, pro-spending pole, and the Conservative party has anchored the right, anti-spending pole, or so Figure 8.1, with data from party manifestos, indicates. The figure plots party positions on social service spending, inferred from the frequency and direction of mentions in each party's platform, for each election since 1945, as coded by the Manifesto

Research Group.[3] The gap between the parties (on average, 9.3 percent more supportive statements in NDP than in Conservative manifestos) is typical of that between parties of the left and right in other countries. Although Figure 8.1 is dominated visually by the spike in 1965, the primary source of variance in the figure is not over time but across parties. There is no evidence of either convergence or divergence.

The fly in the ointment is the Liberal Party, the party of the centre. The Liberals seem to have undergone a long-term shift: whereas in the early postwar years they sometimes found themselves to the right of the Conservatives,[4] since the 1950s this has been true only once. Indeed, in recent years the Liberals have occasionally been farther left than the NDP. Regression of party gaps on years since 1945 confirms the visual impression given by Figure 8.1: whereas in the 1940s, the Liberals were only about half as far from the Conservatives as from the CCF, more recently the NDP and Liberal platforms have been almost indistinguishable. It is also true, however, that the Liberals are quite mobile, exploiting the advantage conferred by their centrist location.[5]

All this would not matter if the Liberal Party were weak. It has not been, of course, and, indeed, was the governing party for forty-four years since the end of the Second World War. Here lies the true peculiarity of the Canadian party system. Although the Liberals might seem to be the natural governing party *because* they are the party of the centre, in no other system with single-member districts and an electoral formula that manufactures single-party majority governments is this true. Dominance by the centre is rare even under proportional representation (PR) systems. Duverger (1954/63, 215) describes the dominant pattern in forceful terms:

> Political choice takes the form of a choice between two alternatives. A duality of parties does not always exist, but there is almost always a duality of tendencies ... This is equivalent to saying that the center does not exist in politics ... The term "center" is applied to the geometrical spot at which the moderates of opposed tendencies meet ... Every Center is divided against itself and remains separated into two halves, Left-Center and Right-Center. For the Center is nothing more than the artificial grouping of the right wing of the Left and the left wing of the Right. The fate of the Center is to be torn asunder.

In places like Canada, where governments are formed by single parties and not by coalitions, the standard form of party competition pits a party with

FIGURE 8.2

The union movement and the CCF/NDP, 1945-2008

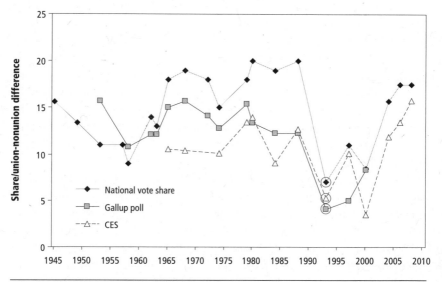

Note: Entries for Gallup Poll and CES are marginal effects estimated by probit, extracted from saturated estimations, non-Quebec respondents only.

links to organized labour against a party of the right whose origins tend to be idiosyncratic. In narratives for other countries, the non-socialist party that survives to fight against the labour-based left may be a party that once was like the Canadian Liberals. But the party crowded out in such a process is a rival on the centre-right, and even if the eventual winner does not start out on the right it ends up there. In Canadian federal politics, such a transition did not happen until 2011, if then.

This left the NDP as the historically weakest among the system's core parties. According to Figure 8.2, it never gained more than 20 percent of the national vote before 2011 and often rather less. Its seat share (not shown) was only about half as large, averaging under 10 percent of the House of Commons. Figure 8.2 also gives an explicit rendering of the electoral salience of organized labour, specifically of the individual-level impact of union membership on NDP support. Values in the figure give the difference, election by election, between union and non-union families in the probability of an NDP vote, holding voters' language, ethnicity, religion, and region of residence constant. Quebec respondents are always excluded, so the effect is overestimated for the country as a whole.[6] The sources are the Gallup Poll for elections from 1953 to 2000 and the Canadian Election Study (CES) for 1965 to 2008. Although the plots differ in detail between the surveys, they tell broadly the same story. Before 1993, union families were ten to fifteen percentage points more supportive of the CCF or NDP than were non-union families. There is little evidence of a qualitative shift after the formalization of the link and the creation of the NDP in 1961. By way of comparison, in the 1950s and 1960s, the impact (not shown) of being a Roman Catholic on the Liberal and Conservative vote was over twice as great, as was the impact of union membership in Australasia and Great Britain. In contrast, in Canada the party of labour has been weak and has never governed at the federal level.

But the NDP's historical levels of support do not tell the whole story. The party grew over the postwar period. It surged in 1945, and this after a provincial victory in Saskatchewan, a near-breakthrough in Ontario, and more than a decade of considerable electoral success in British Columbia. The CCF stalled after 1945, but its refounding in 1961 with explicit support from organized labour initiated a period of modest but steady growth. Whereas the CCF was arguably as much a regional party as a class-based one, the NDP embarked on competition in every region and eventually induced growth outside its western provinces of origin (Johnston and Cutler 2009). By 1980, the party had formed the government in three of the four western provinces. As of 1991, a majority of Canadians lived under NDP provincial governments.

Over the same years, union density also grew, peaking in the 1980s at 36 percent of the labour force. As of 1990, 34 percent of the labour force was unionized, placing Canada roughly in the middle of the OECD pack (OECD 2011). No less important, the movement was no longer divided between craft and industrial unions, thanks to the creation of the Canadian Labour Congress in 1956 (Horowitz 1968).

Moreover, the Liberal Party lost ground after 1960. This is revealed by Figure 8.3, which shows seat shares for governments and the Official Opposition and distinguishes Conservative governments from Liberal ones. Before 1957, the Liberals dominated Parliament utterly: from 1935 to 1957 the party always held a parliamentary majority, usually an overwhelming one. Although from 1963 to 1984 the Liberals governed for all but one year, they did so without a majority for six of the twenty years. When they did attain a majority it was often narrow. And what Figure 8.3 does not show is

FIGURE 8.3

Strength of the government's position, 1945-2008

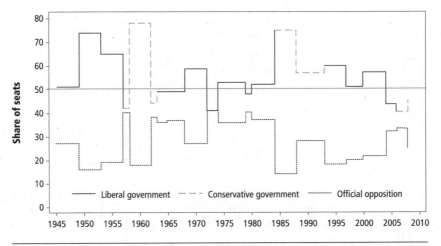

Note: Entries are shares of seats in the House of Commons for the government party and for the Official Opposition.

that those Liberal governments included virtually no western component. In that region, progressive MPs were almost all New Democrats. In 1972-74, the Liberals needed NDP support to survive. In 1963-68, the situation was ambiguous: the Liberals were so close to an outright majority that they could, in principle, have courted either of the small parties, Social Credit on the right or the NDP on the left. As the next section shows, however, tensions internal to the Liberals privileged the NDP.

Power Resources and the Growth of the Welfare State

For the most part, the years before 1960 featured policy stasis, consistent with the Liberal Party's conservatism as revealed by Figure 8.1 and backed by Whitaker (1977). The policy shifts that did occur mostly reflected external pressures. Unemployment insurance was adopted in 1940 by an overwhelmingly dominant Liberal majority but in a period of rising union power reflecting the demand for labour induced by the Second World War. (Growth in demand for labour was also critical to kick-starting the rise in Canadian union densities in the 1940s.) The 1945 Family Allowance Program (FAP) reflected fear of the CCF, stimulated by early Gallup polls, the 1943 Ontario provincial election, and the 1944 CCF victory in Saskatchewan. As a natalist policy, FAP also seems to have been calculated to appeal to the Liberal Party's Quebec base (Kudrle and Marmor 1981).

Less clearly, the results of such pressures were the 1951 Old Age Security pension and the Hospital Insurance and Diagnostic Services Act, 1957. Even though enacted by a Progressive Conservative government, the hospital program seems the less anomalous of the two. This was a minority government anxious to increase its popular vote and led by that most protean of Tories, John Diefenbaker. Diefenbaker's Saskatchewan roots seem relevant, as do his close ties to Emmett Hall, whose royal commission report laid the groundwork for health policy changes in the next decade. This leaves the 1951 enactment of Old Age Security (OAS) entirely outside the power resources model.

The most startling period of policy innovation accompanied the Liberal return to power in 1963 and was a reflection of the party's weakness, not its strength. A two-year span, from 1965 to 1967, saw the enactment of the Canada Pension Plan, the Canada Assistance Plan, medicare, and the Guaranteed Income Supplement. It is tempting to suggest that this flurry of activity is reflected in Figure 8.1's 1965 spike, when the Liberal Party's program featured more pro-welfare state mentions than did any other party's manifesto before or since – with the exception of the NDP in the same year. Accounts of the period make it clear, however, that the Liberal government was divided on the matter, that the Progressive Conservative opposition would not support the measures, and that the NDP was able to channel popular sentiment (McCall-Newman 1982; Smith 1973). The massive expansion of FAP in 1973, in the second (1972 to 1974) stretch of Liberal minority status, followed a similar logic (Mulé 2001, chap. 2). Although the expansion of UI by a Liberal majority government in 1971 might seem to stand outside the power resources logic, the decision reflected electoral calculations incorporating fear of the NDP (Wearing 1981); in this, it was like the enactment of FAP in 1945.

Retrenchment in the 1990s

Outcomes

In 1981, Lars Osberg (1981, 205) could say that "economic inequality has remained roughly constant since the Second World War." This was true notwithstanding the massive changes Canada had undergone over the interval. Even as he was writing, however, the wheel of inequality took another turn.

As Figure 1.2 in Banting and Myles (Chapter 1, this volume) shows, income inequality was about to embark on an upward trajectory. In market income, two rapid shifts stand out, 1981 to 1984 and 1989 to 1993. Each corresponds to the onset of a major economic downturn. Strikingly, the subsequent recoveries only arrested the move towards greater inequality: neither recovery reversed the trend. But if market incomes became more unequal, the system of taxes and transfers fully offset the shifts until 1994. The contrast with the US over the same period is striking. Whereas at the start, according to Kenworthy and Pontusson (2005, fig. 4), Canadian taxes and transfers were less redistributive than were those in the US, at the end they were more so. In a broader perspective, Canada sits in the middle of the Luxembourg Income Study pack for *after-tax* income inequality, with the lowest after-tax Gini among the Anglo-American, or "liberal," welfare states (Kenworthy and Pontusson, fig. 10). But holding the line in those years was not the result of a static tax and transfer system; rather, it required aggressive expansion of the system's redistributive power (Heisz 2007; Frenette, Green, and Milligan 2009, fig. 3). By the 1990s, as Myles (2010, 71) argues, the welfare state may have been "running out of gas." In any case, in 1994, inequality in after-tax income started to climb, and only in 2000 did the rise in inequality cease. Although the system was still more redistributive after 2000 than it had been in 1990, many Canadians lost ground in the interim.

Instruments

How did this happen? Both taxes and transfers contribute to income redistribution, but transfers do most of the heavy lifting. This is true both at any point (as transfers mitigate inequality more than taxes) and over time (as gains and losses in the system's redistributive capacity correspond to the ebb and flow of transfers). Figure 8.4 rearranges the data from Figure 1.2 in Banting and Myles (Chapter 1, this volume) to bring out the redistributive effect of each component. The "cumulative redistributive effect" is simply the Banting-Myles market income Gini coefficient minus the "after-transfers-and-taxes" (disposable income) one; this is the combined effect of taxing and spending. The "redistributive effect of transfers" is the difference between the market income Gini in Figure 1.2 in this volume and the "after transfers" one. The "redistributive effect of taxes" effect is the "after transfers" coefficient minus the "after-transfers-and-taxes" coefficient.[7]

The impact of taxes increased by about 60 percent between 1980 and 1994, and then lost about one-third of the total redistributive gain. But the changes were gradual, and no particular year stands out as a point of

FIGURE 8.4

Components of redistribution, 1980-2006

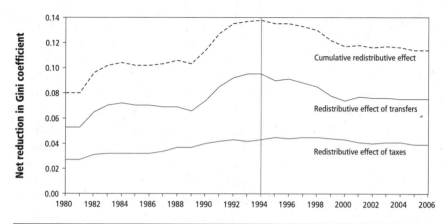

Source: Based on Banting and Myles (this volume), Figure 1.2.

discontinuity.[8] Movement in the transfer component, in contrast, is striking both for its range and its discontinuities. Transfers were responsible for most of the remarkable offsetting of the increased market inequalities induced by the post-1989 cyclical downturn. And whereas the total proportionate increase in the transfer effect between 1980 and 1994 was 80 percent, two-thirds of this occurred between 1989 and 1994. So 1989 stands out as one turning point. Perhaps the jump in market income inequality posed a challenge that the existing system simply met, as in the earlier downturn. If, on the other hand, the system's redistributive parameters had to shift to offset the increased pressure, as Frenette, Green, and Milligan (2009) claim, Figure 8.4 suggests that the critical federal policy change was the 1988 amendment of the Income Tax Act. Battle (2003, figs. 1 and 2) shows that, whereas before 1989 access to elderly benefits was only modestly redistributive in effect, after 1989 it became sharply so. It is worth noting that this increase in redistributive power came as the overall scale of elderly benefits shrank, but with the shrinkage exclusively affecting the well-off.

The policy picture changed dramatically in the 1990s, however, and the critical changes were concentrated right where the transfer component in Figure 8.4 begins its downturn. One key element was Unemployment Insurance, which morphed into Employment Insurance in 1995-96. The most abrupt Unemployment/Employment Insurance (UI/EI) changes were for eligibility: increases in work requirements and reductions of receipt periods.[9] The upshot of this was a precipitous drop in coverage (Battle, Mendelson, and Torjman 2005, 434; Banting 2006, fig. 13.1) with marked variation across labour markets. The rate of income replacement, which had already been dropping by gradual increments from the 1971 high point, also fell; by 1994 the rate was 55 percent (from 1996, 50 percent for repeat claimants) (Banting 2006, 425). The combination of replacement cuts and reduced eligibility made the Canadian system of unemployment compensation scarcely more generous than the US one. As it happened, however, the main impact of UI/EI changes fell on middle-income households and had only a modest effect on the overall distribution (Frenette, Green, and Milligan 2009).

More consequential seem to be shifts in social assistance. Welfare income for single parents with one child dropped about 30 percent in constant dollars from the 1994 peak (Banting 2006, fig. 13.3; Osberg 2007, fig. 8). The drop for single employable persons was smaller, but this group had a smaller welfare entitlement from the start. As a percentage of the average family income, welfare income for single parents dropped 25 to 40 percent, depending on the province. A similar drop affected single employable persons. For both categories, the most abrupt year-on-year drop was from 1995 to 1996. Although it is awkward for my argument that the primary responsibility for social assistance lies with provincial governments, the timing suggests that the federal role was critical: 1995-96 marks the replacement of the Canada Assistance Program with the Canada Health and Social Transfer.[10] The transition to the Canada Health and Social Transfer (CHST) cut overall funding at the same time as it put social assistance into province-level competition with other, more popular programs, notably health care. These cuts were clearly the biggest factor in widening the gap between the top and bottom income groups (Frenette, Green, and Milligan 2009, fig. 8).

As already stated, growth in inequality stopped in 2000. The key may be that no new demands were placed on it by the market economy: market incomes did not become more unequal after that year. It is also true, however, that late in the 1990s the transfer system acquired new elements. The National Child Benefit was authorized in 1998, bringing back a transfer like the old Family Allowance but adding an income test. And, in 2000, the National Child Benefit (NCB) was fully indexed to inflation. As a result, the burden of income maintenance shifted from the provinces to Ottawa, arguably making the system less vulnerable to calls for retrenchment (Battle 2001, 38; Frenette, Green, and Milligan 2009, 402 and fig. 8).[11]

To recapitulate, market inequality began building in the early 1980s and continued to build until the late 1990s; yet, until 1994, taxes and transfers contained the inequality by increased redistributive effort. When the retreat came, it was rapid. It spanned at most five years and rested upon a set of policy changes enacted in one or two years. Why did the change come so quickly? Why did it come in those particular years? And why did it stop?

Electoral Slack

The years between 1993 and 1997 may be close to a perfect example of Pierson's "electoral slack" condition. One piece of evidence is retrospective: in comparison with earlier years, what sort of parliamentary situation did the 1993 election produce? The other looks forward: as of 1994-95, how much retribution should retrenchment-minded policy makers have feared? On each front, the government's position was, or seemed, strong. Yet the 1997 election brought a measure of retribution, not enough to force the undoing of the major retrenchment but enough to block further moves and to hasten course correction.

By postwar standards, according to Figure 8.3, the Liberals' 1993 majority was comfortable. If it did not match the lopsided results of 1949, 1958, or 1984, the government's seat share was still above the median for majority governments and was the fifth largest in postwar history. It was rather larger than the Progressive Conservative share in 1988 and eight points larger than the Liberal majority of 1980. All this was true notwithstanding the weakness in the Liberals' 1993 popular vote, the smallest to that date for any party winning a majority of seats. More important, the gap in seats between the government and the Official Opposition was wide. The latter controlled slightly more than 18 percent of the seats in the House, the fifth smallest since 1945. Likewise, the government-opposition gap, almost 42 percent, was the fifth largest. The 1993 popular vote gap (not shown in the table) between the government and its most plausible rivals was even larger – the largest, bar none, in Canadian history, despite the weakness of the Liberals' own vote share. By implication, the opposition was fragmented both in seats and votes.

No less important, the government's re-election prospects looked astonishingly positive. Figure 8.5 shows this by comparing the government's current standing in Gallup polls with those typical of electoral cycles between 1974 and 1993. Data points are the governing party's month-by-month share of vote intentions in "trial heats," how respondents would vote

FIGURE 8.5

Governing party's electoral prospects, various years

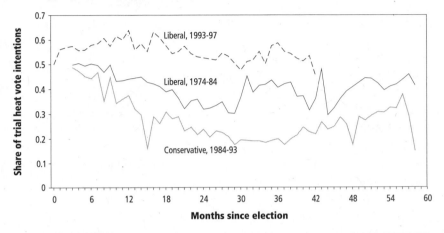

Note: Monthly figures for 1993-97. Median bands for all other years.
Source: Gallup Polls, 1974-97, analyses by the author.

if the election were held "today." In addition to the 1993-97 tracking, plots appear for the Trudeau majority-governments, 1974-79 and 1980-84, and the Mulroney government, 1984-93, averaged across each party's parliaments. All three plots exhibit a post-election "honeymoon" (Nadeau 1990), with early post-election shares in the fifties. Whereas the honeymoon lasted twelve to eighteen months for Trudeau and Mulroney, for Chrétien it never stopped. The 1995 budget's immediate electoral effect, if any, was positive: Liberal vote intentions *jumped* eight points. Not much should be made of the jump as it followed three low readings and the advantage was not sustained. Indeed, the trend in the year following the budget was negative. Even so, the government's standing throughout the period was at historically high levels. The budget may have hurt but not enough, apparently, to put the government at electoral risk.

Electoral slack disappeared with the 1997 election. The last reading in Figure 8.5 (an average of weekly results within the May 1997 campaign) reveals that the comfort level suggested by pre-campaign trial heats was illusory. On election day, the Liberal vote share was 38.5 percent, the smallest vote ever returned by a majority government, smaller than the party's vote shares in its minority wins of 1963 and 1965, and even smaller than the party's share when it was driven from power in 1957 and 1979.[12] Appropriately, its seat majority was, proportionately speaking, the narrowest in history. Liberal losses were greatest in Atlantic Canada, the region hardest hit by EI cuts. The biggest gains in that region were recorded by the NDP.

Power Resources

Electoral slack should diminish a government's normal fear of retribution. But why did the government choose to court electoral risk from the poor and economically vulnerable as opposed to better-off voters? It is not axiomatic that cuts will fall on the poor; if anything, the record of the postwar years points in the opposite direction. The answer takes us back to the "power resources" literature and the balance of electoral forces. In the 1993 election, that balance tilted sharply to the right.

As Figure 8.2 shows, the NDP share had moved up seemingly ineluctably over the 1970s and 1980s, such that, by 1988, the party was pulling one vote in five, not far behind the second-place party. In 1993, however, the NDP collapsed. Proportionally, its drop was as great as was that for the Progressive Conservatives: roughly two votes in three went elsewhere. Its 1993 share was the same as for the CCF in 1935! The union/non-union contrast also collapsed. Depending on the data source, the effect was cut either in half or by two-thirds.

The party system as a whole shifted to the right, as indicated by Figure 8.1. Among the party platforms for 1993, only the NDP kept to the left. The Progressive Conservatives had moved to the right over the preceding decade, and, in 1993, the Liberals also tacked in that direction. Most important, though, was the breakthrough of the Reform Party. In 1993 (and 1997), the Reform manifesto featured more negative references to social spending than positive ones, the only time this happened in the entire postwar period. For its part, the Bloc had little to say about the welfare state; whatever its predilections on social spending, it could hardly be expected to advocate an expansion of the federal role.

Summarily speaking, never in the entire postwar period was there more support for retrenchment than in 1993. Figure 8.1, Panel B, shows this by combining the party-specific data into a reading for the party system as a whole. The system-level reading is the average of the manifesto positions of all competitive parties weighted by each party's proportion of the national popular vote. In 1993, for instance, the unchanged position of the NDP on the left loses value relative to 1988 because of shrinkage in the party's vote.

The arrival of Reform, conversely, pulls the system to the right because of the party's extreme rightist position and its relative electoral success. According to Andersen and Curtis (this volume, Figure 6.1), policy shifts in the party system mirror those in public opinion.

This certainly seems to be how Finance Minister Paul Martin interpreted the situation:

> Challenged about the staying power of the government as it got deeper into the electoral cycle, [Martin] revealed some of the political thinking behind the budget. Pointing out that the Reform Party constituted his main political opposition in most of Canada, he said his challenge lay not in fending off accusations of being too hard but in proving he was not too soft. "We won this election primarily on our votes in Ontario and western Canada. In virtually every one of those ridings, the Reform Party – this is the far-right party – came second. So when I go into my caucus, what they're looking at is who is their opposition in the next election. And that opposition isn't saying cut less; they're saying cut more. So in terms of the electoral cycle, let me tell you there is going to be no let-up on that. The political imperative in this country, in fact, says there can be no let-up on deficit cutting." (Greenspon and Wilson-Smith 1996, 276)

Although in our rendering in Figure 8.1 the 1997 electoral signal tilts to the right, this does not seem to be how the outcome was read. The most startling element in the outcome was the resurgence of the Progressive Conservatives and the NDP, a net gain for the two parties of thirty seats. Reform, in contrast, gained only eight seats. Public opinion data also indicate that the electorate was moving in a pro-spending direction (Soroka and Wlezien 2010, fig. 15.1, 273; Andersen and Curtis, Chapter 6, this volume).

Fiscal Necessity
Why was the retrenchment so dramatic? The answer must start with the fact that the country was on the brink of a fiscal crisis. A Department of Finance document (Canada 1994) that served as backdrop to the 1995 budget highlighted dire statistics: a federal deficit that represented 7 percent of GDP (Chart 29, 74); net debt close to 100 percent of GDP, with three-quarters owed by Ottawa (Chart 31, 75); and over 25 percent of the debt held abroad (Chart 34, 78). On the last point, the language was stark: "The sheer magnitude of Canada's foreign debt in relation to the size of the

economy means that Canada has become excessively vulnerable to the volatile sentiments of global financial markets. We have suffered a tangible loss of economic sovereignty" (Canada 1994, 78).

Subsequent events reaffirmed these fears. By spring 1994, US interest rate rises were undoing the calculations in Martin's first budget:

> By early May, with the budget barely two months old, interest rates stood two percentage points above the supposedly prudent budget assumptions. If the rates didn't fall back fairly quickly, Martin could never reach his 3-per-cent deficit target. Each additional point of interest added $1.7 billion a year to the government's costs – that was the consequence of being $500 billion in hock ... Finance could see the targets for years two and three slipping out of reach. There would be no way to make the 3 percent without additional spending cuts – deep, un-Liberal ones. (Greenspon and Wilson-Smith 1996, 160-61)

The Mexican peso crisis of 20 December gave Martin a further push (ibid., 235). Quite apart from interest rate flux and international exposure, there was the matter of compound interest:

> Martin's increasingly tough talk on the deficit was also motivated by his growing appreciation of the arithmetic of compound interest ... The debt was growing by $85,000 a minute, all of it interest. "Compounding was the fact beyond all others that convinced him of how essential it was to come to grips with the deficit problem," [Peter] Nicholson said. "He became completely seized of the arithmetic of compound interest." (Ibid., 200-1)

This too was a theme in the *Framework* document, which, among other things, included a two-page primer (Box 14: The Arithmetic of Debt, 82-83).

As Pierson (1996) implies, the intellectual and political impetus for the crisis may lay not in the crisis itself but elsewhere. Although the fiscal facts were dire, other aspects of the Canadian case are consistent with Pierson's instrumentalist perspective. For instance, the backdrop document did not dwell solely on deficit, debt, and compound interest. Much of it was devoted to the adverse impact of existing programs, UI in particular, on productivity and on the unemployment rate (Canada 1994). In this, the document mirrored the zeitgeist, as did the general rightward lean of the parties' electoral platforms. Indeed, the party system's shift to the right may have worked with the fiscal crisis to create the scale of the shift. Pierson (1996, 177) again:

Making the claim of crisis credible, however, generally requires collaboration with the political opposition. In turn, the need for consensus makes it difficult to utilize crises to promote radical restructuring. Thus, while the appearance of fiscal stress encourages downward adjustments in social programs, it is far less clear that it provides a platform for a radical overhaul of social policy.

The circumstances of 1995 delivered the basis for cross-party collaboration. It was not that the Chrétien government had to bring a party of the left on side; rather, Paul Martin's primary task was to persuade his own colleagues. The Bloc Québécois might have been unsympathetic to a rightward lurch in social policy (although Figure 8.1 reminds us that the Bloc had little to say in 1993), and the boldness of the policy shift is startling when one considers that the 1995 Quebec referendum was on the horizon. But the main opposition party, Reform, could hardly object to policies for which it had been the chief advocate.

Necessary and Sufficient Conditions: Complementary Perspectives
There is, then, a circumstantial case that elections and the party system played a role in the 1990s surge in after-tax inequality. Arguably, this Parliament was uniquely suited to deliver the shifts. The 1993 election created enough electoral slack to enable a bold move. The policy signal in that election was the most pro-retrenchment in the entire postwar period. And the government's fiscal position was dire. With somewhat more contortion, we can interpret the 1997 election as the evaporation of electoral slack. It helped that the government's books were back in the black by 1998.

It is awkward that we have a surplus of explanations. If the electoral balance tilts sharply right, why do we need a story about electoral slack? If there truly was so much slack, why invoke a substantive electoral signal? Does the issue not just come down to deficit and debt? Simply stated, none of these explanations is sufficient. All three are jointly necessary to account for the timing, direction, and extent of the shift.

Why did the shift take place when it did? Fiscal necessity was critical, as debt and the rise in interest rates were poised to send Canadian public spending into a hole from which there was no escape. Even so, no other country's government pushed deficit fighting as far as the Canadian government under Chrétien, and Canada's OECD partners are still fighting deficit legacies from the same period. It is arguable that Canada could have escaped the deficit-debt crunch with a less aggressive approach. To enable – if not drive – such aggression, it seems necessary to invoke the strength of the government's electoral position, its electoral slack.

But why did the burden fall so heavily on relatively vulnerable Canadians? Here the electoral signal does seem critical. The breakthrough by Reform, both for its scale and for the uncompromising conservatism of its platform, is the outstanding feature on the landscape. Next in line is the evanescence of the NDP. In addition, the Liberals and the Progressive Conservatives shifted to the right. Although the Liberals' Red Book is commonly read as a left-leaning document, it has plenty of text on welfare "reform" and deficit fighting.

Future Directions?

In the first decade of the twenty-first century, not much seemed to change, at least not on the surface. Parties' vote shares shifted but with offsetting implications. Relative to the 1990s, the right was strengthened strategically by the merger of the Progressive Conservatives with the Alliance (formerly Reform). If the left's deconsolidation worked to its collective strategic disadvantage, this was somewhat offset by the "rebirth" of the NDP, the historic anchor of the left side of the policy spectrum. Putting this together, Figure 8.1 suggests that the party system moved left relative to the 1990s but not relative to earlier decades and not relative to 2000 in particular. The return of minority government in 2004 probably blocked sharp rightward shifts in actual policy. Indeed, the eighteen months following the 2004 election – with a Liberal government looking to a rejuvenated NDP for support – reproduced the pro-welfare state circumstances of 1963-68 and 1972-74, with concomitant increases in health spending. The minority Conservative government formed in 2006 could move the spending system to the right by playing chicken on its budgets but had to be careful not to overplay its hand. The 2008 financial crisis was a further restraint on retrenchment, although by putting the government back in the red (helped by earlier, tactically motivated tax cuts) it may have set the stage for a replay of the mid-1990s.

History also expanded the Conservatives' room to manoeuvre. Underneath the postwar narrative of Liberal dominance was the slow decay of the party's popular base. The massive Liberal majorities that Figure 8.3 records for the 1950s rested on vote shares of close to 50 percent. The weaker position of Liberal governments from 1963 to 1984 – minority governments or narrow majorities – reflected the consolidation of the opposition into two powerful blocks and the drop in Liberal winning shares to the low forties. The handsome Liberal majorities of 1993 and 2000 rested on own-party shares that, in earlier decades, would have consigned the party to opposition. When, in 2008, the Liberals were reduced to a vote share in the same league as the NDP, the fact was masked by the electoral system.

In 2011, the electoral-system logic went into reverse. The Liberals were outflanked by the NDP much as the Progressive Conservatives had been by Reform in 1993. Surprisingly, the electoral catalyst for the NDP was its appeal in Quebec. This gave the NDP a magnificent tranche of seats and created a dilemma for Liberal voters outside Quebec – especially in seat-rich Ontario. Liberals on the left felt pressure to vote NDP to block the Conservatives; Liberals on the right felt pressure to vote Conservative to block the NDP. Duverger's description of the general inanity of the centre came true, and the net result was a Conservative majority.

The majority seems likely to persist, partly because of the incoherence of the NDP caucus, dominated for the first time in history by MPs from Quebec but with a strongly pro-Ottawa legacy in the rest of the caucus. The NDP may struggle to hold its gains in Quebec, even as it plunges into internal existential turmoil. For now, however, the NDP's fate is in its own hands. The same cannot be said for the Liberals, whose prospects, history suggests, are dim. If Canada settles into a party system with the Conservatives and the NDP as the rival coordination points, then the future direction of the welfare state is cloudy at best. Canada may now exhibit the form of party competition that is normal under the single-member plurality setup, indeed, under majoritarian (as opposed to proportional) systems more generally. But that standard form is not defined solely by a left-right axis; rather, it features the *dominance* of the right (Iversen and Soskice 2006). Why this is so is a matter of dispute, but the empirical regularity seems clear. In the power resources context, Canada has never been governed by a party of the left; but neither, uniquely among majoritarian systems, has it been dominated by a party of the right. That part of Canada's electoral history seems to have ended.

NOTES

Support for research and writing has come from the University of British Columbia, the University of Pennsylvania, and the Social Sciences and Humanities Research Council of Canada. Comments and advice came from many members of the New Politics of Inequality group, but special mention must be made of Keith Banting, John Myles, Robert Andersen, Carolyn Tuohy, Jingjing Huo, and George Ross.

Benoît Collette and François Pétry supplied party manifesto data for recent elections. None of these institutions or persons bears responsibility for any remaining errors of fact or interpretation.

1 Korpi and Palme (2003) remain unpersuaded by "new politics" arguments and claim that retrenchment follows lines of enactment. Universal programs and universalistic systems seem more resistant to retrenchment than do residualist ones.
2 This understates Canada's peculiarity. Of the other three countries, two, Trinidad and the Bahamas, are preindustrial; and the third, the United States, may be misclassified.
3 Manifesto data come from Budge et al. (2001), Klingemann et al. (2006), and a file furnished by Benoît Collette and François Pétry, who have assumed responsibility for updating the Canadian component. Support for social spending is captured by issue areas 504 ("Favourable mentions of need to introduce or expand any social service or social security scheme; support for social services such as health service or social housing. Note: this category excludes education") and 505 ("Limiting expenditure on social services or social security; otherwise as 504, but negative"). The party's value in 505 is subtracted from its value in 504 to arrive at the net position. In the coding, all "quasi-sentences" mentioning one of these considerations are counted towards the party's position. A quasi-sentence is a sentence, clause, or phrase referring to a single component of policy; in the total coding scheme, components are mutually exclusive. The party position appears in the data file as a percentage of the total number of quasi-sentences in the party's election manifesto. For instance, in 1945, according to Figure 8.1, 22 percent of all statements in the CCF manifesto referred to increases in social spending.
4 This is consistent with accounts of the period based on internal documents (Whitaker 1977).
5 The postwar range and standard deviation in Liberal positions are one-and-a-half to two times larger for the Liberals than for the Conservatives. The NDP is the most mobile of all, reflecting the party's massive 1965 and 2000 spikes. Most often, however, the NDP stays in place with a solid ongoing pro-welfare-state commitment.
6 The labour movement in Quebec has never aligned itself in partisan terms with the movement in the rest of Canada. Before 1993, Quebec union families tended to vote disproportionately Conservative or Social Credit and now strongly support the Bloc Québécois. Both patterns reflect the Quebec labour movement's alignment with Quebec nationalism.
7 The logic is the same as in Heisz (2007, fig. 14-2a), although the signs are reversed.
8 Frenette, Green, and Milligan (2009, 402-3) say: "First the tax system became more redistributive over the 1980-95 period, reflecting a mix of fiscal factors from de-indexation to the 1988 tax reform to provincial and federal surtaxes. Second, the large increase in after-tax income at higher income percentiles ... was driven primarily by provincial base rate changes, with some assistance from the removal of federal and provincial surtaxes." Eyeballing their simulation of tax impacts on income at the 95th percentile (their Figure 7), the turning point actually seems to be 1993.
9 In 1993, voluntarily unemployed persons were denied access to benefits, although this draconian step was "softened somewhat in later years" (Frenette, Green, and Milligan 2009, 22).

10 The provinces' jurisdictional primacy may also have helped the federal government play this role. According to Pierson (1996, 177): "Governments in more fragmented systems must fashion strategies that minimize the need to force multiple policy changes through institutional veto points. However, they may find it easier to duck accountability for unpopular policies. Federalism, for example, opened up considerable possibilities for Reagan to shift blame for cuts in some programs, a tactic that is central to the current efforts of congressional Republicans." The Canadian combination of decentralization in the federation and concentrated power within the national government may have doubly facilitated retrenchment.

11 According to Osberg (2007, fig. 8), by 2005 the federal transfer represented 32 percent of Alberta welfare income, double its 1995 share. The Alberta case is probably fairly typical.

12 For a more detailed appreciation of the unravelling of the Liberal advantage in 1997, see Andersen and Fox (2001).

REFERENCES

Andersen, Robert, and John Fox. 2001. "Pre-election Polls and the Dynamics of the 1997 Canadian Federal Election." *Electoral Studies* 20: 87-108.

Banting, Keith G. 2006. "Dis-embedding Liberalism? The New Social Policy Paradigm in Canada." In David A. Green and Jonathan R. Kesselman, eds., *Dimensions of Inequality in Canada*, 417-52. Vancouver: UBC Press.

Bartolini, Stefano. 2000. *The Political Mobilization of the European Left, 1860-1980*. Cambridge: Cambridge University Press.

Battle, Ken. 2001. *Relentless Incrementalism: Deconstructing and Reconstructing Canadian Income Security Policy*. Ottawa: Caledon Institute of Social Policy.

–. 2003. *Sustaining Public Pensions in Canada: A Tale of Two Reforms*. Ottawa: Caledon Institute of Social Policy.

Battle, Ken, Michael Mendelson, and Sherri Torjman. 2005. "The Modernization Mantra: Toward a New Architecture for Canada's Adult Benefits." *Canadian Public Policy/Analyse de Politiques* 31: 431-37.

Budge, Ian, Hans-Dieter Klingemann, Andrea Volkens, Judith Bara, and Eric Tanenbaum. 2001. *Mapping Policy Preferences: Estimates for Parties, Electors, and Governments, 1945-98*. Oxford: Oxford University Press.

Canada. 1994. *A New Framework for Economic Policy*. Ottawa: Finance Canada.

Duverger, Maurice. (1954) 1963. *Political Parties: Their Organization and Activity in the Modern State*. Trans. Barbara North and Robert North. New York: Wiley.

Esping-Andersen, Gøsta. 1990. *The Three Worlds of Welfare Capitalism*. Princeton, NJ: Princeton University Press.

Frenette, Marc, David A. Green, and Kevin Milligan. 2009. "Taxes, Transfers, and Canadian Income Inequality." *Canadian Public Policy/Analyse de Politiques* 35: 389-411.

Greenspon, Edward, and Anthony Wilson-Smith. 1996. *Double Vision: The Inside Story of the Liberals in Power*. Toronto: Doubleday Canada.

Heisz, Andrew. 2007. "Income Inequality and Redistribution in Canada: 1976 to 2004." In *Analytic Studies Branch Paper Series*. Ottawa: Statistics Canada.

Horowitz, Gad. 1968. *Canadian Labour in Politics.* Toronto: University of Toronto Press.
Huber, Evelyne, and John D. Stephens. 2001. *Development and Crisis of the Welfare State: Parties and Policies in Global Markets.* Chicago: University of Chicago Press.
Iversen, Torben, and David Soskice. 2006. "Electoral Institutions, Parties and the Politics of Class: Why Some Democracies Distribute More Than Others." *American Political Science Review* 100: 165-81.
Johnston, Richard, and Fred Cutler. 2009. "Canada: The Puzzle of Local Three-Party Competition." In Bernard Grofman, André Blais, and Shaun Bowler, eds., *Duverger's Law of Plurality Voting: The Logic of Party Competition in Canada, India, the United Kingdom and the United States,* 83-96. New York: Springer.
Kenworthy, Lane, and Jonas Pontusson. 2005. "Rising Inequality and the Politics of Redistribution in Affluent Countries." *Perspectives on Politics* 3: 449-71.
Klingemann, Hans-Dieter, Andrea Volkens, Judith Bara, Ian Budge, and Michael McDonald. 2006. *Mapping Policy Preferences II: Estimates for Parties, Electors, and Governments in Eastern Europe, European Union and OECD, 1990-2003.* Oxford: Oxford University Press.
Korpi, Walter. 1983. *The Democratic Class Struggle.* London: Routledge.
–. 1989. "Power, Politics, and State Autonomy in the Development of Social Citizenship: Social Rights during Sickness in Eighteen OECD Countries since 1930." *American Sociological Review* 54: 309-28.
Korpi, Walter, and Joakim Palme. 2003. "New Politics and Class Politics in the Context of Austerity and Globalization: Welfare State Regress in 18 Countries, 1975-95." *American Political Science Review* 97: 425-46.
Kudrle, Robert T., and Theodore R. Marmor 1981. "The Development of Welfare States in North America." In Peter Flora and Arnold Heidenheimer, eds., *The Development of Welfare States in Europe and America.* New Brunswick, NJ: Transaction Books.
Lijphart, Arend. 1999. *Patterns of Democracy: Government Forms and Performance in Thirty-Six Countries.* New Haven: Yale University Press.
McCall-Newman, Christina. 1982. *Grits: An Intimate Portrait of the Liberal Party.* Toronto: Macmillan.
Mulé, Rosa. 2001. *Political Parties, Games and Redistribution.* Cambridge: Cambridge University Press.
Myles, John. 2010. "The Inequality Surge: Changes in the Family Life Course Are the Main Cause." *Inroads: The Canadian Journal of Opinion* 26: 66-73.
Nadeau, Richard. 1990. "L'effet lune de miel dans un contexte parlementaire: le cas canadien." *Canadian Journal of Political Science* 23: 483-97.
Organisation for Economic Cooperation and Development (OECD). 2011. *OECDStatExtracts.* http://stats.oecd.org/Index.aspx?DataSetCode=UN_DEN.
Osberg, Lars. 1981. *Economic Inequality in Canada.* Toronto: Butterworths.
–. 2007. "A Quarter Century of Economic Inequality in Canada 1981-2006." Halifax: Dalhousie University, unpublished manuscript.

Pierson, Paul. 1994. *Dismantling the Welfare State? Reagan, Thatcher, and the Politics of Retrenchment.* Cambridge: Cambridge University Press.

—. 1996. "The New Politics of the Welfare State." *World Politics* 48: 143-79.

Smith, Denis. 1973. *Gentle Patriot: A Political Biography of Walter Gordon.* Edmonton: Hurtig.

Soroka, Stuart, and Christopher Wlezien. 2010. "Public Opinion and Public Policy." In John Courtney and David Smith, eds., *Oxford Handbook of Canadian Politics,* 263-80. Oxford: Oxford University Press.

Stephens, John D. 1979. *The Transition from Capitalism to Socialism.* London: Macmillan.

Wearing, John. 1981. *The L-Shaped Party: The Liberal Party of Canada, 1958-80.* Toronto: McGraw-Hill.

Whitaker, Reginald. 1977. *The Government Party: Organizing and Financing the Liberal Party of Canada, 1930-58.* Toronto: University of Toronto Press.

9 The New Bureaucratic Politics of Redistribution

DAVID A. GOOD

This chapter examines the changing nature of bureaucratic politics in the Canadian federal government and the implications for redistributive policy making.[1] The focus is not on how much bureaucratic politics matters but in what ways. Briefly stated, the changing nature of bureaucratic politics affects how redistributive policies are made, and the changing nature of redistributive policies provides different opportunities for, and places different constraints on, various public servants and their organizations in the policy-making process.[2]

No single institution in government is responsible for redistributive policies or for monitoring and managing the Gini coefficient. Indeed, the most important characteristics of redistributive policies lie beyond the capacity of any one institution and level of government. Redistributive policies involve big money and, hence, significantly affect the government's fiscal framework. For the most part, the politics of redistribution rests on the shoulders of those who know where the money is and are able to get it. Redistributive policies require management by "big politics" because they usually result in highly visible winners and losers; what is redistributed to one group gets taken from another. Their complexity and uncertainty require simplified calculations, skilful policy adjustments, and proactive public communications. Hard trade-offs are often necessary: something must be sacrificed to achieve something else – for example, targeted distribution with steep tax back rates and disincentives versus gradual tax back rates with stronger incentives but less targeting. The implementation of redistributive policies requires an efficient administrative apparatus for "sending out cheques," something increasingly integrated with the revenue/tax system. Finally, redistributive policies involve interaction among federal and provincial governments (Boychuk, Chapter 10, this volume), often with divergent political agendas and facing different pressures and accountabilities; yet some level of cooperation is necessary since each government relies upon the same taxpayers and serves the same citizens.

There has been a fundamental transformation in the roles and influence of the key players in the bureaucratic process. Traditionally, three players in redistributive policy making performed different stylized institutional roles: the *advocates*, the ministers and senior officials in the social departments such as Human Resources and Skills Development Canada or, in previous decades, National Health and Welfare and their provincial counterparts; the *restrainers*, the minister and officials in the Department of Finance; and the *gatekeepers*, working in tandem, but from different perspectives, in the Prime Minister's Office and the Privy Council Office.

This pattern of bureaucratic politics has disappeared, replaced by a centralized and politicized process. Line ministers and departments who once were policy advocates and policy developers are now *policy supporters* and delivery agents. Today, the Department of Finance not only continues to set the fiscal parameters for initiatives but is also the undisputed principal *policy designer* of the initiatives. The PCO (Privy Council Office) and, especially, the PMO (Prime Minister's Office), which once served as gatekeepers of priorities and central processes, have become the *political communicators*, interpreting and determining priorities, and being preoccupied with providing political communications through the central formulation and management of public communication strategies and messages.

This transformation has implications for the politics of redistribution. Inside government, redistributive policies are driven by fiscal and tax policy considerations, not by program departments and their political advocates. More of the redistributive benefits, whether federal or provincial, are being delivered to Canadians through the tax-transfer system administered by the increasingly "national" Canada Revenue Agency and less by line departments. More important, redistributive policy making focuses more on correcting past programs and policies and less on responding to new and unmet needs.

Redistributive policy making is opportunistic, incremental, fragmented, and obscure. Political conflict is not exposed in government debates but obfuscated and managed by centrally controlled, proactive public communications strategies. As a result, redistributive policy making is about quietly and incrementally adjusting current directions and existing programs, not debating new responses to growing levels of inequality in Canadian society.

All of this goes on in relative obscurity. Despite a significant increase in government reporting and a new-found emphasis on accountability (Lindquist 2009), performance on income redistribution is not regularly reported by government or reviewed by auditors. It is not part of the government's reporting and accountability framework. The "whole of government performance framework" reports annually on the government's performance for thirteen outcome areas, 220+ departments and agencies, and 400+ program activities, but provides no information on income distribution (President of the Treasury Board of Canada 2009). Nor is there any regular reporting of a related but different measure – the poverty rate (Fortin 2010). While family after-tax-income inequality might not change rapidly – remaining stable across the 1980s but rising between 1989 and 2004 – in the absence of ongoing reporting, there is no regular public information and hence little appreciation by citizens that, since 2004, the government's after-tax-income redistribution policies have failed to keep up with the rapid growth in family market income inequality (Heisz 2007). Canadians get more regular information about who senior public servants lunch with and how much is spent than about the distribution of income in society before and after tax transfers.

The Old Bureaucratic Politics

To understand in what ways changing bureaucratic influence has affected redistributive policy making, we need to examine the changes in the roles of the key players. As the roles have changed, so too has their relative influence. Traditionally, there have been the three players mentioned above: the advocates, the restrainers, and the gatekeepers. When it came to policy making in general and redistributive policy in particular, their interaction was conditioned by a set of behavioural norms reflecting a shared understanding between politicians and the public service (Prince 2007), first, about how things were done in Ottawa and, by extension, in provinces and, second, about the nature of bureaucratic politics.

More than a generation ago as the welfare state was being developed and refined, major redistributive policy development was driven from national blueprints, inspired and developed by royal commissions reflecting a broadly shared consensus in society. The focus of policy making was departmentally centred with strong departmental and regional ministers forcefully advocating policy positions with the professional support, expertise, and experience of their departmental officials. Policy coordination was simple and handled *ad seriatim* through the regular coordinating mechanisms of interdepartmental committees, ministerial speeches, cabinet decision making, speeches from the throne, budgets, and cooperative federalism. Initial public commitments on policy were general, with campaign promises setting out only the broad lines of policy intent. The actual program designs were developed after elections, with public servants playing a significant role in advising their respective ministers on the design and implementation of various redistributive programs.

Senior public servants were experienced departmental officials with extensive policy-sector expertise and history. There were strong partnerships between ministers and their deputies in the preparation and advocacy of policy proposals, with ministers trusting and taking advice from officials. Policy advice was confidential and candid, offered in a neutral and detached manner but designed to advocate a particular position and to counter the arguments of internal adversaries such as the Department of Finance. The public profile of officials was one of anonymity, with limited visibility to interest groups, parliamentarians, and the media. Senior officials operated as confidential and trusted advisors inside government and as neutral observers outside government.

In this environment, advocacy for redistribution was strong and focused. Concentrated in social departments, it supported powerful, high-profile political ministers who actively promoted social and redistributive policies both inside government and in public through their speeches and public appearances. Social departments with analytical support from Statistics Canada and other government agencies and advisory councils, and periodic royal commissions (there were few competing external policy think tanks), assisted their ministers in publicly framing and defining the redistributive policy issues that required attention. Central gatekeepers occasionally opened the redistributive policy gate, narrowly for particular interests (mothers, children, elderly, unemployed), but more broadly in efforts at comprehensive reform. Gatekeepers ensured a special degree of autonomy and influence for social ministers, articulating political priorities on the basis of party ideology in terms of specific groups or interests (the elderly, the poor, youth, women), managing federal-provincial relations through the accepted approach of executive federalism, and, on behalf of the prime minister, working with, through, and on restrainers in the Department of Finance.

Restraint was led by the Department of Finance, which operated as "guardian of the public purse," pushing back vigorously on advocates for redistribution through powerful internal arguments supported by centrally controlled economic and financial information. The finance argumentation stressed the importance of economic growth (increasing the size of the economic pie) over income redistribution (distributing a smaller economic pie); portrayed economic policy as the engine for social policy; emphasized a tight fiscal situation and broad array of competing demands to preclude large and ongoing expenditures on redistribution; and, whenever necessary, or as opportunities arose, played an exclusive role in the design of tax expenditure initiatives and a "challenge role" in the design of direct expenditure programs to protect their central interests, to control costs, and to ensure targeting of redistributive benefits.

The Canada Assistance Plan, adopted in 1966, best epitomizes the old bureaucratic politics of redistribution. The advocates for this cost-shared welfare assistance program included a group of federal and provincial welfare administrators whose cooperative work was facilitated by mutual acquaintanceship, often friendship, and shared professional norms. The norms were established in a blueprint for the program developed by the Canadian Welfare Council in its 1958 document, *Social Security for Canada*. The consensus among welfare administrators on the key elements of the plan was rapidly agreed to by their federal and provincial ministers, who absorbed the norms and attitudes of their departments. Complexity was handled through an extensive and open consultative process involving federal and provincial officials. Federal officials recognized the need to tread lightly in expanding their role in an area of provincial jurisdiction. With limited federal experience and information in welfare delivery, the practical advice of provincial officials was essential to ensuring smooth and effective implementation. The gatekeepers in the PMO, who were particularly sensitive to provincial demands, saw this as an opportunity to "complete the welfare state," as Prime Minister Pearson sometimes put it. The restrainers – the Department of Finance and the Treasury Board – believed that maximum effectiveness could be achieved by avoiding stringent federal standards and rigid program controls and that the measures should contain few conditions – only enough to satisfy Parliament and to maintain an element of federal financial control (Dyck 1976; Splane 2003).

While inherent conflict was built into the distinct roles among these advocates, restrainers, and gatekeepers, cooperation and negotiation ensured that the contentious issues could be momentarily resolved and policy formulated. Mutual expectations reduced the conflicts and the burden of complex calculations, and curtailed and channelled the extent of policy change. Change was a mix of periodic major policy reform, such as CAP, interspersed with regular and ongoing policy adjustments and improvements drawing upon the precedent of previous innovations. This stable and predictable pattern of bureaucratic politics supported and nurtured the roles and their interactions. It shaped how hard advocates pushed, how hard restrainers pushed back, and the types of pushing and pulling done by the gatekeepers. Over the 1960s and well in to the 1990s, it resulted in a pattern of significant government tax-transfer redistribution policies that kept pace with the growth and change in before-tax family market income (Heisz 2007).

The New Bureaucratic Politics

Over the past generation, and more intensely during the past decade, changes in bureaucratic politics have affected the redistributive policy-making process and changed the roles of the key actors. The most significant and far-reaching changes are noted below. There has been a concentration of authority and influence in the hands of the prime minister and his close advisors, with the prime minister becoming the exclusive political minister of government (Savoie 1999).[3] The number of influential political staffers in the operations of government has increased, which, given the five-year prohibition on former staff from lobbying government, has resulted in younger, less experienced, and more partisan political staff (Zussman 2009; Davis 2010). There has been a growing insistence on the political control of government communications by the centre of government to present a favourable image in the face of a probing and relentless media and the expanded use of access to information. This has been coupled with a more aggressive media in an environment characterized by "spin politics" by governments and "gotya journalism" by reporters.

Inside government there has been a weakening of the policy capacity of line departments and a concentration of the government's policy capacity within the Department of Finance, with the finance minister being the policy minister for major changes, and line departments, including the Canada Revenue Agency, being the delivery agents. There is a greater diversity of informational inputs for policy making from external sources (think tanks, lobbyists, interest groups, special purpose government-appointed commissions, and inquiries, etc.), with deputy ministers and their policy staffs no longer the sole source of policy advice to ministers. In parallel, there has been an expansion and politicizing of independent think tanks with increased capacity, through sophisticated networks and linkages, to influence political parties, governments, and the media (Savoie 2010). There has been a preoccupation with accountability in government, numerous parliamentary watchdogs have been appointed and strengthened, and the anonymity of senior public servants has been reduced and their personal accountability before parliamentarians has been increased. There has been an increasing aversion to risk on the part of public servants and an increased partisanship on the part of politicians. Citizen trust in government has declined and so, too, has public deference to government, its authority, and its institutions (Nevitte 1996). There is an expectation that the public service will be enthusiastic about the government's agenda and will promote it rather than simply explain it. Taken together these changes represent nothing short of a "new political governance" (Aucoin 2008; Bakvis and Jarvis 2012), and they are changing the roles, functions, interactions, and behavioural norms of the key players in the redistributive policy-making process.

The focus of redistributive policy making is increasingly central agency (PMO, PCO, and Department of Finance) centred and driven as a basis for strategically positioning issues, designing programs, and managing political conflict. The Department of Finance is undertaking the policy analysis and design, bypassing social departments, drawing directly upon pre-selected think tanks and external advisors, and engaging directly with provincial governments on the redistributive and other aspects of tax and expenditure proposals. With a larger portion of redistributive policies being implemented through the tax system administered by the Canada Revenue Agency (Boadway and Cuff, Chapter 14, this volume), the reach and grasp of the Department of Finance has expanded considerably.

The most critical issues of policy direction, resources, and program design are being handled directly and exclusively by the central players controlling the major action channels (e.g., the budget preparation process or the prime ministerial decision process), with line departments undertaking the difficult, often frustrating, and time-consuming "horizontal work" of coordinating policy implementation through an interdepartmental and intergovernmental maze. Senior public servants are becoming generalist managers with more expertise in decision processes and systems and less knowledge of the substantive policy issues of redistribution. The relationship between line ministers and their deputies is porous, and alternative policy advice to ministers comes from multiple sources, both inside and outside government. Further, the policy advice of deputy ministers is becoming guarded, provided in a compliant fashion to address predetermined priorities.

While the policy process is tightly controlled internally by central agents, notably the PCO and the Department of Finance, it is more open to outsiders – research institutes, think tanks, consultants, and pollsters – and the profile of officials is less anonymous and more visible to outside groups, parliamentarians, and the media. Perhaps not surprisingly, the turnover of deputy ministers and policy staff in line departments is rapid, with a consequential loss in policy capacity, knowledge, and expertise, the striking exception being the Department of Finance (Axworthy and Burch 2010).

All of this has resulted in the fundamental transformation of the roles of the key players. Line ministers and departments who once were policy advocates and policy developers inside government are now *policy supporters* and delivery agents. Today, the Department of Finance not only continues to set the fiscal parameters for initiatives but has become the undisputed *policy designer* of the initiatives. The PCO and, especially, the PMO, which once served as gatekeepers of priorities and central processes, have become the *political communicators,* interpreting and determining priorities and preoccupied with the formulation and management of public communication strategies and messages.

The changing nature of redistributive policies has led to the ever-more influential role of the Department of Finance and the squeezing out of social departments in the design of redistributive programs. As redistributive programs have become less universal and more targeted,[4] the tax system, with its common definition of family income, has become the exclusive mechanism for the efficient design and delivery of income-tested government programs. Thus, redistributive policy and the tax system have become increasingly intertwined. In contrast to needs-tested social assistance, benefits delivered through the tax system are administratively simple, efficient, fair, and non-stigmatizing. Finance, with its large and expert Tax Policy Branch (165 persons), jealously guards the tax system, and there are no rivals to its tax policy expertise anywhere in government.

Given these new roles, redistributive policy making does not proceed from an explicit comprehensive government-wide framework as in 1985, when it followed the Macdonald Commission on the Economic Union and Development Prospects for Canada. Nor is it a visible public contestation of competing policy frameworks as in the mid-1990s, when the activist social policy visions of Lloyd Axworthy, minister of Human Resources Development Canada, fell victim to the fiscal imperatives and deficit reduction of Finance Minister Paul Martin and his department (Battle and Torjman 1995). Today, the framework is deliberately partial and explicitly political, emerging from the quiet interplay of the political communicators in the PMO and the policy designers in the Department of Finance. To the extent that redistributive policy making is undertaken, it is a by-product of the forces of economics and politics, not a clearly articulated and predetermined set of explicit policy objectives about redistribution. Redistributive benefits are not cast as measures to achieve a more equitable distribution of income in society but, rather, as tax cuts to leave more income in the pockets of certain groups or as initiatives to encourage welfare recipients to seek work.

Today, redistributive policy emerges incrementally through opportunities inherent in the Department of Finance blueprint (the most recent being *Advantage Canada*), with its emphasis on fiscal and tax matters, and from the PMO, with its focus on the political interests and electoral intentions of particular groups – children, mothers, the elderly, immigrants, workers, and the disabled. Even within these groups, as a way of distinguishing, for electoral purposes, the government's policies from those of the opposition parties, there can be further segmentation through political targeting along the lines of ethnicity, constituency, rural versus urban, age, or gender.

What links these roles today is less about designing comprehensive income redistribution policies to reduce an inequitable distribution of market income than it is about correcting problems resulting from past programs. Pierson (1994, 9) notes: "Today's policymakers must operate in an environment fundamentally conditioned by policies inherited from the past. These policy structures influence the resources available to both retrenchment advocates and opponents, and also the prospects for shaping viable political strategies." And, as Heclo (1974, 287 and 303) puts it:

> Anyone willing to follow the detailed twists and turns of contemporary social policy cannot fail to be impressed by the ever changing kaleidoscope of new problems overlooked and/or created by each preceding "solution" ... Social policy has most frequently evolved as a corrective less to social conditions as such and more to the perceived failings of previous policy.

When it comes to policy making, the Department of Finance does not begin with an analysis of the distribution of market income to determine what gap public policy should fill to ensure a more equitable distribution of income; rather, it focuses on correcting specific problems created by past policies. For example, in recent years it became evident that some low-income welfare recipients were caught in a "welfare trap," discouraged from getting and keeping a job because it would mean paying higher taxes and receiving reduced benefits. For the Department of Finance, the practical solution was not to attempt to convince provinces and their welfare agencies to adjust income benefits under their welfare schemes but, rather, to focus on incremental changes in the tax system under the direct control of the department.

To this end, in the early 2000s, the Department of Finance, drawing on the experience of a pilot project in Toronto (Modernizing Income Security for Working-Age Adults [MISWAA]) began working directly on the design of what eventually became the Working Income Tax Benefit. A refundable tax credit, it supplements the earnings of low-income workers to ensure they are better off getting a job. The policy has the support of two different political parties. It was first proposed in 2005 in a discussion paper by Liberal finance minister Ralph Goodale, introduced in the 2007 budget by Conservative finance minister Jim Flaherty, and expanded in the 2009 budget.

Opportunistic, Incremental, Fragmented, and Obscure

How the new bureaucratic politics of redistribution operates is best illustrated by examining how the changing roles of line departments, central agencies (the PCO and the Department of Finance), and the PMO have altered the redistributive policy-making process. One observer describes the process as "relentless incrementalism," in which

> strings of reforms, seemingly small and discrete when made ... accumulate to become more than the sum of their parts. [It] is purposeful and patterned, not haphazard and unintended. The drip drip drip of individual changes over time carve substantial and planned shifts in the structure and objectives of public policy. (Battle 2001, 51)

As noted above, and as illustrated by the policy examples below, the new bureaucratic politics of redistributive policy making has become opportunistic, incremental, fragmented, and obscure.

Policy Making Is Opportunistic

Policy opportunities arise when there is a "fit" between the political, economic, and social events of the external environment and the immediate objectives and capacities of the government. At most times and for most policy areas, the steady stream of diverse and contradictory external events and circumstances provides little or no opportunity for alignment. Periodically, however, there is a potential for alignment, with the actual fit and timing being determined through the interaction of the political communicators in the PMO and the policy designers in the Department of Finance. The calculus of the communicators is political and that of the policy designers is fiscal.

Opportunities last for a limited time. From the early 1980s to the early 1990s, there was considerable opportunity and sufficient fiscal flexibility to make difficult but gradual changes to the major redistributive programs for children and the elderly by moving from universal programs to targeted programs. By reducing direct expenditures, taxing back benefits, and instituting refundable tax credits, universal programs were gradually eliminated, with a substantial part of the savings secured by reducing or eliminating benefits for upper-middle and higher-income Canadians and redirecting them to lower-income individuals and families. However, within a decade, the pool of "upper-end" savings was expended and major redistributive reforms slowed as securing further savings by confronting middle-income recipients or by increasing taxes was politically prohibitive.

Sometimes opportunities are predictable and can be used to secure agreement to important and difficult redistributive policy changes, as with the Canada Pension Plan in the mid-1990s (Myles, Chapter 13, this volume). A 1985 federal-provincial agreement established a twenty-five-year "rolling" schedule of rate increases for the Canada Pension Plan (CPP), with the requirement of reviews by finance ministers every five years. More significantly, and buried more deeply in the agreement, was a powerful default provision designed by a Department of Finance official. If ministers could not agree on a new rate schedule after each review, a formula would be triggered, automatically mandating rate increases large enough to generate, over fifteen years, a fund equal to two years of the following year's expenditures. This default provision became the benchmark for extensive analysis and difficult federal-provincial negotiations, and "without it," concludes one analyst, "the reforms of the mid-1990s might never have occurred" (Little 2008, 64).

Policy Making Is Incremental
Against the backdrop of the failure of past efforts at comprehensive "big bang" reforms – the most recent being the Social Security Review led by

Lloyd Axworthy in the mid-1990s – redistributive policy change has become incremental, involving small, gradual changes over many years. Redistributive policy making in the area of disability benefits is especially incremental, and, while nearly every budget contains new announcements, the overall pattern of achievement is "uneven and incomplete" (Prince 2009). Changes in Employment Insurance (EI) since 1996, when it was converted from UI, moving from "passive" dependence towards "active" employment, have been incremental, with regular changes in entrance requirements for eligibility, hours-based coverage, maximum duration of benefits, extended benefits, and the like. And the recent expansions in maternity and parental leave since 2000 have been gradual and incremental over the past decade.

Even child benefits, the area of redistributive policy boasting the most significant change and increase in benefits over the past two decades, has seen gradual and incremental change. In 1989, there was a clawback on Family Allowances, then full income testing with the 1993 Child Tax Benefit (which replaced Family Allowances). By 1998, the Liberal government replaced the Child Tax Benefit with the Canada Child Tax Benefit, which eliminated the Working Income Supplement for the working poor but increased and equalized the benefits of low-income families. Full indexation of the Canada Child Tax Benefit was restored in 2000. Through federal-provincial agreements under the National Child Benefit, provinces and territories began to redirect savings from reductions in their welfare programs to a range of social service programs for low-income families with children. This was followed by another federal-provincial agreement under which Ottawa provided financial support to the tune of $5 billion over five years to help provinces build early learning and childcare services. In 2003, the Canada Child Tax Benefit received a multi-year series of enrichments, and a Child Disability Benefit, payable on behalf of children with severe disabilities living in low- and modest-income families, was introduced. In 2004, the government announced the Canada Learning Bond to help low-income families save towards their children's postsecondary education.

Even with a change in ideology when, in 2006, the new Conservative government eliminated support for daycare facilities and instituted direct support for parents, the policy changes were incremental and were described by one analyst as "back to the future" (Battle 2008, 20). The government eliminated the $5 billion federal-provincial Early Learning and Child Care agreement and instituted the Universal Child Care Benefit, paying $100 a month for children under six to all families whatever their income. At the same time, the Canada Child Tax Benefit's young child supplement was abolished. Then, in 2007, the non-refundable $2,000 Child Tax Credit, payable on behalf of children under eighteen, was introduced. This non-refundable tax credit has a perverse distribution: non-poor families receive $300 per child, including the very rich; some low-income families receive a smaller amount; and the poorest get nothing at all because they do not owe income tax. Clearly, as new programs are introduced on top of old ones, the problems being created will lead to further incremental policy adjustment in the future.

Incremental change does not mean that policy changes are poorly thought out; rather, it is the result of gradual adjustments and adaptations to existing policies over time. Affordability and the prospect of establishing a precedent are often the limiting factors that determine whether to hold back on a policy, to defer it to the future, or to announce it well in advance of the date at which it will take effect. When it comes to the distribution of the benefits of most redistributive programs, the policy designers in the Department of Finance invariably focus on five key technical decisions: (1) the benefit level; (2) the eligibility criteria; (3) the turning point (the income level at which benefits are taxed back) and whether it will be indexed to inflation; (4) the tax-back rate (which, along with the turning point, determines the break-even point at which benefits are phased out); and (5) whether the tax credit will be refundable (i.e., low-income beneficiaries will receive a positive benefit payment over and above any tax that they may owe). While these decisions need to be considered together, small adjustments to any of them – to extend or reduce benefits or to ramp up or ramp down various provisions – are ongoing over time.

Most programs, for example the Child Tax Credit, the National Child Benefit, the Canada Child Tax Benefit, the Universal Child Care Benefit, and the Disability Tax Savings Account, start small and are slowly ramped up. Increments are determined in terms of how much money is available to spend and on whether it is enough to make a difference rather than on what policy change should be made. Some seemingly technical policy changes are particularly significant for improving the effectiveness of the redistributive program – for example, whether to index the benefit and the turning point or whether to make a tax credit refundable. At the same time, the Department of Finance is worried about the precedent that would be set and the costs that would be involved. For example, despite extensive work with numerous think tanks and interest groups over several years, spanning both Liberal and Conservative governments, the Department of Finance has been reluctant to make the Disability Tax Savings Account refundable.

Indeed, indexation of turning points and making tax credits refundable are often the last incremental changes to be made.

The incremental nature of policy change provides different opportunities and constraints for think tanks in their dealings with the Department of Finance. Those with the capacity and reputation for quantitative and tax analysis, such as the Caledon Institute, the Centre for Policy Alternatives, and the CD Howe Institute, are actively engaged by the Department of Finance; those with an advocacy focus on direct expenditure programs, such as Campaign 2000 and the Childcare Resource and Research Unit, are almost never engaged (Phillips, Chapter 5, this volume). In the case of retirement income, the use of a quantitatively oriented policy analyst such as Jack Mintz, a tax expert at the University of Calgary, avails the Department of Finance and its provincial counterparts of the opportunity to define the actual policy problem, how it differs among income groups, what is and is not "broken," and what steps can be taken by the business community as the country moves out of recession. As these policy problems have become defined and quantified, a consensus has emerged whereby political leaders have "put major pension reform on the back burner in Canada and [will] consider a slower 'incremental' approach over the next 10 years" (McFarland and McNish 2010).

Policy Making Is Fragmented

No organization in government has the responsibility for taking a comprehensive approach to income redistribution, to monitor the overall changes and cumulative effects that emerge from the market income, and to assess the effects of government policy. While Statistics Canada produces occasional studies, it does not regularly report on the distribution of income in the same way as it does, for example, on unemployment rates, which are released monthly in its high profile and widely reported Labour Force Survey. Some continue to press for a single Guaranteed Annual Income (GAI) Program, arguing that it is the only way to ensure that there is a comprehensive, streamlined, understandable, and fully integrated policy that can be regularly monitored. Others counter that there already is a de facto GAI at various stages of maturity in a number of areas – seniors' benefits, children's benefits, low-income workers' benefits, and various refundable tax credits.

Fragmentation is natural, given the complexity inherent in a comprehensive approach to income redistribution. The broader the approach, the more complex the decision making and the greater the risk that the assumed benefits of comprehensiveness will be displaced by the real costs of the "seamless web" of inaction. As a result, redistributive policy-making processes usually tend to be focused on particular interests and recipients, with each process being determined by the particularized programming and shaped by the public service agents who control the program instruments. For example, policy making for elderly benefits, with simple one-time eligibility requirements determined by age and standardized monthly payments delivered as direct deposits to the bank accounts of seniors through a combination of direct expenditures and tax expenditures, is shaped by the Department of Finance. Policy making for employment insurance benefits, a direct expenditure program requiring the application of complex rules and regulations by public servants to determine eligibility and payment levels under changing economic circumstances, is shaped by Human Resources and Skills Development Canada. Policy making for child benefits, determined on the basis of family income as used extensively for income tax purposes, is undertaken by the Department of Finance and delivered by the Canada Revenue Agency through the tax-transfer system.[5] The CPP policy, which involves coordinated decision making on financing – employer and employee contributions – and on benefit levels is shaped by the Department of Finance through negotiations with its provincial counterparts (Myles, Chapter 13, this volume).

At another level, fragmentation results from the political requirement to focus and deliver on priorities, targeting benefits to various political interests and constituencies. Because voters punish governments who renege on their election promises, many of which are general in nature, political parties find it in their best interest to make explicit and detailed campaign commitments and then to deliver on these commitments once in government. In recent years, key government priorities, particularly on matters of major expenditure, are no longer decided through formal cabinet decision-making processes but by prime ministers, usually but not always with their closest advisors (Goldenberg 2006; Good 2007). When Prime Minister Chrétien insisted that children become a government priority in 1997, the focus for action was the Department of Finance, which controls the tax-transfer system.

Fragmentation does not preclude learning. In fact, there has been much policy learning within the bureaucracy through the imitation of policy instruments across the areas of children, elderly, working poor, and persons with disabilities. Experience derived from the introduction of a refundable tax credit for children is applied to the working poor. More broadly, learning across policy areas has included the conversion of regressive tax deductions to progressive refundable tax credits, the introduction of tax clawbacks to target and eventually eliminate universal direct expenditure programs, and the use of grants and tax incentives to encourage various savings plans in the areas of retirement, education, and disability. The locus of this learning is the tax-transfer system, and it centres on the officials in the Department of Finance.

Policy Making Is Obscure
Redistributive policy making is fundamentally divisive and prone to political resistance. In the name of equitable distribution of income, what one group receives from government is paid for by another. Political communicators and policy designers spend much of their time figuring out how best to reduce political resistance through compensation and obfuscation (Pierson 1994). The former involves a side payment to compensate those adversely affected by a proposed policy change. And, while this can be the most effective strategy, it is also the most expensive for government. One form of compensation used extensively and effectively in the late 1970s and early 1980s involved the tax-transfer system. The Department of National Health and Welfare's design and development of the refundable Child Tax Credit in 1978, and the Department of Finance's reluctant acceptance that a tax provision in the form of a highly regressive tax deduction could be redesigned into a progressive refundable tax credit, expanded the scope for compensating low-income families for a reduction in their Family Allowance payments. During periods of social welfare retrenchment in the mid-1980s and 1990s, compensation was used to gradually reduce and eventually to eliminate benefit levels in Family Allowances while refundable tax credits were slowly put in place. Similarly, the universality of Old Age Security (OAS) benefits was eliminated with little public resistance by completely taxing back the benefits of high-income recipients while maintaining the perception of a universal direct payment.

Today, in a more restricted fiscal environment, government's strategy of choice is obfuscation. It involves the manipulation of information concerning the policy change and has become the most important and effective strategy for minimizing political resistance. According to Pierson (1994, 8): "Far more than in the era of welfare state expansion, struggles over social policy become struggles over information about the causes and consequences of policy change." The strategy rests on two components. One is the sheer complexity of the policy field of income redistribution: a myriad of interacting policies and programs; a multiplicity of governments; the provision of benefits through both direct expenditures and tax expenditures; the inherent complexity and multiple purposes of the tax system; the technicalities of benefit levels, tax back rates, turning points, and indexation; the changing definitions and diversity of families and individuals; and the difficulties in determining policy impacts. The policy designers in the Department of Finance deal with this complexity by breaking big issues into manageable problems and incrementally adjusting existing instruments and programs in an effort to bring about modest improvement.

The other component of the strategy of obfuscation is the reconstruction of "causal chains" linking negative or positive events to particular redistributive policy choices and to actions of specific governments and politicians (Arnold 1990). Because causal linkages are uncertain and complex, political communications are used to isolate and link positive events to the government and negative events to the opposition. The benefits of policies are played up, and the costs and negative consequences are played down, if they are played at all. Negative consequences are less likely to be observed by citizens if they are spread widely rather than concentrated and if they are diffused over time rather than set out in a single initiative. The political voice for the reconstruction of causal chains emanates from the thirty-seven-person media staff in the PMO.

At one level, when it comes to obfuscation there is a natural and productive tension between the political communicators in the PMO and the program designers of the Department of Finance. On the one hand, the requirement for certainty and simplicity in the implementation of redistributive programs requires that the program designers in the Department of Finance bring clarity to the program in terms of eligibility criteria, benefit levels, program delivery, and expected results; on the other hand, the considerable uncertainty associated with promised outcomes and worldly events provides opportunities for proactive messaging by political communicators as they attempt to create positive first impressions that will become lasting impressions.

At a broader level, however, there is a complementary relationship as both parties engage in their own forms of obfuscation in order to minimize public resistance. For example, in the 2007 budget, the political communicators in the PMO spun the $2,000 Child Tax Credit as if every parent with a child under eighteen years of age were receiving $2,000 in cash through a tax cut. The program designers in the Department of Finance quietly and obscurely acknowledged in the budget that the tax credit was $2,000 times the lowest tax rate of 15 percent, but they left readers to do their own math.[6]

To be sure, in the past, redistributive policy making has displayed some of these four characteristics – opportunism, incrementalism, fragmentation, and obscurantism – but never all at once and never with such pattern and purpose. The increased complexity of redistributive programs is both a contributor to, and a cause of, this form of policy making. The complexity results from delivery by all three levels of government as well as by private- and voluntary-sector organizations. There are different and competing designs across programs and significant complexities in integrated tax expenditure and direct expenditure programs. There are also the multiple and competing objectives of the tax system itself. As a result, the public is often confused and uncertain about programs – who is responsible for them and who is delivering them. This reinforces a policy process in which change is opportunistic, incremental, fragmented, and obscure. It is policy change "by stealth," whereby each individual change, through a steady stream of continuous announcements, is largely imperceptible to the public (Battle 1990), which, in turn, provides opportunities for political communicators to play up positive benefits and to play down the negative costs. Redistributive policy making is a continuous stream of incremental and fragmented adjustments triggered by opportunities and obscured through political communications in an effort to minimize political resistance and to maximize political benefit.

Getting a Grip

At the broadest level, the public service has played and continues to play an important role in the making of redistributive policy. In general terms, what Heclo (1974, 304) concluded about the United Kingdom a generation ago still applies to Canada:

> In both expansionary and restrictive directions, administrative actors have been crucial in giving concrete substance to new policy initiatives and in elaborating already established approaches. What officials have rarely been able to do is to fire up, by themselves, sufficient political steam to cast new policies *ex nihilo*. This corrective – or if one prefers, reactive – role does not minimize the administrative contribution, for much of social policy development has been and remains an elaboration rather than redirection of the original liberal framework.

At a more particularized level, however, there have been important changes. To say that the public service no longer has a grip on substantive redistributive policy making would be an exaggeration. To say the grip has become increasingly concentrated in the hands of the Department of Finance and in advisors close to the prime minister would be closer to the truth. On matters of substantive policy making the reach and grasp of the 765-person Department of Finance is considerable. When it comes to fiscal policy, tax policy, and federal-provincial fiscal relations, all of which are important levers in redistributive policy making, the Department of Finance is unchallenged. When there is a policy opportunity, such as emerged in 1993 when the government transferred its major social policy responsibilities from the old National Health and Welfare to the new Human Resources Development Canada, the Department of Finance stepped in to fill the void. As one insider put it, "Finance Department's Real Bouchard 'knew as much about the CPP as anyone in HRDC. Part of the Finance takeover was the HRDC vacuum'" (Little 2008, 69).

Compared to line departments, the Department of Finance's policy capacity is considerable – be it policy research, integrated policy frameworks, policy analysis, agenda setting, policy consultations, or policy advice. Policy frameworks such as *Advantage Canada* are Department of Finance-developed, with a reach that extends across the entire government. Policy analysis and advice flow through a budget preparation process that is tightly controlled by the department. Fiscal policy holds a grip on redistributive policy making, and tax policy has become the instrument of choice. As a policy centre with no program delivery responsibilities, the Department of Finance is largely immune from administrative "screw-ups," which have diverted the policy attention and weakened the credibility of line departments (the regular public reporting by auditors and watchdogs has made them political targets of the opposition and the media). Yet when it comes to implementation, the Department of Finance can be assured that redistributive benefits will be delivered through the tax system in a reliable, predictable, and professional manner by its close partner, the Canada Revenue Agency, with responsibility for management and direction vested in the commissioner (a deputy minister-level appointment) rather than in the minister (Brown 2009; Auditor General of Canada 2010).

The other pair of hands with a grip on redistributive policy making are the PMO and the PCO, which hold tightly to political control, priority setting, and political communications. To be sure, the PMO's grip has always been important. But its influence on redistributive policy was usually exercised with and through social ministers by, for example, leveraging the advocacy of the minister and the Department of National Health and Welfare to get the Department of Finance to agree in 1978 to the *refundable child tax credit*. The short-lived Ministry of State for Social Development (1979-84), with its skill in packaging policy proposals, expanded the scope for policy direction from the prime minister and the PCO. As late as 1993, the creation of the "super-ministry" – Human Resources Development Canada – offered a partial and, in some areas, effective policy counterweight to the Department of Finance. Today, however, the influence on policy is from the centre of government; it is direct, political, and focused on the Department of Finance.

Along with less advocacy for redistribution from social and civil society groups outside government (Coleman, Chapter 4, this volume; Phillips, Chapter 5, this volume; Phillips 2010), there has been less advocacy inside. Indeed, the grip on advocacy within government for redistributive policy has been loosened at political and bureaucratic levels. Today, social ministers earn their reputations not for their advocacy of major policy change but for how well they deal with the steady stream of crises at their doorsteps. Traditionally, interactions between the Department of Finance and major social departments on matters of redistributive policy took place at the most senior level of ministers and deputy ministers, involving issues of policy priority and direction as well as program design. Today, any interaction is likely to be at the working level, addressing issues of data, analysis, and program implementation. Tellingly, the clerk of Privy Council has exhorted senior public servants to "think big in your role as ADMs (Assistant Deputy Ministers)" (Wouters 2009). This will be a difficult task for risk-averse public servants in line departments, caught up in a web of rules and facing little ministerial demand for policy ideas in an increasingly diffuse policy-making process.

Looking Ahead

On the one hand, those who yearn for the old bureaucratic politics of redistributive policy making will find little comfort in the future. The fundamental forces of "new political governance" that are changing bureaucratic behaviour inside government are not likely to be reversed or even to abate. On the other hand, those who lament the general decline in the policy capacity of social and other line departments with regard to major issues of redistribution should take some comfort in the concentrated professional, non-partisan policy expertise resident in the Department of Finance. Its well-established internal policy analysis and its new-found ability to reach out directly and selectively to policy think tanks for study and advice in advance of budget preparations provide important counterweights to the centralized and controlled political communications of the PMO. The decline of institutionally based advocacy for income redistribution within government does not preclude productive policy debates within the Department of Finance across its four key branches – economic and fiscal policy, economic development and corporate finance, tax policy, and federal-provincial relations and social policy. Yet the department remains today as it was described thirty-five years ago by an assistant deputy minister: "Neither a mutual admiration society nor a place where you can score debating points" (Good 1980, 64).

Those who wish to hear and to see more substantive policy debate and action on redistributive issues inside government will be disappointed with the new bureaucratic politics. Policy making is ideologically driven and tightly controlled around the internal budget preparation process, with limited ventilation and external challenge on major policy issues. But, as Heclo (1974, 283) reminds us, bureaucratic politics is only one variable that affects redistributive policy making, and, while it does not reside in the "outer darkness of statistical insignificance," it is hardly the principal determinant of policy. This suggests that policy analysis and policy debate on matters of income redistribution need to occur more regularly and with greater focus *outside* government – for example, in and around political parties.

In the face of growing concerns about labour productivity, demographic change, and the effects of world economic recession, policy attention is now being paid separately to issues of EI and retirement income. Those who look to a broader, more comprehensive and integrated approach to what some call "adult benefits" (a better label is yet to emerge), including the working poor, the Working Income Tax Benefit (WITB), EI, workers' compensation benefits, welfare, youth education and employment, and retirement benefits, should not sit back and expect it to come from government any time soon. As a first step, the concept needs to be championed through ongoing analysis and advocacy by citizens and organizations outside government. It will also need a prime minister and government with the political will and requisite skill to make it an explicit priority when the opportunity arises, and a public service with the continued policy and institutional capacity to give concrete substance and practical know-how to a comprehensive policy initiative.

NOTES

1 I broadly interpret bureaucratic politics to encompass significant changes in the way policy is made, the relationships among key institutions, central decision-making processes, the management of programs and resources, and the behavioural norms and culture of the senior public service.
2 In examining a process as complex, multifaceted, and subtle as redistributive policy making, there is risk of giving excessive weight to the perspective under investigation – bureaucratic politics. As Heclo (1974, 283) puts it: "There is sometimes an unfortunate tendency for each discipline, or specialty within a discipline, to develop a proprietary interest in a variable, taking it as a matter of honour to prove that its variable is most important or at the very least is not cast into the outer darkness of statistical insignificance."
3 Even when issues are considered by cabinet, recent prime ministers are comfortable knowing that "Cabinet decisions are the sole prerogative of the prime minister" (Goldenberg 2006, 99).
4 From 1960 to 1992, while the share of targeted direct expenditure benefits as percentage of total income transfers in the United States held steady at around 20 percent, in Canada, selective (targeted) benefits rose from 21 percent to 52 percent of income transfers, rising most rapidly after 1975. Canada now spends considerably more on selective income-tested transfers (almost all delivered through the tax system) than on universal social programs (Banting 1997).
5 One notable exception was the short-lived $5 billion Early Learning and Child Care initiative, developed in 2004 by Human Resources and Skills Development Canada under Liberal minister Ken Dryden. Based upon significant direct expenditures and federal-provincial agreements, in some respects it reflected the "old" bureaucratic politics of redistribution.
6 Ken Battle (2008, 21) points out that the answer is $300. He notes that the child credit was worth $310 when introduced in the 2007 budget as the lowest tax rate was 15.5 percent. However, in the Economic Statement of 2007, the lowest tax rate dropped from 15.5 percent to 15 percent and the credit fell by ten dollars.

REFERENCES

Arnold, R. Douglas. 1990. *The Logic of Congressional Action*. New Haven, CT: Yale University Press.

Aucoin, Peter. 2008. "New Public Management and New Public Governance." In David Siegel and Ken Rasmussen, eds., *Professionalism and Public Service: Essays in Honour of Kenneth Kernaghan*, 16-33. Toronto: University of Toronto Press.

Auditor General of Canada. 2010. *Performance Audit of Services Delivered by Selected Federal Departments*. Ottawa: Public Works and Government Services Canada.

Axworthy, Thomas S., and Julie Burch. 2010. *Closing the Implementation Gap: Improving Capacity, Accountability, Performance and Human Resource Quality in the Canadian and Ontario Public Service*. Kingston: Centre for the Study of Democracy, School of Policy Studies at Queen's University.

Bakvis, Herman, and Mark D. Jarvis. 2012. *From New Public Management to New Political Governance: Essays in Honour of Peter C. Aucoin*. Montreal and Kingston: McGill-Queen's University Press.

Banting, Keith. 1997. "The Social Policy Divide." In Keith Banting, George Hoberg, and Richard Simeon, eds., *Degrees of Freedom: Canada and the United States in a Changing World*, 267-309. Montreal and Kingston: McGill-Queen's University Press.

Battle, Ken (under the pseudonym Grattan Gray). 1990. "Social Policy by Stealth." *Policy Options* 11: 2.

–. 2001. "Relentless Incrementalism." In Keith Banting, Andrew Sharpe, and Frances St-Hilaire, eds., *The Review of Economic Performance and Social Progress*. Montreal and Ottawa: Institute for Research on Public Policy and Centre for the Study of Living Standards.

–. 2008. *A Bigger and Better Child Benefit: A $5,000 Canada Child Tax Benefit*. Ottawa: Caledon Institute of Social Policy.

Battle, Ken, and Sherri Torjman. 1995. *How Finance Re-Formed Social Policy*. Ottawa: Caledon Institute of Social Policy.

Brown, David C.G. 2009. "The Canada Revenue Agency as Separate Employer." *Canadian Public Administration* 52(4): 569-90.

Davis, Jeff. 2010. "Accountability Act Dissuading Experienced Staff from Joining Cabinet Offices." *Hill Times*, 1 February.

Dyck, Rand. 1976. "The Canada Assistance Plan." *Canadian Public Administration* 19(4): 587-602.

Fortin, Pierre. 2010. "Quebec Is Fairer." *Inroads* 26: 58-65.

Goldenberg, Eddie. 2006. *The Way It Works: Inside Ottawa*. Toronto: McClelland and Stewart.

Good, David A. 1980. *The Politics of Anticipation: Making Canadian Federal Tax Policy*. Toronto: James Lorimer Ltd.

–. 2007. *The Politics of Public Money: Spenders, Guardians, Priority Setters, and Financial Watchdogs inside the Canadian Government*. Toronto: University of Toronto Press.

Heclo, Hugh. 1974. *Modern Social Politics in Britain and Sweden*. New Haven: Yale University Press.

Heisz, Andrew. 2007. "Income Inequality and Redistribution in Canada: 1976 to 2004." Analytical Studies Branch Research Paper Series. Ottawa: Statistics Canada.

Lindquist, Evert. 2009. "How Ottawa Assesses Department/Agency Performance." In Allan M. Maslove, ed., *How Ottawa Spends, 2009-2010: Economic Upheaval and Political Dysfunction*, 47-88. Montreal and Kingston: McGill-Queen's University Press.

Little, Bruce. 2008. *Fixing the Future: How Canada's Usually Fractious Governments Worked Together to Rescue the Canada Pension Plan*. Toronto: University of Toronto Press.

McFarland, Janet, and Jacquie McNish. 2010. "Politicians Eye Business-Led Retirement Options." *Globe and Mail*, 14 April.

Nevitte, Neil. 1996. *The Decline of Deference: Canadian Value Change in Cross National Perspective.* Toronto: University of Toronto Press.

Phillips, Susan D. 2010. "Civil Society under Neglect." *The Philanthropist* 23(1): 66-74.

Pierson, Paul. 1994. *Dismantling the Welfare State? Reagan, Thatcher, and the Politics of Retrenchment.* Cambridge: University of Cambridge Press.

President of the Treasury Board of Canada. 2009. *Canada's Performance.* Ottawa: Her Majesty the Queen in Right of Canada.

Prince, Michael J. 2007. "Soft Craft, Hard Choices, Altered Context: Reflections on Twenty-Five Years of Policy Advice in Canada." In Laurent Dobuzinskis, Michael Howlett, and David Laycock, eds., *Policy Analysis in Canada: The State of the Art,* 163-85. Toronto: University of Toronto Press.

–. 2009. *Absent Citizens: Disability Politics and Policy in Canada.* Toronto: University of Toronto Press.

Savoie, Donald J. 1999. *Governing from the Centre: The Concentration of Power in Canadian Politics.* Toronto: University of Toronto Press.

–. 2010. *Power: Where Is It?* Montreal and Kingston: McGill-Queen's University Press.

Splane, Richard B. 2003. *George Davidson: Social Policy and Public Policy Exemplar.* Ottawa: Canadian Council on Social Development.

Wouters, Wayne G. 2009. "Leadership in a Chaotic World." Remarks to the Assistant Deputy Minister's Forum, Ottawa. http://www.clerk.gc.ca/eng/feature.asp?pageId=119.

Zussman, David. 2009. "Political Advisors." Background paper prepared for Expert Group on Conflict of Interest. Paris: OECD.

10

Territorial Politics and the New Politics of Redistribution

GERARD W. BOYCHUK

Canadian redistributive policy has been inextricably bound up in the ongoing struggle to preserve national unity. The politics of territorial integration shaped the development of Canadian social programs as the federal government saw national social programs as part of the glue holding together a vast country divided by linguistic and regional conflicts. Is this still the case today, or has this dynamic faded? Some argue that the retrenchment and decentralization of the last two decades, coupled with the acceptance of growing asymmetry in the position of Quebec in the federation, have made it more difficult for the federal government to appeal to the country as a whole through social policy. At the same time, others, such as Jenson as well as Green and Townsend in this volume, emphasize a new concern with social investment, which, by implication, has supplanted more traditional concerns. But when we look at certain key features of contemporary social policy, we see an ongoing concern for territorial integration. Consider the continuing importance of federal programs in redistribution, the priority federal governments give to particular programs such as child benefits, and the fact that its transfers are increasingly targeted towards the lower middle- and middle-income distribution. Territorial politics also helps explain why the enthusiasm for the social investment approach in the 2000s appeared as a federal political project rather than as the outgrowth of a broader federal-provincial policy consensus. Thus, far from fading away, a sense of nation building informed federal social policy reform efforts throughout the 1990s and continued well into the 2000s. The politics of territorial integration remains central to the politics of social policy.

The introductory section begins by summarizing the redistributive policy dynamics generated by territorial politics, focusing on competitive state building. It then outlines two competing alternative interpretations of redistributive policy change in Canada that lead one to expect that the role of territorial dynamics may be fading: the variants of federalism and the social investment perspectives. Each explanation generates distinct understandings of policy change; to this end, the second section offers a series of empirical expectations related to each regarding the new politics of redistribution and the robustness of the federal role, the diverging fate of various programs, and the differential response to new ideas about social policy at federal and provincial levels. The third section assesses these expectations in light of recent patterns of policy change. The chapter concludes that, while decentralization has occurred in some aspects of redistributive policy, the federal government has not retreated from its redistributive role, nor has its concern with the role of redistributive policy in territorial integration faded.

Explaining Redistributive Policy Change: Three Perspectives

This section begins by outlining the territorial politics perspective and how it understands the links between policy change and territorial tensions in the Canadian federation. It then sketches two additional competing perspectives of policy change and the new politics of redistribution in Canada, each suggesting that territorial dynamics are now less salient.

The Role of Territorial Politics: Competitive State Building

As noted above, historically, social policy in Canada has been heavily influenced by territorial politics. Of central importance has been the emergence of a dynamic that Banting (2005, 90) terms competitive state-building, in which different levels of government compete vigorously to occupy political space:

> For the central government, social policy has been seen as an instrument of territorial integration, part of the social glue holding together a vast country subject to powerful centrifugal tendencies. National social programmes create a network of relations between citizens and central government throughout the country, helping to define the boundaries of the national political community and enhancing the legitimacy of the federal state. However, provincial governments, especially the Québec government, have

also seen social policy as an instrument for building a distinctive community at the regional level, one reflecting the linguistic and cultural dynamics of Québécois society. For both levels of government, therefore, social policy has been an instrument not only of social justice but also of statecraft, to be deployed in the competitive processes of nation-building.

This competitive state-building dynamic has three distinct components. First, the provinces may make defensive attempts to limit state building at the federal level. The politics of Canadian federalism, which dictate in many instances that provincial agreement is either politically or constitutionally required for federal policy initiatives, offer provinces – especially larger ones – ample opportunity to do so. However, due to the political popularity of proposed programs, blocking federal social policy initiatives has not been a primary competitive state-building strategy. And the federal government has been accommodating in allowing Quebec to get ahead with its own programs – the Quebec Parental Insurance Plan being a notable example – thus forestalling potential attempts at defensive state building in that province.

The second dynamic involves "reinforcing the push for policy decentralization as an alternative to centralist schemes" (Béland and Lecours 2006, 78). Again, while other provinces are implicated, Quebec figures prominently. As the Canadian welfare state matured, the most important counterweight to centralization was resurgent Quebec nationalism (Banting 2005, 104). This has often been coupled with "various patterns of asymmetry in the administration of social policy in the country" (Béland and Lecours 2006, 78, 80). The most obvious example is Quebec's separate public pension scheme alongside the Canada Pension Plan.

A third dynamic results from the pressure on the federal government to respond to provincial policy initiatives, especially in Quebec, to reinforce its claim to be the central repository of social rights in Canada. This type of jockeying was highlighted by the role of social policy in the 1980 and 1995 Quebec referendum campaigns. In 1980, federal ministers argued that Quebecers would lose social benefits, especially their pensions, if they left Confederation. In the 1995 referendum, which occurred six months after major federal budget cuts, the federal government found itself vulnerable in the face of continuing sovereignist claims in Quebec that "the only political choice left for Quebeckers who wish[ed] to preserve their social programmes, and therefore their identity, [was] sovereignty" (Béland and Lecours 2006, 87). As Banting (2005, 134) notes: "The two battles highlighted the strategic role that politicians attribute to social policy in the life and death of states."

The Role of Federalism: Variants of Federalism

An alternative perspective on the new politics of redistribution in Canada draws on the institution of federalism – Banting's interpretation being the classic example. In explaining the divergent trajectories of various clusters of programs, he notes the models of intergovernmental relations that dominate each program area, including classical federalism, joint-decision federalism, and shared-cost federalism – each of which "has had remarkably different implications for the expansion and the restructuring of the welfare state" (Banting 2005, 95). Both the degree of influence of the ideology of the governing party and the range of governing parties drawn into decision making are strongly conditioned by the model of federalism informing a given program area. More specifically, under classical federalism, "decisions about exclusively federal programmes reflect the ideological orientation of the governing party" (ibid., 105). The joint-decision model insulates programs from the influence of governing parties; at the same time, it expands the range of parties at the table. The shared-cost model does the same without granting any province a veto, thus shifting "the ideological balances struck in the emerging policies" (ibid., 111).

In explaining change, Banting's account leans on the shifting ideological orientation of governing parties and the conditions that give rise to these shifts, although the primary focus is how they are refracted by federal institutions. The new politics of redistribution have been driven, in part, by economic changes that have contributed to an ideological shift in partisan politics (Banting 2005, 116). But these politics have flowed through the "three distinctive institutional filters created by federal institutions" (ibid., 128) mentioned above. Thus, the three models of federalism can account for variations in the new politics of redistribution across program areas and in patterns of change over time.

The Role of Ideas: The Social Investment Perspective

Another interpretation of the new politics of redistribution involves the social investment perspective, which is, at once, a theory of policy change and a framework within which to interpret a specific set of policy changes. As a theory of policy change, it emphasizes the role of ideas: "To be sure, the actions of provincial and federal actors within the new institutions of intergovernmental relations were driven by their understanding of those institutions, but they were also affected by their ideas about social policy. Both sets of ideas had altered and were pushing policy makers towards taking up new instruments" (Jenson, Chapter 2, this volume). International institutions, policy communities, and networks dominate this version of ideational diffusion. The social investment model takes a prescriptive approach with three main features:

> The first is an emphasis on education and learning to ensure that adults in the present and children in the future will be able to adapt to a knowledge-based economy that demands flexibility in employment relations and that offers many precarious jobs. The second is an orientation to the future: there is greater concern for setting the conditions for future success for individuals and countries as a whole than there is in achieving equality in the present. Finally, it is suggested that successful individuals enrich our common future and that ensuring success in the present is beneficial for the community as a whole, now and into the future. (Jenson, Chapter 2, this volume)

Similarly, Green and Townsend (Chapter 3, this volume) argue that Canadian redistributive policy has been framed in terms of a dominant idea about the causes of rising inequality in the Canadian wage and employment structure. They argue that "Canada adopted a consistent set of policies within the context of this unified theory," by which inequality was understood to be driven by a skills shortage – the policy response to which was increased investment in human capital.

Empirical Expectations Generated by the Territorial Politics Perspective and Alternative Interpretations

The territorial politics perspective and the two alternative interpretations of the new politics of redistribution in Canada sketched above – the latter two implying the faded importance of territorial dynamics in the new politics of redistribution – are not simply divergent interpretations of the same empirical patterns. Rather, they differ in their expectations of the role of the federal government in redistribution – whether it is fading, whether programs marked by distinct variants of federalism experience radically different fates, whether new ideas such as the social investment perspective are part of a cross-governmental consensus about the most desirable forms of social policy, or whether these ideas are seized upon more powerfully by one level of government as part of a political project.

A Fading Federal Role in the New Politics of Redistribution?
Much current analysis starts from the proposition that redistributive policy responsibility has been decentralized over the past two decades and that this represents a reduced federal role in redistribution. Typically drawing on literature related to loss imposition, blame avoidance, and credit-claiming, such analyses presage a fading federal role in income maintenance and redistribution and the "provincialization of social policy" (Osberg 2000, 214).

The federalism perspective points to a number of reasons to assume that the influence of territorial politics on federal policy has faded.[1] The combination of welfare state retrenchment, decentralization, and asymmetry has made it harder for federal politicians to fashion appeals to the country as a whole based on national social programs. Retrenchment means that federal politicians are in "blame avoidance" mode rather than "credit claiming" mode. Decentralization has reduced the federal role in core social programs, and asymmetry makes it more difficult to enforce federal norms not only in Quebec but elsewhere. For example, it may be politically unfeasible for the federal government to vigorously enforce Canada Health Act provisions in provinces such as Alberta when it dare not challenge deviations in Quebec. As a result, the politics of social policy and redistribution may no longer be reinforced by territorial politics. Pro-social policy coalitions were deprived of one of the arrows in their quiver as federal politicians began to look to instruments other than social policy to strengthen a sense of common identity (e.g., the Charter and individual rights). Seen in this light, the above-mentioned contrast between the role of social policy in the 1980 and 1995 Quebec referendums is illustrative of the decline in the traditional role of redistributive policy as an instrument of territorial integration (Banting 2005, 134).

Taking a social investment perspective, Jenson (Chapter 2, this volume) concurs, arguing that the provinces now have the initiative. The social investment perspective offers little theoretical explanation of why the federal government has ceded the social policy initiative to the provinces. This is even more puzzling given that, as we shall see, the federal government was the staunchest proponent of a social investment perspective.

In stark contrast, the territorial politics perspective emphasizes that the federal government is likely to maintain an active redistributive role. This perspective points to powerful reasons why the federal government could not afford to abandon the field during the late 1990s and 2000s. The Quebec government was building a more robust set of income maintenance programs, strengthening its contribution to reducing income inequality through "the continued expansion of social spending, universal drug insurance, low-cost public daycare, increased provincial family allowances, [and] the addition of a working income tax credit" (Fortin 2009, 62; see also Noël, Chapter 11, this volume). If the federal government was to remain a presence in the lives of all Canadians, including Quebecers, it had to engage.

The challenges posed by Quebec's redistributive policy distinctiveness are likely to become magnified in periods of heightened territorially based tensions – as they were in the mid- to late 1990s. The role of territorial politics diminished after the defeat of secessionist forces in the 1980 referendum and intensified following the collapse of the Meech Lake and Charlottetown accords and the 1991 creation of the Bloc Québécois. But this was seriously underappreciated by the federal government in the lead-up to the 1995 referendum on sovereignty in Quebec: fewer than six months before the referendum, the federal budget retrenched and restructured federal-provincial transfers, weakening federal claims to be the primary guarantor of social rights in Canada. Federal complacency was shattered by the closeness of the referendum. Paradoxically, however, the federal cuts and renewed economic growth moved the federal government into budgetary surplus, expanding its fiscal ability to play a reinvigorated role in redistributive policy.

In short, given the federal government's improved fiscal position, the post-referendum strains on the Canadian federation, and the resurgent redistributive policy in Quebec, the competitive state-building dynamic generates strong expectations of an active federal response.

Distinct Fates of Various Programs and Redistributive Implications

Each of the three perspectives generates certain expectations of the fate of specific programs, with implications for overall patterns of redistribution.

In the variants of federalism perspective, the structures of the federal state "help explain a number of puzzles about Canadian social policy," including "the different ideological trajectories of income security and health care; and the uneven impact of restructuring in recent decades" (Banting 2005, 135). In exclusively federal programs operating under the classical federalism model, "the outcomes [have] faithfully reflected the power of different client groups" (ibid., 118). Banting contrasts the fate of OAS (where only very minor restructuring occurred) with UI/EI (Unemployment/ Employment Insurance), which saw major restructuring and retrenchment. Meanwhile, in the area of contributory pensions dominated by the model of joint-decision federalism, "the consensus-driven, incremental logic inherent in joint decision-making helped protect the CPP/QPP" with changes stabilizing the program (ibid., 120). Health and social assistance, both dominated by the shared-cost model, had different outcomes, however: "Shared-cost federalism helped to buffer the basic model of the health care system, but the mild protection afforded to social assistance collapsed, exposing recipients more fully to provincial politics" (ibid., 129). Banting attributes these distinctive impacts in health care and social assistance to differences in "the extent to which the federal government tried to sustain a national policy framework" (ibid., 122), but the federal approach in each field remains unexplained.

For its part, the social investment perspective emphasizes the degree to which different program areas are consistent with very specific policy prescriptions, including removing large portions of early childhood education and care from the market and increasing government funding for these services; emphasizing a policy focus on children; combating child poverty by ensuring maximum labour market participation among parents, including lone-parents; and providing access to benefits and services to parents that are not available to single adults. Those programs that enhance equality of opportunity, establish conditions for future success (especially education), focus on children, and promote labour force participation are favoured over programs that emphasize these goals to a lesser degree.

Contrary to the variants of federalism version in which shifts in redistributive impacts appear, at least in part, as an incidental outcome of external political pressures, the social investment perspective implies increased redistribution to the lower middle and middle of the income distribution rather than to the bottom. One example is the emphasis on provisions that reduce disincentives to labour force participation – the flexible labour market approach taken by the federal government as outlined by Green and Townsend – often by extending benefits further up the income distribution. Indeed, it has been argued that removing the "welfare wall" – the whole point of a negative income tax – enriches transfers to the second and third quintile. As Jenson (2010, 72) crisply notes, "Social investment are for the middle class too."

The territorial politics perspective highlights the breadth of distribution of benefits under different programs, the degree to which programs reinforce the federal redistributive presence within Quebec, and the degree to which they enhance redistributive policy congruity between Quebec and the rest of Canada. From this perspective, programs that leverage the federal policy presence in Quebec are likely to be more politically attractive to federal policy makers than are those that do not. Similarly, federal policy will favour interventions that reduce the degree of policy distinctiveness of Quebec by ensuring that social benefits are provided in the rest of Canada at a level commensurate with provision inside Quebec, thus countering claims that "Québec is fairer" (Fortin 2010).[2] Finally, the incentive to foster direct connections between individual citizens and the government on as broad a base as possible should generate a preference for programs that extend benefits more widely.

In sum, major declines in the overall redistributive effect of programs due to program changes (in the absence of shifts in the targeting of redistribution) are difficult to square with the expectations generated by a focus on competitive state building, especially in periods of heightened territorial tensions. These dynamics also imply a stronger focus on the lower middle and middle of the income distribution, redistributive implications similar to those generated by the social investment perspective. Neither perspective implies that policy makers are necessarily concerned with the degree of redistribution per se, but, rather, that their primary concerns have significant, albeit indirect, implications for redistributive outcomes.

Federal and Provincial Adoption of the Social Investment Perspective
A social investment strategy could be employed in the service of pan-Canadian projects of territorial integration and vice versa. For example, a social investment strategy may be part of a pan-Canadian mechanism of territorial integration as opposed to constituting a primary objective in and of itself. Alternatively, federal policy makers may conclude that a social investment strategy will be most effective if implemented on a pan-Canadian basis, thus casting discussion of social investment-inspired policy initiatives in the language of pan-Canadian appeals. The plausibility of either scenario may depend on the degree to which the promotion of a social investment perspective is a federal political project.

From a social investment perspective, it is reasonable to expect that the ideas, societal pressures, and international influences shaping federal policy will also have considerable impact at the provincial level; if they do not, the pattern requires explanation. However, to the degree that the rhetoric of social investment is primarily a federal tool of competitive state building, it is not particularly puzzling if this approach is less evident at the provincial level.

Developments in the New Politics of Redistribution
How do the conflicting expectations implicit in these three interpretations fare in light of evidence about program changes over the last decade?

The Federal Role in Redistribution
The dominant portrayals of the development of redistributive policy in Canada have focused primarily on the declining federal influence over provincial policy resulting from changes in federal transfers to the provinces such as the elimination of the Canada Assistance Plan and its envelopment under the Canada Health and Social Transfer in 1995. For example, analyses have concluded that the federal government "no longer has any meaningful direct role in the provision of social assistance" (Hobson and St-Hilaire 2000; Noël 2002). And despite the reinvestment in child benefits, newer programs, it is argued, have not achieved the same degree of federal influence over provincial policy as might have been expected, including the lax federal control over provincial reinvestment strategies under the National Child Benefit (see Jenson, Chapter 2, this volume).

Diversity in the redistributive impact of provincial transfers has been increasing, as is evident in the increase in the standard deviation in Gini reduction across provinces (see Table 10.1). But, as of 2007, such differences were no greater than were cross-provincial variations in the redistributive impacts of federal transfers. Moreover, increasing diversity in provincial program impacts is significantly offset by the declining cross-provincial variation in federal program impacts, and direct federal income maintenance transfers are playing a greater role in fostering pan-Canadian uniformity. Decentralization, in the sense of diminished federal influence over provincial redistributive programs, has undoubtedly occurred; however, at issue is the significance of this tendency when weighed against the direct redistributive impacts of federal programs (new or enhanced) that are increasingly uniform across provinces.

Frenette, Green, and Milligan (2009, 405) conclude that "much of the story of both the increase in the redistributiveness of the transfer system in the late 1980s and the decline in its redistributiveness in the late 1990s occurs at the provincial level." Meanwhile, at the federal level, explicit changes in the EI program (which were significant in terms of their visibility) had little or no impact on various inequality ratios across the entire 1980 to 2000

TABLE 10.1

Gini reduction, total provincial transfers, and total federal transfers, by province, 1993-2007

	Provincial transfers			Federal transfers			Ratio of federal to provincial transfer impacts		
	1993	2000	2007	1993	2000	2007	1993	2000	2007
QC	-38	-28	-25	-41	-24	-28	1.08	0.86	1.12
ON	-32	-17	-16	-24	-16	-19	0.75	0.94	1.19
AB	-20	-13	-9	-28	-17	-16	1.40	1.31	1.78
BC	-17	-22	-9	-21	-21	-20	1.24	0.95	2.22
NL	-21	-35	-22	-80	-54	-54	3.81	1.54	2.45
PE	-11	-12	-9	-76	-50	-46	6.91	4.17	5.11
NS	-25	-16	-10	-41	-32	-29	1.64	2.00	2.90
NB	-24	-19	-17	-59	-36	-38	2.46	1.89	2.24
MB	-25	-15	-9	-29	-25	-24	1.16	1.67	2.67
SK	-19	-18	-11	-30	-26	-24	1.58	1.44	2.18
Average	-23.2	-19.5	-13.7	-42.9	-30.1	-29.8	2.20	1.68	2.39
STD/AVG	-0.31	-0.35	-0.41	-0.48	-0.41	-0.40	0.81	0.54	0.45

Notes: Average is the unweighted average of all provinces. All data are for economic families in which the main earner is under 65.

Source: Haddow, Chapter 16, this volume. Ratios in the final three columns are calculated by the author.

period and only limited impact from 1990 to 2000 (405, 410). Explicit policy changes in child tax benefits had limited, albeit progressive, effects from 1980 to 1990, mildly regressive effects from 1990 to 1995, and then strongly progressive effects from 1995 to 2000. Conversely, explicit policy changes in provincial social assistance, which resulted in only moderate change in the 1980s (first less redistributive and then more) and the early 1990s (more redistributive), resulted in a major decline in redistributive impact over the 1995 to 2000 period.[3]

Haddow's analysis of the aggregate impacts of program changes and shifts in market income highlights a similar shift in the relative balance between the two orders of government towards greater federal predominance in redistributive impact (see Table 10.1). The redistributive impacts of federal transfers relative to provincial transfers declined over the period from 1993 to 2000 and, by 2000, were less powerful than were the redistributive impacts of provincial programs in the three largest Canadian provinces. However, in the period from 2000 to 2007, this pattern was powerfully reversed as federal transfer impacts tended to stay constant across provinces (or to increase), while the redistributive impacts of provincial programs declined in all provinces. By 2007, federal programs had stronger redistributive impacts than did provincial programs in all provinces and outstripped provincial transfer impacts to a greater degree across provinces than in 1993.

In terms of Quebec, the distinctiveness of the overall redistributive impact of provincial transfer programs declined moderately over the 1993 to 2000 period, while remaining notable. From 2000 to 2007, the redistributive impact of its programs declined – but not as starkly as in other provinces. As a result, in their redistributive impacts, Quebec's provincial transfer programs in this period became even more distinctive relative to programs in other provinces. Decentralization, thus not only contributed to greater diversity in the redistributive impact of provincial transfers among provinces, but also allowed for greater distinctiveness in Quebec.[4]

Distinct Fates of Various Program and Redistributive Impacts

The variants of the federalism model can explain the distinct politics of different program areas, with the notable exception of federal transfers for health care and social assistance. However, the fate of various programs can also be explained by reference to territorial dynamics. In the late 1990s federal income maintenance policy was being reoriented towards the middle class (Boychuk 2001, 123). The federal imperative for this reorientation included, among other things, the desire "to reassert its visibility in this policy area vis-à-vis the provinces" (ibid., 125).

The divergent trajectories of the development of social assistance and health care can be explained by the federal imperative to focus on broadly distributed benefits, which it either provides directly or in which it has a high level of visibility. If health care and social assistance do not differ in terms of the model of intergovernmental relations dominating them, they clearly differ in the proportion of the population receiving benefits and in the extent of the federal government's visibility in its ostensible enforcement of pan-Canadian norms. So, too, the reach of the UI/EI program is relatively limited, and program changes in the early 1990s made it more so. Thus, an imperative for the federal government to foster a network of connections between itself and individual citizens is unlikely to provide a robust underpinning for a program such as UI/EI. In this sense, UI/EI has suffered a similar fate to social assistance: both have a relatively limited reach and, as a result, an attenuated political appeal.

While the social investment perspective convincingly explains the policy preference for child benefits over either UI/EI or social assistance, competitive federal state building also provides a compelling explanation for the "shift away from federal transfers to the provinces for needs-tested social assistance in favour of direct federally-provided income tested child benefits" in order to reach an expanding portion of the middle class (Boychuk 2001, 124). A shift in favour of broadened children's benefits taking place in Quebec at the provincial level reinforced incentives for the federal government to move in this direction. In this narrative, change is driven by territorial dynamics but occurs within the context of a dominant policy discourse on social investment. The National Child Benefit (NCB) reforms built the framework for – and clearly envisioned – significant future expansion of benefits. But the federal government had to bullet-proof the program against appearing to be simply enriching existing welfare programs and increasing employment disincentives. The rhetorical approach of "taking children off welfare" and "lowering the welfare wall" provided such protection, while leaving to the provinces the tough political choice between clawing back social assistance payments and enriching overall transfers to welfare beneficiaries.

There is powerful consensus in the literature that the shifts in the redistributive impact of transfer programs over the 1990s were primarily the result of changes in market income, not the redistributive capacity of government transfers. As Heisz (2007, 8) states, changes in taxes and transfers between the 1980s and 2000s had "little net effect on overall redistribution, which remained as strong in 2004 as it was in 1989" (see also Frenette, Green, and Milligan 2010; Brzozowski 2010; Myles, Chapter 13, this volume). For their part, Frenette, Green, and Milligan posit that the redistributive effects of taxes and transfers in 2000 (the last year of their analysis) were higher than they were in the late 1980s. These findings are consistent with the conclusion based on recently available aggregate data that, far from declining, the reduction in inequality resulting from government transfers was higher in 2006 than it was at earlier cyclical peaks (see Figure 10.1).

In terms of the quintile-specific distribution of government transfers, distinct patterns of change are evident across the periods 1979-89, 1989-2000, and 2000-07.[5] From 1979 to 1989, there was a general upward shift in government transfers, which, although benefitting all quintiles, disproportionately focused on the lower-income quintiles, making the transfer system more

FIGURE 10.1

Gini reduction, government taxes and transfers, 1979-2006

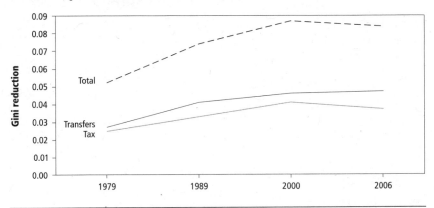

Notes: Gini reduction calculated by author using Gini coefficients for non-elderly economic families of two persons or more.
Source: Statistics Canada, Income Trends in Canada, Table 705: Gini coefficients of market, total and after-tax income by economic family type, annual, Canada and Provinces, 1976-2006.

redistributive (see Table 10.2). This pattern is even clearer when we examine changes in net transfers of taxes (see Table 10.3). In the period from 1989 to 2000, transfers again increased in overall terms; however, none of the increase was captured by the bottom or top quintiles. Rather, increases were disproportionately directed to the middle three quintiles of the income distribution. Transfer increases in the 2000-07 period continued to focus on the middle of the income distribution but were more evenly distributed across quintiles and targeted farther up the income distribution, thus disproportionately favouring the middle and upper-middle of the income distribution. This pattern holds for net transfers (see Table 10.3), and in this case, even the top quintile benefited disproportionately compared to the two lowest quintiles.

The trend toward targeting transfers to the middle of the income distribution is more pronounced in Quebec than across Canada more generally. Fortin (2009, 62) suggests that social policy innovations in Quebec since the mid-1990s have disproportionately benefited the lower ranges of the income distribution. If transfers to the bottom quintile are greater in Quebec than in Ontario and Canada more broadly, this has only been the case since the early 2000s; differences remain moderate, and divergence has been at

TABLE 10.2

Change in government transfers, by market-income quintile, 1979-2007

		Q1	Q2	Q3	Q4	Q5
Constant 2002$	1979-89	3,355	2,655	1,595	1,018	681
	1989-2000	-249	1359	915	317	-46
	2000-7	468	367	729	678	312
	1979-2007	3,575	4,380	3,240	2,013	947
Change as % of total	1979-89	36.7	53.7	51.4	44.6	42.7
transfers to quintile	1989-2000	-2.0	17.9	19.5	9.6	-2.0
	2000-7	3.8	4.1	13.0	18.7	14.0
	1979-2007	39.1	88.6	104.4	88.2	59.4
% of total increase in	1979-89	36	29	17	11	7
transfers	1989-2000	0	52	35	12	0
	2000-7	18	14	29	27	12
	1979-2007	25	31	23	14	7

Notes: Quintiles are constructed using equivalized market income. Data are for all economic families.

Source: Data are from combined Survey of Consumer Finances (SCF) and Survey of Labour Income Dynamics (SLID). Data supplied courtesy of Brian Murphy, Income Statistics Division, Statistics Canada.

least partially driven by declining transfers outside Quebec (see Figure 10.2). In contrast, net transfers in Quebec to the second quintile have remained persistently above those for Ontario and Canada, with no discernible trend towards convergence over time (see Figure 10.3). Similarly, net transfers to the middle quintile in Quebec have remained consistently above those in Ontario and Canada: a period of convergence driven by growth in transfers to this quintile in Ontario was reversed after 2003; at the same time, net transfers grew significantly in Quebec, re-establishing a pattern of distinctiveness (see Figure 10.4). Thus, Quebec is distinctive in its redistribution to the middle ranges instead of the bottom of the income distribution.

Federal/Provincial Adoption of the Social Investment Approach

Why are certain ideas, such as the social investment model, strongly evident at the federal level and not at the provincial level? How can pressures from Canadian society or the influence of international institutions and policy

TABLE 10.3

Change in net government transfers, by market-income quintile, 1979-2007

		Q1	Q2	Q3	Q4	Q5
Constant 2002$	1979–89	3,170	1,800	−80	−2,004	−6,569
	1989–2000	−188	2,292	2,107	869	−5,812
	2000–7	515	585	1756	1889	1737
	1979–2007	3,498	4,676	3,783	754	−10,644
Change as % of net transfers to quintile	1979–89	35.0	67.4	−2.5	−25.3	−34.8
	1989–2000	−1.5	51.3	63.8	8.8	−22.8
	2000–7	4.3	8.7	147.0	20.1	5.6
	1979–2007	38.6	175.1	117.4	9.5	−56.4
% of increase in net transfers	1979–89	64	36	0	0	0
	1989–2000	0	44	40	16	0
	2000–7	8	9	27	29	27
	1979–2007	28	37	30	6	0

Notes: Net transfers are calculated as total transfers minus total taxes.
Source: See Table 10.2.

FIGURE 10.2

Government net transfers (Q1, market income quintiles), Quebec, Ontario, and Canada, 1996-2006

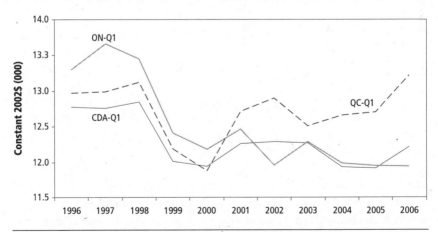

Source: Statistics Canada, Survey of Labour Income Dynamics (SLID).

FIGURE 10.3

Government net transfers (Q2, market income quintiles), Quebec, Ontario, and Canada, 1996-2006

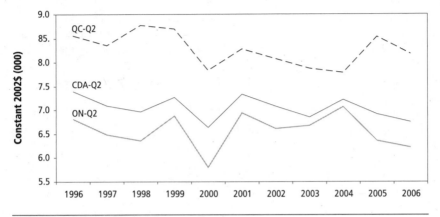

Source: See Figure 10.2.

FIGURE 10.4

Government net transfers (Q3, market income quintiles), Quebec, Ontario, and Canada, 1996-2006

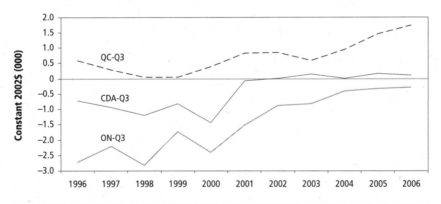

Source: See Figure 10.2.

networks be determinants of the federal adoption of a social investment approach but fail to drive provincial governments in the same direction? It seems that the social investment approach complements federal competitive state-building imperatives. In this interpretation, the social investment approach is a strategic element of a broader federal political project; it does not represent a federal-provincial consensus about appropriate models of redistributive policy.

Under the NCB, the federal government would provide income-tested benefits directly to families with children, and the released provincial funds (as a result of the concomitant reduction of provincial social assistance payments) would be reinvested in benefits designed to ease the transition from welfare to work. From a social investment perspective, the provincial benefit clawbacks and associated reinvestment strategies were the crucial focus of the changes. But Jenson argues that the federal government would have little influence over whether provinces reduced social assistance payments (a central component of the plan); nor could it ensure "even that the initial logic of 'reinvesting in services' was followed" (Jenson, Chapter 2, this volume). Federal inability to ensure appropriate provincial investment strategies has thus been seen as a major policy failure. However, the federal inability – or lack of political will – to ensure that provincial reinvestments adhere to social investment logic indicates that social investment is the weaker element in the federal political equation.

The 1997 Speech from the Throne was unequivocal in its elucidation of territorial concern: "The single most important commitment of the Government is to keep Canada united. The Government of Canada can have no greater duty or responsibility. The overriding goal of the Government of Canada as we approach the 21st century is both simple and ambitious. It is to strengthen and unite this country." The only concrete policy initiative mentioned in the section on "building a stronger Canada" was the NCB: "The federal, provincial and territorial governments have been developing a more collaborative approach to strengthening and modernizing Canada's social union – the new National Child Benefit System is an early result of this new approach" (PCO 1997). Similarly, the 2004 Speech from the Throne called the NCB "the most significant *national* social program since Medicare" (PCO 2004, emphasis added). The National Child Benefit Reports themselves claimed that the initiative transformed the existing unintegrated system "into a national platform of child benefits" (Federal, Provincial, and Territorial Ministers of Social Services 2010, 1).

Early learning and childhood care provide even better evidence of the lack of a federal-provincial consensus on social investment. The federal government has not managed to entice provinces to invest in either. Indeed, federal compromises on the terms of federal-provincial childcare agreements (especially early ones) suggest greater concern with promoting the appearance of a "pan-Canadian child care system" than with vigorously promoting a social investment approach.

The October 2004 Speech from the Throne outlined the government's commitment to "promote the national interest by setting the nation's objectives and building a consensus toward achieving them" (PCO 2004). As one element of doing so, the speech stated boldly that "the time has come for a *truly national* system of early learning and child care." Prime Minister Martin (2004) favourably compared the Liberal plan "to create a nationwide program of early learning and child care" with the Canada Child Tax Benefit of 1997, arguing that the former would "follow the pattern" established by the latter. He further compared the establishment of the childcare program with the initiation of medicare as a "defining moment in Canadian social policy." In discussing childcare and health care and characterizing both as "rank[ing] among the highest priorities of Canadians," Martin said: "[These issues] fall within areas where the provinces and territories have frontline responsibilities and are accountable to their own citizens." While the federal government had "no desire and no intention of infringing in these domains," the commitment to federal action was clear: "Neither do we believe that Canadians want the federal government to be absent on the issues that matter most to us collectively." With considerable rhetorical flourish, Martin concluded:

> There is nothing we cannot achieve if we come together in common purpose – if a strong national government articulates and defends our shared interests, and each of us rallies to national objectives ... Canada is indeed greater than the sum of its parts. True national leadership recognizes the diversity among our provinces and embraces it as an asset, a source of creativity and innovation. But at the same time, true national leadership is about naming a destination down the road and helping to forge the national will and consensus to ensure we get there together.

In closing, he pointed to the 2004 Health Accord as an example of "the importance of national will."

Consequently, in 2005, the federal government negotiated early learning and childcare agreements with all ten provinces. Each agreement (except with Quebec) reiterates the federal government's call for a *"truly* national system of early learning and child care," refers to federal efforts as "charting a national course" emphasizing a "shared national vision for early learning and child care," and commits partner governments to "creat[ing] an overarching early learning and child care framework for all Canadians" with the aim of ensuring high quality, inclusive, and accessible child care and learning programs "across Canada" (Canada and Manitoba 2005, 1-2, emphasis added).

That the Harper Conservatives cancelled these agreements is not surprising; out-of-home childcare is a hot-button issue for social conservatives. Nevertheless, while not predicated on nation-building rhetoric, the Conservative's Universal Child Care Benefit delivered the benefits of pan-Canadian universality without the political risks of appearing to subsidize out-of-home childcare. Certainly, federal government support for a higher-cost program providing universal (as opposed to targeted) benefits to all parents (not limiting benefits to parents providing in-home care) is challenging to explain in terms of Conservative ideology or a social investment model. It is, however, consistent with the imperative of creating connections with individual Canadians through direct federal benefits.

Conclusion

Claims that territorial dynamics are significant in the new politics of redistribution hinge on a number of empirically based propositions: first, the redistributive role of the state in Canada has remained robust rather than declining; second, the federal government has maintained and even strengthened its role and visibility in income maintenance; third, transfers have been increasingly targeted towards the lower middle and middle of the income distribution; fourth, this latter pattern holds at the federal level and also within Quebec.[6] These discernible patterns are consistent with a competitive state-building interpretation, and alternative explanations face challenges in accounting for them. More impressionistic assessments of the politics of redistributive policy corroborate this interpretation, and the social investment approach appears most clearly as a federal political project, not the outgrowth of a broader federal-provincial policy consensus. A sense of nation building informed federal income maintenance reform efforts not only in the 1990s but also into the mid-2000s, and explanations that focus solely on incentives, activation, and employment miss an important part of the enthusiasm for these programs in federal circles.

Assessments of the more recent period must remain mixed. In comparison with earlier periods, territorial politics have waning political salience. Further, the current federal government appears to perceive sharper trade-offs between its own policy preferences and the imperative to use redistributive policy as a mechanism of pan-Canadian integration. Both developments suggest that a competitive state-building dynamic will be less evident. Nevertheless, given Quebec's continuing redistributive policy distinctiveness, should territorial dynamics re-emerge powerfully on the Canadian political scene, as they have historically been wont to do, an interpretation that attributes continued significance to territorial dynamics in the new politics of redistribution leads us to expect the federal government to pay very close attention to its role in redistributive policy – especially its claim to be the primary guarantor of social rights in Canada.

NOTES

1 The following paragraph draws on Banting (2005, esp. 129-37).
2 For a version of this argument with regard to the Canada Health Act, see Boychuk (2008, 137-39).
3 As Frenette, Green, and Milligan (2009, 404) note: "The pattern between 1995 and 2000 might also be partially explained by the social assistance clawback from the National Child Benefit Supplement in most provinces." That is, the decline may not have been the result of changes to provincial redistributive intent. Regardless, the redistributive impact of provincial programs declined relative to the redistributive impact of federal programs.
4 For an impressive overview of recent changes in redistributive policy in Québec, see Noël, Chapter 11, this volume.
5 The following analysis uses equivalized market income quintiles to ensure that the actual composition of the income quintile in question does not change across these measures. The combined SCF/SLID data based on equivalized market income quintiles were kindly supplied by Brian Murphy of the Income Statistics Division of Statistics Canada.
6 If the impacts of territorial politics had not been evident in the late 1990s and early 2000s following the near victory of secessionist forces in Quebec, the claim that territorial dynamics remain central in the new politics of redistribution would be difficult to sustain. At that time, as we noted previously, provincial redistributive policy was resurgent and the federal government was enjoying the recovery of its fiscal wherewithal.

REFERENCES

Banting, Keith G. 2005. "Canada: Nation-Building in a Federal State." In Herbert Obinger, Stephan Liebfried, and Frank G. Castles, eds., *Federalism and the Welfare State: New World and European Experiences*, 89-137. Cambridge: Cambridge University Press.

Béland, Daniel, and André Lecours. 2006. "Sub-State Nationalism and the Welfare State: Québec and Canadian Federalism." *Nations and Nationalism* 12(1): 77-96.

Boychuk, Gerard W. 2001. "Aiming for the Middle: Challenges to Federal Income Maintenance Policy." In Leslie A. Pal, ed., *How Ottawa Spends 2001-02: Power in Transition*, 123-44. Don Mills, ON: Oxford University Press.

–. 2008. *National Health Insurance in the United States and Canada: Race, Territory and the Roots of Difference*. Washington, DC: Georgetown University Press.
Brzozowski, Matthew, Martin Gervais, Paul Klein, and Michio Suzuki. 2010. "Consumption, Income and Wealth Inequality in Canada." *Review of Economic Dynamics* 13: 52-75.
Canada and Manitoba. 2005. *Moving Forward on Early Learning and Child Care: Agreement-in-Principle between the Government of Canada and the Government of Manitoba*. http://www.hrsdc.gc.ca/eng/cs/comm/sd/messages/2005/PCO_Manitoba_e.pdf.
Federal, Provincial, and Territorial Ministers Responsible for Social Services. 2010. *National Child Benefit Progress Report, 2007*. Ottawa. http://www.nationalchildbenefit.ca/eng/pdf/ncb_progress_report_2007.pdf.
Fortin, Pierre. 2009. "Québec Is Fairer." *Inroads* 26 (2009): 58-65.
Frenette, Mark, David Green, and Kevin Milligan. 2009. "Taxes, Transfers and Canadian Income Inequality." *Canadian Public Policy* 35(4): 389-411.
Heisz, Andrew. 2007. "Income Inequality and Redistribution in Canada: 1976 to 2004." Statistics Canada Analytical Studies Branch Research Paper Series. Ottawa: Statistics Canada.
Hobson, Paul, and France St-Hilaire. 2000. "The Evolution of Federal-Provincial Fiscal Arrangements: Putting Humpty Together Again." In Harvey Lazar, ed., *Canada: The State of the Federation, 1999-2000 – Towards a Mission Statement for Fiscal Federalism*, 159-88. Montreal and Kingston: McGill-Queen's University Press.
Jenson, Jane. 2010. "Diffusing Ideas for After Neoliberalism: The Social Investment Perspective in Europe and Latin America." *Global Social Policy* 10(1): 59-84.
Martin, Paul. 2004. *The Prime Minister's Speech in Response to the Speech from the Throne*. http://www.pco-bcp.gc.ca/index.asp?lang=eng&page=information&sub=publications&doc=sft-ddt/2004_2_reply-eng.htm.
Noël, Alain. 2002. "Without Québec: Collaborative Federalism with a Footnote." In Tom McIntosh, ed., *Building the Social Union: Perspectives, Directions, Challenges*, 13-30. Regina: Canadian Plains Research Center.
Osberg, Lars. 2000. "Poverty Trends and the Canadian 'Social Union.'" In Harvey Lazar, ed., *Canada: The State of the Federation 1999-2000 – Toward a New Mission Statement for Canadian Fiscal Federalism*, 212-34. Montreal and Kingston: McGill-Queen's University Press.
–. 2008. *A Quarter Century of Economic Inequality in Canada, 1981-2006*. Toronto: Canadian Centre for Policy Alternatives.
Privy Council Office. 1997. *Speech from the Throne to Open the First Session Thirty-Sixth Parliament of Canada*. Ottawa. http://www.pco-bcp.gc.ca/index.asp?lang=eng&page=information&sub=publications&doc=sft-ddt/1997-eng.htm.
–. 2004. *Speech from the Throne to Open the Third Session of the Thirty-Seventh Parliament of Canada*. Ottawa. http://www.pco-bcp.gc.ca/index.asp?lang=eng&page=information&sub=publications&doc=sft-ddt/2004_2-eng.htm.

11

Quebec's New Politics of Redistribution

ALAIN NOËL

Canadian governments appear increasingly reluctant to compensate for growing market inequalities, and the social and political underpinnings of income redistribution seem less solid. The manifestations of this evolution are multifaceted, as the chapters of this book demonstrate, but the general direction is clear: since the mid-1990s, Canadian politics has become less favourable to equality.

In the late 1990s and early 2000s, many advanced democracies "grew unequal" under the influence of polarizing market forces, new and less stable family and social patterns, and less redistributive policy orientations (OECD 2008). The trend, however, was far from uniform. While market income inequality rose everywhere, the distribution of post-tax income varied significantly across countries. Change was ubiquitous, but its nature, timing, and magnitude were not identical across, and even within, countries. In Canada, for example, Quebec defied the common trend and resisted the rise in inequality and poverty that took place elsewhere, even though many of the same economic and social forces were at work, and roughly half the relevant public policies were federal and thus shared.

Short-term differences in trends could be explained by demographic or market forces as much as by policy choices. The main story, in any case, was less in statistical trends than in policy orientations. In the mid-1990s, when support for redistributive policies began to unravel in Canada, Quebec entered a period of major reforms, which transformed its model of social protection and made it not less but more redistributive.

Not only did Quebec's renewed commitment to redistribution emerge when the rest of the country moved in the other direction, but it unfolded as an unlikely political scenario. Between January 1996 and March 2001, when the main policy innovations were introduced, the centre-left Parti québécois was in power, but the budget deficit headed the political agenda and the premier was Lucien Bouchard, always a small-c conservative. After April 2003, the centre-right Liberal Party came to power under Jean Charest, also a conservative by orientation. Yet, it maintained the new social protection framework and, in fact, completed its implementation.

How could a society with high taxes, a predominant preoccupation with the budget deficit, and relatively conservative political leaders move against the stream to end up with a more progressive arrangement, just as the rest of the country, and indeed the continent, grew more unequal?

Some might point to culture, traditions, or established institutional patterns. There is some truth to this, but Quebec's new politics of redistribution was neither preordained nor path dependent. Indeed, the province's social model was substantially reinvented in the 1990s along lines that were new and unforeseen. Others might appeal to the politics of identity and nationalism, a factor that has encouraged Quebec to compete with the federal government in a never-ending contest to win over the allegiances of citizens. During the years under consideration, however, Ottawa was downsizing, not expanding, social programs, and Quebec nationalism was at a low ebb following the 1995 referendum defeat.

The social and political story behind Quebec's turn towards a new politics of redistribution was not about culture and traditions or identity and nationalism but, rather, about social democracy. In a context defined by the referendum defeat and fiscal austerity, old and new social actors mobilized around common objectives and worked with the Quebec government to chart a progressive path allowing both deficit reduction and the introduction of new social policies. To put it simply, in a difficult context, a new left-of-centre political equilibrium was defined.

Quebec already had a strongly organized society, with powerful trade unions, a solid women's movement, and a dense network of social and community organizations. The ethos of Quebec politics, fashioned by a distinct history of affirmation and reform, was also defined by trust and equality, more so than elsewhere on the continent. Quebec was thus inclined to seek a progressive solution when confronted with the difficulties of the 1990s. This solution, however, had to be created. At a critical juncture, in the aftermath of the 1995 referendum, the province's politicians and social actors had to make a concerted effort to reinvent, together, the Quebec model.

What happened in Quebec was akin to the politics of welfare state reform that took place in many European countries in the late 1990s and early 2000s. European governments were then confronted with a double challenge. On the one hand, they experienced slow economic growth, high levels of unemployment, and important public finance deficits; on the other hand, they faced new demands associated with the development of a post-industrial economy, demographic change, and the transformation of gender and family relationships. Even in hard times, new expectations were voiced concerning, for instance, gender equality, work-family conciliation, or social protection for persons in atypical employment (Haüsermann 2010, 21). Many governments thus sought to engineer a new social pact whereby traditional insiders – notably members of industrial and public-sector unions – accepted concessions in exchange for long-run stability and new initiatives favourable to outsiders such as women or persons in less secure employment. In 1996 and 1997, the Quebec government and its social partners crafted such a reform coalition around innovations in public finance, employment programs, and family policies.

This chapter begins with social foundations to explain how, over time, Quebec developed social structures and public attitudes favourable to equality. It then turns to the politics of the late 1990s and early 2000s to explain how coalition engineering and compromise in a context of austerity helped define Quebec's new politics of redistribution. The resulting work/family model is then presented as a relatively progressive instance of the social investment framework that was on the OECD agenda at the time, and the last section considers its main consequences. The chapter concludes with a cautionary note, pointing to the limits and fragility of the Quebec experiment.

The Ethos of Quebec Politics

In an insightful essay, Yves Vaillancourt argues that Quebec's social policies of the 1960s and 1970s were not all that different from those designed by Ottawa or by other progressive provincial governments. Quebec's main distinction was to seek as much control as possible over these policies. In its basic design, writes Vaillancourt (2003, 162), Quebec's first social model "was not really original." In the 1980s and 1990s, however, the province began to experiment with "a new model of solidarity-based democratic development" anchored in new relationships between the state, the market, and a vigorous and autonomous third sector (163-68). While it remained incomplete and precarious, this model marked a break with the past and a departure from the Canadian mainstream (Vaillancourt and Leclerc 2009, 267).

In the language of comparative social policy, Quebec first developed a "liberal" welfare state, an Anglo-American welfare state *en français,* so to speak. The philosophy and design of most Quebec programs remained close to those of policies implemented elsewhere in Canada, as did their outcomes, in terms of equality, employment, poverty, or access to services. The Quebec Pension Plan, for instance, shared with its Canadian equivalent a liberal design that left a major role to private and individual protection but did reduce poverty among the elderly (Myles 2000; Banting 2005, 110-11). In health care, social services, or social assistance, provincial programs were largely the same, albeit with design variants, and they produced comparable outcomes. Even in education, where the federal government hardly played a role and where cultural differences could have had a stronger impact, Quebec programs often converged with those of other provinces (Wallner 2010).

Contrary to a conventional reading of the Quiet Revolution, this convergence around a liberal type of welfare state was less a case of Quebec's catching up with the rest of Canada than one of common evolution, driven by similar visions and mutual influences. Whether in Regina, Ottawa, or Quebec City, reformists shared a broad outlook informed by Keynes, Beveridge, and the numerous reports and commissions that defined the Canadian postwar order (Vaillancourt 2003, 160).

For Quebec, however, the road to these common programs was distinctive – and not only because the development of social policy was an object of nationalist mobilization (Béland and Lecours 2008). Indeed, to build a Canadian-style welfare state, Quebec society first had to transform itself and undo two social traps that prevented progressive change (Noël 2010). The first was, to use the terms of a recent World Bank (2005, 20-23) report, an "inequality trap," created by the enduring economic disparities between French- and English-speaking Quebeckers. The second was a low-trust trap that stemmed from inequality and the politics of patronage, long important in Quebec.

Consider, first, the inequality trap. Until the 1960s, on average in Quebec, a bilingual francophone earned less than a bilingual anglophone, and both had lower incomes than a monolingual anglophone. "Ethnic origin," noted the Royal Commission on Bilingualism and Biculturalism (1969, 21-23), had "a greater impact on incomes than ... linguistic knowledge." This was hardly exceptional. Inequalities anchored in social categories such as gender, ethnicity, or language are ubiquitous; they endure because categories function as social markers that inform individual decisions and behaviours (Tilly 1998, 7-9). Such inequalities are so difficult to overcome that they create social traps. The only collective solution for members of the subordinate category is to change the rules of the game, and this requires major social and political mobilization (ibid., 227). This is precisely what Quebec's Quiet Revolution was about: the primary aim of Quebec reformists, then, was less catching up, modernizing the state, or building a new nation than eliminating a long-lasting and crippling "inequality trap." One could, of course, debate the relative importance of exogenous economic transformations, investments in education, changes in social and economic policies, or linguistic laws (see Levine 1997). It is the outcome that matters: in a few decades, the linguistic division of labour and incomes disappeared. Quebeckers were no longer paid "for what they were, but rather for what they did" (Béland, Forgues, and Beaudin 2010, 98 [my translation]).

Quebec's social transformation was a rare feat. Categorical inequalities are not often undone, and when they are, the process tends to be long and gradual. Not surprisingly, this achievement left French-speaking Quebeckers with a positive bias towards both equality and state intervention (Mendelsohn, Parkin, and Pinard 2007, 50).

State intervention itself became an object of mobilization during the Quiet Revolution. Indeed, the election of Jean Lesage and the Liberals in 1960 initiated a profound renovation of Quebec politics (Heintzman 1983, 50-51). Until then, the relative poverty of the province and the francophones' lack of access to good jobs in the private sector favoured an intense practice of patronage. In this context, partisan politics worked as an important distributive process, but it was also despised for being skewed and corrupt. Quebec's political culture thus sustained both "a climate of strong party loyalties" and "a profound cynicism about politics and politicians, and deep anxiety about the corroding influence of politics on many areas of national life" (Heintzman 1983, 18). Only political mobilization and institutional reforms could break such a low-trust pattern (Rothstein 2005, 210-11).

In the 1960s, the civil service was reformed and expanded, electoral and campaign finance laws were changed, new departments and Crown corporations were created, and a host of economic and social policies were introduced. The idea was to make politics reputable so that the state could become, in the words of René Lévesque, "one of us, the best of us" (quoted in Levine 1997, 85 [my translation]). In the late 1970s, when the Parti québécois and Lévesque came to power, they moved further in this direction. The 1977 law on political party financing, in particular, which Lévesque saw as his most significant achievement, instituted the strictest rules in the world and made Quebec politics practically scandal-free for decades (Lévesque 1986, 386; Godin 2001, 157; Tremblay 2006, 193).

By the 1980s, the two social traps that plagued Quebec had been undone, and linguistic equality and social trust were solidly anchored. In the process, a society was transformed. Compared to other North Americans, Quebeckers had become more egalitarian and less authoritarian, more supportive of gender equality, and more favourable to trade unions and state intervention. Quebec then stood out as "the most consistently liberal" and "most postmodern" society on the continent (Baer, Grabb, and Johnston 1993, 28; Adams 2003, 82).

Quebeckers also became well organized. Indeed, the mobilization of the 1960s and 1970s gave rise to strong collective organizations. Trade unions, for instance, negotiated collective agreements for 39.6 percent of the labour force in 2010, compared to 28.0 percent in Ontario and 13.1 percent in the United States (Labrosse 2011, 7). Faced with a strong labour movement, business organized as well, facilitating socio-economic collaboration and coordination (see Coleman, Chapter 4, this volume). The Conseil du patronat, notably, became a powerful voice, with "no equivalent elsewhere in Canada" (Haddow and Klassen 2006, 48-49 and 124-26). The feminist movement was also shaped by this context, developing alongside a host of other popular and social movements. Peak associations, networking, and collaborative practices multiplied to encompass most activities, groups, sectors, and regions, and to define a distinct social model anchored in participation and egalitarianism (Laforest 2007, 183; Hamel and Jouve 2006, 7). A comparative study of gender attitudes attributed to this model of organization the fact that Quebec evolved into "the most progressive social space" in North America (Clement and Myles 1994, 234; Adams 2003, 87). The shrinking and reorientation of civil society organizations described by Phillips (Chapter 5, this volume) simply did not take place in Quebec.

Thus, while the social policies developed during the Quiet Revolution were largely those of a liberal welfare state, the road to these policies was unique, and it generated distinct social foundations – social foundations more favourable to equality and state intervention than those found elsewhere in Canada.

As a path-breaking reformist moment, the Quiet Revolution modified the prevailing political representations. Quebeckers undid long-established social traps and renovated their social and political institutions, and, as they did so, they acquired a new collective memory, which linked the construction of the province's welfare state with success and modernity. Emerging state institutions and a strongly organized society reinforced and mobilized this bias, arguably sustained by equality itself as a factor strengthening social trust and fostering a continued demand for equality (Kumlin and Rothstein 2005; Wilkinson and Pickett 2009). In the 1990s, these distinct social foundations began to have policy impacts, allowing Quebec to diverge from other provinces with its own version of the new politics of redistribution.

Coalition Politics

Born between 1996 and 2006, Quebec's new redistribution framework included an ambitious and encompassing family policy, a set of active labour market programs, and a law and a strategy against poverty and social exclusion. These policies did not simply extend the Canadian-style liberal welfare state established in the 1960s and 1970s: they delineated a new, distinctive model for the twenty-first century.

It would be tempting to tie these innovations to the ethos of Quebec politics, defined by a favourable bias towards equality and state intervention. The public opinion maps produced by the CBC Vote Compass after the 2011 federal elections painted a vivid picture of the enduring public policy preferences of Quebeckers. Compared to other Canadians, Quebec respondents were much more likely to favour or accept a carbon tax, higher taxes for the rich, easier rules to qualify for employment insurance, and same-sex marriages. They wished to keep the long-gun registry, abolish the Senate, and spend less on the military. They also expected bilingualism from Supreme Court judges (http://votecompass.ca). Given such tendencies in public opinion and the strength of trade unions and social movements, Quebec's progressive reforms of the late 1990s could seem foreordained.

A necessary condition, however, is not always a sufficient one. Public preferences and the capacities of social movements provide favourable conditions but cannot easily explain a sudden shift. Yves Vaillancourt (2003), for instance, documents the evolution of Quebec's social model in the 1980s and early 1990s, and he observes a gradual transition towards renewed policies and practices constructed jointly by the government and collective actors involved in the social economy. What happened in the late 1990s was of a different order. In just a few years, a raft of legislation transformed the situation of women in the labour market, redesigned the support and services offered to families, changed the working conditions and earnings of low-wage earners, and revised social programs aimed at the poorest.

Partisan politics certainly played a role. The party in power was indeed the Parti québécois and it presented these reforms as inherent to its social-democratic orientations. Quebec's two main parties, however, remained first and foremost divided over the national question, and they did not stand very far apart on social questions (Haddow and Klassen 2006, 128-30 and 276). Many reforms, including those on pay equity, parental leave, and poverty, received the support of both parties. As mentioned earlier, nationalism also failed to offer a satisfactory explanation since most reforms occurred after, not before, the defeated 1995 referendum.

The referendum does provide a key, however. On 30 October 1995, Quebec sovereignty was defeated by a very narrow margin of 54,288 votes. Sovereigntists could have interpreted the unprecedented support received from 49.4 percent of the electorate as a moral victory, but the bitter remarks of Jacques Parizeau on referendum night precluded this possibility. Their project was defeated, and so was the broad alliance of progressive forces behind the idea. When Lucien Bouchard became premier in January 1996, he had to adjust to this defeat and to mend the social divisions left by the referendum. Bouchard was also confronted with an unprecedented fiscal situation. In 1995, the Quebec government had realized its largest-ever budget deficit ($5,814 million), the country's worst provincial deficit as a proportion of GDP (3.4 percent). Other provinces, notably Ontario, had already adopted drastic measures to reduce their deficits, and so had the federal government, which had implemented profound reductions on transfers to the provinces (Imbeau and Leclerc 2002, 68-71). The Bouchard government could not avoid the general turn towards austerity.

In the context of Quebec politics, however, and given the social-democratic orientations of the party in power, unilateral cuts in public programs would have presented major difficulties. The Parti québécois had a majority in the National Assembly, and the opposition Liberal Party was sensitive to the call to restore fiscal balance. Still, Lucien Bouchard needed to reach out to the government's social partners, which were also his allies in the just ended referendum campaign (Savage 2008, 878). Other governments in North America, explained the premier at the opening of the March

1996 socio-economic summit on the deficit and employment, had acted alone, but in Quebec, the government and its social partners had to work together (Bouchard 1996b).

In her study of welfare state reform politics in Continental Europe, Silja Häusermann underlines the importance of coalition engineering for the construction of viable reform paths. In hard times, she writes, "all governments have to engage in coalition engineering," and, in this context, the "modernizing expansion of the welfare state" becomes "a very strong currency for governments to buy agreement for otherwise unpopular changes" (Häusermann 2010, 202-14).

In January 1996, when he became premier, Bouchard immediately announced a socio-economic summit on deficit reduction and employment creation to be held in two steps, first in March in Quebec City and then in October in Montreal, and he called on all major social actors to come together and conclude a "new social pact for Quebec" (Bouchard 1996a). His objective was to bring social partners to accept the need to reduce the deficit and to implement reforms conducive to a higher level of employment. More fundamentally, as he explained in a later speech, the idea was to "heal Quebec's social-democracy" and relieve it of "the weight of public debt, social exclusion and unemployment" (Bouchard 1996c).

The March 1996 Quebec summit was unprecedented because it included representatives from the community sector, alongside business, labour, and the state. The process proved particularly successful since participants agreed not only to eliminate the current account deficit – the government's initial objective – but also to aim for an overall surplus by the end of the decade, with the help of a new anti-deficit law. In exchange, the government promised to reform and improve active labour market programs, support the development of the social economy, and adopt a law on pay equity. The October summit in Montreal added content to this "social pact" and committed the government to a new family policy, reform of social assistance and employment programs, and an effort to recover jurisdictions and funds from Ottawa to integrate active labour market programs and to establish a new parental insurance plan. The Quebec government also formally recognized the role of community organizations and, unexpectedly, agreed to add a zero-impoverishment clause to its zero-deficit objective (Bouchard 1996d).

In less than a year, the government of Lucien Bouchard had reached out to business and labour, brought in the voices of perennial outsiders – women's and youth groups, community and social rights organizations, social economy producers – and redesigned major social programs, even as it placed the state on the road to budgetary surplus. The 1995 referendum defeat and the context of austerity had become an occasion for a concerted *aggiornamento* of the provincial welfare state.

No grand design or elaborate plan prefigured this outcome. The process was nevertheless consonant with many European reforms of the same years. To sell austerity measures, the Bouchard government worked with its social partners and brought in actors who were traditionally weak and underrepresented, responding in the end to many of their preoccupations more so, in fact, than it did to the desires of trade unions (Graefe 2007, 163-66). New programs fostered gender equality, improved childcare services and parental support, complemented low wages, supported less traditional forms of employment, and made room for community organizations and their preoccupations, including an enduring concern for poverty. In effect, Quebec's old "liberal" welfare state was transformed to accommodate new demands. In a context of austerity, the government exchanged retrenchment measures for programs that helped working women, the atypically employed, and the poor (Häusemann 2010, 2-6).

When he was elected in April 2003, Liberal Jean Charest promised his government would be different. In his first speech as premier, Charest claimed that Quebeckers had "turned the page on a model of government," and he promised to initiate the first "reengineering" of the Quebec government since the Quiet Revolution (Charest 2003a). The Quebec state, he added during the June 2003 opening session of the National Assembly, no longer spoke to the reality of the twenty-first century (Charest 2003b).

These radical intentions never translated into major changes. The promised re-engineering rapidly faltered when it met the resistance of the social movements that had concurred in the 1996 social pact (Facal and Bernier 2008, 497-99). Daycare fees were raised from five to seven dollars a day, some public-private partnerships were introduced, as was a modest modernization of public administration, but the page was not turned on recent reforms. If anything, the transformation initiated in the late 1990s was completed. The 2004 budget, in particular, improved transfers to families and low-income households and prepared the ground for the first Action Plan against poverty and social exclusion (Noël 2004). In January 2006, the Liberal government also introduced the Quebec Parental Insurance Plan. Clearly, the Charest government had learned that Quebec could not be governed easily without the support of the broad coalition acknowledged and consolidated by the Bouchard government.

Twice, then, Quebec premiers with conservative leanings and a preference for austerity or market-oriented policies had to concede that the only way forward involved redistributing more, not less. Both Bouchard and Charest acknowledged that governing Quebec required a capacity for coalition engineering and compromise, and reform paths that combined retrenchment with social policy renewal. This requirement was anchored in a strongly mobilized civil society and a consistent public ethos.

A New Work/Family Model

Quebec's new redistribution framework does not have a name, a master frame, or an explicit discourse. It is an assemblage of policies gradually put together by governments of different political persuasion, who often sold change as a means to preserve established practices and institutions (Béland and Lecours 2008, 68-74).

At the same time, the structure and logic of this model are in tune with the recent orientations of international organizations, such as the OECD or the European Union, in their responses to the transformation of women's roles in the labour market and the family. In the early days of the welfare state, in OECD countries, the rate of female employment stood at around 35 percent; in the 2000s, it consistently exceeded 70 percent, and stable one-earner families had largely given place to varied, less stable family arrangements (Esping-Andersen 2009, 5-7). Across the OECD, policy makers sought reforms to facilitate employment and to reconcile work and family life (Jenson 2010; Daly 2010, 143). The main idea, organized around the notion of social investment, was to better recognize and support women's employment and new family forms, and to improve out-of-home care and early education for children. The social investment perspective remained general, however, and policy choices differed significantly across countries (Daly 2011).

At the outset, in the late 1990s, Quebec's emphasis on universality, public provision in childcare, and gender equality appeared at odds with the targeted social programs, market solutions, and children-oriented measures favoured in social investment discourses (Jenson 2002, 309-10 and 327; Jenson 2009). The Quebec government, observed Jane Jenson (2002, 309-10), was a "lone ranger" moving "against the current." Over time, however, the international social investment discourse evolved to encompass more progressive versions of work and family policies (Mahon 2010), and the OECD (2005, 53) acknowledged that, in terms of "policy coherence in the family-friendly policy area," Quebec had moved "way ahead of other provinces and of federal policy development."

At the heart of Quebec's approach was an encompassing family policy. In 1997, Bouchard's government introduced three interrelated programs that redefined public support for families with children: universally accessible regulated daycare spaces at a uniform, modest daily fee (five dollars at first, seven dollars since 2004); a universal family allowance adjusted to family income and designed to equalize child benefits between parents receiving social assistance and those earning low wages; and a projected Quebec-specific parental leave to be negotiated with the federal government.

The expanded funding of early childhood education and care (ECEC) almost instantly became a "sacred trust" in Quebec politics. The number of subsidized places expanded rapidly, to serve more than 200,000 children by 2009 (Gouvernement du Québec 2009, 28). In 2007-08, the Quebec government spent $1,694 per zero-to-twelve-year-old child on ECEC, compared to $414 for Ontario. For families using daycare, this commitment was equivalent to a transfer of $4,691 per child per year, against $3,040 in Ontario. Quebec's total expenditures then rose over $1.7 billion, more than half the total Canadian ECEC investment ($3.1 billion; Beach et al. 2009, tables 23, 27, 28, and 29).

The family allowances introduced in 1997 were restructured and improved in 2004 to become a significant and relatively simple financial support for families with children. Financial assistance is now provided through a child assistance payment delivered every three months. This payment is universal and non-taxable but more generous for the first child, for low- and middle-income families, and for large families. A supplement is provided to single-parent families and to parents of a handicapped child. In 2011, for instance, a couple with one child and an income below $44,788 received $2,204 in child assistance payment. Beyond this income, the payment decreased at a 4 percent rate to a minimum of $619 per year. Payments for the second and third child amounted to $1,102, and they rose to $1,652 for the fourth child and beyond. Above the standard payment, a single-parent family with one child received a supplement ranging between $772 and $309, and parents of a handicapped child obtained a monthly supplement of $174 (Régie des rentes du Québec 2011). Couples with at least one child and an annual income in 2010 of less than $44,788 also received a work premium of up to $2,942. Work premiums were provided as well to single parents and, with less generous conditions, to childless couples and singles (Revenu Québec 2011).

Combined with existing federal programs, these transfers made a significant difference for Quebec families (on the redistributive impact of federal transfer programs, see Boychuk, Chapter 10, this volume). Between 2000 and 2008, a couple with two children and no market income increased its income by more than 28 percent, from $19,325 to $24,779 in constant 2008 dollars. A couple with a $25,000 income saw its transfers go from $7,009 to $14,610; and at $50,000, transfers went from $5,368 to $7,934. In 2000, a Quebec couple with two children began to contribute to the tax and transfer system when its income reached $39,681 (in 2008 dollars); in 2008, the same couple remained a net beneficiary until it reached an income of $53,138 (Godbout and St-Cerny 2008, 168-73). Single-parent families experienced a similar progression.

Finally, in 2006, the Quebec government introduced its own Parental Insurance Plan, which offered more generous income replacement rates, higher maximum insurable earnings, and payments over a longer period than Canadian Employment Insurance. The Quebec plan also covered self-employed workers, offered paternity benefits, and had no penalty period. Quebec's parental leaves and income replacement rates came close to those offered in Scandinavia, with more favourable conditions for self-employed parents (Conseil de gestion de l'assurance-parentale 2009a). Rounding out the family policy package were reforms ensuring the financial responsibility of non-custodial parents and working time release for family obligations.

Altogether, the Quebec government spent $6.5 billion for family policy in 2008. Added to the $3.6 billion contributed by the federal government, these expenditures amounted to 3.2 percent of GDP, a level comparable to that of Denmark or Sweden (Gouvernement du Québec 2009, 1-5). Policy changes of this scale simply could not be interpreted as path dependent. They opened a new avenue, which combined in a distinct way concerns for redistribution and gender equality with an enduring commitment to public service and a focus on employment.

A second and related set of reforms focused on the labour market. First, the government introduced the Public Prescription Drug Insurance Plan, which extended coverage to all citizens not protected by a private plan, to the benefit in particular of low-income, self-employed, and small-company workers. When the plan was created in 1997, about 1.7 million Quebeckers had no drug insurance (Ministère de la Santé et des Services sociaux 2002, 5). This reform was not without flaws. The co-existence of private and public insurance, in particular, raised issues of equity in terms of cost and protection, and, although based on income, contributions to the public plan were not very progressive, the maximum personal contribution being reached rapidly (Union des consommateurs 2009, 9-11). The new plan nevertheless succeeded in reducing inequalities in access to drugs, and it probably made the transition to employment easier for low-income households (Pomey et al. 2007, 492).

Second, in November 1996, a proactive law on pay equity introduced a procedure to correct gender-based discrepancies in earnings. Controversial at its inception, the law eventually gained acceptance from employers and it was maintained by the Liberals (Haddow and Klassen 2006, 146-47). Ten years later, in 2006, the government reached a comprehensive pay equity agreement with its own employees (Artemova 2008, 82). By then, about half of Quebec's employers had gone through a pay equity process, to the benefit of women in traditionally feminine jobs (Commission de l'équité salariale 2006, 93).

Third, active labour market policies were integrated within Emploi-Québec to cover all the unemployed, whether they qualified for employment insurance or not. After a rocky start, this comprehensive approach proved effective and allowed growing investments in training and work integration measures (Saint-Martin 2001; Haddow and Klassen 2006, 139; SOM Recherches et Sondages 2006). In 2008, the federal government acknowledged the success of Quebec's model in reaching persons farther from the labour market, and it signed new bilateral Labour Market Agreements with all provinces and territories to generalize a formula it had previously discouraged (Noël 2012). Finally, employment standards were upgraded in 2002 and the minimum wage was regularly raised, reaching $9.65 an hour in May 2011 (Haddow and Klassen 2006, 147-48).

The third prong of Quebec's new redistribution model came in December 2002 with the adoption of a law against poverty and social exclusion. The product of a collective mobilization spearheaded by the Collectif pour un Québec sans pauvreté, the new law was the first to commit a Canadian government to a strategy against poverty (Noël 2002). In 2004, the first Poverty Action Plan improved the income of families and low-wage earners (Noël 2004). New autonomous institutions were also created in 2005: the Comité consultatif de lutte contre la pauvreté et l'exclusion to advise the government on policies relevant to fight poverty, and the Centre d'étude sur la pauvreté et l'exclusion to measure progress. In June 2010, a second and more modest action plan introduced fiscal measures for low-income households and a strategy to mobilize regions and Aboriginal communities around innovative poverty reduction projects (Ministère de l'Emploi et de la Solidarité sociale 2010).

It is not easy to establish the consequences of this new law. At the very least, it modified the public agenda and brought new, traditionally weak stakeholders into the policy process. The law also helped legitimize and sustain reforms that improved the situation of low-income families. Social assistance penalties for refusing to search or accept a job, for instance, were abolished, and exemptions for assets were increased (Torjman 2010). Along with Newfoundland and Labrador, Quebec became one of the few provinces to improve welfare incomes after 1997, to the extent that, in certain situations, these incomes came close to the low-income threshold (National Council of Welfare 2008). Results were less favourable, however, for single, working-age unemployed persons (Noël 2011). In a report discreetly tabled in the National Assembly in June 2011, the government made clear that it would not follow the main recommendation of its Comité consultatif, namely, that social assistance benefits for childless households be improved to guarantee a minimal income for all (Ministère de l'Emploi et de la Solidarité sociale 2011).

Altogether, Quebec's new work/family model constituted an elaborate framework of innovative measures organized around three interrelated objectives: first, supporting families through services and transfers; second, promoting employment and equity by removing obstacles to employment, countering discriminatory practices, providing training and work opportunities, and making work pay; and third, reducing poverty and empowering persons and communities affected by poverty. These reforms addressed many of the preoccupations associated with the social investment perspective and, more generally, with the social movements typical of postindustrial welfare states, including concerns with female employment and gender equality, childcare and early education services, income security for lone parents or persons in atypical employment, and social protection for working-age adults (Häusermann 2010, 2). In doing so, they developed in tandem with federal initiatives also inspired by the social investment perspective, but the Quebec version proved more ambitious and progressive, and much more sustained compared with the persistent ambiguity of federal policies and the relative inaction of most provincial governments. Unannounced and multifaceted, Quebec's reforms turned out to be remarkably coherent, and, over time, they made a difference.

Growing Not So Unequal

After the mid-1990s, most of the policy changes that mattered for redistribution in Canada took place at the provincial level (Frenette, Green, and

FIGURE 11.1

Gini coefficients, all family units after-tax income, Ontario and Quebec, 1976-2009

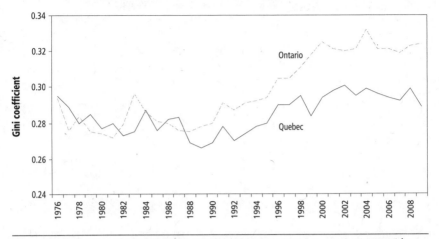

Source: Statistics Canada (CANSIM 202-0709). This is a new series, more consistent with international standards than CANSIM 202-0705.

Milligan 2009, 408). Until then, after-tax income inequalities as measured by the Gini coefficient for all family units evolved at about the same pace and at similar levels in the different provinces. Quebec and Ontario, in particular, stood very close to each other, as is shown in Figure 11.1.

Gini coefficients were also relatively stable over time; this began to change in the 1990s when after-tax inequalities increased and began to diverge. In Ontario, income disparities started rising in the late 1980s and kept growing. In Quebec, they rose more moderately in the early 1990s and stabilized after the late 1990s, leaving a gap between the two provinces. This divergence did not stem from the evolution of market incomes but from differences in redistribution efforts. Indeed, in 2009 market income disparities were more pronounced in Quebec than in Ontario. As explained in the introduction to this volume, after-tax incomes ended up more equal in Quebec because transfers and taxes had a stronger impact.

As Haddow and Boychuk note in their contributions to this book, Quebec's new redistributive policies focused on households with incomes near the median and favoured families with children. Provincial transfers and taxes proved less generous for single persons or those over sixty-five (Crespo 2007, 39-48). In two recent studies, Luc Godbout and his co-authors applied OECD methodology to calculate the effective tax burden in Quebec

FIGURE 11.2

Percentage of population with an after-tax income below 50 percent of the median income (LIM), families and single persons, Canada (including Quebec) and Quebec, 1973-2008

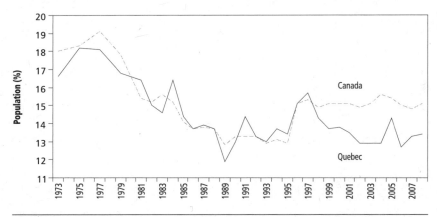

Note: The Canadian rate is based on the Canadian median income (Canada including Quebec), and the Quebec rate on the Quebec median income.
Sources: Crespo (2008, 110-11 and 140-41); Institut de la statistique du Québec (2011a).

and in Canada (including Quebec), that is, the net impact of all transfers and taxes on the income of various types of households (Godbout, St-Cerny, and Amiot 2010; Godbout, St-Cerny, and Robert-Angers 2011; OECD 2009). Between 2000 and 2009, this impact was lowered for all households but more for Quebec families with children. By 2009, low- and average-income Quebec families with children always had a lower effective tax burden than did comparable families in Canada, while households with high incomes ($132,588) contributed more, as did households without children, except when their income was low ($26,597). The Quebec-Canada difference was particularly significant for families at or below the average income. These families were obvious beneficiaries of Quebec's new politics of redistribution. Households with higher incomes, on the other hand, paid more in taxes.

What about persons living in or near poverty? Using the standard international measure of poverty, Figure 11.2 presents the evolution of the Quebec and Canadian poverty rates based on the low-income measure (LIM) at 50 percent of the median for the 1973-2008 period.

Statistics Canada defines provincial LIM rates with reference to the Canadian median income. There are good arguments for doing so, in so far as many policies that determine the earnings of low-income households are pan-Canadian. Yet, such a measure masks important differences in living costs, and it is not helpful to understand redistribution at the provincial scale. For this purpose, it makes more sense to refer to the provincial median income, just as Europeans refer to their national, and not to a European median, income. This is what is done for Quebec in Figure 11.2, using data computed by Crespo (2008). Low-income rates started diminishing in Quebec around 1997, while they remained practically constant in Canada (including Quebec). This turning point is consistent with the evolution of Gini coefficients presented above. Table 11.1 broadens the picture by including data for a few comparable countries and a LIM measure for Canada without Quebec.

Quebec ranked somewhere between the conservative welfare states of Continental Europe and the most redistributive of the Anglo-American welfare states. Canada without Quebec, on the other hand, belonged clearly in the liberal welfare state category, standing roughly between the United Kingdom and the United States.

TABLE 11.1

Percentage of population with an after-tax income below 50 percent of median income (LIM), all persons, Canada, Quebec, and selected OECD countries, 2003-05

Society	LIM (50%)
Sweden, 2005	5.6
Netherlands, 2004	6.3
France, 2005	8.4
Germany, 2004	8.5
Quebec, 2005 (Quebec median)	*10.0*
United Kingdom, 2004	11.6
Italy, 2004	12.1
Australia, 2003	12.2
Canada, 2005	*12.9*
Ireland, 2004	13.2
Canada without Quebec, 2004 (Canada without Quebec median)	*13.9*
United States, 2004	17.3

Note: These rates are based on the international definition and cannot be compared directly with those in Figure 11.2 (see Murphy, Zhang, and Dionne 2010).
Sources: OECD countries: Luxembourg Income Study (http://www.lisdatacenter.org); Canada and Quebec: Centre d'étude sur la pauvreté et l'exclusion (2009, 43).

In interpreting these international comparisons, one must remember that Quebec is not a country. The federal government receives 32 percent of all government revenues in Quebec and 47 percent of personal income taxes, the tax field with the most impact on redistribution (data for 2008, from Statistics Canada 2010, Quebec tables 6 and 7). Ottawa also provides, Old Age Security, the Guaranteed Income Supplement, EI, the GST/HST Credit, the Canada Child Tax Benefit, the Universal Child Care Benefit, the Working Income Tax Benefit, and a host of other tax-based credits and benefits that encourage saving for retirement, education, or other purposes and support educational activities or daycare for children. When Quebec low-income rates diverge from Canadian rates, then, it is in spite of a common policy framework and because provincial labour market trends and policies push in a different direction. A recent study indicates that, indeed, Quebec's relatively generous transfers to families were effective in alleviating poverty (Bibi and Duclos 2011).

To sum up, both inequality and poverty have diminished or levelled out in Quebec since the mid-1990s, going against the tendency elsewhere in Canada. This was likely due to provincial public policies favouring low- and median-income families (with one or two parents), probably at the expense of persons living alone, who paid more taxes or gained less from transfers. This redistributive effort did not seem to hurt labour market participation. At 80 percent in 2009, the employment rate of Quebec women aged between twenty-five and forty-four was higher than ever and above the Canadian rate (Gouvernement du Québec 2010, 153). The overall employment rate also increased, gradually closing the historical gap between Quebec and the rest of Canada. In 1989, there was a six point difference between the Quebec and Ontario employment rates; in May 2011, this difference had dwindled to 1.5 percentage points (Institut de la statistique du Québec 2011b). The number of persons receiving social assistance declined as well, particularly among families with children, despite significantly improved welfare incomes (Comité consultatif de lutte contre la pauvreté et l'exclusion sociale 2009, 14). In 1996, 813,200 persons, or 11.2 percent of Quebec's population, received social assistance (Roy 2004); by April 2011, this number was down to 488,346, or 7.3 percent of the population (Ministère de l'Emploi et de la solidarité 2011b). The general improvement in the employment situation, along with the new family benefits and expanded childcare provision, seemed responsible for the reduction in social assistance beneficiaries and increased labour supply (Blouin 2005; Lefebvre and Merrigan 2008; Baker,

Gruber, and Milligan 2008). In addition, Quebec's birth rate progressed in the last fifteen years to engender something like a minor baby boom, in good part because of supportive family policies (Gouvernement du Québec 2010, 150-52; Beaujot and Wang 2010).

Is this new redistribution model sustainable within a less redistributive Canada? In fact, the Quebec model may influence other governments, as can be seen in public pressures for better early childhood education and care policies, in the diffusion of strategies against poverty across provinces in the 2000s, or in the influence of Quebec's integrated active labour market measures on federal programs (Mahon 2009; Standing Committee 2010, 63-79; Noël 2012). As Mahon explains in her chapter (this volume), however, outside Quebec civil society organizations often fail to mobilize at the provincial scale. In fact, Quebec's initiatives may even fuel resentment in other provinces. A discourse popular in Alberta and Ontario, for instance, associates, wrongly, Quebec's more generous social services with the federal equalization program (Essen and Milke 2010; MacKinnon 2011).

Redistribution and state intervention remain popular in Quebec, and the ethos of Quebec politics continues to anchor public debates somewhere left of the centre. The political context could be changing, however, and the traditional parameters of Quebec politics may not hold.

Conclusion

When he resigned as premier in 2001, Lucien Bouchard had few fans on the Quebec left, partly because his government was associated with severe austerity policies. It remained that, in a difficult context – after a political defeat and with record-high public deficits – he succeeded in bringing together the key actors of Quebec society, including many that were traditionally excluded from such deliberations, to reach a new social pact addressing the deficit and employment and, more important, introducing a new redistribution model for the twenty-first century. Bouchard was not alone in this endeavour; the ethos of Quebec politics – favourable to equality and state intervention – strong trade unions, a dynamic women's movement, and a mobilized network of community organizations, all contributed to an innovative, positive-sum outcome.

Endowed since the 1960s with an Anglo-American, liberal welfare state, Quebec then developed a new and progressive work/family model that addressed the ubiquitous postindustrial issues raised by women's employment, new family patterns, a polarized and unstable labour market, and recurrent problems of poverty. With a reconfigured coalition of social forces, Quebec opened a new progressive path, well suited to meet the demands of a post-industrial society (Huo 2009; Esping-Andersen 2009).

In a world context inimical to social democracy, in a country governed by a conservative government with little interest in equality, and in a society in which trust in politics is now at a low ebb, maintaining and expanding a distinctive redistribution model will not be easy. The new Quebec model, however, remains well anchored in public opinion and in social institutions, and seems better suited for the challenges of the new century than does the standard liberal option. Only time will tell if this original and progressive version of the new politics of redistribution will prove resilient.

NOTE
I am grateful to the editors for their patient and helpful guidance as well as to the other book contributors and workshop participants for their comments and suggestions. I also thank Stéphane Crespo for his help with low-income statistics.

REFERENCES
Adams, Michael. 2003. *Fire and Ice: The United States, Canada and the Myth of Converging Values.* Toronto: Penguin.

Artemova, Olga. 2008. "La lutte pour l'équité salariale au Québec." Cahiers du CRISES, MS0804, Montréal, Centre de recherche sur les innovations sociales, April. http://www.crises.uqam.ca/upload/files/publications/mouvements-sociaux/MS0804.pdf.

Baer, Douglas, Edward Grabb, and William Johnston. 1993. "National Character, Regional Culture, and the Values of Canadians and Americans." *Canadian Review of Sociology and Anthropology* 30(1): 13-36.

Baker, Michael, Jonathan Gruber, and Kevin Milligan. 2008. "Universal Child Care, Maternal Labor Supply, and Family Well-Being." *Journal of Political Economy* 116(4): 709-45.

Banting, Keith. 2005. "Canada: Nation-Building in a Federal Welfare State." In Herbert Obinger, Stephan Leibfried, and Francis G. Castles, eds., *Federalism and the Welfare State: New World and European Experiences,* 89-137. Cambridge: Cambridge University Press.

Beach, Jane, Martha Friendly, Carolyn Ferns, Nina Prabhu, and Barry Forer. 2009. *Early Childhood Education and Care in Canada 2008.* 8th ed. Toronto: Early Childhood Resource and Research Unit.

Beaujot, Roderic, and Juyan Wang. 2010. "Low Fertility in Canada: The Nordic Model in Quebec and the US Model in Alberta." *Canadian Studies in Population* 37(3-4): 411-43.

Béland, Daniel, and André Lecours. 2008. *Nationalism and Social Policy: The Politics of Territorial Solidarity.* Oxford: Oxford University Press.

Béland, Nicolas, Éric Forgues, and Maurice Beaudin. 2010. "Inégalités salariales et bilinguisme au Québec et au Nouveau-Brunswick, 1970 à 2000." *Recherches sociographiques* 51(1-2): 75-101.
Bibi, Sami, and Jean-Yves Duclos. 2011. "L'effet des prélèvements fiscaux et des transferts aux particuliers sur la pauvreté au Québec et au Canada." *Canadian Public Policy* 37(1): 1-24.
Blouin, Olivier. 2005. "L'impact de la politique familiale de 1997 sur la dépendance à l'aide sociale des familles monoparentales." Mémoire de maîtrise en économie, Université Laval.
Bouchard, Lucien. 1996a. "Discours d'assermentation." Québec, Assemblée nationale, 29 January. http://www.archivespolitiquesduquebec.com/Bouchard.off.html.
–. 1996b. "Ouverture de la conférence sur le devenir économique et social du Québec." Québec, 18 March. http://www.archivespolitiquesduquebec.com/Bouchard.off.html.
–. 1996c. "Allocution devant la Chambre de commerce de Laval." Laval, 8 October. http://www.archivespolitiquesduquebec.com/Bouchard.off.html.
–. 1996d. "Clôture du sommet sur l'économie et l'emploi." Montréal, 1 November. http://www.archivespolitiquesduquebec.com/Bouchard.off.html.
Centre d'étude sur la pauvreté et l'exclusion. 2009. *Taking the Measure of Poverty: Proposed Indicators of Poverty, Inequality and Social Exclusion to Measure Progress in Quebec – Advice to the Minister*. Québec: Centre d'étude sur la pauvreté et l'exclusion.
Charest, Jean. 2003a. "Discours d'assermentation." Québec, 29 April. http://www.archivespolitiquesduquebec.com/Charestoff.html.
–. 2003b. "Discours d'ouverture." Québec, Assemblée nationale, 4 June. http://www.archivespolitiquesduquebec.com/Charestoff.html.
Clement, Wallace, and John Myles. 1994. *Relations of Ruling: Class and Gender in Postindustrial Societies*. Montreal and Kingston: McGill-Queen's University Press.
Comité consultatif de lutte contre la pauvreté et l'exclusion sociale. 2009. *Individual and Family Income Improvement Targets: On Optimal Means for Achieving Them, and on Baseline Financial Support*. Québec: CCLP.
Commission de l'équité salariale. 2006. *La loi sur l'équité salariale, un acquis à maintenir: Rapport du ministre du Travail sur la mise en œuvre de la Loi sur l'équité salariale*. Québec: Commission de l'équité salariale.
Conseil de gestion de l'assurance parentale. 2009a. *Dispositions des régimes d'assurance parentale dans certains pays d'Europe: Comparaison avec le Québec*. Québec: Conseil de gestion de l'assurance parentale.
Crespo, Stéphane. 2008. *Annuaire de statistiques sur l'inégalité de revenu et le faible revenu*. Québec: Institut de la statistique du Québec, December.
Daly, Mary. 2010. "Families versus State and Market." In Francis Castles, Stephan Leibfried, Jane Lewis, Herbert Obinger, and Christopher Pierson eds., *The Oxford Handbook of the Welfare State*, 139-51. Oxford: Oxford University Press.

–. 2011. "What Adult Worker Model? A Critical Look at Recent Social Policy Reform in Europe from a Gender and Family Perspective." *Social Politics* 18(1): 1-23.

Esping-Andersen, Gøsta. 2009. *The Incomplete Revolution: Adapting to Women's New Roles*. Cambridge, UK: Polity Press.

Essen, Ben, and Mark Milke. 2010. *The Real Have-Nots in Confederation: Ontario, Alberta and British Columbia: How Canada's Equalization Program Creates Generous Programs and Large Governments in Have-Not Provinces*. Winnipeg: Frontier Centre for Public Policy, FCPP Policy Series, 83, February.

Facal, Joseph, and Luc Bernier. 2008. "Réformes administratives, structures sociales et représentations collectives au Québec." *Revue française d'administration publique* 127(3): 493-510.

Frenette, Marc, David A. Green, and Kevin Milligan. 2009. "Taxes, Transfers, and Canadian Income Inequality." *Canadian Public Policy* 35(4): 389-411.

Godbout, Luc, Diana Darilus, and Suzie St-Cerny. 2010. "Fiscalité comparée: Une utilisation prédominante des assiettes fiscales au Québec." Document de travail 2010/05, Chaire de recherche en fiscalité et en finances publiques, Sherbrooke, Université de Sherbrooke, December.

Godbout, Luc, and Suzie St-Cerny. 2008. *Le Québec, un paradis pour les familles? Regards sur la famille et la fiscalité*. Québec: Presses de l'Université Laval.

Godbout, Luc, Suzie St-Cerny, and Chantal Amiot. 2010. "Année d'imposition 2008: Une charge fiscale nette plus faible et des impôts sur le revenu plus élevés qu'ailleurs, est-ce possible?" Document de travail 2010/03, Chaire de recherché en fiscalité et en finances publiques, Sherbrooke, Université de Sherbrooke, 17 March.

Godbout, Luc, Suzie St-Cerny, and Michaël Robert-Angers. 2011. "La charge fiscale nette en 2009: Une position compétitive pour le Québec combinée à une forte progressivité et à une prise en compte de la situation familiale." Document de travail 2011/0X, Chaire de recherché en fiscalité et en finances publiques, Sherbrooke, Université de Sherbrooke, 20 June.

Godin, Pierre. 2001. *René Lévesque*. Tome 3: *L'espoir et le chagrin 1976-80*. Montréal: Boréal.

Gouvernement du Québec. 2009. *Budget 2009-10: Status Report on Quebec's Family Policy*. Québec: Ministère des Finances, March.

–. 2010. *Budget 2010-11: Choices for the Future – Economic and Budgetary Action Plan*. Québec: Ministère des Finances, March.

Graefe, Peter. 2007. "State Restructuring and the Failure of Competitive Nationalism: Trying Times for Quebec Labour." In Michael Murphy, ed., *Canada: The State of the Federation 2005; Quebec and Canada in the New Century – New Dynamics, New Opportunities*, 153-76. Montreal and Kingston: McGill-Queen's University Press.

Haddow, Rodney, and Thomas Klassen. 2006. *Partisanship, Globalization, and Canadian Labour Market Policy: Four Provinces in Comparative Perspective*. Toronto: University of Toronto Press.

Hamel, Pierre, and Bernard Jouve. 2006. *Un modèle québécois? Gouvernance et participation dans la gestion publique*. Montréal: Presses de l'Université de Montréal.

Häusermann, Silja. 2010. *The Politics of Welfare State Reform in Continental Europe: Modernization in Hard Times*. Cambridge: Cambridge University Press.
Heintzman, Ralph. 1983. "The Political Culture of Quebec, 1840-60." *Canadian Journal of Political Science* 16(1): 3-59.
Huo, Jingjing. 2009. *Third Way Reforms: Social Democracy after the Golden Age*. Cambridge: Cambridge University Press.
Imbeau, Louis M., and Mélisa Leclerc. 2002. "L'élimination du déficit budgétaire au Québec: contexte et réalisation d'un engagement électoral." In François Pétry, ed., *Le Parti québécois: Bilan des engagements électoraux, 1994-2000*, 67-81. Québec: Presses de l'Université Laval.
Institut de la statistique du Québec. 2011a. *Income, Income Inequality and Low Income*. Québec: Institut de la statistique du Québec.
–. 2011b. *Comparaisons interprovinciales*. Tome 6: *La main d'oeuvre*. Québec: Institut de la statistique du Québec.
Jenson, Jane. 2002. "Against the Current: Child Care and Family Policy in Quebec." In Sonya Michel and Rianne Mahon, eds., *Child Care Policy at the Crossroads: Gender and Welfare State Restructuring*, 309-32. New York: Routledge.
–. 2009. "Lost in Translation: The Social Investment Perspective and Gender Equality." *Social Politics* 16(4): 446-83.
–. 2010. "Diffusing Ideas for After Neoliberalim: The Social Investment Perspective in Europe and Latin America." *Global Social Policy* 10(1): 59-84.
Kumlin, Staffan, and Bo Rothstein. 2005. "Making and Breaking Social Capital: The Impact of Welfare-State Institutions." *Comparative Political Studies* 38(4): 339-65.
Labrosse, Alexis. 2011. *La présence syndicale au Québec en 2010*. Québec: Ministère du Travail, Direction de l'information sur le travail, April. http://www.bdso.gouv.qc.ca/docs-ken/multimedia/PB01500FR_presence_syndicale2010 A00F01.pdf.
Laforest, Rachel. 2007. "The Politics of State/Civil Society Relationships in Quebec." In Michael Murphy, ed., *Canada: The State of the Federation 2005; Quebec and Canada in the New Century – New Dynamics, New Opportunities*, 177-98. Montreal and Kingston: McGill-Queen's University Press.
Lefebvre, Pierre, and Philip Merrigan. 2008. "Child-Care Policy and the Labor Supply of Mothers with Young Children: A Natural Experiment from Canada." *Journal of Labor Economics* 26(3): 519-48.
Lévesque, René. 1986. *Attendez que je me rappelle ...* Montréal: Québec/Amérique.
Levine, Marc V. 1997. *La reconquête de Montréal*. Montréal: VLB éditeur.
MacKinnon, David. 2011. *Dollars and Sense: A Case for Modernizing Canada's Transfer Agreements*. Toronto: Ontario Chamber of Commerce, February.
Mahon, Rianne. 2009. "Canada's Early Childhood Education and Care Policy: Still a Laggard?" *International Journal of Child Care and Education Policy* 3(1): 27-42.
–. 2010. "After Neo-Liberalism? The OECD, the World Bank and the Child." *Global Social Policy* 10(2): 172-92.
Mendelsohn, Matthew, Andrew Parkin, and Maurice Pinard. 2007. "A New Chapter or the Same Old Story? Public Opinion in Quebec from 1996-2003." In Michael

Murphy, ed., *Canada: The State of the Federation 2005; Quebec and Canada in the New Century – New Dynamics, New Opportunities*, 25-52. Montreal and Kingston: McGill-Queen's University Press.
Ministère de l'Emploi et de la Solidarité sociale. 2010. *Québec's Combat against Poverty: Government Action Plan for Solidarity and Social Inclusion, 2010-15*. Québec: Ministère de l'Emploi et de la Solidarité sociale, June.
–. 2011a. *Améliorer la situation économique des personnes: Un engagement continu – Rapport de la ministre de l'Emploi et de la Solidarité sociale en vertu de l'article 60 de la Loi visant à lutter contre la pauvreté et l'exclusion sociale*. Québec: Ministère de l'Emploi et de la Solidarité sociale, April.
–. 2011b. *Rapport statistique sur la clientèle des programmes d'assistance sociale*. Québec: Ministère de l'Emploi et de la Solidarité sociale, April.
Ministère de la Santé et des Services sociaux. 2002. *L'assurance-médicaments: Un acquis social à préserver*. Québec: Ministère de la Santé et des Services sociaux.
Murphy, Brian, Xuelin Zhang, and Claude Dionne. 2010. "Revising Statistics Canada's Low Income Measure (LIM)." Income Research Paper Series, Ottawa, Statistics Canada, Catalogue 75F0002M, 004, June.
Myles, John. 2000. "The Maturation of Canada's Retirement Income System: Income Levels, Income Inequality, and Low Income among the Elderly." Statistics Canada Working Paper, 147, Ottawa, Statistics Canada, March.
National Council of Welfare. 2008. *Welfare Incomes, 2006 and 2007*. Ottawa: National Council of Welfare.
Noël, Alain. 2002. "A Law against Poverty: Quebec's New Approach to Combating Poverty and Social Exclusion." Background Paper – Family Network, Ottawa, Canadian Policy Research Networks, December. http://www.cprn.org/documents/16409_en.pdf.
–. 2004. "A Focus on Income Support: Implementing Quebec's Law against Poverty and Social Exclusion." Commentary – Family Network, Ottawa, Canadian Policy Research Networks, May. http://www.cprn.org/documents/29659_en.pdf.
–. 2010. "Quebec." In John C. Courtney and David E. Smith, eds., *The Oxford Handbook of Canadian Politics*, 92-110. Oxford: Oxford University Press.
–. 2011. "Une lutte inégale contre la pauvreté et l'exclusion sociale." In Miriam Fahmy, ed., *L'état du Québec 2011*, 103-10. Montréal: Boréal.
–. 2012. "Asymmetry at Work: Quebec's Distinct Implementation of Programs for the Unemployed." In Keith Banting and Jon Medow, eds., *Making EI Work: Research from the Mowat Centre Employment Insurance Task Force*, 421-48. Montreal and Kingston: McGill-Queen's University Press. http://mowateitaskforce.ca/sites/default/files/Noel.pdf.
OECD. 2005. *Babies and Bosses: Reconciling Work and Family Life*. Vol. 4: *Canada, Finland, Sweden and the United Kingdom*. Paris: OECD.
–. 2008. *Growing Unequal: Income Distribution and Poverty in OECD Countries*. Paris: OECD.
–. 2009. *Taxing Wages, 2007-08*. Paris, OECD.
Pomey, Marie-Pascale, Pierre-Gerlier Forest, Howard A. Palley, and Elisabeth Martin. 2007. "Public/Private Partnerships for Prescription Drug Coverage:

Policy Formulation and Outcomes in Quebec's Universal Drug Insurance Program, with Comparisons to the Medicare Prescription Drug Program in the United States." *Milbank Quarterly* 85(3): 469-98.

Régie des rentes du Québec. 2011. "Amount of the Child Assistance Payment." Québec, Régie des rentes du Québec. http://www.rrq.gouv.qc.ca/en/enfants/naissance/paiement_soutien_enfants/Pages/montant.aspx.

Revenu Québec. 2011. "Work Premium." Québec, Revenu Québec. http://www.revenu.gouv.qc.ca/en/citoyen/credits/credits/credit_remb/prime_travail/.

Rothstein, Bo. 2005. *Social Traps and the Problem of Trust.* Cambridge: Cambridge University Press.

Roy, F. 2004. "Social Assistance by Province, 1993-2003." *Canadian Economic Observer,* Ottawa, Statistics Canada, November. http://www.statcan.gc.ca/ads-annonces/11-010-x/6000774-eng.pdf.

Royal Commission on Bilingualism and Biculturalism. 1969. *Report.* Vol. 3A. Ottawa: Queen's Printer.

Saint-Martin, Denis. 2001. "Guichet unique et reconfiguration des réseaux de politiques publiques: Le cas d'Emploi-Québec." *Politique et sociétés* 20(2-3): 117-39.

Savage, Larry. 2008. "Quebec Labour and the Referendums." *Canadian Journal of Political Science* 41(4): 861-87.

SOM Recherches et Sondages. 2006. *Étude sur le rendement de l'investissement relié à la participation aux mesures actives offertes aux individus par Emploi-Québec: Rapport d'évaluation présenté à la Direction de l'évaluation, Direction générale adjointe de la recherche, de l'évaluation et de la statistique.* Québec: Ministère de l'Emploi et de la Solidarité sociale.

Standing Committee on Human Resources, Skills and Social Development and the Status of Persons with Disabilities. 2010. *Federal Poverty Reduction Plan: Working in Partnership towards Reducing Poverty in Canada.* Ottawa, House of Commons, 40th Parliament, 3rd Session, November.

Statistics Canada. 2010. *Provincial and Territorial Economic Accounts: Data Tables, 2009.* 13-018-XWE, Ottawa, Statistics Canada.

Tilly, Charles. 1998. *Durable Inequality.* Berkeley: University of California Press.

Torjman, Sherri. 2010. *Poverty Reduction in Quebec: The First Five Years.* Ottawa: Caledon Institute of Social Policy, December.

Tremblay, Martine. 2006. *Derrière les portes closes: René Lévesque et l'exercice du pouvoir, 1976-85.* Montréal: Québec/Amérique.

Union des consommateurs. 2009. "Pour un régime public universel d'assurance-médicaments au Québec." Montréal, Union des consommateurs, June. http://www.consommateur.qc.ca/union-des-consommateurs/docu/sante/MemAssurRxJuin2009UC.pdf.

Vaillancourt, Yves. 2003. "The Quebec Model in Social Policy and Its Interface with Canada's Social Union." In Sarah Fortin, Alain Noël, and France St-Hilaire, eds., *Forging the Canadian Social Union: SUFA and Beyond,* 157-95. Montreal: Institute for Research on Public Policy.

Vaillancourt, Yves, with Philippe Leclerc. 2009. "Vers un État stratège partenaire de la société civile." In Louis Côté, Benoît Lévesque, and Guy Morneau, eds., *État stratège et participation citoyenne*, 235-74. Québec: Presses de l'Université du Québec.

Wallner, Jennifer. 2010. "Beyond National Standards: Reconciling Tension between Federalism and the Welfare State." *Publius: The Journal of Federalism* 40(4): 646-71.

Wilkinson, Richard, and Kate Pickett. 2009. *The Spirit Level: Why Greater Equality Makes Societies Stronger.* New York: Bloomsbury Press.

World Bank. 2005. *World Development Report 2006: Equity and Development.* Washington, DC: World Bank.

PART 2

POLICY

12

Health Care Policy after Universality
Canada in Comparative Perspective

CAROLYN HUGHES TUOHY

Together with public pensions, treated in the following chapter, health care forms one of the "rocks of stability" in an otherwise turbulent Canadian welfare state. Why this should be so presents an interesting puzzle. A possible explanation is that, at any given point in time, these programs disproportionately benefit a powerful voting bloc: the elderly. But this is also the case in other nations in which policy related to health care and/or pensions has been much more volatile. Rather, the keys to the relative lack of change in health care and pensions policy in Canada lie in the way these programs have been embedded in federal-provincial relations and the design of the programs themselves. Even while the core was being reinforced, however, health care was not immune from policy drift at the margins.

The Political Trajectory of the Health Care State in Advanced Nations

Universal health care is a pillar of the welfare state in most advanced nations. As a principal channel of redistribution, it follows a similar political trajectory across nations. Initially, establishing universal coverage sets off the classic *redistributive* form of politics described by Lowi (1964), marked by class conflict, ideological debate, and contests among peak associations representing powerful interests (business coalitions, labour federations, professional associations).[1] Once a significant proportion of health care costs is borne by public budgets, increases in health costs lead governments to seek ways to constrain cost increases, triggering a phase (or phases) of *retrenchment* (Pierson 1994), the timing of which varies according to a nation's fiscal climate. Marked by blunt across-the-board cuts, this phase focuses on the supply and remuneration of providers of health care as well as on stealthy, less visible strategies designed to reduce government expenditures. Retrenchment, however, encounters strong opposition from now-entrenched interests, both providers and beneficiaries, and governments seek ways to reinvest in health care that will make cost-effective changes in the design of the health care system. This third stage generates a politics of *hybridization,* in which strategic alliances between the state and key actors in the health delivery system play a pivotal role. As the fiscal climate shifts, governments may cycle back and forth between these last two phases.

In Canada, this process has played out with some important differences. The establishment of the universal "single-payer" policy framework for hospital and medical insurance in the 1950s and 1960s exemplified the high politics of redistribution (particularly when pioneered in Saskatchewan) and had clearly redistributive effects. But Canada's modern health care state was a hybrid from its conception. The now-iconic single-payer framework (which relies exclusively on universal tax-funded public finance) covers only hospital and physician services. Beyond those areas lies a realm of mixed public and private finance that varies across provinces and health care sectors. Over time, technological change has produced alternatives to hospitalization and occasionally to physician services. Thus, a further hybridization through policy drift (i.e., in the absence of action by governments) has occurred with the expansion of the share of non-hospital-based and non-physician services (Hacker 2004). Accordingly, the relative size of Canada's single-payer system has shrunk from about 60 percent of total health care expenditures in the 1970s to about 40 percent today, inverting the ratio of the single-payer system to the mixed-finance system.

In this process, both federal-provincial relations and the core accommodation between the medical profession and the state within the "single-payer" design of Canadian medicare limited the range of change possible in the physician and hospital sectors and also limited the possibilities for change in other interrelated areas such as long-term care. The 1990s featured blunt budget cuts to federal-provincial transfers and provincial health budgets, driven entirely by deficit-reduction agendas. When public budgetary balances were restored, retrenchment was quickly superseded by a "catch-up" phase of reinvestment. Unlike other nations, however, in Canada health care was privileged as an area of reinvestment, and innovation in finance and delivery was limited.

Overall, the marginal dollars spent in the era of reinvestment in Canadian health care have been less redistributive than have those spent in the era of medicare's establishment and have come at the expense of dollars that might have been spent to more redistributive effect outside the health care system. Health care has become not a pillar of the Canadian welfare state but a citadel: self-contained, impenetrable, and dominating.

Canadian Health Policy in Comparative Perspective

The Design of the Canadian Health Care State

Canada is the quintessential example of a "single-payer" system for physician and hospital services: the bulk of spending on physician and hospital services comes from a single source – government – and is financed from general tax revenue.[2] Physicians and hospitals remain "privately" organized; they are not employed or owned by government but are independent practitioners and not-for-profit institutions, respectively. For all other services, including prescription drugs and medical devices, the Canadian system is close to a "residual" welfare-state model (classically represented by the United States), in which most of the population relies on the private market, and government programs exist only for certain groups for whom the private market is considered to fail. (Residual systems also leave a significant minority of the population lacking coverage either through the market or government programs.) Some provinces operate universal programs for non-physician and non-hospital services such as home care and prescription drugs. The terms and conditions of these programs vary by province and may involve considerable private finance in the form of high co-payments and deductibles, often on an income-scaled basis. Non-universal public subsidies for lower-income and/or elderly individuals, with varying terms and conditions, are the norm for home care and prescription drugs in other provinces and for other services such as dental and eye care in all provinces.

These features of the policy framework result in a striking anomaly: Canada's single-payer system is the strictest one in the OECD,[3] yet the private share of total health spending is among the top third of OECD nations. Moreover, unlike other nations in which private financing is regulated and integrated into an overall financing framework, Canada leaves the privately financed area unregulated beyond basic safety provisions.

The single-payer and residual models represent two ways to organize the public/private boundary in health care. Other possibilities include the "national health service" model, in which the state employs physicians and other health care providers and owns hospitals and other health care institutions.[4] In the "social insurance" model,[5] financing is accomplished primarily through "sickness funds" funded by mandatory contributions from beneficiaries or employers. These sickness funds negotiate with health care providers for the provision of service to their beneficiaries.

Regardless of the basic design of health care financing and delivery, fiscal pressures bear strongly on the health care state. In response to these pressures, and given the policy goals of ensuring access to and quality of health services, these classic models of the health care state are becoming hybridized.

Health Care and the Fiscal Squeeze

Over the past three decades (1975 to 2007), public health spending as a proportion of GDP increased in all OECD nations for which we have consistent data (OECD 2010).[6] Various nations went through periods of constraint in public spending on health. In most cases, however, these constraints were blunt and disruptive and were quickly followed by significant public reinvestment.

For most of this period, increases in health care spending took place in the context of substantial growth in public revenues as a proportion of GDP. But the limits of tolerance for such increases were reached by the mid-1990s in most nations. Tax revenue as a proportion of GDP increased on average from 30.7 percent in 1975 to 36.8 percent in 1995 across twenty-one democratic OECD nations for which data are available,[7] then rose more slowly over the next decade to reach 37.5 percent by 2005. This pattern of levelling-off (or decline) varied across nations but held in thirteen of the twenty-one nations – including Canada, where tax revenues rose from 32 percent of GDP to 35.6 percent between 1975 and 1995, and declined to 33.4 percent by 2005 (see Figure 12.1). Over this time, health care spending accounted for an increasing share of total public spending. While it can be argued that the growth of health costs per se is not alarming and that the "sustainability" of public spending on health care is a matter of political will to maintain the necessary levels of taxation,[8] the waning of political will is a cross-national phenomenon.

In Canada, more than in any other of these nations, the increase in health care spending from 1995 to 2004 contrasted with declines in other areas of social spending (Table 12.1). The pride of place for health care in the Canadian welfare state is reflected in the high proportion of social expenditure

FIGURE 12.1

The fiscal context: Public health spending and government revenue as percentage of GDP, Canada and 21-nation OECD mean, 1975-2005

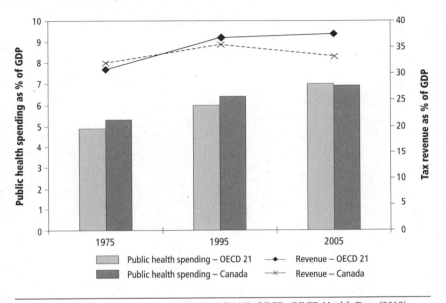

Sources: OECD, Revenue Statistics, 1965-2007 (2008); OECD, OECD Health Data (2012); Schieber and Poullier (1986); Huber (1999).

devoted to health care compared to other nations. Relative to other social services, health care spending rebounded faster from the fiscal austerity of the mid-1990s and benefited most from renewed spending in subsequent years.

The New Politics of Hybridization

Faced with increases in health care spending and with the non-sustainability of blunt budgetary restraint, governments across the OECD sought more focused strategies of structural change. The design of these strategies depended on political circumstances beyond the health care arena. The three leading examples of major health policy change in the past twenty years are the UK, the Netherlands, and the US. Elsewhere, I analyze the different strategies of change adopted in each of these nations and find one factor common to all: in the *implementation* phase, changes to mechanisms of health care delivery and finance were shaped by strategic alliances between

TABLE 12.1

Social expenditure as percentage of total government expenditure, Canada and 19-nation OECD mean, 1980-2007

	Canada	19-nation OECD mean
Total social spending as percentage of government spending		
1980	32.7	39.3
1995	39.4	44.5
2007	43.3	54.5
% point change, 1980-95	6.7	5.2
% point change, 1995-2007	3.9	10.0
% point change, 1980-2007	10.6	15.2
Health spending as percentage of government spending		
1980	12.3	11.6
1995	13.3	11.7
2007	17.8	15.1
% point change, 1980-95	1.0	0.1
% point change, 1995-2007	4.5	3.4
% point change, 1980-2007	5.5	3.5
Social spending other than health as percentage of government spending		
1980	20.4	27.7
1995	26.1	32.8
2007	25.5	39.4
% point change, 1980-95	5.7	5.1
% point change, 1995-2007	-0.6	6.6
% point change, 1980-2007	5.1	11.7

Source: OECD Social Expenditure Database (SOCX). http://www.oecd.org/social/soc/socialexpendituredatabasesocx.htm.

government reformers and certain actors in the health care arena (Tuohy 2010).

This phase of strategic redesign is marked by what I have termed the new politics of hybridization. By hybridization, I mean the mutation of systems that once represented welfare-state ideal types (national health service, social insurance, single-payer, and residual) to incorporate elements from other models. These mutations change the lines of accountability, instruments of control, and/or sources of finance within the system. For example, the UK's national health service model now incorporates elements of contracting among "purchasers" and "providers" that are more characteristic of markets than of hierarchies. The recent US reforms, as and when implemented, will leave the architecture of the residual system (private market, public safety nets) in place but graft a new element onto the private market (state-based health insurance exchanges, discussed below) to move the system closer to universal coverage.

The politics of this hybridization phase differ from both the "high politics" of welfare-state establishment and the stealth politics and short-term budgetary unilateralism of welfare-state retrenchment. In the hybridization phase, opportunities for reallocation and reinvestment are seized upon by certain actors within the health care system who see the potential to benefit from them. These may be commercial actors who seek financial profit or "social entrepreneurs" who hope to benefit a specific community. These actors determine the shape of reforms, either by joining forces with policy makers to influence the design of policy or simply by using newly available resources to innovate within the existing framework.

From the perspective of other policy arenas, the politics of hybridization (opportunistic alliances between state and other actors) is "politics as normal." But in health care it marks a change from the typical dominance of peak associations and occasional short-term statism. While the timing varies across nations, this type of politics tends to follow periods of retrenchment when blunt measures fail to stick. The advent of another period of retrenchment in the second decade of the twenty-first century, however, reminds us that mature health care states are likely to alternate between periods of retrenchment and periods of reinvestment.

Hybridization in Other Nations
In Britain, the "internal market" reforms adopted under Conservative governments in the 1990s separated the National Health Service hierarchy into "purchaser" and "provider" units who were henceforth to contract with each other within the publicly funded system. In the Netherlands, a twenty-year transition through a succession of coalition governments moved the system from a social insurance model to universal mandatory private insurance under an umbrella of regulated competition. In the US, recent reforms under a Democratic administration and Congress have adjusted the system of employer-based private insurance, moving from a residual model to universal

mandatory coverage. The residual gap is to be filled (albeit with some exemptions for "affordability") by a managed market for the purchase of private insurance by individuals and small employers, with income-scaled government subsidies.

In the British and Dutch cases, reforms were shaped during implementation by alliances of key actors who saw entrepreneurial advantages in certain reform elements. In the British (particularly the English) case, unexpected allies emerged in the form of general practitioners who embraced an initially small aspect of the reforms, a new "funding-holding" model giving them budgets from which to purchase a range of hospital and community services on behalf of their patients. The involvement of GPs in purchasing services gradually took on greater significance and was ultimately universalized. Concerns that fund-holders had better access to hospital services for their patients, thus creating a "two-tier" system, led the Labour government elected in 1997 to abolish the model. Soon thereafter, however, Labour adopted a universal model of purchasing ("commissioning") by Primary Care Groups (later Primary Care Trusts) – regionally based purchasing bodies advised by Professional Executive Committees composed of local GPs. In 2012, legislation enacted under the Conservative/Liberal-Democrat coalition government introduced a comprehensive and powerful model of purchasing by consortia of GP practices. Throughout all of these reforms, the entrepreneurial GPs who had emerged in the 1990s continued to play important political roles.

In the Netherlands, entrepreneurial managers of social insurance funds used the abolition of occupationally and regionally based monopolies to compete on a nationwide basis, laying the groundwork for a system of competition in a market encompassing all insurers. Policy entrepreneurs arose to develop the regulatory tools necessary for this "managed competition" model.[9]

In the US, after the establishment of public programs for the elderly and the poor in the 1960s, change was driven by entrepreneurs in the private sector. Public policy was reactive, fuelling a cycle of regulation and response that dramatically increased the sector's complexity and made comprehensive policy change more difficult. Although the strategic alliances that will drive the implementation of current reforms have yet to coalesce, the complexity of the US health care arena and the multiple provisions of the enabling legislation provide numerous opportunities for entrepreneurs to advance various elements of the reform framework (and potential veto points for opponents of change).

In other nations, such as France, Germany, Australia, and New Zealand, a more modest degree of hybridization has occurred in the absence of major system reform, again driven by strategic alliances within the health care arena. France and Germany have built upon their social insurance frameworks to achieve universal coverage by establishing public programs for those not covered by social insurance, and Germany has adopted a universal mandate for health insurance (Hassenteufel and Palier 2008). Australia has progressively integrated private health insurance into its health care financing regime by subsidizing and regulating it. In New Zealand, after a short-lived attempt in the 1990s to establish an "internal market" on the British model, "Independent Practitioner Associations" were established by GPs in the context of the internal market reforms and embraced by the centre-right government. These private physician-led IPAs survived attempts by the subsequent centre-left government to replace them with community-governed Primary Health Organizations, and they remained a strong element in an uneasy IPA-PHO amalgam (Gauld 2008; Thorlby et al. 2012).

Health Care Policy in Canada: Hybridization through Drift

In Canada, the opportunities for strategic alliances to drive reform are limited by the nature of the Canadian version of the single-payer model. Unlike the UK, the Netherlands, and the US, in the past four decades Canada has not experienced an episode of major change in health policy. Instead, incrementalism has been the hallmark of the "two worlds" of Canadian health policy: (1) the physician and hospital sectors, and (2) the rest of the health care system. For physician and hospital services, the limited range of variation has included differing provincial approaches to horizontal and vertical integration in the hospital and community sectors and limited experimentation with modes of physician remuneration.[10] In other sectors, provincial economies, political cultures, and structures of interest have driven more significant variations in coverage for drugs, long-term care, and other health care goods and services (Tuohy 2009).

Overall, however, the scope of the single-payer model has been reduced as policy change did not keep pace with technological and demographic change. Spending on areas such as prescription drugs (as a result of technological change) and long-term care (as a result of population aging) grew faster than did spending on physician and hospital services.[11] But while the scope of the single-payer system accordingly shrank from about 60 percent to just over 40 percent from 1975 to 2008, the overall public share of health care expenditure decreased only from 76 percent to 70 percent (Canadian Institute for Health Information 2011, 114, 118-19). This was true for two reasons. First, population aging actually counteracted the effects of technological change with regard to drug coverage. Most provinces at least initially based eligibility for their programs of coverage for prescription drugs on age, and crossing the sixty-five-year age threshold moved people *into* public programs. Second, most provincial governments expanded public programs of long-term care (including home care), as well as those for prescription drugs. As a result, the degree of privatization of the system was less for the elderly than it was for other age cohorts,[12] and, as more people moved into the elderly category, the extent of privatization was moderated. But it was not eliminated: in the face of technological change and the complex effects of population aging, the politics of drift have shrunk not only the single-payer system but also, at the margins, the role of the state itself.

To cite an example, the public share of drug spending more than doubled from 21 percent to 46 percent between 1975 and 2008. But because of the growth of the drug share of *total* health spending, private expenditures on drugs went from 5 percent of total health spending in 1975 to 7.5 percent in 2008, accounting for 2.5 percentage points of the 6 percentage point increase in the total private share. Furthermore, recent changes in public drug programs have been less redistributive than have earlier interventions. Programs of universal coverage for "catastrophic" expenditures on prescription drugs (expenditures exceeding a specified amount or a specified proportion of household income) introduced in the western provinces in the 1970s and 1980s and Ontario in the 1990s had a modestly redistributive effect for seniors but a larger effect for non-seniors, probably because of the greater equalization of seniors' incomes (Alan et al. 2002, 2005). In the 1990s and 2000s, the policy focus shifted from age-based to income-based eligibility for public coverage in some provinces, including British Columbia and Quebec,[13] but these programs have had little redistributive effect on equity in the share of household budgets spent on prescription drugs (Grootendorst and Racine 2005), in part because they also increased requirements for co-payments and deductibles.

To explain Canada's persistent incrementalism, we must look to the political dynamics of the single-payer model. Canada's health care system is politically dominated by two principal axes: first, the federal-provincial relationship under federal legislation establishes the model's basic principles (Canada Health Act); second, the profession-state relationship that governs the operation of the model in each province.

Federal-Provincial Relations and the Single-Payer Model

Canada comprises not one but thirteen single-payer systems; each of Canada's ten provinces and three territories operates its own health insurance plan within the framework of federal legislation. The Hospital and Diagnostic Services Insurance Act, 1958, and the Medical Care Act, 1966, provided universal public insurance for hospital and physician services. By 1971 all provinces had enacted legislation establishing universal programs in compliance with federal legislation. The two earlier pieces of federal legislation were consolidated and reinforced in the Canada Health Act, 1984.

Essentially, the federal single-payer framework has remained unchanged since the 1960s. The implications of this stability are twofold. First, no additional services have been brought into federal legislation, despite growth in sectors such as prescription drugs. Second, provinces have had few incentives to innovate in the delivery of physician and hospital services. Individual provinces have done so, depending on the nature of the profession-state relationship as discussed below.

The propitious climate of federal-provincial relations that enabled the framework's establishment in the late 1950s and 1960s was followed by three decades of constitutional wrangling that cast changes in the medicare framework as jurisdictional issues. Health care negotiations became fixated on federal transfers rather than on system change (Tuohy 1999). Intergovernmental relations were dominated by unilateral actions by the federal government, involving the progressive reduction of federal transfers. Despite a provincial-federal stalemate in health care, one significant action affected the policy framework – the enactment of the Canada Health Act, 1984; this reinforced the five principles for federal transfers: universality, comprehensiveness, accessibility, portability, and public administration. The act reinforced the "accessibility" criterion, providing for dollar-for-dollar penalties for any provinces allowing any charges to patients over and above the publicly insured benefit, but the federal government proved reluctant to exercise the sanctions available to it. Despite the occasional highly publicized showdown between the federal health minister and her provincial counterparts, penalties have been miniscule, amounting to $9 million *in total* from 1984 to 2007, while *annual* cash transfers rose from about $6 billion to $20 billion. Penalties concerned charges to patients by private clinics (cataract surgery, abortion, etc.) in BC, Alberta, Manitoba, Nova Scotia, and Newfoundland and Labrador. Given the politically sensitive aspects of the exercise of federal jurisdiction, Quebec was not penalized, despite practices similar to those in BC. The act gives the minister of health discretionary authority to withhold payment for non-compliance with any other principle, but that authority has never been exercised.

Federal transfers continued to decline as a share of provincial health expenditures over the 1980s and early 1990s. Then, in 1995, driven by a deficit- and tax-reduction agenda, the federal Liberal government consolidated transfers for health, social assistance, and postsecondary education to create a new Canada Health and Social Transfer, drawing up a schedule for the reduction of those transfers. The agenda of tax reduction and fiscal prudence was shared by the provinces (Conference Board of Canada 2001, 85-95), some of whom had already begun to reduce real per capita spending on health care.

As a result of fiscal constraint at both levels of government, between 1992 and 1996, real per capita public health care spending declined by about 8 percent. As budgets were brought into balance between 1996 and 2000, spending rebounded, increasing by 16 percent. These fiscal swings shook public confidence in the health care system and the ability of governments to manage it. Polls in the late 1990s and early 2000s consistently demonstrated this erosion of faith (Tuohy 2009). The proportion of Canadians in a cross-national survey reporting that the health care system needed "only minor change" plunged between 1988 and 1998 and did not rebound proportionately with increased public investment. Conversely, those believing that the system needed to be "rebuilt completely" soared from a miniscule 5 percent to 23 percent between 1988 and 1998. That proportion declined steadily as spending increased but still stood at twice the 1988 level in 2010.[14] In light of this public sentiment and the intergovernmental blame-shifting that accompanied the fiscal restraint of the 1990s, health care dominated the intergovernmental agenda.

The first few years of the twenty-first century were a time of ferment in health policy. Federal and provincial commissions (Alberta, Quebec, and Saskatchewan) explored a greater range of options than had been in play since the inception of medicare. The system seemed poised for significant change. The question was whether this change would occur within the parameters of the Canadian single-payer model or whether the model would be changed. The debate centred on increased roles for market instruments (opening up competition between private clinics and public hospitals for the provision of publicly funded services) and private finance (allowing privately purchased alternatives to publicly funded services and/or for medical savings accounts). Nonetheless, although the rhetoric varied considerably, the commissions all recommended maintaining and enhancing the essential features of the Canadian model.

In short, the Canadian model of health care finance passed a crucial test in the early 2000s. Some conditions for major change coalesced – including a more propitious federal-provincial climate dominated by health care and a rising sense of public concern that might have strengthened the political will to act. Yet the essential features of the single-payer system were reaffirmed and maintained.

While the tone of federal-provincial relations remained acrimonious in the wake of intergovernmental blame-shifting, health care dominated the intergovernmental agenda. As the fiscal situation turned around, health care remained a high reinvestment priority. In 2000, 2003, and 2004, the federal government committed, at first unilaterally and then through federal-provincial agreement, to higher cash transfers to the provinces for health care.

Most of the increased funding went to the federal base transfer to the provinces, for which accountability mechanisms are weak, from $15.5 billion (for health and social services) in 2000-01, to $19 billion (health services only) in 2005-06, to be escalated by 6 percent annually thereafter to 2013-14. In 2000 and 2003, $16.8 billion was provided for specific priorities (primary care, home care, and catastrophic drugs), but, as of 2005, $13.5 billion of this was simply folded into the base transfer. In 2004, a ten-year "Accord" was reached, under which the Canada Health and Social Transfer (CHST) was split into separate transfers for health and social services. The Canada Health Transfer (CHT) was set at a base of $19 billion and escalated at 6 percent thereafter (Canada 2008a, 2008b, 2008c). The base for the Canada Social Transfer, covering federal contributions for social assistance and postsecondary education, was set at $8.28 billion, to be increased to $10.85 billion by 2009-10, and thereafter to increase by 3 percent annually to 2013-14 (Gauthier and Fard 2009). By 2011-12, the cash transfer stood at $27 billion, about 20 percent of total provincial health expenditures.

Attention to reducing waiting times for health services, principally elective surgery and diagnostic services, figured prominently in the 2004 accord and thereafter. Frustrated by the failure of spending increases to allay public concerns, politicians sought to direct marginal expenditures to areas that could yield measurable and publicly demonstrable improvements. The targeted initiative receiving the single largest infusion was a wait times reduction fund, allocated $5.5 billion under the 2004 accord and enhanced by another $612 million in the federal 2007 budget. The services to be targeted were left to the provinces and shaped by profession-state relations in each province, as discussed below.

Evidence of the impact of these new federal investments is sparse. As a condition for their receipt, the provinces undertook to report publicly on comparable measures of performance, to be facilitated by the Health Council of Canada. The council was initially conceived as an impartial body, but its membership became determined by federal/provincial/territorial ministers of health. The reporting commitments made by provincial governments had, by and large, not been met four years later. A progress report issued by the council in 2008 was lukewarm, noting that implementation of the federal-provincial accords and agreements of 2003 and 2004 represented a "glass half full" (Health Council of Canada 2008). Even reductions in waiting times showed little consistency across provinces, as noted below.

Waiting times also featured prominently in an unprecedented ruling by the Supreme Court of Canada in 2005, which overturned lower court decisions and struck down Quebec legislation banning private insurance for publicly covered services as contrary to the Quebec Charter of Rights and Freedoms.[15] In response, the Quebec government took measures to establish "wait time guarantees" for specified services and to allow private insurance for a restricted scope of services to permit faster access than in the public system. No private insurance sector for these services has, in fact, arisen.

The federal-provincial "accord" of 2004 was a ten-year agreement. In December 2011, as provincial governments were preparing for a round of negotiations for a new agreement to take effect in 2014, the federal finance minister unilaterally announced that the 6 percent annual increase to the CHT would continue for three additional years, to 2017-18, after which the transfer would be escalated on a straight per capita basis by the rate of growth in GDP, or 3 percent, whichever is greater, annually to 2024-25. The federal government did not seek to influence provincial expenditure through the establishment of targeted funds as in the past, although federal spokespersons indicated that violations of the Canada Health Act would continue to be penalized. Given the very limited use of federal sanctions in the past, it is doubtful that enforcement of the CHA's provisions will be any more aggressive in the future.

The hands-off approach of the federal government, culminating in the December 2011 announcement, has, on the one hand, meant that the provinces have had considerable latitude to experiment with delivery modes; on the other hand, the provinces have had no federal backing in their negotiations with providers, and the dynamics of those negotiations militate against change.[16]

The Profession-State Accommodation within the Single-Payer Model

On the profession-state plane, the bilateral monopoly implied by a single-payer system draws governments and physicians into a tight accommodation that constrains both the scale and the pace of change. That accommodation, in turn, is shaped by internal politics, particularly the partisan cast of provincial governments and the general practitioner-specialist power balance within the provincial medical associations.

The fiscal contraction of the 1990s had serious effects on the profession-state accommodation. The design of the Canadian system meant that the impact of restraint was felt most sharply in areas with the greatest share of public spending: physician and hospital services. The nature of the founding bargain between the profession and the state placed the system's control levers in professional hands, leaving the state with access only to blunt measures of supply and budget control. These were exercised more vigorously than in the past: physician and hospital budgets were capped, and, in most provinces, caps on remuneration were instituted at the individual physician level. The number of practising physicians per capita remained unchanged, and the number of nurses per capita declined. In other OECD nations, these ratios continued to rise, albeit at a slower pace than in past years (OECD 2001).[17] Hospital beds per one thousand population also declined over the 1990s, as in most OECD nations.[18]

The fiscal swings of the 1990s and 2000s further concentrated the bilateral monopoly of the single-payer framework. In the early decades of Canadian medicare, the profession-state accommodation played out in multi-nodal networks in which academically based physicians had key strategic roles in some provinces (such as Ontario). But under the pressure of budgetary restraint in the 1990s, the negotiation table for remuneration supplanted other forums of profession-state interaction, and the bilateral relationship between governments and medical associations defined the politics of medicare (Tuohy 1999, 228-31). Although the internal politics of organized medicine varied across provinces, it was dominated by specialist groups who mobilized to protect their relatively high incomes in the negotiation process. The most substantial changes within the single-payer system involved the reorganization of the hospital sector in most provinces over the

1990s and 2000s. Each province chose a different model of regionalization, and regional structures have undergone considerable reorganization over the course of their existence: policies have cycled through different permutations in the number of regional authorities, their functional scope, the size of population served, and the mechanism of appointment or election to their boards. Common to all models, however, are a focus on the horizontal and vertical integration of hospital and community services (including social services in Quebec and PEI) and an exclusion of physician services and prescription drugs from the purview of regional authorities. All derive their budgets from the province; none has an independent revenue base, although some have increased flexibility to acquire capital. In all provinces except Ontario and Quebec, ownership and operation of hospitals has been shifted from local to regional not-for-profit corporations. In those two provinces, regional authorities have responsibilities for planning and allocation but not direct ownership and management.

In the era of "reinvestment" after the constraint of the 1990s, priorities in the physician sector were driven by demands for catch-up in remuneration within the context of negotiations between provincial governments and medical associations. More attention was paid to alternative (fee-for-service) forms of remuneration but to different degrees and with different results across provinces. In the wake of the federal-provincial accord of 2004, significant attention was paid to reducing wait times. Areas targeted for wait time reduction varied across provinces but overwhelmingly focused on specialist services, reflecting the power of specialist groups. In December 2005, the premiers agreed to establish pan-Canadian benchmarks for medically acceptable wait times. The priority areas identified at the national level were cancer and cardiac care, diagnostic imaging, joint replacement, and cataract surgery.

Both policy and action have varied considerably across provinces. Partly as a result of different intra-professional balances of power, provinces have targeted different procedures for wait time reduction and have used such different measures that cross-provincial comparison is difficult, even impossible. Identification of trends in wait times is hobbled by changes in definitions and measurement. By 2010, only Ontario and BC had reported that at least 75 percent of patients were receiving care within the specified benchmark for radiation therapy for cancer, hip replacement, hip fracture repair, knee replacement, and cataract surgery (Canadian Institute for Health Information 2010).

These policy developments have opened up limited space for entrepreneurial innovation within the single-payer model. In the hospital sector, some hospital CEOs saw opportunities within the new regional frameworks and experimented with market-oriented business models, contracting mechanisms, and capital acquisition strategies. But even here, politics constrained the range of innovation. In Alberta, for example, after developing a sophisticated, entrepreneurial, and mature regional structure, the provincial government abruptly consolidated all regional authorities into one provincewide board in 2008. The reasons for this decision are unclear, but arguably the entrepreneurial competition between regional hospital systems in Calgary and Edmonton mobilized political opposition within the provincial government (Donaldson 2010).

Another type of entrepreneurial activity within the single-payer system was spurred by the focus on reducing wait times for diagnostic imaging and elective surgery. In some provinces, privately capitalized, specialized clinics were established by entrepreneurs (usually specialist physicians) to contract with public authorities for the provision of their services on a publicly funded basis. Outside the hospital sector, experimentation with "primary care reform" encouraged entrepreneurial family practitioners to establish multi-provider practices and networks. Entrepreneurial activity in each of these areas may yet drive change in the single-payer system to include a broader range of providers than traditional medical practices on an internal market model. To date, however, changes have been held hostage to comprehensive profession-state negotiations over remuneration and the protection of a fee-for-service "pot."

Outside the Single-Payer Model: Prescription Drugs

Greater cross-provincial variation has prevailed in areas outside physician and hospital services that were never incorporated into the single-payer model (Tuohy 2009). All provinces offer coverage for out-of-hospital drugs, long-term care, and home care to some segments of their populations, and varying degrees of coverage are provided for non-physician services such as dental care, eye care, physiotherapy, and chiropractic care. Because terms of eligibility and scope of benefits vary widely, the public share of total expenditures shows sharp cross-provincial differences. From the 1980s through the 2000s, this variation increased through incremental changes in provincial policies – most relating to eligibility for public subsidies.

Provincial programs for out-of-hospital prescription drug coverage illustrate this cross-provincial variation (Grootendorst and Racine 2006; Morgan

2008; Standing Senate Committee on Social Affairs, Science and Technology 2002, 130-37). Since the 1970s, all provinces have operated plans covering social assistance recipients, although some require co-payments and/or deductibles. In the past thirty years, there have been numerous extensions and clawbacks of eligibility for public coverage. Most provinces introduced coverage of those aged sixty-five and older, and most increased these co-payments over time. In the past decade, three provinces (BC, Saskatchewan, and Manitoba) shifted from age-based to income-based coverage for the entire population. Ontario added "catastrophic" coverage for the entire population to its more comprehensive programs for the elderly and social assistance recipients in the 1990s. The most substantial change occurred in Quebec. Since 1998, all residents are required to have comprehensive insurance for prescription drugs, integrating employer-based coverage into an overall regime of public and private financing and offering a public program with an income-based premium for those without access to employer-based coverage.

Redistribution in the Canadian Health Care State

Comparisons of Canadian provinces before and after the introduction of universal hospital and medical insurance, as well as Canada-US comparisons, show that the introduction of universal insurance has redistributive effects (Enterline et al. 1973; Greenhill and Hawthorne 1972; Beck 1974; McDonald et al. 1974; Siemiatycki, Richardson, and Pless 1980; Manga 1978; Barer, Manga, and Shillington 1982; Blackwell et al. 2009; Schoen et al. 2000; Decker and Remler 2004).[19] Nonetheless, universal coverage does not remove all income-related effects. A "pro-rich" bias continues to exist for specialist services (elective surgery and diagnostic imaging) such as those targeted in Canada in the 2000s by the focus on reducing wait times. The use of specialist services, cardiac care, and diagnostic imaging is associated with income, even under universal insurance (Allin 2006; Alter et al. 1999; Demeter et al. 2005; Dunlop, Coyte, and McIsaac 2000; Hutchison 2007). These findings are consistent with cross-national results showing a "pro-rich" bias in access to specialist services, controlling for health need, across twenty-one OECD nations, most of which have universal coverage (van Doorslaer, Masseria, and Koolman 2006). Findings with regard to GP services are more mixed (Allin 2006; Dunlop, Coyte, and McIsaac 2000; Schoen et al. 2000; Van Doorslaer, Masseria, and Koolman 2006). Most international and Canadian studies find no bias or a pro-poor bias in the use of hospital services (Allin 2006). Studies in both Canada and the US show that emergency room utilization is associated with low income, even when individuals have government health insurance (DeLia and Cantor 2009; Ionescu-Ittu et al., 2007; Mustard et al. 1998).

These findings dovetail with more general cross-national findings about the redistributiveness of spending on various social programs. There is considerable variation across OECD nations in the relative weight of in-kind versus cash benefits in reducing income inequality and the in-kind benefits provided. On balance, Marical et al. (2006) show that in-kind health benefits are redistributive in nature, albeit less so than cash benefits. Controlling for variation in health care prices across nations, Garfinkel, Rainwater, and Smeeding (2006) find that valuing health benefits at their average cost across nations (to take out the effect of cross-national price differences and represent the "inherent" value of benefits) reduces their redistributive effect in several nations, notably the US. Glied (2008) takes this analysis further, adopting a "lifecycle" approach to draw attention to the fact that upper-income individuals are likely to live longer past age sixty-five and, hence, to populate disproportionately the highest-utilization age demographic for health care services. Glied argues that marginal investments in primary care are less likely to suffer from this pro-rich bias – a point to which I return below.

Access to health care is not a good in itself. Health care services represent only one contributor to health status,[20] and not the most powerful. A growing literature suggests a linkage not only of income to health at the individual level but also (more controversially) of income inequality and social exclusion to the health status of populations (Evans, Barer, and Marmor 1994; House 2001; Wilkinson and Pickett 2009). Spending on primary education, meanwhile, is considerably more redistributive than is spending on health care (Garfinkel, Rainwater, and Smeeding 2006). If increased health spending comes at the expense of income transfers and education spending, the implications may be negative in the longer term for health status overall. This is, of course, hypothetical: there is no guarantee that reducing the fiscal pressure of health care on public budgets would result in increased spending in these more redistributive areas. Nonetheless, the fiscal pressure of health care makes spending in other areas less possible in the foreseeable fiscal climate.

A Policy Envoi

The most effective redistributive measure within Canada's single-payer system for physician and hospital services would be to accelerate the adoption of new models of primary care, given their pro-poor bias. True gatekeeping in primary care establishes first contacts, points of referral, and sources of continuity, with the potential to improve the quality and efficiency of care and to reduce the rate of escalation in health care costs. As noted by Hutchison, Ableson, and Lavis (2001), policy legacies limit options; a focus on cumulative incremental change with a pluralism of models across provinces is not only unavoidable but also desirable. To this, I add the importance of identifying strategic allies by developing enhanced models with greater purchasing authority to attract the entrepreneurialism of GPs on the British model.

Moving in this direction would mean building on developments under way in all provinces, albeit at greatly varying paces. To date, the limited restructuring has involved group-based funding arrangements for certain specialists in certain hospitals (beginning with teaching hospitals) and primary care reform. All provinces have tentatively established new models for the provision of primary care through community clinics, group practices, networks, and teams, including family physicians and nurses. Most but not all require patients to enrol with the providing practice, clinic, or network; they are funded on a composite basis, taking account of the population served and provide 24/7 access to a comprehensive range of primary care services. Ontario has established "Family Health Groups" and "Family Health Networks" (family physicians entering into group contracts to provide extended hours of service and off-hours telephone advice to enrolled patient populations), and "Family Health Teams" (interdisciplinary practices comprising non-physicians and physicians). In Quebec, Family Medicine Groups are being established under the planning auspices (but not the financial purview) of regional health agencies. In both Ontario and Quebec, the contracts and agreements show considerable variety with regard to the terms for remunerating physicians and the mechanisms for integrating service provision. Notably, in none do family practitioners play a purchasing role for services beyond primary care (unlike Primary Care Trusts in the UK). These gradual moves have involved intensive negotiations with provincial medical associations and have proceeded on a voluntary basis, unlike the horizontal and vertical restructuring in hospital and community care.

The second priority lies outside the single-payer model. The area of greatest promise is coverage for prescription drugs. Not only have prescription drug costs grown faster than have physician and hospital services, but coverage remains uneven across provinces. Various models for achieving universal coverage for prescription drugs have been proposed, and their relative merits are beyond the scope of this chapter (Evans, Hertzman, and Morgan 2007; Flood, Stabile, and Tuohy 2008; National Forum on Health 1997; Standing Senate Committee on Social Affairs, Science and Technology 2002). While moving to universal drug coverage could improve the equitableness of the Canadian system, the degree of redistribution depends on the program's design, especially its intersection with other public programs and private insurance. Another area of highly uneven coverage (and looming larger than prescription drugs in public consciousness) is long-term care for the elderly. This area is ripe for innovation, as developments in other nations such as Britain are demonstrating.

Summary

The modern Canadian health care system of finance and delivery has always been hybrid, combining a single-payer model for physician and hospital services with a residual model for everything else. The hybridization dynamic found in other nations is driven by strategic alliances between policy makers and certain actors in the health care arena who see entrepreneurial advantages in certain reforms. While such alliances are inhibited in Canada by the bilateral monopoly of the single-payer system, further hybridization has occurred "passively" as technology has moved goods and services (notably drugs) outside the boundaries of the single-payer system into a world of mixed finance, causing the scope of the single-payer model to shrink from 60 percent to 40 percent.

To shift the focus of health care spending in Canada to areas with the greatest redistributive potential and to reduce budgetary pressures on other redistributive programs, policy makers must become active participants in a Canadian version of the "politics of hybridization" that characterize other mature heath care states. There is no necessary connection, either positive or negative, between the entrepreneurial activity typical of hybridization politics and redistributive spending. The challenge for policy makers is to identify entrepreneurial allies within the health care arena and to create opportunities for those allies within the public system. In the case of primary care reform, the family practitioner community is a potential locus of allies. In the case of prescription drug coverage, models that incorporate the existing base of private insurance into an integrated model of public and private finance could make private insurers allies of reform (as in Quebec and the Netherlands). No dramatic course correction is likely in Canadian health care policy. But these reforms in primary care and drug coverage are consistent with Canada's pattern of incrementalism. If carefully crafted and strategically implemented, they can nudge the trajectory of change towards greater equity and efficiency.

NOTES

1. These politics were in full play during the 2009-10 health reform episode in the US.
2. In 2012, about 99 percent of total spending on physician services and 90 percent of total spending on hospital services came from public sources (Canadian Institute for Health Information 2012, Table C.1.4).
3. The federal framework legislation establishes penalties for provinces that allow co-payments or extra charges to patients for physician and hospital services, and private markets for health insurance for these services are either banned or tightly constrained in all provinces
4. Often called the "Beveridge" model after its author, who successfully proposed a version of it in the UK in the mid-twentieth century.
5. Often called the "Bismarck" model after the German chancellor who introduced it in the late nineteenth century.
6. The only nations to increase public health spending by less than two percentage points of GDP over the full 1975-2007 period were Denmark and Sweden (two of the highest spenders at the beginning of the period) and Ireland (the result of its rapid and dramatic GDP increase).
7. Iceland and Luxembourg should not be included in calculations of means, given their small size.
8. See, for example, Evans, Hertzman, and Morgan (2007, 292-93, 301-3).
9. This label overstates the degree of management and the degree of competition. The market is dominated by relatively few large insurers, functioning on a not-for-profit basis (although the largest is part of a large for-profit corporate structure). The Dutch developed "risk-adjustment" mechanisms aimed at preventing insurers from selecting only healthier individuals, but competition on quality is emerging only slowly (Maarse and Paulus 2011).
10. "Horizontal integration" refers to bringing individual hospitals under a common umbrella. "Vertical integration" refers to combining hospitals with other types of providers within a common organizational framework.
11. Between 1980 and 2008, total health care spending grew at an annual average of 7.4 percent for non-hospital (principally long-term care) institutions and 11 percent for drugs, as compared with 6.5 percent for hospitals. (Calculated from Canadian Institute for Health Information 2011, 143).
12. Private expenditure as a share of total health expenditure rose by 4.5 percentage points (from 16.8 to 21.3 percent) between 1980 and 2000 for those over sixty-five, in contrast to a 9.4 point shift (from 29.4 to 38.8 percent) for those in the forty-five to fifty-four-year age bracket (Health Canada 2001).
13. Ontario's program extends only catastrophic insurance to the general population as well as to the elderly.

14 The third possible response is that the system "has some good things but needs fundamental changes." For full results, see Blendon et al. (2002); Schoen et al. (2004, 2007, 2010).
15 The case was brought by a physician and a patient who claimed that the ban on purchasing insurance to obtain faster access to services on a privately financed basis constituted an undue infringement on the claimant's constitutional right to "security of person."
16 To be fair, the provinces have not explicitly sought such backing, preferring always that federal transfers be as unconditional as possible.
17 OECD reference is to the 1992-97 period.
18 The hospital beds/1000 population ratio declined by 22.5 percent in Canada from 1991 to 2001, the eighth largest decline among the twenty-three OECD nations for which data are available for both years.
19 Although cross-national studies of utilization need to be treated with caution because of many possible confounding variables, the linkage of higher socio-economic status with higher levels of utilization of certain health care services has been found to be stronger in the US than in Canada (Blackwell et al. 2009; Schoen et al. 2000; Decker and Remler 2004). Other Canada-US studies focusing on particular health care services and/or health conditions have shown mixed results, a reminder of the fraught nature of cross-national comparisons of multi-factoral causal effects (O'Neill and O'Neill 2007).
20 The contribution may not always be positive. The incidence and consequences of "medical error" and in-hospital "adverse incidents" are receiving policy attention in several nations.

REFERENCES

Alan, Sule, Thomas F. Crossley, Paul Grootendorst, and Michael R. Veall. 2002. "The Effects of Drug Subsidies on Out-of-Pocket Prescription Drug Expenditures by Seniors: Regional Evidence from Canada." *Journal of Health Economics* 21: 805-26.

–. 2005. "Distributional Effects of 'General Population' Prescription Drug Programs in Canada." *Canadian Journal of Economics* 38(1): 128-48.

Allin, Sara. 2006. "Equity in the Use of Health Services in Canada and Its Provinces." Working Paper No: 3/2006. October. London: London School of Economics and Political Science.

Alter, D.A., C.D. Naylor, P. Austin, and J.V. Tu. 1999. "Effects of Socioeconomic Status on Access to Invasive Cardiac Procedures and on Mortality after Acute Myocardial Infarction." *New England Journal of Medicine* 341(18): 1359-67.

Barer, M., P. Manga, and R. Shillington. 1982. *Income Class and Hospital Use in Ontario*. Toronto: Ontario Economic Council.

Beck, R.G. 1974. "Economic Class and Access to Physician Services under Public Medical Care Insurance." *International Journal of Health Services* 3(3): 341-55.

Blackwell, D.L., M.E. Martinez, J.F. Gentleman, C. Sanmartin, and J.M. Berthelot. 2009. "Socioeconomic Status and Utilization of Health Care Services in

Canada and the United States: Findings from a Binational Health Survey." *Medical Care* 47(11): 1136-46.

Blendon, Robert J., Cathy Schoen, Catherine M. DesRoches, Robin Osborn, and Kimberly L. Scoles. 2002. "Trends: Inequities in Health Care – A Five-Country Survey." *Health Affairs* 21: 182-91.

Canada. Department of Finance. 2008a. *Federal Investments in Support of the 2003 Accord on Health Care Renewal.* http://www.fin.gc.ca/fedprov/2003a-eng.asp.

–. 2008b. *Federal Transfers in Support of the 2000/2003/2004 First Ministers' Accords.* http://www.fin.gc.ca/fedprov/fmAcc-eng.asp.

–. 2008c. *Federal Investments in Support of the 10-Year Plan to Strengthen Health Care.* http://www.fin.gc.ca/fedprov/typhc_-eng.asp.

Canadian Institute for Health Information. 2010. *Wait Times Tables: A Comparison by Province, 2010.* http://secure.cihi.ca/cihiweb/products/wait_times_tables_2010_e.pdf.

–. 2011. *National Health Expenditure Trends, 1975-2010.* http://secure.cihi.ca/cihiweb/products/NHEX_Trends_Report_2010_final_ENG_web.pdf.

–. 2012. NHEX Datatables 2012. https://secure.cihi.ca/estore/productFamily.htm?locale=en&lang=en&pf=PFC1952

Conference Board of Canada. 2001. *Performance and Potential, 2001-02.* Ottawa: Conference Board of Canada.

Decker, Sandra L., and Dahlia K. Remler. 2004. "How Much Might Universal Health Insurance Reduce Socioeconomic Disparities in Health? A Comparison of the US and Canada." Working Paper 10715. August. Cambridge, MA: National Bureau of Economic Research. http://www.nber.org/papers/w10715.

DeLia, Derek, and Joel Cantor. 2009. "Emergency Department Utilization and Capacity." Research Synthesis Report 17. July. Princeton, NJ: Robert Wood Johnson Foundation. http://www.rwjf.org/files/research/072109policysynthesis17.emergencyutilization.pdf.

Demeter, Sandor, Martin Reed, Lisa Lix, Leonard MacWilliam, and William D. Leslie. 2005. "Socioeconomic Status and the Utilization of Diagnostic Imaging in an Urban Setting." *Canadian Medical Association Journal* 173(10): 1173-77.

Donaldson, Cam. 2010. "Fire, Aim ... Ready? Alberta's Big Bang Approach to Healthcare Disintegration." *Healthcare Policy* 6(1): 22-31.

Dunlop, S., P.C. Coyte, and W. McIsaac. 2000. "Socio-Economic Status and the Utilisation of Physicians' Services: Results from the Canadian National Population Health Survey." *Social Science and Medicine* 51(1): 123-33.

Enterline, P.E., V. Salter, A.D. McDonald, and J.C. McDonald 1973. "The Distribution of Medical Services before and after 'Free' Medical Care: The Quebec Experience." *New England Journal of Medicine* 289(22): 1174-78.

Evans, Robert G., Morris L. Barer, and Theodore R. Marmor, eds. 1994. *Why Are Some People Healthy and Others Not?* New York: Aldine de Gruyter.

Evans, Robert G., Clyde Hertzman, and Steve Morgan. 2007. "Improving Health Outcomes in Canada." In Jeremy Leonard, Christopher Ragan, and France St-Hilaire, eds., *A Canadian Priorities Agenda: Policy Choices to Improve Economic*

and Social Well-Being, 291-326. Montreal: Institute for Research on Public Policy.
Flood, Colleen, Mark Stabile, and Carolyn Hughes Tuohy, eds. 2008. *Exploring Social Insurance: Can a Dose of Europe Cure Canadian Health Care Finance?* Montreal and Kingston: McGill-Queen's University Press.
Garfinkel, Irwin, Lee Rainwater, and Timothy M. Smeeding. 2006. "A Re-examination of Welfare States and Inequality in Rich Nations: How In-Kind Transfers and Indirect Taxes Change the Story." *Journal of Policy Analysis and Management* 25(4): 897-919.
Gauld, Robin. 2008. "The Unintended Consequences of New Zealand's Primary Health Care Reforms." *Journal of Health Politics, Policy and Law* 33(1): 93-115.
Gauthier, James, and Shahrzad Mobasher Fard. 2009. *The Canada Social Transfer.* Ottawa: Parliamentary Information and Research Service, Library of Parliament, 23 July. http://www2.parl.gc.ca/content/LOP/ResearchPublications/prb0857-e.pdf.
Glied, Sherry. 2008. "Health Care Financing, Efficiency and Equity." In Colleen Flood, Mark Stabile, and Carolyn Hughes Tuohy, eds., *Exploring Social Insurance: Can a Dose of Europe Cure Canadian Health Care Finance?*, 37-58. Montreal and Kingston: McGill-Queen's University Press.
Greenhill, J., and D. Hawthorne. 1972. *Health Care Utilization Patterns of Albertans, 1968 and 1970.* Edmonton: Department of Community Medicine, University of Alberta.
Grootendorst, Paul, and Jeffrey S. Racine. 2006. "Distributional Effects of 'Needs-Based' Drug Subsidies: Regional Evidence from Canada." Working Paper, University of Toronto, 29 June. http://individual.utoronto.ca/grootendorst/pdf/rxshare_eur_workshop.pdf.
Hacker, Jacob S. 2004. "Review Article: Dismantling the Health Care State? Political Institutions, Public Policies and the Comparative Politics of Health Reform." *British Journal of Political Science* 34: 693-724.
Hassenteufel, Patrick, and Bruno Palier. 2008. "Towards Neo-Bismarckian Health Care States? Comparing Health Insurance Reforms in Bismarckian Welfare Systems." In Bruno Palier and Claude Martin, eds., *Reforming the Bismarckian Welfare Systems*, 40-61. Oxford: Blackwell.
Health Canada. 2001. *Health Expenditures by Age and Sex, 1980-81 to 2000-01* Ottawa: Health Canada. http://www.hc-sc.gc.ca/hcs-sss/pubs/expen-depens/2001-exp-depen-1980a/index-eng.php.
Health Council of Canada. 2008. *Rekindling Reform: Health Care Renewal in Canada 2003-2008.* Toronto: Health Council of Canada. http://www.healthcouncilcanada.ca/rpt_det.php?id=331.
House, James S. 2001. "Commentary: Relating Social Inequalities in Health and Income." *Journal of Health Politics, Policy and Law* 26(3): 523-32.
Huber, Manfred. 1999. "Health Expenditure Trends in OECD Countries, 1970-1997." *Health Care Financing Review* 21(2): 99-117.

Hutchison, Brian. 2007. "Disparities and Healthcare Access and Use: Yackety-Yack, Yackety-Yack." *Healthcare Policy* 3(2): 10-18.
Hutchison, Brian, Julia Abelson, and John Lavis. 2001. "Primary Care in Canada: So Much Innovation, So Little Change." *Health Affairs* 20(3): 16-31.
Ionescu-Ittu, Raluca, Jane McCusker, Antonio Ciampi, Alain-Michel Vadeboncoeur, Danièle Roberge, Danielle Larouche, Josée Verdon, and Raynald Pineault. 2007. "Continuity of Primary Care and Emergency Department Utilization among Elderly People." *Canadian Medical Association Journal* 177(11): 1362-68.
Lowi, Theodore J. 1964. "American Business, Public Policy, Case Studies, and Political Theory." *World Politics* 16: 677-715.
Maarse, Hans, and Aggie Paulus. 2011. "The Politics of Health-Care Reform in the Netherlands since 2006." *Health Economics, Policy and Law* 6: 125-34.
Manga, P. 1978. "The Income Distribution Effect of Medical Insurance in Ontario." Occasional Paper 6, Ontario Economic Council.
Marical, François, Marco Mira d'Ercole, Maria Vaalavuo, and Gerlinde Verbist. 2006. "Publicly Provided Services and the Distribution of Resources." Social, Employment and Migration Working Paper #45. Paris: Organisation for Economic Cooperation and Development
McDonald, A.D., J.C. McDonald, V. Salter, and P.E. Enterline. 1974. "Effects of Quebec Medicare on Physician Consultation for Selected Symptoms." *New England Journal of Medicine* 291(13): 649-52.
Morgan, Steve. 2008. "Grails, Veils, Shale and a Sail: Thoughts on Social Insurance for Canadian Pharmacare." In Colleen Flood, Mark Stabile and Carolyn Hughes Tuohy, eds., *Exploring Social Insurance: Can a Dose of Europe Cure Canadian Health Care Finance?*, 199-220. Montreal-Kingston: McGill-Queen's University Press.
Mustard, Cameron A., Anita L. Kozyrskyj, Morris L. Barer, and Sam Sheps. 1998. "Emergency Department Use as a Component of Total Ambulatory Care: A Population Perspective." *Canadian Medical Association Journal* 158(1): 49-55.
National Forum on Health. 1997. *Canada Health Action: Building on the Legacy*. Ottawa: Minister of Public Works and Government Services.
O'Neill, June E., and Dave M. O'Neill. 2007. "Health Status, Health Care and Inequality: Canada vs. the US." NBER Working Paper 13429. September. Cambridge, MA: National Bureau of Economic Research. http://www.nber.org/papers/w13429.
Organisation for Economic Cooperation and Development. 2001. *OECD Health at a Glance: How Canada Compares*. Policy Brief, October. http://www.oecd.org/dataoecd/5/25/2465559.pdf.
–. 2008. *Revenue Statistics 1965-2007, 2008 edition*. http://www.oecd.org/document/32/0,3343,en_2649_34533_44108128_1_1_1_1,00.html.
–. 2010. *OECD Health Data 2010*. http://www.oecd.org/document/16/0,3343,en_2649_34631_2085200_1_1_1_37407,00.html.
Pierson, Paul D. 1994. *Dismantling the Welfare State? Reagan, Thatcher and the Politics of Retrenchment*. New York: Cambridge University Press.

Schieber, George J. and Jean-Pierre Poullier. 1986. "International Health Care Spending." *Health Affairs* 5(3): 111-22.

Schoen, Cathy, Karen Davis, Catherine DesRoches, Karen Donelan, and Robert Blendon. 2000. "Health Insurance Markets and Income Inequality: Findings from an International Health Policy Survey." *Health Policy* 51: 67-85.

Schoen, C., Robin Osborn, Michelle M. Doty, Meghan Bishop, Jordan Peugh, and Nadita Murukutla. 2007. "Toward Higher-Performance Health Systems: Adults' Health Care Experiences in Seven Countries, 2007." Health Affairs, Web Exclusive: 26 (6): w717-w734. http://content.healthaffairs.org/cgi/reprint/26/6/w717

Schoen, Cathy, Robin Osborn, Phuong Trang Huynh, Michelle Doty, Karen Davis, Kinga Zapert, and Jordan Peugh. 2004. "Primary Care and Health System Performance: Adult's Experiences in Five Countries." Health Affairs, Web Exclusive W4: 487-503. October 28. http://content.healthaffairs.org/cgi/reprint/hlthaff.w4.487v1

Schoen, Cathy, R. Osborn, D. Squires, M. M. Doty, R. Pierson, and S. Applebaum. 2010. "How Health Insurance Design Affects Access to Care and Costs, by Income, in Eleven Countries." Health Affairs, Web First, 18 November. http://www.commonwealthfund.org/~/media/Files/Publications/In%20the%20Literature/2010/Nov/Int%20Survey/1457_Schoen_how_hlt_ins_design_2010_intl_survey_HA_WebFirst_11182010_ITL_v2.pdf.

Siemiatycki, J., L. Richardson, and I.B. Pless. 1980. "Equality in Medical Care under National Health insurance in Montreal." *New England Journal of Medicine* 303(1): 10-15.

Standing Senate Committee on Social Affairs, Science and Technology. 2002. *The Health of Canadians: The Federal Role.* October. Ottawa: Parliament of Canada.

Thorlby, Ruth, Judith Smith, Pauline Barnett, and Nicholas Mays. 2012. *Primary Care for the 21st Century: Learning from New Zealand's Independent Practitioner Associations.* London: Nuffield Trust

Tuohy, Carolyn Hughes. 1999. *Accidental Logics: The Dynamics of Change in the Health Care Arena in the United States, Britain and Canada.* New York: Oxford University Press.

—. 2009. "Single Payers, Multiple Systems: The Scope and Limits of Subnational Variation under a Federal Health Policy Framework." *Journal of Health Politics, Policy and Law* 34(4): 453-96.

—. 2010. "Paths of Progress in Healthcare Reform: The Scale and Pace of Change in Four Advanced Nations." Paper presented at the American Political Science Association annual meeting, Washington, DC, 2-5 September. http://ssrn.com/abstract=1642790.

van Doorslaer, Eddy, Cristina Masseria, and Xander Koolman. 2006. "Inequalities in Access to Medical Care by Income in Developed Countries." *Canadian Medical Association Journal* 174(2): 177-83.

Wilkinson, Richard G., and Kate E. Pickett. 2009. "Income Inequality and Social Dysfunction." *Annual Review of Sociology* 35: 493-512.

13

Income Security for Seniors
System Maintenance and Policy Drift

JOHN MYLES

The Canadian experience in pension policy poses two puzzles. First, unlike many other affluent democracies, the Canadian pension design has been relatively stable; major reforms have been "system-maintaining" rather than "system-changing." Second, in comparison to other social programs (such as unemployment insurance and social assistance) old age pensions emerged relatively unscathed from Canada's "neoliberal" 1990s. And, by 2010, there was serious discussion at both federal and provincial levels of expanding the role of *public* pension institutions. This chapter looks at these puzzles, seeking to explain why public pensions have (thus far) been so stable in Canada.

By international standards, the core of Canada's public old age security system was left untouched by retrenchment efforts in the 1980s and 1990s. As with health care (Tuohy, Chapter 12, this volume), the Canada/Quebec Pension Plans were reinforced in the late 1990s with major new investments. Efforts to "retrench" Old Age Security (OAS) in the 1980s and 1990s were broadly resisted and largely turned back.[1] In both decades, cuts were made, but, by international standards, these were marginal. The core architecture that has reduced poverty and maintained retirement living standards among Canadian seniors remains largely intact.

Indeed, Canada's old age security system could be a "poster child" for Paul Pierson's (1994) thesis of "path dependency" and the relative rigidity of well-established welfare state institutions in the face of pressures to adopt major innovations. The Pierson thesis has not fared as well in other countries. The "Bismarckian" pension systems of Continental Europe, once viewed as virtually immune to "big reforms," are now described as having been through "paradigmatic" change (Bonoli and Palier 2007; Palier 2010) in both financing and benefit models. By 2011, leading German (Hinrichs 2011) and Italian (Jessoula 2011) scholars were forecasting gloomy scenarios for future retirees in their respective nations. How to explain these differences?

I argue that differences in pension reform outcomes are the result of differences in welfare state *design*. In Canada, the choices made by policy makers in the now distant 1950s and 1960s had long-term effects on the policy options available after 1980. I emphasize three key features: (1) the design and distribution of public pension *benefits* and the political coalitions they create; (2) the distinctive *financing* mechanisms for the different bits of the pension system and their effects on incentives for reform; and (3) differences in the *locus of control* over pension reforms in Canada's complex federal decision-making structure. The long-term implications of policy choices made in the 1960s were not, and could not, be foreseen by the policy makers of the day. Yet their choices had comparatively benign implications for Canadian policy makers facing new constraints several decades later, partly because, by international standards, Canada's income retirement system is both cheap and effective.

The picture is very different when we turn to the other side of Canada's retirement income system, namely, workplace pensions and personal retirement savings, where there is a severe case of "policy drift." Though often identified as the "private" part of the system, workplace pensions and personal savings accounts are highly subsidized by government (with tax deductions) and regulated by both federal and provincial governments. As Canadians entered the 2000s, there were growing concerns about the absence of workplace coverage (60 percent of workers lack workplace pensions), declining participation rates among younger workers, risk-shifting from employers to workers, and the high administrative overhead costs of "private" plans. The concern was not about today but about retirees of the future. A variety of innovative proposals for reform appeared – including, once again, expansion of the Canada/Quebec Pension Plans (C/QPP). Yet the result has been disappointing. In November 2011, the Harper government introduced a modest proposal to introduce PRSPs (pooled retirement savings plans), a "solution" that leaves observers sceptical.

Now, at the time of writing, retrenchment is back on the agenda. In February 2012, the Harper government announced its intention to raise the age of eligibility for OAS and the Guaranteed Income Supplement from sixty-five to sixty-seven, phasing in the increase between 2023 and 2029. OAS is an easy target for deficit cutting, but previous governments have failed in such efforts. The outcome of the current effort remains to be seen.

Welfare State Design

As in most countries, Canada's national pension system is a product of the welfare state expansion that extended from the 1950s to the 1970s. The resulting public system might be characterized as a small-scale version of the traditional Swedish design: a universal flat benefit for all seniors (OAS), supplemented by a guaranteed minimum income-tested pension (the GIS), and a modest second tier of earnings-related pensions (Canada/QPP). Middle- and upper-income families supplement these benefits with employment-based pensions (Registered Pension Plans) and personal retirement accounts (Registered Retirement Savings Plans). These elements were all in place by the end of the 1960s. Understanding their implications for the politics of restructuring since 1980 requires attention to the design of benefits, the financing of those benefits, and the decision-making process.

The Benefit Side

Recent studies of pension reform in the OECD countries have reached conclusions that, retrospectively, seem obvious. Juan Fernandez's (2010) analysis of pension policy retrenchments in fourteen nations, for example, concludes that major pension retrenchments were most likely in *large* (i.e., expensive) public pension systems. This conclusion fits the Canadian case: by international standards, Canadian public spending on old age pensions has always been modest. Until 2000, Canada was spending about 5 percent of GDP on public old age pensions (now slightly over 4 percent), well below levels of eight to 13 percent in most of Europe and also well under American and Australian levels.

The claim that bigger welfare states are more vulnerable to big cuts is not self-evident, however, since cuts to bigger welfare states are also more likely to meet greater electoral and popular resistance. Esping-Andersen's "liberal" welfare state regimes (including the UK and US) are modest welfare spenders by international standards but have hardly been immune to major retrenchment initiatives. "Cheap" welfare states are usually cheap because they offer targeted benefits that cater to a narrow, politically weak sector of the population (the "poor"); hence, they are politically vulnerable in periods of austerity. Social assistance in Canada is a good example.

"Big" welfare states, in contrast, are typically big because they are "encompassing" (Korpi and Palme 1998); they provide significant benefits to broad sectors of the politically influential "middle classes" – and higher income earners too. The result is what Korpi and Palme call the "paradox of redistribution": targeting benefits on the most disadvantaged may be economically *efficient* but is politically *ineffective*. The "poor" will be better protected when the more affluent have strong incentives to defend public programs

Canada's old age security system provides an important counter-example as it is both "cheap" and "effective." Measured against the usual benchmarks, Canada's income security system for seniors is a major international success story. Old age poverty rates in Canada (about 7 percent) are among the lowest among the OECD nations, comparable to levels in the Scandinavian countries (OECD 2009, 64) where public expenditures are very high. Canada is usually included among the "liberal" welfare regimes in international comparisons, countries in which government intervention is weak and targeted on lower-income groups. As I argue below, Canadian old age benefits are indeed "targeted" by international standards and hence "cheap." But they are targeted in a particular way, a design that generated political coalitions strong enough to resist retrenchment efforts in both the 1980s and 1990s.

The basic components of the Canadian retirement income system comprise three distinct pillars:

- *Pillar One* is focused on basic security and consists of the OAS, a quasi-universal, flat rate benefit, and the GIS, an income-tested supplement. Together the OAS and the GIS provided a guaranteed annual income of about $23,000 for singles and $34,000 for couples in 2010.[2] In the US, by contrast, Supplemental Security Income, a classic means-tested program, pays a maximum of $8,088 for singles and $12,132 for couples.
- *Pillar Two* consists of earnings-related public pension plans, the C/QPP. The aim is to ensure income continuity in old age, not just to avoid poverty during retirement. Canada's earnings-related plan is modest by international standards, even compared to the US, and helps account for its low cost. Nevertheless, the C/QPP has a large impact on low-income earners and is a major factor in accounting for Canada's low poverty rate

among seniors (Myles 2000). In 2011, the maximum yearly benefit was $11,520.
- *Pillar Three* consists of tax-subsidized occupational plans (RPPs) and individual retirement accounts (RRSPs). Middle- and upper-income retirees get a disproportionate amount of their income from these sources, and they have been the main source of recent policy concern. These plans are highly sensitive to fluctuations in the stock and bond markets, and, relative to public plans, they are expensive to administer. Firms have been changing their plans to shift risk to beneficiaries (the shift from defined benefit to defined contribution plans).

Though highly targeted by European and even US standards, Canadian OAS programs reach well beyond the ranks of the "poor." *Classical* targeting involves "means-testing," whereby beneficiary eligibility is determined not only by an income test but also by an asset test. Individuals must reduce their assets (savings, home ownership) to a minimum, in effect impoverishing themselves, to qualify. Tax-back rates on benefits are high: benefits are usually reduced dollar for dollar when there are additional income sources. This traditional "poor law" method of targeting is operative in provincial social assistance programs in Canada but entirely absent in its three old-age security pillars. While the GIS is tested against annual income, there is no asset test: low-income seniors do not need to spend their way into poverty to qualify. Benefits fall as income rises, but the tax-back rate is only 50 cents on the dollar; thus, benefits reach recipients well above the poverty line.

OAS was established in 1951 as a universal flat rate benefit available to all who meet age and residency requirements. "Targeting" in this case simply means that low-income earners receive much more in relative terms than do high-income earners. Since OAS is financed from general taxation, it also means low earners contribute much less to financing the program. A modest income test on high-income earners was introduced in 1989 but full benefits still go to 96 percent of eligible seniors.

The C/QPP is an earnings-related benefit based on payroll contributions that provides higher benefits to higher earners. However, the maximum C/QPP benefit was deliberately set low – geared to the average wage earner and those lower in the earnings distribution. In this sense, C/QPP benefits are "targeted" on workers in the bottom half of the earnings distribution.

Despite the redistributive character of Canada's old age security system, however, the public pension system's importance for seniors' incomes reaches well up the income distribution. By the mid-1990s, public transfers from OAS/GIS and C/QPP accounted for 92 percent of disposable income of bottom quintile seniors but also accounted for 62 percent of middle (third) quintile seniors and 47 percent of after-tax income among the fourth quintile. Canada's old age security system, while "targeted," is not for the poor alone. As a result, threats of cuts trigger widely based opposition.

Given the target population of Canada's old age security system (roughly the "bottom half" of the earnings distribution), financial institutions have had little incentive to lobby for cutbacks. Standard economic models demonstrate that the bottom half do not save a lot; therefore, the top half are the main target of financial institutions selling retirement insurance. Older public- and private-sector firms with well-established defined benefit plans also have had strong incentives to maintain the status quo. "Integrated" defined benefit plans that guarantee a fixed percentage of final earnings were designed on the assumption that OAS and the C/QPP would partially underwrite their pension costs. Cuts to OAS and/or the C/QPP could potentially raise firm pension costs.

Funding Mechanisms

How old age security systems are funded matters. The "big" pension systems of Western Europe have been funded on a "pay-as-you-go" basis with benefits paid by payroll contributions from younger, active workers. Countries leading the move towards large state-run earnings-related schemes (Belgium, Germany, France, Sweden, Italy) have faced the biggest challenge and have led the way in restructuring and "retrenchment" efforts, especially after 1990, often collaborating with left parties and the labour movement (Myles and Pierson 2001).

The adjective "large" is important. In these countries, pay-as-you-go earnings-related schemes were designed to provide most or all of the retirement income (70 percent of pre-retirement earnings) considered necessary to meet the income security needs of the "average worker." The benefits are financed almost exclusively from payroll contributions, taxing the earnings of the working-age population. In most schemes, this tax is imposed on only the bottom half or two-thirds of the earnings distribution. Consequently, virtually *all* of the expenditure increase that results from population aging must be financed by higher payroll taxes, driving down the relative wages of active (younger) workers. Thus, even labour unions are concerned with finding alternatives.

The problem is usually framed by comparing implicit "rates of return" in a pay-as-you-go scheme to those in a fully funded scheme financed out of

TABLE 13.1

Real growth in total wages and salaries and real interest rates, Canada, 1960s-90s

	1960-69	1970-79	1980-89	1990-94
Total wages and salaries	5.1	4.8	2.1	0.0
Real interest rates	2.4	3.6	6.3	4.6

Source: Canada, *An Information Paper for Consultations on the Canada Pension Plan* (Ottawa: Department of Finance, 1996).

returns on investments. The return in a *funded* model depends on long-term rates of return to capital (real interest rates). The implicit "rate of return" in schemes financed from a payroll tax, in contrast, is the annual percentage growth in total real wages and salaries ("returns to labour"). Total real-wage growth is a function of the growth in the average wage multiplied by the growth in the number of wage earners. The latter term is, in turn, a function of population growth and the rate of labour force participation.

Simply, then, the financial viability of "paygo" pensions financed from *payroll* taxes depends on high wage growth, high fertility, and rising rates of labour force participation. Given the values of these parameters in the 1960s, most treasury officials would have advised their ministers to opt for a paygo design. By the 1990s, everything had changed. Data produced by the Canadian Department of Finance illustrate the turnaround (Table 13.1).

Clearly, by the 1980s, a treasury official would be advising her minister that the 1960s model was in difficulty: the parameters that made it the model of choice – rising wage rates, an expanding labour force, and comparatively high fertility – had changed dramatically.

The C/QPP introduced a paygo pension scheme in 1965 but at very modest levels. The C/QPP replaces only 25 percent of average earnings, while OAS adds an additional 15 percent. The C/QPP was also partially funded. As a result, when pension reform surged onto the political agenda in the 1980s and 1990s, Canada faced a very different situation than did most European countries and even the US. In the mid-1990s, Germans, for example, were paying 19 percent of covered wages, with this figure projected to rise to as high as 38 percent (Table 13.2). Canadian payroll taxes for the C/QPP were enviably low (5.4 percent) by comparison. While Canada's payroll tax rate had considerable room for growth, in Continental Europe

TABLE 13.2
Pension contribution rates in selected countries, 1995

	Percent of average earnings
Canada	5.4
UK	13.9
US	12.4
France	19.8
Germany	18.6
Italy	29.6
Norway	22.0
Sweden	19.8

Source: Sveinbjörn Blöndal and Stefano Scarpetta, *The Retirement Decision in OECD Countries*, OECD Economics Department Working Paper no. 202, 1998.

and the Nordic countries, high and rising payroll taxes on the working-age population created strong incentives for business, government, and labour to bring payroll contributions rates under control (see Myles and Pierson 2002).

Canada's low payroll contribution rate reflected the modest scale of the C/QPP and a reliance on general revenue financing, not payroll taxes, to fund OAS and the GIS. General revenue provides a much broader tax base (including income and consumption taxes paid by retirees) and hence is more stable and less subject to intergenerational trade-offs. This combination of low payroll taxes and greater reliance on general revenue financing placed Canadian policy makers in a more benign position than their European and US counterparts as population aging loomed.

The Locus of Decision Making

A third feature of Canada's welfare state design is the locus of decision making. Canadian federalism takes a variety of forms (Banting 2005). OAS and the GIS are entirely subject to decisions made by Ottawa – "classical federalism" in Banting's typology. As a result, the federal government gets the electoral credit for positive reforms and takes the heat for negative reforms.

Reforms to the C/QPP are subject to very different political dynamics, the result of what Banting calls "joint decision federalism": nothing happens without the consent of federal *and* provincial governments. In the case of the C/QPP, nothing happens unless two-thirds of the provinces with two-thirds of the population consent. In short, under "joint decision federalism," when things go well, Ottawa can take credit, but when things go badly, "blame" can be shared with the provinces.

Reform Efforts in the 1980s and 1990s

Rereading Kenneth Bryden's (1974) classic study of the foundational years of pension policy formation in Canada is a wake-up call for those convinced that welfare state politics is fundamentally different today. His distinction between "cost-conscious" and "welfare conscious" actors continues to ring true: the Department of Finance and the business community still worry about costs; the "social" departments of government, the labour unions, welfare advocates, and seniors groups are concerned with benefits and their adequacy; federal-provincial relations are at the centre of considerations of pension policy; the role of Quebec remains crucial; and the financial industry seeks to protect its turf against encroachments by government in the marketing and regulation of retirement savings instruments.

But things have changed as well. The reforms that launched Canada's old age income security system occurred against the backdrop of the baby boom of the 1950s and 1960s and the postwar economic boom. A growing labour force and rising real wages generated windfall gains for government revenues, making policy expansion easy. Income could be transferred away from the working age population, and their earnings, net of taxes, would still go up – something harder to accomplish in a slow growth environment.

Since the 1980s, the decline in fertility, or "baby bust"; the prospect of population aging; slow real wage growth; rising deficits; and periodic economic "crises" have generated what Paul Pierson (1996) aptly describes as the "politics of austerity." As Coleman, Good, and Phillips note in this volume, the influence and bargaining power of the traditional "welfare conscious" institutions have waned. By the 1980s, as Bruce Little (2008, 68) writes, the cost-conscious Department of Finance had "taken over the file." Nevertheless, things did not go well for the "cost-conscious" in the 1980s and 1990s.

The Failed Assault on "Universality"

"Universality" is a central element of Canada's political culture and is historically associated with three major programs: universal flat rate child benefits (family allowances established in 1944), universal flat rate old age benefits

(OAS, established in 1951), and national health insurance (established in 1966). "Universality," in this context, simply means that, while the rich pay more, all citizens who qualify receive the same amount in benefits. Benefits do not reflect contributions, hence the term "flat rate."

Unlike Europe, where the threat of high and rising payroll taxes was real, Canadian officials in the 1980s and 1990s were facing high and rising public deficits and a rising debt load. The deficit had a powerful impact on their choice of targets in the pension sector. Reforming the C/QPP, financed with payroll contributions, would not help with the deficit, but cutting OAS and GIS expenditures – financed from general revenue – could. OAS became the primary target for the Department of Finance of the 1980s Mulroney and 1990s Chretien governments.

Virtue seemed to be on their side. OAS benefits do not reflect "need." The same OAS benefit goes to the poor widow of a retired factory worker and, in Prime Minister Brian Mulroney's catch-phrase, to "the wealthy banker's wife." Both governments tried, mostly in vain, to cut OAS benefits for higher-income Canadians. Whether universal flat rate benefits "make sense" from a redistributive point of view has long been highly contested by technical experts. But in this case, political reactions, not technical arguments, won the day.

In May 1985, Mulroney's Conservatives launched the first serious retrenchment attempt in the field of pension reform. The new government's first budget proposed the "partial deindexation" of OAS.[3] De-indexation was aimed at saving the federal treasury approximately $4 billion over the next five years. Unfortunately for Mulroney and Finance Minister Michael Wilson, the de-indexation issue created a countrywide political tempest. Labour unions, anti-poverty groups, and old-age organizations participated in a two-month-long campaign that finally forced Mulroney to discard the proposal. A televised encounter between the tall prime minister and a petite but vocal French-Canadian woman named Solange Denis became a national symbol of the conflict between "greedy politicians" and the "deprived elderly," and, in this instance, the politicians backed down.

During the second half of the 1980s, the Progressive Conservative government enjoyed a partial, if temporary, success, implementing a 1989 "clawback" of OAS benefits from high-income seniors that was largely ignored by the media and the public. Benefits for individuals with incomes greater than $51,765 were reduced by 15 percent for every dollar of income above the threshold, with all benefits disappearing at approximately $89,000 per year. However, the cut-off point ($51,765) at which the clawback would come into effect, was only indexed to inflation in excess of 3 percent, so that, in real terms, a growing share of seniors could be affected with the passage of time. Since the huge majority of the elderly were not immediately affected, and few politicians or journalists understood the longer-term implications of the reform, the clawback was identified as "social policy by stealth." Low inflation and slow income growth during the 1990s, however, meant that, by 2001, fewer than 5 percent of all seniors were affected by the 1989 income test. In 2000, the subsequent Liberal government restored full indexation of the cut-off point: future savings from the clawback will only occur if and when there is a large increase in the numbers of very high-income retirees.

Nevertheless, the issue did not go away. For David Dodge, who took over as deputy minister of finance under the newly installed 1993 Chretien government, the rising debt load was a central fact of life and his first target was OAS. "If we are looking for one issue," he warned, "OAS is it" (Greenspon and Wilson Smith 1996, 54). The 1995 budget represented a big step in social policy restructuring; a key issue in the run-up to budget day was whether pensions would be included. With the "war on deficit" and demographic fears as a background, the budget formulated five principles for the reform of public pensions (Battle 1997, 539). Far from departing from the Progressive Conservative agenda, these design criteria reinforced the logic of pension reform that emerged during the 1980s, namely, the erosion of universal flat rate pensions. Henceforth, OAS benefits would be "targeted" rather than "universal."

The question was whether the 1995 budget would go beyond enunciating principles to taking action. Targeting remained controversial, but the Liberals carefully avoided the mistake of the first Mulroney government and its questioning of the full indexation of benefits. Solange Denis's unforgettable encounter with Brian Mulroney was a source of "political learning."

The 1995 Quebec referendum on separation from Canada also lurked in the background. The potential loss of pension benefits for Quebeckers if Quebec declared independence was an important weapon in Ottawa's arsenal in the first referendum debate in 1980. As a result, cutting OAS before the 1995 referendum would be a risky step.

Finance Minister Paul Martin pressed for action. But Prime Minister Chretien, conscious not only of Solange Denis but also of his cabinet colleagues, continued to put on the brakes (Greenspon and Wilson Smith 1996, 257-67; Goldenberg 2006, 147). The result was a compromise; Martin would not get his reform in the 1995 budget but he could return to it in 1996.

In 1996, the Liberals unveiled their reform proposals. The government proposed to replace both OAS and GIS programs with a new seniors benefit that would integrate the two in a single income-tested scheme. Generally speaking, low- and even middle-income families could benefit while higher-income retirees would bear the brunt of reform (see Prince 1997). For example, a family receiving $20,000 per year on top of the Seniors Benefit would gain $500 per year under the new system. But families with $50,000 per year of other retirement income would lose more than $4,000 per year (Geddes 1998, 13). Unlike the 1989 clawback, which was calculated on the basis of individual income, this one was to be based on family income, thus affecting a much larger pool of retirees. In particular, women who had low earnings during their working lives but who were married to high-income partners would lose much or all of their pension.

To minimize political backlash among the wealthiest segment of the elderly population, Martin stressed that *current* OAS/GIS beneficiaries would not be affected by the reform. Later, this commitment was expanded to "apply to everyone age 60 and over as of December 31, 1995, as well as their spouses, regardless of their age."[4] Martin spent an afternoon with Mulroney's erstwhile critic, Solange Denis, and apparently won her support (Greenspon and Wilson-Smith 1996, 261)

Despite these efforts, groups representing not only the elderly but also professional associations and investment firms slowly united against the proposal. At the beginning of 1997, the Retirement Income Coalition sealed an alliance between twenty-one such groups, including the Canadian Teachers' Federation, the Investment Dealers Association, and the Canadian Association of Retired Persons. This coalition generated considerable media attention on the potentially negative impact of the reform on savings behaviour (Geddes 1998). The Seniors Benefit was opposed, as expected, by the NDP. But as Reform Party MP Keith Martin (1997) argued:

> This new Seniors Benefit is obviously not much of a benefit at all, but a seniors tax. It penalizes those who have sacrificed and saved for their retirements. Ultimately, it will make more people dependent on taxpayer-funded, low return, government controlled pensions instead of enabling people to earn a more lucrative pension through their investments, such as RRSP's.

From this perspective, income-testing the Seniors Benefit would discourage personal savings and encourage "welfare dependency." But, as Michael

Prince (1997, 227) notes, it was ironic that the financial community was "bemoaning" the effects of selectivity, a principle it had long promoted.

Facing considerable pressure from the Retirement Income Coalition and right-wing opposition parties, the government withdrew the controversial reform proposal. Referring to renewed economic prosperity and a shrinking federal deficit, Finance Minister Martin (1998) retreated, arguing that new economic conditions made the cuts unnecessary. Now that the federal government was expecting long-term fiscal surpluses, the idea that future retirees had to make significant economic sacrifices in the name of fiscal austerity was difficult to justify.

Martin's backdown was not easy, an unhappy result for the Department of Finance and the "cost conscious" generally. He undoubtedly saw the Seniors Benefit as the right way to go on both moral and fiscal grounds (Greenspon and Wilson-Smith 1996, 257). The Seniors Benefit could give more to the elderly poor and less to the middle class and the affluent while saving billions for the treasury.

In short, Pierson's (1994) thesis that, once established, welfare state programs create new political constituencies that make policy reform difficult appears well supported by these two decades of assaults on OAS. Despite its new-found powers and whatever the technical "virtues" of its position, the Department of Finance lost the debate and popular "politics" won.

The Institutional Logic of CPP Reform

If the reform of OAS/GIS failed because of strong opposition from the left and the right, as well as the advent of budget surpluses, why did Canada Pension Plan (CPP) reform materialize so quickly in the mid-1990s? The answer is that it had to: reform was institutionally "locked in" by earlier federal-provincial agreements.

The key event was the commitment by federal and provincial governments in 1985 to return to the CPP negotiating table every five years to review CPP expenditures and to adjust contributions and benefits accordingly. The agreement meant that they could not ignore any future problem. Little (2008, 65) writes:

> Tucked into the federal-provincial deal was a little-noticed twist in the form of a powerful default provision. If ministers could not agree on a new schedule of rate increases after each review, their failure would trigger a formula that would mandate rate increases large enough to generate, over 15 years, a fund equal to two years of the following year's expenditures.

Having agreed to a two-year fund, the ministers had, in effect, committed themselves to rate increases (or, hypothetically, cuts to benefits) that would deliver a fund that large.

The default provision meant that, when the chief actuary submitted his gloomy fifteenth report on the CPP in February 1995 (Battle 1997, 537), the outcome was certain: federal and provincial ministers would soon be at the bargaining table either to cut benefits or to raise contributions. Should they fail to act, the payroll contribution rate was projected to rise to 13.9 percent in 2030 and to 14.2 percent in 2040.

For Finance Minister Martin and the Department of Finance, the challenge was how to distribute the additional CPP costs generated by increased longevity and low fertility across current and future generations, a problem of intergenerational equity. Maintaining the benefit rate (and allowing contributions to rise to 14.2 percent) meant that future cohorts would experience lower living standards during the working years but maintain their benefits in retirement. Freezing the contribution rate (then at 5.4 percent), in contrast, would mean that the living standards of future generations would be preserved during their working years but that benefits would decline in their retirement years.

The Department of Finance's strategy was to raise contribution rates before it was necessary to generate a capital pool to finance future benefits; this involved "splitting the difference" between generations (see Myles 2002). Ramping up contribution rates to 9.9 percent in the short run raised costs for the current generation of contributors but stabilized contribution rates at that level, reducing costs for future generations.

Policy makers opted for this strategy, partly because they had been pleasantly surprised by the lack of negative reaction to previous rate hikes that resulted from CPP reviews in 1985 and 1991-92. The main response "had been praise, not criticism" (Little 2008, 72). The praise might have been considerably more muted, of course, if the C/QPP were facing increases of up to 25 or 30 percent of payroll as was common in Europe.

While the decision to increase "funding" with a large capital investment pool under government control would have been much more controversial in the US, in Canada, policy learning played an important role in muting opposition. The experience of the Caisse de dépôt et placement du Québec, which had been investing the funds of the Quebec Pension Plan in the financial markets since the QPP began in the late 1960s, was influential, but the experience of the Ontario Municipal Employees Retirement System and the

Ontario Teachers' Pension Plan, run by arm's-length government-controlled pension investment boards, became the preferred model (Weaver 2003).

By European standards, benefit cuts provided a relatively modest part of the CPP reform package. The radical push for the replacement of CPP by individual retirement accounts (super-RRSPs) advocated by the Reform Party, the editorial board of the *Globe and Mail*, and a number of conservative think tanks, never gained serious leverage (Béland and Myles 2005; Little 2008). South of the border, a similar approach, known as "Social Security privatization," became widely debated during the second Clinton mandate as conservative think tanks and other policy actors successfully reframed the policy agenda to make room for this controversial idea (Béland 2005). Interestingly, it never gained traction in mainstream Canadian debates during the Chrétien years, simply because Finance Minister Paul Martin and his advisors, as well as most of the provincial leaders involved, did not think that CPP was a problematic program in itself. It required "fixing," not "demolition." This relative consensus around the CPP's goals and structure contrasts with the dissatisfaction of many federal policy makers concerning Unemployment Insurance (Little 2008; Hale 1998).

Nevertheless, at various moments, serious benefit reductions for future retirees were discussed. According to Bruce Little (2008, 108), early in the CPP debate (1995) it would be easy to get the impression from reading newspaper articles "that a higher retirement age was the single biggest solution to the CPP's woes, almost to the exclusion of other possible ways of rescuing the CPP." Canada could play "follow the leader" and move the retirement age to sixty-seven as the US was already doing, a strategy justified by dramatic gains (about four years) in longevity since the 1960s.

As Béland and Myles (2005) emphasize, federalism and (especially) Quebec were critical in shaping reform. By law, CPP reform requires the consent of at least two-thirds of the provinces representing two-thirds of the Canadian population. In addition, pension planners have tried to maintain parallelism between the Canada and Quebec plans, giving Quebec added leverage in the intergovernmental bargaining process. Quebec made it clear that it would oppose any significant benefit cuts. Moreover, Quebec would be backed by Saskatchewan and BC, then ruled by the New Democrats. Quebec's stance removed the option of drastic erosion of CPP old-age benefits during the 1990s. At the same time, the unusual character of the CPP decision-making rules provided Ottawa with a built-in mechanism for reaching a "negotiated settlement" with provincial leaders representing a variety of partisan preferences and regional divisions.

Benefit cuts were part of the reform package but were modest by European standards and mainly the result of poorly understood technical redesign rather than substantial restructuring. The single largest measure added late in the process was the decision to alter the final earnings formula to calculate benefits on the basis of average earnings in the last five years rather than in the last three years. This type of change, widely adopted in Europe in the 1990s, is generally assumed to reduce benefits for higher-income workers. However, low-income workers also took a hit: the Yearly Basic Exemption was frozen (i.e., de-indexed) at $3,500 a year so that future cohorts of low-wage workers will end up paying more for their CPP retirement benefits.

Overall, the politics of CPP reform in the mid-1990s did not lead to path-departing reforms, at least not on the benefit side; instead, parametric changes in contribution rates helped reproduce a program in which basic features remained the same. While institutional factors both constrained and facilitated pension reform in the mid-1990s, the fact that most policy makers saw CPP as a legitimate and adequate program, and that CPP reform had little role to play in debt reduction, explains this strategy.

Policy Drift: Reforming Workplace Pensions and Individual Retirement Savings Accounts in the 2000s

The 2008 worldwide economic crisis again brought pension issues to the forefront, but this time attention had shifted from the public retirement income system to private-sector plans and RRSPs. Individual savers saw their retirement savings in RRSPs and defined contribution plans erode by 30 percent or more in a few months. Defined-benefit employer pension schemes suddenly became massively underfunded. Wide swathes of the middle class rediscovered the perils of the market.

Between November 2008 and January 2009, three reports on workplace pensions in Canada were released by four provincial governments. On 21 November 2008, the Ontario minister of finance released a report prepared by the Ontario Expert Commission on Pensions, *A Fine Balance: Safe Pensions, Affordable Plans, Fair Rules*. A week later, the governments of Alberta and British Columbia released the report of the Joint Expert Panel on Pension Standards, *Getting Our Acts Together: Pension Reform in Alberta and British Columbia*. On 27 January 2009, the report of the Nova Scotia Pension Review Panel, *Promises to Keep*, was released.

The economic crisis was not the source of this new concern. Workplace pensions are under provincial jurisdiction, and the four provincial governments had initiated reviews of what were considered to be major challenges facing the industry well before 2008. Rather, the crisis accentuated the problems facing the private pension sector, bringing calls for new forms of regulation and possibly an expanded role for governments (including expansion of the C/QPP and/or a federally administered RRSP plan).

As Baldwin and Fitzgerald (2009) note, the initiative for these reviews stemmed from long simmering unresolved issues in the scope and regulation of workplace pensions in Canada. The share of the workforce covered by workplace pensions has been declining since the 1980s (especially among younger workers). More than 60 percent of working Canadians do not have workplace pensions. And there has been a shift from defined benefit to defined contribution plans that will result in less secure futures for retirees. The "big story" from recent discussions is well summarized in Hansen's (British Columbia 2010) report to the Steering Committee of Ministers on Pension Coverage and Retirement Income Adequacy. Hansen's summary, which might well be described as the view of the "welfare conscious," highlights two major reform options.

1. A Canada Supplementary Pension Plan (CSPP) – a voluntary, defined contribution "tier" added to the CPP. This variant, advocated by Keith Ambachtsheer (2008), is similar in concept to the proposals advanced by the BC and Alberta governments.
2. CPP Expansion – an expansion of the existing mandatory, defined benefit plan through an increase in the replacement rate, or the upper limit on income on which the pension is calculated, or both.

The second option has been called for by traditional "welfare conscious" groups, including the Canadian Association of Retired Persons, the Canadian Labour Congress, and the Federal Superannuities Association. Both the federal NDP and Liberal parties have announced support for some expansion of the CPP, and prominent public finance economist Jonathan Kesselman (2009) also argues for this solution.

The first option is rather more modest. As Keith Ambachtsheer (2008) argues, a national RRSP program administered by the federal government could increase coverage with "automatic" enrolment of all workers and employers (with an option to opt out) and dramatically reduce costs (and raise returns) associated with smaller employer plans and RRSPs.

Both the Alberta/BC and Nova Scotia reports cited above proposed the creation of provincially administered retirement savings plans. In the

Alberta/BC version, enrolment in the plan would be automatic for all employers and employees but would allow individual employers and workers to "opt out." Automatic enrolment is widely thought to provide a partial cure for declining coverage rates. Workers must choose *not* to be enrolled rather than choose to "opt in." The Nova Scotia report proposed a province-wide plan that would be mandatory for places of employment with more than fifty employees that do not now offer a pension plan, and voluntary for smaller places of employment and the self-employed. Large provincially administered pension plans of this sort would have much lower administrative costs and hence higher returns.

The Harper government's reaction towards significant new government administered plans was "cool," as is indicated by the selection of Jack Mintz, a noted critic of government-run "super pension funds," to chair the Federal-Provincial Task Force on this issue.[5]

The striking contrast between the Hansen (2010) and Mintz (2009) reports highlights the division between the welfare and cost-conscious factions. The Mintz report plays to the low poverty rates and high-income replacement rates of current seniors to argue that Canada is doing well and that radical reforms should be approached with caution. Some seniors are having financial difficulties, but we need "more research" to discover why and we need to adopt modest regulatory interventions. The Hansen report emphasizes the future. Pension coverage and savings rates have been falling, so future elderly cohorts are likely to fare less well than current ones. Much inefficiency in the current private pension system, such as the high cost of "retail" retirement savings plans, could be overcome by public policy innovations.

Strikingly, in 2010, Canadian policy elites were discussing an expansion of the role of the state in old age income security. Seniors were no longer at the top of the poverty statistics. Policy makers had to deal with strong competing claims (e.g., early childhood education) and another round of rising deficits.

Even so, the result was a severe case of policy drift: a proposal from Finance Minister James Flaherty in November 2011 to introduce Pooled Retirement Savings Plans (PRSPs), an incremental step aimed at lowering pension costs and raising coverage for the self-employed and employees in small firms by freeing employers from the administrative complexity and costs associated with running a pension plan. Critics from the left, right, and centre have been sceptical about the outcome (Brown and Meredith 2012; Ambatchtsheer and Waltzer 2011; Townson 2011). As Brown and

Meredith highlight, employer contributions are entirely voluntary, thus reducing incentives for employees to contribute and making PRSPs little different from already existing group RRSPs. The mode of implementation is left to the provinces (Ambatchtsheer and Waltzer 2011), potentially creating wide disparities between regions and provinces. In brief, PRSPs are a minimalist response to the national problem faced by today's workers and future retirees.

Back to Retrenchment? Raising the Age for OAS and GIS Benefits

In February 2012, Prime Minister Harper put retrenchment back on the agenda by indicating that Canada should raise the age of eligibility for OAS and the GIS from sixty-five to sixty-seven. In a classic case of blame mitigation, the government's budget announced plans to phase in the increases between 2023 and 2029. If these changes are not reversed by a subsequent government, they will represent the first significant retrenchment in the pension sector.

As I argue elsewhere (Esping-Andersen and Myles 2006), there is good reason for encouraging later retirement in a population that lives longer and is healthier than in the past. There are huge equity choices involved, however. The main beneficiaries of OAS/GIS are workers in the bottom half of the earnings distribution; many enter retirement without workplace pensions or adequate savings. Their life expectancy is also much less than is that of high-income workers. As noted earlier, however, unlike the C/QPP, OAS is financed by general revenues making both programs juicy targets for deficit-reduction exercises. Unlike C/QPP reform, Ottawa cannot share the "blame" of cutbacks with the provinces since both programs are under the exclusive jurisdiction of the federal government. Neither the Mulroney nor the Chretien governments were prepared to take the electoral heat for unilateral OAS reforms. At the time of writing, it remains to be seen whether the Harper government will do so.

Conclusion

Compared to those of many other affluent democracies, Canadian pension politics have been tranquil, arguably because the Canadian public pension system has effectively reduced old age poverty and is cheap by international standards. The policy makers and technocrats who designed the system in the 1950s and 1960s could not have anticipated this outcome. Rather, contemporary Canadian policy elites have been lucky: the multi-tiered pension system created in the 1950s was working well fifty years later, despite new circumstances.

The benefit structure includes a basic security system – OAS and the GIS. Together, these two programs provide the majority of citizens who meet residency requirements with a guaranteed retirement income at or close to conventional poverty lines.

The funding source for this basic security system – general revenue – is both a strength and a source of vulnerability. On the one hand, general revenue financing – from income, consumption, and other taxes – is more broadly based than payroll taxes and more immune to the intergenerational trade-offs that result from population aging. Retirees also pay income and consumption taxes while only active workers contribute payroll taxes. On the other hand, general revenue financing is also a source of vulnerability since, unlike the C/QPP, which is self-financing, expenditures show up on the government books. Cuts to OAS have been a target for deficit reduction over the decades but thus far have failed. Prime Minister Harper's proposal to raise the age of eligibility for OAS and the GIS from sixty-five to sixty-seven is merely the most recent example. As experts agree that "working longer" is the most effective antidote to population aging, the scheme may pass into legislation. However, it will be a decade before it takes effect. Since the incentive effects from changes to OAS/GIS will mainly affect lower and middle wage-earners, equity considerations mean that political debate on this issue will be contentious over the next decade.

Basic security against poverty in old age is only one of two key goals of all national pension systems. The second goal is income security – providing middle-income retirees with continuity in living standards during retirement. Like the Nordic countries, Canada met this challenge with the creation of the C/QPP in 1965; however, compared to Nordic, European, and even US efforts, the C/QPP was a modest initiative with low benefits and low contribution rates. The expectation at the time was that middle- and upper-income retirees would meet their retirement income goals with workplace pensions, RRSPs, and other savings. Although most experts, including government experts and the author, challenged this assumption, the original expectations were largely realized. By the 1990s (LaRochelle-Côté, Myles, and Picot 2009), middle-income retirees were doing well by international standards.

In sum, while policy elites in a number of provinces have noted the erosion, declining quality, and high costs of workplace pensions and individual retirement accounts, the result has been policy drift rather than innovation. We can expect this issue to return to the political agenda.

NOTES

1 In reaching this conclusion, I ignore changes to disability benefits provided by the C/QPP, an important topic for a separate chapter. For a concise overview of this issue see Prince (2010).
2 In 2009, "welfare incomes" (social assistance plus child benefits) for a single parent with one child ranged from a low of $14,929 in Manitoba to a high of $19,297 in Newfoundland and Labrador (National Council of Welfare 2011).
3 According to the plan, OAS benefits would increase by the amount that inflation surpassed 3 percent: "If inflation were 3 percent or higher a year, then OAS benefits would automatically lose 3 percent of their value. Even if inflation were less than 3 percent, benefits would decline by the amount of inflation (e.g., an inflation rate of 2 percent would reduce the value of OAS by 2 percent)" (Battle 1997, 530-31).
4 The same strategy has been used in the US, with the gradual change in retirement age enacted as part of the 1983 amendments to the Social Security Act (Light 1995).
5 See Jack Mintz at http://network.nationalpost.com/np/blogs/fpcomment/archive/ 2009/04/21/jack-mintz-beware-of-the-super-pension-fund.aspx.

REFERENCES

Ambachtscheer, Keith. 2008. *The Canadian Supplementary Pension Plan (CSPP): Towards an Adequate, Affordable Pension for All Canadians.* Toronto: C.D. Howe Institute.
Ambachtscheer, Keith, and Edward Waitzer. 2011. *Saving Pooled Registered Pension Plans: It's Up To the Provinces.* Toronto: C.D. Howe Institute.
Baldwin, Bob, and Brian Fitzgerald. 2010. *Seeking Certainty in Uncertain Times: A Review of Recent Government Studies on the Regulation of Canadian Pension Plans.* Toronto: C.D. Howe Institute.
Banting, Keith. 2005. "Canada: Nation-Building in a Federal Welfare State." In Herbert Obinger, Stephan Leibfried, and Frank G. Castles, eds., *Federalism and the Welfare State: New World and European Experiences*, 89-137. Cambridge: Cambridge University Press.
Battle, K. 1997. "Pension Reform in Canada." *Canadian Journal on Aging* 16: 519-52.
Béland, Daniel. 2005. *Social Security: History and Politics from the New Deal to the Privatization Debate.* Lawrence: University Press of Kansas.
Béland, Daniel, and John Myles. 2005. "Stasis amidst Change: Canadian Pension Reform in an Age of Retrenchment." In G. Bonoli and T. Shinkawa, eds., *Ageing and Pension Reform around the World*, 252-72. Cheltenham: Edward Elgar.
Bonoli, Giuliano, and Bruno Palier. 2007. "When Past Reforms Open Up New Opportunities: Comparing Old Age Insurance Reforms in Bismarckian Welfare Systems." *Social Policy and Administration* 41: 555-73.
British Columbia. 2010. "Options for Increasing Pension Coverage among Private Sector Workers." Vancouver: Ministry of Finance.

Brown, Robert, and Tyler Meredith. 2012. *Pooled Target-Benefit Plans: Building on PRPPs.* Montreal: Institute for Research on Public Policy.
Bryden, Kenneth. 1974. *Old Age Pensions and Policy-Making in Canada.* Montreal and Kingston: McGill-Queen's University Press.
Esping-Andersen, Gøsta, and John Myles. 2006. "Sustainable and Equitable Retirement in a Life Course Perspective." In G. Clark, A. Munnell, and J.M. Orszag, eds., *Oxford Handbook of Pensions and Retirement Income,* 639-64. Oxford: Oxford University Press.
Fernandez, Juan. 2010. "Economic Crises, High Public Pension Spending and Blame Avoidance Strategies: Pension Policy Retrenchment in 14 Social-Insurance Countries." MPlfG Discussion Paper. Cologne: Max Planck Institute for the Study of Societies.
Geddes, John. 1998. "Citizen's Revolt." *Maclean's,* 20 April, 12-13.
Goldenberg, Eddie. 2006. *The Way it Works: Inside Ottawa.* Toronto: McClelland and Stewart.
Greenspon, Edward, and Anthony William Smith. 1996. *Double Vision: The Inside Story of the Liberals in Power.* Toronto: Doubleday.
Hale, Geoffrey E. 1998. "Reforming Employment Insurance: Transcending the Politics of the Status Quo." *Canadian Public Policy* 24(4): 429-51.
Hansen, Colin. 2010. "Options for Increasing Pension Coverage among Private Sector Workers in Canada." Steering Committee of Provincial/Territorial Ministers on Pension Coverage and Retirement Income Adequacy. Vancouver: British Columbia Ministry of Finance.
Hinrichs, Karl. 2011. "Germany: A Flexible Labour Market Plus Pension Reforms Makes Old-Age Poverty." Conference on Work and Welfare in Europe: New Compromises or Ongoing Demise? Brussels.
Jessoula, Matteo. 2011. "A Risky Combination in Italy: 'Selective Flexibility' and Defined Contribution Pensions." Conference on Work and Welfare in Europe: New Compromises or Ongoing Demise? Brussels.
Kesselman, Jonathan. 2009. "Impending Battle over Pension Reform: Case for Big CPP." *Globe and Mail,* 19 December.
Korpi, Walter, and Joachim Palme. 1998. "The Paradox of Redistribution and Strategies of Equality: Welfare State Institutions, Inequality and Poverty in Western Countries." *American Sociological Review* 63: 661-87.
LaRochelle-Côté, Sébastien, John Myles, and Garnett Picot. 2009. "Income Security and Stability during Retirement in Canada during Retirement." In M. Abbott, C. Beach, R. Boadway, and J. MacKinnon, eds., *Retirement Policy Issues in Canada,* 65-96. Montreal and Kingston: McGill-Queen's University Press.
Light, Paul. 1995. *Still Artful Work: the Continuing Politics of Social Security Reform.* New York: McGraw-Hill.
Little, Bruce. 2008. *Fixing the Future: How Canada's Usually Fractious Governments Worked Together to Rescue the Canada Pension Plan.* Toronto: University of Toronto Press.
Martin, Keith. 1997. "No Benefits under the Seniors' Benefit." Ottawa, 20 July. http://www.keithmartin.org/policy/hrd/hrd_seniorsbenefit.shtml.

Martin, Paul. 1998. "Finance Minister's Statement on the Seniors Benefit." Ottawa, Government of Canada, 28 July. http://www.fin.gc.ca/news98/98-071e.html.

Mintz, Jack. 2009. *Summary Report on Retirement Income Adequacy Research.* Ottawa: Government of Canada, Department of Finance.

Myles, John. 2000. "The Maturation of Canada's Retirement Income System: Income Levels, Income Inequality and Low Income among the Elderly." *Canadian Journal on Aging* 19: 287-316.

—. 2002. "A New Social Contract for the Elderly?" In G. Esping-Andersen, D. Gallie, A. Hemerijck, and J. Myles, eds., *Why We Need a New Welfare State,* 130-72. Oxford: Oxford University Press.

Myles, John, and Paul Pierson. 2001. "The Comparative Political Economy of Pension Reform." In P. Pierson, ed., *The New Politics of the Welfare State,* 305-33. Oxford: Oxford University Press.

National Council of Welfare. 2011. *Welfare Incomes 2009.* Ottawa: National Council of Welfare.

Organisation for Economic Cooperation and Development. 2009. *Pensions at a Glance: Retirement Income Systems in OECD Countries.* Paris: OECD.

Palier, Bruno ed. 2010. *A Long Goodbye to Bismarck? The Politics of Welfare Reform in Continental Europe.* Amsterdam: Amsterdam University Press.

Pierson, Paul. 1994. *Dismantling the Welfare State? Reagan, Thatcher and the Politics of Retrenchment.* Cambridge: Cambridge University Press.

—. 1996. "The New Politics of the Welfare State." *World Politics* 48: 143-79.

Prince, Michael. 1997. "Lowering the Boom on the Boomers: Replacing Old Age Security with the New Seniors Benefit and Reforming the Canada Pension Plan." In G. Swimmer, ed., *How Ottawa Spends, 1997-98: Seeing Red – A Liberal Report Card,* 211-34. Ottawa: Carleton University Press.

—. 2010. "Avoiding Blame, Doing Good, and Claiming Credit: Reforming Canadian Income Security." *Canadian Public Administration* 53: 293-332.

Townson, Monica. 2011. *How the Finance Ministers Bungled Pension Reform.* Toronto: Canadian Centre for Policy Alternatives.

Weaver, R. Kent. 2003. *Whose Money Is It Anyhow? Governance and Social Investment in Collective Investment Funds.* Chestnut Hill, MA, Center for Retirement Research. http://www.bc.edu/centers/crr/wp_2003-07.shtml.

14 The Recent Evolution of Tax-Transfer Policies

ROBIN BOADWAY AND KATHERINE CUFF

Market-based inequality has grown in Canada in the past three decades, and the government seems increasingly unable to address the situation through redistribution policies (OECD 2008a; Frenette, Green, and Milligan 2007; Heisz 2007). There are many reasons for the growing inequality (see Boudarbat, Riddell, and Lemieux 2006; Lu et al. 2010; Brzozowski et al. 2010). For one thing, increased competition from low-wage countries contributes to the stagnation of earnings at the bottom of the income distribution. This may be exacerbated by changes in the composition of the labour force, such as an increased number of unskilled single parents or an increase in part-time workers and the self-employed whose earnings exhibit variability. At higher income levels, earnings differentials between high- and low-skilled workers might have increased as a result of changes in the comparative importance of skilled labour. The skill mix of the labour force might also be growing more unequal as more persons acquire postsecondary education. And, as in many other OECD countries, earnings of those in the top 1 percent of the population have been increasing rapidly because of pay patterns for upper management in the financial sector and elsewhere (Saez and Veall 2005; Piketty and Saez 2007; Lemieux, MacLeod, and Parent 2009).

The sources of market-based inequality have been discussed elsewhere (e.g., Beaudry and Green 2005), and our interest in this chapter lies in the concomitant changes in Canadian redistributive policy: not only has it failed to respond to the growth of inequality but it has also become less effective in its own right. While it is difficult to pinpoint the precise reasons, there are a number of suggestive explanations. An intriguing one from the economics literature concerns the role of ideas that have informed the policy process; as we show, some directions of change are compatible with findings in the normative literature on redistribution policy. Another important influence is the response to policy changes elsewhere. More specifically, a number of major changes in redistribution policy in Canada mimic those adopted by OECD countries whose economies are interdependent with ours. These changes stem from responses to international competitiveness, ideas about optimal redistributive policy, and political ideology, the latter being most apparent in the US and UK. A factor unique to Canada is the contribution of the provinces to redistribution policy; in certain key areas, provincial redistribution has flagged, exacerbated by the growing decentralization from federal to provincial governments in response to financial stringencies.

Admittedly, not all policy changes have been bad. In fact, some significant innovations in redistribution policy may go on to shape future policy; we discuss this at more length in the final section of the chapter.

In the next section, we recount the evolution of ideas about redistribution in the economics literature and the policy arena, noting the links between the two. We go on to document the extent to which Canadian policies have and have not followed the evolution of these ideas and suggest reasons for the apparent deterioration in the effectiveness of these policies. After indicating possible directions for policy reform, we offer a conclusion. Our discussion about the evolution of economic ideas of redistribution complements those found in Part 1 of this volume that focus on political ideas.

The Evolution of Ideas about Redistribution

Before the 1970s, redistribution policies were underpinned by a few influential ideas. Universality was the norm in social protection policies, including health care, pensions, and family allowances. More targeted redistribution was largely the responsibility of the progressive tax-transfer system. The anchor of the system was the income tax, whose ideal was a progressive comprehensive system promoted by the Carter Report (Royal Commission on Taxation 1966) and whose rallying cry was: "A dollar is a dollar no matter what its source." The income tax system was the government's main revenue-raiser and was characterized by a highly progressive rate structure. The transfer side of the tax-transfer equation was less progressive, relying on a combination of broad-based transfers and welfare payments to the disabled and the long-term unemployed. The ideal of a negative income tax, whereby transfers to low-income persons would be conditioned on their incomes, was not pursued, despite being advocated by economists and policy advisors. Corporate income tax rates were high, and an inheritance tax served as the ultimate wealth equalizer.

Despite the apparent progressivity of the income tax, tax incidence studies of the time found the tax system to be surprisingly non-progressive, except at the bottom end (Vermaeten, Gillespie, and Vermaeten 1994). Such findings, however, were sensitive to the incidence assumptions made, especially the treatment of capital income (Whalley 1984).

The 1970s ushered in some major rethinking about redistributive policy. Influential tax reform documents in the US (US Treasury 1977) and the UK (Report of a Committee Chaired by Professor James Meade 1978) advocated replacing the income tax with a progressive consumption tax, a position also taken in Canada by the Royal Commission on the Economic Union and Development Prospects for Canada (1985) and the Economic Council of Canada (1987). Public finance economists now thought capital income ought not to be taxed at the same rate as earnings, if at all, following the influential argument of Kaldor (1955) that one ought to be taxed on what one takes from the social pot (consumption), not on what one contributes (income).[1]

While there has been some retraction of the idea that capital income ought not to be taxed at all, the persuasive view remains that it should be taxed at a much lower rate than earnings. The case for taxing capital income is complex. Simply stated, it rests on capital income being correlated with either individual earnings abilities or with sources of unearned income, such as inheritances or other windfall gains, that would otherwise go untaxed under an income tax system. Taxing capital income at a preferential rate reflects the following: (1) much capital income reflects saving to smooth consumption over the lifecycle; (2) capital income is more responsive than labour income to tax rates; and (3) in the absence of incentives, people save too little for retirement.[2]

The tax treatment of capital income has particular relevance for retirement savings. To the extent that such savings are a means of smoothing one's consumption over the lifecycle, the case for tax-preferred treatment of saving is strong. Recent behavioural economics literature has supported encouraging saving for retirement since there is considerable evidence that individuals set aside much less for their retirement than the standard lifecycle saving approach would predict. Experimental and other evidence attributes this, in part, to systematic short-sightedness in current choices that have long-term consequences, called time-inconsistent preferences or preference reversals (Laibson 1997). Moreover, personal decisions are sometimes subject to framing effects, whereby choices are made based on how alternatives are framed, even though the alternatives are equivalent. When a pension savings plan is available, for example, the proportion of those opting in when the default option is not to participate is much lower than is the proportion choosing to remain in when that is the default option. In these circumstances, "nudge policies" (Thaler and Sunstein 2008) encourage individuals to make the decision that is in their long-run best interest – like supplementary voluntary public pensions with an opt-out option.

Favouring capital income, either by a dual income tax or by consumption taxation, does not preclude highly progressive taxes on earnings. On the contrary, with capital income removed, it should be possible, at least in principle, to increase the progressivity of the tax on earnings or, equivalently, consumption. Yet, following an important paper by Nobel Laureate James Mirrlees (1971), the influential optimal income tax literature argues that the progressivity of a tax system may be limited by the disincentive effects it creates, especially at the top of the earnings distribution. The argument, which has recently been carefully outlined in Diamond and Saez (2011), is based on standard trade-offs between efficiency and equity, as well as considerations of tax avoidance and evasion, and has been taken to apply even if the government objective is highly egalitarian. It assumes that high earnings are significantly influenced by effort, not luck. The case in favour of limited progressivity has been fairly widely accepted by dominant countries and imitated in others.

Progressivity at the bottom of the earnings distribution is more nuanced. In the standard normative approach, it is optimal to have those at the very bottom not employed but receiving generous transfers. Those working would receive transfers (negative income taxes), while facing positive marginal tax rates on their earnings, possibly steeply rising ones. Recently, Saez (2002) (drawing on Diamond [1980]) has argued convincingly for an earnings subsidy at the bottom: because labour supply choices by low-income persons are typically participation decisions rather than hours of work decisions, an optimal redistribution scheme should have negative marginal tax rates at the bottom to encourage participation.

The normative tax literature has lessons for other elements of the tax-transfer system (Boadway, Cuff, Marceau 2008; Boadway 2011). A stand-alone transfer system that selects recipients using personal monitoring to determine eligibility is an accepted way to alleviate information problems that plague redistribution. Stand-alone transfers, such as welfare and disability assistance, can supplement transfers delivered through the tax system, which relies on self-reporting. Stand-alone transfer recipients, especially those who are unable to work, should receive greater transfer incomes than others; otherwise, there would be little point in administering such a system. Similarly, in-kind transfers as part of a redistributive system have been widely studied and advocated; in many circumstances, they effectively target those most in need. More generally, the redistribution literature has emphasized the value of targeting assistance to those most deserving. Universality, whatever its justification in terms of political and ethical acceptability (Korpi and Palme 1998), necessarily entails less redistribution to those persons and greater cost.

Finally, much literature has been devoted to alternative rationales for redistribution. In the standard arguments of welfarism, premised on the notion that social welfare should be based on aggregating individual welfare into a social welfare function, redistribution is conceptually based on redistributing from the better off to the less well off. Some scholars argue that this view of redistribution is too narrow and is challenging to implement, given the difficulty of indexing personal well-being. Roemer (1998) argues that equality of opportunity should be an objective of redistribution, while Sen (1999) argues that all persons should have the opportunity to participate in society and to exploit their capabilities. Such ideas have led to the creation of policy instruments besides the standard income-based tax-transfer system. Wealth transfer (inheritance) taxes can be justified on this basis, as can redistributive schemes directed towards children raised in difficult circumstances. Redistribution policies also have a special role to play when persons face volatility in circumstances for which insurance is not readily available, and for which self-insurance may be costly.

The literature notes other factors that compromise redistribution. For example, fiscal competition constrains redistribution by reinforcing the argument against taxing capital income, both personal and corporate, because of capital's mobility. It also makes it more difficult to tax earnings of high-income persons regarded as mobile. These pressures apply especially at the provincial level, where progressivity might induce both an outflow of high-income people and attract transfer recipients with little or no income. Even in the absence of mobility, some argue that yardstick competition causes some countries to follow other countries, especially economically dominant ones, in reforming their tax systems. Thus, the supply-side revolutions of the Reagan administration in the US and the Thatcher government in the UK may have had copy-cat effects. But why did supply-side policies take hold in these countries? Pure ideology played a role, but circumstances would have had to make supply-side changes politically palatable. One such circumstance was the perception of a wasteful public sector in which redistribution was costly given the universality of transfer systems. There was also some political acceptance of the idea that inequality was related to a lack of effort, not bad luck (Alesina and La Ferrara 2005; Alesina and Angeletos 2005; Alesina and Giuliano 2010).

The form of redistribution policy is also influenced by notions about sources of inequality. As Green and Townsend emphasize elsewhere in this volume, policies aimed at making labour markets more flexible and improving incentives for workers to improve their skills were natural responses to the presumption that inequality was heavily driven by the belief, right or wrong, that globalization and technological pressures favoured skilled over unskilled workers.

Policy changes over the past three decades have reflected many of the above ideas on differential tax treatment of capital income, negative marginal tax rates, and targeting of redistribution; interestingly, the ideas have not all pre-dated the policy innovations.

The Evolution of Redistribution Policy in Canada

To begin, it is important to note that redistribution policies contain a large number of elements, reflecting the many circumstances in which individuals find themselves. In Canada, redistribution is complicated by the fact that some policies are delivered by the federal government, some by the provinces, and some by both. To the extent that the two levels face different pressures and accountabilities, this can affect redistribution. Redistributive equity is a constitutionally sanctioned responsibility of both levels of government. Section 36 (1) commits them jointly to equality of opportunity, economic development, and the provision of essential public services. Furthermore, most government fiscal policies, regardless of level, have redistributive effects, whether intentional or not. Yet each level assumes primary responsibility for different programs and, therefore, for different groups of transfer recipients. There is evidence that this division of responsibilities has worked to the disadvantage of some groups.

Redistribution in the Income Tax-Transfer System

Much redistribution takes place through the income tax-transfer system at both federal and provincial levels. Over the past forty years, the income tax rate structure at both levels has become considerably less progressive, especially at the top.

The federal graduated marginal income tax rate system was significantly flattened in the 1980s, first with a reduction in the number of income tax brackets from thirteen to eleven, accompanied by a significant reduction in the top marginal tax rates in the early 1980s, then with a shift to three income tax brackets and a further reduction in the top rate to 29 percent in 1988. Since then, the federal income tax system has remained relatively stable, with some reduction in the bottom marginal tax rate. Over the same time period, significant changes were made at the provincial level. The gradual devolving of tax room to the provinces, along with the 2001 change in the Tax Collection Agreements to allow provinces to set their own rate structures, reduced the progressivity of provincial income taxes. Alberta went so far as to opt for a flat rate structure, while all other provinces have adopted less progressive rate structures than the federal income tax, contributing to a less progressive system overall. An important question is the extent to which fiscal competition pressures have contributed to this, as suggested by the literature. The fate of the inheritance tax might answer this question: when it was devolved to the provinces, it was gradually eliminated by all provinces, suggesting that fiscal competition is a reality.[3]

Combined with a flatter rate structure, the progressivity of the tax system at the top has eroded considerably while earnings inequalities have increased. At the same time, the relatively generous sheltering of capital income has been maintained and enhanced. Savings for retirement through employment-based Registered Pension Plans are fully sheltered, Registered Retirement Savings Plans for those not covered by employers have been enhanced, and both have been supplemented by modest Tax-Free Savings Accounts. Corporate tax rates have fallen at least as much in Canada as elsewhere, and equity in home ownership continues to be tax-free (although subject to significant property taxes for local services). Revenue from personal income taxes as a percentage of total tax revenue fell from 40.8 percent to 35.7 percent from 1990 to 2005 (OECD 2008b). More importantly, the introduction of the Goods and Services Tax (GST) in 1991, and its harmonization with several provincial counterparts, foreshadowed a shift in the tax mix from income to consumption taxes over the longer run (despite the recent reduction in the GST by the federal government),[4] explicitly following what happened in many other OECD countries (Department of Finance 1983). The move further reduced the progressivity of the overall tax system, except to the extent that the refundable GST credit offset it for lower-income families. Overall, the role of the income tax-transfer system as a device for addressing inequality over most of the income distribution has been muted.

Recent reforms, though, have made the income tax-transfer system more effective at the lower end of the income distribution. The system of exemptions and deductions that existed through the 1970s has been largely replaced by credits, enhancing their value to low-income taxpayers, at least those with taxable incomes large enough to benefit. More recently, the innovation of refundable tax credits has added a transfer, or negative income tax, element to the income tax system. In addition to offsetting the burden of the GST on low-income persons, income-tested refundable tax credits have assisted low-income families with children through the Canadian Child Tax Benefit, which replaced family allowances, and subsidize the earnings of low-income workers with the Working Income Tax Benefit. Being income-conditioned as well as available to non-taxpayers, refundable tax credits are much more progressive than are their non-refundable counterparts and have been reasonably successful at redistributing in favour of children in low-income families and low-income employed persons. Whether the Working Income Tax Benefit (WITB) has induced greater participation in the labour force, its main economic rationale, as discussed above, remains unknown.

Redistribution in Social Programs

The income tax system that redistributes among income-earners is accompanied by other redistribution programs for those who are not working. The federal government is primarily responsible for public pensions and transfers to the elderly, although the former is a shared responsibility that can be assumed by any province, as in Quebec with the Quebec Pension Plan. The federal government also has exclusive responsibility for the temporarily unemployed through its stand-alone employment insurance system. The record in public pensions and employment insurance has been mixed, with relatively greater success in the former program.

The provinces are responsible for delivering important social services like education, health care, and social assistance, although, as mentioned, the federal government shares the commitment. The long-term unemployed, the sick, and the unemployable (the disabled) rely on provincial services. The federal government has exercised its commitment in the case of health, social assistance, and postsecondary education through its spending power, although the extent of federal conditionality varies among the programs, ranging from non-existent for postsecondary education to reasonably explicit for health. These differences partly account for the heterogeneity of program standards among provinces.

We begin with a review of the changes to the federal programs of retirement and unemployment benefits before turning to the programs handled by the provinces. Some of these programs are treated in more detail elsewhere in this volume: labour market policies in Green and Townsend, social assistance in Haddow, childcare in Mahon, and public pensions in Myles.

Retirement Benefits

For the most part, the federal programs of retirement benefits have been successful at lifting the elderly poor from poverty. Retired individuals with inadequate retirement incomes rely on federal Old Age Security (OAS) and the Guaranteed Income Supplement (GIS), as well as the Canada/Quebec Pension Plans for those who contributed during their working lives. Both Old Age Security and the Guaranteed Income Supplement are family-income-conditioned and are well-targeted to retired persons with the greatest financial need, for example, single women with no other means of support. In combination with in-kind transfers available in the provinces, these two programs contributed to the decline in poverty among the elderly in the 1980s (Milligan 2008). The maturation of the Canada/Quebec Pension Plans (C/QPP) also reduced seniors' income inequality (Myles 2000). Both family income targeting and the indexing of the OAS/GIS benefit levels to inflation have made OAS and the GIS more responsive to need than are provincial social assistance programs. Indeed, the contrast between the relative success of transfers to the elderly poor, which is a federal responsibility, and welfare transfers, which are provincial, is suggestive of a problem resulting from the distribution of responsibilities within the federation, especially with the elimination of the federal contribution through the Canada Assistance Plan. We return to this issue below.

Public assistance for retirement income in Canada follows the so-called three-pillar system: transfers to the needy elderly (OAS/GIS), a mandatory employment-based public pension system (C/QPP), and tax-assisted private saving for retirement, including RRPs and RRSPs, housing, and the recent Tax Free Savings Accounts (TFSAs). Adequate retirement incomes require a significant element of personal saving, with OAS/GIS and C/QPP acting as a backstop. In recent years, however, there has been a significant decline in the proportion of the population covered by private pensions, particularly defined-benefit ones (Gougeon 2009). Unless those affected offset this shortfall by increasing their private saving for retirement, and there is limited evidence that this is happening, this will have adverse consequences for income inequality among the retired and will put budgetary pressures on the OAS and GIS systems, especially in light of the aging population. In a later section of the chapter, we offer suggestions for dealing with this situation, including public-sector alternatives to private retirement savings systems.

Unemployment Benefits

The success of the unemployment system is less clear. The temporarily unemployed in Canada are generally eligible for the federally administered Employment Insurance program. Starting in 2007, like the OAS/GIS and C/QPP systems, the base of eligible earnings that determine Employment Insurance (EI) rates began to change automatically each year – in the case of EI, with average industrial weekly earnings. Before that, the maximum insurable amount had not exceeded the limit established by the Employment Insurance Act. In addition, the EI system was made more flexible by being based on cumulative hours rather than on full-time work weeks. Even so, the benefit replacement rate has remained at 55 percent since 1994, down from 66 percent in the 1970s.

The program's structural features have increasingly restricted the coverage and led to differential treatment across provinces. Thus, eligibility requirements and the length of the benefit period vary according to local unemployment rates. While this may reflect actuarial considerations, it does so arbitrarily as other relevant actuarial considerations are avoided (such as experience rating).

Moreover, some classes of self-employed (e.g., fishers) are allowed to participate while others are not. More generally, given that most self-employed and part-time workers are not eligible, a substantial proportion of the involuntary unemployed are ineligible for EI and have to rely on other means of support, such as self-insurance and family members or welfare. While the problem with providing EI to self-employed and part-time workers has been around a long time (and the solution is not obvious),[5] it has become more pressing as the nature of the labour force has changed. In fact, the self-employed are excluded from unemployment insurance in most countries, even though they face considerable income uncertainty.

Social Assistance

The provinces are responsible for social assistance or welfare, but the federal government provides financial support to the provinces. The move to unconditional federal grants, the overall decline in federal support, and increased health care costs have all put the provincial welfare programs under considerable strain. Further, the administrative structure of these provincial programs and lack of provincial/federal coordination have been detrimental to potential recipients. Consequently, those on social assistance have fared poorly over the last twenty years.

Federal support has gone from the 50 percent shared-cost CAP program with eligibility based on needs to the bloc funding approach of the current Canada Social Transfer (CST) with much less financial support and only a mobility condition remaining. Under the CAP program, the percentage of total federal cash transfers targeted for social assistance increased fourteen percentage points from 1980 to 42 percent of total federal transfers in 1995; during this time, the real value of the federal cash transfers remained relatively unchanged. Between 1996 and 2004, all federal cash transfers were delivered via the Canada Social and Health Transfer (CHST). With the implementation of the CHST, the real value of federal cash transfers fell by 21 percent and did not recover their lost value until 2004 with the implementation of the Canada Social Transfer (CST) and Canada Health Transfer. After the implementation of the CST, the percentage of federal cash transfers notionally targeted to social assistance dropped precipitously from the early 1990s and currently stands at 20 percent of total federal cash transfers.[6] Not surprisingly, provincial coffers have felt the strain.

The federal government's commitment to the provinces' provision of basic public services includes equalization payments to ensure that the provinces can provide reasonably comparable levels of public services at reasonably comparable levels of taxation. Since the 1950s, this has been accomplished by a system of revenue equalization. Recently, this system has come under some strain, forcing provinces to rely more on own-source revenues. Consequently, horizontal imbalances are growing, a trend exacerbated by greater imbalances in natural resource revenues. This has resulted in various restrictions on equalization, including capping the rate of program growth and limiting the extent to which natural resources are equalized. Per capita social transfers are also implicitly equalizing, but, as we have seen, they, too, have been restricted from time to time.

Given that growing shares of provincial budgets are devoted to health and education expenditures, the amount left for welfare has come under particular strain, with most of the squeeze coming from health expenditures. The fraction of total provincial expenditure on health grew seven percentage points during the past two decades and currently makes up over one-third of total provincial spending.[7] Increases in federal cash transfers have largely gone to health. Since 2004, the CST has grown by 20 percent in constant dollars, whereas the Canada Health Transfer (CHT) has grown by 43 percent. Recent increases in federal cash transfers for health have not offset the growth in provincial spending; the fraction of provincial spending on health, social assistance, and education covered by federal cash transfers in 2009 is still lower by six percentage points than it was in 1989.

The federal government also contributes directly to provincial welfare recipients through refundable tax credits that vary according to the type of recipient. All welfare recipients benefit from the refundable GST tax credit, the only federal refundable tax credit available on a universal basis (albeit relatively small in size). In addition, as mentioned, families with children benefit from refundable tax credits targeted to children; these are family-income tested. Non-refundable tax credits are of no use to welfare recipients, nor do they receive the WITB even if they earn modest working incomes.

Most welfare incomes peaked in real terms in 1994 or earlier and have been falling since then, with some regional variation. In Ontario, between 1994 and 2007, the real welfare income fell by 35 percent for a single employable, by 19 percent for a person with a disability, and by 25 percent for a lone parent with one child. In Alberta over the same period, the percentage declines were smaller, at 21 percent for a single employable, 4.2 percent for a person with a disability, and 2.6 percent for a lone parent with one child (National Welfare Council 2008). This is a result of government passivity and the fact that welfare payments are indexed neither to inflation nor to market wages nor again to poverty levels. While some welfare recipient groups have fared better than others, such as those with children who obtain refundable tax credits versus single unemployables, all have fallen behind in real absolute terms and relative to others in society as measured by relative poverty levels (National Welfare Council 2008).

On a broader scale, the decline of welfare incomes coincided, perhaps not surprisingly, with the replacement of CAP and its federal shared financing of welfare by the system of bloc transfers (now the CST), with minimal conditions attached. The fact that the provinces independently set their own welfare rates discourages unilateral increases in the absence of harmonization.[8] Welfare rates vary widely across provinces and, as mentioned, are typically well below poverty rates (and below provincial minimum wage incomes, for that matter). Moreover, they are administered separately, not only from programs in other provinces but also from the federal EI system. This is in sharp contrast to income and sales taxes, where there is a considerable amount of harmonization in terms of bases and collection. Given that many persons move between welfare and EI, this absence of harmonization increases the administrative inefficiency and the ability to move persons from welfare into employment. No doubt it also gives rise to the potential for provinces to take actions that induce persons who would otherwise be on welfare to become eligible for EI

Certain structural features of provincial welfare systems discourage people from helping themselves or from self-insuring, including strict limits on asset ownership (typically about $1,000 for singles and $2,000 for couples), and on the amount of earnings allowed before full clawbacks take effect ($100 to $200 per month). The asset rules also apply to savings in RRSPs and TFSAs, but not to Registered Disability Savings Plans and Registered Education Savings Plans, an inconsistency noted by Stapleton (2010). In the mid-1990s, some provincial social assistance programs began instituting welfare-to-work or workfare programs requiring mandatory participation in employment programs with possible reductions in benefits for non-compliance. Such requirements were prohibited under CAP.

At the same time, to deal with rising program costs, public debt, and cuts to federal transfers, all provinces reduced real social assistance benefits. Several implemented new administrative procedures determining eligibility of social assistance recipients, thereby significantly reducing the number receiving social assistance, with the single employables being the hardest hit (Kneebone and White 2009). Interestingly, those welfare recipients with the least federal support have fared least well in the past two decades (the disabled and the single unemployed), while other categories of low-income persons receiving federal transfers have done better (low-income families with children, the elderly, the temporary unemployed). Of course, this may have encouraged some single employables to seek employment, especially given the inducement of the WITB.

Education Policy

An area of redistribution policy relevant for social mobility is education, particularly postsecondary education. The responsibility for universities and colleges is provincial. The provinces provide operating funds, regulate these institutions, provide varying forms of student financial assistance through loans and grants, and, in some cases, operate research and scholarship programs. As in other provincial spending programs, there is virtually no harmonization across provinces, partly due to the form of federal support. In fact, there is increasing evidence of beggar-thy-neighbour provincial policies, such as discriminatory fees for out-of-province students, preferential admissions for professional programs, and financial incentives for graduates to remain in-province. There is limited harmonization of programs and mobility among institutions of the sort now emerging in Europe with the Bologna agreement.[9]

The federal CST is nominally intended to provide federal transfers to provinces in support of postsecondary education, along with welfare. However, since these funds are untied and impose no conditions on provincial postsecondary education spending, they cannot be regarded as federal contributions to postsecondary education as opposed to federal support for general provincial program spending. The federal government provides direct research funding to institutions and scholars through the granting councils and other means. It also provides direct support for infrastructure from time to time. In recent years, the federal government has provided financing for faculty positions in the form of Canada Research Chairs, a direct intervention in university policy.

The federal and provincial tax systems provide relatively generous treatment for investment in human capital and take specific measures to make higher education more accessible to those with limited family means. To the extent that the costs of education are deductible from the tax base, human capital investment is treated on a cash-flow basis similar to savings for retirement in RRSPs. Thus, forgone earnings are implicitly deductions from taxable income, albeit when tax rates are low. Financial costs are not deductible but are subject to a series of tax credits for tuition, textbooks, and education costs that are not refundable but that can be carried forward or passed on to relatives. These credits are not progressive like refundable tax credits, nor do they come near to matching the costs of postsecondary education. In addition, the Registered Education Savings Plan (RESP) allows parents to save in a tax-sheltered form for their child's education. Interest on RESP contributions accumulates tax-free until the child enters postsecondary education, at which point the accumulated interest becomes taxable income for the child (though not the original contribution). But neither education tax credits nor RESPs are well-targeted; much of their benefit goes to middle- and upper-income families (Milligan 2005). In any case, the amounts are not sufficient to address accessibility problems of children from low-income families.

Two other programs are somewhat better targeted: student loans and the new federal Canada Student Grant Program, which replaced Millennium Grants. The latter is a needs-based grant that depends on family income and lasts for the duration of a student's program, although at relatively low levels considering the cost of university education. The Canada Student Grant has the potential to address equality of opportunity in higher education, but it constitutes a limited amount of support in a broader system that is not particularly well targeted to those likely to face the greatest barriers to postsecondary education (Finnie, Usher, and Vossensteyn 2004).

Child Benefits

The treatment of children has also evolved considerably in recent years, seemingly motivated by two considerations. One is the rapid increase in female participation in the labour market and the barriers that childbearing impose on that; the other is the objective of equality of opportunity, which suggests particular attention be paid to children in lower-income families. An array of programs addresses the needs of children and their parents, the most obvious and costly of which is the system of public education, which is being extended in some provinces to include early childhood education.

Within the tax-transfer system, there are various child-benefit initiatives, many relatively recent. Some facilitate the participation of mothers in the workforce, such as maternity leave provisions of the EI system and deductions for daycare under the income tax. These are available for all mothers and are not targeted to lower-income families. Refundable tax credits for children – the Canada Child Tax Benefit and the National Child Benefit Supplement and provincial counterparts – are reasonably well targeted to children in low-income families. Additional tax credits are available for low-income families with disabled children under the Child Disability Benefit.

The significant decline in the poverty rates of children, from 18 percent in 1995 to 9 percent in 2008,[10] may be partly attributed to the federal government's deliberate shift towards policies targeting children. Other elements are much less targeted and probably contribute relatively little to equality of opportunity or redistribution more generally. The Universal Child Care Benefit is widely available whether parents work or not and, as such, is a relatively weak instrument for enhancing daycare for working mothers. Similarly, the new Fitness Tax Credit, however much weight one attaches to children's physical fitness, is not a particularly effective policy instrument for that purpose.

The Policy Reform Agenda

Possible directions for reform include the increased use of refundable tax credits, a dual income tax system, administrative reform in current programs, tax-saving incentives, and equality of opportunity initiatives. These suggestions are motivated by the demonstrated inadequacy of current policies in dealing with inequality, especially poverty, and by the budget constraints of governments at all levels. The latter are due not only to the debt incurred in addressing the recent international financial crisis but also to the rising public expenditures on health and postsecondary education that crowd out welfare and other anti-poverty programs. Redistribution has to be smarter, and much better targeted to those most in need.

The increased reliance on refundable tax credits in the income tax system has had a clear impact on those receiving such credits, particularly families with children. Greater targeting in the income tax system could be achieved by making all tax credits refundable, especially those for eligible dependents, children, and employment. Moreover, they could be made income-contingent for further progressivity. Enhancing the use of refundable tax credits would turn the income tax system into a negative income tax and allow the federal government to complement provincial welfare systems by making a real contribution to non-taxpayers, including welfare recipients and poor pensioners.

Another way to increase the progressivity of the individual income tax system would be to move to a dual income tax system with more progressive rates on labour income earnings. Such systems were adopted in several Nordic countries in the 1990s, and recent tax reforms in a number of European countries have moved their respective tax systems in this direction. Under a dual income tax system, any income earnings from non-capital (labour/pension/transfer) sources are subject to a progressive tax schedule, whereas capital income earnings are taxed at a flat rate, generally at the lowest rate of the non-capital income tax schedule and at the same rate as corporate income. One advantage of such a system is that it treats capital and labour income as two different tax bases, and, thus, differentiated rates can be applied. It is not clear whether the same tax schedule should be applied to both bases as is currently done in the income tax system, with some allowances for retirement saving. The potential ease of administrating a flat tax and possible cost-savings are appealing features of this type of dual income system. In addition, a low flat tax on capital income could reduce the incentive for capital to move abroad, an ever-growing concern with the increased mobility of capital. Finally, separating capital income from earnings in the personal income tax system could lead to greater progressivity.

The administration of programs aimed at helping those who are out of work calls for reform. For example, individuals could be better sorted by considering the reasons for unemployment: disability, long-term unemployment, and involuntary unemployment. Doing so would allow the improved targeting of transfers to social assistance and disability recipients with the intent of increasing these transfers relative to the poverty lines. The current system is failing certain individuals, particularly unattached singles. By and large, those receiving social assistance have either exhausted benefits in the EI system or were never eligible for EI benefits. Improved accessibility to EI by part-time workers, and possibly by the self-employed and those with limited attachment to the labour market, might address the latter problem, although how to do so remains unclear.

Improvements in the EI system in terms of higher benefits, longer qualifying periods, and greater training opportunities could help with the former problem. Greater harmonization between the federally run EI system and the provincially run social assistance programs would go a long way towards ensuring individuals do not slip through the cracks. Further, a harmonized system could improve the responsiveness of social insurance programs to sudden income changes experienced by the most vulnerable in our society – the importance of timely response cannot be overstated. One imaginative approach sees EI as a two-tier system in which benefits differ for those who have been unemployed for a long period of time and are needs-based, as in many European systems. Integrating EI with welfare systems would facilitate such a reform but would require federal-provincial collaboration. Finally, more advantage could be taken of the non-profit and charitable sector by enhancing tax credits for charitable giving.

With the reduction in coverage of private pension plans, some fear that working individuals will not save enough for their retirement. To this end, the government has introduced limited new tax-savings incentives. Alternatively, the government could act on the insights of behavioural economics literature, which show that individuals do not always choose actions that are in their own self-interest if they do not fully understand the options or are short-sighted. Both may limit an individual's ability to save on his/her own for retirement. However, policies may be designed to influence savings decisions. For example, changing the default enrolment option on private retirement savings plans from not being automatically enrolled to being automatically enrolled and setting a default contribution rate can increase both participation in and contributions to the retirement savings plan (Madrian and Shea 2001). Such changes have already been implemented in the UK and New Zealand. Some suggest that the public sector could set up a broad-based fully funded defined-benefit pension scheme as an alternative to private employer-based plans. A public scheme could avoid the high management fees faced by private savers – if it is efficiently managed (Ambachtscheer 2007). Those preferring to remain with their current employer-based schemes would be free to do so.

The government could also seek out equality of opportunity initiatives. Increased equality of opportunity could be achieved by the better targeting of student aid, enhancing the Canada Student Grant program, which is well structured but of limited size, and reforming education tax credits and the RESP. To increase the use of RESPs by lower-income families, financial incentives could be targeted to those with low household incomes. Better information, increased subsidy rates, or even lump-sum payments to initiate the opening of an RESP might increase RESP use by such families (Milligan 2005). Another equality of opportunity initiative could mimic the Child Trust Fund, used in the UK until recently to ensure a more equal start for children at the beginning of their adult lives. The Child Trust Fund provided every child born in the UK with £250 in a savings account that could only be used by the child after s/he turned eighteen. The scheme need not be universal as in the UK but, rather, could be targeted to less advantaged children. At the provincial level, governments could imitate the Bologna agreement in Europe by harmonizing postsecondary education policies, for example, by eliminating out-of-province fees and preferential admissions for professional programs to increase the mobility of students across provincial lines and establishing common professional education standards to enhance employment opportunities.

Another suggestion is to provide increased support to working families by expanding available childcare options, increasing the maximum allowable childcare deductions (perhaps linking them to actual childcare costs that typically vary by the age of the child), increasing the child tax credits, and reducing provincial clawbacks. Perhaps a better approach than using a taxable universal childcare grant to support working families would be to increase the use of targeted childcare subsidies. The recent Working Income Tax Benefit could be enhanced; for example, it only applies to those earning a minimum of three thousand dollars, thus ruling out welfare recipients whose work limits constrain the amount they can earn.

Concluding Remarks

Market inequality has increased over the past three decades, especially at the upper and lower ends of the income distribution, and the policy response to this has been mixed. Far from undoing the increase in market inequality, redistribution policy has become, if anything, less redistributive. Even so, a few notable innovations have improved outcomes in some dimensions, setting a basis for further improvements. Transfers to the elderly and families have been converted from universal to income-based, and most income tax deductions have been converted to tax credits. Refundable tax credits have been introduced to shelter low- and zero-income earners from GST liabilities to support low-income families with children and to encourage the participation of low-income workers in the labour force; these refundable credits are super-progressive since they decline with income. The recently introduced federal grants for postsecondary education target students with the most financial need. Generally speaking, two of the main components of social policy – health care and education – remain solid pillars of the system of social insurance and equality of opportunity.

While these changes get resources into the hands of those who need it most, they are timid and selective in terms of the broader population of the needy. The replacement of credits for deductions, although potentially an effective redistributive instrument, is compromised by the absence of refundability; this makes them of limited use to the lowest-income persons. Refundable credits are limited in size and focus on certain target groups. Overall, the income tax system has become much less progressive, especially at the upper end and at the provincial level where an increasing share of tax revenue is collected. The elimination of the inheritance tax has also reduced progressivity at the upper end. The various measures for sheltering asset income from taxation (RRSPs, RPPs, RESPs, housing, TFSAs), although beneficial as a means of encouraging saving for retirement, are largely taken up by middle- and upper-income households. The lowest-income households who rely on social assistance still face strong disincentives to save.

For the neediest persons in society, redistributive policy has been particularly harsh. Real welfare incomes have fallen significantly over the past two decades, especially for the disabled and single employable persons. They are well below both conventional poverty lines' minimum wage incomes.

The ability of the social protection system to respond to economic shocks has also been compromised. Those least able to self-insure and the most exposed to employment shocks are afforded minimal protection under the EI system, whose generosity has been limited and whose eligibility conditions leave a high proportion of the unemployed without coverage. Active labour market policies, such as the WITB, training and workfare programs, and employment services, combined with less generous transfers to the short- and long-term unemployed, might have had a positive effect on labour market participation for those able to find work, but they have left those unable to find work further behind.

Why has the effectiveness of redistribution policy eroded? There is no simple answer, but we can discern a number of contributing factors. Decentralization has undoubtedly played a role. While federal initiatives such as refundable tax credits have been promising, provincial transfer systems have languished, particularly for single persons and the disabled. Provincial income taxes have become notably less progressive as provinces have taken on more revenue-raising responsibility. Globalization and the cross-border influence of ideologies seem to have been important as well. Canada is one of many countries whose rate structure has flattened out and who have reduced their reliance on the income tax for less progressive options. This may partly reflect fiscal competition as countries compete to retain capital, businesses, and mobile persons; countries are also imitating policies of other countries through a sort of yardstick competition. Ideas might have influenced the flatter rate structure, along with other policy outcomes. Most notably, the hope that persons could be encouraged into the workplace by a combination of financial incentives and active labour market policies has coincided with more punitive welfare and EI provisions. Finally, financial stringencies must be considered: redistributive policies were ratcheted down in the 1990s, and there has been no initiative for reversal. This reflects the fact that major fiscal changes often occur as a result of big shocks, and, given the inertia in the system, many of these changes are irreversible.

Redistribution policy has evolved through a number of piecemeal changes, interrupted by responses to major fiscal shocks. Broad-based reforms are rarely undertaken. It is not surprising, therefore, that the result is uneven. Perhaps it is time to contemplate rationalizing the whole system.

NOTES

We are very grateful for helpful comments and suggestions on earlier versions by the editors, David Green, and participants in the preparatory workshop for this project.

1 A tax on consumption is equivalent to a tax on earnings in present value terms, and both involve equivalent ways of sheltering capital income from taxation. Arguments involve equity, efficiency, and administrative simplicity rather than simply Kaldor's slogan. A key assumption is that progressivity can be maintained when capital income taxation is eliminated by suitable revision of the structure of tax rates. The Meade Report also argued strongly for a tax on inheritances.
2 These views are reflected in the President's Advisory Panel on Federal Tax Reform (2005) and in recent work for the Mirrlees Review in the UK (Banks and Diamond 2010). The former advocated a dual income tax of the sort pioneered in some Scandinavian countries, whereby earnings are taxed at a progressive rate while capital income faces a low fixed tax rate.
3 Canada is one of the few developed countries in the world without a tax on bequests or inheritances (or wealth).
4 The GST reduction apparently reflected populist sentiment and a commitment to tax reduction rather than intending to change the structure of taxes. The VAT has continually expanded worldwide and has seen rate increases in European countries. The forthcoming Mirrlees review in the UK is recommending the maintenance of the role of the VAT there, as well as a broadening of its base.
5 Changes to the EI system in 2010 allow the self-employed to make voluntary contributions to qualify for EI maternity, parental, sickness, and compassionate care benefits. Participation obliges contributors to continue paying premiums on self-employed earnings for the duration of the self-employed career once benefits have been drawn.
6 Data obtained from the Department of Finance (2013). The CST is a transfer for both social assistance and postsecondary education.
7 Data obtained from Statistic Canada on Consolidated Government Revenue and Expenditures, CANSIM Table 3850002.
8 It is interesting to note that, in 1996, the federal government began setting the federal minimum wage according to provincial legislation. Although there is some variation in the federal/provincial minimum wages across the country, real minimum wages declined in all provinces for the decade before the late 1980s and have remained fairly constant or increased slightly since then (Murray and Mackenzie 2007).
9 The "Joint declaration of the European Ministers of Education convened in Bologna on the 19th of June 1999" was a pledge signed by twenty-nine countries to reform their structures of higher education in a convergent way.
10 As calculated by the National Council of Welfare, http://www.ncw.gc.ca/d.1tas.2t1@-eng.jsp?chrtid=3.

REFERENCES

Alesina, Alberto, and George-Marios Angeletos. 2005. "Fairness and Redistribution." *American Economic Review* 95(4): 960-80.

Alesina, Alberto, and Paola Giuliano. 2010. "Preferences for Redistribution." In Alberto Bisin, Jess Benhabib, and Matthew Jackson, eds., *Handbook of Social Economics*, 93-131. Amsterdam: North Holland.

Alesina, Alberto, and Eliana La Ferrara. 2005. "Preferences for Redistribution in the Land of Opportunities." *Journal of Public Economics* 89: 897-931.

Ambachtscheer, Keith P. 2007. *Pension Revolution: A Solution to the Pensions Crisis.* Hoboken, NJ: John Wiley and Company.

Banks, James, and Peter Diamond. 2010. "The Base for Direct Taxation." In Stuart Adam, Timothy Besley, Richard Blundell, Stephen Bond, Robert Chote, Malcolm Gammie, Paul Johnson, Gareth Myles, and James Poterba, eds., *Dimensions of Tax Design: The Mirrlees Review*, 548-648. Oxford: Oxford University Press.

Beaudry, Paul, and David Green. 2005. "Changes in US Wages, 1976-2000: Ongoing Skill Bias or Major Technological Change?" *Journal of Labor Economics* 23(3): 609-48.

Boadway, Robin. 2011. "Viewpoint: Innovations in the Theory and Practice of Redistribution Policy." *Canadian Journal of Economics* 44(4): 1138-83.

Boadway, Robin, Katherine Cuff, and Nicolas Marceau. 2008. "Design of Assistance Programs to Address Real Income Volatility." In Dean Jolliffe and James Ziliak, eds., *Income Volatility and Food Assistance in the United States*, 217-58. Kalamazoo, MI: W.E. Upjohn Institute.

Boudarbat, Brahim, W. Craig Riddell, and Thomas Lemieux. 2006. "Recent Trends in Wage Inequality and the Wage Structure in Canada." In David A. Green and Jonathan R. Kesselman, eds., *Dimensions of Inequality in Canada*. Vancouver: UBC Press.

Brzozowski, Matthew, Martin Gervais, Paul Klein, and Michio Suzuki. 2010. "Consumption, Income and Wealth Inequality in Canada." *Review of Economic Dynamics* 13(1): 52-75.

Department of Finance. 1983. *Report of the Federal Sales Tax Review Committee.* Ottawa: Government of Canada.

–. 2013. "Federal Support to Provinces and Territories." http://www.fin.gc.ca/fedprov/mtp-eng.asp.

Diamond, Peter A. 1980. "Income Taxation with Fixed Hours of Work." *Journal of Public Economics* 13: 101-10.

Diamond, Peter, and Emmanuel Saez. 2011. "The Case for a Progressive Tax: From Basic Research to Policy Recommendations." *Journal of Economic Perspectives* 25(4): 165-90.

Economic Council of Canada. 1987. *Road Map for Tax Reform: The Taxation of Savings and Investment.* Ottawa: Economic Council of Canada.

Finnie, Ross, Alex Usher, and Hans Vossensteyn. 2004. "Meeting the Need: A New Architecture for Canada's Student Financial Aid System." In Charles Beach, Robin Boadway, and Marvin McInnis, eds., *Higher Education in Canada*, 495-538. Montreal and Kingston: McGill-Queen's University Press.

Frenette, Marc, David Green, and Kevin Milligan. 2007. "The Tale of the Tails: Canadian Income Inequality in the 1980s and 1990s." *Canadian Journal of Economics* 40(3): 734-64.

Gougeon, Philippe. 2009. "Shifting Pensions." *Perspectives*, May 2009, Statistics Canada Catalogue 75-001-X.

Heisz, Andrew. 2007. "Income Inequality and Redistribution in Canada: 1976 to 2004." In Analytical Studies Branch Paper Series, 298. Ottawa: Statistics Canada.

Kaldor, Nicholas. 1955. *An Expenditure Tax*. London: Allen and Unwin.

Kneebone, Ronald, and Katherine White. 2009. "Fiscal Retrenchment and Social Assistance in Canada." *Canadian Public Policy* 35(1): 21-40.

Korpi, Walter, and Joakim Palme. 1998. "The Paradox of Redistribution and Strategies of Inequality: Welfare State Institutions, Inequality, and Poverty in the Western Countries." *American Sociological Review* 63(5): 661-87.

Laibson, David. 1997. "Golden Eggs and Hyperbolic Discounting." *Quarterly Journal of Economics* 112: 443-77.

Lemieux, Thomas, W. Bentley MacLeod, and Daniel Parent. 2009. "Performance Pay and Wage Inequality." *Quarterly Journal of Economics* 124(1): 1-49.

Lu, Yuqian, Rene Morissette, and Tammy Schirle. 2010. "The Growth of Family Earnings Inequality in Canada, 1980-2005." *Review of Income and Wealth* 57: 23-39.

Madrian, Bridgette, and Dennis F. Shea. 2001. "The Power of Suggestion: Inertia in 401(k) Participation and Savings Behavior." *Quarterly Journal of Economics* 116(4): 1149-87.

Milligan, Kevin. 2005. "Who Uses RESPs and Why." In Charles Beach, Robin Boadway, and Marvin McInnis, eds., *Higher Education in Canada*, 467-94. Montreal and Kingston: McGill-Queen's University Press.

–. 2008. "The Evolution of Elderly Poverty in Canada." *Canadian Public Policy* 34 (Supplement): 79-94.

Mirrlees, James. 1971. "An Exploration in the Theory of Optimum Income Taxation." *Review of Economic Studies* 38: 175-208.

Murray, S., and H. Mackenzie. 2007. *Bringing Minimum Wages above the Poverty Line*. March. Ottawa: Canadian Centre for Policy Alternatives.

Myles, John. 2000. "The Maturation of Canada's Retirement Income System: Income Levels, Income Inequality and Low Income among the Elderly." *Canadian Journal on Aging* 19(3): 287-316.

National Welfare Council. 2008. *Welfare Incomes, 2006 and 2007*. Ottawa: National Welfare Council.

Organisation for Economic Cooperation and Development. 2008a. *Growing Unequal: Income Distribution and Poverty in OECD Countries*. Paris: OECD.

–. 2008b. *Revenue Statistics: 1965-2007*. Paris: OECD.

Piketty, Thomas, and Emmanuel Saez. 2007. "How Progressive Is the US Federal Tax System: A Historical and International Perspective." *Journal of Economic Perspectives* 21(1): 3-24.

President's Advisory Panel on Federal Tax Reform. 2005. *Simple, Fair and Pro-Growth: Proposals to Fix America's Tax System*. Washington, DC.

Report of a Committee Chaired by Professor James Meade. 1978. *The Structure and Reform of Direct Taxation*. London: Allen and Unwin.

Roemer, John E. 1998. *Equality of Opportunity*. Cambridge: Harvard University Press.

Royal Commission on Taxation. 1966. *Report of the Royal Commission on Taxation.* Ottawa: Queen's Printer.

Royal Commission on the Economic Union and Development Prospects for Canada. 1985. *Report of the Royal Commission on the Economic Union and Development Prospects for Canada.* Ottawa: The Commission.

Saez, Emmanuel. 2002. "Optimal Income Transfer Programs: Intensive vs. Extensive Labor Supply Responses." *Quarterly Journal of Economics* 117: 1039-73.

Saez, Emmanuel, and Michael Veall. 2005. "The Evolution of High Incomes in Northern America: Lessons from Canadian Evidence." *American Economic Review* 95(3): 831-49.

Sen, Amartya. 1999. *Commodities and Capabilities.* New Delhi: Oxford University Press.

Stapleton, John. 2010. "Down But Not Out: Reforming Social Assistance Rules that Punish the Poor for Saving." Toronto: C.D. Howe Institute e-brief, 2 March.

Thaler, Richard H., and Cass R. Sunstein. 2008. *Nudge: Improving Decisions about Health, Wealth, and Happiness.* New Haven, CT: Yale University Press.

US Treasury. 1977. *Blueprints for Basic Tax Reform.* Washington, DC: Treasury of the United States.

Vermaeten, Frank, W. Irwin Gillespie, and Arndt Vermaeten. 1994. "Tax Incidence in Canada." *Canadian Tax Journal* 42: 348-416.

Whalley, John. 1984. "Regression or Progression: The Taxing Question of Incidence Analysis." *Canadian Journal of Economics* 17(4): 654-82.

# 15 Childcare, New Social Risks, and the New Politics of Redistribution in Ontario

RIANNE MAHON

Changes in labour markets (precarious work, income polarization) and in families (adult earner, lone-parent families) have generated a series of social risks that drive the new politics of redistribution. The old politics of redistribution reflected the economic and social structures of the postwar period, generating a particular understanding of the kind of social programs needed to protect the population from the social risks to which these structures gave rise. Nevertheless, changes in the structure of families and women's increased participation in the labour force and their concomitant social risks present a new set of challenges for the politics of redistribution.

This is not to suggest that the "old" risks have disappeared. The spread of precarious work and the increase in lone parenthood have contributed to the resurfacing of poverty, one of the oldest of social risks. Nor does it imply that the "old" politics no longer matters. As in the past, centre-left governments – at least those who work to integrate the demands of women and young people into their platforms and party organization – are more likely to develop effective, equality-promoting policy responses to new social risks (Bonoli 2006, 19). Yet the new social risks highlight the inadequacy of the social policy mixes developed to meet the old social risks; the former require a new (or redesigned) social architecture (Jenson, Chapter 2, this volume). While the architects may be inspired by the principles that guided policy development in the past, the new challenges may stimulate the development of path-breaking designs.

Public support for childcare constitutes an important feature of the new blueprint. Well-designed childcare policies contribute to the reconciliation of work and family life for the time-pressed adult-earner family, while making it possible for lone parents to improve their economic situation through paid work. Universally accessible early childhood education and care can also lay the foundations for life-long learning, indispensable in the knowledge-based, postindustrial economy. Finally, adequate public support for such a system helps generate good postindustrial jobs as early childhood educators, working in publicly financed and regulated settings, replace low-paid, informal caregivers.

Although Canada began to experience political pressure to provide public support for childcare in the 1960s (Finkel 1995; Mahon 2000), the Canadian government's responses – the childcare expense deduction (1971) and federal-provincial cost-sharing of subsidized spaces through the Canada Assistance Plan (1966) – were consistent with the liberal, pro-market bias of the broader social policy architecture in which they were embedded. Reliance on these policies, in turn, left many without access to regulated childcare spaces and did little to promote the formation of a universally accessible early childhood education and care (ECEC) system across the country.

Yet in assessing responses to new social risks in a country like Canada, where federalism allows for substantial diversity in social policy design, it is important to move beyond the pan-Canadian level and to examine provincial responses. In other words, while federalism can be seen as a barrier to social policy expansion (Obinger, Leibfried, and Castles 2005), it also affords opportunities for the federal government to indulge in pan-Canadian state building (Boychuk, Chapter 10, this volume) as well as openings for provinces to respond to the new social risks in innovative ways. For example, Quebec architects followed a bolder blueprint in developing their "five dollars a day" childcare plan. Some, including Noel (Chapter 11, this volume), have analyzed the forces behind this innovative turn. Rather than repeating the story, this chapter asks why Ontario has fallen so far behind Quebec. After all, Ontario, Canada's most populous province, pioneered the public financing and regulation of childcare in Canada (Prentice 2003) and is home to Toronto, where the idea of childcare as a public service available to all took root in the 1980s (Mahon 2005). Moreover, ideas very similar to those underpinning the Quebec government's childcare policy have been present in Ontario since the 1980s. Nevertheless, progress has been, at best, incremental.

Part of the explanation for the difference has to do with "old politics," in the sense of left-right shifts in partisan alignment. Jenson (2006) and Noel (Chapter 11, this volume) also suggest the need to examine the pattern of institutionalized relations between provincial states and business, labour, and other social movements. An explanation based on such differences is not without merit. Even so, a straight province-to-province comparison between Quebec and Ontario would miss a critical difference – their respective positions within Canadian federalism, which have shaped the horizons of civil society actors. It is not just that Quebec has sought to assert its social policy autonomy vis-à-vis the federal government while Ontario has served as "the linchpin of Canadian federation and one of the provinces most strongly committed to the Canadian project" (Cameron 2002, 1). Rather, in Quebec, civil society actors look primarily to "their" state for solutions, while Ontario-based actors (including politicians) play a multi-level politics, seeking pan-Canadian solutions even as they pursue their claims at the provincial – and, in the case of childcare, municipal – levels. Thus, while both partisan and state-civil society politics matters, in Ontario the outcome has been contingent on developments at the federal level.

The first section of this chapter discusses the relationship between new social risks and the new politics of redistribution and fleshes out a way to think about the politics of childcare in Ontario relative to Quebec. Section two reviews the advances made under centre-left Ontario governments between 1985 and 1995, highlighting the ways in which provincial initiatives remained contingent on federal policies. The third section focuses on the giant step backwards under the neoliberal Progressive Conservative governments from 1995-2003, while the final section examines what happened when federal and provincial policies were aligned (2003-06), the rupture introduced by the federal Conservative government in 2006, and the provincial Liberal government's response.

New Social Risks and the New Politics of Redistribution: Quebec versus Ontario

The link between the new social risks and the new politics of redistribution is clearest with regard to the growing earnings inequality and employment instability associated with deindustrialization and the tertiarization of employment, but it also concerns changes in gender relations, as reflected in the increasing incidence of lone-parent families and the rise in women's labour force participation. Thus, the new social architecture involves policies to facilitate the reconciliation of work and family life, including childcare, as well as those designed to mitigate income inequality. Just as there are different ways of addressing rising income inequality, however, so are there different childcare designs. One, inspired by social-democratic ideals, builds on investment on the supply-side to facilitate universal access to a high-quality system; in this design, centre-based care under public or non-profit auspice predominates. Care is provided by skilled employees who are paid equitable wages and offered decent employment conditions. Provision is made for democratic control, including parental voice. In contrast, the liberal design supports the development of a childcare market, in which commercial operations play an important role. Instrument choice favours the demand side (e.g., provision of information and subsidies for low-income families, supplemented by regulation or quality assurance programs). The tax system can also be used to reimburse better-off families for childcare expenses or to encourage employers to provide places for their employees.

For Bonoli (2006, 5), responses to the new social risks "can be explained using the same independent variables that are known to have influenced the development of post-war welfare states: socio-economic developments, political mobilisation and institutional effects." In line with the dominant approach to comparative social policy, he emphasizes the nature of the existing welfare regime; that is, various ways in which responsibilities have come to be allocated among states, families, markets, and civil society.[1] Yet, while regime theory predicts path-dependent responses to new challenges, new risks also create opportunities for path-breaking policies. In examining responses to new social risks, therefore, greater weight needs to be given to the *politics* of new social risks and to the institutional context in which it occurs.

To do so in a federal country like Canada means going beyond politics at the pan-Canadian level to examine provincial responses and the particular power resources underpinning these. Jenson's account of Quebec's break with the liberal path notes that it was indeed a centre-left Parti québécois (PQ) government that introduced five-dollar-a-day childcare, but feminists in civil society, the PQ, and the Quebec state apparatus played an important part in making the case. Their voices could be heard because the old tripartite structure of political representation had expanded to include other social movements (Jenson 2002, 2006). Ideas mattered too: the development of a conception of ECEC as a solution to a number of issues on the political agenda facilitated the construction of a consensus bringing pro-family forces, the anti-poverty movement, and experts in child development together with feminists and PQ party officials (Jenson 2006,

9-10). Noel (Chapter 11, this volume) places less emphasis on ideas but concurs with Jenson's emphasis on political mobilization – or power resources understood as reflected not only in partisan alignments but also more generally in civil society.

Ideas favouring a universal ECEC system were also to be found in Ontario. Moreover, in the decade from 1985 to 1995, successive centre-left governments attempted to forge stronger state-civil society relations (Bradford 1998). There was also a vibrant women's movement, developing its points of contact in the Ontario state (Collier 2006). For the most part, these experiments proved ineffective because Ontario associations of business and labour were not very representative. Unlike Quebec, Ontario lacks an umbrella organization of business, and the Ontario Federation of Labour represents less than 30 percent of the workforce. More broadly, until the mid-1980s,

> there was no distinctive "Ontario model" that focused policy resources or mobilized private sector commitment along the lines of the various active employment regimes distinguishing some European countries. In addition, Ontario's bureaucracy was neither corporatist in style, nor statist in its developmental aspirations or modes of intervention. (Bradford 1998, 543)

There is another reason for this difference: the institutional context for political mobilization in Canada is marked by the federal structure of the Canadian state system, and the two provinces relate in very different ways to the federal government. Since Quebec's "Quiet Revolution" in the 1960s,[2] successive Quebec governments have sought to embed a distinctive national model, and Quebec social movements have learned to look to "their" government for solutions, not to Ottawa. This is in marked contrast to Ontario, the "linchpin" of Confederation.

For most of the twentieth century, Ontario, the province that accounts for 40 percent of Canada's GDP, has stood as the centre of the federation and, with slightly more than one-third of the seats in the federal House of Commons, Ontario "could be assured that whatever party was in power in Ottawa, a large proportion of that party's seats would come from the province" (Cameron and Simeon 1997, 158). As a result of this and because of the tendency to allocate key economic posts to Ontario MPs, federal policies reinforced Ontario's central position within the economy. Therefore, Courchene (2002, Table 1) suggests:

Since Ontario could generally count on the federal government to further the province's interests, Heartland Ontario was in favour of a strong central government. For example, Queen's Park did not assume the role of economic policy maker that l'Assemblée Nationale did for Quebec. There was no need for this since Rideau Street was essentially an extension of Bay Street, and Ottawa delivered.

Nor did Ontario try to gain control over social policies the way Quebec did. Under successive centre-right governments throughout the postwar years it was, at best, a reluctant follower of federal initiatives (White 2002).

Ontario's place within federalism has had an impact on Ontario's political culture, contributing to the multi-level horizons of Ontario-based actors. Therefore, Ontarians have traditionally identified more with the federal than with the provincial government, something that is reflected in higher voter turnout rates for federal elections (Cameron 2002, 1). Moreover, Ontarians have been "the most likely to think of the federal government as being more important to them than their provincial government," and they lead in describing themselves as "Canadians first" (Wiseman 1997, 435). This orientation shapes the political horizons of Ontario-based actors. Thus, since the early 1980s, Ontario has had an effective provincially based childcare advocacy movement, the Ontario Coalition for Better Child Care (OCBCC), but the latter's strategic horizons have always been multi-level. Childcare advocates in Ontario seek to influence debate at the pan-Canadian level, and both state and civil society actors are prepared to jump levels – below to municipal or above to federal politics – according to the political opportunity structure. The province matters, especially in areas under provincial jurisdiction like childcare, but it is not the sole, nor even the primary, site of political engagement.

This is not to suggest that Ontario's position within the federal system has remained unchanged. In fact, since the 1980s, pressures produced by the restructuring of its manufacturing base have combined with important shifts in federal policy to prompt centre-left governments to forge Ontario's own "quiet revolution." Even then, they have found it difficult to imagine developing provincial childcare policy in the absence of federal support. Although the election of governments with a neoliberal agenda in Ottawa induced Ontario-based actors to pay more attention to the provincial (as well as municipal) level, again, the achievement of a pan-Canadian childcare policy remained the ne plus ultra.

As the following analysis of childcare politics in Ontario shows, ideas highlighting the importance of ECEC have been present since the 1980s and, in the decade from 1985 to 1995, under pressure from childcare advocates and their allies in the labour and women's movements, successive centre-left governments sought to lay the foundations for such a system. Yet, in contrast to Quebec, both Queen's Park and the childcare advocates continued to see the development of a pan-Canadian policy as critical to the successful development of a provincial program. Ontario activists hold onto the longer-term goal of securing a pan-Canadian policy.

Childcare in Ontario's "Quiet Revolution"

The story of childcare politics in Ontario before 1985 has been told elsewhere (Prentice 1988; Mahon 2005). This chapter picks up the story as Ontario politics began to change in important ways. The election in 1985 of a minority Liberal government marked the end of over forty years of successive centre-right Progressive Conservative governments. Yet, although the government took office in the midst of an economic boom, beneath the surface southern Ontario's manufacturing base was under increasing pressure (Albo and MacDermid 2000; Wolfe and Gertler 2001). This intensified as the decade wore on, and boom turned to bust. It was also becoming clear that Ontario could no longer leave economic policy to the federal government. The Progressive Conservative government's high-dollar policy and the Canada-US Free Trade Agreement concluded in 1987 put pressure on Ontario's branch plant economy, while its embrace of neoliberal economics was reflected in its abandonment of an active industrial policy. In response, the Ontario government established a new institution – the Premier's Council – to promote the development of an Ontario-centred innovation policy and took the first step towards the creation of an associative form of governance. The agenda included an important "investing in people" component that listed childcare as the first stage in the development of a highly qualified labour force.

In fact, childcare was already on the federal and Ontario agendas before the provincial Liberals' breakthrough. Initially raised in federal politics by the Royal Commission on the Status of Women (1970), the issue was kept on the federal agenda by the National Action Committee on the Status of Women and its allies.[3] In Ontario, the struggle to defeat the Progressive Conservative government's proposal had given rise to an alliance of feminists and early childhood educators (Mahon 2005). In 1981, the Ontario

Coalition for Better Day Care (now Ontario Coalition for Better Child Care [OCBCC]) brought together organizations on the left and from the mainstream; throughout the 1980s, it carried on a provincial campaign for universal childcare under non-profit auspices (Collier 2006, 89). At the same time, Ontario activists looked to the federal government. As Collier notes, "Calls for a national childcare program became a central lobbying point for the OCBDC, along with demands aimed at the provincial state to improve service delivery and provide more childcare space" (91). Ontario childcare activists also played a central role in the formation of the Canadian Day Care Advocacy Association (now Childcare Advocacy Alliance of Canada [CCAAC]).

In the early 1980s, childcare was framed as essential for women's equality, a frame reinforced by strong ties between the National Action Committee on the Status of Women (NAC) and the CCAAC and sustained within the federal government by the Abella Commission (1984) and the Cooke Task Force. In the spirit of the times, the centre-right government of Ontario created the Ontario Women's Directorate (Collier 2006, 57) and seemed poised to move beyond the liberal principles that had hitherto guided its childcare policies. Accordingly, in his address to the intergovernmental meeting of ministers responsible for the status of women,[4] Ontario's minister, Robert Welch (1984, 9.10), declared:

> Childcare is no longer a welfare issue, concerning only the needy. It is as well an employment and economic issue concerning all working parents of all income levels. Either we take the action required to ensure the provision of a range of reliable childcare services at an affordable price or we risk losing many of the gains women have won, and endangering the economic independence of families.

The concept of childcare as a public service was enshrined in the 1985 Liberal-NDP Accord, which committed the minority Liberal government to the "reform of day care policy and funding to recognize childcare as a basic public service and not a form of welfare" (cited in Courchene 1998, 119). Support for universal preschool also came from within the Ministry of Education from George Radwanski, whose report on preschool education rehearsed arguments that became prominent in the 1990s. Radwanski (1987, 125) eschewed the targeted approach of well-known American preschool programs, noting that even the children of well-educated parents stood to benefit from preschool education: "Rather than viewing day care shortages and pre-school education as separate issues, the two should be combined by making early childhood education available free of charge in public and separate schools province-wide for all children at the age of three."

The provincial government's *New Directions for Childcare* (Ontario 1987) outlined plans for a universally accessible system. In addition to increased funds for subsidies, it promised to replace the intrusive means test with an income test. The province also expanded capital funding, and, in 1989, it announced that, within five years, all school boards would offer junior kindergarten to four-year-olds. This encouraged the ministries of education (kindergarten) and community and social services (childcare) to promote new school-based programs and to allocate funds to support the requirement that all new schools include childcare space. Finally, the provincial government introduced direct operating grants for non-profit centres. This step recognized the government's commitment to non-profit provision and the need to improve staff salaries – a critical step towards turning jobs in this sector into "good" postindustrial jobs.

From the outset, however, the provincial government indicated implementation of its new vision was contingent on federal support:

> A new national partnership is critical for the success of the Ontario government's new directions. Improved cost-sharing arrangements are necessary to realize fully the provincial objective of delivering quality childcare services to all who require them. Indeed the extent and timing of the provincial plan will depend on the level of federal commitment. (Ontario 1987, 9)

At the beginning of 1987, prospects for such a new partnership still seemed promising. The Cooke Task Force had submitted its recommendations, which, if implemented, would have meant a substantial change in federal funding. In addition, the federal Progressive Conservative government had appointed its own special parliamentary committee, which received strong input from the childcare movement and its allies across the country (Friendly 1994). Yet the Progressive Conservatives' childcare act met substantial opposition from the childcare movement, which was critical of the absence of pan-Canadian standards. Of particular concern was the opening to federal funding of commercial childcare on equal terms with the private sector. In addition, the bill would have put a ceiling on the federal government's commitment, whereas, at the time, there was no cap on CAP dollars. Finally, the broader package included a child tax credit, an important concession to anti-feminist forces (Family Caucus) within the federal Progressive Conservative Party (Mahon and Phillips 2002). In the face of strong opposition, the federal government let the bill die on the order papers and, following its re-election, did not revive it. In response, the Ontario government scaled back its plans.

The 1990 election of the first social-democratic government of Ontario raised the hopes of childcare advocates and their allies. Although the government was elected as the Ontario economy began to slide into the worst recession since the 1930s, the new government's ECEC plans were bolder than were those of its Liberal predecessors. Nevertheless, the NDP government was hobbled by mounting fiscal restraints, exacerbated by the federal Progressive Conservatives' imposition of a cap on CAP transfers to Ontario and the other two "have" provinces (British Columbia and Alberta), while changes to the federal unemployment insurance program forced many newly unemployed Ontarians onto swelling provincial social assistance rolls. In addition, the federal Liberal's promise of new federal funds for childcare was postponed and later abandoned as it sought to eliminate the federal deficit by downloading to the provinces. Even though these and other moves strained Ontario's relationship with the federal government, they were not enough to drive the province into the decentralist camp; rather, the NDP "wanted Ottawa to change, not to take down additional powers" (Courchene 1998, 160).

Faced with mounting social assistance claims, the Ontario NDP government embraced the federal activation agenda with the launch of Jobs Ontario in 1992. Consistent with its emphasis on providing opportunities, however, the program included plans to create twenty thousand new subsidised childcare spaces for participants and to set up a special fund of $77 million to help cover capital costs associated therewith. Its commitment did not stop there. In response to a provincewide campaign by childcare advocates eager to move forward now that "their" party was in office,[5] the government developed even bolder plans. In addition to more childcare subsidies, it agreed to promote the conversion of commercial auspices to non-profit. It also sought to turn childcare jobs into good jobs by expanding the direct grant to cover all those working in childcare centres and introducing pay equity by proxy, which meant childcare workers could benefit.

Of particular importance, in 1991, it launched two studies: an external consultation process that resulted in *Childcare Reform in Ontario: Setting the Stage*, guided by the Ministry of Community and Social Services, and an internal study, led by the Ministry of Education, called the Early Years

Initiative (OCBCC 1994, 50). The planned childcare reforms built on the foundations laid in *New Directions,* aiming at the creation of a high-quality, affordable, and accessible service delivered by non-profit community partners and managed at the local level. As well as making improvements in demand-side policies, the government planned to directly fund operating costs. The Early Years Initiative went further, aiming at the integration of early childhood education and care for all children aged three to five, to be provided by a team led by a certified school teacher with a specialization in early childhood education and backed up by an early childhood educator and a trained assistant. Preschool children would receive wrap-around care at the beginning and end of the day and over school holidays, provided by an early childhood educator and a trained assistant. This vision was reiterated by the Royal Commission on Learning, whose report was released just months before the 1995 election. Like the earlier Radwanski report, the latter argued: "The equity question, which is most often raised when young people are in secondary school, must also be addressed in social policies and practices that have an impact on what happened before birth and in the first years of life" (Ontario 1995, 118).

In 1993, the cabinet rejected the idea of preschool for children aged three to five as, given the tight fiscal constraints under which the government was operating, the proposal was seen as too radical. Instead, it decided to build on already existing kindergarten programs for four- and five-year-olds – programs that most boards in the province already had in place. Staffing requirements matched those suggested in the initial report – requirements identical to those proposed by the advisor to a subsequent Liberal government.[6] At the same time, staff in the Ministry of Community and Social Services worked on a complementary ECEC program for children aged zero to four, to be strengthened by the introduction of a more stable system for funding operating costs, and the income test. While the debt crisis of 1994 forced these plans onto the back burner, a scaled-down version of the kindergarten proposal moved forward, given added impetus by the Royal Commission report. Thus, just before the NDP went to the polls in 1995, school boards were asked to submit proposals for pilot "seamless day" programs for four- to five-year-olds.

These setbacks were affected not only by the government's attempt to control its deficit – a task aggravated by federal downloading – but also by the federal government's failure to deliver on its promises. The NDP made it clear that implementation of its plans was contingent on promised federal support; the premier noted that the government would "not be making any decision ... until we hear from Ottawa" (*Toronto Star*, 19 February 1994). When the NDP government drew back in April 1994, childcare advocates criticized it for failing to take advantage of federal funds, which the minister in charge of childcare had indicated could be forthcoming (*Toronto Star*, 15 April 1994).[7] The premier replied:

> What was being proposed was not part of a coherent federal strategy with respect to transfers to the provinces. Instead it was a mug's game ... The federal government, on the one hand, asked for a leadership role in childcare, and on the other, chopped off every source of funding that Ontario had to run the childcare programs that we had already started. (Rae 2001, 64)

While OCBCC and its allies became more focused on the provincial government in this period, they did not abandon the idea of a pan-Canadian policy in which the federal government would play a role. In fact, they wanted the NDP government to "do for childcare what Douglas did for health care" (*Globe and Mail*, 2 June 1992); in other words, to implement a childcare policy that would force the federal government to adopt a pan-Canadian policy. Instead, that leadership role was taken by Quebec several years later – a province whose government and social movements did not aspire to pan-Canadian scale.

Ontario's Quiet Revolution Undone? 1995-2003

While Ontario's Quiet Revolution was constrained by a severe economic downturn and adverse federal policy developments, the government elected in 1995 faced a more favourable situation. The Ontario economy had begun to recover (Wolfe and Gertler 2001), and, while relations with the federal government reached a nadir with the decision to roll CAP into a reduced block fund (the Canada Health and Social Transfer), by the latter part of the 1990s the federal government seemed ready to support provincial social policy initiatives, especially those related to child development. Had the Liberals won the 1995 provincial election as expected, it is quite possible that Ontario's Quiet Revolution, including implementation of a "seamless day" for preschool children, would have continued. This was not to be. The Conservative Party, whose leader was committed to a neoliberal counter-revolution and was definitely opposed to implementing an ECEC policy, won the election. The political situation was now the reverse of what it had been in the previous decade: with the federal (Liberal) government increasingly keen to support ECEC, the Ontario government embraced an "anything but childcare" position.

The premier's position was evident even before his election when he dismissed preschool for three- to five-year-olds as "foolish." As he later noted, when it comes to childcare, "there is a role for family, for relatives, for neighbours, for the private sector. In fact, 8 or 9 out of 10 actually choose that form of childcare as opposed to formal, subsidized care" (*Globe and Mail*, 29 September 1999). Accordingly, his government made childcare an early target of the counter-revolution. In 1995, the fund to support pay equity was capped;[8] the minor capital and start-up fund was eliminated; the major capital fund was cancelled; funding for junior kindergarten was cut and the fund for childcare spaces in new schools eliminated; the NDP's policy of limiting new subsidies to non-profit providers was cancelled; and municipalities were required to pay 20 percent of Jobs Ontario childcare subsidies (Friendly et al. 2007, 88). In 1996, Jobs Ontario was replaced by the Conservative government's "work first" workfare program. Rather than subsidizing spaces in regulated childcare, Ontario Works shared the premier's bias towards informal care. That same year, the Conservative government's childcare review recommended reduced wage subsidies and promotion of commercial childcare. It also introduced a workplace tax incentive for business to invest in childcare spaces while wreaking havoc on the non-profit sector through changes to funding education that forced many boards to impose rent on childcare centres located in their schools. Expenditure on childcare fell from a peak of nearly $600 million in 1994-95 to $516.4 million in 2001-02 (Cleveland and Colley 2003).

Thus, within a very short time, the Conservative government not only reversed earlier moves toward an ECEC system for pre-school children but undermined the foundations of quality childcare for all children. It also undercut efforts to make childcare part of the "good jobs" postindustrial sector by introducing substantial cuts in pay for childcare workers and, through Ontario Works, encouraging the growth of informal care. Childcare advocates did not sit idly by, however, while the system was dismantled. OCBCC organized a one-day strike and major demonstration at Queen's Park in the fall of 1995, but, faced with provincial intransigence, it shifted its attention to local governments hard hit by the provincial government's downloading of the costs of childcare (McCuaig 1998, 14).

The federal government proved an increasingly attractive target as the Liberals moved to establish their children's agenda, encouraged by research on the importance of the "early years" and the newly formed National Children's Alliance, which brought together a wide range of child and family voluntary organizations. The National Child Benefit, which included a tax credit for low-income families, allowed the provinces to claw back the equivalent from social assistance beneficiaries to invest in child-related services. The Ontario government's response was characteristic: its so-called childcare supplement for working families went to low- and modest-income parents, whether or not such families included a stay-at-home parent. The next federal initiative, the Early Childhood Development Fund, explicitly included childcare in its menu of options.[9] Yet, "although Ontario received $844 million or 38 percent of the total allocation from the 2000 Early Childhood Development Agreement, it did not create one new childcare space" (Jeffrey 2006, 140).

This is not to suggest that the Conservative government remained untouched by the growing consensus on the social investment paradigm. Courchene (2002, Table 1), an advisor to the Conservative government, warned: "With human capital at the cutting edge of competitiveness and with skills and education the key to a high wage economy, an integrated approach to this subsystem must become a defining characteristic of Ontario as a region-state. Ontario is not yet on track here." A government-commissioned report on the "early years" strongly recommended provincial leadership in the development of a coherent early child development system and envisioned an important role for schools as accessible "hubs" for such a system. The premier also established an expert panel on the role of government. The panel's final report, *Investing in People: Creating a Human Capital Society for Ontario* (Ontario 2004b), reiterated earlier recommendations for a "seamless" preschool day for four- and five-year-olds, supplemented by an affordable, high-quality ECEC system for younger children. The government, however, did little to follow up on this. For instance, its primary response to the Early Years report was to establish one "early years centre" per riding; contrary to the report's recommendations, the centres did not make schools hubs for children's services, and the centres terms of reference explicitly excluded childcare.

Ontario was increasingly out of phase with developments at the federal level, where pressure was building for a renewed commitment to ECEC. As Jeffrey (2006, 138) notes: "With the heightened federal profile on the social policy agenda well established, and a third majority government in hand after the 2000 election, the Chrétien Liberals were even prepared to tackle the issues of childcare and social housing once more." Federal Liberal backbenchers, led by a Toronto-area MP, produced a report (2002) that called for a national childcare plan, while the influential (especially in Ontario) *Toronto Star* campaigned for a new federal initiative that would force the province to invest in regulated childcare. A *Star* editorial notes: "Already the plan has run into a snag with Ontario,[10] which is balking at being told how to spend the funds. Ottawa must hang tough. Ontario's record shows it can't be trusted to spend that money on regulated day care" (20 February 2003). In January, the executive director of (Toronto-based) Campaign 2000 reinforced the message with the federal finance minister: the federal government needed to insist all provinces invest in ECEC.

Back on Track?

The Multilateral Framework Agreement on Early Learning and Childcare concluded between the federal and provincial governments in 2003 committed $1.05 billion in federal transfers to improve access to ECEC for children under six. Yet, while the money had to be used for childcare, the provinces were not required to invest matching funds, as they had under the old system, and were free to select from a broad menu of programs and funding models. Had the Conservatives been re-elected in the fall of 2003, the Ontario government might have used these options to promote the expansion of a childcare market. The election, however, was won by the Liberals, who came to office on a promise "to take us back to an era when provincial leaders ... believed it was their duty to invest heavily in children's education, health care, public transit and the environment" (*Toronto Star*, 27 September 2003). Federal and provincial agendas were in alignment again – at least for a while.

Although the new government's main focus was schools, its election platform included a "Best Start" program to prepare Ontario children for school start, and, in November 2004, it announced its plan to begin with full-day programs for children aged four to five as part of a long-term goal of extending this to children from age 2.5, with schools as the preferred site for delivery. In addition, Ontario used its share of funds from the multilateral agreement to create four thousand new spaces, with priority given to preschool children. It also promised to introduce a sliding fee scale and to enhance the professional status of early childhood educators by establishing a college of early childhood educators (Beach et al. 2009, 78-80) – promises on which it soon made good.

In 2004, prospects for moving ahead on this agenda with adequate support from the federal government looked promising. The OECD had released its report on the poor state of ECEC in Canada, and the federal Liberal government, which went to the polls in 2004 promising to invest in a pan-Canadian ECEC system, moved quickly to act on this, negotiating bilateral agreements with all ten provinces.[11] Ontario was one of the first to conclude an agreement and, in November 2005, received $271.9 million of a promised $1.9 billion over five years (Beach et al. 2009, 79). Yet the happy alignment of federal and Ontario objectives proved short-lived. The minority Liberal government fell, ceding office to an avowedly neoliberal Conservative government in January 2006, and the latter was quick to give the required one-year notice of its withdrawal from the agreements. In their stead, it introduced the so-called universal childcare benefit – an (expensive) taxable benefit of $100 a month for each child under six, whether or not the parents chose to use it for childcare.[12]

The Ontario government opted to spread its share of the remaining $650 million over four years, yielding $63.5 million per annum. This, plus Ontario's share of the multilateral framework agreement, helped finance its next steps – $105.7 million to sustain licensed childcare centres and $24.8 million to fund an average wage increase of 3 percent for staff plus incentives for staff to upgrade their credentials. It appointed an early learning advisor to report on how best to implement its long-term plan; the report's core recommendations (Ontario 2009) revived the NDP government's Early Years Project, including starting with a "seamless day" for children from ages four to five, to be followed by out-of-school-hours care for children aged six to twelve, and the development of an ECEC curriculum and financial support for children from ages 2.5 to four. The decision to start with four- and five-year-olds accorded with the stance taken by childcare advocates in their pan-Canadian campaign to move things forward at the provincial level in the face of the federal government's intransigence.

In the absence of federal support, the Liberal government might have gone the way of the earlier Liberal and NDP governments, especially as it had to deal with a deteriorating economy. Between October 2008 and June 2009, manufacturing employment was particularly hard-hit, and the provincial unemployment rate surged to over 9 percent.[13] As in the 1990s, this contributed to the province's rising deficit as many of the newly unemployed were not eligible for (federal) unemployment insurance. Despite the fiscal pressure, the provincial government launched its all-day program for four- to five-year-olds (albeit more slowly than recommended), and, faced with the closure of 7,600 childcare spaces when the last of the bilateral money had been spent, it agreed to replace it with its own money on an annual basis, despite its $24.7 billion deficit (*Toronto Star*, 24 March 2010).

Ontario may have been prepared to "go it alone" this time because of the broad consensus on investment in "the early years," a consensus that childcare advocates and their allies were well-placed to utilize. Nevertheless, the government's commitment was reinforced by the emergence of an antipoverty movement that brought together "social democratic and liberal social policy thinkers with reformist elements of the business community" (Graefe and Hudson 2009, 11). Throughout the decade, various organizations had been documenting the growth of poverty in a province in which the destruction of Fordist jobs had contributed to the rise of low-wage work.[14] In 2006, the Toronto City Summit Alliance enlisted a group of social policy experts to produce a report on the poverty of working-age adults and to identify federal and provincial initiatives to combat this. Graefe and Hudson (2009, 14) note: "Throughout the summer of 2007, loosely coordinated by Campaign 2000, a push for poverty reduction was being developed both inside and outside the [provincial] government ... helped along considerably by McGuinty's formal commitment to develop a set of strategies to fight poverty during the provincial election."

The province's commitment to poverty reduction added impetus to its ECEC agenda because its strategy, like that of earlier federal Liberal programs, focused on child poverty. Yet this focus did not undermine the province's commitment to a universal program, partly because of the steadfast support that Ontario's anti-poverty advocates of all stripes offer for universal ECEC. Influential experts in the neuroscience of the brain, like Fraser Mustard, also support the universality principle.[15]

Although the province's policy will be rolled out gradually, with $200 million allocated for the start-up of a "seamless day" for four and five-year-olds in selected sites, a further $700 million has been promised for 2011. The province has also sought to mitigate any adverse impact on the childcare sector, providing capital funding and an increase in subsidies. More broadly, as the *Globe*'s Queen's Park correspondent notes, the premier has come to regard the seamless day for four- to five-year-olds as "a landmark policy that future governments will find hard to undo" (*Globe and Mail*, 28 October 2009). With at least two years until the next provincial election, there may be enough time to ensure that this part of the ECEC system will be available to the majority of Ontario families. Should the McGuinty government, however, give in to pressure to eliminate the program as part of the broader program of expenditure cuts considered "essential" to tackling the province's deficits, it could face the kind of popular resistance the Charest government encountered when it sought to roll-back the PQ's childcare policy (Jenson 2006; Noel, Chapter 11, this volume). That said, the programs for children aged 2.5 to four and for out-of-school-hours care for school-aged children that are part of the government's long-term plans remain vulnerable.

Conclusion

New social risks associated with women's increased labour market participation and changes in the structure of families in Canada have given rise to pressures for social policy redesign, especially in the field of childcare. Canadian governments have responded, albeit intermittently, and shifts in childcare policy have by and large reflected the political orientation of the governing party, with the Liberals more open to a larger public role and the Conservatives stressing family "choice." Whichever party has been in power, federal childcare policies have always remained within the liberal mould that characterized the postwar system. To this extent, the story of childcare in Canada fits with Bonoli's account of the politics of new social risks. Yet the federal structure of the Canadian state complicates the picture, forcing analysts to go beyond the national level to probe developments at the provincial scale.

This chapter focuses on childcare politics in Ontario, Canada's most populous and richest province. The development of a universal ECEC system has been on the agenda in Ontario for three decades or more. Yet, unlike Quebec, which introduced its five-dollars-a-day policy in 1997, Ontario's progress has been uneven, reflecting differences in the economic situations faced by the two provincial governments. Yet, it was not simply economic circumstances that dictated the outcome: politics also played a part. Quebec's childcare policy was forged in the dense networks linking Quebec civil servants and politicians with associations in civil society. In Ontario, centre-left governments were hampered by the institutional legacy of years of Conservative rule.

There is another critical difference between Quebec and Ontario: whereas Quebec political actors expect the provincial government to forge its own policies, Ontarians see the provincial government as just one part of a broader federal system and often look to the latter to achieve their principal aims. This was reflected in the Liberal and NDP governments' childcare plans, the expansion of which remained contingent upon federal support. Nor is it only provincial governments who look to the federal government for leadership; rather, this stance has been shared by Ontario-based childcare advocates who brought pressure to bear on the federal government directly via OCBCC and through their support for CCAAC. Similarly, a multi-level orientation characterized their allies in the women's movement (NAC in the 1980s) and the anti-poverty movement (Campaign 2000). For Ontarians the accumulation of power resources in support of childcare in the province thus continues to be seen as insufficient: they must be developed at the federal scale if an adequate childcare policy framework is to be secured.

NOTES

This chapter could not have been written without the financial support provided by the Swedish research council through the Kerstin Hesselgren professorship and the incredible research skills of Emre Uckardesler.

1 Welfare regime theory is most closely identified with the typology developed by Esping-Anderson (1990, 1999): liberal, market-centred regimes; social democratic regimes in which the state mitigates the impact of the market and reduces the burden on families through generous and comprehensive social policies based on the principles of universality; and the conservative corporatist regimes, which, though they may offer generous public benefits, do so in a way that reinforces social stratification.
2 The Quiet Revolution refers to the dramatic changes launched by the victory of the Lesage Liberal government, which were designed to rapidly "modernize" Quebec society.
3 For several decades, NAC acted as an umbrella organization for the pan-Canadian women's movement. The Quebec women's movement, as represented by the Fédération des Femmes du Québec (FFQ), was initially part of NAC but withdrew, partly because of differences in their views of federalism, which, in turn, reflected the impact of competing (Quebec and Canadian) nationalisms. See Vickers (2008).
4 While even under the centre-right Conservative government, Ontario seemed prepared to support a new federal program; Quebec resisted, insisting that childcare fell within an area of exclusive provincial jurisdiction (Findlay 2008, 231-32).
5 Although officially non-partisan, OCBCC's ties to the labour movement made it closer to the NDP than to the Liberals.
6 Interestingly, Charles Pascal was deputy minister of education during this period.
7 Apparently, the key issue blocking such an agreement was the federal government's insistence that federal dollars be used to create new spaces, while Ontario sought help to sustain the thousands of spaces it had created since 1990. (Interview: source withheld upon request.)
8 The next year the government sought to eliminate the proxy mechanism, but court action by OCBCC and others forced its reinstatement several years later.
9 The federal government had attempted to require the provinces to invest something in each of the areas but backed off in the face of provincial intransigence led by Alberta and Ontario.

10 For example, the multilateral framework agreement on early learning and childcare, then being negotiated between the federal government and the provinces – minus Quebec, which stayed out of this and the earlier agreements to pursue its own policies.
11 It is important to underline that Quebec had not been party to the Early Childhood Development and Multilateral Framework agreements.
12 For an insightful account of the Harper government's policy, see Prince and Teghtsoonian (2007).
13 http://www.statcan.gc.ca/subjects-sujet/labour-letravail/lfs-epa-eng.htm.
14 The incidence of low-wage work in Ontario (7.7 percent) is above the national average of 5.6 percent (Statistics Canada 2010, 15).
15 Fraser Mustard, unlike his American counterparts, has long stressed the importance of universality.

REFERENCES

Albo, Greg, and Robert MacDermid. 2000. "Divided Province, Growing Protests: Ontario Moves Right." In Keith Brownsey and Michael Howlett, eds., *The Provincial State in Canada: Politics in the Provinces and Territories*, 163-202. Peterborough, ON: Broadview Press

Beach, Jane, Martha Friendly, Carolyn Ferns, Nina Prabhu, and Barry Forer. 2009. *Early Childhood Education and Care in Canada, 2008*. Toronto: Childcare Resource and Research Unit.

Bonoli, Guiliano. 2006. "New Social Risks and the Politics of Post-Industrial Social Policies." In K. Armingeon and G. Bonoli, eds., *The Politics of Post-Industrial Welfare States: Adapting Post-War Social Policies to New Social Risks*, 3-26. New York: Routledge.

Bradford, Neil. 1998. "Prospects for Associative Governance: Lessons from Ontario, Canada." *Politics and Society* 26: 539-73.

Cameron, David. 2002. "The Landscape of Civic Engagement in Ontario." Paper written for the Panel on the Role of Government, Toronto, October.

Cameron, David, and Richard Simeon. 1997. "Ontario in Confederation: The Not So Friendly Giant." In Graham White, ed., *The Government and Politics of Ontario*, 158-88. Toronto: University of Toronto Press.

Cleveland, Gordon, and Sue Colley. 2003. "The Future of Government in Supporting Early Childhood Education and Care in Ontario." Report to the Panel on the Role of Government in Ontario, 4 June.

Collier, Cheryl. 2006. "Governments and Women's Movements: Explaining Childcare and Anti-Violence Policy in Ontario and British Columbia, 1970-2000." PhD diss., University of Toronto.

Courchene, Thomas J. 1998 (with Colin R. Telmer). "From Heartland to North American Region-State: The Social, Fiscal, and Federal Evolution of Ontario." University of Toronto School of Management.

–. 2002. "Ontario as North American Region State." Comments prepared for Borderlines: Canada in North America, Calgary, 12-13 September.

Esping-Andersen, Gøsta. 1990. *The Three Worlds of Welfare Capitalism*. Cambridge, UK: Polity Press.

—. 1999. *Social Foundations of Post-Industrial Economies.* Oxford: Oxford University Press
Findlay, Tammy. 2008. "Femocratic Administration: Gender, Democracy and the Ontario State." PhD diss., York University.
Finkel, Alvin. 2006. *Social Policy and Practice in Canada.* Waterloo: Wilfrid Laurier University Press
Friendly, Martha. 1994. *Childcare Policy in Canada: Putting the Pieces Together.* Don Mills, ON: Addison Wesley.
Friendly, Martha, Jane Beach, Carolyn Ferns, and Michelle Turiano. 2007. *Early Childhood Education and Care in Canada, 2006.* Toronto: Childcare Resource and Research Unit.
Graefe, Peter, and Carol-Anne Hudson. 2009. "Social Policy Renewal in Ontario: Narrowly Inclusive Liberalism?" Paper presented at the annual meeting of the Canadian Political Science Association, Carleton University, Ottawa.
Jeffrey, Brooke. 2006. "From Collaborative Federalism to the New Unilateralism: Implications for the Welfare State." In Hans J. Michelman and Cristine de Clercy, eds., *Continuity and Change in Canadian Politics,* 117-46. Toronto: University of Toronto Press.
Jenson, Jane. 2002. "Against the Current: Childcare and Family Policy in Quebec." In Sonya Michel and Rianne Mahon, eds., *Childcare Policy at the Crossroads: Gender and Welfare State Restructuring,* 309-32. New York: Routledge.
—. 2006. "Rolling Out or Back Tracking on Quebec's Childcare System? Ideology matters." Paper prepared for the annual meeting of the Canadian Political Science Association, York University, Toronto.
Mahon, Rianne. 2000. "The Never-Ending Story: Canadian Feminist Struggles for Universal Childcare in the 1970s." *Canadian Historical Review* 81(4): 582-615.
—. 2005. "Childcare as Citizenship Right? Toronto in the 1970s and 1980s." *Canadian Historical Review* 86(2): 285-316.
Mahon, Rianne, and Susan Phillips. 2002. "Dual-Earner Families Caught in a Liberal Welfare Regime? The Politics of Child Care Policy in Canada." In S. Michel and R. Mahon, eds., *Child Care Policy at the Crossroads: Gender and Welfare State Restructuring.* 191-218. New York: Routledge.
McCuaig, Kerry. 1998. "The Fight for a National Childcare Program." *Ginger: Bulletin of Socialist Debate* 2: 13-14.
Obinger, Hebert, Stephan Leibfried, and Francis Castles. 2005. *Federalism and the Welfare State: New World and European Experiences.* Cambridge: Cambridge University Press
Ontario. 1987. *New Directions for Childcare.* Toronto: Ministry of Community and Social Services.
—. 1995. *Report of the Royal Commission on Learning.* Toronto: Government of Ontario.
—. 2004a. *Ontario Baseline Report on Early Learning and Childcare 2004.* Toronto: Government of Ontario.
—. 2004b. *Investing in People: Creating a Human Capital Society for Ontario – Final Report of the Panel on the Role of Government.* Toronto: Queen's Park.

–. 2009. *With Our Best Future in Mind: Implementing Early Learning in Ontario.* Report to the premier by the special advisor on early learning, Charles Pascal. Toronto: Queen's Park.

Ontario Coalition for Better Childcare. 1994. *A Guide to Childcare in Ontario.* Toronto: The Coalition.

Prentice, Susan. 1988. "'Kids Are Not for Profit:' The Politics of Child Care." In Frank Cunningham, Sue Findlay, Marlene Kadar, Allan Lennon, and Ed Silva, eds., *Social Movements/Social Change: the Politics and Practice of Organizing,* 98-128. Toronto: Between the Lines.

–, ed. 2003. *Changing Child Care: Five Decades of Child Care Advocacy and Policy in Canada.* Halifax: Fernwood

Prince, Michael J., and Katherine Teghtsoonian. 2007. "The Harper Government's Universal Child Care Plan: Paradoxical or Purposeful Social Policy?" In G. Bruce Doern, ed., *How Ottawa Spends, 2007-2008: The Harper Conservatives – Climate for Change* 180-99. Montreal and Kingston: McGill-Queen's University Press.

Radwanski, George. 1987. *Ontario Study of the Relevance of Education.* Toronto: Ontario Ministry of Education.

Rae, Bob. 2001. "The Politics of Childcare in Canada: Provincial and Federal Governments." In Gordon Cleveland and Michael Krashinksy, eds., *Our Children's Future: Childcare Policy in Canada,* 62-68. Toronto: University of Toronto Press.

Vickers, Jill. 2008. "Do Women's Movements Need a 'Peak Agency' to Influence State Policy in a Federation? Or Should We Invent a New NAC?" Paper presented at the annual meetings of the Canadian Political Science Association, Vancouver.

Welch, Robert. 2004. "Childcare in Ontario: Understanding the Present for the Future." Presentation on childcare at the third annual meeting of federal, provincial, and territorial ministers responsible for the status of women, Niagara on the Lake, 9-10, Toronto Reference Library.

White, Randall. 1998. *Ontario since 1985.* Toronto: Eastend Books.

Wiseman, Nelson. 1997. "Change in Provincial Politics." In Graham White, ed., *The Government and Politics of Ontario,* 418-42. Toronto: University of Toronto Press.

Wolfe, David, and Meric Gertler. 2001. "Globalization and Economic Restructuring in Ontario: From Industrial Heartland to Learning Region?" *European Planning Studies* 9(5): 575-92.

16 Labour Market Income Transfers and Redistribution
National Themes and Provincial Variations

RODNEY HADDOW

Inequality in rich capitalist democracies is shaped by how much governments use taxes and transfers to reduce disparities (Kenworthy and Pontusson 2005, 454-56). This chapter examines the role that labour market transfer programs, traditionally an important source of redistribution, have played in reducing income inequality among economic families since the 1980s, a conventional definition of the beginning of the current globalization era. Simply stated, labour market transfers, sometimes termed "passive labour market policies," provide individuals with income support while they are absent from the labour market (Organisation for Economic Cooperation and Development 1994, 36, 52). In Canada, the main labour market transfers are Employment Insurance, administered by the federal government, and social assistance and workers' compensation for which the provinces are responsible. The federal government and most provinces also deliver child tax benefits. Because receipt of these does not depend on a family's labour market status, they are not categorized as labour market transfers here; nevertheless, they are an important part of the redistributive landscape in Canada, and I discuss their impact in detail.[1]

The following discussion situates the redistributive role of these measures in relation to Canada's overall tax and transfer system. It addresses interprovincial variations in the extent of these redistributive patterns and asks whether these can be explained by political variables.

I make three arguments, each addressing a misconception or oversight in the existing scholarly literature. First, in the wake of cuts in program coverage since the 1990s, Employment Insurance (EI) and social assistance redistribute less than they did in the late 1980s. However, contrary to claims made by observers who stress one or the other of these measures in curtailing redistribution, EI and assistance probably contributed about equally to this decline, making it difficult to assign to either Ottawa or the provinces the primary "blame" for the curtailed redistributive role of labour market transfers. Furthermore, this reduced impact has been offset by increased redistribution by other elements of the tax and transfer system. In contrast to what some authors have suggested (Teeple 2000), Canada's welfare state has not been emaciated in recent years. Redistribution by taxes and transfers has not noticeably diminished, let alone collapsed. Governments reduce inequality by about as much today as they did during the 1980s but from a significantly higher initial level of market inequality. As Myles and Banting note in the introduction to this volume, this outcome nevertheless suggests that the redistributive capacity of Canada's welfare state is diminishing; its overall design has not been adjusted adequately since the 1990s to compensate for ever-growing market inequality.

Second, the provinces play an important redistributive role in Canada, but they vary in how much they use taxes and transfers to reduce inequality. These differences are not diminishing in the face of supposedly homogenizing globalization. It is widely observed that Canada's federation assigns important powers to the provinces and that this results in policy variations. But the fact that provincial authority is associated with persistently and significantly different redistributive results – what I term distinct "redistributive regimes" – remains unaddressed. Measured by the Gini coefficient, a commonly used measure of inequality, the impact on inequality of provincial measures alone in Canada's most and least redistributive provinces differs by at least half as much as it does for non-pension transfers between Europe's most redistributive welfare states, on the one hand, and the United States, on the other.

Third, consistent with the long-established "brokerage" theory of the federal party system in Canada, changes in the federal EI program since the 1980s have been little affected by ideological differences among governing federal parties. In the provinces, however, the picture is different. The impact of what is sometimes termed "democratic class struggle" – by left parties and strong labour movements – is much greater than the literature acknowledges. Quantitative evidence indicates that union density and left-party government are strongly associated with a higher redistributive impact of transfers and income taxes in the Canadian provinces over the past fifteen years. And qualitative examination of developments in the larger provinces also suggests the impact of partisanship and union density on labour market policy reform. Variables highlighted by the "power resources" perspective are more relevant to the Canadian setting than conventional wisdom suggests. This perspective also features prominently in Richard Johnson's (Chapter 8, this volume) discussion of federal politics but heretofore has not received adequate attention in Canadian welfare state scholarship.

This chapter comprises five sections. The first describes the federal and provincial labour market transfers and reviews their evolution since the 1980s. Only the four most populous provinces are treated here: Alberta, British Columbia, Ontario, and Quebec. After reviewing recent scholarship, the second section describes the data that form the basis of the quantitative interpretations provided thereafter. The next section uses these data to evaluate whether Canada's taxes and transfers have become less redistributive since the 1980s. The fourth section turns from changes over time to variations across space. The final substantive section returns to the political context of redistributive policy, addressed qualitatively in the first section.

Canadian Labour Market Transfers and their Evolution

Ottawa launched its Unemployment Insurance program in 1940; in 1996 it was renamed Employment Insurance, and this is how I refer to it throughout this chapter. Initially this program provided narrow coverage, but a series of extensions, culminating in a major expansion in 1971, created one of the most generous of such measures in the world. As Canada was governed by the Liberal Party for all but six years between 1940 and the late 1970s, that party presided over EI's creation and expansion. Yet the Progressive Conservatives did not reverse this course when in power between 1957 and 1963, instead using this interlude to introduce enhancements.

If the growth of EI was little affected by ideological division between Canada's two main federal parties, neither was its subsequent curtailment. It was restricted several times during the 1970s by Liberal governments and then by the Progressive Conservatives between 1984 and 1993. Individually modest, their cumulative effect was large. The Liberals returned to power in 1993; their 1996 legislation, the most significant since 1971, restricted eligibility and reduced benefits. Between 1971 and 1996, the replacement rate for EI (the percentage of previous earnings that an unemployed worker could expect in benefits) fell from 66 percent to between 50 and 55 percent. (A subsequent reversal eliminated the 50 percent level, which had been designed to penalize frequent users.) In 1990, about 90 percent of the total number of unemployed received benefits during the year; in 1999, this figure had fallen to about 50 percent. By the latter year, Canada's EI was less generous, at least in the more affluent provinces where the program's more ample benefits for high unemployment areas were less available, than were comparable unemployment insurance schemes in many American states (Banting 2006, 424-26).

Though criticized by the centre-left NDP (reduced to a marginal position in the federal House of Commons during the 1990s) and by organized labour, the EI cuts occasioned little debate between the major parties and did not preclude the Liberals from being comfortably re-elected in 1997 and 2000. This substantial lack of left/right ideological contention throughout most of EI's history is consistent with the "brokerage" theory of Canada's national party system, first advanced by historian Frank Underhill. By seeking to integrate sufficiently large coalitions of diverse interests to win elections, rather than to articulate distinctive principles, the major parties avoid ideological confrontation (Underhill 1960 [1935], chap. 1).

By contrast, partisan influences have played an important role in provincial social assistance and workers' compensation reform since the 1980s.[2] Social assistance long predates EI in Canada; referred to as "relief," or "welfare," it dates back centuries and is the original form of social security in most developed societies. After the Second World War, Ottawa began to cover about half of the costs of provincial social assistance programs. When the legislation that authorized these transfers, the Canada Assistance Plan of 1966, was abolished by Ottawa in 1995, the provinces were left with less money to fund assistance and with few impediments to cutting benefits to make up for the lost revenue.

Of the four provinces considered here, only Alberta introduced major social assistance cuts before the termination of CAP. This province has been governed by its centre-right Progressive Conservative Party since 1971, with very weak electoral challenges coming from its left. Alberta curtailed access to benefits and reduced levels in 1990 to help eliminate a severe budgetary deficit. Even considering the many cuts made elsewhere over the next decade, Alberta's stand out as severe. By 2003, the percentage of the provincial population receiving assistance was less than half that in Ontario,

Quebec, or BC, and about one-third of the ten-province average. In the context of the province's right-dominated party system, these cuts encountered much less resistance than would have been likely elsewhere and have not been reversed.

In Ontario and BC, major cuts did not begin until the mid-1990s. In each case, restraint began under a centre-left government and was extended by a centre-right one. Even though both left and right cut assistance, partisan differences are evident.

In Ontario, a centrist Liberal government introduced significant benefit increases during the late 1980s. When the centre-left NDP came to power in 1990, it took further steps in this direction. A large budgetary deficit forced the NDP to reverse course, however, and, by 1992, it was imposing restrictions and encouraging recipients to seek training. But substantial cuts and a major reduction in program participation did not happen until the centre-right Progressive Conservatives came to power in 1995. The PCs cut benefits by 20 percent; they also introduced "workfare" (as had Alberta), potentially requiring beneficiaries to work in exchange for their benefits. While the NDP's post-1993 reforms imposed restraint, these new changes were more severe and were implemented in a highly partisan political atmosphere.

BC's NDP government increased benefits in the early 1990s. Even though it introduced restrictions shortly before the vote, the NDP was re-elected in 1996 in a campaign in which assistance was a contentious issue. These restrictions went beyond those enacted by Ontario's NDP, curtailing benefits and encouraging re-employment. Enrolment subsequently fell, as did costs. Spending nevertheless fell proportionately much less than it did in the other three provinces examined here. More severe restraint awaited the arrival in power of a centre-right BC Liberal government in 2001. It introduced a controversial time limit for receipt of assistance, albeit with exemptions. The per capita caseload, still 12 percent above its 1990 level in 2001, quickly fell to 16 percent below. Now in opposition, the NDP strongly opposed the changes.

Social policy making in Quebec resembles the collaborative arrangements found in some European countries that reduce left/right polarization. Contention between the centre-left Parti québécois and the centrist Liberal Party, sharp on sovereignty, is muted regarding the welfare state, though the PQ generally advocates more generous measures. In 1989, a Liberal government passed new assistance legislation designed to encourage recipients to return to work; the caseload nevertheless rose during the subsequent recession and remained high when the PQ came to power in 1994. In this atmosphere, the new government abandoned an initial desire to expand benefits and, in 1997, introduced more reforms to stabilize the caseload and to foster re-employment. In 2003, the re-elected Liberals contemplated substantial cuts. But these plans were quickly abandoned; by 2004, they were introducing yet another program to encourage recipients to prepare for work. Unlike their counterparts in the other large provinces, the main parties in Quebec's more collaborative setting seem to converge when in office.

Child tax credits are closely related to social assistance, although as noted in the introduction, they do not fit into the conventional definition of labour market transfers. As with EI, there is little evidence that partisanship has played an important role in their development at the federal level. In 1993, the federal Progressive Conservative government replaced a universal family allowance with an income-tested child tax benefit, concentrating its benefits on low-income families. In 1998, a federal Liberal government provided additional funds to this program, now termed the National Child Benefit. Provinces could "claw back" the additional money from assistance recipients, leaving the latter with no more (and no less) income; but, if they did, provinces were expected to spend the savings on alternative measures for needy families. Initially, most did claw back the benefit, but, over the next decade, they reversed this decision. Even so, assistance benefit levels implicitly take the National Child Benefit (NCB) into account. When we look at the inequality-reduction figures for social assistance given below, therefore, we must remember that part of the decline in this statistic since the 1990s reflects the impact of these child benefits, not an overall reduction in the income of assistance families. Since the early 1990s, moreover, some provinces have introduced their own child tax benefits, but only in Quebec have the resulting payments become sizable.

Provincial workers' compensation programs emerged in the early twentieth century.[3] Designed to recompense workers for work-related injuries and funded by employer premiums, their administration always occasions friction between the unions who wish to ensure adequate benefits and the businesses that have to pay for them. As Tables 16.A and 16.B in the appendix to this chapter reveal, workers' compensation is always much less redistributive than are other measures considered here; hence, I give it less attention. Conflict is common in this field, but labour federations and business associations are at the forefront of contestation, not political parties. In Alberta, where union density is the lowest in Canada, the Progressive

Conservative government's decision to restrain costs during the 1990s encountered little effective organized resistance but was fought vociferously and generally in vain by loosely organized groups. In Ontario and BC, the transition from a centre-left to a centre-right government, in 1995 and 2001, respectively, coincided with substantial policy changes. Relatively generous and labour-friendly benefit levels and administrative practices were replaced by more restrictive alternatives that closely reflected business views. Quebec labour and business also diverge on this issue, but successive Liberal and PQ governments have, after extensive consultation, managed to introduce piecemeal reforms deemed acceptable by the largest and most mainstream union and business groups, though not by smaller and more militant unions or small business groups. Here again, conflict is attenuated by Quebec's distinctively concerted institutions.

Literature Review and Data Selection

The research discussed in this section uses two definitions of income: *market income* is a family's income before governments deduct taxes from it and supplement it with transfer payments (it includes employment earnings, returns on investments, income from private pensions, and so forth); *final income* is what families have after their market income is altered by these taxes and transfers. The difference between the two tells us how much redistribution has been accomplished by government taxes and transfers.

Research published during the 1990s told us that, while market inequality rose significantly during the 1980s, final (or "after tax") income inequality did not; during this period, Canada's tax and transfer system effectively compensated for the rise in market inequality (Morissette, Myles, and Picot 1995, 24). In the 1990s, however, both market and after-tax inequality rose, indicating that taxes and transfers did not become more redistributive in that decade (Frenette, Green, and Picot 2006, 65-66, 93-95; Heisz 2007, 4-9). In perhaps the most innovative recent contribution to Canadian inequality research, Frenette, Green, and Milligan (2009), using census and tax data, employ simulations to estimate how changes in the tax and transfer system between 1980 and 2000 affected its redistributive potential independently of the changing economic conjuncture. They conclude that the design of both income taxes and transfers became significantly more redistributive during the 1980s. During the 1990s, by contrast, the overall redistributive potential of these measures was not changed much by governments (15). Some transfer measures were made more redistributive during the latter decade, especially child tax benefits, but this was offset by curtailments in the redistributive potential of provincial income taxes and, above all, of social assistance. Changes in federal measures including EI, in spite of its substantial redesign, had few observable implications for inequality (23-24).

As noted at the outset, I wish to draw attention to the extent to which inequality and redistribution vary among the provinces, a theme given little consideration in Canadian inequality research, including the research discussed above. Therefore, to update the inequality research, this chapter presents observational data on a province-by-province basis to detect interprovincial variations. Data are derived from the two main Statistics Canada surveys of income, the Survey of Consumer Finances (SCF) from 1980 to 1992, and the Survey of Labour and Income Dynamics (SLID) from 1993, when it first became available, until 2007, the most recent year for which figures are available.[4] We can only measure variations in redistribution associated exclusively with provincial taxes and transfers after 1993.

The inequality measure used is the Gini coefficient – a comprehensive measure because it calculates inequality using the entire distribution of incomes. If the Gini coefficient rises over time, inequality is considered to have risen. Incomes are compared among economic families and are measured on an adult-equivalent basis to account for the economies of scale achieved in larger families.[5]

Because the main focus is on Canadians with a high likelihood of labour market attachment, the sample is restricted to families whose "head" or "major earner" is under the age of sixty-five, though such families may include members who are over that age. To capture the effects of labour market transfers, I pay particular attention to redistribution by EI, social assistance, and, where possible, workers' compensation.

Table 16.A in the appendix reports inequality data for 1980 and 1989 from the SCF survey. Table 16.B, also in the appendix, does the same for 1993, 2000, and 2007 using SLID figures. Four of these years – 1980, 1989, 2000, and 2007 – coincide with economic peaks, when unemployment reached a low point before rising again. In discussing changing redistributive impact between the 1980s and the 2000s, this section uses only data from these four years. The 1993 data, which coincide with an economic trough, are used in the next section. In Tables 16.A and 16.B, the Gini coefficient for market income appears at the left beside the respective province's name. Each column to the right reports the number of digits by which the identified measure (social assistance, EI, child benefits, income tax) reduced Gini inequality below the market income figure. For instance, in 1989, the market income Gini for Quebec was 361; when EI benefits are added to market income (and all other transfers and taxes remain excluded), the Gini coefficient falls by eighteen points (to 343). The column on the far right in each table reports the Gini for final or after tax income; in other words, after the impact of all taxes and transfers is accounted for, including federal measures such as public pensions that are not reported separately in the intervening columns. Column 9 in each table represents the combined redistributive impact of all federal and provincial measures. Column 5 in Table 16.B does the same for the combined impact of provincial taxes and transfers alone. To aid comparisons, all columns reporting the redistributive impact of the same measure have the same number. Where the SCF combines two measures reported separately by SLID, Table 16.A indicates this by listing both column numbers together.

Has Redistribution Atrophied in Canada? What Has Been the Trend for Labour Market Transfers?

Consistent with the findings reported above, Tables 16.A and 16.B indicate that total redistribution by taxes and transfers (column 9) rose significantly during the 1980s, preventing rising market inequality from translating into higher after-tax inequality during that decade. The ten-province average of total redistribution was 71 points in 1980 and 92 in 1989; thus, while the average market Gini coefficient across the ten provinces rose from 345 to 365 between 1980 and 1989, the average after-tax Gini remained essentially unchanged: 274 in 1980 and 273 in 1989.

Between 1989 and either 2000 or 2007, the redistributive impact of all taxes and transfers changed little, averaging 97 points in 2000 and 95 in 2007. Since market inequality continued to rise between 1989 and 2000 (though not thereafter), this translated into higher after-tax inequality in Canada during the 2000s than in the 1980s: the average market Gini climbed to 405 in 2000 and 401 in 2007, and the after-tax coefficient rose from 273 in 1989 to 308 in 2000 and 306 in 2007.

On the one hand, globalization has not emasculated the state's redistributive capacity in Canada, if this is understood to mean a reduction in the ability of its taxes and transfers to curtail market inequality. On the other hand, this capacity may have reached its limits by the early 1990s: taxes and transfers have not "coped" with the continued rise of market inequality for working-age families since then by redistributing ever more vigorously in compensation.

Yet this picture of overall redistributive stasis since 1989 masks important changes in the impact of different components of the tax and transfer system. Labour market transfers (EI, social assistance, and workers' compensation) have become less redistributive since the 1980s. About half of this erosion, as measured by the Gini coefficient, was compensated for by enhanced redistribution from federal and provincial income taxes (Tables 16.A and 16.B, columns 4 and 8) and, to a lesser extent, child tax benefits (columns 3 and 7). The rest was made up by increased redistribution through measures not reported separately in the tables, such as public pensions.

The impact of child tax benefits is modest in this context, but its role in reducing inequality is revealed to be more extensive if one uses a measure, such as the P10/P50 ratio, that emphasizes the bottom of the income distribution. Because they involved transforming universal benefits into selective ones, the redistributive impact of the 1990s child benefits reforms was much greater for families with very low incomes than it was for those in the middle of the income distribution, who have a particularly strong impact on the Gini coefficient.[6]

In discussing the data reported in Tables 16.A and 16.B for social assistance and EI, a qualification is required. Both the SCF and SLID surveys under-report the *level of income* that respondents received from EI and social assistance, the latter to a greater extent than the former. Consequently, one cannot use these reported levels to assess the absolute redistributive impact of these measures relative to others identified in the tables. There is less reason to be concerned about the comparative accuracy of the SCF and SLID surveys in reporting these levels *over time*, that is, between the 1980s and 2000s. Finally, there is no evident problem with comparing these figures *across provinces* in the same year, the purpose for which they are used in the next two sections.[7]

Table 16.A tells us that the combined redistributive impact of social assistance (Column 1) and EI (Column 6) averaged twenty-six Gini points across the provinces in 1980 and thirty-seven points in 1989; in other words, the two main labour market transfers made important contributions to the enhancement of the entire tax and transfer system's redistributive impact during the 1980s. But their combined impact fell to about twenty-nine points in 2000 and to twenty-five points in 2007. Average redistribution by social assistance was lower in 2007 than any of the earlier years. EI's decline is most evident earlier; its redistributive impact fell by one-third between the 1989 and 2000 economic peaks. Even without an adjustment to account for the possibility that the SCF understates these measures' impact compared to SLID, their combined impact fell by about one-third between 1989 and 2007; given the possibility of such an adjustment, we might suppose that it declined by more.

A majority of the observed decline between 1989 and 2007 can be attributed to EI (about 6.5 points) rather than social assistance (approximately five points). Again, as the latter figure may understate the decline more than the former due to greater under-reporting of assistance income, it is prudent just to surmise that both EI and assistance made a major contribution to the reduction in their combined impact on inequality. This conclusion is not what one might expect in light of Frenette, Green, and Picot's (2009) simulation-based conclusion that the potential for redistribution, at least until 2000, fell significantly for social assistance alone; it is more consistent with a common-sense intuition that the major EI cuts in the early- to mid-1990s are likely to have had some measurable implications for inequality.

Heightened redistribution by non-labour market measures compensated for curtailed social assistance and EI when we consider overall inequality. We have already seen that, among non-labour market measures, enhanced child benefits were particularly important for the bottom end of the income distribution. Not surprisingly, then, the shift away from labour market transfers had different consequences for poverty rates among distinct types of Canadian families, benefitting those with children, above all single mothers, while disadvantaging those without.

Table 16.1 reports poverty rates in the four most populous provinces for four time periods since 1980.[8] The first row of data for each province indicates that the poverty rate for all economic families rose moderately in most, though not Quebec, after 1980-82. For single mothers (reported in the third row for each province), however, poverty rates fell slightly in Ontario and Alberta and by more than one-third in Quebec and BC. For detached individuals, by contrast, the record was worse than the average: poverty rose by at least one-third in three provinces and by a smaller margin in Quebec.

To further clarify the sources of the decline of poverty for single mothers, Table 16.2 disaggregates their income. In all provinces, child benefits increased substantially as a share of single mothers' income; they rose most in BC and Quebec, where the poverty decline was dramatic. Child benefits largely displaced social assistance income for single mothers, causing the latter to decline by more than two-thirds, except in Ontario. In general, then, the relative displacement of responsibility for redistribution in Canada's tax and transfer system away from labour market transfers, while not associated with a significant change in overall rates of inequality reduction

TABLE 16.1

Incidence of family poverty by family type, four largest provinces and four time periods

Province		Incidence (%)			
		1980-82	1988-90	1999-2001	2005-07
Quebec	All economic families	14	15	16	14
	Detached individuals	33	37	38	36
	Single mothers	54	54	45	34
	Two-parent families	11	10	11	7
Ontario	All economic families	14	16	18	18
	Detached individuals	29	33	40	41
	Single mothers	55	60	52	49
	Two-parent families	11	13	15	15
Alberta	All economic families	16	18	17	18
	Detached individuals	27	34	41	36
	Single mothers	52	63	48	50
	Two-parent families	13	14	14	14
British Columbia	All economic families	16	17	20	18
	Detached individuals	29	32	41	39
	Single mothers	65	66	55	44
	Two-parent families	12	12	14	14

Source: Calculations by the author based on data from the Survey of Consumer Finances (SCF) and the Survey of Labour and Income Dynamics (SLID).

TABLE 16.2

Source of income for single mothers, four largest provinces

	Income percentage							
	Quebec		Ontario		Alberta		BC	
Income source	1979-81	2005-07	1979-81	2005-07	1979-81	2005-07	1979-81	2005-07
Market	73	70	81	79	83	84	80	78
Social assistance	14	4	8	6	8	2	11	2
EI	3	2	2	2	1	2	2	3
Federal child benefits	6	10	5	9	5	8	5	12
Provincial child benefits	–	8	–	0	–	1	–	1
Other	4	6	4	4	3	3	2	4
Total	100	100	100	100	100	100	100	100

Source: Calculations by the author based on data from the SCF and SLID.

and poverty, was to the advantage of single mothers, while exposing other Canadians, especially unattached individuals, to greater poverty.

Are There Different "Redistributive Regimes" in Canada?

Poverty rates have not only followed divergent paths for different family types since the 1980s; as we have just seen, they have also tracked distinctive trajectories across the provinces. These differences and those revealed by provincial-level inequality data rival the often-noted contrast between the egalitarian welfare states of "social Europe" and the market-oriented alternative of "liberal America" (Pontusson 2005, chap. 2). I therefore refer to the provinces as having divergent "redistributive regimes."

Quebec is alone among the larger provinces in not witnessing a rise in the overall poverty rate for working-age economic families since 1980 (Table 16.1). Its poverty rate for two-parent families is half that of Ontario, Alberta, and BC, even though rates were comparable during the early 1980s. Even for unattached individuals, where Quebec's much-noted family policies are less relevant, the trajectory has been distinctive, albeit less so: it has moved from having the highest poverty rate for this cohort to the lowest. For single mothers, its poverty rate has fallen, in relative terms, by 37 percent. The figure for BC (about 32 percent) rivals this impressive result, but provincial spending has been much more relevant to Quebec's result than to BC's. Results for Ontario and Alberta have been much more modest, with falls, respectively, of 11 and 4 percent.

These variable provincial poverty rates are not the exclusive result of differences in provincial taxes and transfers; rather, they are conditioned by market poverty levels and by federal programs that redistribute more in some provinces than in others. For example, Quebec benefits from much greater redistribution by EI than Ontario, Alberta, and BC. Data from the SLID survey offer us one way to distinguish variations in redistributive consequences that result entirely from provincial policy "effort" and are discussed here. A more formal approach, based on regression analysis, is provided below.

A calculation for the redistributive impact of all provincial taxes and transfers, excluding federal ones, appears in Table 16.B, Column 5 (in the appendix). This impact varies substantially across the provinces for the three years reported, and, in many cases, the extent of interprovincial variation does not change much over the fifteen-year period covered by the data. In other words, the disparities are persistent, not eroding over time in the face of common international competitive pressures, as globalization theorists suggest. Nor can these variations, unlike those for EI's impact, be clearly associated with levels of affluence or employment in any province. For instance, Newfoundland and Prince Edward Island were among Canada's poorest in most years; Newfoundland chronically redistributes about twice as much as does PEI.

Among the three most affluent provinces, Ontario typically redistributes much more than either Alberta or BC. For the most part, Ontario's rate roughly matches or exceeds the national average; Alberta is always among the least redistributive provinces, as was BC in 1993 and 2007. Quebec is not alone, then, in having a distinctive redistributive pattern, but it stands out. It redistributed more than any other province, by at least ten points in absolute terms in 1993 and 2007, and was a close second to Newfoundland in 2000. Its taxes and transfers reduced Gini-measured inequality by at least twenty points more than the average province in 1993 and 2007, and this premium shows no signs of diminishing over time. This represents strong evidence of the "new politics of redistribution" that Alain Noël (this volume) identifies in Quebec.

Is provincial redistribution falling over time, and are provinces converging in their rate of redistribution (both outcomes predicted by some globalization theorists)? In fact, average redistribution fell between the 1993 economic trough and the 2000 peak, but this result was likely affected by the business cycle and is therefore inconclusive.

Of more relevance, average provincial redistribution fell from 31.3 Gini points to 25.5 between the 2000 and 2007 business peaks. While consistent with a "race-to-the-bottom" scenario, this result must be treated with caution: it is entirely accounted for by reduced redistribution by social assistance during this period, a development that, as we know, is linked to an expansion of child tax credits whose impact is not well registered by the Gini coefficient. Provincial workers' compensation and income taxes also became more redistributive, arguing against broad-based provincial redistributive retrenchment. Even so, this trend warrants observation in future years.

Regarding the second part of the question – interprovincial convergence – the evidence is emphatically negative. The average province diverged from the mean level of total provincial redistribution by 7.5 Gini points in 1993, 7.8 points in 2000, and 8.0 points in 2007. In short, interprovincial distinctions show no sign of erosion, at least since the early 1990s.

How important are these interprovincial variations when compared to those long identified by comparative welfare state research on advanced capitalist nations? By this standard, the differences are important. Mahler and Jesuit's (2006, 490) recent study of redistribution in thirteen Western European and North American welfare states identifies four countries – Sweden, Denmark, Belgium, and the Netherlands – whose non-pension tax and transfer programs' redistribution exceeded 110 Gini points; their average Gini impact of 113 points is forty-four points higher than the equivalent figure (sixty-nine points) for the US, the most commonly cited welfare state laggard.

In comparison, Quebec's redistribution exceeded that of Alberta, the least redistributive province, by about thirty-five points in 2000 and 2007 – about three-quarters of the gap between Europe's most generous welfare states and the US. A comparison of the interprovincial redistributive variances reported above to an equivalent figure calculated from Mahler and Jesuit's data highlights the significance of the Canadian differences. If the anomalous case of Switzerland is excluded from the calculation, the remaining twelve nations vary from the mean redistributive level by an average of 14.5 Gini points for non-pension measures. In Canada, the interprovincial variance figure of eight for 2007 is more than half of this level.

Canadian provinces produced these divergent results while gaining access to only a part of the fiscal and legal resources available to a sovereign state (the rest are in Ottawa's hands); by contrast, the cross-national differences detected by Mahler and Jesuit reflect the impact of taxes and transfers administered by all levels of government in each country.

What caused the emergence and persistence of distinctive redistributive regimes in the provinces? While a full response cannot be provided here, I argue elsewhere that variations in labour market policy arrangements across the most populous Canadian provinces reflect historically enduring differences in the political economies, political cultures, and party systems of these jurisdictions (Haddow and Klassen 2006, chap. 2). These features of a province's policy-making setting are difficult to measure quantitatively; proof of their importance is likely to depend on the careful use of comparative qualitative case studies.

Quantitative analysis can, however, measure whether interjurisdictional differences are statistically significant and whether they remain so once we control for the influence of various quantifiable influences commonly considered important policy determinants, including trade openness (a measure of globalization), economic growth, the budget balance, and a number of other fiscal, social, and political factors. This kind of analysis, widespread in the comparative welfare state literature, has not been applied to interprovincial variations in redistributive outcomes in Canada. Table 16.3 begins to fill this gap.[9] It reports the results of "fixed effect" regressions in which the dependent variables are the Gini coefficient-reduction figures for provincial taxes and transfers between 1993 and 2007 as summarized in columns 1 to 5 of Table 16.B.[10] For social assistance alone (Column 1), the provincial coefficients in the bottom half of the table indicate no statistically significant differences between Quebec (the absent, or "omitted," case in these calculations) and any other province, after controlling for other variables listed at the bottom of the table. For this fifteen-year period as a whole, there were no distinctive "redistributive regimes" for social assistance. An alternative regression (not shown here), using inequality-reduction data for 1981 to 1992 from the SCF survey, finds that Quebec redistributed more with social assistance than all other provinces – and to a degree that was statistically significant at 1 percent for all but one province.

The remaining columns of Table 16.3 indicate that Quebec's redistributive "premium" remains very much alive, having persisted in – or migrated to – the mostly non-labour market components of its tax and transfer system. Although workers' compensation is a modest source of redistribution, Quebec's coefficient is higher than that for all other provinces for this measure (Column 2), and the difference is significant at the 5 percent level or higher for seven provinces. Not surprisingly, Quebec's redistributive impact via child tax benefits (Column 3), net of the control variables, is also higher than that for all other provinces; and only in BC, Quebec's main rival in reducing poverty among single mothers, is the level of statistical significance for this difference lower than 5 percent. Since these credits only emerged in the 1990s, they may have replaced social assistance as the main transfer-based source of Quebec's premium since the early 1990s.

Yet this premium is most evident in redistribution by the income tax (Column 4). All but one of the negative coefficients for the other provinces exceeds ten, and all are significant at the 1 percent level. For the comprehensive measure of provincial redistribution (Column 5), the negative coefficients for all provinces again are very high, only falling below the 1 percent significance level (to 5 percent) for Ontario and Newfoundland.

Quebec redistributes to a fundamentally different degree than do other Canadian provinces, though social assistance is no longer a source for this difference. The regressions, as modelled here, do not report the significance of differences among the other provinces. But an alternative model for total provincial redistributive effect (not shown here), selecting Ontario as the omitted case, found that five provinces' redistributive levels were

TABLE 16.3

Correlates of Gini coefficient (inequality) reduction by provincial transfers and income taxes, 1993-2007

	Fixed effects models, partial results				
	(1) Social assistance	(2) Workers' compensation	(3) Child benefits	(4) Income taxes	(5) All (including 1-4)
Ontario	6.242	−1.652	−4.467**	−13.06***	−12.44**
	(1.59)	(−1.14)	(−2.48)	(−6.79)	(−2.44)
Newfoundland	−0.815	−2.499	−6.112***	−4.686***	−12.60**
	(−0.17)	(−1.60)	(−4.05)	(−2.73)	(−2.19)
PEI	−5.969	−5.061***	−6.388***	−11.95***	−30.29***
	(−1.25)	(−3.07)	(−3.90)	(−6.51)	(−5.55)
Nova Scotia	3.547	−3.651***	−5.129***	−10.90***	−17.27***
	(1.03)	(−2.65)	(−3.12)	(−6.91)	(−3.91)
New Brunswick	3.168	−4.423**	−5.600***	−12.07***	−22.35***
	(0.67)	(−2.54)	(−3.26)	(−6.92)	(−4.00)
Manitoba	−0.353	−3.569***	−5.917***	−12.74***	−22.55***
	(−0.10)	(−3.15)	(−3.84)	(−7.29)	(−4.90)
Saskatchewan	3.710	−3.336**	−5.987***	−14.86***	−22.12***
	(0.80)	(−2.14)	(−3.12)	(−6.91)	(−3.67)
Alberta	3.807	−3.863**	−4.824**	−17.75***	−23.23***
	(0.76)	(−2.14)	(−2.34)	(−7.52)	(−3.74)
British Columbia	0.972	−2.813**	−3.423*	−17.27***	−20.81***
	(0.24)	(−2.27)	(−1.80)	(−8.47)	(−3.82)
N	150	150	150	150	150
r^2	0.751	0.553	0.441	0.809	0.788

z statistics in parentheses.
*$p < .10$, **$p < .05$, ***$p < .01$
Prais-Winsten (OLS) regression, with panels correlated standard errors (PCSEs).
Note: The following variables were also included in the model presented here, but their coefficients are excluded to conserve space: trade openness, growth, budget balance, federal transfers, industrialism, per capita immigration, unemployment, union density, left party, centre party, and year. Results for all of these variables are reported for the pooled regression in Table 16.4. Results for these variables for this fixed model are available from the author upon request.
Source: Calculations by the author based on data from SLID.

significantly below Ontario's (Quebec's was, of course, significantly above). This shows that there are also important differences in redistribution among the English-speaking provinces. The strongest case for this variability, nevertheless, is the descriptive analysis provided above and the evidence reported therein of the extent to which interprovincial variations in general compare well with the international variations identified by other researchers. The case is, I believe, a strong one.

Does Politics Matter?

There is a quantitative literature on the impact of party ideology on provincial policy outcomes in Canada based on studies of spending and taxation, but the brokerage party theory discussed above does not have the central position in this provincial literature that it has in studies of the federal party system.[11] While the literature reports some ideologically based differences among provincial parties in power, the association is usually found to be modest and intermittent; these results do not suggest a consistent and strong impact for party ideology on welfare state outcomes. For example, Petry et al. (1999, 285, 290) found that left/right differences mattered for spending in five provinces, but modestly. Overall, partisan differences were not associated with spending unless pre-election and non-election periods were distinguished.

Tellier (2006, 375-79) did not find an association between party ideology and spending levels unless variables for the governing party's popularity were included in models. Tellier's (2009, 603-4) later study of revenue-raising found no impact for party ideology on overall revenue levels, though differences existed for the use of different kinds of revenue. In his examination of changes in spending levels, Pickup (2006, 909-12) detected a tendency to raise spending in the face of globalization, except that Social Credit and NDP governments cut spending if union density was high.

Above all, this literature is affected by its preoccupation with spending and taxation levels, whereas an emerging literature in welfare state research points out that spending is not always the best way to evaluate such pivotal outcomes as the protection of social rights and redistribution (Siegel 2007). The data used here go some distance towards addressing this objection.

Table 16.4 shows the results of pooled regressions.[12] These results strongly suggest that a combination of influences traditionally associated with working-class politics – government by left parties and strong labour unions – is associated with greater redistribution for each of the provincial tax and

TABLE 16.4
Correlates of Gini coefficient (inequality) reduction by provincial transfers and income taxes, 1993-2007

	Pooled models				
	(1) Social assistance	(2) Workers' compensation	(3) Child benefits	(4) Income taxes	(5) All (including 1-4)
Trade openness	0.0929***	-0.00313	-0.0166*	0.0334**	0.106**
	(2.63)	(-0.28)	(-1.74)	(2.00)	(2.38)
Growth	-0.0000777	-0.0000910	-0.0000593	0.0000261	-0.000222
	(-0.42)	(-1.16)	(-1.04)	(0.27)	(-0.88)
Budget balance	7.596	11.41**	2.692	-14.03*	6.590
	(0.44)	(2.16)	(0.61)	(-1.68)	(0.30)
Federal transfers	-19.07	6.568	-8.151*	8.736	-11.80
	(-1.04)	(0.91)	(-1.77)	(1.21)	(-0.48)
Industrialism	0.266	0.153**	0.187*	0.523***	1.503***
	(1.22)	(2.30)	(1.71)	(3.49)	(4.74)
Immigrants/pc	21.12	-20.25	-98.53	-90.87	-221.5
	(0.14)	(-0.39)	(-1.56)	(-0.89)	(-1.06)
Unemployment	0.713**	0.239***	-0.0491	-0.221**	0.193
	(2.36)	(2.92)	(-0.71)	(-2.01)	(0.52)
Union density	0.620***	0.0665**	0.154***	0.452***	1.228***
	(6.02)	(2.34)	(3.18)	(7.77)	(9.00)
Left party	0.0230	0.468	0.327	0.601	1.556
	(0.02)	(1.41)	(0.56)	(0.89)	(1.01)
Centre party	1.970*	0.294	0.476*	0.871*	3.219**
	(1.91)	(0.97)	(1.70)	(1.93)	(2.34)
Year	-0.744***	0.113***	0.138***	0.146*	-0.447**
	(-4.46)	(2.94)	(2.80)	(1.77)	(-1.98)
Constant	1463.2***	-228.9***	-279.2***	-305.2*	850.4*
	(4.38)	(-2.99)	(-2.84)	(-1.83)	(1.87)
N	150	150	150	150	150
r^2	0.668	0.426	0.180	0.525	0.677

z statistics in parentheses.
*$p < .10$, **$p < .05$, ***$p < .01$
Prais-Winsten (OLS) regression, with panels correlated standard errors (PCSEs).
Source: Calculations by the author based on data from SLID.

TABLE 16.5

Political party correlates of Gini coefficient reduction with "union density" variable absent from pooled models, 1993-2007, partial results

	(1) Social assistance	(2) Workers' compensation	(3) Child benefits	(4) Income taxes	(5) All (including 1-4)
Left party	2.416** (2.35)	0.877*** (3.10)	1.207** (2.27)	2.414*** (2.84)	5.569*** (3.07)
Centre party	2.285** (2.16)	0.359 (1.16)	0.666** (2.17)	1.134* (2.25)	3.630** (2.54)

z statistics in parentheses.
*$p < .10$, **$p < .05$, ***$p < .01$
Prais-Winsten (OLS) regression, with panels correlated standard errors (PCSEs).
Note: The regression for which results are reported here included all variables in the Table 6.4 model, except for union density.
Source: Calculations by the author based on data from SLID.

transfer measures discussed here. Unlike fixed effects models, pooled regressions do not calculate separate coefficients for each panel (province). But they allow us to measure the impact of these ten variables more fully.

Union density is strongly associated with higher redistribution in all five models, as shown in Table 16.4. The relationship is significant at the 1 percent level in all models except for workers' compensation, but it reaches the 5 percent level even there. The role of parties is modest, in contrast, and not what one might expect: left parties are significantly associated with redistribution in none of these models, though the left variable is always positively signed. The results for centre parties are stronger – positive and significant for all models except workers' compensation, albeit only at the 10 percent level for the individual programs. If working-class politics matters, these results suggest, it is workers' economic organizations that matter most, not their legislative allies.

The notion that organized labour alone plays a central role in shaping redistributive politics is inconsistent with received Canadian scholarly opinion, though William Coleman (Chapter 4, this volume) makes a strong case for the relevance of organized labour. It also runs counter to the international evidence that left parties advance social reform much more than do unions (for instance, Huber and Stephens 2001; Boix 1998). To explore this issue, Table 16.5 reports the coefficients for left and centre parties from an alternative pooled model from which the union density variable is dropped.

FIGURE 16.1

Union density, partisanship, and inequality reduction: An interpretation

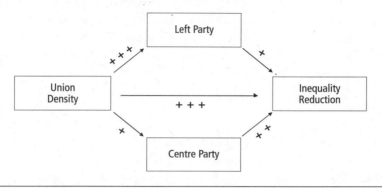

Note: Strength of relationship: +++ strong, ++ moderate, + weak

Here, the results for the partisan variables, especially the left party one, change dramatically. The left variable is now significantly associated with all inequality-reduction variables at the 5 percent level for social assistance and child benefits, and at the 1 percent level for workers' compensation, income taxes, and the comprehensive measure. Coefficients for the centre party variable also rise in the absence of union density but not nearly as much. The centre variable is now significant at the 5 percent level in all cases except workers' compensation. Its coefficient is always now lower than that for the left variable, though not by a great deal.

These results point to the possibility of a more complex relationship between union power and the partisan arena than can be captured by OLS regressions of the kind presented here. However, in non-statistical terms, the alternative results reported in Table 16.5 are consistent with the relationship portrayed in Figure 16.1. Union density has a strong impact independently of the value of either party variable. The left party variable, by contrast, looks much more like an intervening influence. When the density variable is in models, its observed impact is weak; when density is absent, the left coefficient is very strong, suggesting that it is "standing in" for an influence that lies ultimately with union density. A definitive test of this interpretation requires more complex, non-OLS modelling.

More modestly, we can note that the results in each case point to a strong influence for the political variables included in the models in Tables 16.4 and 16.5: the main model suggests a substantively large and highly significant impact for union strength on the politics of redistribution in the provinces; the alternative formulation, in Table 16.5, transfers this influence to centre and, to a greater extent, to left political parties. The strength of the union density and left party variables in alternative models points to a powerful component of "democratic class politics" in provincial redistributive politics. This is not the currently accepted view of things among Canadian politics scholars.

Conclusion

This chapter traces changes in redistribution in Canada since the 1980s, with particular attention to labour market transfers. As in other welfare states, such transfers are part of a broader redistributive system, and access to this broader system does not necessarily depend on a recipient's labour market status. Since the 1980s, the redistributive role of the main labour market transfers – federal EI and provincial social assistance – has declined relative to non-labour market transfers and income taxes. The imperfect nature of our data on recipiency rates for these transfers means that we cannot be sure which one is most to blame – most likely they are equally responsible. In the case of social assistance, this loss of redistributive power cannot be understood fully without paying attention to increases in child tax transfers, which are an important part of the income of assistance recipients with children.

Other transfers have become more redistributive during these years, so that the overall level of redistribution for working-age families in Canada has remained about the same since 1989. But the reduced role of labour market transfers within the entire system has specific consequences: although poverty rates for single mothers are lower than in earlier decades, those for other groups, especially unattached individuals, have risen. Moreover, Canada's tax and transfer system has failed to keep up with the continued rise in market income inequality so that final income inequality is now significantly higher than it was a quarter century ago.

As well as tracing these changes, this chapter argues that Canadian provinces diverge substantially in the extent to which they redistribute income. Quebec is something of an outlier, a fact confirmed by fixed effects regressions. While social assistance once played an important role in its "distinct" redistributive status, this has shifted elsewhere, especially to child tax credits and income taxes. But variations among the other provinces are also large; interprovincial differences in redistribution, by different measures, are equal to about half or about three-quarters of the variation that exists among the most commonly studied welfare states. Provinces produce this outcome, moreover, while controlling only part of Canada's entire complex of tax and transfer measures. In view of their magnitude, these interprovincial differences deserve more scholarly attention.

Finally, a strong current within comparative welfare state scholarship, the "power resources" perspective, argues that the conflict between organized representatives of working-class power and their business and middle-class opponents drives much welfare state change, causing the differentiation of relatively strong and weak systems of social provision (e.g., Korpi 2006; Allen and Scruggs 2004); this perspective is not taken up by Canadian welfare state scholarship. But, after controlling for the influence of the leading non-political variables typically used in comparative research, the influence of "working-class" power (union density and left party governance) on redistributive impact is consistently very strong. It is my contention that the alternative pooled regression models presented here suggest an interactive relationship among these variables; more specifically, union density is strongly associated with higher redistribution both directly and indirectly through its influence on left party government. Centre parties also have an important impact on most measures of redistribution. Qualitative case study evidence also indicates a strong role for political influences in shaping provincial policy making. Of course, this question requires additional research, and I encourage Canadian welfare state scholarship to take power resources approaches more seriously in this context.

TABLE 16.A

Sources of Gini coefficient (inequality) reduction for 1980 and 1989

Province	Market income Gini	Reduction of Gini coefficient measure of inequality associated with ...					After tax income Gini
		(1) Social assistance	(6) EI	(3/7) All child benefits	(4/8) All income taxes	(9) All (inc. 1-8)	
1980							
QC	360	−19	−14	−13	−36	−88	271
ON	317	−4	−6	−8	−21	−48	269
NF	419	−19	−42	−24	−27	−118	301
PE	340	−16	−26	−16	−25	−94	246
NS	340	−11	−19	−14	−26	−80	260
NB	376	−22	−35	−17	−26	−105	271
MB	336	−3	−5	−10	−24	−51	286
SK	315	−4	−3	−10	−22	−43	272
AB	336	−1	−3	−5	−23	−41	295
BC	309	−6	−4	−6	−15	−37	272
Mean	345	−10.5	−15.7	−12.3	−24.5	−70.5	274
1989							
QC	361	−18	−18	−11	−41	−98	263
ON	336	−6	−5	−6	−28	−58	278
NF	409	−13	−70	−18	−36	−145	264
PE	366	−14	−44	−16	−30	−112	254
NS	368	−17	−17	−12	−33	−93	275
NB	382	−23	−33	−14	−32	−110	271
MB	369	−12	−11	−12	−41	−90	279
SK	377	−11	−11	−15	−35	−83	295
AB	351	−12	−9	−10	−31	−66	285
BC	330	−10	−11	−8	−28	−65	265
Mean	365	−13.6	−22.9	−12.2	−33.5	−92	273

Note: Numbers in italics indicate summary results.
Source: Calculations by the author based on data from the SCF.

TABLE 16.B

Sources of Gini coefficient (inequality) reduction for 1993, 2000, and 2007

		Reduction of Gini coefficient measure of inequality associated with ...								
		Provincial transfers and income taxes					Federal transfers and income taxes			Provincial + federal	
Province	Market income Gini	(1) Social assistance	(2) Workers' compensation	(3) Child benefits	(4) Income tax	(5) All (1-4)	(6) EI	(7) Child benefits	(8) Income tax	(9) Combined (inc. 5-8)	After tax income Gini
1993											
QC	407	-33	-6	-3	-19	-56	-29	-12	-23	-132	275
ON	387	-28	-5	0	-12	-44	-13	-9	-22	-99	289
NF	409	-21	-6	0	-12	-32	-71	-17	-20	-161	248
PE	360	-8	-2	0	-9	-15	-63	-13	-19	-126	234
NS	383	-22	-7	0	-9	-34	-30	-13	-17	-111	272
NB	390	-24	-2	0	-8	-31	-45	-15	-18	-121	269
MB	369	-25	-2	0	-13	-38	-13	-15	-19	-94	275
SK	383	-19	-1	0	-13	-31	-11	-16	-19	-87	296
AB	369	-19	-2	0	-9	-29	-12	-13	-20	-84	285
BC	354	-16	-2	0	-9	-25	-10	-10	-19	-73	281
Mean	381	-21.5	-3.5	-0.3	-11.3	-33.6	-29.7	-13.3	-19.6	-109	272
2000											
QC	412	-18	-3	-4	-24	-50	-10	-12	-24	-110	302
ON	400	-11	-2	0	-12	-28	-3	-9	-21	-72	328
NF	462	-30	-7	-1	-16	-51	-40	-17	-27	-156	306
PE	397	-9	-3	0	-12	-22	-34	-15	-25	-109	288

▼ TABLE 16.B: YEAR 2000

Reduction of Gini coefficient measure of inequality associated with ...

Province	Market income Gini	Provincial transfers and income taxes					Federal transfers and income taxes			Provincial + federal	After tax income Gini
		(1) Social assistance	(2) Workers' compensation	(3) Child benefits	(4) Income tax	(5) All (1-4)	(6) EI	(7) Child benefits	(8) Income tax	(9) Combined (inc. 5-8)	
NS	400	-13	-2	-1	-12	-27	-17	-13	-23	-100	300
NB	400	-15	-3	-1	-11	-29	-22	-13	-25	-104	296
MB	377	-11	-2	0	-13	-27	-6	-15	-21	-78	299
SK	399	-14	-3	-3	-14	-32	-8	-16	-25	-90	309
AB	390	-7	-1	0	-5	-16	-3	-10	-26	-66	324
BC	411	-13	-2	-5	-10	-31	-7	-11	-28	-88	323
Mean	*405*	*-14.1*	*-2.8*	*-1.5*	*-12.9*	*-31.3*	*-15.0*	*-13.1*	*-24.5*	*-97*	*308*
						2007					
QC	412	-11	-4	-10	-23	-47	-16	-12	-23	-115	298
ON	404	-10	-4	-1	-13	-28	-7	-10	-25	-84	320
NF	436	-17	-8	-1	-16	-37	-43	-13	-27	-138	298
PE	367	-8	-2	0	-13	-19	-35	-13	-22	-110	257
NS	396	-6	-4	-1	-15	-24	-16	-12	-25	-95	302
NB	412	-14	-4	-1	-15	-30	-23	-15	-25	-112	300
MB	405	-6	-2	0	-15	-23	-8	-14	-29	-89	316
SK	403	-10	-2	0	-12	-22	-7	-15	-24	-82	322
AB	385	-2	-2	0	-5	-11	-4	-8	-23	-57	328
BC	390	-4	-2	0	-7	-14	-6	-11	-23	-69	321
Mean	*401*	*-8.8*	*-3.4*	*-1.4*	*-13.4*	*-25.5*	*-16.5*	*-12.3*	*-24.6*	*-95*	*306*

Note: Numbers in italics indicate summary results.
Source: Calculations by the author based on data from SLID.

NOTES

1 The federal Working Income Tax Benefit is another tax credit for low-income families, but its recent creation means that its impact on inequality cannot yet be measured empirically.
2 This discussion draws substantially from Haddow and Klassen (2006): chapter 8 (for social assistance) and pages 110-14, 140-45, 161-66, and 187-91 (for workers' compensation).
3 The federal Conservative government introduced another tax credit, the Working Income Tax Benefit (WITB), in 2007. Unlike child tax credits, receipt of which is contingent on a family's including eligible children, the WITB is available to low-income working families. Although, as noted in the introduction, it is too soon to come to any conclusions about its impact, it is likely to play a role in reducing inequality in the future.
4 A version of this chapter available from the author expands upon the technical aspects of the data and methods. Because SLID does not report child tax benefits separately for the provinces and Ottawa for 1993-95, a formula divides these expenditures between the two levels of government.
5 Besides the adult-equivalent adjustment, the data used here were amended in three other ways to be consistent with the internationally standard methodology outlined by Heisz (2007, 15).
6 Calculations not reproduced here indicate that the redistributive impact of all taxes and transfers increased in the most populous provinces between 1980 and 2007 when measured by the P10/P50 ratio. Increased redistribution by child tax benefits accounted for almost 100 percent of this improvement in Quebec, Alberta, and British Columbia, and for about half in Ontario.
7 Kapsalis (2001, 1-2) has determined that SLID underreports incomes from EI and (by as much as 50 percent) from social assistance.
8 Economic families are identified as poor in these calculations when their income falls below 50 percent of the median family income.
9 The independent variables included in the models reported in tables 16.2 and 16.3 (but only displayed in Table 16.3) encompass most of those typically used in contemporary comparative political economy research, provided they are not obviously irrelevant to interprovincial comparisons within Canada or unavailable. A data imputation method reconciled two different sets of union density data used in the regressions reported here.
10 Fixed effects regressions estimate the intercept level of each dependent variable (the five measures of inequality reduction) separately for each panel (province), controlling for the influence of the other variables included in the model. One panel must be selected as the "omitted category"; its level is not reported in the regression results, but those for all other provinces are reported in relation to it. The estimator used in all calculations in Tables 16.3, 16.4, and 16.5 is the Panel Corrected Standard Errors (PCSEs) approach pioneered by Beck and Katz (1995). It is explicitly designed for smaller panel data sets where t exceeds n, and where there is evidence of panel-level heteroskedasticity and causal dependence in the data (as tests show is true of the models examined here); serial correlation is addressed by an autocorrelation (ar1) correction.

11 Although "at the provincial level ... the nature of party competition remains largely under-studied," the brokerage theory is a strong current in this setting as well (Wesley 2009, 212, 215).
12 For all models, F tests identified the fixed effects model as the most appropriate, though test results were not usually overwhelming. Consistent with common practice, I nevertheless present both fixed effect and pooled models.

REFERENCES

Allen, James, and Lyle Scruggs. 2004. "Political Partisanship and Welfare State Reform in Advanced Industrial Societies." *American Journal of Political Science* 48: 496-512.

Banting, Keith. 2006. "Dis-embedding Liberalism? The New Social Policy Paradigm in Canada." In David A. Green and Jonathan Kesselman, eds., *Dimensions of Inequality in Canada*, 417-52. Vancouver: UBC Press.

Beck, Nathaniel, and Jonathan Katz. 1995. "What to Do (and Not Do) with Time-Series Cross-Section Data." *American Political Science Review* 89: 634-47.

Boix, Carles. 1998. *Political Parties, Growth and Equality*. Cambridge: Cambridge University Press.

Frenette, Marc, David A. Green, and Kevin Milligan. 2009. "Looking for Smoking Guns: The Impact of Taxes and Transfers on Canadian Income Inequality." Manuscript, Statistics Canada.

Frenette, Marc, David A. Green, and Garnett Picot. 2006. "Rising Income Inequality in the 1990s: An Exploration of Three Data Sources." In David A. Green and Jonathan Kesselman, eds., *Dimensions of Inequality in Canada*, 65-100. Vancouver: UBC Press.

Haddow, Rodney, and Thomas Klassen. 2006. *Partisanship, Globalization and Canadian Labour Market Policy*. Toronto: University of Toronto Press.

Heisz, Andrew. 2007. "Income Inequality and Redistribution in Canada: 1976 to 2004." In *Analytical Studies Branch Research Paper Series 298*. Ottawa: Statistics Canada.

Huber, Evelyne, and John Stephens. 2001. *Development and Crisis in the Welfare State*. Chicago: University of Chicago Press.

Kapsalis, Constantine. 2001. "An Assessment of EI and SA Reporting in SLID." Business and Labour Market Analysis Division, 166. Ottawa: Statistics Canada.

Kenworthy, Lane, and Jonas Pontusson. 2005. "Rising Inequality and the Politics of Redistribution in Affluent Countries." *Perspectives on Politics* 3: 449-71.

Korpi, Walter. 2006. "Power Resources and Employer-Centred Approaches to Explanations of Welfare States and Varieties of Capitalism." *World Politics* 58: 167-206.

Mahler, Vincent, and David Jesuit. 2006. "Fiscal Redistribution in the Developed Countries: New Insights from the Luxembourg Income Study." *Socio-Economic Review* 4: 483-511.

Morissette, René, John Myles, and Garnett Picot. 1995. "Earnings Polarization in Canada, 1969-91." In Keith Banting and Charles Beach, eds., *Labour Market*

Polarization and Social Policy Reform, 23-50. Kingston: School of Policy Studies, Queen's University.

Organisation for Economic Cooperation and Development. 1994. *The OECD Jobs Study: Facts, Analysis, Strategies.* http://www.oecd.org/dataoecd/42/51/1941679.pdf.

Petry, François, Louis M. Imbeau, Jean Crête, and Michel Clavet. 1999. "Electoral and Partisan Cycles in the Canadian Provinces." *Canadian Journal of Political Science* 32: 273-92.

Pickup, Mark. 2006. "Globalization, Politics and Provincial Government Spending in Canada." *Canadian Journal of Political Science* 39: 883-917.

Pontusson, Jonas. 2005. *Inequality and Prosperity: Social Europe vs. Liberal America.* Ithaca, NY: Cornell University Press.

Siegel, Nico. 2007. "When (Only) Money Matters: the Pros and Cons of Expenditure Analysis." In Jochen Clasen and Nico Siegel, eds., *Investigating Welfare State Change: The "Dependent Variable Problem" in Comparative Analysis,* 43-71. Cheltenham, UK: Edward Elgar.

Teeple, Gary. 2000. *Globalization and the Decline of Social Reform.* 2nd ed. Aurora, ON: Garamond Press.

Tellier, Genevieve. 2006. "Public Expenditures in Canadian Provinces: An Empirical Study of Political-Economic Interactions." *Public Choice* 126: 367-85.

—. 2009. "Les Déterminants des Recettes Fiscales des Gouvernements Provinciaux Canadien." *Canadian Public Administration* 52: 591-612.

Underhill, Frank. 1960. *In Search of Canadian Liberalism.* Toronto: Macmillan.

Wesley, Jared. 2009. "In Search of Brokerage and Responsibility: Party Politics in Manitoba." *Canadian Journal of Political Science* 42: 211-36.

PART 3

CONCLUSION

17

Canadian Social Futures
Concluding Reflections

KEITH BANTING AND JOHN MYLES

The redistributive state is fading in Canada. As we have seen, although the tax-transfer system offset rising inequality in the market incomes of families through the 1980s and the harsh recession of the early 1990s, taxes and transfers are no longer offsetting the growth in inequality generated by the market, and Canadian society has become more unequal. Politics has been critical to the redistributive fade. Advanced democracies almost everywhere have faced higher levels of inequality in market incomes. But countries have responded differently, reflecting differences in their domestic politics. In some countries, public policy mitigated the growth of inequality; in others, policy has accentuated it. Canada is one of those in which politics and policy have contributed to the weakening of the redistributive role of the state.

As we argue in the Introduction, there is no smoking gun that fully explains the redistributive fade in Canada. According to our authors, a complex mix of forces have reshaped the politics of social policy: global economic pressures, ideological change, a yawning imbalance in the political influence of business groups and unions, the decline of equality-seeking civil society organizations and think tanks, the cyclical pattern of public support for welfare, negative public attitudes towards Aboriginal peoples, realignment in the party system, a new bureaucratic politics, and decentralization in the federation. While it is impossible to disentangle the independent effect of these diverse changes, their cumulative impact has redefined the politics of redistribution. The new politics has two prongs. On one side, organizations that speak for the economic interests of lower-income Canadians, mobilizing resources, expertise, and attention on their behalf, have weakened; on the other side, changes in the distribution of power within our political institutions have made concerted action to tackle inequality more difficult. The result is a mutually reinforcing political syndrome that is less sensitive to the economic needs of individuals and families with modest and low incomes.

This new political landscape has sharp edges. Universal programs such as pensions and health care that benefit the entire population, including the broad middle classes, have largely been maintained. But elsewhere policy changes have weakened redistribution. Changes in tax policy have reduced both the progressivity of the tax system and the public revenue available to governments to support social purposes. The restructuring of the transfer system, especially retrenchment in unemployment benefits and social assistance, have reduced support for vulnerable Canadians. The few expansions of transfer programs that did occur in recent decades, such as the expansion of child benefits, were not large enough to offset the cumulative impact of retrenchment elsewhere. Finally, policy drift has compounded the problem. Governments have failed to modernize the policy architecture in light of new social risks confronting Canadian families.

None of this was inevitable. Globalization did not impose these outcomes on Canada. Other countries chose to mute the impact of global economic and technological change through strong policy choices.[1] In Canada, Quebec chose a separate path. Distinctive politics produced distinctive policies that stabilized the distribution of income in *la belle province*.

This story has been documented in considerable detail in the Introduction and the chapters of this book. This concluding chapter reflects on the importance of the findings. The first section examines the implications for scholarly research on the politics of social policy both in Canada and in advanced democracies more generally. The second section examines the implications for the future of Canadian social policy, asking whether Canada is likely to go further down the path towards higher inequality. The third section then asks whether growing inequality matters, surveying the economic, social, and politics risks that Canada would be courting by going further down that path. A short final section pulls the implications together.

Understanding the Politics of Social Policy

The findings of this book have important implications for the literature on Canadian social policy and the comparative literature on the welfare state.

The literature on Canadian social policy has explored the implications of major tectonic shifts, such as globalization and the advance of neoliberalism, and has traced the evolution of social programs in rich and nuanced ways. But the role of politics in mediating between large structural and ideational changes, on the one hand, and the redesign of social programs, on the other, has been analyzed less thoroughly. Although much has been written about federalism and social policy, the implications of other dimensions of the country's political institutions remain less studied: the relative political clout of business associations and organized labour, the restructuring of the party system, the evolution of public attitudes about politics and the state, the implications of the electoral system, and changes in bureaucratic politics. These institutions have been examined by specialists in those fields, but – with honourable exceptions – the implications for social policy have not been analyzed in depth. Moreover, a clear message of this book is that it is the cumulative impact of diverse changes in different corners of the political system that alters the representation of economic interests and redistributes power in ways that matter. This book has not developed a comprehensive view of the linkages, but we hope that it will contribute to future research agendas.

The Canadian case also has implications for the comparative literature on the welfare state. As the Introduction demonstrates, the Canadian case is generally consistent with comparative analyses of the politics of social policy. But several distinctive strands in the Canadian pattern stand out. One is the importance of the territorial dimension of the welfare state. In most countries, attention focuses on the role of social policy in mediating class divisions. In Canada, however, territorial divisions cross-cut class-based politics at the national level, and the politics of equality have always centred as much on regional inequalities as on class inequalities. As the chapters by Jenson and Boychuk emphasize, social programs in Canada have been seen as an instrument of territorial integration (also Banting 1995, 2005). The potential of the welfare state as an instrument of territorial integration has attracted some attention in the context of the European Union (e.g., Ferrara 2005), but its role within many individual countries remains understudied. Canadian experience also speaks to the intense international controversy about immigration and ethnic diversity. Here, Canada represents a counter-narrative, challenging some of the more alarmist predictions that multicultural diversity will undermine the welfare state. The finding that negative attitudes towards Aboriginal peoples weakens support for redistribution is troubling. But the evidence that immigrant diversity actually strengthens support for redistribution is important to international debates.

Further, the Canadian trajectory expands our understanding of stability and change in welfare states. The concept of path dependency has advanced our understanding about the nature and processes of institutional change. But the evidence here emphasizes that path dependency is not simply the quiet persistence of programs inherited from the past. Pensions and health care have represented large rocks in the landscape of Canadian social policy, but their stability is deceptive. Stability has been the product of active "system maintenance," a process requiring major political effort and the injection of significant new resources. The preservation of the Canada/Quebec Pension Plans, for example, depended not simply on the mobilization of old allies and beneficiaries but also on the construction of a complex political coalition that crossed levels of government and partisan lines. It also required the political will to impose a doubling of the associated payroll taxes over a decade, which the opposition party in the House of Commons labelled the biggest tax grab in Canadian history.

Potentially, however, the most interesting point of contact with the comparative literature centres on the politics of liberal welfare states. There are striking similarities between the conclusions of this book and those of recent studies of the politics of social policy in the United States. Jacob Hacker and Paul Pierson also emphasize the weakening of groups that speak for people of modest incomes, institutional changes in the distribution of political power that limit the prospects for redistributive politics, and policy drift in the face of growing inequality. The details differ. In examining what they call "the politics of organized combat," Hacker and Pierson (2010, chap. 5) place primary weight on the weakening of organized labour, the expansion of business lobbies, and the role of money in electoral politics, and pay less attention to the erosion of social movements and related think tanks, reflecting important differences in the role of civil society in the two countries. Similarly, their analysis of institutional change focuses on congressional politics and the cloture rule in the Senate, and it pays less attention to the shifting balance between bureaucratic agencies and the federal-state interface. But the underlying logic is similar. Organizations that speak on behalf of the poor are weaker, and power has moved to institutional niches less responsive to redistributive interests.

Such trends are hardly unique to liberal welfare states. But there may be structural features of the politics of liberal welfare states that make this political syndrome more likely. The lack of corporatist structures, the weaknesses of left parties, first-past-the-post electoral systems, and majoritarian as opposed to consensual policy making make shifts in organized politics and the institutional distribution of power easier. Moreover, in liberal welfare states, where the redistributive role of the state has always been less developed, the ability to block action may be sufficient for anti-redistributive interests. In societies with more robust redistributive traditions, those committed to a neoliberal order need to actively dismantle programs inherited from the past. In liberal welfare states, mere drift in social policy can represent a victory for conservative interests.

The Future of Redistributive Politics

The future will undoubtedly surprise us. But does the analysis of the recent past help to anticipate the pressures on Canadian social policy in the years to come?

At least since Elizabethan times, poverty – and, by extension, the poor – have been a focus of public policy debates. But rarely, if ever, has inequality per se been an explicit target of government policy making. Statistics Canada has published a historical series on income inequality and, less often, wealth inequality for many years. But as David Good points out in his chapter, no government department is responsible for the Gini coefficient in policy terms. Nevertheless, suddenly inequality per se is emerging in policy debates. The OECD (2008, 2011) and the IMF (Berg and Ostry 2011) have expressed concern about the inequality surge and point to the reduced redistributive capacity of tax-benefit systems, hinting that some rethinking is in order (OECD 2011). All this is a far cry from the OECD's (1994) *Jobs Study*, in which more inequality was construed as the necessary price for returning to high employment levels. In 2011, the "Occupy Movement" injected inequality into the popular agenda, with its dramatic "99/1" metaphor, even winning some approval from the governor of the Bank of Canada. The discourse of redistributive politics in Canada has long been dominated by an "anti-poverty" rhetoric. The fact that "inequality" has raised its discursive head is a relatively new phenomenon. Is Canada likely to change course as a result?

In answering this question, it is important to consider both inequality in market incomes and inequality in income after taxes and transfers. Are there reasons to assume that inequality in market incomes will decline? That seems unlikely in the short term. As Fortin et al. (2012) note, inequality rises sharply in recessions because low-income earners bear the brunt of hard times. What is striking, however, is that during the 1980s and 1990s inequality did not decline again as the economy recovered. While there was a modest decline in inequality in the early 2000s, it rose again in the recession that began in 2008, and it remains to be seen if the increase persists: "If recent history is any guide, we could be witnessing another ratcheting up in inequality" (ibid., 4).

Are there longer-term factors that might work in the opposite direction? For example, is demographic change likely to reduce inequality in market incomes? Given the retirement of the postwar baby-boom generation and the dramatic drop in fertility rates, we can anticipate labour shortages and stronger wage growth over the next decade. However, the most acute shortages will be among skilled workers, and real wage growth for unskilled workers is likely to depend in part on changes in labour market institutions. As LaRochelle-Côté and Dionne (2009) show, the Canadian labour market produces an unusually high number of low-wage jobs. About 24 percent of full-time earners in Canada (and the US) earn less than two-thirds of the median earner compared to less than 15 percent in Continental Europe and less than 10 percent in Scandinavian countries. Differences in wage structures of this sort account for a large share of cross-national differences in both poverty and income inequality and are the product of long-standing national differences in wage-bargaining institutions that resist change. As Coleman notes in his chapter, Canada lacks the cooperative (i.e., "corporatist") wage-bargaining systems that have led to wage levelling elsewhere. The labour market is not often thought of as a major part of Canada's "social policy" agenda, but policies that affect the labour market (largely under provincial jurisdiction) are especially subject to policy drift and inaction. Moreover, federal changes in the immigration program to admit more temporary workers and allow employers to pay them less than prevailing wage rates, coupled with requirements that Employment Insurance (EI) recipients accept a wider range of alternative employment at lower wages, will tend to dampen any upward pressures at the bottom end of the wage distribution.

If inequality in market incomes is unlikely to decline on its own, what are the prospects for a reinvigoration of the redistributive role of government? Such a reinvigoration would require that two conditions be met: (1) rising political demand and (2) new policy paradigms. By rising political demand, we mean a change in what people demand from their political leaders. Where will such demand come from if our labour unions and equality-seeking civil society organizations are as weak as our authors say? Recent research on Europe suggests that the politics of social protection in the future is unlikely to resemble that of the past. The social policy domain is increasingly multidimensional, and major social policy innovations have depended on the ability of policy makers to construct encompassing "cross-class" coalitions that go well beyond the historic champions of the welfare state (Häusermann 2010). These coalitions have embraced groups on the margins of society or facing new social risks – the atypically employed, immigrants, working women – but they have also incorporated the concerns of elements of the broad middle class.

Such strategies would seem especially important in Canada. As we have seen, programs that matter to the middle class, such as pensions and health care, have been handled with a delicacy not evident in the restructuring of social assistance and EI. In addition, the contemporary form of inequality points in the same direction. As we saw in Chapter 1, the rich have gotten richer and upper-income groups generally have done well; the middle and especially the lower-middle classes have struggled; but there is little evidence to indicate that the poor have gotten poorer. Egalitarians in Canada have traditionally relied on an anti-poverty discourse and surges in poverty levels to mobilize supporters. For egalitarians, this new pattern of inequality creates a material base for new political coalitions between the middle and the bottom, coalitions that have traditionally been absent from our redistributive discourse.

The response of the middle class will be critical. The key difference between the politics of liberal welfare states and the politics of European welfare states has been the alignment of the middle class. In liberal welfare states, the middle class tends to support a limited safety net for the poor and to be less enthusiastic about a broader displacement of market mechanisms. In European welfare states, the middle class sees the welfare state as serving its needs as well and supports a wider array of expansive programs that also benefit the poor. As we saw in the Introduction, the nature of the electoral system is important in shaping these alignments. In majoritarian ("first-past the post") electoral systems, as in Canada, the "middle" tends to align with the top. In proportional systems of representation, the middle is more likely to align with the bottom against the top.[2]

Will the middle classes in Canada rethink their view of the social role of the state? The new inequality does have the potential to unsettle parts of the middle class and challenge the social policy ideas that gained currency in the 1980s and 1990s. Encouraged by neoliberal economic policy thinking, earnings levels and taxation policies at the "top" have been moving in opposite directions: rapidly rising earnings and declining taxes. In contrast, the middle class in general and young adults and families in particular are under pressure. Average real incomes have been stagnant for decades; the relative earnings and savings of young adults have fallen in the past thirty years with no significant policy response; and students increasingly graduate with heavy debt loads. Fortin et al. (2012) sum up the impact of the forces driving inequality in the following terms: "The young and the poorly educated have borne the brunt of these forces, but significant numbers of those previously in the middle and lower middle of the occupational skill and wage distribution have also been adversely affected."

In addition, certain weaknesses of neoliberal social policy ideas are becoming clear, creating problems for the middle class in particular. In the retirement-income sector, for example, the emphasis on market mechanisms is hitting limits. The proportion of the labour force enrolled in occupational pensions is declining, especially among younger workers, and personal savings such as RRSP savings are not filling the gap. Moreover, private pensions and savings represent an uncertain base for retirement planning, given low rates of return on savings and volatile capital markets. Globalization may not represent a powerful constraint on the redistributive role of the state, as we saw in the Introduction, but it clearly constrains the capacity of private corporations to provide assured benefits to their workers. The combination of rising inequality, stagnant average incomes, declining relative earnings for the young, and weakening private benefits represent potential fuel for a debate on the balance between market and state in meeting the social needs of the middle class.

These cross-currents would seem to create opportunities for strategic coalition builders. But the reinvigoration of reformist politics also requires a shift in the dominant ideas among policy elites. Policy elites who came of age in the 1980s and 1990s still carry elements of the conventional economic "wisdom" of those decades. As the chapter by Boadway and Cuff documents, for this generation, progressive taxation systems discourage entrepreneurship and incentives to invest, and higher wages and more job security for those at the bottom discourage employment. More inequality was the price to be paid for maintaining high employment and economic growth. These claims have been increasingly discredited because of the lack of systematic supporting evidence. Nonetheless, they have not been superseded by an economic policy paradigm that provides a clear mandate for governments to challenge the new inequality in a serious way.

Will electoral politics force governments to look for new conceptual roadmaps? Political parties of all stripes require strong incentives to take on the inequality issue in its contemporary form. A swing in the popular vote for the CCF (predecessor to the NDP) in 1944 provided a strong incentive to the Liberal government of the day to move forward with a social agenda in the early postwar years. Many believe that the 2011 election ushered in a new party system at the federal level; the centre-dominated system of the past is gone, and Canada is evolving towards a party system divided in left-right terms. This is uncharted terrain at the national level. Haddow's chapter indicates that the balance between left and right matters for redistribution at the provincial level, and much would seem to depend on which party dominates a polarized federal party system in the longer term. The chapter by Richard Johnston addresses this question most explicitly. Canada, he agrees, seems to be moving to the left-right form of party competition that is common under majoritarian as opposed to proportional electoral systems. But comparative evidence also demonstrates that such party systems tend to be dominated by parties of the right; conservative governments are three times more likely under such electoral systems (Iversen and Soskice 2006). Johnston concludes: "Canada has never been governed (at the federal level) by a party of the left; but neither, uniquely among majoritarian systems, has it been dominated by a party of the right. That part of Canada's electoral history seems to have ended."

This suggests that the Conservative Party's approach to social policy will be critical over the years to come. The Conservatives have governed since 2006, but they have not had the electoral flexibility enjoyed by the Liberals in the mid-1990s. For the first five years, they were a minority government, and, although they won a majority in 2011, they face a resurgent NDP, which became the Official Opposition for the first time. The prospects are therefore for the continued erosion of redistributive instruments on an incremental rather than on a radical basis. Changes in income security programs, as we saw in the Introduction, have been incremental or, in the case of Old Age Security, are to be phased in beginning a decade from now. The biggest impact has undoubtedly been on taxation. The Conservatives have consistently given priority to reductions in taxes, especially the GST and corporate income taxes, draining the federal treasury of resources that might otherwise have been devoted to social ends.

The 2011 election also shook up the territorial axis of social politics. Unlike their Liberal predecessors, the Conservatives do not see social programs as an instrument of pan-Canadian unity, preferring to build a common identity by celebrating older symbols such as the monarchy and the military. But the massive change on the opposition benches poses intriguing questions. During the building of the postwar welfare state, members of Parliament from Quebec represented a powerful block within Liberal governments fighting for progressive causes; and the Quebec provincial government often sided with NDP provinces in federal-provincial negotiations. Although Quebec always defended its jurisdiction, cabinet ministers such as Jean Marchand, Marc Lalonde, and Monique Bégin supported an expansive conception of social policy. Recently, Quebec's focus has been more internal. During the dominance of the Bloc Québécois at the federal level, Quebec MPs stood on guard against an expansionist federal social policy; and the Quebec government frequently chose to be an observer in federal-provincial meetings. This limited engagement in pan-Canadian social politics weakened collectivist forces at the federal level. Will the dramatic shift of Quebec voters to the New Democratic Party in 2011 fuel pan-Canadian debates on social policy? Quebec members will undoubtedly continue to defend an asymmetrical role for Quebec in new initiatives. But Quebec's policy culture may have a more direct bearing on social policy debates in the years to come.

Nonetheless, the future of redistribution will be increasingly determined at the provincial level and will be shaped by differences in provincial politics. While there is interprovincial convergence in some fields, such as primary and secondary education (Wallner 2010), the evidence in this volume points to the persistence of distinctive provincial regimes in redistribution. As a country, Canada seems comfortable with greater regional variation in the terms of social citizenship than do most federations. But the capacity of poorer provinces to sustain their social programs depends in part on intergovernmental fiscal arrangements, especially the equalization program due for renewal in 2014. The equalization program has traditionally helped poorer provinces provide average levels of services without having to resort to above average taxes. However, the program is coming under increasing strain. The uneven distribution of resource wealth across the country and the weakening of the Ontario economy have triggered a significant economic rebalancing of the federation, and the equalization program has not kept pace. Federal spending on the equalization program is declining as a proportion of GDP and is narrowing inter-regional differences in fiscal capacity less than in the past. Inter-regional fiscal solidarity is fraying at the edges.

In the short and intermediate future, the prospects for a revival of redistributive politics thus seem limited. At the time of writing, Canada is in a period of slow growth and a new round of deficit reductions. In the near term, the prospects are for continued policy drift and/or incremental movement along the path to rising inequality.

Does Rising Inequality Matter?

Should we worry? Whether we should worry about rising inequality and how much inequality we should tolerate are highly contested and confused issues in Western social thought.

Normative debates give different answers to this question. In a well-cited article, the prominent American economist Martin Feldstein (1998) argues that we should be concerned about increasing inequality in the form of rising poverty but that concern over the rising incomes of the rich is simply the result of envy. His normative foundation is the Pareto principle, which holds that anything that makes some people better off without making anyone worse off is morally acceptable. In contrast, John Rawls (1972), the most prominent political philosopher of the past half century, argues that increases in inequality are ethically acceptable only when such gains increase the well-being of the poor (the "maximin" principle). Rawls's argument rests on the empirical claim that most inequality is the result of "luck," not "effort." Much of what determines people's earnings and income – intelligence, creativity, persistence, good looks – is a product of genetics, parental assets, and traits, or the quality of neighbourhoods and schools in which they grew up. The counter-argument is that we should be rewarded in terms of what we make of our luck (Nozick 1974): individuals are responsible for what they do with their endowments and should be rewarded accordingly. Parsing out the differences between luck and effort has preoccupied scholars for many decades and will undoubtedly continue into the future.[3]

Policy makers, however, usually make choices based on *consequential*, not normative, arguments. The core question centres on the risks that Canada faces if it goes further down the road to greater inequality. The Gini coefficient in disposable income in Canada rose from .28 to .32 between the 1990s and the 2000s, a rather large change in an index that is hard to move. As Lars Osberg (2012) asks, what if this was not just a one-time event but the first stage in a longer-term trend? What are the implications of a continued upward drift in inequality, with the Gini reaching .40? What are the *effects* of rising inequality on the economy, on the polity, and on social outcomes for individuals?

Does inequality pose risks for the economy? In recent years, the dominant policy discourse has insisted that inequality encourages growth, and even the most robust egalitarians are unlikely today to argue in favour of perfect equality (where the Gini coefficient is zero) because of incentive issues. But claims that differential rewards are necessary to provide individuals with incentives to develop and use their talents, or for the efficient allocation of societal resources, tell us nothing about how large or how small these incentives should be in order to achieve high levels of employment or economic growth. Cross-national studies demonstrate that market economies can flourish at very different levels of national income inequality (Kenworthy 2004). Over the past quarter century, a number of countries have combined high levels of economic growth with low levels of inequality (Gini coefficients as low as .22). Moreover, there may be economic risks inherent in continued growth in inequality. The International Monetary Fund and economists such as Joseph Stiglitz, a Nobel prize winner, question the effect of high inequality on long-term growth (Berg and Ostry 2011; Stiglitz 2012). The OECD (2008, 2011) questions the effects of high inequality on social and political stability, key prerequisites of economic growth. Among Canadian economists, Lars Osberg (2012) agrees that continually increasing inequality cannot be a steady state; that is, the trend cannot go on forever without inducing serious instability. Even if the income gap does not trigger riots in the streets, Fortin et al. (2012) worry that, "if economic gains from growth continue to accrue in a lopsided fashion, public support for pro-growth policies is likely to wane" (see also Conference Board of Canada 2011).

Are there social risks inherent in continuing growth in inequality? Numerous studies have demonstrated a relationship between higher levels of inequality and poorer social outcomes. Across OECD countries, for example, high-inequality countries have, on average, lower levels of life expectancy, higher levels of infant mortality, and weaker educational performance among children. Social mobility between generations is lower in high-inequality countries, raising questions about the extent to which equality of opportunity is realized in practice. The quality of community relations also seems to be at stake; interpersonal trust tends to be lower in more unequal countries. These lower averages tend to result from a steeper social gradient within high-inequality countries: the gap between rich and poor in educational performance and health status tends to be greater in countries with higher levels of economic inequality. The links between economic inequality and social outcomes are intensely debated.[4] They are undoubtedly complex and probably differ from one social outcome to another. Moreover, the causal relationships are likely to run in both directions: for example, high levels of economic inequality may well contribute to inequality in the educational attainment of children; but highly unequal educational outcomes are also likely to reinforce unequal economic outcomes. However, the fact that social scientists debate the precise nature of the linkages does not mean that the issues can be ignored. We know enough to say that if Canada continues down the road to growing inequality, it will be courting significant social risks.

Finally, inequality poses risks for the quality of democracy. Here we run into what political scientists refer to as the "endogeneity" problem. Politics not only affect inequality; inequality also affects politics. Political parties worry about elections, and elections are expensive – more so with each electoral cycle. Like bank-robbers, political parties tend to go where the money is. As a result, political scientists have long worried about the fate of democratic politics under conditions of high and rising inequality (see Beramendi and Andersen 2008). A simple indicator is political participation: as we saw in the Introduction, the affluent tend to vote more than the less affluent; they are also more likely to engage in other forms of political participation. The issue is one of political "voice." As our authors document, institutions that provide political voice to the less advantaged have been seriously weakened over the last several decades. The experience of the United States also stands as a warning about the tension between high levels of inequality and democracy. Sophisticated students of the links between public opinion and public policy have demonstrated the much greater responsiveness of policy outcomes in that country to the preferences of the affluent than to the preferences of the much more numerous low- and middle-income Americans (Bartels 2010; Gilens 2012). Such studies represent a sobering assessment of the corrosive effects of high levels of inequality on a nation's capacity to live up to its democratic ideals.

Despite the limited prospects for a re-energized reformist politics in the short term, we hesitate to be gloomy. Writing in the nineteenth century, Karl Marx, spokesperson for the left, was gloomy about the future of capitalism. Writing almost a century later, Frederick Hayek, spokesperson for the right, was equally gloomy. Both proved to be wrong. Contra Marx, capitalist economies did not collapse into a polarized war between rich and poor. Contra Hayek, welfare states did not destroy market economies. The reason is that both capitalism and democracy are full of surprises. Viewed in the long term, capitalism has brought economic growth while political democracy has provided a recurring counterfoil to capitalism's inegalitarian tendencies.

The cumulative message of this volume is that retrenchment has mattered but inaction has mattered more. A critical part of the story has been the quiet indifference to new social risks and rising inequality. Policy drift – living off the social policy accomplishments of an earlier generation – is not enough. This is the challenge awaiting a new generation of strategic coalition builders in Canada.

NOTES

1 Lane Kenworthy (2011, 9-16) shows that transfers to low-end households (bottom decile) increased significantly between 1979 and 2007 in Denmark, Norway, the Netherlands, and Finland, more than offsetting stagnant or declining earnings. Under Blair, in the UK, transfers rose between 1995 and 2005. In the US, transfers remained constant, with increases in the Earned Income Tax Credit (EITC) offsetting reductions in social assistance.
2 Given the power of this relationship, the most decisive recent choices for social policy may have been the rejection of moves towards more proportional electoral systems in referenda held in British Columbia, Ontario, and Prince Edward Island.
3 For a concise review of recent egalitarian and anti-egalitarian debates in political philosophy, see Roemer (2009).
4 A "strong" view of the negative impact of inequality on social outcomes can be found in Wilkinson and Pickett (2009). However, these views are contested, largely for methodological reasons that remain unresolved. For more qualified views, see Burtless and Jencks (2003); and Leigh, Jencks, and Smeeding (2009). On social mobility, see Corak (2004).

REFERENCES

Banting, Keith. 1995. "The Welfare State as Statescraft: Territorial Politics and Canadian Social Policy." In Stephan Leibfried and Paul Pierson, eds., *European Social Policy: Between Fragmentation and Integration*, 269-300. Washington, DC: Brookings Institution.

–. 2005. "Canada: Nation-Building in a Federal Welfare State." In Herbert Obinger, Stephan Leibfried, and Frank G. Castles, eds., *Federalism and the Welfare State: New World and European Experiences*, 89-137. Cambridge: Cambridge University Press.

Bartels, Larry M. 2010. *Unequal Democracy: The Political Economy of the New Gilded Age*. Princeton, NJ: Princeton University Press.

Berg, Andrew, and Jonathan Ostry. 2011. "Inequality and Unsustainable Growth: Two Sides of the Same Coin." IMF Discussion Note, 8 April. Washington, DC: International Monetary Fund.

Burtless, Gary, and Christopher Jencks. 2003. "American Inequality and Its Consequences." In Henry Aaron, James Lindsay, and Pietro Nivola, eds., *Agenda for the Nation*, 43-108. Washington, DC: Brookings Institution.

Conference Board of Canada. 2011. *How Canada Performs: A Report Card on Canada*. http://www.conferenceboard.ca/hcp/default.aspx.

Corak, Miles, ed. 2004. *Generational Income Mobility in North America and Europe.* Cambridge: Cambridge University Press.
Feldstein, Martin. 1998. "Income Inequality and Poverty." Working Paper 6770. Cambridge, MA: National Bureau of Economic Research.
Ferrara, Maurizio. 2005. *The Boundaries of Welfare: European Integration and the New Spatial Politics of Social Protection.* Oxford: Oxford University Press.
Fortin, Nicole, David A. Green, Thomas Lemieux, Kevin Milligan, and W. Craig Riddell. 2012. "Canadian Inequality: Recent Development and Policy Options." *Canadian Public Policy* 38(2): 121-45.
Gilens, Martin. 2012. *Affluence and Influence: Economic Inequality and Political Power in America.* Princeton, NJ: Princeton University Press.
Hacker, Jacob, and Paul Pierson. 2010. *Winner Take All Politics: How Washington Made the Rich Richer – and Turned Its Back on the Middle Class.* New York: Simon and Schuster.
Häusermann, Silja. 2010. *The Politics of Welfare State Reform in Continental Europe: Modernization in Hard Times.* Cambridge: Cambridge University Press.
Iverson, Torben, and David Soskice. 2006. "Electoral Institutions and the Politics of Coalitions: Why Some Democracies Redistribute More than Others." *American Political Science Review* 100(2): 165-81.
Kenworthy, Lane. 2004. *Egalitarian Capitalism.* New York: Russell Sage Foundation.
–. 2011. *Progress for the Poor.* Oxford: Oxford University Press.
LaRochelle-Côté, Sébastien, and Claude Dionne. 2009. "International Differences in Low-Paid Work." *Perspectives on Labour and Income* 10(6): 5-13.
Leigh, Andrew, Christopher Jencks, and Timothy Smeeding. 2009. "Health and Economic Inequality." In Wiemer Salverda, Brian Nolan, and Timothy Smeeding, eds., *Oxford Handbook of Economic Inequality*, 384-404. Oxford: Oxford University Press.
Nozick, Robert. 1974. *Anarchy, State and Utopia.* New York: Basic Books.
Organisation for Economic Cooperation and Development. 1994. *The OECD Jobs Study: Facts, Analysis, Strategies.* Paris: OECD.
–. 2008. *Growing Unequal? Income Distribution and Poverty in OECD Countries.* Paris: OECD.
–. 2011. *Divided We Stand: Why Inequality Keeps Rising.* Paris: OECD.
Osberg, Lars. 2012. *Instability Implications of Increasing Inequality: What Can Be Learned from North America.* Toronto: Canadian Centre for Policy Alternatives.
Rawls, John. 1972. *A Theory of Social Justice.* Cambridge: Harvard University Press.
Roemer, John. 2009. "Equality: Its Justification, Nature and Domain." In Wiemer Salverda, Brian Nolan, and Timothy Smeeding, eds., *Oxford Handbook of Economic Inequality*, 23-39. Oxford: Oxford University Press.
Stiglitz, Joseph. 2012. *The Price of Inequality: How Today's Divided Society Endangers Our Future.* New York: W.W. Norton and Company.
Wallner, Jennifer. 2010. "Beyond National Standards: Reconciling Tension between Federalism and the Welfare State." *Publius: The Journal of Federalism* 40(4): 646-71.
Wilkinson, Richard, and Kate Pickett. 2009. *The Spirit Level: Why Greater Equality Makes Societies Stronger.* New York: Bloomsbury Press.

Contributors

Robert Andersen is Distinguished Professor of Social Science and Chair of the Department of Sociology at the University of Toronto. His recent research explores the interaction between national-level economic conditions and individual-level economic position, as measured by social class or income, in their effects on various outcomes considered important to democracy, such as tolerance, redistribution and inequality, support for social and political freedoms, and civic participation. He is the author of *Modern Methods for Robust Regression* (2008) and more than fifty research articles.

Keith Banting is a professor and holder of the Queen's Research Chair in Public Policy in the Department of Political Studies and the School of Policy Studies at Queen's University. His research interests focus on the politics of social policy and the politics of immigration, multiculturalism, and integration.

Robin Boadway is David Chadwick Smith Chair in Economics at Queen's University. His research interests include taxation, redistribution, and fiscal federalism.

Gerard W. Boychuk is Chair of the Department of Political Science, University of Waterloo, and Professor in the Balsillie School of International Affairs. He is co-editor of the journal *Global Social Policy,* and his current research interests include the domestic politics of redistribution in Canada from a comparative perspective, as well as transnational initiatives relating to social protection, including the global social protection floor.

William D. Coleman is a professor of Political Science at the University of Waterloo and at the Balsillie School of International Affairs. With Dr. Alina Sajed, he published *Fifty Key Thinkers on Globalization* in 2013.

Katherine Cuff is an associate professor of Economics at McMaster University and a Canada Research Chair in Public Economic Theory. Her main research interests include taxation and redistribution.

Josh Curtis is a PhD candidate in sociology at the University of Toronto. His current research explores the sources and effects of class identification and awareness. Specifically, he is interested in how conditions at both the individual and national level influence class awareness, and concomitantly the link between class and political behaviour. His research has been published in several sociology journals.

David A. Good is a professor of Public Administration at the University of Victoria and a former federal assistant deputy minister. He has authored numerous articles and books on public administration and public policy, the most recent, *The Politics of Public Money* (2nd ed.). He is the recipient of the Donald Smiley Prize awarded by the Canadian Political Science Association for his book, *The Politics of Public Management: The HRDC Audit of Grants and Contributions* (2003).

David A. Green is a professor in the Vancouver School of Economics at the University of British Columbia and is the current editor of the *Canadian Journal of Economics*. His research interests are primarily related to the interaction of technological change and social policy in determining wage and employment outcomes.

Rodney Haddow is a political scientist at the University of Toronto. His current research project is a comparative study of social and economic policy in Quebec and Ontario since the 1990s.

Jane Jenson was awarded the Canada Research Chair in Citizenship and Governance in 2001 at the Université de Montréal, where she is a professor of Political Science. Since 2004, she has also been a Senior Fellow of the Successful Societies program of the Canadian Institute for Advanced Research. Her research focuses on the politics of social policy in Canada and Europe.

Richard Johnston is a professor of Political Science and Canada Research Chair at the University of British Columbia. He is a specialist in public opinion, elections, and representation.

Edward Koning is an assistant professor of Political Science at the University of Guelph. His research centres on the politics of immigration and integration, with a particular focus on North America and Western Europe. His interests also include social policies, minority politics, and institutionalist theory. His recent publications have appeared in *Comparative Political Studies, Ethnic and Racial Studies, Canadian Public Policy,* and *Acta Politica*.

Rianne Mahon holds a CIGI Chair in Comparative Social Policy at the Balsillie School of International Affairs and is a professor in the Department of Political Science at Wilfrid Laurier University in Waterloo. She has co-edited several books, most recently *The OECD and Transnational Governance* (with S. McBride), *Leviathan Undone?* (with R. Keil), and *Feminist Ethics and Social Politics* (with F. Robinson), and has written numerous articles and book chapters on the politics of childcare, as part of a broader process of redesigning welfare regimes. Her current work focuses on the role of international organizations in disseminating social policy discourses.

John Myles is emeritus professor of Sociology and Senior Fellow in the School of Public Policy and Governance at the University of Toronto. He has written widely on topics related to the comparative politics of the welfare state and on topics related to poverty, earnings, and income inequality in Canada.

Alain Noël is a professor of Political Science at the Université de Montréal. He works on social policy in a comparative perspective, as well as on federalism and on Quebec and Canadian politics. He is the author, with Jean-Philippe Thérien, of *Left and Right in Global Politics* (2008).

Susan D. Phillips is a professor and director of the School of Public Policy and Administration, Carleton University. She is currently co-editing a major handbook, the *Routledge Companion to Philanthropy*, as well as conducting comparative studies of place-based philanthropy and of regulatory frameworks for the third sector.

Stuart Soroka is an associate professor and William Dawson Scholar in the Department of Political Science at McGill University. His research focuses on the relationships between public opinion and public policy.

James Townsend is an associate professor of Economics at the University of Winnipeg. His research interests include the economics of immigration and economic inequality.

Carolyn Hughes Tuohy is Professor Emeritus of Political Science and Senior Fellow in the School of Public Policy and Governance at the University of Toronto, and a Fellow of the Royal Society of Canada. She works in the area of comparative health and social policy and is the author of *Accidental Logics: the Dynamics of Change in the Health Care Arena in the United States, Britain and Canada* (1999). She is currently completely a study of strategies of policy change in health care in the US, the UK, the Netherlands, and Canada over the past twenty years.

Index

Note: page numbers in *italics* refer to figure or tables.

Abella Commission (1984), 366
Aboriginal peoples
   government transfers as percentage of income of Aboriginals, by area of residence, 171, *172*
   housing and poverty reduction programs (Quebec), 269
   negative attitudes towards, as weakening support for redistribution, 414
   as percentage of Canadian population, 170-71
   poverty, and need for welfare support, 171
   public perception, and racial stereotypes of, 172, 173, 180
   viewed as more reliant on welfare than immigrants, 166, 173-74, *176*
   welfare rates, general and on-reserve, *172*
Access for Ontarians with Disabilities Act (2005), 131-32
"active labour-market policies" (ALMPs)
   purpose, 55
   as replacement for passive unemployment benefits, 53-54
   and shift from Unemployment Insurance (UI) to Employment Insurance (EI), 82
Advantage Canada (Dept. of Finance), 83, 218, 228
Alberta
   correlates of Gini coefficient reduction by provincial transfers and income taxes (1993-2007), *397*
   poverty rates (1982-2007), *392*
   welfare cuts, before abolishment of CAP, 384-85
   workers' compensation, restraint (1990s), 386-87
Ambachtsheer, Keith, 328
American Association of Retired Persons (AARP), 127
American Federation of Labor–Congress of Industrial Organizations, 102

Annual Work Patterns Survey (AWPS) (Statistics Canada), 67
Australia
  health care hybridization, driven by strategic alliances, 293
  poverty rates, compared with Canada, 30
  total public social expenditure as percentage of GDP, 1960-2007, 5
Austria
  poverty rates, compared with Canada, 30
  total public social expenditure as percentage of GDP, 1960-2007, 5
Axworthy, Lloyd, 218, 220-21

Battle, Ken, 123-24
Bégin, Monique, 422
Belgium
  poverty rates, compared with Canada, 30
  total public social expenditure as percentage of GDP, 1960-2007, 5
Best Start program (Ontario), 59, 373
Bismarck, Otto von, 7
Bloc Québécois, 200, 203, 24, 422
Bologna agreement, 348, 352
Bonoli, Guiliano, 362, 376
Bouchard, Lucien, 257, 263, 264, 266, 275
British Columbia
  correlates of Gini coefficient reduction by provincial transfers and income taxes (1993-2007), 397
  poverty rates (1982-2007), 392
  welfare cuts (mid-1990s), 385
  workers' compensation, restrictions on, 387
British North America Act (1967), 47, 48
Bryden, Kenneth, 320
Bulloch, John, 103
bureaucratic politics
  new policy making, as centralized in PMO office and politicized, 215-30
  old policy making, as departmentally centred, 212-15
  public service, expected to support government agenda, 216
business
  advantage of centralized decision making by PMO and premiers, 94-95
  associations, as pluralistic, 103-4
  globalization, as exacerbation of differences between business and labour in Canada, 94
  and labour, absence of cooperation in Canada, 93-94, 111
  lobbying difficulty, of regional and global networks, 105-6
  and policy making, under neoliberalism and globalization, 99, 109-111
  See also globalization; *names of business organizations;* unions
Business Council of Australia, 111
Business Council on National Issues (BCNI), 103, 104, 109
Business Roundtable (US), 111

Caisse de dépôt et placement du Québec, 325
Caledon Institute of Social Policy, 108, 223
Campaign 2000, 127-28, 129, 223, 373
Canada
  decentralization, and politics of redistribution, 16-19
  economic gains, disproportionate to high-income earners, 2
  government orientation, from centrist to right, 205
  immigrants, percentage of population, 169
  multiculturalism, and redistribution, 165-91
  neoliberal policies, 12-13
  as "pluralist" economic system, 101

Index 435

political party system, and social policy, 188-93
poverty, population with after-tax income below 50 percent of median income (Quebec and Canada), 272-73
public opinion on social spending (1980-2005), 145-57
redistribution, new politics of, 1, 2, 12-19, 187
social policy, decentralization of, 17
territorial politics, 6-7
total public social expenditure as percentage of GDP, 1960-2007, 5
See also names of specific provinces; political party system, Canada; provinces
Canada Assistance Plan (CAP)
cancellation of, 53, 56, 384
childcare subsidies, 51, 360
disintegration of, 22-23, 52-53, 147
as example of old bureaucratic politics of redistribution, 214-15
as federal social program, 17
as Liberal Party social policy, 194
replacement by Canada Health and Social Transfer (CHST), 53, 147, 197, 243, 296, 345, 346, 370
and social service reform (1966), 49
Canada Child Tax Benefit (CCTB)
creation of (1997), 252
criteria for, 57
as federal benefit, 274
incremental change to, 222
purpose of, 23
as refundable tax credit, 342, 349
as replacement for Child Tax Benefit, 221
Canada Health Act (1984), 8, 295, 298
Canada Health and Social Transfer (CHST)
as replacement of Canada Assistance Program (CAP), 53, 147, 197, 243, 296, 345, 346, 370
split into Canada Health Transfer (CHT) and Canada Social Transfer (CST), 297
Canada Health Transfer (CHT), 297, 298, 345, 346
Canada Learning Bond, 221
Canada Pension Plan (CPP). See Canada/Quebec Pension Plan (C/QPP)
Canada Research Chairs, 348
Canada Revenue Agency (CRA)
delivery of redistributive benefits, 216, 228
See also tax-transfer system
Canada Social Transfer (CST), 345, 346
Canada Student Grant program, 352
Canada Supplementary Pension Plan (CSPP) (proposed), 328
Canada/Quebec Pension Plan (C/QPP)
creation of (1966), 49
as earnings-related pensions, 314
funding of, 319-20, 331
as income security programs, 7, 315-16
labour lobbying for increase in, 108
as Liberal Party social policy, 194
as percentage of seniors' income, 317
preservation, due to complex political coalition, 416
rate increases, 220, 324-27
as redistribution policy, 343
reform proposals, 313, 328
reinforcement with new investments (1990s), 312
retirement age, move to age 67, 326
shaped by Dept. of Finance, 224
shared characteristics, 259
Canada-US Free Trade Agreement (CUSFTA) (1987), 12, 76-77, 103, 365
Canadian Advisory Council on the Status of Women (CACSW), 120, 122
Canadian Association of Retired Persons (CARP), 108, 323, 328

Canadian Auto Workers (CAW), 102
Canadian Centre for Policy Alternatives (CCPA), 108
Canadian Chamber of Commerce (CCC), 103, 104
Canadian Council of Chief Executives (CCCE), 94, 101, 104, 106, 109-11
Canadian Council on Fair Taxation, 103
Canadian Council on Social Development (CCSD), 14, 108, 122, 124, 125, 127
Canadian Day Care Advocacy Association, 366
Canadian Election Study (CES), 192
Canadian Export Association, 104
Canadian Federation of Independent Business (CFIB), 94, 103, 104-5, 109
Canadian Federation of Voluntary Sector Networks, 132
Canadian Labour Congress (CLC)
 and Canadian Centre for Policy Alternatives (CCPA), 108
 and coalitions of citizen groups in municipal elections, 131
 on connection between government and corporate leaders, 110
 creation of (1956), 192
 lobby for expansion of C/QPP, 328
 loss of influence in policy making, 106
 "Municipalities Matters" campaign, 107-8
 relation with Quebec unions, 101-2
 "Retirement Security for Everyone" campaign, 108
 and "social movement unionism," 107
Canadian Labour Market and Productivity Centre, 106
Canadian Manufacturers and Exporters (CME), 104
Canadian Manufacturers Association (CMA), 103

Canadian Policy Research Networks, 14, 132
Canadian Teachers' Federation, 323
Canadian Volunteerism Initiative, 132
Canadian Welfare Council, 214
Carter Report (Canada, 1966), 336
CBC Vote Compass, 262
CCF. *See* Co-operative Commonwealth Federation (CCF)
CD Howe Institute, 223
Centre d'étude sur la pauvreté et l'exclusion, 269
Centre for Civic Governance, 108
Centre for Policy Alternatives, 223
Change to Win (CtW) federation, 102
Charest, Jean, 257, 265, 266
Charlottetown Accord, 124-25, 240
Charter of Rights and Freedoms, 123
Child and Elderly Benefits, Consultation Paper, 121
child benefits
 changes in (after 1993), 221-22
 correlates of Gini coefficient reduction by provincial transfers and income taxes (1993-2007), 397, 399
 correlates of Gini coefficient reduction with "union density" variable absent (1993-2007), 400
 determined by Dept. of Finance and Canada Revenue Agency, 224
 as displacing welfare for single mothers, 391
 emphasis on, 54
 importance of federal programs in redistribution, 234
 provinces, reduction of Gini co-efficient associated with, 404-6
 reasons for, 349
 and social investment perspective, 26
 tax benefits, progressive effects of (1990-2000), 244
 tax benefits, provinces with highest redistributive impact, 396

Index

tax benefits, role in reducing inequality, 390
tax credits, 346, 349-50, 386
See also Canada Child Tax Benefit (CCTB); childcare; children; National Child Benefit (NCB); Universal Child Care Benefit (UCCB)
child care. *See* childcare
Child Care Expense Deduction (CCED), 51
Child Disability Benefit, 221, 349
Child Poverty Action Group, 126-27
Child Tax Benefit (CCTB), 221
Child Tax Credit, 222, 226
childcare
    attempts at creation of universal access, 58-59
    Canadian public opinion on social spending, 142, *146*
    childcare bill (1988), killed by CSO collective action, 122
    facilities, support eliminated in favour of direct support to parents, 221
    federal-provincial bilateral agreements on early learning and, 128, 129
    as lagging behind economically advanced countries, 26
    liberal approach, and commercial operations, 362
    Liberal-NDP Accord (1985), on childcare as public service, 366
    Ontario, downloading of costs to municipalities, 127
    Ontario, "seamless day" for 4-5 year olds, 374, 375
    policies, possible reform directions, 352
    policies, social investment perspective on, 241
    Progressive Conservative bill (1987) not implemented, 122, 367-68
    public opinion on social spending on, 154, 156, *158, 159, 160*
    Quebec and Ontario, reasons for different approaches to, 361
    Quebec, daycare fees, 265
    social democratic approach, and universal access, 362
    tax deductions, 349, 360
    universal daycare (Quebec), 26, 266, 267, 360
    universal preschool, support for, 366-67
    universally accessible, advantages of, 360
    See also early childhood education and care (ECEC)
Childcare Advocacy Alliance of Canada (CCAAC), 366
Childcare Reform in Ontario: Setting the Stage (1991), 368
Childcare Resource and Research Unit, 223
children
    early learning and childcare (ELCC), 58, 59, 267
    education, emphasis on, 55
    and EI Family Supplement, 54
    government focus on child poverty, 128-29
    Ontario, commitment to ECEC agenda, 375
    poverty rates, compared with European countries, *30*
    poverty rates, decline of, 349
    Quebec social policy reforms, 266
    See also child benefits; childcare
Chrétien, Jean, 224, 322
Christian Democrats, 46
Christian right groups
    and Conservative social policy, 122, 131
    opposition to same-sex marriage, 131
Citizens' Forum on Canadian Unity (Spicer Commission), 125

Citizenship Branch, Dept. of Secretary of State, 119
civil society organizations (CSO)
  advocacy groups, viewed as "special interests," 125
  child poverty concerns, 134
  coalitions, limited capacity of, 130
  federal funding cuts, 116, 118, 120, 124, 129, 132-33, 134
  "golden" age (1970s-1985), 118-120
  government disregard of (1990-99), 124-28
  government lack of consultation on social policy (1985-89), 121-24
  immigrant services groups, 119
  lack of large mass membership advocacy organizations, 120-21, 124
  lack of media interest in, 123-24, 132
  Quebec, and implementation of ELEC program, 362-63
  role of, in democracy, 117
  schism between advocacy and service-providing groups, 118, 119
  service delivery by, 125, 132, 133
  shift of attention to provincial and urban governments, 131
  social enterprise by, 133
  vertical *vs.* horizontal dimension of representation, 117
  weakening of impact on social policy, 2-3, 14-15, 116, 117-18, 134, 416
Collectif pour un Québec sans pauvreté, 269
Columbia Institute, 108
Comité consultatif de lutte contre la pauvreté, 269, 270
comparative perspectives
  on Canadian health care policy, 287-94
  on conflict between unions and business, 403
  on new politics of redistribution, 9-12
  on policy change, 19-27
  on politics of social policy in welfare state, 415-17
  power resources in the Canadian party system (1940-93), 188-93
  redistribution rate (Gini coefficients) of Canadian provinces, 394-98
  on redistributive role of state, 9-12
Concerned Christians Canada, 131
Conseil du patronat du Québec (CPQ), 103, 104, 261
Consejo Mexicano de Hombres de Negocios, 111
Conservative governments, federal
  cap on Canada Assistance Plan (CAP), 22, 52
  changes to unemployment benefits, 23, 383
  child benefits, 59, 128, 129, 221, 372, 386
  and dominant theory approach to labour market policy, 83
  extension of Spouse's Allowance (1985), 8
  federal-provincial agreements on childcare, withdrawal of (2007), 26, 59, 129, 253, 374
  free trade agreements, 365
  funding cuts to advocacy organizations, 124, 134
  initiation of Hospital Insurance and Diagnostic Services Act (1957)
  initiation of Old Age Security (OAS) (1951), 194
  initiation of Working Income Tax Benefit (WITB), 219
  non-implementation of childcare bill, 122, 367-68
  party funding rule changes, 103
  policy drift under, 417
  proposed partial deindexation of Old Age Security (OAS) (1985), 21, 121-22, 321-22
  social programs not viewed as instrument of pan-Canadian unity, 421

Index

social spending compared with
 other parties, 149, *189*
strength of government's position
 (parliamentary seats), *193*, 198,
 201, 205
support of Christian right, 122, 131
tax cuts as priority, 24, 421
See also Conservative Party; Progressive Conservative Party
Conservative governments, provincial
 Alberta, social assistance cuts, 384
 Ontario, Best Start ELCC program initiative, 385
 Ontario, restrictions on funding of childcare, 370-71, 372
 Ontario, "workfare" imposition and welfare cuts, 371, 385
Conservative Party
 merger with Alliance (formerly Reform), 204
 policy shift to right, 200, 204
 viewed as right, anti-spending pole of political parties, 189
 See also Conservative governments, federal; Conservative governments, provincial; Progressive Conservative Party
Cooke Task Force, 366, 367
Co-operative Commonwealth Federation (CCF), 6, 45, 421
corporatism
 institutionalized horizontal bridges between associations, 101
 institutions, and resistance to retrenchment, 11
 and Organization of Business Interests project, 99
 policy making, cooperative role of labour, 96-97
Council of Canadians, 108
Council of Canadians with Disabilities, 108
Courchene, Thomas J., 363-64, 368, 372
Court Challenges Program, 123, 132

Denis, Solange, 321, 322, 323
Denmark
 poverty rates, compared with Canada, 30
 total public social expenditure as percentage of GDP, 1960-2007, 5
Department of Finance
 concentration of policy capacity within, under new bureaucratic politics, 215, 228
 cost containment, and domination of social policy by, 122
 on fiscal crisis due to federal deficit (1995), 201
 as focus of redistributive policy making, 216-17
 non-partisan policy expertise of, 229-30
 as policy designer in politics of redistribution, 16, 211, 217, 218-19, 220, 222, 223
 as policy restrainer, in old bureaucratic politics of policy making, 211, 214
 Tax Policy Branch, intertwining of redistributive policy and tax system, 217
Department of Health and Welfare, 120
Department of National Health and Welfare, 229
Dept. of Secretary of State, Citizenship Branch, 119
Diefenbaker, John, 194
Disability Tax Savings Account, 222
disabled persons. *See* persons with disabilities
doctors. *See* health care, Canada
Dodge, David, 322
drugs, prescription
 changes in public drug programs to less redistributive, 294
 cost, and lack of coverage by universal program, 24-25
 drug share of total health spending, 294

as outside single-payer health care model, 52, 301-2
Quebec "pharmacare," 25

Early Childhood Development Fund (Ontario), 372
Early Childhood Development Initiative, 128
early childhood education and care (ECEC)
- Ontario, insufficient political support for, 363
- Ontario, politics of, 365-76
- public support for, 360
- Quebec, expanded funding for, 267
- Quebec, political mobilization of implementation of, 362-63
- Quebec, supported by coalition of government and social groups, 362
- as social investment, 55

early learning and child care (ELCC)
- Ontario, Best Start program, 59
- proposed federal-provincial agreement, unsuccessful, 58, 59, 221, 251-53

Early Years Initiative (Ontario), 368-69, 374
Economic Council of Canada, 337
"economic utilitarian" hypothesis, 144
education
- differentials in wages and employment, 69-71
- federal research funding, 348
- policies, possible reform directions, 352
- postsecondary, as provincial responsibility, 347-48
- postsecondary, student grants, 353
- preschool, universal, 366-67
- and redistribution policies, 348-49
- Registered Education Savings Plan (RESP), 348
- tax credits, 348

unionization rates of industries, and education level, 75
See also human capital; social investment perspective
elderly. *See* seniors
electoral slack
- definition, 16
- effect on social policy, 23
- as factor in retrenchment of welfare state, 188, 203
- Liberal government (1993-97), 198-99

electoral systems, effect on welfare state
- first-past-the-post, 11, 419
- majoritarian, 421
- proportional representation, 11, 419

employment
- education, differentials in wages and employment, 69-71
- employment rates, Canada *vs.* US (1980-2008), 69
- female (Quebec), 266
- instability, 69
- and life-long learning, 83
- non-standard, 69, *70*, 79, 85
- pay equity, to correct gender-based earning discrepancies (Quebec), 269
- reduced demand for unskilled workers, 84-86
- skill-based demand shift in US (1980s), 78-79
- skilled worker shortage, anticipated, 418
- technological change, and skill-based demand, 80-81
- training and work integration measures (Quebec), 269
- unemployment rates, Canada *vs.* US (1980-2008), 67-68
- work experience, and employment rates, 72
- *See also* Employment Insurance (EI); labour market; technological

change; Unemployment Insurance (UI)
Employment Insurance (EI)
"active labour-market policies" (ALMPs), emphasis on, 53, 54-55, 82
changes, limited impact on inequality ratios, 243-44
compared with Quebec's Parental Insurance Plan, 268
creation of, 53
critique of "passive" benefits of, 53
cuts to, 22
disparity in redistributive impact in different provinces, 393-95
education and training policy, 66, 67
eligibility changes (1995), 197, 354
Family Supplement, 54
as federal responsibility, 60, 274
as focus of policy attention, 230
as income security program, 7
increasing restrictions of, 344
as less redistributive since 1980s, 390, 402
maternity benefits (1971), 51
policies, and assumed effect of technological change on labour force, 66
policies, possible reform directions, 351
policies, shaped by Human Resources and Skills Development Canada, 224
by province, reduction of Gini coefficient associated with, 390, *404-6*
as redistribution policy, 342
reduced impact offset by other elements of tax-transfer system, 382
replacement rate reduction (1971-96), 384
retrenchment, and requirements relating to alternative employment, 23
self-employed, inconsistency of coverage, 344
shift from Unemployment Insurance (UI), 81, 82, 88, 196-97
Environics
on trends in Canadian public opinion on social spending, 145-47
Equality, Security, and Community Survey (ESCS) (2002-3), 173
Esping-Anderson, Gøsta
on allocation of welfare production, 46
on Canada as "liberal" welfare state, 4
factors shaping welfare regimes, 44
on the "Good Society," 54
typology of welfare state, 97, 142, 314-15
ethnic diversity. *See* multicultural diversity
Europe
Gini coefficient for selected countries, compared with US, 395
negative attitudes towards immigrants receiving welfare, 167-68
total public social expenditure as percentage of GDP, 1960-2007, 5
European Roundtable of Industrialists, 111
evangelical groups. *See* Christian right groups

families
decline in earnings, effect on, 25-26
EI Family Supplement, 54
family policy (Quebec), 267-70
median incomes (1980-2003), 148, *149*
parental leave (Quebec), 267
universal family allowance (Quebec), 267
See also children; women
Family Allowance Program (FAP) clawback, 221

as income security program, 7
as Liberal Party social policy, 193-94
reduction, and compensation through progressive refundable tax credits, 225
universal flat-rate, 48
Federal Superannuities Association, 328
federalism
   classical, 237, 240-41
   joint-decision model, 237, 241
   predominance in redistributive impact of policies, 244-45
   shared-cost model, 237, 241
   See also provinces; territorial politics
Federation of Canadian Municipalities, 108
Feldstein, Martin, 423
feminist movement
   Ontario, support for childcare, 365-66
   Quebec, and coalition of social movements, 261
Fernandez, Juan, 314
A Fine Balance: Safe Pensions, Affordable Plans, Fair Rules (Ontario Expert Commission on Pensions), 327
Finland
   poverty rates, compared with Canada, *30*
   support for redistribution, 143-44
   total public social expenditure as percentage of GDP, 1960-2007, *5*
Fitness Tax Credit, 349
Flaherty, Jim, 219, 329
food banks, 53
France
   as corporatist welfare state, difficulty of integrating immigrants into economy, 167
   health care hybridization, driven by strategic alliances, 293
   poverty rates, compared with Canada, *30*
   support for redistribution, 144

   total public social expenditure as percentage of GDP, 1960-2007, *5*
   unemployment rates, compared with US and Germany, *77*, 78
From Bronze to Gold: A Blueprint for Canadian Leadership in a Transforming World (CCCE, 2006), 109-10
From Unemployment Insurance to Employment Insurance (Human Resources Development Canada), 81

Germany
   Bismarckian pension plan, 313
   as corporatist welfare state, difficulty of integrating immigrants into economy, 167
   health care hybridization, driven by strategic alliances, 293
   and introduction of welfare state by Bismarck, 7
   poverty rates, compared with Canada, *30*
   support for redistribution, 144
   total public social expenditure as percentage of GDP, 1960-2007, *5*
   unemployment rates, compared with France and US, *77*, 78
Getting Our Acts Together: Pension Reform in Alberta and British Columbia (Joint Expert Panel on Pension Standards), 327
Gini coefficient
   after tax income of family units (Ontario and Quebec), *271*
   and "cumulative redistributive effect," 195, *196*
   definition, 382, 388
   disposable income, Canada, 423
   income inequality and redistribution in Canada and Quebec (1979-2004), *33*
   lack of monitoring and management of, by government, 26-27, 417

poverty rates and inequality, selected OECD countries (2004), *30*
reduction, through government taxes and transfers (1979-2006), *247*
Global Champion or Falling Star? The Choice Canada Must Make (CCCE, 2000), 109
globalization
  Canada, vulnerability to, 12
  and dominant theory of employment demand shift, 83
  economic policy making under, 98-99
  as exacerbation of differences between business and labour in Canada, 94
  government approach to, 105
  influence on redistribution policies, 354
  and marginalization of labour from policy process, 13
  and neoliberal assault on welfare state, 9, 45-47
  policy making, by regional and global networks of public officials, 105-6, 111
  resistance to retrenchment, in countries with corporatist institutions, 11
  trade, as explanation for employment demand shift, 82, 87, 88
  See also North American Free Trade Agreement (NAFTA) (1994); technological change
Godbout, Luc, 271-72
Goodale, Ralph, 219
Goods and Services Tax (GST), 24, 341
GST/HST Credit, 274
Guaranteed Annual Income (GAI) Program, 223
Guaranteed Income Supplement (GIS)
  age of eligibility raised to 67, 330
  funding of, 319
  as income security program, 7, 49, 274, 314, 315, 331
  labour lobbying for increase in, 108
  as Liberal Party social policy, 194
  as likely target for deficit-reduction, 330
  as redistribution policy, 343
Guelph Civic League, 108

Hacker, Jacob, 416
Hall, Emmett, 194
Häusermann, Silja, 264
Hayek, Frederick, 425
Health Accord (2004), 252
health care
  as core program in Canadian welfare state, 285
  cuts to federal-provincial transfers and provincial budgets (1990s), 286
  design of Canadian health care state, 287-88
  entrepreneurial innovation, 301, 305
  fixated on federal transfers rather than system change, 295
  government spending on, 21, 288-89, *290*
  as hybrid system, 286, 289-94, 305
  income, and health status, 302-3
  increasing costs of, at expense of other social programs, 345-46
  long-term care, 293, 294
  "national health service" model, 288
  new models of primary care, 304, 305
  non-universal public subsidies, 287
  policy drift, 293-94
  policy priorities, 303-6
  prescription drugs, 268-69, 294, 301-2, 304-5
  private clinics, 295
  reinvestment and innovation in, 286-87
  as residual welfare-state model, 287
  separate provincial/territorial health insurance plans, 295
  and shared-cost federalism, 241

single-payer system, and federal-provincial relations, 294-99
single-payer system, profession-state accommodation, 298-301
"social insurance" model, 288, 291
support for, and impact of perceptions of immigrants and Aboriginals, 178, *179*
universal, as Liberal Party social policy, 194
universal, creation of, 7-8, 48, 49, 50, 302
universal, in contrast with US privatized care, 142
waiting times, 297, 298, 300, 301, 302
See also Canada Health Act (1984); Canada Health and Social Transfer (CHST); Canada Health Transfer (CHT)
Health Council of Canada, 298
Healy, Teresa, 110
Hospital Insurance and Diagnostic Services Act (Canada, 1957), 50, 194, 295
human capital
building, 10
early childhood education and care, investing in, 55, 56, 59, 128
education and training of workers, 66, 82-83, 86, 88, 238, 372
higher education, tax credits for, 348
and parental employment, investing in, 55
physical capital, complementary investing in, 67
See also education; social investment perspective
Human Resources and Skills Development Canada
as advocates of redistribution policies, 211
data on economic trends, correlated with public opinion on social spending, 148-54
responsible for employment benefit policies, 224
as successor to National Health and Welfare, 16
Human Resources Development Canada (HRDC), 129, 228, 229

ideas/ideational change
and Canadian policy response, 81-83, 88
and federalism, 43, 56-57
and new politics of redistribution in Canada, 9-10, 12-13, 26, 45-47, 59, 60, 336-40
defined, 9
problems with, 83-85
and technological change, 80-81, 87, 88
See also liberalism; neoliberalism; social investment perspective
identity politics, growth of, 14
immigrants
Canada, percentage of population, 169
economic immigrants, 170
ethnic diversity, and sense of common community, 165
ethnic diversity, as strengthening support for redistribution, 415-16
immigration, as federal responsibility, 60
welfare use by, 169-70, *174*
income
capital, taxing of, 337
distribution, lack of government information on, 212, 223
family market income, and disposable income (1976-2010), 28, *29*
family market income, by percentile (1976-2007), *28*
family market income, Canada and Quebec, *33*
final, definition, 387
Gini coefficients, after-tax income of Ontario and Quebec families, *271*

Index 445

linked to health, 302-3
market, definition, 387
market inequality, reduction of Gini coefficient associated with specific social programs, *404-6*
percentage of population with after-tax income below 50 percent of median income (Canada and Quebec), 272-73
redistribution effect, as difference between market and final income, 387
redistribution, fragmented policies on, 223
redistributive impact of transfer programs, shift from lower to middle quintiles, 246-248
See also income tax; inequality; tax-transfer system

income tax
capital income, possible reform directions, 350-51
deductions, conversion to refundable tax credits, 353
negative income tax, 241, 336, 338, 342, 350
provincial, devolving of tax room to, 341
rate structure evolution to less progressive, 341, 414
taxes, correlates of Gini coefficient reduction by provincial transfers and income taxes (1993-2007), *397, 399*
taxes, correlates of Gini coefficient reduction with "union density" variable absent (1993-2007), *400*
tax-preferred treatment of savings, 337-38
See also tax-transfer system

Income Tax Act (Canada, 1980 amendment), 196

inequality
acceptance by business community, 110

and alignment of middle class with top or bottom of economic ladder, 419
avoiding, through investment in human and physical capital, 86-87, 88
continued growth in, possible risks, 424
and democracy, risks for quality of, 425
diminishment of (Quebec), 274
and dominant theory of employment demand shift, 82-83, 420, 423-24
education and training, effect on, 67
family market income, and disposable income (1976-2010), 28, *29*
family market income, by percentile (1976-2007), *28*
family market income, Canada and Quebec, *33*
growth, inability to address through redistribution policies, 335
higher after-tax income inequality after 2000, 389
income, of Canadian families (1980-2003), 148, *149*
increase, and erosion of progressivity of tax system at top, 341, 353
increase, causes of, 32-33
increase, in both market and after-tax income during 1990s, 387
increase, in 1990s, 27
lack of government response to, 3, 26
market income, changes contained by taxes and transfers (1980s-1994), 195, 198
market income, increase in, 417-18
and "Occupy Movement," 417
Pareto *vs.* maximin principles, 423
Quebec, economic disparities between French and English Quebeckers, 259-60
reasons for, 27, 335
reduction, resulting from government transfers, 246-47

and skilled-unskilled wage differential, 83-84
and supply-side policies, 339-40
use of tax transfers to reduce disparities, 381, 382
viewed as driven by skills shortage, 238, 340
See also Gini coefficient; poverty
inheritance taxes, 337, 339, 341, 353
Institute for Christian Values, 131
International Monetary Fund, 424
Investing in People: Creating a Human Capital Society for Ontario (2004), 372
Investment Dealers Association, 323
Italy
    pension plan, 313
    poverty rates, compared with Canada, *30*
    total public social expenditure as percentage of GDP, 1960-2007, *5*

Jobs Ontario, 368, 371
Jobs Study (OECD, 1994), 10, 417
Joint Expert Panel on Pension Standards, 327
"Just Society," 119

Kesselman, Jonathan, 328
"Krugman/OECD" hypothesis, 81

labour
    and business, absence of cooperation in Canada, 93-94
    changes in engagement with state, under neoliberalism and globalization, 106-9
    collective action against capitalist class, in power resources theory (PRT), 97
    cooperative role, in corporatist policy making, 97
    engagement in direct action initiatives with relevant social partners, 111
    labour market policies, subject to policy drift and inaction, 418
    labour market reforms (Quebec), 268-70
    lack of cooperation with business on redistribution, 111
    lobbying difficulty, of regional and global networks, 105-6
    opposition to neoliberal globalization, 94, 106
    policy reforms, impact of partisanship and union density on, 383
    and policy making, under globalization, 99
    shift to "social movement unionism," 106-7
    skill premium and employment rates, 70, *71*
    See also unions
Labour Force Survey (LFS) (Statistics Canada), 67, 223
labour market
    Canada, unemployment rates, 67-68
    de-unionization, and decline in real wages, 74-76
    dominant theory, alternative views to, 85-87
    dominant theory, of employment demand shift, 80-85
    education, differentials in wages and employment, 69-71, 72-74
    globalization and technological change, assumed effect on, 65-66
    US, unemployment rates, 67-68
    work experience, and employment rates, 72
    See also employment; unions
Labour Market Activity Surveys (LMAS), 67
Labour Market Agreements, federal-provincial, 269
labour unions. *See* unions
Lalonde, Marc, 422
Law Reform Commission, 132
Lesage, Jean, 260

Lévesque, René, 261
Liberal governments, federal
   abolishment of Canada Assistance Plan (CAP), 22-23, 53
   child benefits, 221, 386
   creation of Canada Health and Social Transfer (CHST), 296
   creation of Employment Insurance (EI), 383
   economic policies (Purple Book) and dominant theory, 81-82
   federal-provincial agreements on childcare, 58, 128, 252-53, 372-74
   proposed replacement of OAS and GIS, 21, 323-24
   restoration of full indexation of OAS and GIS, 322
   social program cuts by, 16, 200-3
   social program reforms, 44-45, 49
   social programs and nation building, 7
   social spending compared with other parties, 149, 189-90
   unemployment policy reforms, 53, 383-84
Liberal governments, provincial
   British Columbia, unemployment reforms, 385
   Ontario, Best Start ELCC program, 53, 59
   Ontario, childcare proposals, 365-68, 373-74
   Quebec, and redistribution policy, 257, 260, 265-66
   Quebec, as centre-right, 257
   Quebec, unemployment policy reforms, 385
Liberal Party
   centre role in Canadian party system, 190
   decline of, 192-93, 204-5
   parliamentary role (seats) (1945-2008), 192-93, 198-99
   shift to right on social policy, 204
   social policies, 193-94
   See also Liberal governments, federal; Liberal governments, provincial
liberal welfare state. *See* welfare state regimes
liberalism
   classical, 10
   social, 10
   See also neoliberalism
Little, Bruce, 324-25, 326
Luxembourg Income Study, 195

Macdonald Commission on the Economic Union and Development Prospects for Canada, 217
Maioni, Antonia, 45
Manitoba
   correlates of Gini coefficient reduction by provincial transfers and income taxes (1993-2007), *397*
Manley, John, 109
Marchand, Jean, 422
Marsh Report (Canada, 1943), 48
Marshall, T.H., 165
Martin, Keith, 323
Martin, Paul, 201, 203, 218, 252, 322, 324, 325
Marx, Karl, 425
maternity leave, 221
"maximin" principle, 423
McDonald, Marci, 131
Medical Care Act (Canada, 1966), 50, 295
medicare. *See* health care
Meech Lake Accord, 123, 240
middle class
   and federal income maintenance policy (late 1990s), 245
   inequality, and real income stagnation, 2, 419-20
   redistributive politics, and alignment with top or bottom of economic ladder, 419
Miller, David, 168
minimum wages, Canada, 30

Ministry of State for Social
  Development, 229
Mintz, Jack, 223, 329
Mirrlees, James, 338
Modernizing Income Security for
  Working-Age Adults (MISWAA),
  219
Monty, Jean C., 104
multicultural diversity
  difference in Canadian attitudes towards immigrants and Aboriginal
    peoples, 166
  impact on public attitudes towards
    redistribution, 15
  interpersonal trust, decline in ethnically diverse neighbourhoods,
    168
  national identity, as cultural glue,
    168-69
  and sustainability of welfare state,
    165
  See also Aboriginal peoples
Multilateral Framework Agreement on
  Early Learning and Child Care
  (2003), 58, 59, 104, 128, 221, 251-53, 373, 374
Mustard, Fraser, 375

National Aboriginal Health Organization, 14
National Action Committee on the
  Status of Women (NAC)
  and anti-poverty coalitions, 122
  funding cuts, 125
  internal challenge by women of colour, 126
  lobby for childcare as necessary for
    women's equality, 365, 366
  opposition to Charlottetown Accord,
    125
  opposition to Meech Lake Accord,
    123
National Anti-Poverty Organization
  (NAPO), 122, 124, 125, 127

National Child Benefit (NCB)
  creation of (1999), 128
  features, 128
  as federal social program, 17
  and incremental change to child
    benefits, 222
  indexing to inflation (2000), 197
  and intergovernmental relations,
    56-57, 221
  and interprovincial relations, 243,
    246
  and provincial clawback of social
    assistance, 372, 386
  and social investment perspective,
    26, 250-51
National Child Benefit Supplement
  (NCBS), 57-58, 349
National Children's Agenda, 128
National Children's Alliance, 128, 130,
  372
National Council of Welfare (NCW),
  14, 120, 121
National Health and Welfare (Canada),
  16, 211, 228
National Welfare Grants, 120
NDP. *See* New Democratic Party
  (NDP)
neoliberalism
  branding of social policy groups as
    "special interests," 116
  Canada, vulnerability to, 12-13
  globalization, and assault on welfare
    state, 45-47
  and inequality, 419
  Ontario, opposed to ECEC policy,
    370
  resistance to retrenchment, in
    countries with corporatist institutions, 11
  and restructuring of welfare state,
    9-10
  viewed by labour as threat to policies
    aimed at reducing inequality, 94,
    107

weaknesses of social policy of, particularly for middle class, 420
See also Conservative governments; social investment perspective
neoliberalism, social investment perspective
  lack of federal response to, 26
  to meet challenges of globalization and technological change, 10
  as varying by country, 10
Netherlands
  health care reform, by alliances of key actors, 292
  health care, transition from social insurance to universal mandatory private insurance model, 291, 292
  negative attitude towards immigrants receiving welfare, 167
  poverty rates, compared with Canada, 30
  total public social expenditure as percentage of GDP, 1960-2007, 5
New Brunswick
  correlates of Gini coefficient reduction by provincial transfers and income taxes (1993-2007), 397
New Democratic Party (NDP)
  collapse of support for (1993), 200, 204
  declining support of labour, 102
  electoral resurgence (1997, 2111), 201, 205
  emphasis on social spending, 148
  historical levels of support, 191-92
  Ontario, ECEC plans restricted by fiscal restraints, 368, 369-70
  opposed to new seniors benefit to replace OAS and GIS (1996), 323
  and power resource theory of welfare state in Canada, 6, 45
  as successor to Co-operative Commonwealth Federation (CCF), 102
  and union movement, *191*, 192
  viewed as left, pro-spending pole of political parties, 189
New Directions for Childcare (Ontario, 1987), 367, 369
A New Framework for Economic Policy (Purple Book) (Canada, Dept. of Finance), 81, 82-83, 202
New Frontiers: Building a 21st Century Canada-United States Partnership in North America (CCCE, 2004), 110
"New Social Movements," 119
New Zealand
  health care hybridization, driven by strategic alliances, 293
Newfoundland
  correlates of Gini coefficient reduction by provincial transfers and income taxes (1993-2007), *397*
Nippon Keidanren (Japan), 111
North American Competitiveness Council, 110
North American Free Trade Agreement (NAFTA) (1994)
  and economic changes due to globalization, 103
  effect of imports on Canadian employment rates and wages, 76-77
  and neoliberalism, 106
  and new politics of redistribution, 12
  opposition to, by civil society organizations, 123
North American Security and Prosperity Initiative (SPI), 110
Norway
  poverty rates, compared with Canada, 30
  total public social expenditure as percentage of GDP, 1960-2007, 5
Nova Scotia
  correlates of Gini coefficient reduction by provincial transfers and income taxes (1993-2007), *397*

Occupy Movement
  focus on income of top one percent, 27, 417
  on gap in wealth, 2
OECD. *See* Organisation for Economic Cooperation and Development (OECD)
Old Age Security (OAS)
  age of eligibility, 49, 330
  clawback of benefits, from high-income seniors (1989), 321-22
  creation of (1952), 48
  funding of, 319
  as income security program, 7, 274
  labour lobbying for increase in, 108
  as Liberal Party social policy, 194
  as likely target for deficit-reduction, 330
  as part of first pillar of Canadian retirement income system, 315, 331
  as percentage of seniors' income, 317
  proposal to replace OAS and GIS with new seniors benefit (1996), 323
  as redistribution policy, 343
  resistance to efforts to retrench (1980s, 1990s), 312
  as universal benefit, 314
  universality, assaults on, 225, 321-24
Ontario
  assumption of federal solutions to social issues, 363-64
  childcare, politics of, 18, 363-77
  correlates of Gini coefficient reduction by provincial transfers and income taxes (1993-2007), *397*
  early childhood education and care (ECEC), reasons for lack of implementation by, 363
  poverty rates (1982-2007), *392*
  Premier's Council, 365
  tax transfers, favouring middle income quintiles, *249, 250*
  welfare benefit increases (1980s), 385
  workers' compensation, restrictions on, 387
  "workfare" imposition and welfare cuts, 385
Ontario Coalition for Better Childcare (OCBCC), 363-64, 366, 370, 371, 377
Ontario Expert Commission on Pensions, 327
Ontario Federation of Labour, 363
Ontario Municipal Employees Retirement System, 325
Ontario Teachers' Pension Plan, 326
Ontario Women's Directorate, 366
Ontario Works, 371
Organisation for Economic Cooperation and Development (OECD)
  critique of passive social benefits, such as UI and welfare, 53
  on effects of high inequality on social and political stability, 424-25
  on inequality surge, and reduced redistributive capacity of tax-benefit systems, 417
  Jobs Strategy, 66
  Jobs Study, 10, 82
  neoliberal philosophy of, 10, 12
  promotion of tax credits for low-income earners, 59
  public social expenditure, impact of recession of 2008, 5-6
  and Quebec social policy reforms, 266
  on redistributive impact of tax-transfer system, mid-1980s to mid-1990s, 1
  total public social expenditure as percentage of GDP, 1960-2007, *5*
Organization of Business Interests project, 99-100
Osberg, Lars, 194, 239, 423, 424

Panel on Violence against Women, 125
Parental Insurance Plan (Quebec), 268
parental leave, 221
Pareto principle, 423
Parizeau, Jacques, 263
Parti québécois, 17, 257, 263
path dependency
    inability to explain decline of influence of civil society organizations, 118
    and nature and processes of institutional change, 416
    Old Age Security (OAS) as example of, 312
    and resilience of policy structures, 19
    See also Pierson, Paul
pensions
    Bismarckian systems, Europe, 313
    constraint on provision by private corporations, under globalization, 420
    contributions in selected countries (1995), *319*
    funding models, 317-19
    retrenchment, more likely in large public pension systems, 314
    workplace, decline in, 344
    See also Canada/Quebec Pension Plan (C/QPP); Old Age Security (OAS); pensions, Canada; seniors
pensions, Canada
    expectation of senior supplementation with workplace pensions and own savings, 331
    incremental approach to reform, 223
    as international success story, 315
    and joint-decision federalism, 241
    OAS and GIS funded from general revenues, 331
    policies, possible reform directions, 351-52
    pooled retirement savings plans (PRSP), 313
    redistributive character of, 316-17, 342
    reform efforts (1980-90s), 320-24
    resistance to retrenchment efforts (1980-1990s), 315
    retrenchment, raising age of eligibility for OAS and GIS to 67, 314
    as security against poverty and income security, 331
    shift from defined benefit to defined contribution, 328
    stability, and system maintenance, 19, 21-22, 312
    three pillars of, 315-16
    workplace, decline of, 25, 313, 328
persons with disabilities
    benefits, changes to, 221
    Child Disability Benefit, 221, 349
    disability benefits, as stand-alone tax transfer system, 339
    disability support, creation of, 48
    Disability Tax Savings Account, 222
    Ontario, movement of, 131-32
pharmaceuticals. See drugs, prescription
physicians. See health care, Canada
Pierson, Paul, 416
    on "locked-in" social programs, 19
    on "path dependency," of well-established welfare state institutions, 312-13, 324
    on "politics of austerity," 320
    on power resource theory and the welfare state, 10
    See also path dependency
policy change
    defined, 3
    federal transfer programs, and mitigation of impact of retrenchment, 23
    political contestation, 20
    "punctuated equilibrium," 20
    and role of federalism, 237
    social assistance, cuts to, 22-23
    social investment perspective, 237-38, 239
    "social policy by stealth," 322
    tax system, as less progressive, 24

and territorial politics, 235-37, 239-40
See also names of specific programs
policy drift
  as compounding problem of redistributive fade, 414
  defined, 3
  effect on family market income inequality, 32
  effect on social programs, 24-27
  fading of program effectiveness through, 20
  health care (Canada), 286, 293-94
  of labour market policies, 418
  pension reform, 327-30
  in workplace pensions and personal retirement savings, 313
policy making
  advocates, 16, 211, 212, 213, 215
  communicators, 211, 215, 217
  as confusing for public, 227
  corporatist approach, 95, 96-97
  delivery agents, 217
  designers, 211, 217, 218
  fragmented, 223-25
  gatekeepers, 16, 211, 212, 213-14, 215
  as ideologically driven, 230
  incremental, 218, 220-23
  under new bureaucratic politics, 215-30
  new social risks, and dominant approach, 362
  obscure, to reduce political resistance, 225
  old bureaucratic politics, as departmentally centred, 212-215
  opportunistic, 218, 219-20
  outside influences on, 216, 217
  pluralist approach, 95-96
  power resources theory approach, 97-98, 187-88
  restrainers, 16, 211, 212, 214, 215
  supporters, 211, 217
  See also policy change; policy drift; redistribution policies

political party system, Canada
  "brokerage" theory, 382, 384
  correlates of Gini coefficient reduction with "union density" variable absent, *400*
  evolution towards left-right division, 421
  impact of political party ideology on redistribution policies, 398-402, 403
  left political parties, resistance to retrenchment of welfare state, 10
  shift to right, 15-16
  See also electoral systems, effect on welfare state; *names of political parties*
Polyani, Karl, 9
Pooled Retirement Savings Plans (PRSP), 313, 329-30
poverty
  child poverty, shift of focus by advocacy groups, 126-27
  cycle of, and "active labour market policies" (ALMPs), 55, 57
  decline in 1970s, 4
  diminishment of (Quebec), 274
  low-income cut-off (LICO), 29-31, *31*
  low-income measure (LIM), 29, *31*
  Ontario, civil society organization push for poverty reduction, 375
  percentage of population with after-tax income below 50 percent of median income (Quebec and Canada), 272-73
  public opinion on social spending on, 152, 153, *158, 159, 160*
  rates, compared with European countries, 28-29, *30*
  rates for largest provinces (1982-2007), *392*
  rates, impact of non-labour market transfers, 391-93
  rates, measurement of, 212
  rates of Canadian seniors, as among lowest of OECD nations, 315

single-parent families, 359
stability of, 2
See also Campaign 2000
Poverty Action Plan (Quebec), 269
power resource theory (PRT)
  and Canadian labour market reform policies, 383
  characteristics, 44, 187-88
  and collective action of labour against capitalist class, 97
  as explanation for expansive welfare states, 6
  on importance of labour movement relationship with political party, 102
  on reasons for resistance to retrenchment of welfare state, 10
Prime Minister's Office (PMO)
  and centralization of authority, 105, 215
  centralized decision making as advantage to business, 94-95
  decisions on major expenditures made by, not formal Cabinet decision-making processes, 224
  as focus of redistributive policy making, 216-17, 228
  as "gatekeeper" in politics of redistribution, 16, 211, 214
  as political communicator of policies, 211, 217, 218, 220, 228
Prince Edward Island
  correlates of Gini coefficient reduction by provincial transfers and income taxes (1993-2007), *397*
Prince, Michael, 323-24
Privy Council Office (PCO)
  and centralization of authority, 105
  as focus of redistributive policy making, 216-17
  as "gatekeeper" in politics of redistribution, 16
  as political communicator of policies, 217
  as redistribution policy communicator, 211
  as redistribution policy gatekeeper, 16, 211
Progressive Conservative Party
  government position (1945-2008), 204
  merger with Alliance (formerly Reform Party), 204
  resurgence in 1997 election, 201
  See also Conservative government; Conservative Party
Promises to Keep (Nova Scotia Pension Review Panel), 327, 329
provinces
  centralized decision making as advantage to business, 94-95
  correlates of Gini coefficient reduction by provincial transfers and income taxes (1993-2007), *397*
  decentralization and "provincialization" of social policy, 239
  "democratic class struggle" by left parties and labour movements, 382-83
  federal transfers for welfare, health, and education, 345-46
  Gini coefficient standard deviation, reduction across provinces, 243, *244*
  inequality, reduction of Gini coefficient associated with specific social programs, *404-6*
  inequality, variance in use of tax-transfer system for reduction of, 382
  postsecondary education, responsibility for, 347-48
  redistributive impact of provincial transfers, increasing diversity of, 243
  reduction of Gini coefficient associated with specific social programs, *404-6*
  social program responsibilities, 342

taxes, as less progressive, 354
territorial politics, and competitive state building, 235-37
variance in public support for welfare, 177
public opinion
  contextual effects on, 143
  influences on attitudes towards redistribution, 143-45
  on social spending, 142-57
Public Prescription Drug Insurance Plan (Quebec), 268-69
public service. *See* bureaucratic politics
Purple Book. *See A New Framework for Economic Policy* (Purple Book) (Canada, Dept. of Finance)
Putnam, Robert, 168

Quebec
  birth rate increases, 275
  child benefits, broadening of, 246
  childcare, political mobilization of implementation, 362-63, 376
  childcare, universal, 26
  civil society organizations, strength of, 257-58, 261
  Employment Insurance (EI) benefits, greater redistribution compared with other provinces, 393, 394
  employment rate, overall and women, 274
  family policy, reforms in, 267-70
  and federal social policy, 422
  feminist movement, 261
  Gini coefficient (1989), 389
  inequality, Gini coefficient (1989), 389
  inequality, state intervention in addressing, 260
  labour market reforms, 268-70
  linguistic equality, 260, 261
  new redistribution framework (1996-2006), 262
  objection to C/QPP cuts (1990s), 326

Old Age Security, acceptance of (1952), 48
patronage, addressing, 259, 260-61
perceptions of immigrants as welfare-dependent, 176
"pharmacare," 25
politics of identity, and competition with federal government over allegiance of citizens, 257
population with after-tax income below 50 percent of median income (Quebec and Canada), 272-73
poverty alleviation, though tax transfers to families, 274
poverty and social exclusion law, 269
poverty rates (1982-2007), *392*
poverty rates, lack of increase since 1980, 393
poverty, resistance to rise of inequality and, 256
and power resource theory of welfare state in Canada, 45
Quebec Pension Plan (QPP), establishment of (1966), 49, 236, 259
redistribution, comparison with other provinces, 395, 396
redistribution policies, challenges posed to federal government, 239, 240
redistribution policies, focussed on families with children, 271
redistributive impact of provincial transfer programs (2000-7), 244-45
redistributive reforms (from mid-1990s), 256-58
referendum (1995), 239, 240, 263, 265, 322
reformation of political institutions, 262
social democracy, and new social policies, 25, 259
social policy, autonomy of, 17, 236-37, 239, 240, 258-59, 363

social policy reform, and coalition politics, 263-66, 275-76
tax policies, as offset to increase in income market inequality, 32, *33*
tax transfers, favouring middle-income quintiles, 247-48, *249, 250*
taxes, lower tax burden for families with children, 272
territorial politics, and policy change, 236-37
unions, 101, 107
welfare benefits and criteria, collaboration between successive governments, 385-86
workers' compensation, reforms, 387
See also Quiet Revolution (Quebec)
Quebec Parental Insurance Plan, 236, 265
Quebec Pension Plan (QPP), 49, 236, 259
Quebec summit (March 1996), 264
Quebec summit (October 1996), 264
Quiet Revolution (Quebec), 50, 259, 260-62

Radwanski, George, 366
Rawls, John, 423
Reagan, Ronald, 8, 10, 339
REAL Women, 122, 125
redistribution
  alternative rationales, 339
  benefits, delivered through tax-transfer system, 211
  business community, acceptance of inequality by, 110
  children, emphasis on benefits for, 54
  civil society, weakening of impact on social policy, 116, 117-18
  corporatist approach, 95, 96-97
  dominant theory, 80-81
  "economic utilitarian" hypothesis, 144
  factors in changes in, 2-3
  federal institutions and instruments of social policy, 45
  functionalist approach to social policy, 44
  globalization and neoliberal assault on welfare state, 45-47
  and multiculturalism, 165-91
  "paradox of redistribution," 145, 315
  power resource approach, 44-45
  provincial responsibility, 50-51, 56
  public opinion on social spending, 142-57
  social investment perspective, 54-56
  taxes, credits and transfers, effect of, 56, 195, *196*
  See also inequality; *names of specific programs*; redistribution policies; redistributive politics; tax-transfer system
redistribution policies
  administrative requirements, 210-11
  and bureaucratic politics, 210-30
  as centralized, under new bureaucratic politics, 216, 217-18
  change from universal to targeted programs, 220
  as correction of previous policy problems, 218-19
  driven by fiscal and tax policy, not program departments, 211, 228
  effect, measured as difference between market and final income, 387
  "provincialization of social policy," 239
  universality *vs.* targeted assistance, 339
  See also policy change; policy drift; policy making; redistribution policies, Canada; redistributive politics
redistribution policies, Canada
  as benefit to mostly middle and upper-income households, 353

complexity of federal-provincial
responsibilities, 340
conversions from universal to
income-based, 353
decentralization of responsibility,
and erosion of effectiveness, 354
evolution of, 340-50
federal responsibilities, 342-43
federal transfers, reduction of Gini
coefficient associated with specific social programs, *404-6*
inability to respond to growth of
inequality, 335-36
policy reform agenda, 350-54
provincial redistributive regimes,
393-98
provincial responsibilities, 342
provincial transfers, reduction of
Gini coefficient associated with
specific social programs, *404-6*
social programs, 342-50
trends (1980s to 2000s), 389-93
*See also names of specific social
programs*
redistributive politics
and alignment of middle class, with
top or bottom of economic ladder,
419
Canada, future of, 417-23
changes in distribution of power,
impact on inequality, 414
disparity of redistributive impact in
different provinces, 393-94, 402
federal role, as mechanism for panCanadian integration, 253-54
federal role in redistribution, 243-45
impact of political party ideology on
redistribution policies, 398-402,
403
"new politics," approaches to childcare, 361-62
power shift to institutions less responsive to redistributive interests, 416-17
regional variations, and equalization
programs, 422

and retrenchment, 286
universal coverage and, 285
See also civil society organizations
(CSO); federalism; provinces;
retrenchment; territorial politics
Reform Party, 125, 200, 201, 203, 204,
323, 326
Registered Education Savings Plan
(RESP), 348, 352
Registered Pension Plan (RPP), 25, 314,
316, 341, 343
Registered Retirement Savings Plan
(RRSP), 25, 314, 316, 328, 341, 343
retirement benefits. *See names of
specific programs;* pensions
Retirement Income Coalition, 323
retrenchment
and hybridization, 286
opposition to, 286
See also redistributive politics
Rights and Democracy (Canada), 14
Rothstein, Bo, 168
Rowell-Sirois Royal Commission (1940),
48
Royal Commission on Bilingualism and
Biculturalism, 260
Royal Commission on DominionProvincial Relations. *See* RowellSirois Royal Commission (1940)
Royal Commission on Equality in
Employment (1984), 366
Royal Commission on Health Services
(1964), 52
Royal Commission on Learning (1995),
369
Royal Commission on New Reproductive
Technologies (1994), 125-26
Royal Commission on Taxation (1966),
336
Royal Commission on the Economic
Union and Development Prospects for Canada (1985), 337
Royal Commission on the Status of
Women (1970), 51, 365

same-sex marriage debate, 131

Saskatchewan
    correlates of Gini coefficient reduction by provincial transfers and income taxes (1993-2007), *397*
Scandinavian countries
    total public social expenditure as percentage of GDP, 1960-2007, 5
Schmitter, Philippe, 99
Security and Prosperity Initiative (SPI), 110
seniors
    erosion of benefits by policy drift, 24-25
    financial reasons for later retirement, 330, 331
    income security programs, 7
    lack of consistent advocacy voice for, 127
    long-term care, 293, 294, 305
    policies on benefits, 224, 320-24
    poverty, decline of, 29
    retirement income, and weaknesses of neoliberal social policy, 420
    retirement income, as focus of policy attention, 230
    support for health care programs, 285
    See also names of specific programs; pensions
Seniors' Benefit (proposed), 323-24
social architecture
    federal social benefits, 48, 50
    federal-provincial cost-sharing of social benefits, 48-49
    liberal welfare regime, 47
    provincial social benefits, 51, 52-53, 59-60
    social investment perspective, 54-56
social assistance. *See* welfare
Social Democrats
    Scandinavian policy-making model of cooperation between labour, political parties and business, 98
    social policy influences, 46
social investment perspective
    and child benefits, 26, 56-59, 241, 245, 246
    as complementary to federal competitive state-building imperatives, 250-51
    features, 10
    federal/provincial adoption of, 43, 242-43, 246, 248-53
    Ontario, report *Investing in People* (2004), 372
    and pan-Canadian projects of territorial integration, 241-42
    and policy change, 128-29, 234-35, 237-38, 239, 241
    Quebec, and new politics of distribution, 258, 266, 270
    and redistribution politics, 54-56
    as response to transformation of women's roles in labour market and family, 266
    shaping, by civil society organizations, 134
    and social architecture, 54-56
    See also early childhood education and care (ECEC); early learning and child care (ELCC); education; human capital
social policy
    and Canadian political party system, 188-93
    cumulative impact of diverse changes in political system affecting redistribution, 414
    functional approach to, 44
    innovations, increasingly dependent on "cross-class" coalitions, 419
    social expenditure, as percentage of total government expenditure, *290*
Social Policy Reform Group, 122
Social Security for Canada (1958), 214
Social Security Review, 126, 220-21
Spain
    poverty rates, compared with Canada, 30
    support for redistribution, 144
    total public social expenditure as percentage of GDP, 1960-2007, 5

Spicer Commission, 125
Spouse's Allowance, 8
Statistics Canada
    cuts to, 14
    See also names of specific studies and reports
Steering Committee of Ministers on Pension Coverage and Retirement Income Adequacy, 328
Stiglitz, Joseph, 424
Streeck, Wolfgang, 99
supply-side policies, 339-40
Survey of Consumer Finance (SCF), 83-84, 388, 390
Survey of Labour and Income Dynamics (SLID), *248, 249*, 388, 389, 390, 391, *392, 393, 397*, 399, 400, *405-6*
Survey of Union Membership (SUM), 67
Survey of Work Arrangements (SWA), 67
Sweden
    poverty rates, compared with Canada, *30*
    support for redistribution, 144
    total public social expenditure as percentage of GDP, 1960-2007, *5*
Switzerland
    negative attitude towards immigrants receiving welfare, 167
    support for redistribution, 144
system maintenance
    defined, 3
    health care, 21
    pensions, 19, 21
    of social programs, 19

Tax-Free Savings Accounts (TFSA), 341, 343
tax-transfer system
    change in net government transfers, by market-income quintile (1979-2007), *248, 249, 250*
    as compensation for rise in market income inequality until 1990s, 387, 389
    de-indexing debate, 121, 122
    failure to offset growth in market inequality, 413
    as mechanism for design and delivery of income-tested government programs, 217
    under old bureaucratic politics of policy making, 215
    policies, evolution of, 335-54
    policy learning within bureaucracy from existing programs, 224-25
    as progressive (1970s), 336-37
    and redistribution, 13, 18, 31-32, *33*, 246-50, 340-42, 389, 402
    stand-alone, 338-39
    tax credits, as policy instrument, 54, 56, 342, 350
    used to reduce and eliminate benefits, 225
    See also Canada Revenue Agency; income tax; *names of specific tax credits and benefits*
technological change
    blamed for eroding welfare state, 9
    dominant theory, 80-81
    and inequality, avoiding through investment in human and physical capital, 86-87, 88
    and life-long learning, 83
    and skill-based employment demand, 80-81
    skills, and labour market benefits, 74
    See also employment
territorial politics
    federalism, predominance in redistributive impact of policies, 244
    as highlighting national breadth of distribution of benefits, 241-42
    and shaping of Canadian social programs, 234-54
    See also federalism; provinces; Quebec
Thatcher, Margaret, 8, 10, 339
think tanks
    dearth of, in Canada, 120
    influence in policy making, 216, 217

and policy design by Dept. of
Finance, 223
Toronto City Summit Alliance, 375
Treasury Board
as restrainer in old bureaucratic politics of policy making, 214
trust
in government institutions, and support for redistribution to immigrants, 168
interpersonal, decline in ethnically diverse neighbourhoods, 168

Underhill, Frank, 384
unemployment
and effect of free trade agreements, 76-77
and public opinion on social spending, 148-49, 150
rate, Canada (1980-2003), 148, *149*
See also Employment Insurance (EI); Unemployment Insurance (UI)
Unemployment Assistance Act (1956), 48
Unemployment Insurance (UI)
change from "passive" dependence to active employment, 221
creation of (1940), 48, 383
as Liberal Party social policy, 193, 194
shift to Employment Insurance (EI), 81, 82, 88, 196-97
viewed as having adverse impact on productivity, 201
See also Employment Insurance (EI)
unions
collective agreement benefits, as private welfare state, 51
competition for members, 101
coverage, not mandated by Canadian law, 100
decline of, and wages in low-skilled labour markets, 78-79
decline of influence on social policy, 13, 124
density, associated with higher redistribution, 400-2, 403
density, decline in Canada, 100-101
de-unionization, and decline in real wages, 74-76
lack of effective collective voice, 101-2
and power resource theory of welfare state, 6
Quebec, 257, 261
and resistance to retrenchment of welfare state, 10
as "social partners" with business and government, and protection of social programs, 11
support for New Democratic Party, 191-92
union density and left-party government, associated with high redistributive impact, 383
unionization rates, education, and industry composition of employment, 75
weakening of, 13-14
See also labour market
United Kingdom
Conservative government health care system reforms, 291-92
health care, separation of "purchasers" and "providers," 291, 292
health care, "social insurance" model, 291
poverty rates, compared with Canada, *30*
support for redistribution, 144
total public social expenditure as percentage of GDP, 1960-2007, *5*
United States
education, differentials in wages and employment, 78-79
Gini coefficient, compared with selected European countries, 395
health care, opportunities for entrepreneurs, 292
health care, transition from residual model to universal mandatory coverage, 291-92
as liberal social welfare regime, 142

percentage of population with after-tax income below 50 percent of median income, 273
poverty rates, compared with Canada, 30
public attitudes towards government social responsibility, 155, 156, 157
Supplemental Security Income, for seniors, 315
total public social expenditure as percentage of GDP, 1960-2007, 5
unemployment rates, compared with France and Germany, 77, 78
welfare, racialization of, 166-67
United Way, 120
Universal Child Care Benefit (UCCB), 59, 221, 222, 253, 274, 349

Vaillancourt, Yves, 258, 262
Vital Signs, 129
Voluntary Sector Initiative (VSI), 130-31
Voluntary Sector Roundtable (VSR), 130

Weiss, Linda, 98
Welch, Robert, 366
welfare
  asset rules, 347
  changes to benefits (1994-2006), 197
  correlates of Gini coefficient reduction by provincial transfers and income taxes (1993-2007), 397, 399
  correlates of Gini coefficient reduction with "union density" variable absent (1993-2007), 400
  creation of, 48
  critique of "passive" benefits of, 53
  cuts to, 22-23
  decline in numbers of recipients (Quebec), 274
  decline in redistributive impact (1995-2000), 244
  as income security program, 7
  as less redistributive since 1980s, 390, 402
  perceptions of recipients, and support for welfare, 169, 175-76, 177, 179, 181
  by province, reduction of Gini coefficient associated with, 390, 404-6
  provincial responsibilities, 51, 52-53, 345
  public opinion on social spending on, 146, 150-51, 153, 156, 157, 158, 159, 160
  rate raises (Quebec, Newfoundland and Labrador), 270
  rates, decline of, 24, 53, 346, 353-54
  rates, variation across provinces, 347
  recipients, and refundable tax credits, 346
  reduced impact offset by other elements of tax-transfer system, 382
  shift to pressure to participate in employability programs, 23
  as stand-alone tax transfer system, 339
  See also Canada Assistance Plan (CAP)
welfare state
  "big," characteristics, 315
  challenges to, 8
  "cheap," characteristics, 314-15
  electoral systems, effect on, 11
  evolution, theoretical approaches to policy change, 19-20
  and government policy, 47
  "new politics" model, 187
  new politics of, 188
  path dependency, and resilience of policy structures, 19
  and pension plan design, 313
  power resource theory, 6, 187-88
  resistance to retrenchment, in countries with corporatist institutions, 11
  restructuring of, views on, 9-12

retrenchment of, factors, 188
and social integration, 7
sustainability factors, 165
union collective agreement benefits, as private welfare state, 51
vulnerability, due to governmental debt, 9, 12
"welfare diamond," as four sources of well-being, 46-47
See also welfare state, Canada; welfare state regimes
welfare state, Canada
design, and pensions for seniors, 314
erosion of, 141
federal responsibility, 48
globalization and neoliberalism, effect on, 45
government policy, history of, 47-53
as hybrid version of liberal welfare state, 7, 8
as "liberal," 43
as liberal social welfare regime, 142, 315
political party system, and power resources (1940-93), 188-93
postwar creation of, 4
power resource theory, 6, 44-45
as power resources model, 187
provincial responsibility, 47
public opinion on social spending, 142-57
social programs as instrument of territorial integration, 7, 414
welfare state regimes
conservative, characteristics, 142
liberal, characteristics, 4-5, 142, 143, 314
liberal, exemplified by Quebec, 259
liberal, structural features enabling power shift away from redistributive interests, 416-17
social democratic, characteristics, 142, 143
welfarism, 339
Wilson, Michael, 321

women
and "active labour-market policies" (ALMPs), 54
childcare framed as essential for women's equality, 366
education, differentials in wages and employment, 73
employment (Quebec), 266
labour market participation, and need for childcare, 376
pay equity, to correct gender-based earning discrepancies (Quebec), 269
single mothers, decline of poverty rates due to impact of non-labour market transfers, 391-93, 402
single mothers, sources of income in four largest provinces (1979-2007), 391
skill premium and employment rates, 70, *71*
universal childcare, and gender equality (Quebec), 266
women's groups
as connecting diverse civil society organizations, 122-23
decline of influence on social policy, 124
See also Canadian Advisory Council on the Status of Women (CACSW); feminist movement; National Action Committee on the Status of Women (NAC); women
Women's Legal and Education Action Fund (LEAF), 123
workers' compensation
correlates of Gini coefficient reduction by provincial transfers and income taxes (1993-2007), *397, 399*
correlates of Gini coefficient reduction with "union density" variable absent (1993-2007), *400*
as less redistributive since 1980s, 390

by province, reduction of Gini coefficient associated with, *404-6*
variance in provincial programs, 386-87
Working Income Supplement, 221
Working Income Tax Benefit (WITB), 26, 59, 219, 230, 274, 342, 347, 352-53, 354

World Trade Organization (WTO), 111
World Values Survey (WVS)
effect of income on attitudes towards government social responsibility, 154-55, *161*

Printed and bound in Canada by Friesens

Set in Futura Condensed and Warnock by Artegraphica Design Co.Ltd.

Copy editor: Joanne Richardson

Proofreader: Stephen Ullstrom

Indexer: Annette Lorek